Reappraisals in Canadian History
Post-Confederation

A. D. Gilbert
C. M. Wallace
R. M. Bray

Laurentian University

Prentice Hall Canada Inc., Scarborough, Ontario

Canadian Cataloguing in Publication Data

Main entry under title:

Reappraisals in Canadian history, post-confederation

ISBN 0-13-768797-4

1. Canada – History – 1867- . 2. Canada -
History – 1867- - Historiography. I. Gilbert,
Angus Duncan, 1941- . II. Wallace, Carl Murray.
III. Bray, Robert Matthew.

FC500.R42 1992   971.05   C92-094436-1
F1033.R42 1992

Prentice Hall, Inc., Englewood Cliffs, New Jersey
Prentice-Hall International, Inc., London
Prentice-Hall of Australia, Pty., Ltd., Sydney
Prentice-Hall of India Pvt., Ltd., New Delhi
Prentice-Hall of Japan, Inc., Tokyo
Prentice-Hall of Southeast Asia (Pte.) Ltd., Singapore
Editora Prentice-Hall do Brasil Ltda., Rio de Janeiro
Prentice-Hall Hispanoamericana, S.A., Mexico

ISBN: 0-13-768797-4

Acquisitions Editor: Michael Bickerstaff
Developmental Editor: Linda Gorman
Production Editor: Norman Bernard
Production Coordinator: Anna Orodi
Cover Design: Monica Kompter
Cover Image Credit: Colville, *Ocean Limited*
Royal Ontario Museum.
Page Layout: Anita Macklin

1 2 3 4 5   RRD   96 95 94 93 92

Printed and bound in the U.S.A. by R.R. Donnelley & Sons.

Table of Contents

Preface

Reappraisals in Canadian History is designed for use in university-level survey courses. It is, however, neither a textbook nor a traditional reader. Each of the units in the two volumes focuses on differing or complementary interpretations of a particular historical problem. A brief introduction to each unit establishes the context for the selected readings, and suggestions for relevant additional sources are included.

The vitality in Canadian historical studies over the past two decades has been outstanding, resulting in a profusion of new periodicals and monographs. Few organizations, groups, or regions are now without a journal. This has created both opportunities and challenges in fashioning a collection such as this. Although much recent historical writing is included, we have not neglected the important contributions of the previous generation of historians. In assembling these volumes we have consciously rejected the popular trend of trying to satisfy every region and province, every interest group, every minority, everybody. Instead we attempted to find common threads pointing to the integration of the exploding body of literature and interests. This topical approach demanded that all interests, including such disparate ones as regions, women, politics, the underclasses, and minorities, be part of the total fabric rather than segregated ghettoes.

In assembling this collection we have incurred a number of obligations. Faye Kennedy, formerly of Prentice Hall Canada, first persuaded us that there was a need for such a collection. We wish also to thank the Dean of the Faculty of Social Science and the Institute of Northern Ontario Research and Development at Laurentian University for financial assistance. Two of our students, Ross Danaher and Michael Stevenson, gave us logistical support. The students in HIST 1406/1407 participated cheerfully as we experimented with the classroom use of these materials in tutorials. Leo Larivière created the maps. Rose-May Demoré, our departmental secretary, responded to every call for help.

Finally we must thank the dozens of historians, editors and publishers who have generously given us permission to reprint this material. It is both ironic and troubling that the only rebuff we encountered was at the hands of an agency of the federal government, the Canadian War Museum, whose refusal to allow us to reprint material by George F.G. Stanley resulted in a unit on the War of 1812 representing two American but no Canadian historians.

A.D. Gilbert
C.M. Wallace
R.M. Bray

Laurentian University Sudbury, Ontario

Introduction

Canadian History and Historians

History is misunderstood more often than not. At a superficial level it appears to be one of the few immutables in an ever-changing world. That the past itself can never be altered is irrefutable, and students frequently choose history as an option at university believing that at least one subject will provide security when others mystify with unique concepts, vocabulary and content. That cozy view of history never lasts long, for as a discipline history is complex, malleable, and imprecise, subject to changing conditions and perspectives. Far from being set in cement, history is continuously being recast by each generations's need to find its own past. If R.G. Collingwood was correct, then "every new generation must rewrite history in its own way." The past that he, Winston Churchill and others found meaningful differs dramatically from that of today's leaders and their societies.

This charactersitic of history causes much confusion for students and academics alike. A psychology professor at lunch with several historians recently declared that, after she had taken world history in grade eight, further study was irrelevant. The subject, like Napoleon, was dead. One of the historians ventured the opinion that history had possibly changed more in the past twenty years than psychology. At that point she threw up her hands and left, unable to entertain such a ludicrous proposition. Yet it may be true.

That dynamic nature of the discipline of history, when compared to the permanence of past events such as the death of Napoleon, is the apparent paradox the psychology professor never unravelled. Over the past three decades a revolution has taken place in historical scholarship. In the era after the Second World War a sort of plateau, encompassing a broad consensus about the nature of the discipline, was reached. The traditional scholar worked for months or years in archives, poring over primary sources, and producing "revisionist" books or articles published in the handful of journals that all historians of Canada read. Triumphs were achieved with the discovery of new source material or a new angle on a known subject. Politics and biography were favoured, though economic, religious, military and international topics found their specialists. The overall nature of history as the study of the activities and ideas of elites, however, was rarely questioned. This view from the "court," or top-down, became the textbook version of the Canadian past, and while there were divisions over some interpretations based on ideology, religion, or even personal hostility, there was no division on what history itself was.

In Canada the small coterie of academics dominating the field included Marcel Trudel, Donald Creighton, A.R.M. Lower, W.L. Morton, Hilda Neatby, C.P. Stacey, W.S. MacNutt, Frank Underhill, Guy Frégault, and Margaret Ormsby. A younger generation of "revisionists" from the same mould was expanding the content without challenging the structures. Among them were J.M.S. Careless, Peter Waite, Margaret Prang, W.J. Eccles, Ramsay Cook, Jean Hamelin, Ken McNaught, Blair Neatby, and Jacques Monet. These people all knew each other personally, frequently comparing notes at the Public Archives of Canada, then located on Sussex Drive beside the Royal Mint in Ottawa. At the annual meetings of the Canadian Historical Association they read papers to each other, and were never short of advice. The *Canadian Historical Review*, published by the University of Toronto Press, was the final authority in English Canada, while Abbé Groulx reigned over French Canada with the *Revue d'histoire de l'Amérique française*. It was from this more or less homogeneous group that the dominant view of Canada, as presented in school textbooks, emerged. The comfortable unity of this well-written version of Canada's past permitted it to survive its generation, which many regard as the "Golden Age" of Canadian historical scholarship.

By the late 1960s, however, several younger scholars reacted against that veneration of the images of a previous generation. To them the historical imagination had been crippled by consistency. More than that, the consensus version of the past, in their view, had no relevance for the current generation. One may admire a Rolls Royce Silver Ghost, a 1955 Chevrolet, or even a Model T, the argument goes, but one must not confuse an abacus with a computer, a museum piece with modern needs.

It is the nature of history that the status quo does not survive long, and in the upheaval that characterized the whole mentality of the 1960s, several academics began to search for a more "usable past," one that abandoned the impressionistic views from the "court," and aimed at the reconstruction of a more meaningful society. The "New Social History" was the umbrella under which most of the innovations may be grouped. The dissatisfaction with a Canadian past dominated by political and economic factors led to a renovation with new methodologies, different approaches and alternate subject matter muscling in on the old-school-tie network. Subjects once ignored moved to centre stage, including work on classes and class relations, demography, literacy, the family, leisure, mobility, immigration, religion and education, though there was little cohesion among the disparate activities. Quantification and the computer found their place in the historian's baggage. *Histoire sociale / Social History*, co-sponsored by the University of Ottawa and Carleton University in 1968, eventually provided a focus and emerged as an alternate journal, though its lack of coherent editorial policy was simply a reflection of the diversity of opinion within the discipline. In a sense each historian could become a different school. The *Annales* of France, for example, were the source of inspiration for many French Canadians, while most English Canadians turned to American sociology for their models. Although there was considerable resentment over this "invasion of the barbarians" among the traditional historians, their own anecdotal approach invited criticism from those who asked different questions of sources and approached the past from new perspectives.

By the 1970s a veritable floodgate had opened. The annual meetings of the Canadian Historical Association became not one but a dozen or more fragments meeting separately. There was the ethnic group, the labour, the Atlantic, the Western, the Arctic, the Native, the women, the urban, the local, the material, the oral—the divisions were endless. Each of these had the capacity to subdivide. Labour quickly separated into the "old-fashioned" and the "New Left," with the latter winning the day and mounting its own journal, *Labour/Le Travailleur*. Each segment, in fact, launched one or more journals, such as *Urban History Review*, *Canadian Ethnic Studies*, *Polyphony*, *Canadian Woman Studies*, *Journal of Canadian Studies*, *B C Studies*, and *The American Review of Canadian Studies*. The range of topics and quality of scholarship were like the rainbow. Some, like *Acadiensis: Journal of the History of the Atlantic Region*, founded in 1971 at the University of New Brunswick, established and maintained an enviable reputation. Others have been less successful.

As a consequence of this fragmentation over recent decades, a student is faced with not one but many versions of Canadian history. This confusion may be considered an unnecessary encumbrance to those who are content with the "good old stuff," but that implies the study of a dead subject. The reappraisal is never-ending, and the challenge for the student is not to learn a few facts and dates but to sample the literature and to recognize what the authors are doing with the subject and trying to do to the reader. This requires an agile and a critical mind.

Reappraisals in Canadian History is intended to reflect this diversity of interpretation in Canadian history and to present it in such a way as to enable a student to make sense of it. This is not a "textbook" history of Canada, and makes no attempt to survey all of the main developments in that history. Nor is it simply a collection of readings, randomly selected and with little or no relationship one to another. Rather, each of the chapters is devoted to a particular historical problem and the different ways in which historians have approached that problem. In some cases their conclusions stand in sharp contradiction to each other; in others they are complementary. In every case students should attempt not merely to grasp the author's conclusions, but, of even greater importance, to understand how they were reached.

In order to do this it is useful to understand the variety of reasons that may lead different historians to reach different conclusions about what appears to be the same historical problem. In one sense, of course, there is nothing new about this. The debate over "historical relativism" is an old one, and it is now a truism that historians are influenced by the context in which they themselves live. It is, after all, hardly surprising that their view of the past is, to some degree at least, relative to their own time and place and circumstance, to their own preferences and prejudices. This may mean that they view historical evidence in a new light, or that they pose different questions of the past. It has long been accepted, therefore, that there will be differences of emphasis and interpretation, not only between different generations of historians, but also between historians of the same era.

The present fragmentation of the discipline, however, goes far beyond the traditional recognition of the relativity of historical knowledge. Implicit in it is fundamental disagreement over content and methodology, the meaning of history and its purpose. The one point on which historians do agree, however, is that not all historical interpretations are of equal validity. Certainly historians are less inclined than scholars in other disciplines to claim to have discovered any final "truths." This is understandable, given the nature of the evidence with which they deal and the problems with which they are concerned. The readings in this volume are in themselves testimony to the elusiveness of any final answers in history. Despite these limitations, historians do insist that historical scholarship can and must be subjected to critical scrutiny, that historical evidence and the use to which that evidence is put can be evaluated. The study of history at any kind of advanced level requires the development of these analytical skills, and never more so than with its current fragmentation. It is this, rather than the mastery of voluminous detail, that distinguishes the historian from the mere antiquarian. One of the purposes of this collection of readings is to assist students to develop their critical skills. Within each chapter, therefore, students should attempt to identify the interpretative thrust of each author, how the interpretation of one author differs from or complements that of another, what sources and methodologies have been employed, and, finally, how convincingly each author has based his or her interpretation on the historical evidence.

There are a number of fairly obvious points to look for. Has an author found new evidence which calls into question previous work on the subject? Is a new methodology being applied? Is anecdotal evidence, for example, being challenged by statistical analysis? Is a new type of historical evidence being brought to bear on an old problem? Is the historical problem itself being defined in an entirely new way?

For the period in Canadian history since 1867 the student is faced not only with the entirely new nation that was created that year, but with an amalgam of the several histories that were brought together and the complexity of a large nation state in a rapidly changing world. The tensions of the pre-Confederation era survived into the union, many of them being magnified in the new state. These included the regional, linguistic, religious, political and class divisions that were both obvious and divisive. These became even more complicated as

Canada emerged from the pre-industrial world of small cities and towns nestled among the dominant rural society that made up over 85 percent of the population. In the decades after 1867 massive technological innovation, combined with rapid urbanization and industrialization, drastically altered the world. Large factory cities emerged in the wilderness and on the prairies, displacing previous inhabitants and creating a dominant urban culture to replace the rural folk. The history of the era, therefore, reflects the reality of a rapidly changing world.

The fourteen chapters in this volume are a selection from that dynamic history. An attempt has been made to strike a balance among the traditional subjects, such as politics, and the several newer fragments. There are three chapters centred directly on politics, though this subject appears in several others. Chapter 1 is somewhat traditional in that it offers two versions of the centralist/regionalist dichotomy that remains a constant throughout Canadian history. Sir John A. Macdonald and his system are examined in chapter 4, and W.L.M. King is encountered in chapter 10. Not surprisingly King has attracted a diversity of opinion and the three readings in this unit move from a traditional examination of his leadership to psycho-history.

The diversity of Canadian society is examined in several chapters. Chapter 3, "Old and New Definitions," offers the student two selections, a traditional anecdotal version and an examination of society through sport. Women are central to chapter 5 in which there are three positions on women and work, a traditional, a "new left", and a feminist perspective which emphasizes gender. Class is the glue for chapter 12 on Quebec. The fumbling unemployment policies of the government in the 1930s are central to chapter 9, while the long shadow of McCarthyism in Canada during the 1940s and 1950s is the problem in chapter 13. Other units look at a variety of subjects, including Riel, the working class, and ethnic diversity.

The wars of the twentieth century have scarred Canada in a number of ways, and these are discussed in chapter 7, "The Great War", and chapter 11, "The Evacuation of the Japanese Canadians." Different questions are examined for those wars, especially on the home front, though the contribution of the soldiers at the front in World War I is emphasized in one reading.

Any rigid categorization of the chapters is bound to be misleading since politics, economics, social dynamics and regional aspects pervade most studies about Canada in one way or another. The student must learn to stride through the variety, identifying the interpretations, the mind-sets, the methodologies, and the mythologies. Each chapter in this collection offers a variety of interpretations which are frequently contradictory. At the same time, each chapter has a coherence which explains something about Canada, its history and its historians. Since history is what historians say it is, the student has both the opportunity and the responsibility to identify those views and the objectives of the historians. History will continue to be misunderstood, and the student must know why.

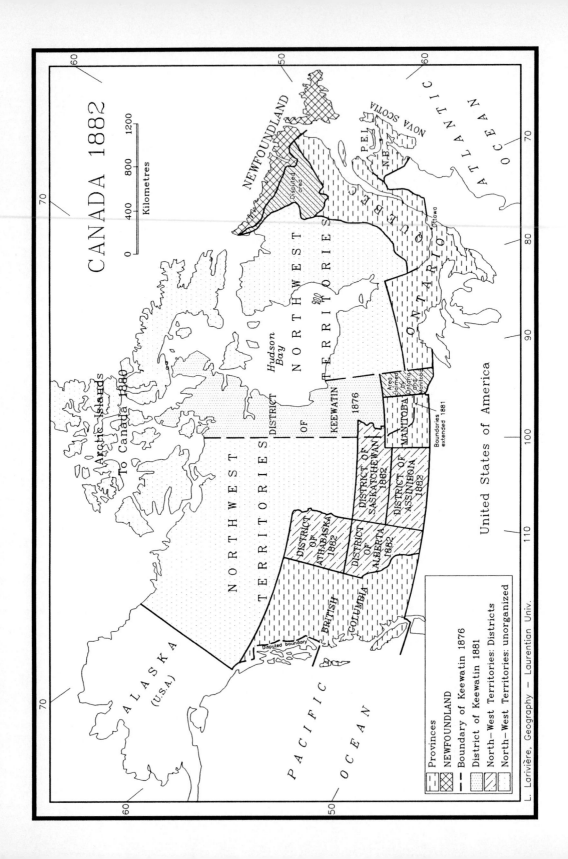

CANADA 1882

Kilometres

0   400   800   1200

NEWFOUNDLAND

Disputed area

NORTHWEST TERRITORIES

Arctic Islands
To Canada 1880

Hudson Bay

DISTRICT OF KEEWATIN 1876

NORTHWEST TERRITORIES

QUEBEC

ONTARIO

Ottawa

Area claimed by Ontario and Manitoba

MANITOBA

Boundaries extended 1881

DISTRICT OF SASKATCHEWAN 1882

DISTRICT OF ASSINIBOIA 1882

DISTRICT OF ATHABASKA 1882

DISTRICT OF ALBERTA 1882

BRITISH COLUMBIA

Disputed boundary

ALASKA (U.S.A.)

P.E.I.
N.B.
NOVA SCOTIA

ATLANTIC OCEAN

United States of America

PACIFIC OCEAN

Provinces

NEWFOUNDLAND

Boundary of Keewatin 1876

District of Keewatin 1881

North-West Territories: Districts

North-West Territories: unorganized

L. Larivière, Geography — Laurentian Univ.

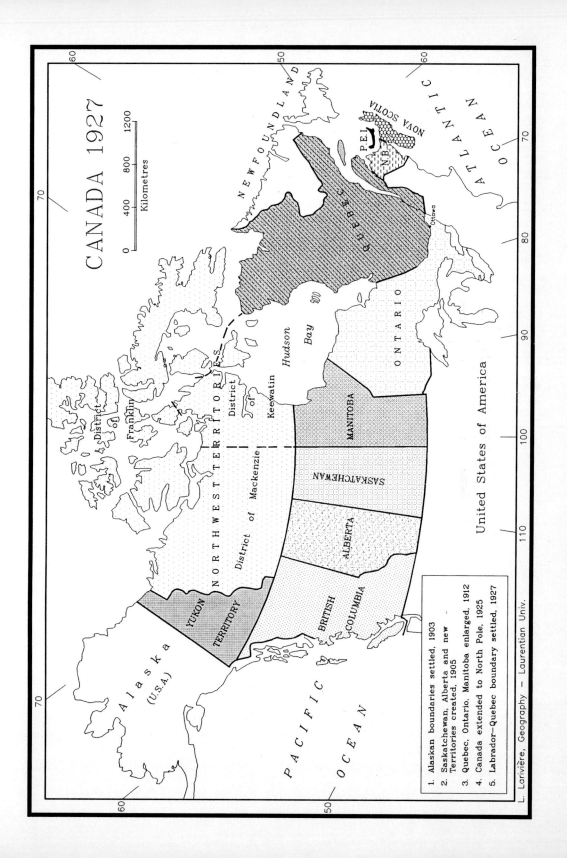

CANADA 1927

Kilometres

0 400 800 1200

ATLANTIC OCEAN

NEWFOUNDLAND

NOVA SCOTIA

P.E.I.

N.B.

QUEBEC

Ottawa

District of Franklin

NORTHWEST TERRITORIES

District of Keewatin

Hudson Bay

District of Mackenzie

ONTARIO

MANITOBA

SASKATCHEWAN

ALBERTA

YUKON TERRITORY

BRITISH COLUMBIA

Alaska (U.S.A.)

United States of America

PACIFIC OCEAN

1. Alaskan boundaries settled, 1903
2. Saskatchewan, Alberta and new Territories created, 1905
3. Quebec, Ontario, Manitoba enlarged, 1912
4. Canada extended to North Pole, 1925
5. Labrador–Quebec boundary settled, 1927

L. Larivière, Geography – Laurentian Univ.

CHAPTER
1 THE FIRST YEARS AFTER CONFEDERATION: CENTRALISM VS. REGIONALISM

The enthusiasm generated by the July 1, 1867, celebrations had barely subsided when the complexity of governing and nation building became obvious to the Fathers. "Everyone knows of course," wrote Peter Waite, "that Confederation began badly." Difficulties arose at every turn, especially in matters of power sharing. Every act of the new federal government infringed in one way or another on rights and privileges previously held by the provinces or claimed by them. The national tariff, for example, infuriated Maritimers by imposing the higher rates of the old province of Canada across the new Dominion. Antagonisms over language and religion in both New Brunswick and the West led to armed conflict. Domineering and disdainful Ontario, with its increasingly large population, responded negatively to most federal initiatives while pursuing its own imperial dreams. All the while Sir John A. Macdonald and his government were nation building with breathless haste. Between 1867 and 1873 they annexed half a continent, a record of expansionism with few parallels in history. They began constructing the Intercolonial Railway from Quebec to Halifax and agreed to build a line to the Pacific. In the process they certainly overreached the capacity of the fragile young nation, adding to the normal stress of the new relationship.

Donald Creighton, in *Canada's First Century* (1972), elaborated on his centralist view of Canadian history developed over many years, most notably in the second volume of his biography of John A. Macdonald, *The Old Chieftain* (1955). In "Confederation and Expansion," included here, he described the working out of the early kinks in the system and the inevitable expansion of Canada across the continent. The opposition of Joseph Howe and the Nova Scotia "Antis," in Creighton's world view, was the story of people out of step with the future. Despite Creighton's images, Maritimers were at a significant disadvantage in the Dominion. The old Canadian civil service administered the new nation with something less than sensitivity to the Atlantic provinces, carrying out what the Halifax *Morning Chronicle* called a "miniature reign of terror." The ineffectual Maritime representatives in the House of Commons failed to protect the interests of their electorate, while those from Quebec and Ontario, which permitted their members to sit in both federal and provincial houses, had continuity and numbers in the first Parliament. Quebec appeared to be the most conciliated province in the new Dominion, while Maritimers came to regard the sacrifices of becoming Canadian as far greater than the benefits. Peter Waite, who like Creighton has written on Confederation and Macdonald, explained the position of the Atlantic Provinces in "Becoming Canadian: Ottawa's Relations with Maritimers in the First Twenty-Five Years of Confederation."

Suggestions for Further Reading

Armstrong, Christopher, "Remoulding the Constitution," in *The Politics of Federalism: Ontario's Relations with the Federal Government, 1867-1942*. Toronto: University of Toronto Press, 1981.

Bercuson, D.J., ed., *Canada and the Burden of Unity*. Toronto: Macmillan, 1977.

Forbes, E.R., *Aspects of Maritime Regionalism, 1867-1927*. Ottawa: Canadian Historical Association, 1983.

Friesen, Gerald, *The Canadian Prairies: A History*. Toronto: University of Toronto Press, 1984.

Hodgins, Bruce W., Don Wright and W.H. Heick eds., *Federalism in Canada and Australia: The Early Years*. Waterloo: Wilfrid Laurier Press, 1978.

Hynes, Maureen, "A History of the Rise of Women's Consciousness in Canada and Quebec," in *The Hidden History of the Female*, ed. M. Atkins. Toronto: New Hogtown Press, 1971.

Rawlyk, George ed., *The Atlantic Provinces and the Problems of Confederation*. St.John's: Breakwater Press, 1979.

Shelton, George, ed., *British Columbia and Confederation*. Victoria: University of Victoria, 1967.

Silver, Arthur, *The French Canadian Idea of Confederation, 1864-1900*. Toronto: University of Toronto, 1982.

Stanley, George, "The Caraquet Riots of 1875," *Acadiensis*, II, no. 1 (Autumn 1972), 21-38.

CONFEDERATION AND EXPANSION

Donald Creighton

The British North America Act of 1867, the act which laid the constitutional framework for the federal union of four British American provinces, Ontario, Quebec, New Brunswick, and Nova Scotia, was a characteristic expression of their collective political experience. Its authors were the thirty-six delegates, known subsequently as the Fathers of Confederation—though some of them did not deserve the title and would, in fact, have indignantly repudiated it—who had met in conference at Charlottetown, Quebec, and London and framed the bases of the union. They were typical mid-Victorian colonial politicians who were intellectually as remote from the eighteenth-century preoccupation with first political principles as they were from the twentieth-century obsession with ethnic and cultural values. They thought of themselves as British subjects, and assumed that they were legitimate heirs of the British constitutional heritage and full participants in the British political experience. Alone among all the colonies that European nations had founded in the New World, the British American provinces had never sought to separate themselves from the Motherland. They had not followed the path through revolution to republicanism which had been first blazed by the United States and worn smooth and commonplace by a long string of slatternly South and Central American republics.

Constitutional monarchy, parliamentary institutions, and responsible government made up a political tradition which was not only British but also British American. The Fathers of Confederation assumed, without question, that this political tradition must be continued unimpaired in the nation they were creating. The calamities that had overtaken republicanism in the past twenty-five years had simply confirmed and strengthened their belief in the wisdom and efficacy of parliamentary institutions on the British model. In western Europe, the republican and liberal governments which had been born of the revolutions of 1848 had weakened and yielded to much more authoritarian and arbitrary régimes; and, in the United States, a terrible civil war had seemed to cast discredit, not only on American federalism, but also on American democracy. In sharp contrast with this tragic republican record of defeat and dishonour, the British constitution, which Walter Bagehot had just celebrated in a new book, had apparently adapted itself to new, more democratic circumstances, without ever sacrificing the continuity of its development. The Fathers of Confederation had good reason for believing that constitutional

From *Canada's First Century, 1867-1967* (Toronto: Macmillan, 1970), 8-22. Reprinted by permission of the estate of Donald Creighton.

monarchy on the British model was the best government for free men that had yet been devised. They regarded the British Empire as the greatest association of free states that had ever existed.

There remained, however, the business of adapting British institutions to a union of British provinces—a union which, it was firmly intended, would ultimately extend from ocean to ocean and over a half of the North American continent. Constitutional monarchy on the British model meant parliamentary sovereignty—the concentration of political power in a single, sovereign legislature; and, if a great many British Americans, including certainly such prominent political leaders as John A. Macdonald and Charles Tupper, could have had their way, they would have preferred to see the whole of British America united in a single Parliament and government. But legislative union, however politically desirable, was not thought to be politically possible. The Fathers of Confederation believed that one legislature would be incapable of coping with the diverse needs of a number of varied and widely separated communities. The French-speaking majority of one of those regions, the future province of Quebec, wished to protect its distinctive culture with a measure of local autonomy; and the provinces of the Atlantic region, which had not developed any system of municipal institutions, would have been left without any local government at all, if their provincial legislatures had been taken away.

No, the union could not be legislative. It would have to be federal. But, though the Fathers of Confederation recognized the inevitability of federalism, they could not help regarding it as a suspect and sinister form of government. There had never yet been a federal union in the British Empire; the United States of America was the only federal union in the English-speaking world; and in 1864-7, when the Fathers of Confederation were planning to unite British America, the United States could scarcely be considered a convincing advertisement for federalism. The republic was, in fact, convulsed by a fearful civil war, a war which seemed to prove that a federal union was a divisive form of government which might very readily break up as a result of its own centrifugal pressures. The 'federal principle', as British Americans called it then, was usually regarded as a highly potent political drug, which might prove efficacious in the cure of certain constitutions, but which must be administered in small doses, with great precautions, and never without a readily available antidote. The obvious corrective to the disruptive forces of 'states rights' was a strong central government; and this the Fathers of Confederation were determined to create. British American union, they admitted, would have to be federal in character; but at the same time it must also be the most strongly centralized union that was possible under federal forms.

This basic principle guided all the planning whose end result was the British North America Act of 1867. The Fathers of Confederation openly declared that they proposed to correct the mistakes and remedy the weaknesses of the American federal union. 'The primary error at the formation of their constitution,' John A. Macdonald said at the Quebec Conference, 'was that each state reserved to itself all sovereign rights, save the small portion delegated. We must reverse this process by strengthening the general government and conferring on the provincial bodies only such powers as may be required for local purposes.' While, in the United States, residuary legislative powers were retained by the State, or by the people, in the new Dominion of Canada they were to be held by the federal Parliament. The Provinces and the Dominion were not to be coordinate in authority, as a purist definition of federalism would have required them to be; on the contrary, as Macdonald frankly explained, the provincial governments were to be subordinate to the central government. Their responsibilities and functions, it was generally expected, would be relatively small and unimportant; and their legislative authority, even within the field of provincial powers, was not to be absolute. The chief provincial executive officer, the lieutenant-governor, who was to be appointed by the federal government, could reserve provincial bills for the federal government's consideration, and the federal government could disallow provincial acts. 'We thereby strengthen the central parliament,' said Macdonald in the Canadian legislature after he had finished describing federal powers, 'and make the Confederation one people and one government, instead of five peoples and five governments with merely a point of authority connecting us to a limited and insufficient extent.'

The primary aim of Confederation was political—the creation of a great 'new nationality'; and the British North America Act was the result of a political agreement among several provinces, not of a cultural compact of two ethnic groups, English and French. Before 1867, British America still remained, and was still regarded, not as a cultural duality but, in the words of George Cartier, as 'a diversity of races'. 'In our own federation,' Cartier declared, 'we should have Catholic and Protestant, English, French, Irish, and Scotch, and each by his efforts and his success would increase the prosperity and glory of the new confederacy.' Language was only one of the many components that made up the curious cultural medley that was British America before Confederation. National origin and national tradition—Irish, Scotch, and English, as well as French—might be equally influential, and religion, so often sharpened by sectarian bitterness, was perhaps the most important of all. The Fathers of Confederation had to take account of these differences; but their great aim was not the perpetuation of cultural diversity but the establishment of a united nation. At the Quebec and London conferences they gave, on the whole, relatively little time to the discussion of ethnic and cultural questions; and the resolutions they adopted on these matters, though important and essential, were few, precise in their wording, and limited in their scope.

The British North America Act contained no general declaration of principle that Canada was to be a bilingual and bicultural nation—or, for that matter, that it would remain 'a diversity of races'. The Fathers of Confederation were as little inclined to lay down the law about the cultural purpose and future of their new nation as they were to issue a general pronouncement on the nature and probable destiny of mankind. The English and French languages were given equal official status in the Parliament and the courts of Canada, and in the legislature and courts of Quebec. Canada was to establish only two federal courts, the Supreme Court and the Exchequer Court, at Ottawa; and all the other courts in the country were to be provincial courts, constituted and maintained by the provinces. The French language had thus no official standing in the courts of any of the provinces except Quebec; and, perhaps even more important, it was given no protected place in any of the nation's schools. The Fathers of Confederation showed a fair amount of interest in education and its legislative control; but it was very characteristic of these typical British Americans, with their strong denominational affiliations and frequent sectarian biases, that what concerned them was not the role of language, but the place of religion, in the schools. The provinces were given the power to legislate in respect of education; but this authority was limited by some rather complicated provisions designed to protect any rights or privileges concerning separate or denominational schools.

In sum, the distinctive cultural features of French Canada—its language, civil code, and educational system—were confirmed in those parts of the new Dominion in which they had already become established by law or custom. They were not extended in their application to Ontario and the Atlantic provinces. They were given no protected position in the nation as a whole.

II

The making and inauguration of the new federal constitution, embodied in the British North America Act, was only the first, theoretical stage in the building of the new nation; the far greater task of its territorial completion and integration still lay ahead. The Canada that celebrated the first Dominion Day on the 1st of July, 1867, was composed of only four provinces, Ontario, Quebec (the two former Canadas), New Brunswick, and Nova Scotia; and, in Nova Scotia, Joseph Howe was leading a popular movement for secession from the Dominion. Beyond the restricted boundaries of the original Dominion, the rest of British America, immense, vulnerable, and largely uninhabited, stretched away, east, west, and north, and far into the distance. In the east, the two island provinces, Newfoundland and Prince Edward Island, still held stubbornly aloof from the union. In the far west, the now united province of British Columbia was a likely candidate for admission to Confederation; but she was separated from Canada by Rupert's Land and the North-West Territories, a vast expanse of almost empty country, still owned or controlled by the Hudson's Bay Company.

A formidable task of national expansion and unification confronted the new federal government, appointed on the 1st of July, 1867. The first cabinet was a coalition of former Confederates, drawn from both parties and all four provinces, and representing every important interest—provincial, ethnic, and religious—in nicely graduated numbers. Its leader, the first Prime Minister of the new Canada, was John Alexander Macdonald. At fifty-two, he seemed oddly youthful in appearance. His dark, curly hair was thick, his eyes amused and friendly, his smile genially sardonic. The long oval of his face was spare, and almost as unlined as a young man's; and, unlike most of his contemporaries, who followed the mid-Victorian fashion of beards, whiskers, and moustaches, he was invariably clean-shaven. There was no sign of the heaviness of age in his tall, slight figure, and no hint of the pride of position in the easy, rather jaunty fashion in which he carried himself. He had always been something of a dandy, and he wore his clothes well. He seemed to take life very easily and to find it continually entertaining; and for a long time people had refused to take him very seriously. They had admitted his great expertise in all the devices and stratagems of party politics; but they were inclined to write him down as an accomplished political manipulator, with few ideas and even fewer principles. The events of the past ten years had gradually but effectively altered this early impression; and the movement for federal union had enabled him to reveal his exceptional gifts to the full. The success of Confederation was largely the result of his expert leadership. The British North America Act was, in the main, the expression of his political theory.

Macdonald and his cabinet were anxious to complete the work of union—to appease Nova Scotia, bring Newfoundland and Prince Edward Island into Confederation, and acquire Canada's great inheritance in the north-west. As it chanced, the political circumstances, both hostile and friendly, of the first few years that followed 1867 helped to hasten the completion of their design. The native Canadian drive towards continentalism was strengthened by two external forces—the same forces that had aided the union movement of 1864-7: the urgency of Great Britain and the pressure of the United States. Ever since the beginning of the American Civil War, Great Britain had been moving purposefully towards an honourable withdrawal from British America. It was not that she hoped or intended to cut the imperial connection with Canada, certainly not until Canada was fully prepared to accept separation; but she was anxious to recall her isolated military garrisons, and to escape from her remaining territorial obligation in North America—her ultimate responsibility for the future of the Hudson's Bay Company lands. If Canada took over Rupert's Land and the North-West Territories, not only would England be relieved of an unwanted burden, but Canada would also be better able to endure. Great Britain had supported Confederation because it seemed likely to create a colonial nation strong enough to take over imperial responsibilities. But, so long as Canada remained a mere fragment of a still disunited British America, it would remain vulnerable. If it could acquire all remaining British territory and reach its destined continental limits, it would have its best chance to survive.

The anxious encouragement of Great Britain was the first of the two external forces hastening national expansion; the second was the pressure of a resentful and predatory United States. The Civil War was over; but peace had not brought a settlement of those angry wartime grievances that the North had come to nurse against Great Britain and British America. The triumphant republic could not easily forget or forgive the sympathy which both British and colonials had shown for the Southern cause; and the American government insistently demanded enormous reparations for the losses inflicted by the *Alabama* (a Southern cruiser built in a British shipyard) on American shipping during the war. It was seriously proposed that the whole of Rupert's Land and the North-West Territories should be ceded to the United States in satisfaction of the *Alabama* claims; and both the new American President, Ulysses S. Grant, and his Secretary of State, Hamilton Fish, were expansionists who were prepared to use almost any method, short of armed force, to acquire all or part of British America. In the east, where there were established colonies, the danger was less; but, so long as Nova Scotia was dissatisfied and Newfoundland and Prince Edward Island remained outside the union, there was at least a chance of American intervention. The likelihood was much greater in the west where the politicians and journalists of the frontier state of Minnesota were casting covetous glances upon a vast and almost empty territory which seemed as if it might be theirs for the taking. 'It is quite evident to me,' Macdonald wrote in January 1870, '... that the United States government are resolved to do all they can, short of war, to get possession of our western territory, and we must take immediate and vigorous steps to counteract them.'

III

There were dangers everywhere. But the pacification of Nova Scotia was, without any doubt, the immediate and most urgent task. Joseph Howe and the Nova Scotian Anti-Confederates had failed to persuade the British government to exclude their province from the union of 1867; but they refused to believe that this first rebuff was final. In their eyes, the sweeping Anti-Confederate successes in both the federal and provincial elections of 1867 seemed an irrefutable proof, which even the unwilling British government must recognize, of Nova Scotia's unanimous determination to escape from Confederation. Howe led a second delegation to England to ask for repeal of the union; and Charles Tupper, Nova Scotia's leading supporter of Confederation, was dispatched by the Canadian government to counteract his old rival's propaganda. 'Repeal is not even a matter of discussion,' Macdonald declared bluntly; and this was very much the way in which the British government looked at it. Neither Conservatives nor Liberals were willing to undo the work of Confederation. To break up the newly formed union would simply protract and perhaps perpetuate the fragmentation of British America. It might mean the indefinite pro-longation of Britain's responsibilities in the region and the indefinite postponement of her military withdrawal from North America.

This second British refusal meant the end of the repeal movement. What were the Nova Scotian Anti-Confederates to do? Two extreme, heroic courses—open rebellion or annexation to the United States—were conceivable; but no Nova Scotian politician, least of all Joseph Howe, could bring himself to advocate such desperate policies. A species of political 'sit-down' strike, in which the Anti-Confederate majority in the provincial legislature would refuse to govern and prevent their opponents from doing so, was perhaps a more feasible plan; but, though Howe suggested this course, his Anti-Confederate associates declined to consider it seriously. The movement had obviously reached a dead end: and Howe came to the conclusion that submission, on the best terms possible, was inevitable. At first he hoped vaguely that he might obtain some amendments of real substance in the British North America Act; but the Canadian and British governments were adamant in their refusal to consider any constitutional changes. Better financial terms—a larger federal subsidy to the provincial government—was all that Macdonald was willing to grant; and in the end this became the basis of an agreement by which Howe renounced repeal and, in January 1869, entered the federal cabinet.

Long before Howe had made his great renunciation and accepted federal office, two of his new colleagues in the Canadian cabinet, Sir George Cartier and William McDougall, had gone to England to make a start on the next and more ambitious phase of the nationalist programme, the acquisition of Rupert's Land and the North-West Territories. With the help of some heavy persuasion from the British government, the Hudson's Bay Company was induced to cede its lands to Canada in return for a payment of £300,000, and a grant of one-twentieth of the western 'fertile belt'. The Canadian government proceeded very cautiously with the political organization of its nearly empty domain. Rupert's Land was to be governed provisionally as a territory with a small nominated council, rather than as a province; representative institutions and responsible government would come later, when they were warranted by the spread of settlement. William McDougall, the Lieutenant-Governor designate, went west early with the intention of familiarizing himself with the country and its people before the transfer of authority actually took place on the 1st of December, 1869. He never reached his future 'capital', the tiny Red River settlement. On the 30th of October, he was stopped at the Canadian border by a roadblock, held by an armed force of *Métis* or French-speaking half-breeds.

Undoubtedly, a fair number of people at Red River awaited the coming of the Canadians without enthusiasm, or with doubt and misgiving. But it was the initiative of the *Métis* which alone inspired the resistance and gave it force and direction. They were 'a peculiar people', conscious of their distinctive corporate identity and grandiloquently styling themselves 'the new nation'; in fact, their slow ascent from nomadism to civilization was far from complete. Reluctant and indifferent farmers, expert horsemen and hunters, born and bred to a long tradition of direct and violent action, they had built up a semi-military organization through the comradeship of the buffalo hunt. Their uniquely gifted son, Louis Riel, was an able but temperamental and dictatorial man, full of delusions of grandeur, quickly infuriated when his will was crossed, and quite without compunction in the use of force. He and his *Métis* seized Fort Garry, the Hudson's Bay Company's fortified post at Red River, and proclaimed a provisional government for the region.

Riel's immediate object was to prevent the automatic and unconditional transfer of the north-west to Canada; he was determined to obtain safeguards which would ensure the survival of his *Métis* against the peril of Protestant and Anglo-Saxon immigration and settlement. His ultimate aim remains uncertain; he may seriously have considered the alternative of annexation to the United States. Certainly, during the first months of the resistance, the principal advisers of his provisional government were a small group of Americans resident at Red River, one of whom was a government agent and the others avowed annexationists. These men joined forces with the annexationist politicians, journalists, and railway men of Minnesota and the American north-west—'the Yankee wire-pullers', Macdonald called them; and both groups tried, in their various ways, to persuade the American government to exploit Canada's difficulties, to take advantage of the temporary suspension of British and Canadian authority at Red River, and to press forward the territorial aggrandizement of the United States.

This prospect appalled Macdonald. He was determined that 'the United States should not get behind us by right or by force and intercept our route to the Pacific'; and he realized that, as long as the effective acquisition of Rupert's Land was delayed, the whole of his great design for national expansion was in jeopardy. The resistance at Red River must be appeased as quickly as possible. He knew that he would have to make terms for the union of the north-west with Canada; but he was determined that Canada would negotiate, not with Riel's dictatorship, the provisional government with its American and clerical advisers, but with the Red River community as a whole. Donald Smith, sent west as a federal commissioner, succeeded in calling an assembly or 'convention' of elected delegates from all the parishes of the settlement, French and English; and the 'convention', in its 'list of rights', drew up reasonable terms for the admission of the north-west, as a territory, into Confederation.

This was a sensible settlement; but it was not to be. Riel was resolved to prevent it. The democratically expressed wishes of the Red River community, where they differed from his private plans for his own people, the *Métis,* meant nothing to him; and the very generosity and goodwill of the settlement gave him his chance of thwarting its intentions. The 'convention', in a final gesture of conciliation, had confirmed the provisional government and elected Riel as president. Once back in control, Riel took the negotiations with Canada into his own hands. He appointed the delegates who were to go to Ottawa, and he made short work of the 'list of rights' of the 'convention.' Two new 'lists of rights', drawn up in private by Riel and his clerical advisers, demanded provincial status, which the convention had expressly rejected, and separate or confessional schools, which the convention had not even discussed.

Macdonald was compelled to yield. So long as Riel's provisional government lasted, the threat of American intervention in the north-west remained. A quick settlement was the only solution; but a quick settlement meant, in fact, acceptance of Riel's terms, now strongly backed by French-Canadian influence in the federal government. Macdonald was caught in a squeeze-play with Riel and his clerical and American advisers on the one hand, and Sir George Cartier and the French and Roman Catholic M.P.s at Ottawa on the other. 'The French,' Sir Stafford Northcote, the governor of the Hudson's Bay Company, candidly observed, 'are earnestly bent upon the establishment of a French and Catholic power in the north-west to counteract the great preponderance of Ontario.' 'Manitoba,' the name given to the first political division of the north-west, entered Confederation as a province with a top-heavy bicameral legislature, modelled on that of Quebec, two official languages, and confessional schools.

IV

With the creation of Manitoba, the most serious danger threatening Macdonald's expansionist plans had ended. It was now nearly certain that Canada would acquire the whole of the British north-west and that a new transcontinental nation would come into being in North America. It was also fairly clear that the United States, however reluctantly and disapprovingly, was prepared to accept this situation. In the early spring of 1871 a Joint High Commission met at long last in Washington and proceeded to settle all the wartime grievances and controversies—including the dispute over the *Alabama* claims—which had grown up between Great Britain and the United States.

In the meantime, Canada's onward expansionist march had already been resumed. The acquisition of Rupert's Land and the North-West Territories cleared the way for the union with British Columbia. British Columbia had never seriously considered any other destiny; and a petition, circulated in 1869, for annexation to the United States, collected only a few score signatures. The British Columbia Legislative Council, partly elected and partly appointed, agreed to send a delegation to Canada to negotiate for union on terms proposed by the Executive Council; and the three delegates, R. W. Carrall, J. W. Trutch, and J. S. Helmcken, reached Ottawa in June 1870, just after the passage of the Manitoba Act. Their first request was for provincial status with a fully elected legislative assembly and responsible government; they also wanted a generous debt settlement and lavish federal subsidies. But their most interesting—and, as it turned out, their most controversial—proposals had to do with communications with Canada. They asked for the construction of a coach road between Fort Garry and British Columbia, the commencement of a railway within three years, and thereafter an annual expenditure of $1,000,000 on the British Columbia section of the line. The requests were stiff, almost exorbitant; but to the amazement, almost the incredulity, of the delegates, the terms voluntarily offered by the Dominion government vastly exceeded anything they had ever dreamed of asking. The coach road was dropped; instead, Canada offered to begin a railway within two years, and finish it in ten.

In 1873, two years after the entrance of British Columbia, Prince Edward Island followed and became the seventh province in Confederation. Prince Edward Island had rejected 'better terms' in 1869; she might have gone on almost indefinitely considering and declining 'better terms', every few years, in the vague hope of getting a superlative bargain; but in the early 1870s a series of events occurred which stopped this temperamental shilly-shallying. An expensive, badly designed, and corruptly managed railway-building programme ended the Island's state of financial innocence and her proud sense of self-sufficiency. In 1864, at the time of the Quebec Conference, she had had a debt of less than $250,000; in 1874, it had risen to a little over $4,000,000. Canada agreed to assume the debt and to buy up the land of the remaining absentee proprietors; and, reluctantly, through sheer necessity, Prince Edward Island overcame her complacent parochialism and entered Confederation. On the 17th of May, the day S. L. Tilley, the new Minister of Finance, presented the terms of union to the Canadian House of Commons, a daughter was born to Lady Dufferin, the Governor General's wife. 'This, with Prince Edward's Island, makes *twins,*' Dufferin wrote to Macdonald.

In the first six years of its existence, the new Dominion had nearly attained its appointed natural limits. Newfoundland, alone of all the British North American territories, remained outside Confederation. The generous terms of union which the Carter government negotiated with Canada in 1869 were rejected in the Newfoundland general election of the autumn of that year; and the defeat was so decisive that all hope of Newfoundland's admission was abandoned for another quarter-century. Apart from this important limitation, the great work of nation building was complete; but the process of expansion had been troubled and hurried, and Canada had incurred costs, the full extent of which could not then be foreseen. In Manitoba the Dominion had been forced to impose an elaborate, highly unsuitable constitution upon an immature province which had not yet developed its real and permanent character. To British Columbia, the Dominion had promised, on its own initiative, to begin a Pacific railway within two years and to finish it within ten. The burden of the railway was to strain Canada's financial resources to their limit; and the enforced and hasty appeasement of the north-west was to provoke a reaction which would seriously divide the Canadian people.

BECOMING CANADIANS: OTTAWA'S RELATIONS WITH MARITIMERS IN THE FIRST AND TWENTY-FIRST YEARS OF CONFEDERATION

P.B. Waite

The traditional view of the early years of Confederation is curious. It is well known that New Brunswick history stops utterly after 30 June 1867. Nova Scotia ceases to be of much interest after the Hants by-election and better terms in 1869; it rises briefly above the horizon in 1886, and thereafter it sinks, never to be seen again. Newfoundland history subsists until the autumn election of 1869 when it too goes out of sight, to be seen occasionally in storms, like the Flying Dutchman, a ghost that appears over the sea in bad economic weather. For in 1869 it is time to go west; the Atlantic provinces are consigned to their own devices. By the time Riel has been got safely out of Manitoba in 1870, there is just time to quickly glance at the British Columbians before we head east for the first act of the now famous Prince Edward Island play, "How much did you say the debt allowance was?" Then, after 1 July 1873, Prince Edward Island disappears too, debt allowance, railway and all, and what is left, out there on the Cavendish shore, is the smile of Anne of Green Gables, like the smile of the Cheshire Cat. We have just time to get to Montreal in time for the splendid and latest consignment of correspondence in the Montreal *Herald*, 18 July 1873, on the Pacific Scandal. Thus are we launched into national life.

Everyone knows of course that Confederation began badly; its first year was worse than most people imagine. There was a litany of complaints, and not just Nova Scotia chafed, angry over having been dragooned in: New Brunswick was restless, unhappy, and painfully surprised over the new legislation of 1867-68; Prince Edward Island continued to preen herself on her independence; and Newfoundland had already been inoculated against Confederation by the bitterness of the Nova Scotians and the disappointments of the New Brunswickers.

The first year or, rather, years of Confederation were not easy, not for the dominion government nor for the new provinces. Macdonald's plan for the Northwest Territories, in the act of 1869, was symptomatic of attitudes that had to be refashioned, even partly unlearned. There was more truth than jocularity in the remark of Alexander Campbell, Macdonald's new minister of the interior in 1873, that he was now "Secretary for the Colonies."[1] This perspective—the view from Parliament Hill one might call it—saw the Dominion mainly

---

Waite, P.B., "Becoming Canadians: Ottawa's Relations with Maritimers in the First and Twenty-first Years of Confederation" in R. Kenneth Carty and W. Peter Ward (eds.), *National Politics and Community in Canada* (Vancouver: University of British Columbia Press, 1986), 153–168. Copyright University of British Columbia Press. All rights reserved.

in terms of the 65 MP's from Quebec and the 82 from Ontario. That there were 19 from Nova Scotia and 15 from New Brunswick was a palpable fact, for there they were, and room had literally to be made for them; the House of Commons chamber had originally been designed for the 130 members of the Legislative Assembly of the Province of Canada; it had now to be stretched to include the 17 MP's that "rep. by pop." added to Ontario, and the 34 from Nova Scotia and New Brunswick. But that stretching of the House of Commons chamber was symptomatic.

The old Province of Canada, though dead, was resurrected. The old officialdom, the officers of the old Legislative Council and of the House of Commons, and the civil service stayed on in Ottawa. Why not? That's where they were already. There would be a few Maritime appointments, but only a few. The new provinces of Ontario and Quebec appointed their own staff; the old civil service of the Province of Canada stayed on with the Dominion of Canada, some five hundred of them, many familiar with the ways of the MP's from Quebec and Ontario. No provision was made to compensate Nova Scotian or New Brunswick civil servants whose offices had been abolished by Confederation; it seems not to have been thought of, or expected. Any Province of Canada employees so affected were pensioned. A debate arose in March 1868 in the Senate on this topic. Senator Holmes of Nova Scotia said he could not consider the officers of the old Legislative Council of the Province of Canada as being proper officers of the Senate. What right, asked his Nova Scotian colleague, W. J. Ritchie, had "most of these employees to be here at all? ... Why not bring our officials from Fredericton and Halifax at the same time? ... What would be said if we should come to the House and ask for pensions for the old servants of the Maritime Provinces[?]"[2] The Parliament Hill of 30 June 1867 was nearly the same Parliament Hill 1 July 1867, with scarcely a perceptible shift in thought, deed, or emphasis.

The first session of the Canadian Parliament only made things worse. All the new changes seemed to be dictated by what had previously been done in central Canada, in tariffs, postage, law, systems of administration even, almost all unknown in Nova Scotia and New Brunswick, and some of them distinctly retrograde in character. It was a set of issues that made pro-Confederate New Brunswickers despair and Nova Scotians say venomously, "I told you so."

Prior to 1867 the closest approach the British North American provinces had made to a *Zollverein* was in 1854-66, during the American Reciprocity Treaty. Customs lines between the provinces in natural products were then obliterated by concurrent legislation. The complete interprovincial free trade proposed by Confederation was the system that existed up until March 1866, but now it was expanded to include manufactured goods. After 1 July 1867, the new Dominion of Canada tariff was mainly tariff assimilation to the old Province of

Canada model. True, downward revision of the Province of Canada tariff in 1866 had reduced nonpreference, or general rate tariffs, to 15 per cent, a concession to Maritime opinion. It is difficult to gauge the effects of the new Canadian duties technically, since old Province of Canada duties had been largely *ad valorem,* the Maritime ones specific. At the very beginning of the new tariff regime, there was some complacency on both sides, Nova Scotia and New Brunswick turning over their tariff administrations to the Dominion of Canada apparently without much regret. That did not last long. The central Canadian style of administration came as a shock. One has the impression that the old colonial administration in Nova Scotia, and especially in New Brunswick, had been rather easygoing. The new and more rigorous dominion customs-house procedures were mightily resented. These included the retention of the original invoices by the customs department; the actual examination of one package in every ten; the refusal to allow cash discounts as deductions from dutiable value; and even the charging of duty on the casks in which molasses and rum came. Thomas Worthington, the commissioner of customs, replied to complaints about these practices loftily, "Experience has taught us that, in order to be effective, laws for the collection of our revenues can hardly fail to be inquisitorial in their action ... and exceedingly annoying to those who are subject to their operations."[3]

The first tariff bill brought in by Tilley, the new minister of customs, in 1867 was the act that had been in force in the Province of Canada with only minor alterations.[4] The effect was to produce very extensive changes from old New Brunswick and Nova Scotia tariff structures, especially the latter. Tea, molasses, and sugar would go up to about double the tariff it had been before; flour would be twenty-five cents a barrel, where in New Brunswick it had been free.[5] The duty on spirits was set at eighty cents a gallon for brandy, rum, gin, and whisky. This was not a serious inconvenience for Nova Scotia, where the duty on rum had been forty cents but was raised just prior to Confederation to seventy-five cents. Jones of Halifax proposed that the duty should be sixty-three cents, exactly the excise tax on a gallon of Canadian rye. Most Nova Scotians and New Brunswickers drank rum, not rye, and it seemed sensible to Jones, who was an importer, to make the respective taxes equal. It did not work. Rose's tax was not unreasonable, but he might have avoided rubbing in the five-cent increase on rum. He said that if New Brunswick and Nova Scotia did not like it, they should "accustom themselves to Upper Canada rye."[6]

On 16 December 1867, Finance Minister John Rose brought in the stamp tax—stamps on cheques, promissory notes, and official documents—a tax familiar in the Province of Canada, but unknown in the Maritimes. It was a tax, as E. M. McDonald of Lunenburg observed, that "had cost England half this continent." It seemed to stir up memories in Nova Scotia of the stamp-tax agitation in Halifax of 1765. Nor was Rose very accommodating to objections. The stamp tax, he said, would be in force—he used the word "continue"—and the government "intended putting it in force in the Maritime Provinces at the earliest possible moment."[7]

On top of that was piled postage for newspapers. Nova Scotia and New Brunswick made no charge for the transmission of newspapers through the mail; the Province of Canada did. The Macdonald government's strategy was to reduce existing rates of newspaper postage in Ontario and Quebec while imposing it on New Brunswick and Nova Scotia. In vain did even Charles Tupper urge that it be postponed:

> If ever there ever was a time when it was necessary for the interests of the whole Dominion that just the sort of information which newspapers conveyed, should be disseminated through all the Provinces, it was now. He was most averse from touching upon local or sectional prejudices, but it could not be denied that there was a considerable amount of mutual hostility existing between different portions of the country.[8]

Tupper was joined by D'Arcy McGee. "This tax on the public intelligence," said McGee, "would do the public mind an injury.... It was a tax upon a form of knowledge most essential to the people.... There was never a time when such knowledge was of greater importance to the country."[9] Brown Chamberlin of the Montreal *Gazette,* MP for Missisquoi, moved that the tax be abolished, whereupon Macdonald threatened to throw over all the proposed post office legislation, thus taking Ontario and Quebec back to its older, and higher, newspaper postage. Two attempts were made to stop newspaper postage and both were defeated, twenty-two to forty, and twenty-three to thirty-six, the last on 20 December, when nearly every Maritime MP had gone home for Christmas.[10] In the Senate, Miller, Bourinot, and Dickey, proGovernment senators from Nova Scotia, opposed newspaper postage; their amendment too was lost.[11]

As Edward Blake pointed out when Parliament resumed in mid-March 1868, Confederation could not be maintained if there existed a permanent feeling of discontent. There was little use "in attempting to prolong such an unwilling Union." Bad as things had been in July 1867, they were now, in 1868, much worse, simply because of the Macdonald government's legislation. No interest required the imposition of the tariff on flour, and, in fact, it was rescinded in May 1868.[12] Senator R. D. Wilmot, who had been a Father of Confederation (having been a delegate to the London Conference), complained in March that instead of being able to go back to New Brunswick and congratulate himself and his fellow citizens on Confederation, he had to admit "the prognostications of its enemies had been fulfilled."[13]

In April 1868 came a series of bills on the assimilation of the criminal law. Macdonald, the minister of justice, did not introduce a code, but following British practice, brought down eleven bills dealing with injuries to property, crimes against persons, criminal procedure, and so on. The bills were based on the common law, of course; but different colonies differed in their views of, and their ameliorations of, the English common law. In the Maritimes, reforms and improvements of old common law penalties had proceeded much further than in the Province of Canada. For example, in England and in the Province of Canada, rape was a capital offence. In Nova Scotia it was not, the change having been made in 1853; in Nova Scotia a jury would not convict if rape were made a capital crime. Senator McCully, another Father of Confederation, objected that by the new bills brought down by Macdonald, men were being sentenced to hard labour for what Nova Scotians would regard as trivial offences. There was not a jail in Nova Scotia, and hardly any in New Brunswick, adapted for such penalties. In fact, Maritime criminal law was much more concise, much less specific; an amendment to postpone application of these wide-ranging changes in criminal law, notably in the Act respecting offences against the Person, was moved in the Senate, and passed, twenty-five to twenty-two, 16 May 1868. Thus, the principal act of criminal law was defeated.[14] In a pique, the government withdrew all the criminal law bills of that session. The Senate earned itself some criticism in central Canada for this action; but far from apologizing, those responsible reiterated their position in 1869, when the Offences against the Person Act again came up. McCully, and Senator J. W. Ritchie (later Justice of the Supreme Court of Nova Scotia), both argued that rape punishable by death was too severe. Nevertheless, this second time it carried in the Senate, twenty-nine to twenty.[15]

Toward the end of 1868, results of this line of action began to show up. In New Brunswick, in York County's by-election in October 1868, J. L. Pickard, a well-known antiConfederate, was elected, replacing Charles Fisher, a Confederate appointed to the bench; in Northumberland, R. L. Hutchinson, another antiConfederate, was elected in December 1868.[16] New Brunswick did not look promising.

Nor was the Intercolonial Railway helping very much. John Bolton, MP for Charlotte, roundly asserted in 1869 that if Confederation had been offered to New Brunswick with the North Shore route attached, it would not have been accepted. He was not the only New Brunswick MP who ascribed the government's insistence on the North Shore route to the political exigencies of Sir George Etienne Cartier.[17] The absurdity of the route recalled to W. H. Chipman, MP for Kings, N.S., the story of the volunteer officer who, practising war manoeuvres in the cabbage garden, tumbled backwards into the cellar. His wife came to get him out; the would-be officer said, "Go away with you, woman, what do you know about war?" Richard Cartwright, still a Conservative at that time, proposed a clever amendment that deplored all discussion about the Intercolonial route, adding that it would only prejudice Canadian credit at home and abroad. This carried one hundred and fourteen to twenty-eight, and the North Shore route stood.[18]

Better terms for Nova Scotia did not pass easily either. Hon. E. B. Wood, treasurer of Ontario, 1867-71, MP for Brant South, boldly asserted that since Ontario paid 60 per cent of the dominion revenue, there was no reason to give in to Nova Scotia. Per capita Ontario paid in twenty-seven cents to the dominion pot and got back six cents; Quebec paid in nine cents and got back six cents; but Nova Scotia, even before better terms, put in five and a half cents and took out eighteen cents, and New Brunswick was much the same. Nova Scotia was doing beautifully as she was. Luther Holton objected strongly to changing the terms of Confederation. "Our Constitution was of the nature of a compact between the Provinces, and could only be violated, disturbed, changed or modified with the consent of all the contracting parties."[19] Better terms did get through the House of Commons by ninety-six to fifty-seven, that is, the government majority plus the Nova Scotians, none of whom had the hardihood to oppose better terms for their own province.

Then, slowly, by fits and starts, things began to get better. The government felt strongly enough to reimpose the flour tariff in 1870; it had Tupper's new name attached to it, "the National Policy," the *quid pro quo* for the tariff on flour being a tariff on coal.[20] Popular disapproval of the 1870 tariff was widespread, but the government backed off only to the tune of 5 per cent in 1871. Nova Scotia had begun to respond. They were still bitter at having been forced into Confederation; but when Tupper entered the cabinet in June 1870, he won his by-election by acclamation. Four months later Colchester was carried by an antiConfederate now willing to support the Ottawa government. By 1871, with the Washington Treaty negotiated by Macdonald, Nova Scotians seemed to think there might be some good in Confederation after all.[21]

What was making the change? Prosperity was, something A. T. Galt, now in 1871 an Independent, was happy to congratulate the government upon.[22] The gradual education in national issues and national questions was another. Political education, not to say ductility, of national parties was a significant part of the process of education. The Liberals had made some effort to establish links with their Nova Scotian and New Brunswick brethren. Alexander Mackenzie visited the Maritimes in the summer of 1870, taking up an acquaintance with A. G. Jones, MP for Halifax, the ablest of the Nova Scotian Liberal contingent in Ottawa. Mackenzie even promised to support the local government in their argument with Ottawa over the provincial building that Ottawa claimed was theirs and which the local government refused to give up. (That was settled by negotiation in 1872) During the session of 1871 in Ottawa, opposition MP's from Ontario made definite efforts to help ameliorate Nova Scotian bitterness. The local government still remained recalcitrant; not the least of their actions was to disenfranchise, in 1871, all dominion employees from voting in provincial elections. As Wilkins, the Nova Scotia attorney-general delicately put it, "every person who had the smell of Canada upon them."

This was aimed especially at the provincial election to take place in May 1871. In fact, it meant that the provincial governments were no longer so confident that antiConfederation was as much use as it had once been. There was feverishness in the shrill call to arms of the *Morning Chronicle* the day after dissolution was announced: the antiConfederates in Nova Scotia were becoming too faint hearted! What was needed was straight, "out and out" antiConfederation:

> No surrender; let each man stick to his post.... We have gained much by stubborn and unyielding resistance to Canada.... This is no time to speak of "harmony."[23]

But that did not stop the change. A dozen or more Confederates were elected provincially, and in the federal election the following year, Conservatives won ten of twenty-one seats in Nova Scotia, seven of sixteen in New Brunswick. This gain could not be held in the face of the Pacific Scandal, and in 1874 the Conservatives took only three and five respectively. By that time the Mackenzie government was trying its hand at making political accommodation work and, in the process, was finding that the Liberal Nova Scotians provided it with rather green cabinet timber.

Maritimers discovered that central Canadian manufactured goods were in many cases cheaper than American and just as good. Between 1867 and 1874 the central Canadians also discovered there was a Maritime market. By the latter date, over half the agricultural tools used in the Maritimes came from Ontario or Quebec. Manufacturers of heavy equipment, like reapers, had also succeeded in driving the Americans out of the Maritime market, a process that started as early as 1871, the machines arriving by the Gulf of St. Lawrence ports or Portland, Maine. Canadian manufacturers were underselling the Americans by about 25 per cent. A Guelph manufacturer of woollen knit goods said that in fact Confederation had given him the Maritime market. Just as this evidence was being taken by the Mills Committee in 1876, the Intercolonial Railway was being finished. The first through train from Halifax to Quebec left Halifax on 5 July 1876. In 1879 Nova Scotia adopted the National Policy with such enthusiasm, so rapidly did capital and human resources move from staple industries, that between 1880 and 1890 Nova Scotian industry grew more proportionately than Ontario or Quebec.[24]

By the end of the 1880's the problems of Nova Scotia, New Brunswick, and perhaps to a degree even Prince Edward Island, were of quite a different order. The National Policy was a success if judged by the milltowns of St. Stephen or Marysville, New Brunswick, the industrial towns of Amherst, Truro, and New Glasgow in Nova Scotia. The railway policy of the Dominion had had considerable effects. It was noticeable that the Conservative vote tended to follow the dominion railway lines. Railways made good politics; when he was minister of railways, Macdonald had to tell one anxious Nova Scotian MP that the railway the MP was proposing would not carry enough traffic to justify construction. The MP replied with some heat, "Traffic be damned! I wanted the road to carry me back to Parliament."[25]

Nearly all the government railways were in eastern Nova Scotia. If a line were drawn from Moncton to Halifax, east of the line would be found all but one of Nova Scotia's ten senators and the two members of the federal cabinet; and all the railways east of that line were owned and operated by the Dominion and had lower rates. The railways west of the line were company railways. So complained W. C. Bill, the Conservative candidate who lost Kings to Frederick Borden in 1891.[26] The Dominion owned and ran not only the Intercolonial, but the eastern extension, Pictou to the Strait of Canso, and it contracted and built the railway from the Strait of Canso to Sydney. One of Macdonald's very last notes as minister of railways was about a report on the hard-pan problem on the Cape Breton railway.[27]

Not the least part of this process of political accommodation was patronage, in all its many variations. From the Macdonald and the Thompson Papers there emerges the picture of an extensive network of patronage, well defined and highly developed. So much so that one has the impression that Antigonish County, for example, lived by its wharves, breakwaters, and railways. Dominion wharfmasters, Intercolonial railway employees, customs collectors, lighthouse keepers, and postmasters formed part of a well-ramified system of dominion patronage, organization, and administration.

Of all the provinces of Canada, the Maritimes seem to have developed the arts of patronage in the most sincere, unblushing, naked enthusiasm. Nova Scotia had had a fair running start in the practice of it, ever since 1749. There is an interesting perspective about this from J. S. D. Thompson in 1888. Bishop McDonald of St. John's, Newfoundland, was to be in Halifax, and Thompson was asked by Sir John Macdonald and Sir Charles Tupper to write to T. E. Kenny, a Catholic MP in Halifax, to get Kenny to interview the bishop about Newfoundland entering Confederation. Thompson sketched out the advantages of Confederation for Newfoundland and presented them to Kenny as useful arguments to the bishop. What Thompson said was very suggestive of the basis of accommodation that had been arrived at in the Maritime provinces over the previous twenty years. There was, said Thompson, dominion government spending on railways; Newfoundland's resources had been exhausted by 1888 in an ineffective attempt to complete the transNewfoundland railway. Besides railways there were lighthouses, post offices, even militia appropriations. Indeed, said Thompson to Kenny, look at the general position of the smaller provinces in Canada:

> The fear of the smaller provinces in 1867 was that they would be overpowered and disregarded by the larger ones, [but] the result has been that the smaller provinces have obtained a far larger share of consideration (including expen-

diture) than the larger [provinces], and have more influence than could be claimed on account either of territorial extent or population. The fact that they have always been more troublesome than the larger ones is perhaps one of the reasons.[28]

These arrangements were well known by the late 1880's. Newfoundland's revived interest in Confederation was some kind of a benchmark of the success of Confederation in the three other Atlantic provinces.

The sequence of events in Maritime patronage went like this. A Conservative worthy in, let us say, Pictou County, thought X should have the job of collector of customs in Pugwash. He would recommend X to C. H. Tupper, the Conservative MP, who would in turn mention it to the responsible minister, Mackenzie Bowell. It could go the other way around, that Bowell would ask the Conservative MP in whose riding the vacancy occurred, whom he would recommend. If there were no Conservative MP for the constituency, then the recently defeated Conservative candidate would be approached. As a rule the minister did not need to make too many enquiries, for a cloud of applications would descend upon him the moment the post was known to be open. Indeed, the body of the newly deceased incumbent of the office would be still warm when the letters would be off to Ottawa. With judges, the letters would often arrive before the judge was dead. If Judge Y was very ill, a candidate would write to Sir John Thompson: "Judge Y's illness is almost certainly mortal," the candidate would add cheerfully, "and please consider me a candidate."

Thompson's own constituents in Antigonish County ate and drank patronage. The long winters and the halcyon summers seemed only to nourish that delightful preoccupation. Thompson himself was not proud of this unpleasant and important side of his work as MP for Antigonish. His constituency seemed to him greedy, rapacious, impatient, unforgiving, with alarmingly tenacious Scotch memories that kept past rights (and wrongs) clearly in the world of present reality. "I revolt against Antigonish the more I think of it," Thompson grumbled to his wife Annie in 1887.[29]

One day in October 1886, Archie A. McGillivray, an Antigonish constituent, vain, brash and greedy, heard that the Intercolonial Railway stationmaster at Antigonish town had died. "May his soul rest in peace," said Archie piously, "I hereby apply for the situation ... and finding that this situation would suit me, I demand it. All I want from you is a decided answer." Thompson said no, in a letter written, Archie claimed, "in that cool faraway tone." It made Archie furious. He railed against Thompson's rank ingratitude for all that Archie had done for him over the years in Antigonish County; Thompson's "dark, ungrateful heart" would rue the day that he refused the modest exigencies of Archie A. McGillivray.[30]

B. F. Power, another constituent with more brains and more clout than Archie, preferred telegrams. The Antigonish stationmaster died on 11 October

1886; B. F. Power reminded Thompson that very day that the stationmaster was, happily or unhappily, very dead and that B. F. Power's brother Henry was quite available. When the new stationmaster was appointed, it was neither Archie McGillivray nor Power's brother, but D. H. McDonald, promoted from being stationmaster at Tracadie, eighteen miles eastward along the line. B. F. Power kept a watchful eye on D. H. McDonald, however, and two months later came the following telegram:

> If stationmaster here be dismissed for drunkenness you have a right to confer that office on me. I pay all telegrams answer before sixteenth as I will be away state salary.

That was certainly brash enough. Thompson did not ignore it, however; he telegraphed his cousin, David Pottinger, chief superintendent of the Intercolonial Railway at Moncton (1879-92) for information. The pay, said Pottinger, was forty dollars a month; but he added that D. H. McDonald was not in any trouble so far as Pottinger knew.[31] But McDonald was in trouble, and the chief superintendent soon found out.

The Intercolonial Railway rules about drinking by employees were strict and specific. In the rule book of 22 November 1886, Rule No. 59 was that only men of known careful and sober habits were to be employed in the movement of trains. Rule No. 60 was even more specific: any employee drunk on *or* off duty would not be kept on the Intercolonial Railway service.[32] What had actually happened to D. H. McDonald is not altogether clear—it seldom is on such occasions. On the nights of 6 and 7 December he and some friends had something of a party, which included McDonald getting pitched out of a sleigh into an adjacent snowbank, followed by some good-natured but very drunken wrestling in the snowdrifts in front of Antigonish's main hotel. This was not drunkenness, McDonald told Thompson, but only animal energy; all he had had to drink was whisky and milk, taken for strictly medicinal purposes. Whatever McDonald's explanations, he was dismissed for drunkenness. B. F. Power was given the position, even though he could not yet use the telegraph key and would have to learn. It was a clear patronage appointment, and David Pottinger did not altogether relish it. "The usual and proper course," he wrote to his cousin, "would be to promote some experienced person to a station like this, but I suppose we can't."[33]

It can be added that it was also virtually impossible to appoint a man from outside the county to such a position. A Pictou County man, however competent, might even be, *horribile dictu,* a Protestant; in any case being from outside the county, he could not be given an important patronage preferment in Antigonish. The reverse would also be true in Pictou County.

Thompson was less susceptible to patronage pressures outside his own constituency. In his own department, Justice, he preferred to encourage the *esprit de corps* of the civil service. The warden of Dorchester Penitentiary, New Brunswick, as indeed other wardens, had been a patronage appointment when Thompson became minister of justice in 1885. The incumbent in Dorchester, Warden Botsford, was the brother of Senator Amos Botsford (1804-94). Warden Botsford died in April 1887. Within twenty-four hours Thompson had fifteen telegrams about four possible candidates, plus a letter from Sir Charles Tupper. Senator Botsford had his own ideas who should replace his dead brother. The director of penitentiaries, J. G. Moylan, also had a candidate in mind.

Thompson cut all that off. He promoted the deputy-warden, J. B. Forster. Politely, firmly, he told an irate Conservative in Dorchester that promotion of good men to the highest positions in the service was the stuff of which a good service was made. "If these officers find the higher positions disposed of according to political claims, some political advantage may result but the Service will soon be in a useless condition."[34]

Thompson was also concerned to redress the imbalance he observed in Nova Scotian appointments in the inside service. Across the whole inside service, he told Macdonald, Nova Scotia's share of the five hundred or so appointments should have been seventy; she had in 1887 only twenty-six. No Nova Scotian was deputy-minister, none was chief clerk. This argued the more cogently why Thompson should have a free hand in the choice of his deputy-minister, consequent upon the appointment of his former deputy, J. W. Burbidge, to the Exchequer Court of Canada.

> My choice would however be very limited as I could not afford to take a man about whose fitness I could entertain a doubt and I am not at all sanguine that any of the best men would accept. If not I should want to look to Ontario. New Brunswick has far more than her share now.[35]

Tilley and Costigan had clearly been doing their work! Thompson, after inviting Robert Borden of Halifax (who was tempted but said no), appointed Robert Sedgwick of Halifax.

Many of the little Maritime towns, and doubtless others in Quebec, Ontario, and elsewhere, presented curious mixtures of dominion-provincial relations, some seldom explored, or not even known. It was a process of accommodation at its most basic. In Antigonish town, by 1887, there was a small dominion public building, housing the customs office and the post office, but it had room for more than these. It so happened that the postmaster of Antigonish was also the caretaker of the building; besides these offices, he was also sheriff of Antigonish County. The county found the space convenient; it was also cheap since it cost nothing. Thus were accommodated county officials, the registrar of deeds, registrar of probate, and others. The registrar of probate was also a magistrate and did his magistrate's business there, rather to the discomfiture of the other occupants of the building. Since the Municipality of Antigonish County contributed nothing to the building, neither to cost nor upkeep, should not the situation be regularized in some way? It seemed so to Thompson. There was surely no objection, he suggested to Sir Hector Langevin, the minister of public works, to housing municipal officers in dominion public buildings, but they ought to have some regular system of tenure. Otherwise, there would be all kinds of similar demands on dominion public buildings elsewhere.

There was an odd consequence to this. The town of Antigonish discovered that much the best place to hang the town's fire bell was on that dominion building, on the northeast corner. Thompson thought that would do no harm. But the postmaster-caretaker-sheriff thought differently. He objected; he said that the process of hanging that fire bell there on that northeast corner would ruin, positively ruin, his flower garden! It took the bishop and a peremptory telegram from Thompson to get the fire bell placed where the town wanted it.[36]

Such was the infinitude of questions, little and big, that filled so much of the life of Thompson, the conscientious administrator.

At election time the story is more familiar, noticeable from the beginning: the importing of campaign funds from central Canada. Both Nova Scotia and New Brunswick raised roughly half of their own campaign funds, but they seemed to expect, and to get, assistance from outside. This seems to have been especially the case in 1891, where it was known that American money had been imported into both provinces by the Liberals. Both Thompson and young C. H. Tupper found Nova Scotians very canny with their own money; the Halifax merchants and manufacturers never seemed enthusiastic when the time came to dig into their pockets. Senators, who did not have to fight any elections at all, were not very responsive in shelling out money for MP's who did.

In 1891 Maritime money seems to have been channelled, some of it at least, through John Haggart, the postmaster general from Ontario. There were some frank pleas. L. deV. Chipman in Kentville, trying to help W. C. Bill defeat Frederick Borden in Kings County, wrote anxiously that they had raised $1,500 in the Annapolis valley, had got $1,000 more (presumably from Ottawa), but needed a further $2,000. Chipman promised to raise this extra $2,000 himself, provided he were promised the vacant Nova Scotia seat in the senate. Thompson's response was not helpful. F. W. Borden won by 161 votes; Chipman claimed afterward that had Thompson come through with the promise of the senate seat, W. C. Bill would have won by fifty to one hundred votes. Chipman never did get a seat in the Senate.[37] Joseph Pope telegraphed Thompson from Kingston that if more ammunition were needed in Nova Scotia, Thompson could draw up to $2,500 from W. A. Allan of Ottawa. Sir John Macdonald suggested leaving Cumberland to its own devices (where Dickey, Sir Charles Tupper's successor, seemed a certainty) and sending $500 to John McDonald in Victoria, Cape Breton (who won), and $500 to J. N. Freeman in Queens (who did not).[38]

The result of the federal election in 1891 in Nova Scotia surprised everyone, Liberals and Conservatives alike. Thompson won Antigonish by 227 votes, a much bigger majority than either 1885 or 1887. In the province as a whole, the Conservatives took sixteen of twenty-one seats compared to fourteen seats in 1887. In New Brunswick, they took thirteen of sixteen seats. In both provinces it was the best Sir John A. Macdonald's Conservative government had ever done. Even Prince Edward Island, which had given its six seats to the Liberals in 1874 and in 1887, had elected two Conservatives. Indeed, twenty-one seats of the Macdonald government's twenty-seven-seat majority, coming into the new session of 1891, were created by New Brunswick and Nova Scotia. No wonder Sir Richard Cartwright was cross; the Macdonald government, he said, was nothing but a patchwork "made up of the ragged remnants from half a dozen minor provinces, the great majority of whom do not even pretend to be actuated by any principle save ... a good slice of booty."[39] There was some truth in that. The ragged remnants were New Brunswick and Nova Scotia, joined with Manitoba, British Columbia, and the Northwest Territories. The five together had presented a thirty-four-seat majority to help the Conservative government. There was not a little irony in the fact that by 1891 the shreds and patches of Confederation had won their own victory over the central Canadians who had run things so much their own way only twenty years before.

It was not the end of antiConfederation in the Maritimes or the West. That would come again, like delirium, when the patient ran a fever from economic illness. But it was clear that there were many and widely ramified changes. Even W. S. Fielding, the premier of Nova Scotia, who could not attend a Dominion Day dinner in London in 1892 for fear of hearing speeches that he would have had publicly to disagree with, joined Laurier in Ottawa in 1896. By that time, the process of national accommodation by both political parties was well under way. Perhaps that function, that achievement, has been underestimated.

It is obvious that some of this can be set down in terms of "incentive systems," an expression dear to political scientists. Even mere historians can realize that the party organization by 1888 provided forms of satisfaction familiar enough; power, a sense of national identity, prestige, to say nothing of the ordinary delights of a regular, if modest, salary. In all of this party organizations were shaped by individuals and forces that often went in ways tangential to the apparent or formal purposes of party organization. As Antigonish County showed Thompson, Pictou showed C. H. Tupper, and Kings County, New Brunswick, revealed to G. E. Foster to say nothing of the other forty or so Maritime MP's, failure to meet constituency exigencies frequently led to what sociologists sometimes call intraorganizational conflict.[40] As E. R. Black, a political scientist, put it, "Particular configurations of centripetal and centrifugal forces within the federation may still be expected to be closely related to the vitality of individual concepts."[41] One may prefer André Siegfried:

Dans la vide voulu des programmes, les questions d'intérêts matériels, de travaux publics à exécuter prennent vraiment une place trep importante. Il y a certes d'autres problèmes plus brûlants; on y pense toujours, mais les grands chefs voudraient qu'on n'en parlât jamais ... ce n'est pas le parti qui est au service de l'idée, mais bien l'idée qui est au service du parti.[a] [42]

Notes

1. Campbell to Macdonald, 27 July 1873, cited in L. H. Thomas, *The Struggle for Responsible Government in the North-West Territories, 1870-1897* (Toronto, 1956), p. 61.

2. Canada, Senate, *Debates, 1867-1868,* 26 March 1868 (Ottawa, 1968), p. 145.

3. Cited in Gordon Blake, *Customs Administration in Canada* (Toronto, 1957), p. 70.

4. Canada, House of Commons, *Debates, 1867-1968,* 10 December 1867 (Ottawa, 1967), p. 231.

5. Ibid., 16 December 1867, pp. 292-93.

6. Ibid., 30 April 1868, p. 598.

7. Ibid., 16 December 1867, p. 287.

8. Ibid., 20 December 1867, p. 335.

9. Ibid., p. 337.

10. Ibid., p. 338.

11. Senate, *Debates, 1867-1868,* 6 December 1867, pp. 79-80.

12. House of Commons, *Debates, 1867-1868,* 19 March 1868, p. 372. The tariff on flour was eventually taken off late in the session, ibid., 18 May 1868, pp. 731-33. Macdonald wrote the archbishop of Halifax to tell him about the removal of the duty on flour, corn, and corn meal. Joseph Pope, *Correspondence of Sir John Macdonald* (Toronto, 1921), p. 68, Macdonald to Connolly, 1 June 1868. The tariff on flour was reimposed in 1870.

13. Senate, *Debates, 1867-1868,* 23 March 1868, p. 130.

14. Ibid., 15 May 1868, p. 321: 16 May 1868, p. 328.

15. Ibid., *Debates, 1869* (Ottawa, 1975), 16 April 1869, p. 14; 26 April 1869, pp. 36-37, 1 June 1869; p. 247-48; 4 June 1869, p. 277.

16. Noted by Senator Wilmot, Ibid., 4 June 1869, p. 273.

17. House of Commons, *Debates, 1869,* (Ottawa, 1975), 17 May 1869, p. 348.

18. Ibid., 17 May 1869, p. 365.

---

[a] In the vacuum intended by the programs, questions of material interests and of public works to be carried out truly take on excessive importance. Of course, there are other more burning issues that people constantly have on their minds. The leaders, however, wanted no one to speak about them...it isn't that the party serves the idea but rather that the idea serves the party.

19. Ibid., 12 June 1869, p. 756; 16 June 1869, p. 806.

20. Ibid., 14 May 1869, p. 335, for the original locus of the phrase.

21. O. J. McDiarmid, *Commercial Policy in the Canadian Economy* (Cambridge, 1946), p. 139; K. G. Pryke, *Nova Scotia and Confederation, 1864-74* (Toronto, 1979), pp. 114-15, 136.

22. Library of Parliament, *Scrapbook Debates 1871,* 10 March 1871.

23. Nova Scotia, Assembly, *Debates 1871,* p. 273; Halifax *Morning Chronicle,* 18 April 1871. This editorial was used by the Conservative Montreal *Gazette* to show the folly of the conciliatory courses followed by the Ontario Liberals (22 April 1871).

24. The Report of the Mills Committee is in Canada, House of Commons, *Journals,* 1876, Appendix 3; T. W. Acheson, "The National Policy and the Industrialization of the Maritimers, 1880-1910." *Acadiensis* 1, no. 2 (Spring 1972): 3.

25. J. S. Willison, "Reminiscences, Political and Otherwise," *Canadian Magazine* 52, no. 6 (April 1919): 1028.

26. W. C. Bill to Thompson, Macdonald and Tupper, 6 April 1891, confidential, J. S. D. Thompson Papers (hereafter JSDT), vol. 126.

27. Macdonald to Thompson, 18 May 1891, ibid., vol. 128. The issue concerned the underestimate by contractors—good Conservatives—of the cost of excavation along a section of the Cape Breton Railway. Hard-pan is firm heavy clay and gravel compressed into a rocklike consistency.

28. Thompson to T. E. Kenny, 22 February 1888, private and confidential, ibid., vol. 233.

29. Thompson to Annie, 22 September 1887, ibid., vol. 290.

30. McGillivray to Thompson, 18 October 1886, ibid., vol. 45; 13 November 1886, ibid., vol. 46.

31. Power to Thompson, 9 December 1886, telegram, ibid., vol. 47; Pottinger to Thompson, 11 December 1886, telegram.

32. D. H. McDonald to Thompson, 17 January 1887, ibid., vol. 48. A condensed version of the Antigonish story is in P. B. Waite, *The Man from Halifax: Sir John Thompson, Prime Minister* (Toronto, 1985), pp. 176-77.

33. Pottinger to Thompson, n.d., endorsed on Thompson to Pottinger, 29 May 1887, private, ibid., vol. 52.

34. Thompson to Michaud, 15 April 1887, ibid., vol. 229; vol. 52 contains the incoming correspondence on this question.

35. Thompson to Macdonald, 21 September 1887, Macdonald Papers, vol. 273.

36. Thompson to Langevin, 23 August 1888, private; JSDT, vol. 235; vol. 76, Whidden to Thompson, 24 October 1888, telegram; same, 25 October 1888, telegram.

37. L. deV. Chipman to Thompson n.d., private and confidential, ibid., vol. 124; 19 March 1891, private, ibid., vol. 125.

38. Pope to Thompson, 1 March 1891, telegram, ibid., vol. 124.

39. Toronto *Globe,* 9 March 1891.

40. These concepts are outlined in Peter Clark and J. Q. Wilson, "Incentive systems," *Administrative Studies Quarterly* 6 (1961): 129-66.

41. E. R. Black, *Divided loyalties: Canadian Concepts of Federalism* (Montreal, 1975), p. 222.

42. André Siegfried, *Le Canada, les deux races: problèmes politiques contemporains* (Paris, 1906), pp. 180, 182. The references in the F. H. Underhill edition (Toronto, 1966) are on pp. 113, 114.

CHAPTER
2 LOUIS RIEL

There is no more controversial figure in Canadian history than Louis "David" Riel, who twice led his *Métis* followers in armed resistance against the federal government. Riel has been both lauded and vilified, seen by some as a heroic figure defending a downtrodden people and by others as a traitor who richly deserved his fate. One of the unusual aspects of the large historical literature which exists on this subject is its wide variety of broad interpretative contexts. Thus the Riel agitations can be seen as both resulting from and significantly contributing to divisions between French and English Canada. Alternatively, they may be viewed as the result of a clash between civilization and the frontier. Or they may be placed within the context of regional discontent, the western hinterland protesting against real or prospective exploitation by the east.

The readings which are reprinted in this unit focus on the role of individual participants in the 1885 crisis. The first selection is by Thomas Flanagan who has written widely on Riel. In this reading, a chapter from his book *Riel and the Rebellion: 1885 Reconsidered*, Flanagan places the responsibility for the North West Rebellion on the shoulders of Riel himself. Arguing that the grievances of the *Métis* had been sufficiently remedied, that they could no longer constitute the cause of an armed uprising, Flanagan looks for the answer in Riel's personal—and mistaken—belief that the *Métis* owned the North West by virtue of aboriginal title. This was entirely contrary to Ottawa's position.

In the second reading, D.N. Sprague rejects the view that the Canadian government had moved to remedy *Métis* grievances and presents the provocative thesis that the 1885 uprising was consciously and deliberately provoked by the Canadian prime minister, Sir John A. Macdonald. In his biography of Macdonald, Donald Creighton had linked the 1885 uprising with the successful completion of the Canadian Pacific Railway. The practical demonstration of the railway's usefulness in transporting troops to the North West, so the argument ran, made it possible for the government once again to approach Parliament with a request for further subsidies. Sprague takes this linkage much further, suggesting that circumstantial evidence supports the view that by late August 1884, Macdonald preferred an "angry Riel" and to that end he thereafter followed a policy of "provocative inaction" deliberately designed to bring about an "exploitable crisis"—all in aid of the Canadian Pacific Railway.

Suggestions for Further Reading

Beal, Bob, and Rod Macleod, *Prairie Fire: The 1885 North-West Rebellion*. Edmonton: Hurtig Publishers, 1984.

Creighton, D.G., *John A. Macdonald: The Old Chieftain*. Toronto: Macmillan, 1955.

Ens, Gerhard, "Dispossession or Adaptation: Migration and Persistence of the Red River Métis, 1835-1890," CHA *Historical Papers*, 1988, 120-144.

Flanagan, Thomas, *Louis 'David' Riel: 'Prophet of the New World'*. Toronto: University of Toronto Press, 1979.

_____, "Métis Land Claims at St. Laurent: Old Arguments and New Evidence," *Prairie Forum*, XII, no. 2 (1987), 245-255.

Martel, Gilles, *Le messianisme de Louis Riel*. Waterloo: Wilfrid Laurier University Press, 1984.

Miller, J.R., "From Riel to the Métis," *Canadian Historical Review*, LXIX, no. 1 (March 1988), 1-20.

Morton, W.L., ed., *Alexander Begg's Red River Journal and Other Papers Relative to the Red River Resistance of 1869-70*. Toronto: The Champlain Society, 1956.

Owram, Douglas, "The Myth of Louis Riel," *Canadian Historical Review*, LXIII, no. 3 (September 1982), 315-336.

Silver, A.I., "Ontario's Alleged Fanaticism in the Riel Affair," *Canadian Historical Review*, LXIX, no. 1 (March 1988), 21-50.

Stanley, G.F.G., *The Birth of Western Canada: A History of the Riel Rebellions*. Toronto: University of Toronto Press, 1961.

_____, *Louis Riel*. Toronto: Ryerson Press, 1963.

ABORIGINAL TITLE

Thomas Flanagan

Why then did the North-West Rebellion occur at all, if the objective grievances of the *Métis* were remedied by the government? In this connection, it must be remembered that many other factors contributed to the *Métis'* sense of alienation. They were still bitter over the events in Manitoba, which, in spite of the seeming success of the movement of 1869-70, had left them a marginal minority in their own homeland. Having moved farther west to escape this status, they could see themselves once again faced with being outnumbered by white settlers. Another long-range consideration was the decline of the *Métis* economy. The buffalo withdrew from the Canadian prairies during the 1870s and vanished altogether after 1878, adversely affecting numerous trades in which the *Métis* had been prominent: buffalo hunting, trading with the Indians for pemmican and

From *Riel and the Rebellion: 1885 Reconsidered* (Saskatoon: Western Producer Prairie Books), 1983, 75-100, 161-163. Reprinted by permission of Douglas & McIntyre Ltd.

robes, and transporting these goods to market. The *Métis* cart trains and boat brigades also suffered from the advent of railways and steamboats in the Canadian West. Deprived of much of the income from traditional occupations, the *Métis* had to rely more on agriculture. As they began to make this transition, they were struck, as were all western farmers, by the economic depression and fall in grain prices which began in 1883. For the *Métis* of St. Laurent, this economic malaise was aggravated by the decision to build the Canadian Pacific Railway along the southern route through Regina instead of along the northern route through Prince Albert. The *Métis* lost out on the jobs and contracts that would have been created by a construction boom in northern Saskatchewan.

All these factors help to explain the prevailing mood in St. Laurent, yet none really accounts for the outbreak of the Rebellion; for similar factors were equally at work in other *Métis* settlements which did not turn to violence. The unique fact about St. Laurent was the presence of Louis Riel. His great prestige made him a prism through which all information from the outside world was refracted to the *Métis*. His interpretation of the government's concessions made them seem like provocations. Any explanation of why the rising occurred must focus on Riel. What motivated him to take up arms? Such questions can never be answered with total certainty, but one can make a reasonable estimation of the forces at work in his mind at this time.

First was Riel's brooding resentment over the aftermath of 1869-70. Thinking himself the natural leader of his people, he had expected a quick amnesty followed by a successful career in politics. Instead he received exile, loss of his Commons seat, and penniless obscurity. His own misfortunes paralleled those of the *Métis* as they were submerged in Manitoba politics and went into voluntary emigration. Riel's bitterness lay behind the efforts he would make in the winter of 1884-85 to obtain a cash payment from the federal government. In his mind, this was fair compensation for the wrongs he had suffered. The failure of these efforts to show any tangible result must have strengthened his readiness to undertake extreme measures.

A second factor was Riel's religious "mission." As I have shown at length in *Louis "David" Riel: "Prophet of the New World,"* he believed himself to be a divinely inspired prophet, even after his "cure" in the insane asylums of Quebec. His mission of religious reform was only in abeyance, awaiting a signal from God to be made public. The longer he stayed with the *Métis,* the more ostentatious became Riel's piety. He began to argue with the Oblate missionaries over points of politics and theology, until the exasperated priests threatened him with excommunication. The notebook of prayers he kept over the winter of 1884-85 shows an ascending curve of spiritual confidence culminating in readiness for action. Riel launched the Rebellion convinced it was the occasion to reveal his new religion to the world. That is why he began his first major speech to the *Métis* with the words, "Rome has fallen."

In spite of this religious dimension, Riel's rising was a political phenomenon whose causes must also be sought at the political level. If the *Métis* grievances over river lots and land scrip do not furnish an adequate explanation, more insight can be found through examining Riel's views on aboriginal rights. For reasons explained below, he held that the *Métis* were the true owners of the North-West; that their entry into Confederation had been conditional upon fulfillment of the Manitoba "treaty"; and that they were legally and morally free to secede from Canada since (in his view) the "treaty" had not been kept by Canada. In this sweeping perspective, the grievances of river lots and scrip were petty complaints, useful in mobilizing local support but peripheral to the real issues. Study of the course of the agitation, from July 1884, when Riel arrived at St. Laurent, to February 1885, the eve of the Rebellion, demonstrates that his strategy was built upon his radical view of aboriginal rights. Preexisting local grievances were only pawns in a complex series of maneuvers aimed at vindicating *Métis* ownership of the North-West as a whole. To understand this is to explain the apparent paradox that the *Métis* launched an insurrection immediately after the government granted their demands. Under Riel's leadership, they were fighting for stakes which far transcended river lots and scrip. They may have only dimly perceived what the real goals were, but these are plain enough in Riel's writings.

Conflicting Views of Aboriginal Rights

Riel's political views can only be appreciated against the background of the events of 1869-70 and their aftermath. In his interpretation of these events he was quite different from official circles in Ottawa or London. To see the magnitude of this difference, we must first sketch the official view. Here, a word of caution is required. What I call the "official view" was not articulated until the *St. Catherine's Milling Case,* decided in 1889. But the theory of aboriginal rights developed in this case was, I believe, implicit in the practice of the previous decades, including the acquisition of Rupert's Land by Canada and subsequent dealings with Indians and half-breeds in that territory. Naturally, there is room for debate over the exact contours of an implicit, unarticulated view.

To the rulers of Britain and Canada as well as to the proprietors of the Hudson's Bay Company, the acquisition by Canada of Rupert's Land and the Northwestern Territories was a complicated real estate conveyance. In return for compensation from Canada, the Company surrendered its land to the Crown, which in turn passed it to Canada by Act of Parliament and Royal Proclamation. The transaction was founded on the property rights conferred on the Company by the royal charter of 1670:

> ... the sole trade and commerce of all those seas, straights, bays, rivers, creeks
> and sounds in whatsoever latitude they shall be that lie within the entrance of

the straights commonly called Hudson's Straights together with all the lands and territories upon the countries, coasts, and confines of the seas, bays, lakes, rivers, creeks, and sounds aforesaid that are not already actually possessed by or granted to any of our subjects or possessed by the subjects of any other Christian prince or state.[1]

It is true that Canada had accepted the Company's ownership rights only reluctantly and after years of protest, putting forward the different theory that most of Rupert's Land ought to belong to Canada because of the explorations undertaken from New France. But the Colonial Office refused any measures that might diminish the Company's rights, and in the end the sale went through on the assumption that the Company was the rightful owner of this immense territory.

When the *Métis* of Red River, who had never been consulted about the sale, showed signs of resistance, the Canadian government refused to take possession, much as a purchaser might refuse to take possession of a house which had undergone damage in the period between signing of contract and date of transfer. The Imperial government doubted the legality of Canada's position but did not force the issue. Canada invited the inhabitants of Red River to send a delegation to Ottawa to make their concerns known. Having discussed matters with the three delegates (Father N.-J. Ritchot, Alfred Scott, John Black), the Canadian government drafted the Manitoba Act to respond to the desires of Red River: provincial status, responsible government, official bilingualism, protection of customary land rights, etc. Importantly, the Manitoba Act was a unilateral action of the Canadian Parliament, not a treaty between independent partners (although it was probably *ultra vires* of the Canadian Parliament and had later to be confirmed by Imperial statute). Payment for Rupert's Land was made in London after the Company delivered the Deed of Surrender to the Colonial Office; and the Imperial government, by order-in-council of 23 June 1870, annexed Rupert's Land to Canada, effective 15 July.

It was always assumed by both governments that aboriginal rights of the Indians would be respected. Indeed section 14 of the order-in-council of 23 June 1870 specified that "any claims of Indians to compensation for lands required for purposes of settlement shall be disposed of by the Canadian Government in communication with the Imperial Government."[2] The *Métis* were not explicitly mentioned, but the Canadian government had already recognized their aboriginal rights in the Manitoba Act.

Native title was not seen as sovereignty in the European sense. Only a state could claim sovereignty, and the North American Indian tribes had never been organized as states. Hence the validity of claims to sovereignty made by European states on the basis of discovery, settlement, and conquest. Nor was Indian title understood as ownership in fee simple, for the nomadic tribes of North America had never marked off plots of land in a way compatible with

European notions of private property. Indian title was interpreted as an encumbrance upon the underlying title to the land held by the sovereign. Indians had a real and enforceable right to support themselves on this land as they had from time immemorial. This right could be surrendered only to the sovereign, not to private parties; and compensation had to be paid for surrender, according to the ancient principle of common law that there should be no expropriation without compensation.

This understanding was legally articulated in the *St. Catherine's Milling Case,* decided by the Supreme Court of Canada in 1887 and the Judicial Committee of the Privy Council in 1889. There aboriginal title was defined in the context of a dispute between the governments of Ontario and Canada over who owned the lands ceded by the Ojibway in Treaty No. 3: the Crown in right of Canada or the Crown in right of Ontario? We can ignore this aspect of the dispute to concentrate on the issue of aboriginal title. To explain this concept, the judges resorted to the concept of usufruct, which in Roman law was the right to use and enjoy the fruits of property—usually slaves or a landed estate—without actually owning it. The holder of usufructuary rights could enjoy the property undisturbed during the life of those rights, but could not sell or otherwise alienate the property. At the expiration of the usufruct, the property reverted to the owner. The Canadian and British courts, seeking to interpret aboriginal title as it had developed over the centuries, used the concept of usufruct as an analogy. They cast the sovereign in the role of owner and the natives in the role of holders of "a personal and usufructuary right"[3] to occupy the land and support themselves from its produce. This limited right stemmed from the benevolence of the sovereign, who had not yet chosen to make use of the land in other ways. It was an internal concession made by the sovereign as part of Indian policy; it was not a right to be claimed under the law of nations by Indian tribes as if they were sovereign nations.

Title, thus, was vested in the Crown. The aboriginal right to use the land was an encumbrance on that title which had to be extinguished before the Crown could alienate the land to private owners. Extinguishment required compensation, which might take the form of land reserves, money payments, educational or medical services, etc. Logically, the situation was not different from other real estate conveyances where an encumbrance existed upon a title, as from mortgage or other debt. Title had to be cleared before alienation through sale or donation was possible.

The Canadian government acted on this basis to extinguish aboriginal rights in Rupert's Land. The Indians were dealt with in the numbered treaties of the 1870s, and a land grant of 1,400,000 acres was divided among the *Métis* of Manitoba. The only anomaly concerned the *Métis* of the North-West Territories, where delay had ensued for various reasons. But on the eve of the Rebellion, the government announced that it would also deal with them, although the precise form that compensation would take was apparently still undecided. This sequence of actions should have wiped the slate clean, according to the official view. All encumbrances to title should have been removed, all aboriginal rights extinguished. Without injustice to Indian or *Métis,* the government could open the land for homesteading, make land grants to railways or colonization companies, and in general act as a landlord with a clear title.

It is crucial to appreciate the intellectual framework within which the government acted. From offer to purchase through taking possession and finally clearing title, everything was based on the validity of the Hudson's Bay Company's charter and on the contemporary understanding of aboriginal rights. The quarrel with Riel arose in large part because he had a view of the situation which diverged at fundamental points. This view was never expressed completely and systematically, but it may be put together from various writings and utterances. Since many of these statements come from the months after the Rebellion was put down, there may be some question as to whether they adequately represent Riel's earlier ideas. We must presume they do; otherwise there is not enough material to analyze Riel's thinking at the pivotal moment of the Rebellion's outbreak. Apart from this one assumption, we will try not to impose an artificial consistency upon the thoughts of a man who was not a political philosopher.

Riel explicitly denied the validity of the Hudson's Bay charter because of its monopolistic provisions. The Company's sole right to trade "unjustly deprived the Northwest of the advantages of international trade and the rest of humanity, especially neighboring peoples, of the benefit of the commercial relations with the North-West to which they were entitled."[4] The result was impoverishment and oppression of the native inhabitants, both Indians and *Métis.* Riel coined the term *haute trahison internationale*[5] to describe the situation, which we might translate into today's idiom as "a crime against humanity." The charter was void, as was any sale based upon it; for the Company could not sell what it did not own. The most Riel would admit was that the Company had an interest in the land which it had sold to Canada;[6] but that transaction did not affect the natives, who were the true owners of the land. Aboriginal rights were clearly in Riel's mind not a mere encumbrance on the title but actual ownership—not individual ownership in fee simple, perhaps, but a collective ownership by the *Métis* as a nation and by the Indians as tribes. In effect, he reversed the official view according to which the Hudson's Bay Company was the true owner of lands in which the natives possessed an interest consisting of the usufructuary right of subsistence. Riel made the natives the owners of lands in which the Company possessed the interest of being allowed to trade. They owned their land in the same way as all other nations owned their lands under the law of nations; their title was not merely a limited right of occupancy dependent on the grace of the sovereign. He stood in the tradition of *Métis* nationalism which stretched back to the conflict with the Hudson's Bay Company about the Selkirk Settlement. Traders of the Northwest Company had suggested to the *Métis* that the land was theirs, not the Company's, and the idea had persisted across the generations.

Riel had argued in a slightly different way when he established the Provisional Government on 8 December 1869. He issued a Declaration which somewhat grudgingly conceded the legitimacy of the Company's regime while remaining silent about the question of ownership:

> This Company consisting of many persons required a certain constitution. But as there was a question of commerce only their constitution was framed in reference thereto. Yet since there was at that time no government to see to the interests of a people already existing in the country, it became necessary for judicial affairs to have recourse to the officers of the Hudson's Bay Company. Thus inaugurated that species of government which, slightly modified by subsequent circumstances, ruled this country up to a recent date.

Although this government "was far from answering to the wants of the people," the *Métis* "had generously supported" it. But now the Company was abandoning its people by "subjugat[ing] it without its consent to a foreign power"; and according to the law of nations, a people abandoned by its government "is at liberty to establish any form of government it may consider suitable to its wants."[7] Thus the Provisional Government was legitimate according to the law of nations, and the Hudson's Bay Company had no right to transfer to Canada the land and people it had abandoned. Canada would have to deal with the Provisional Government if it was going to annex Rupert's Land.

Riel's original position of 1869 was that it violated that law of nations (or "international law" as we would say today) to transfer a population without seeking its consent. In 1885 he added the argument that the Company did not own Rupert's Land because its charter was void. Both arguments led to the same conclusions, that the sale to Canada was invalid until the inhabitants of Rupert's Land gave their consent, and that, living in a political vacuum, they certainly had the right to form their own government to negotiate the terms of sale on their behalf.

Riel not only sought to demonstrate the legitimacy of the Provisional Government through abstract reasoning, but also tried to show that the Provisional Government had been recognized by both Britain and Canada. He formulated the facts slightly differently on various occasions, but the main line of argument was always the same: ministers of the Canadian government had invited the insurgents to send delegates to Ottawa and had conducted negotiations with them. An amnesty had been promised by the governor general himself, both directly and through intermediaries. Thus both Canada and Britain had recognized the Provisional Government *de facto,* even if there had not been a formal exchange of ambassadors according to international protocol.[8]

The legitimacy of the Provisional Government was essential to Riel because it determined his interpretation of the Manitoba Act and of the entry of Manitoba into Confederation. His frame of reference was the law of nations (*droit des gens*), because negotiations had been carried out between independent entities, Canada and Red River. Rupert's Land had not been purchased; rather its inhabitants, acting through their government, had decided to join Canada. Union with Canada was not the result of unilateral action in Ottawa; it had required the assent of the Provisional Government, which was formally given after Father Ritchot returned from Ottawa to report on the terms offered by Canada. After the vote, Riel's "secretary of state" wrote to Canada's secretary of state to inform him that

> ... the Provisional Government and the Legislative Assembly, in the name of the people of the North-West, do accept the "Manitoba Act," and consent to enter into Confederation on the terms entered into with our delegates.... The Provisional Government and the Legislative Assembly have consented to enter into Confederation in the belief, and on the understanding, that in the above mentioned terms a general amnesty is contemplated.[9]

The arrangement was a "treaty" in the sense of an international agreement between states. The treaty had two parts: the written text of the Manitoba Act and the oral promise of amnesty for all actions committed over the winter of 1869-70. This explains the final lines of Riel's pamphlet on the amnesty question:

> Ce que nous demandons, c'est l'amnistie: c'est l'exécution loyale de l'acte de Manitoba. Rien de plus, mais aussi rien de moins. [What we demand is amnesty—the fulfillment in good faith of the Manitoba Act—nothing more, but also nothing less.][10]

Riel literally meant that the annexation of Rupert's Land was the result of a "solemn treaty"[11] which, like all treaties, would become void if it were not observed. Ergo the annexation was reversible. The people of Rupert's Land, which had become the Province of Manitoba and the North-West Territories, could remove themselves from Canada if the treaty was broken in either of its branches: the amnesty or the Manitoba Act.

In Riel's view, Canada had betrayed its obligations under both headings. We will not go into the amnesty question here. It was certainly never far from Riel's mind, but it would not have sufficed to raise the flag of revolt among the *Métis* in 1885. This purpose was served by Riel's interpretation of the Manitoba Act, particularly of section 31, which authorized the half-breed land grant. At its time of entry into Confederation, Manitoba consisted of approximately 9,500,000 acres. With the 1,400,000 acres set aside by section 31 for the "children of half breed heads of families," the government clearly thought to equip each young *Métis* with enough land to make him economically self-sufficient. It was the same principle as the one by which Indian reserves were calculated at the rate of a quarter-section of land per family of five. The government was thinking in terms of the future needs of a special group among the population.

Riel, on the contrary, viewed the 1,400,000 acres as the sale price of the 9,500,000 acres comprised in Manitoba. This ratio set a precedent for the rest of the land of the North-West. As subsequent acres were opened for settlement, the *Métis* of those areas should receive a similar price, in order to extinguish their aboriginal title, namely one-seventh of the land or the financial value of the one-seventh. This would amount to about 176,000,000 acres for the North-West outside the original boundaries of Manitoba.[12]

Riel's single best explanation of this theory was given in his final trial speech. It must be read carefully, for his phrasing in English is sometimes awkward, even though the ideas are clear and logically developed:

> But somebody will say, on what grounds do you ask one-seventh of the lands? In England, in France, the French and the English have lands, the first was in England, they were the owners of the soil and they transmitted to generations. Now, by the soil they have had their start as a nation. Who starts the nations? The very one who creates them, God. God is the master of the universe, our planet is his land, and the nation and the tribes are members of His family, and as a good father, he gives a portion of his lands to that nation, to that tribe, to everyone, that is his heritage, that is his share of the inheritance, of the people, or nation or tribe. Now, here is a nation strong as it may be, it has its inheritance from God. When they have crowded their country because they had no room to stay anymore at home, it does not give them the right to come and take the share of all tribes besides them. When they come they ought to say, well, my little sister, the Cree tribe, you have a great territory, but that territory has been given to you as our own land, it has been given to our fathers in England or in France and of course you cannot exist without having that spot of land. This is the principle God cannot create a tribe without locating it. We are not birds. We have to walk on the ground, and that ground is encircled of many things, which besides its own value, increases its value in another manner, and when we cultivate it we still increase that value. Well, on what principle can it be that the Canadian Government have given one-seventh to the half-breeds of Manitoba? I say it must be on this ground, civilization has the means of improving life that Indians or half-breeds have not. So when they come in our savage country, in our uncultivated land, they come and help us with their civilization, but we helped them with our lands, so the question comes: Your land, you Cree or you half-breed, your land is worth to day one-seventh of what it will be when the civilization will have opened it? Your country unopened is worth to you only one-seventh of what it will be when opened. I think it is a fair share to acknowledge the genius of civilization to such an extent as to give, when I have seven pair of socks, six, to keep one. They made the treaty with us. As they made the treaty, I say they have to observe it, and did they observe the treaty? No.[13]

The statement accepts and justifies the surrender of land by aboriginal peoples in return for compensation. To that extent, it is compatible with the official Indian policy of Britain and Canada. Beyond that, however, lie some marked differences. Riel seems to challenge the unilateral assumption of sovereignty which was the foundation of British rule in North America. (I say "seems to challenge" because his language is ambiguous; he does not distinguish between sovereignty and ownership). In any case, he certainly does not accept the principle of unilateral extinguishment of aboriginal title through legislation. The land grant of section 31 was valid compensation for surrender of land only inasmuch as it was part of a treaty approved by both sides. Furthermore, the basis of compensation was a *quid pro quo* as in any sale. Because the advantages of civilization could multiply the value of land seven times or more, the *Métis* would be at least as well off by surrendering six-sevenths of their land and adopting civilized ways while retaining one-seventh (or its money equivalent). It was most decidedly not a matter of government allocating a certain amount of land to each *Métis* individual. In another text, Riel derided this approach as a "sophism" designed to let the government "evade its obligations" and "frustrate the *Métis,* as a group or nationality, of their seventh of the lands."[14]

Riel's insistence on the principle of "the seventh" nicely illustrates the theoretical difference between his position and the official view. According to the latter, aboriginal title was only a "personal and usufructuary right" of the natives to gather subsistence from the land. If it was to be extinguished, it was logical to compute compensation on the basis of the number of persons who would now have to subsist in other ways. Riel, however, maintained that the natives were the true proprietors of the soil in the full sense of ownership. Thus compensation for expropriation should be based on the value of the land, not on the number of people affected. To use a modern analogy, if a provincial government has to expropriate land for, say, a hydroelectric transmission line, it would compensate owners according to the fair market value of the asset, not according to the size of their families. Riel's understanding of the nature of aboriginal title drove him to demand analogous treatment for the *Métis*.

The government grudgingly agreed to a new issue of scrip to provide for the relatively few *Métis* who had not participated in the Manitoba land grant. But in Riel's mind, the whole North-West outside Manitoba still belonged to the *Métis*. The Hudson's Bay Company had sold whatever interest it had, and the Indians, at least in the fertile belt, had signed land surrender treaties. It was still necessary to extinguish the *Métis* title, and that could not be done with a few pieces of scrip. It would require payment of the value of one-seventh of the whole North-West, following the precedent solemnly established in the "Manitoba Treaty." And if that treaty continued to be broken, the *Métis* would no longer be part of Canada. According to the law of nations, they could once again form a

Provisional Government and undertake negotiations with other governments. There might be a new treaty with Canada, or perhaps the North-West would become a separate colony within the Empire, or perhaps it would even ask for annexation to the United States, as Riel did after his trial. Everything was possible. It is this train of thought, and only this, which makes the North-West Rebellion intelligible.

The Agitation

When Riel came to Saskatchewan on 1 July 1884, it was expected that his work would last only a brief time. The people knew what they wanted; all they needed from Riel was advice on the best way of pressing their demands within constitutional limits. But nothing was sent to the government until 16 December 1884, and that petition was only a preliminary draft. Work on further declarations continued well into February 1885. Why did things drag on for such a long time? Probably because Riel was trying to unite several incompatible points of view:

1. His own radical theory that the North-West Territories were free to leave Confederation if Canada continued to refuse large-scale compensation for extinguishment of *Métis* aboriginal rights.

2. The desire of the *Métis* for an issue of scrip and settlement of their disputes with the Department of the Interior. Their aims were moderate; but, as events would show, many of them were willing to resort to arms to achieve their goals.

3. The desire of the English half-breeds for the same goals as the *Métis*. The difference was that the half-breeds were not willing to take up arms.

4. The intention of a group of white businessmen in Prince Albert, mostly allied to the Liberal Party, to win provincial status and responsible government for the North-West. Their most active figure, William Henry Jackson, was willing to consider separation from Canada, but it is not known whether there was much support for his extreme position.

5. The demand of the more militant Indians, whose most prominent spokesman was Big Bear, for a renegotiation of treaties on more favorable terms.

Riel tried to coalesce all these groups around his own views, but irreconcilable differences made the coalition unstable. The *Métis* were willing to follow him, except for those, particularly of the merchant class, who disapproved of armed force. The English half-breeds could accept his demand for a massive settlement of aboriginal rights, but they also disapproved of force. William Henry Jackson and perhaps others among the whites were willing to consider a rupture with Canada, but they were put off by Riel's ideas on aboriginal rights, which would have enriched the *Métis,* half-breeds, and Indians at the expense of the white community.

In the nine months between his return to Canada and the outbreak of the Rebellion, Riel grappled with this political problem. He wrote or collaborated on the writing of several documents, but none was completed. Those which expressed his own views could not command universal support among the different groups, while those which could be supported did not express his own radical theory. Thus no single text was produced which adequately expressed all the demands which led to the Rebellion.

Let us now follow the course of the agitation from Riel's return to Canada up to the eve of the Rebellion. This is not a general history of these months, which has been well written by Stanley and others. It is a study of the intellectual difficulties faced by Riel in melding his own views with those of the groups he hoped to organize under his leadership. The analysis is sometimes speculative because very little written by Riel during the period of the agitation has been found. However, there is abundant material in the papers of Riel's collaborator, William Henry Jackson, with which to fill the gaps.[15]

Riel was received at Fish Creek on 1 July. He made public appearances to the *Métis* and half-breeds within the next two weeks, but we do not know what he said. His first major appearance was a speech in Prince Albert, 19 July. His own notes, and the various transcripts of the speech, show that he stressed provincial status and responsible government, themes dear to that audience. "Let the people of Assiniboia, of Alberta, of Saskatchewan petition in the proper manner for immediat[e] admission as provinces in the confederation." Riel also admonished his listeners to insist on provincial control of public lands, which had been denied Manitoba. But they were to strive for all this strictly "within the bonds of constitutional energy."[16] One account reports a brief reference to aboriginal rights;[17] but the reporter garbled what Riel said, and probably its full significance was not apparent to the audience.

Shortly after this meeting Jackson circulated an open letter to residents of Prince Albert and the surrounding area. It began: "We are starting a movement in this settlement with a view to attaining Provincial Legislatures for the North-West Territories and if possible the control of our own resources, that we may build our railroads and other works to aid our own interests rather than those of the Eastern Provinces." Readers were asked to send delegates to the executive committee, "which will be called together in a few days to put our own statement of rights in final shape." The petition would be sent to Ottawa for action by the Canadian government, though Jackson also mentioned a more radical option: "Possibly we may settle up with the East and form a separate Federation of our own in direct connection with the crown." There was no mention of the *Métis,* except to say that Riel had united them "solidly in our favour"; nor was there mention of Riel's special theories.[18]

Jackson's reference to "a few days" shows he was thinking of quick action. This is confirmed by a letter he wrote to Riel the same day: "Today I shall finish up work in town and tomorrow start for the Lower Flat etc. I will try and get out to your place toward end of week. Please be working up the petition into shape and we will get it in neat form before the committee is called to endorse or alter it."[19] This sense of urgency was apparently shared by Riel, for he wrote at this time that he intended to return to Montana around September.

The petition which Jackson expected to finish in a few days has been preserved among his papers. It chided the British government for having permitted the North-West Territories to be governed by men "chosen by and responsible to not the people of the said Territories but the people of the Eastern Provinces."[20] A long list of grievances mentioned public works and services, taxation, tariffs, monopolies, and other topics of interest to local businessmen. Homestead regulations got only a few lines, and aboriginal rights were barely mentioned. It was clearly a Prince Albert document, one that would have little appeal to the *Métis* or to Riel, except that he would have been in accord with its closing demand that the Territories "be forthwith formed into Provinces, each Province having full control of its own resources and internal administration, and having power to send a just number of representatives to the Federal legislature."[21]

Another and much more radical draft seems to be connected with Jackson's idea of "settling up with the East." Alleging that the "Government of Eastern Canada hath grossly exceeded and abused" its trusteeship over the North-West, it calls upon Great Britain

> to assert its suspended Guardianship and remove the Trusteeship of the said lands from the hands of the Gov't of Eastern Canada and place it in the hands of a council composed partly of members elected by the actual residents to protect interests of actual settlers, and partly of members nominated by Brit. Gov't. to protect interests of future settlers.[22]

August brought two reasons for delay. When a visit from Minister of Public Works Sir Hector Langevin was announced, it was decided to present a list of grievances to him; but he cancelled his trip late in the month. The second reason for delay was a broadening of the movement to include the Indians. In the first ten days of August there was a council of several Cree bands at the Duck Lake reserve. Several speakers denounced the treaties and called for renegotiation. Jackson seems to have been present and taken notes, for the speeches are recorded in his hand. Riel apparently did not attend, but he was in contact with the chiefs through intermediaries. Later in August Riel and Big Bear met at Jackson's house in Prince Albert.[23] These delays caused resentment among the English half-breeds. James Isbister wrote to Riel on 4 September: "I cannot for a moment, understand what is your delay, in not having our Committee meeting, sitting and working.... I must say we the people of the Ridge, Red

Deer Hill, Halcro's Settlement, and St. Catherine Parish find you are too slow, or does the delay rest with W. Jackson and his people?"[24] Isbister, one of those who had gone to Montana to fetch Riel, had been the earliest farmer around Prince Albert, and his opinion carried great weight. But even as Riel received this letter, he was off on another tack, this time particularly concerned with the *Métis*.

On 5 September the *Métis* held a large meeting at St. Laurent to discuss their grievances with Bishop Grandin, who was making a pastoral visit. Riel read aloud a memorandum of eleven points. Two days later, as Grandin left for Regina, Riel gave him a slightly abridged written version containing eight items.

It is not clear why the list was reduced from eleven to eight. Perhaps it was only because Riel was writing in haste under awkward conditions. One of the three omitted points was a demand for better rations for the Indians. Riel, complaining that the *Métis* and other settlers were forced to support the Indians, had called on the government to "make the Indians work as Pharaoh had made the Jews work"—a proposal that may lift some eyebrows among those who now regard him as a humanitarian. A second point was a request that the government should pay a thousand dollars to build a convent wherever there were enough *Métis* to justify the nuns in coming to found a school. The third point was a demand for provincial status for the districts of the North-West as soon as their populations equalled that of Manitoba in 1870. Provincial status "should be accompanied by all the advantages of responsible government, including the administration of public lands."[25] The first two of the omitted points were rather peripheral to the agitation and to Riel's long-term goals, but the third was absolutely fundamental, so its omission is curious.

Its main idea was, however, partially included in the first item of the eight-point list given to Grandin, which called for "the inauguration of responsible government." Four other points on the list covered long-standing grievances of the local *Métis*. Riel wanted "the same guarantees ... as those accorded to the old settlers of Manitoba," which implied several things such as river lots, hay and wood privilege, and squatter's rights. He demanded patents for the plots of land along the Saskatchewan on which the *Métis* had settled, often in disregard of homestead rules. A land grant similar to that in Manitoba would of course be required. Finally Riel requested that more contracts for public works be let to local inhabitants. These were all old items of complaint, and Riel's document added nothing new to their formulation.

The list did, however, contain three points, stemming directly from Riel, which added a whole new dimension to the *Métis* demands.

5. That two million acres be set apart by the government for the benefit of the half breeds, both Protestant and Catholic. That the government sell these lands; that it deposit the money in the bank, and that the interest on that money serve for the support of schools, for the construction of or-

phanages and hospitals, for the support of institutions of this type already constructed, and to obtain carts for poor half breeds as well as seed for the annual spring planting.

6. That a hundred townships, selected from swampy lands which do not appear habitable at the moment, be set aside by the government and that every eighteen years there take place a distribution of these lands to the half breed children of the new generation. This to last 120 years.

7. The Province of Manitoba has been enlarged since 1870. The half breed title to the lands by which it was enlarged has not yet been extinguished. Let that title be extinguished in favour of the half breed children born in the province since the transfer [i.e. since 15 July 1870] and in favour of the children born there for the next four generations.[26]

Item 5 amounted to a *Métis* trust fund designed to promote their economic and social advancement, while item 6 would have insured the availability of land to several new generations of *Métis*. Item 7, although vague, had the most radical implications, for it hinted at Riel's theory that *Métis* ownership rights to the North-West were still alive. All these points flow from his idea of collective ownership of the North-West by the *Métis* nation. Riel was asking for a two million acre reserve, plus a hundred townships (2,304,000 acres), plus something for the expansion of Manitoba: a considerable amount in all, but far less than one-seventh of the North-West. These demands were moderate because they were only a first instalment, as shown by Riel's postscript to the document: "This is what we ask while we wait for Canada to become able to pay us the annual interest on the sum that our land is worth and while we wait for public opinion to agree to recognize our rights to the land in their fullest extent *(dans toute leur étendue)*."[27] Grandin gave a copy of Riel's text to Governor Dewdney, who forwarded an English translation to Sir John A. Macdonald. The bishop stated that he supported the traditional demands of the *Métis* but that he could not speak to the political questions of responsible government and aboriginal title.[28] Macdonald received additional information about Riel's postscript from A.-E. Forget, who had accompanied Grandin. Forget reported that Riel's document

> only purports to contain such requests as need an immediate settlement. In addition to these advantages, they claim that their right to land can only be fully extinguished by the annual payment of the interest on a capital representing the value of land in the Territories estimated to be worth at the time of transfer twenty-five cents an acre for the halfbreeds and fifteen cents for the Indians. This is the claim alluded to in the post-scriptum of Riel's memo to His Lordship.[29]

Forget added that the *Métis* were planning to draw up a memorial on this basis and send it to the House of Commons. He tried to persuade them to direct it to the governor general in council through Governor Dewdney.

A draft of such a memorial exists in Riel's hand, addressed to "Your Excellency in Council." The heading suggests it was written out after the conversation with Forget on 7 September, although earlier drafts must have preceded this neatly written text. Unaccountably long overlooked, this document is an invaluable statement of Riel's true objectives.[30]

The text began by denouncing the Indian treaties as a swindle because they "are not based on a reasonable estimation of the value of their lands." The Indians would not be content until they receive this value. "It is the opinion of your humble petitioners that the land in its uncultivated state, with its natural wealth of game, fish, and berries cannot be worth less to the Indian than twelve and a half cents per acre." The same principle applied to the *Métis,* except that the land was worth twenty-five cents an acre to them because their usage of it was "fairly civilized." Then followed some calculations, based on certain assumptions:

—1,100,000,000 acres of land in the North-West
—100,000 Indians
—100,000 *Métis*
—5% interest rate

The result of these assumptions was an annuity of $68.75 for each Indian and $137.50 for each *Métis.* However, not too much importance was attached to these calculations, which were "only approximate." They were offered only to give "a fair idea" of *Métis* rights and to suggest "the profound distress in which the Dominion of Canada plunges us by taking possession of our lands and not giving us the adequate compensation we expect of it."[31]

The line of reasoning embodied in this petition was not a temporary aberration on Riel's part. He reproduced exactly the same argument in his last major piece of writing, published posthumously as "Les Métis du Nord-Ouest," except that he used figures of fifteen cents an acre for the Indians and thirty cents an acre for the *Métis.*[32] Furthermore, the total amounts of money involved were of the same magnitude as the value of the one-seventh of the North-West demanded at the trial.[33] The notion of a trust fund based on the value of the land surrendered flowed directly from Riel's conception of aboriginal title as collective ownership, not a mere encumbrance on the sovereign's title, and was in direct contrast to the official policy of calculating compensation proportionally to numbers of individuals rather than to the area of land involved.

Why this petition dropped completely from sight is one of the riddles of the agitation. One may conjecture that its radical theory of aboriginal rights was unacceptable to the white settlers whose support was indispensable to a joint movement. Collaboration with the white settlers and English half-breeds became very active in September. An important meeting was held 10 September at the home of Andrew Spence of Red Deer Hill. A brief minute of that meeting in the hand of Jackson shows the internal strains to which the movement was subject: "Committee met at Red Deer Hill, Andrew Spence's residence Wednesday afternoon, dispute whether Bill of Rights or petition. Committee appointed to prepare samples of both."[34]

As will be shown below, the "petition" was to be a list of grievances submitted to the government for redress. Compiling such a document was a purely constitutional action. The "Bill of Rights" was to be a more sweeping statement of the right of the people of the North-West to self-determination. To speak in such terms would at least be to border on sedition, and the committee was still undecided whether to go that far.

Not surprisingly, it was easier to compile the petition than the Bill of Rights. A draft seems to have been completed as early as 22 September,[35] and two days later a copy was sent to Archbishop Taché.[36] Further copies were mailed on 1 October to Father Constantine Scollen, an Oblate missionary in Alberta, and to J. W. Taylor, American Consul in Winnipeg.[37]

Of the three copies sent out, the only one to have been found is Taylor's. Written entirely in Riel's hand, it is very little different from the later draft sent to the secretary of state on 16 December. It was mostly concerned with the redress of specific grievances without challenging the government's authority. But the final paragraph showed a larger strategy:

> Your humble petitioners are of opinion that the shortest and most effectual methods of remedying these grievances would be to grant the N.W.T. responsible government with control of its own resources [*sic*] and just representation in the federal Parliament and Cabinet. Wherefor[e] your petitioners humbly pray that your excellency in council would be pleased to cause the introduction, at the coming session of Parliament, of a measure providing for the complete organization of the District of Saskatchewan as a province; and that they be allowed, as in 70, to send delegates to Ottawa with their Bill of Rights, whereby an understanding may be arrived at as to their entry into confederation with the constitution of a free Province.[38]

The dispute over whether to prepare a petition or a Bill of Rights had been resolved by deciding to submit the petition first, followed by a Bill of Rights.

The document's meaning is not fully apparent until one recalls Riel's interpretation of the events of 1870. He was not merely calling for the government to hear and act upon complaints; he was proposing a new "treaty" in the international framework of the law of nations. This analysis is confirmed by Riel's covering letter to Taylor, which made the point emphatically:

> The people of the Northwest are poor. They are not happy under the Canadian rule; not only because their public affairs are improperly administered by the federal government, but because they are practically denied by that government the enjoyment *of the right of people.* [Riel's emphasis] That is principally what is ruining them.[39]

Another mystery of the agitation is that nothing further happened for two and a half months after this burst of activity in September. It may be that Riel and the others were waiting for signatures to be gathered. We know little about this, but efforts to obtain signatures in other parts of the Territories seem to have been made.[40] It may also be that they were waiting for reactions to the copies they had sent out.

Taché's reply was not slow in coming, nor was it encouraging. He told Riel to "give up useless agitation, give up certain ambiguities of language whose true meaning would not escape those who reflect."[41] He had obviously divined the implications of allusions to a Bill of Rights. Father Scollen, less politically sophisticated, was more positive. He passed the petition on to Dan Maloney, a political figure of St. Albert who had befriended the *Métis* on other occasions. Maloney promised to do what he could to intercede with the government on their behalf.[42]

The final version of the petition, hardly changed from the text of late September, was sent on 16 December to the secretary of state. There were several odd things about the submission which could not but detract from the impression it made in Ottawa. Although the petition was written out in longhand by Riel, his name did not appear anywhere. The petition in fact is unsigned, although earlier researchers, confusing the petition with the covering letter, have claimed it bore the names of W. H. Jackson and Andrew Spence.[43] There certainly is no long list of signatures of the kind one would expect to accompany such a petition. It seems that this submission was only preliminary, for Jackson was occupied after the New Year in collecting signatures. Apparently he intended to resubmit the signed petition directly to the governor general. A covering letter, rather bold in tone, was provided by Jackson, who signed himself "Secretary General Committee," without explaining the nature of the committee:

> the petition is an extremely moderate one.... to the Canadian and English wing of the movement a more searching exposition of the situation would have been much more satisfactory. The opinion has been freely expressed that our appeal should be directed to the Privy Council of England and to the general public rather than to the federal authorities.[44]

Jackson's choice of words was deliberately disingenuous. He admitted elsewhere that the petition "was purposely made weak, as a blind," because the agitators were not yet ready to show their hand to the government.[45] The petition gave the impression that it was one last attempt at moderation, which might be followed by more extreme measures if concessions were not made immediately; yet Jackson and Riel were already preparing their next steps even before the petition could have reached its target. On 18 December, Jackson, back in Prince Albert, wrote to Riel that he would be down to see him in ten days or so, adding, "In the meantime please work away at your proclamation," probably a reference to the Bill of Rights.[46]

It cannot be emphasized too strongly that this petition was only secondarily an appeal to the Canadian government for redress of grievances, although it has generally been presented that way in the historical literature. It was

primarily a step in a bigger campaign whose objectives, although not absolutely certain, were on a grand scale. Immediate provincial status, control of
natural resources, renegotiation of the terms of Confederation, separation from
Canada, and a vast settlement of aboriginal claims were all possible outcomes.
The concrete grievances of the *Métis* had become merely a means to these ends.

The petition's ulterior purpose helps explain its peculiar structure. It was
divided into two parts of roughly equal size: sixteen particular items of complaint, followed by a seventeenth item of great length rehearsing the events of
1870 and the government's subsequent failure to observe the "treaty." The sixteen points corresponded to specific grievances; the seventeenth laid the
foundation of a demand for self-determination under the law of nations.

The specific grievances fell into several categories. One demand called for
better rations for the Indians. Another called for a half-breed land grant as in
Manitoba. Eight items concerned the complicated issues of survey and homestead
requirements. The remaining six are readily identifiable as standard tenets of
western Liberalism: greater efficiency and economy in public works and buildings, a Hudson's Bay railway, strict liquor laws, secret ballot, and free trade. This
part of the petition was truly a comprehensive, if miscellaneous, catalog of local
dissatisfactions.

The seventeenth point was in contrast a long, tightly reasoned chain of argument: the people of the North-West in 1870 had sent representatives to
Ottawa who were recognized "as the Delegates of the North-West." Even as
Canada negotiated with them, she was preparing a military expedition. Promises
of amnesty were made and not fulfilled. The Imperial order-in-council annexing
Rupert's Land to Canada was passed before the people of the North-West had
a chance to ratify the agreement. Since that time Canada had continued to vi-
olate the "treaty" by denying provincial status to the North-West, by excluding
Westerners from the cabinet, and by retaining control of natural resources.
Riel did not openly state the conclusion of the argument, namely that the broken "treaty" had released the people of the North-West from allegiance to
Canada, but he hinted at it obliquely, stating that inhabitants of the North-
West "are treated neither according to their privileges as British subjects nor
according to the rights of people." The implication is clear to anyone familiar with
Riel's thinking. The petition closed with virtually the same words as those of the
draft of October, calling for delegates to take a Bill of Rights to Ottawa and
negotiate entry into Confederation.

Not much came of this petition. A formal acknowledgment was sent to
Jackson, while the document was sent to William Pearce for comment. In a
point-by-point analysis, he argued that the specific grievances were based on misconceptions or were being dealt with.[47] Indeed the government had already
made an inquiry into the homestead problems of St. Laurent and had decided
to do something about scrip. Ironically, the petition had arrived after the major
problems of the *Métis* were on the way to resolution.

However, the long-range plans of Riel and Jackson were very much alive, as we may deduce from a letter of 27 January. Having received a formal acknowledgment of the petition, Jackson wrote:

> I think with you [Riel] that the mere fact of an answer is a very good sign considering the bold tone of my letter and our audacious assumption that we are not yet in Confederation, an assumption which it seems to me, they have conceded in their letter.[48]

This was surely building on air, for the acknowledgment had only stated that "the matter will receive due consideration." But Jackson was looking for favorable signs for his work. His letter spoke rather confusingly of several documents he had drawn up. There was a reference to a petition for which he was collecting signatures, probably the petition which had already been submitted without signatures to the secretary of state. He may have planned to get it signed and resubmit it with more publicity. Also mentioned were

> a memorial suitable to catch the [Parliamentary] opposition in case the Council [i.e. cabinet] pay no attention—a stronger memorial for the Imperial sec'y of state for the Colonies in case the Federal Parliament pays no attention—and the Declaration of Rights for private circulation, and use if necessary. I will get all these documents signed along with the petition.[49]

The order of the documents suggests a strategy of appeals to cabinet, Parliament, and Great Britain, followed by a unilateral declaration of independence, if necessary. Jackson anticipated quick action as the parliamentary session was about to open, but he was also prepared for delays: "I will have the councillors in good heart for an unlimited period of quietness if found unavoidable. They must learn that quietness does not necessarily mean stagnation."

The description of the strategy was amplified in an undated note by Jackson. The plan was

> to organize every settlement & the N.W.T. convene a central congress in about two months and take our case direct to the throne. In the meantime we will send down a softly worded petition which will leave them under the impression that if they remove some of our present grievances, we will cease to agitate for the power to prevent other grievances. They will therefore ease the present situation by giving us a greater share of grain contract and an order to float cash among us, and we will then have the sinews of war to go for stronger measures. The Bill of Rights is composed so as to cover the whole North West. The various examples of the resolution of those rights will be collected in each settlement, and we will then have a clear case for the Privy Council.[50]

And more radical still:

> Platform
> 1. In regard to Government:
>   Petition Brit. Govt. to appoint Commit. & transfer Govt. to council.
>   In case of refusal declare Independence and appoint Council & assume control.[51]

The most interesting document to recover would be the Bill of Rights, but it was deliberately burnt shortly before the battle of Duck Lake.[52] No one has stated why it was destroyed, but perhaps Riel felt it to be incriminating. His explanation of the revolt was that the *Métis* had taken up arms in self-defense, fearing they were about to be attacked by the Mounted Police.[53] That theory would have been seriously compromised by a Bill of Rights showing that an uprising had long been posited as a possible last step if other measures failed.

Some idea of the Bill of Rights can be gleaned from Jackson's letter of 27 January. As the Bill was an English document, Riel had left the writing to Jackson, who had looked up precedents in law books; but the thought came from Riel. His central principle was that "the world is governed by justice." It was unjust "that the inhabitants of any section of the Globe should possess the right of irresponsible and infallible authority over the inhabitants of some other section of the Globe." Such rule from afar would despoil its subjects, subjecting them to injustice. The aboriginal inhabitants had self-government, and this "consistency between their institutions and natural law ... resulted in fair play & prosperity to each member of the community." But the introduction by the colonial powers of "irresponsible authority" had led to general misery. The declaration concluded "with the assertion of the natural right of self-government thus proven." It was obviously meant not as a theoretical statement but a call to action; Jackson was putting it "into such a simple shape that any ordinary man could catch the main drift of the argument at first reading."[54]

Although Riel and Jackson seemed agreed on strategy, signs of strain were already beginning to show in their alliance. A bizarre episode took place on 14 or 15 January when Riel was having dinner at the Jackson home in Prince Albert. He was served an end cut of roast beef, rather heavily seasoned with salt and pepper. After he tasted it, he ran outside and made himself vomit. Then he went to Father André's residence to fetch Charles Nolin, whom he mysteriously informed that attempts were being made to poison him. The incident, improbable as it sounds, is attested in several independent sources.[55] A few days later, Jackson wrote to the Edmonton newspaperman Frank Oliver: "Efforts are being made to separate Riel and myself, but though we differ on certain theoretical points we have too much confidence in each other's honesty of purpose for such attempts to succeed."[56]

In the first two weeks of February Jackson made the round of the English settlements, collecting signatures for the petition, memorials, and Bill of Rights. According to one report, he also had people sign an authorization for him to be their delegate to Canada.[57] On 14 February, he went upriver to the French parishes to collect more signatures. It was on this trip that he and Riel came into open conflict. According to the subsequent account of T. Eastwood Jackson, William's brother, "[Riel] opposed the petition, attacking it on the basis of Halfbreed ownership, and my brother being equally determined on the other side, the argument lasted all night, and became so fierce that Riel lost his self-control."[58] If Eastwood may be believed, William was kept under house arrest, from which he twice tried unsuccessfully to escape. Whatever the precise details, it was definitely the end of the collaboration between Riel and Jackson as equal partners.

After the Rebellion was over and Jackson had been sent to a lunatic asylum, he briefly explained what had caused the argument. He had maintained his conviction

> that the particles of matter composing the Earth were the property of whosoever first chose to develop them into articles of utility except in case of the express allocation of land as in the case of Canaan, while Mr. Riel was, if I remember, pursuing the argument which I see he advanced on the occasion of his trial of Regina—that *every* nation is allotted its means of existence in the shape of a *land*.[59]

Since it hinges on the idea of uniting one's labor to the land to form property, Jackson's view may loosely be called Lockean. His report of his opinions corresponds substantially to a letter he wrote on 2 February 1885 to Albert Monkman, a leader of the agitation who moved in both the *Métis* and English half-breed communities.

> Let this be our aim. Let us sink all distinctions of race and religion. Let the white man delight in seeing the Indian helped forward to fill his place as a producer of wealth, and let the Indian and Halfbreed scorn to charge a rent for the soil which God has given to man, upon the settler who comes in to help to build up the country.... and let both unite in seeing that the fur country be managed for the benefit of the Indians who live by hunting, not for the good of a grasping company. Direct the attention of the Indian to the H.B.Co. monopoly, and to the necessity of providing schools for those who wish to learn productive arts, and turn them aside from the idea of being landlords. Why should God give a whole continent to 40,000 Indians and coop up 40,000,000 Englishmen in on a little island? The Indians are the same race; they, too, once lived in Europe. America was once without a man in it, why should a part of the human race go into that empty continent, and as soon as they have got there, turn round and forbid any more to come in, unless they pay for the privilege?[60]

It is not hard to see why Riel would have been enraged by such a cogent critique of the very idea of aboriginal title. It contradicted the basis of the agitation as he saw it. The agreement between Jackson and Riel on provincial status and responsible government was superficial compared to this profound disagreement about who really owned the North-West.

Riel began to assume a belligerent stance in public from 24 February onwards. Did the recent break with Jackson help steer him in that direction? Perhaps it made him feel that, if he continued the collaboration with the English, he would never be able to make his theory of aboriginal rights prevail.

Absence of documents, particularly on Riel's side, makes it likely that much will always remain obscure about the North-West agitation. But we know enough to realize how false is the naive version of events so often found in the contemporary literature. It would be more nearly true to tell the story thus: Riel saw in the grievances of the *Métis* an opportunity to implement his theory that the Manitoba "treaty" had been broken; that the *Métis* were the real owners of the North-West; that they could renegotiate entry into Confederation; that they must receive a seventh of the value of the land of the North-West as compensation for letting others live there; and that they could seek an independent political destiny if these terms were not met. Collaborating with white agitators like Jackson who were chiefly interested in provincial status and responsible government, he embarked upon a complex and deliberately deceptive strategy of making successively more radical demands. A Bill of Rights amounting to a Declaration of Independence was envisioned almost from the beginning. Finally, when Riel realized there was an unbridgeable gap between himself and Jackson, he determined to go it alone, as he had in 1869. The *Métis* would take the lead, rise in arms, and carry the English half-breeds and white settlers with them.

Notes

1. Cited in Peter A. Cumming and Neil H. Mickenberg, *Native Rights in Canada* (Toronto: General Publishing, 1972; second edition), p. 138. I have modernized the orthography.

2. Ibid., p. 148.

3. See ibid., pp. 13-50.

4. Louis Riel, [Mémoire sur les troubles du Nord-Ouest], *Le Canadien*, 26 December 1885. Ms. missing.

5. Ibid.

6. Interview with C. B. Pitblado, *Winnipeg Sun,* 3 July 1885.

7. Thomas Flanagan, ed., "Political Theory of the Red River Resistance: The Declaration of December 8, 1869," *Canadian Journal of Political Science* 11 (1978): 154.

8. *Le Canadien,* 26 December 1885; and Petition "To His Excellency [Grover] Cleveland ...," [August-September 1885], NARS, Despatches from U.S. Consuls in Winnipeg, No. 441.

9. Cited in Stanley, *Birth of Western Canada,* p. 124.

10. Louis Riel, *L`Amnistie* (Montréal: Bureau du "Nouveau Monde," 1874), p. 22.

11. Ibid.

12. Louis Riel to J. W. Taylor, [2-3 August 1885], NARS, Despatches from U.S. Consuls in Winnipeg, 1869-1906, No. 433; [Manifeste à ses concitoyens américains], [August-November 1885], PAC, MG 27 IC4, 2150-56, 2159-60.

13. Desmond Morton, ed., *The Queen v. Louis Riel* (Toronto: University of Toronto Press, 1974), pp. 358-59.

14. Riel, [Manifeste à ses concitoyens américains], 2150-56, 2159-60.

15. I am indebted to the new research on Jackson carried out by Donald B. Smith and Miriam Carey, although my interpretation differs somewhat from theirs. See Smith, "William Henry Jackson: Riel's Secretary," *The Beaver* 311 (Spring 1981): 10-19; *idem,* "Honoré Joseph Jaxon: A Man Who Lived for Others," *Saskatchewan History* 34 (Autumn 1981): 81-101; Carey, "The Role of W. H. Jackson in the North-West Agitation of 1884-85," Honors Thesis, University of Calgary, Political Science, 1980.

16. [Notes for Speech in Prince Albert], [19 July 1885], PAC, RG 13 B2, 2359, 2345.

17. Prince Albert *Times,* 25 July 1884.

18. W. H. Jackson to "Gentlemen," 23 July 1884, PAC, RG 13 B2, 512-17.

19. W. H. Jackson to Louis Riel, 23 July 1884, PAC, RG 13 B2, 503-9.

20. Louis Riel to Joseph Riel and Louis Lavallée, [25?] [July 1884], PAM, MG 3 D1, No. 418.

21. USL, A. S. Morton Mss. Collection, C555/2/13.9v. Typescript, original missing. Several other typed drafts are in the same collection. None is dated, but the contents match the description of the petition given by Jackson in his letter to "Gentlemen," note 18 *supra.*

22. Ibid., C555/2/13.9q.

23. Sgt. W. A. Brooks to L. N. F. Crozier, 21 August 1884, PAC, RG 13 B2, 522-23. Typed copy.

24. James Isbister to Louis Riel, 4 September 1885, PAM, MG 3 D1, No. 412.

25. A copy of the memorandum in the hand of Louis Schmidt is included in his "Notes: Mouvement des Métis à St-Laurent Sask. TNO en 1884," AASB, T 29799-80. The original has not been found.

26. Louis Riel to J.-V. Grandin, [7 September 1884], ACAE, Correspondence of Vital Grandin.

27. Ibid.

28. Edgar Dewdney to J. A. Macdonald, 19 September 1884, PAC, MG 26 A, 42897-905. The English translations are in ibid., 42935-41.

29. A.E. Forget to Edgar Dewdney, 18 September 1884. Ibid., 42921-34.

30. Gilles Martel, "Le Messianisme de Louis Riel (1844-1885)," Thèse de doctorat, Paris, 1976, p. 393.

31. Pétition à "votre excellence en conseil," [September 1884], PAC, RG 13 B2, 42-43.

32. "Les Métis du Nord-Ouest," Montreal *Daily Star,* 28 November 1885.

33. Riel's petition requested a total compensation to natives of 37 1/2 cents per acre, slightly more than one-seventh of the current preemption price of $2.00 per acre.

34. W. H. Jackson, [Note], [September 1884], PAC, RG 13 B2, 159 The date of the meeting is taken from Jackson to J. Isbister, 8 September 1884, PAC, RG 13 B2, 528.

35. Louis Riel to W. H. Jackson, 22 September 1884. USL, A. S. Morton Mss. Collection, C555/2/13.7d.

36. Enclosed in Louis Riel to A. A. Taché, 24 September 1884. AD, W206.M62F, No. 744, p. 7. Microfilm; the original, once at AASB, is now lost.

37. There are two drafts of a letter from Riel to Scollen, 1 October 1884, PAC, RG 13 B2, 77 and 531-32. The final letter has not been recovered. The letter to Taylor, 1 October 1884, is in DAMMHS, J. W. Taylor Papers. A partial draft, [1 October 1884], is in PAC, RG 13 B2, 74-76.

38. Petition "To His Excellency the Governor General in Council, etc." [1 October 1884]. DAMMHS, J. W. Taylor Papers.

39. Louis Riel to J. W. Taylor, 1 October 1884, DAMMHS, J. W. Taylor Papers.

40. A trip to Battleford is mentioned in Louis Riel to T. E. Jackson, 29 September 1884. USL, A. S. Morton Mss. Collection, C555/2/13.7e.

41. A. A. Taché to Louis Riel, 4 October 1884. AASB, T 29742.

42. Constantine Scollen to Louis Riel, 10 November 1884. PAM, MG 3 D1, No. 415; Dan Maloney to Louis Riel, 17 November 1884, ibid., No. 416.

43. Petition "To His Excellency the Governor General in Council," [16 December 1884]. PAC, RG 15, Dominion Lands Branch Correspondence, File 83808. Assertions that the petition was signed by Andrew Spence and W. H. Jackson are made by Stanley, *Louis Riel,* p. 291; and Lewis H. Thomas, "Louis Riel's Petition of Rights, 1884," *Saskatchewan History* 23 (1970): 16-26.

44. W. H. Jackson to J. A. Chapleau, 16 December 1884. PAC, RG 15, Dominion Lands Branch Correspondence, File 83808.

45. W. H. Jackson to Frank Oliver, 21 January 1885. USL, A. S. Morton Mss. Collection, C555/2/13.9e. Typescript, original not found.

46. W. H. Jackson to Louis Riel, 18 December 1885. PAM, MG 3 D1, No. 417.

47. H. J. Morgan to W. H. Jackson, 5 January 1885; memo by William Pearce, n.d.; PAC, RG 15, Dominion Lands Branch Correspondence, File 83808.

48. W. H. Jackson to Louis Riel, 27 January 1885. PAC, RG 13 B2, 568-79.

49. Ibid.

50. W. H. Jackson, "Summary," n.d. USL, A. S. Morton Mss. Collection, C555/2/13.9o. Typescript, original missing.

51. W. H. Jackson, "Platform," ibid.

52. W. H. Jackson to "Dear Michel," 6 September 1886. AASB, T 53009-11.

53. Louis Riel to Romuald Fiset, 16 June 1885. PAC, RG 13 B2, 1036-43.

54. W. H. Jackson to Louis Riel, 27 January 1885. PAC, RG 13 B2, 568-79.

55. Louis Schmidt "Notes," AASB T 29811. It was described in very similar terms by Cicely Jackson to A. S. Morton, 25 June 1932; USL, A. S. Morton Mss. Collection, C555/2/13.5. W. H. Jackson obliquely refers to it in his letter to Riel, 27 January 1885; PAC, RG 13 B2, 579. It is also mentioned in Louis Riel to Julie Riel, 9 June 1885; PAM, MG 3 D1, No. 420.

56. W. H. Jackson to Frank Oliver, 21 January 1885. USL, A. S. Morton Mss. Collection, C555/2/13.9e.

57. Affidavit of John Slater, 28 July 1885. USL, A. S. Morton Mss. Collection, C555/2/13.9h.

58. T. E. Jackson, Letter to the Editor, Toronto *Globe,* 2 July 1885.

59. W. H. Jackson to "My dear Family," 19 September 1885. PAM, Selkirk Asylum Medical Records, MG 3 C20.

60. Cited in T. E. Jackson to the Toronto *Globe,* 2 July 1885. Original missing.

CONFRONTING RIEL AND COMPLETING THE CPR

D.N. Sprague

As the construction of Stephen's railway proceeded across the Prairies, the largest exodus of Red River Métis moved from Manitoba towards Saskatchewan. The most frequent destination was the district of Prince Albert, attractive because of employment by the Hudson's Bay Company (distributing freight to or from nearby Fort Carlton) and because the vacant land fronting the south branch of the Saskatchewan River closely resembled that of the old Red River colony. As positive reports from the first migrants reached discouraged relatives and former neighbours still in the large Métis parishes of St Norbert, St Franois Xavier, and Baie St. Paul, one relative followed another with increasing frequency in 1882 and 1883.[1]

In the new colony, called St Laurent, the many settlers of the early 1880s were careful to avoid trespassing on the claims of their countrymen,[2] but normally they paid little attention to the settlement status of particular parcels as designated by the Department of the Interior. The Métis were not concerned with the grid pattern of townships, sections, and ranges, and whether the parcel on which they landed happened to fit into an even-numbered section (potentially open for homesteading) or was odd-numbered (reserved for some system of sale).[3] And even if they had been careful to settle exclusively on even-numbered sections fronting on the river, they would still have encountered difficulty with the Dominion Lands Branch because, although the basic sectional survey had been completed in 1879 (and in the normal course of events would have been open to homestead entry within one year), there was an inexplicable delay in the case of St Laurent.[4]

Part of the delay is attributable to the effect of Macdonald's land policy: on the south branch of the Saskatchewan, portions of several townships amounting to more than 50,000 acres had been reserved for the Prince Albert

From *Canada and the Métis, 1869-1885* (Waterloo: Wilfrid Laurier University Press, 1988), 157-177. Reprinted by permission of Wilfrid Laurier University Press.

Colonization Company in April 1882; and the area underwent an inspection nearly equivalent to resurvey in 1883 before the final reservation occurred in November 1883.[5] Homestead entries became acceptable in February 1884.[6]

In the interim, almost 300 Métis families had come into the territory and settled mainly on river lots they laid out for themselves. Periodically, the Métis settlers asked George Duck, the Dominion Lands Agent at Prince Albert, to record their claims and to recognize the emerging river-lot pattern. Of course all such requests were frustrated, at first because the land was not open to entry of any kind; then, after February 1884, the Métis found their claims were complicated by the distinction between river lots and section land, and whether the land was odd or even-numbered in the sectional survey.[7] A few residents complied with the legal complexities; more than ninety per cent of the population held out for their own pattern of settlement and for the demand for patents immediately. What made claimants all the more persistent was seeing that approximately one-fifth of the area of new settlement had been laid out as river-lots as the Métis had wanted (in 1878 to take account of the observed pattern of occupancy at the time of original survey),[8] but even the occupants of the regularly surveyed river lots were deemed to be "squatters" until they made legal entry and completed the settlement duties that would make them eligible for patents.[9]

The Minister of the Interior might have recommended use of the sweeping powers in section 125 of the Dominion Lands Act to cut through the complexities depicted on Map 1. He might have exempted the St Laurent Métis from the odd circumstances that made their case so complicated, but there was no political advantage to be gained by moving boldly on the matter. Sir John A. Macdonald preferred continuing doing nothing, a position he had chosen deliberately in the spring of 1879 after Métis land claims first came to his attention as the Minister of the Interior following the Conservatives' return to power in September 1878.

Early in 1878, the North West "half breeds" had petitioned for land, seed grain, and implements to ease their transition to farming as the extinction of the buffalo became more and more evident in the late "1870s."[10] But none of the pleas for assistance had found favour with Macdonald's predecessor, David Mills, who dismissed all such appeals with a peculiar contradiction that was frequently evident in the utterances of officials writing on the subject of "half breeds." On the one hand, they denounced the allegedly inherent aversion of the Métis to field agriculture. On the other hand (in response to explicit requests for aid to make the transition to the way of life for which priests and certain government officials seemed to have prayed so fervently), they were told that non-Indians need not apply. In Mills' case, a letter went to the territorial governor explaining that the Métis were either Indians or not. If non-Indian, Mills could "not see upon what grounds the half breeds can claim to be treated in this particular differently from the white settlers in the territories."[11]

FIGURE 1 Conflicting Claims to the Colony of St. Laurent

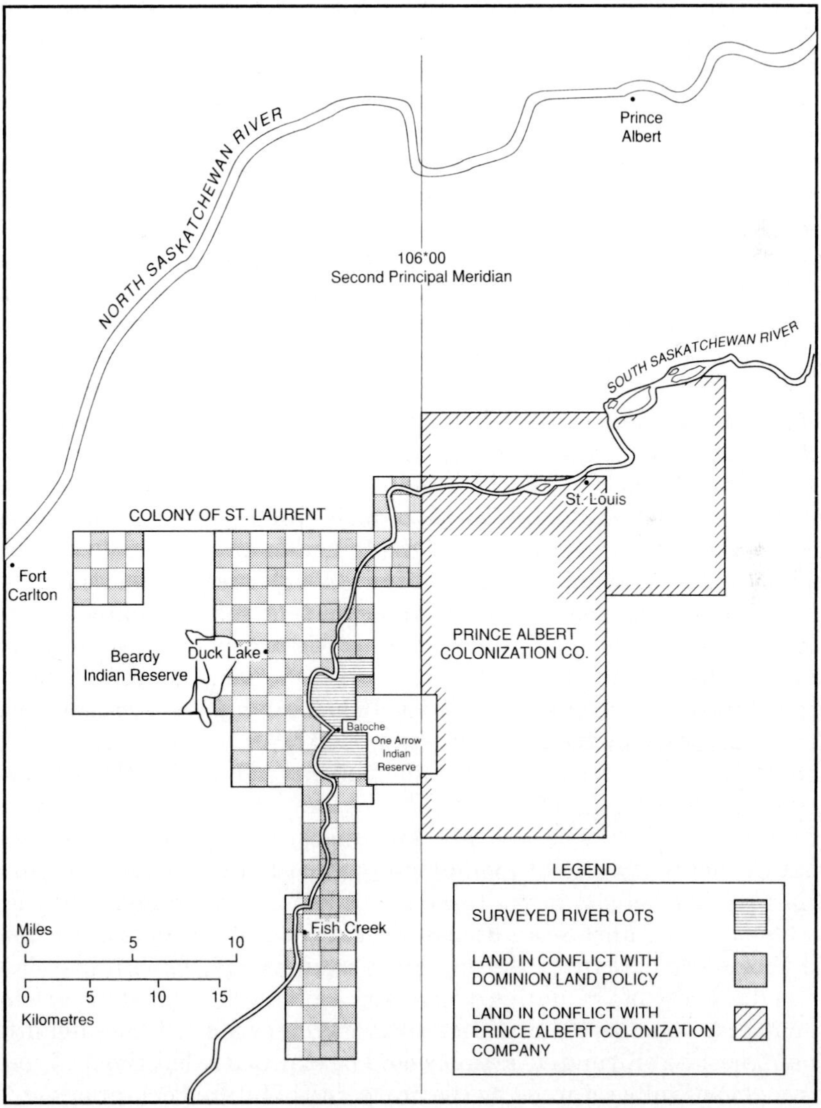

NORTH SASKATCHEWAN RIVER

Prince Albert

106°00
Second Principal Meridian

SOUTH SASKATCHEWAN RIVER

COLONY OF ST. LAURENT

St. Louis

Fort Carlton

Beardy Indian Reserve

Duck Lake

PRINCE ALBERT COLONIZATION CO.

Batoche

One Arrow Indian Reserve

Fish Creek

LEGEND

SURVEYED RIVER LOTS

LAND IN CONFLICT WITH DOMINION LAND POLICY

LAND IN CONFLICT WITH PRINCE ALBERT COLONIZATION COMPANY

Miles
0   5   10

0   5   10   15
Kilometres

But the North West Territorial Council (the appointed committee advising the Lieutenant Governor) saw the matter rather differently. In its view, all native people previously dependent on the buffalo were entitled to aid. Council members recommended an assistance programme in August 1878 that was remarkably similar to the scheme adopted by the British for the resettlement of Loyalists in Canada after the American Revolution. They proposed that a "nontransferable location ticket" entitling the recipient to 160 acres should be issued to every "half breed" left without land in the North West. Once located on plots of their own choosing, each family could then make free use of government supplied seed-grain and farm implements for up to three years, just as the British had resettled their displaced persons in North America a century before. Then the Métis settlements would be carefully monitored in their agricultural development. The council members recommended a ten-year period of probation for each assisted claimant of a free grant. It was not recommended that they should receive their land automatically. The "half breeds" would have to perform settlement duties in their first three years, then continue in residence for seven more years before they would be eligible to claim patents for their farms.[12]

Such was the policy recommended by the persons closest to the scene. Since the North West was a kind of crown colony ruled from Ottawa, one delay followed another. After Sir John A. Macdonald replaced David Mills in the Interior Ministry, he neither accepted nor rejected the advice of the Territorial Council, preferring instead to refer the matter to his Deputy Minister, J.S. Dennis, for more study. Dennis, in his turn, did draft a broader range of alternatives, adding two other possibilities to the council's proposal late in December 1878. One was extending the provisions of the Indian treaties to the Métis and native English, to "treat them as wards of the Government ... and look forward to their remaining for many years in their present semi-barbarous state." The other possibility was giving them an issue of scrip as had been done with the Manitoba "half breed heads of families" with the same doubtful benefit to the nominal recipients in the North West. Reluctantly, Dennis recommended the package proposed by the North West Council.[13]

Macdonald still hesitated. He disliked rewarding the Métis for what he considered their own improvidence—it was they who spoiled their opportunities in Manitoba, and they as well who killed most of the buffalo.[14] Not worrying about further delay, the Prime Minister instructed Dennis to send his memorandum on the subject to the three bishops most acquainted with the Métis. The two Roman Catholic consultants added their endorsements to the Territorial Council's scheme, saying, "the half breed cannot compete with the White man in the discharge of the duties of civilized life unless some steps are taken at the outset to equalize the conditions on which they start. " They admitted that the appropriate affirmative action would be expensive, but the first costs were expected to be fully returned by the prosperity of future generations of Métis.[15]

Later, the Anglican bishop contributed more muted approval to the growing chorus of promoters of aid, saying that he thought that the free land, seed grain, and implements would be "necessary at first." Still, because he believed that fear of starvation was God's way of teaching respect for civilization, Bishop Machray added that "the less of such gifts the better. They are apt to do mischief."[16]

The result of Macdonald's fruitless quest for a cheap and simple alternative to the proposal of the North West Council was the addition of a few phrases to the Dominion Lands Act in the spring of 1879. The new words appeared to recognize that the North West "half breeds" had a claim to a share of the Indian title to the territory and that the Cabinet was empowered to set aside land "to such extent, and on such terms and conditions, as may be deemed expedient" to satisfy such claims.[17] But in 1879, 1880, 1881, 1882, and 1883 nothing was done towards implementing the new authority to deal with the Métis. Not surprisingly, Macdonald was no more inclined to respond favourably to the new demands of the Métis reinforced in number and resolve by the large migrations from Manitoba. Consequently, the St Laurent claims underwent the same rigour of evaluation as those of any other group of complaining homesteaders. Of the more than 250 persons demanding patents in 1884, less than 10 were considered legally entitled to what they claimed.[18] Then a new factor suddenly caused Macdonald to reassess his sense of political profit and loss in "half breed" claims. He received an alarming assessment of the situation in June 1884.

Lawrence Clarke, Chief Factor of Fort Carlton, had informed James Grahame (Clarke's superior officer in Winnipeg) that a pattern of escalating discontent was reaching a point of crisis; "repressive measures" were needed. Clarke explained that as "half breeds" in the District of Saskatchewan were losing freighting employment to the railway and steamboats, they were becoming poorer and poorer, and were pressing extravagant claims on the government in the hope of getting something they might readily sell for cash. As their first appeals were failing, they were on the point of taking extreme action—threatening to repeat the events of 1869-70. A delegation had gone to Montana intending to bring Louis Riel back. The repression Clarke proposed was arresting Riel at the border if he accepted the offer of leadership. Otherwise his presence among hundreds of armed Métis and native English might involve the Indians and even some of the disgruntled white settlers who resented having been bypassed by the CPR. Clarke admitted that taking Riel prisoner would anger some people, but he said a "strong detachment" of police near St Laurent could deter the most militant. The others would be calmed by judicious use of the "influence" at Clarke's disposal and that of the Catholic priests in the area.[19]

Receiving the alarm via Grahame,[20] Macdonald reacted immediately by seeking more information. On the one hand, he asked his man on the spot,

Edgar Dewdney, for his assessment. The Lieutenant Governor replied in a matter of days that the "half breeds" had been "ventilating their grievances" in secret meetings, and Dewdney also agreed that the principal reason for their discontent was economic because the Hudson's Bay Company had drastically cut both the volume and the rate of pay for overland freighting. But Dewdney added that a little group of Prince Albert speculators (including Clarke) had suffered from the collapse of the recent land boom. They welcomed the idea of a larger police garrison for the money it would bring into the district. Indeed, Lawrence Clarke was playing a double game. Having goaded the "half breeds" to bold protest, his "very sensational" letter now played to his speculator's interest more than to a real crisis.[21]

Dewdney's reassuring letter was not confirmed by the result of the police inquiries that Macdonald requested at the same time. He wanted to know the overall number of "half breeds" in the North West, how many were disaffected Manitobans, where they lived, and their probability of following Riel in the event of his attempting to form a second provisional government. Macdonald had also asked the Deputy Minister in charge of the police, Fred White, to go west for his own first hand impressions.

Before his departure, Comptroller White ordered Superintendent Crozier and Commissioner Irvine (the field officers in the North West Mounted Police with military ranks of major and colonel, respectively) to collect the statistical data. On June 10, White ordered Irvine to make discreet inquiries while travelling from community to community under some improvised purpose—"with some object ... other than the real one."[22] On the same day, White sent identical instructions to Crozier, ordering him to "visit the settlements and ... form an opinion which you can communicate to me confidentially."[23]

Thus, Macdonald did not ignore Clarke's warning. He moved quickly for a comprehensive view and from diverse sources, even though he rejected the appeal for immediate "repressive measures." Riel and the delegation were not arrested when they reached the Canadian border in late June, but the police did "shadow" the progress of Riel and his entourage closely, and kept the Prime Minister fully informed of what followed.

While Dewdney continued to report that Riel's return was a political nuisance but no threat (not unless the Métis leader "tampered" with Indian discontents),[24] White's report was remarkably consistent with the original alarm sounded by Clarke. Canada's most senior policeman was certain that, despite peaceful appearances, Louis Riel did aim for something like a second provisional government. "I am convinced that there is an illegal movement of some kind in contemplation."[25] A detailed statistical report substantiating the danger of such a development suggested that, of the 5,400 "half breeds" in the North West, 4,400 were Manitoba emigrants. Although they were found in twenty-one separate localities, almost half were settled near the forks of the

Saskatchewan. There Riel could expect support from an estimated force of 600 men capable of bearing arms in the event of trouble. St Laurent was the true centre of "disloyalty" because its population was "chiefly from White Horse Plains, Baie St Paul, etc. in Manitoba. A hard lot, were Riel's supporters in 1869."[26] Other communities were either too small or too far away from St Laurent to pose any serious difficulty. "They would take no steps unless Riel's party was fairly certain of being successful," or "not ... mixed up, but if Indians were once on the warpath they would likely join them."[27]

On July 10, Macdonald reported the disturbing news to the vacationing Governor General, Lord Lansdowne, saying that the situation was serious but manageable. He believed land was the key. "Some of the Half breeds have land claims which are in the process of adjustment. The claims are for the most part invalid, but they will be liberally treated."[28] Then, as the news continued to be "disquieting," Macdonald outlined a broader programme of conciliation in more correspondence with the absent representative of the Queen. On August 5, the Prime Minister repeated the idea that he was prepared to honour the land claims of Riel's followers, and something special might be offered to Riel himself:

> In his answer to the invitation sent him which was a temperate and unobjectionable paper, he spoke of some claims he had against the Gov't. I presume these refer to his land claims which he forfeited on conviction and banishment, [but] I think we shall deal liberally with him and make him a good subject again.
>
> If I don't mistake his character, he will make a good Moral Agent or Detective for the Gov't and keep the metis in order.[29]

Lansdowne replied the same day with a note stating that the idea of conciliating the leader was the key factor, and urged Macdonald to "make every endeavour to obtain touch' " with Riel and offer him a bribe; "it might be intimated to him that you were prepared to deal generously with him in so far as his private requirements seem concerned, and that you were ready to consider in a general conciliatory spirit the demands put forward by the half breeds."[30] In the arrangement envisioned by Lansdowne, the people would get their land, and Riel could receive at least an appointment to the North West Council if not to the Canadian Senate.

In Macdonald's opinion, the contemplated patronage for Riel was excessive. Macdonald protested that Louis Riel had "committed a cold-blooded murder in `69, which will never be forgotten by the whites either in Manitoba or Ontario."[31] A less extravagant offer was more appropriate, but the rest of Macdonald's answer did make clear that he was still committed to conciliation in principle. Emissaries of good will would see Riel and his lieutenants as in 1869 and "encourage them to specify their grievances in Memorials and send them with or without delegations to Ottawa." Such a course would "allow time for the present effervescence to subside—and on the approach of winter—the climate will keep things quiet until next spring." Meanwhile officials in the Department of the Interior could use the respite bought by the promise of conciliation to go over the land claims and concede patents to any with "a semblance of foundation."[32]

Lansdowne approved. He appreciated that the problem of Riel and his people was "intricate," and Macdonald's proposed method of handling Riel would make him "understand that he has more to gain, personally and as a public man, by confining himself to the legitimate ventilation of the grievances of his clients, than by leading a disorderly movement."[33]

The first person recruited to have a private word with the Métis leader was C.B. Rouleau, a French-Canadian lawyer recently appointed to judicial responsibilities at nearby Battleford, Saskatchewan. A second, more prominent prospective emissary was Sir Hector Langevin, the Minister of Public Works in the federal Cabinet and already committed to tour the West on other errands. Here as well the Governor General gave unqualified approval. On August 13, he agreed that Rouleau could "gauge the situation pretty accurately"[34] and on August 23 Lansdowne expressed special satisfaction that Langevin was going on his errand to "set Riel's head the right way."[35]

All was arranged by the end of August for avoiding the political liability of Riel leading several hundred families into a second provisional government. Macdonald had reliable intelligence from diverse sources that such a development was possible, and he had a plausible plan for undercutting the basis of the "foolish plot"[36] and for buying Riel's loyalty. Should conciliation fail, the safety of the government was still assured by a planned expansion of police power. Macdonald told Lansdowne that he intended to increase the police force in the West by thirty per cent with a flying column of 100 to be garrisoned at Fort Carlton.[37] If there was a second "Riel rebellion," it could be checked quickly by a mounted constabulary already on the scene. Still, timely conciliation was expected to prevent such a development.

The policy Macdonald described to the Governor General in July and August flowed from the obvious calculation that an "outbreak" in the North West was an avoidable political liability. The cost would be land that the Métis already occupied and money or patronage to be invested in Riel with the expectation of larger dividends in more general native pacification. In this sense, Macdonald had to agree with Lansdowne that Riel's return was "anything but a misfortune."[38] Yet Macdonald appears to have decided near the end of August 1884 that an angry Riel could be even more useful in the broader field of Canadian politics. For some reason, the Langevin visit was mysteriously[39] cancelled; the land claims were handled more in conformity with the Dominion Lands Act than with what the "half breeds" demanded; and none of Riel's personal claims received favourable consideration. In the context of escalating discontent the Métis did become more militant; Riel did lead them into an illegal government;

and the Government of Canada did respond with force—with the mobilization of militia from as far away as Halifax, as well as with the police power already on the scene. What were the political advantages of the sequence of events as they actually occurred?

The political problem that made provocative inaction ultimately worthwhile was renewed difficulty with Stephen's railway. At the time that Macdonald was first thinking about his programme of Métis conciliation, Stephen had begun to hint that he might need more assistance from Canada.[40] Macdonald's reaction was so swift and completely discouraging on July 18[41] that the railway president promised not to say another word on the subject, then violated his own promise in the same letter: "I will only say here that I cannot under the existing condition of affairs, any longer, look forward to the land grant as affording an available asset ... and our 35 million capital is equally useless...."[42]

Concurrent with Macdonald's corresponding with Lansdowne, Macdonald and Stephen exchanged eight letters[43] (which have survived) and held at least two meetings (mentioned in the correspondence). The Prime Minister fretted about the "many threads" of crisis he had to attend to personally and showed the railway president the papers documenting developments in the North West.[44] Stephen assured Macdonald that the railway construction was proceeding better than expected but continued to complain about a serious deficiency of capital for other needs. Macdonald could not agree to what Stephen thought essential, but he did agree to help in recruiting $5 million from private bankers in London and to accompany the railway president on his Atlantic crossing.

Unfortunately for Stephen, neither a letter of recommendation[45] from Canada's Prime Minister nor Macdonald's presence in London was sufficient to persuade Baring Brothers that the railway was a safe risk, and Stephen's need for the additional $5 million from Parliament matured before anything else to convince Macdonald's colleagues (or the country) that additional legislative assistance was warranted. Then, once Macdonald returned to Ottawa, Sir David Macpherson complained that Langevin had returned from the West as the perfect champion of "dead beats."[46]

Langevin's position even without seeing Riel was that the Métis leader was too dangerous to ignore. "We must take care not to make a martyr of him and thus increase his popularity." The solution was "good treatment of the half breeds." Langevin believed even a little would "go a long way to settle matters."[47] Macpherson tried to convince Langevin that every land claim had been "fully considered and equitably disposed of," but Sir David believed Sir Hector remained unconvinced. A meeting with Sir John was needed.[48] That appears to have ended the matter. At least there were no more memoranda advocating concessions such as Langevin had proposed early in November.

Macdonald's greater difficulty was calming Stephen. By mid-January the railway president was insisting that the survival of his company absolutely depended on aid from the government, but Macdonald insisted that the proposition was still "hopeless." A telegram from the Prime Minister on January 20 urged Stephen to "postpone matter to eighteen eight six can carry it in Council."[49] Stephen replied that postponement was "impossible" and begged for a meeting the next day to "decide finally on course am forced to take."[50] They did meet, but the only surviving record of what was apparently agreed to was a letter from Stephen in mid-April alluding to maturing obligations that "three months ago were postponed till now on the faith that by this time we should be in a position to meet them."[51] Further contextual evidence that something had been agreed to in late January was a more optimistic tone and shift in Stephen's correspondence on the subject in February and early March as he devoted most of his letters to the terms of the rescue he was clearly expecting.[52] Conversely, Macdonald seemed more depressed than ever. On January 24 he reported to his old friend Tupper that the situation was nearly as bad as the worst the two had imagined in the previous autumn. "Geo Stephen says the CPR must go down unless sustained," and he enumerated the key personnel in Cabinet who were adamantly opposed to any such additional aid. "How it will end I don't know."[53]

Nothing had happened to change "the thing"[54] in Ottawa. Yet the abandonment of straightforward conciliation had meant that Métis discontent was maturing into an exploitable crisis. Riel had spent the entire autumn and early winter writing—and rewriting—the draft of a comprehensive statement of grievances covering claims. The most preliminary statement specified: territorial self-government; land rights similar to the assurances in section 32 of the Manitoba Act; a 2-million-acre trust (the income from which would provide long-term development capital for the Métis); 64,000 acres of "swamp lands" to be reserved for the children of Métis heads of families (to be distributed every eighteen years over seven generations); reconsideration of the land rights of the Manitoba Métis; and preferential consideration of "half breeds" for "works and contracts" in the Territories.[55]

After consulting Bishops Taché and Grandin, Riel dropped some of the demands that the clerical consultants and his own close advisors considered "extravagant."[56] The petition that the St Laurent Métis finally mailed to the Governor General on December 16 was more limited in its focus upon land titles, home rule, and compensation for alleged maladministration of the Manitoba Act. Considering the last point, it was not surprising that the document was addressed to the Governor General with a covering letter requesting that the Queen's representative should forward the document directly to England in the hope that the British would compel Canada to act as in 1870.[57]

Given the direct parallel that the Métis drew between their present situation and the events of 1869, the alarms that kept streaming in from the North West might have led Macdonald to expect the formation of a provisional government at almost any moment in January. The police reports of the previous summer had indicated that delay would almost certainly result in some "illegal combination," and six months had passed without meeting any of the agitators' principal demands or taking steps to break up the agitation with police power. But nothing had happened. In late January Riel was still not acting according to prediction even as Stephen's financial crisis reached new, more frightening proportions, and nothing had altered Macdonald's inability to deliver his partner the promised aid.

Here was the context and perhaps also the explanation for the peculiarly provocative content of an important Order in Council that was adopted on January 28. Telegraphed to Dewdney, the news was that Canada would "investigate claims of Half Breeds and with that view [Cabinet] had decided [to make an] enumeration of those who did not participate in Grant under Manitoba Act."[58] The provocation was that only a small minority of the residents of St Laurent could benefit from awards to non-Manitobans. Moreover, the government already had the figures: 200 of 1,300 potential claimants.[59] Dewdney was so stunned by the news he refused to pass on the information without alteration. Imagining the purpose of the Order in Council was conciliation rather than provocation, he changed the announcement before transmitting the telegram to St Laurent: "Government has decided to investigate claims of Half Breeds and with that view has already taken preliminary steps." Then Dewdney reminded Macdonald that "the bulk of the French Half Breeds" had "nothing to expect" from the unrevised text. The original news would "start a fresh agitation."[60]

No prime ministerial congratulation came back over the wire thanking Dewdney for his editorial intervention, and Dewdney's text was still far short of the news the Métis wanted. They demanded recognition of their aboriginal title demand, not additional consideration of the matter. Equally important, they wanted news that their claims to river lots were recognized. Here too the telegram from Dewdney was silent. Then on February 6, the Dominion Lands Agent at Prince Albert learned from the Deputy Minister of the Department of the Interior that the river-lot question was about to be disposed of. He could expect instructions "in the course of a few days."[61]

The claims reported to Winnipeg in June 1884 had passed from Winnipeg to Ottawa in October, and finally back from headquarters to Prince Albert near the end of February 1885. The news the Lands Agent was to report to the claimants was an enormous disappointment to the vast majority of the families hoping for confirmation of titles.[62] They felt they had done their part. All but a small non-co-operating group of forty-five had compromised their original demand for river lots laid out in the old Manitoba pattern. More than 200 settlers had provided evidence of compliance with the boundaries of subdivisions as laid out in the government survey. Eight such claimants received notification that their periods of settlement, extent of cultivation, and value of improvements entitled them to patents. The others were processed as applications for "entry." Consequently, more than sixty per cent of the settlers expecting patent were confronted with an infuriating contradiction: their claims were allowed;

patents were denied. They would not become the owners of their land in the eyes of Canada until paying fees, performing more settlement duties, and going through another process of application, inspection, and consideration by the local agent, by the Winnipeg Lands Board, and by the Dominion Lands Branch in Ottawa. Even then they would have to pay for any acreage in excess of the 160-acre maximum allowable "free grant" (some claimants were told that the pre-emption part of their claim would cost $1 per acre, for others the price was $2). Finally, the question of trespass on the lands of the Prince Albert Colonization Company was unresolved; thirty families were excluded from "entry" as well as from patents.[63]

Canada's handling of the river-lot question was far from conciliatory, but the government could defend itself by saying that the claimants received all the consideration they were entitled to expect under the Dominion Lands Act. Indeed, in one respect—waiving the distinction between odd- and even-numbered sections (except in the vicinity of the Prince Albert Colonization Company)—the government could say that the Métis claimants were treated more liberally than the law required.

One last provocation was similarly defensible from the standpoint of rigid adherence to principle. On February 20 the Prime Minister informed Lieutenant Governor Dewdney that the answer to Riel's private claims was a definite no. With uncharacteristic moral outrage Macdonald declared: "We have no money to give Riel. He has a right to remain in Canada and if he conspires we must punish him. That's all."[64]

The last two provocations together—the personal disappointment of Riel and the general frustration of the land claimants—finally broke Métis patience the day after Lands Agent Duck sent out the last disturbing notification on March 7. On March 8, Riel announced that he thought that the time had come to form a provisional government.

Three days later, Lieutenant Governor Dewdney telegraphed the latest development to the Prime Minister, saying there was a possibility that the declaration was no more than a "bluff" but "if the Half breeds mean business, the sooner they are put down the better." Dewdney advised taking them by surprise. "They are like Indians. When they gather and get excited it is difficult to handle them, but if they are taken unawares there is little difficulty in arresting the leader."[65]

On the same day, March 11, Stephen demanded bold action for the railway, complaining that his finances were "getting beyond all control." Stephen expressed sympathy for Macdonald's political problems, but the CPR president insisted that the time had come for the Prime Minister to do whatever was necessary to alter the current political impasse. "I know and appreciate fully the reason for delaying consideration of our matters till the proper and most favourable time arrives but I am really concerned about ways and means to carry us along in the meantime.... I hope you will think of this and bring things to a head as soon as possible."[66]

True to his favourite maxim, "He who waits wins,"[67] Macdonald did nothing, but not with any evident comfort. On March 17, he informed Tupper that "Stephen asks a loan for a year of 5 millions (that Tilley [the Minister of Finance] can't face)" and complained that everyone was reaching the limits of endurance. "How it will end God knows—but I wish I were well out of it."[68] No doubt Stephen and Dewdney were equally perplexed. Unable to get a satisfactory answer to his letters and telegrams, Dewdney pursued his own initiative.

On March 12, the Lieutenant Governor convened a meeting to consider the Riel crisis with four other people in Regina: Hayter Reed (the Indian Commissioner), A.G. Irvine (the Police Commissioner), Hugh Richardson (the Stipendiary Magistrate of the district), and Lawrence Clarke (still Chief Factor at Fort Carlton). The primary concern was Riel's proclamation of intent: whether it was genuine or "a mere matter of bluff ... to frighten the government into making concessions." Clarke suggested that since the total force at Riel's command was probably no more than 350 poorly armed men "with their wives and children, who must be exposed to extreme peril should they be so foolish as to resort to arms," and since the government force "already on the spot" numbered 120 well-armed police backed by artillery, the Hudson's Bay Company officer thought that the "only danger to be apprehended ... would be in the event of Riel attempting to tamper with the loyalty of the Indians." In that event, it was agreed that they should arrest the Métis leader "no matter at what risk." And even without Riel's moving towards alliances with the Indians, it was considered that "Mr. Riel and his band of discontents should not be allowed to keep up senseless agitation, destroying all faith in the country and ruining its peaceable inhabitants." Sooner or later they would have to "settle this matter once for all." In Clarke's opinion the question was "whether this was not the time." Under the circumstances of the moment, it was agreed that Clarke should return to Fort Carlton at once, and Irvine would "start for the `seat of war' " several days later, about the time Clarke reached Fort Carlton from Regina.[69]

Arriving at his destination on the evening of March 17,[70] Clarke reported that Riel's movement had "apparently flattened out" but there was no doubt as to his "tampering with Indians." Clarke did not think Riel would win many over, but advised the immediate arrest of Riel to prevent any further mischief. "No better time to deal with leader and followers."[71] Dewdney responded that he had still "heard nothing from Ottawa" and reported that Irvine was departing for Fort Carlton the next day with 100 reinforcements.[72] Then, as rather an afterthought, Dewdney sent Clarke a second telegram on March 17 advising him to make the government's intentions public. "Put in PA Times that an additional force is being sent.... Get paper to enlarge and state scattered that government intend to have peace in the district."[73]

Clarke passed the instruction on to his new superior officer in Winnipeg, Joseph Wrigley, who responded by telegram that he opposed the newspaper advertisement, at least as a Hudson's Bay Company announcement. Perhaps Wrigley feared that such information would be interpreted as a provocative gesture and lead to criticism of the company later. "Better for you not to act publicly but leave responsibility on Government."[74] As a result, the action that pushed Riel to take the next step was not a printed word, but verbal communication that Clarke subsequently denied he had ever spoken.

The story Lawrence Clarke later denounced as a "tissue of lies"[75] was that he had encountered a group of Métis near Fort Carlton some time before March 19 and had given them information resembling the news that Dewdney instructed him to spread through the district on March 17. According to popular legend, the Métis asked Clarke if there was any answer yet to their petitions and protest. "His reply was that the only answer they would get would be bullets, and that, indeed, on his way northward, he had passed a camp of 500 policemen who were coming up to capture the Half breed agitators."[76] It is possible that Clarke said only that more police were on the way with the intention of arresting Riel. The rest may have been nothing more than the result of exaggeration in retelling the news at Batoche.

What is certain is that the Métis reacted to Clarke's news as the final provocation. The provisional government emerged on March 19 (with eighty-eight per cent support from the inhabitants of the colony of St Laurent).[77] Despite the risk of police intervention, Riel did not foresee any great danger because the newspapers were full of reports of the possibility of war between England and Russia. With British (and Canadian) forces occupied in a foreign war, surely Canada would dispose of a small domestic crisis peacefully as in 1870. Riel miscalculated. The mobilization for conflict overseas did not occur. Instead, Canada mobilized militia from Halifax to Winnipeg to deal with the Métis, even though Dewdney's dispatches indicated that he thought the police were competent to deal with the situation unfolding in late March.

Macdonald did not anticipate a war against the Métis. At the time of the mobilization (March 23), he cautioned the Minister of Militia, J.P.R.A. Caron, to "remind General Middleton that the [NWMP] Commissioner and Officers are magistrates and well acquainted with the character of the Half-breeds and Indians and must understand the best mode of dealing with them and inducing them to lay down their arms and submit to legal authority."[78] A massive show of force would compel surrender without a fight. Although Dewdney preferred resolving the problem with local resources ("I would have rather seen the trouble stopped entirely by the police"), the Governor had to concede that the Métis were even less likely to resist if thousands of troops suddenly appeared on the scene, especially if the government met Riel's price and whisked him out of the country before the troops arrived. "How far can I go?" Dewdney asked on March 23.[79]

What Macdonald seems to have envisioned was a sudden dash to the Prairies, a mysterious "escape" of Riel back to the United States, conciliatory gestures to the surrendering Métis, and aid for the railway after it played such a key role in breaking up the "outbreak" so "speedily and gallantly."[80]

On March 26, however, the situation became unexpectedly complicated by bloodshed. Since the Métis believed 500 police were en route to arrest Riel, they prepared to fend off the NWMP in a long siege by sending a force to seize supplies from a store at Duck Lake. Simultaneously, a party of police went to the same place to spoil the attempt. When the two groups came face to face, both sides sent out spokesmen to talk under a flag of truce, but the meeting soon deteriorated into single-champion combat with two men dead, then into general shooting with twelve fallen on the Canadian side and five Métis killed.[81]

The confrontation between police and "half breeds" was followed by sporadic Indian action and raised the spectre of war such as the Americans had fought in the 1860s and 1870s. After March 26, greater prospects of danger and longer delays filled Macdonald with increased dread. "This insurrection is a bad business," Macdonald wrote Dewdney on March 29, "but we must face it as best we may."[82]

Since the Americans were almost as worried as some Canadians that the "outbreak" would become a general Indian war, they offered full cooperation in the movement of troops and supplies and their own cavalry for patrolling the border.[83] Macdonald accepted the transport offer for shipping equipment, but he insisted on the CPR as the vehicle for transporting the unfortunate Canadian volunteers, the first contingent of whom left Toronto on March 30 in two separate trains. When the men reached the north shore of Lake Superior in the first week of April, they discovered that there were four gaps in the line that had to be crossed by sleigh or on foot. The worst part, however, was one section of isolated railway where the men had to ride on flat cars in the open, bitter cold.[84] Still, in less than two weeks, more than 3,000 troops did reach the Territories ready to be deployed against the "half breeds" and their few Indian allies.

In the fighting that occurred here and there in late April and early May there were several encounters that could be called battles.[85] For more than fifty Canadians and a similar number of "half breeds" and Indians, death was a final as in any global conflict. And yet Macdonald did not exaggerate later when he dismissed most of the military side of the "North West Rebellion" as a "mere riot."

From Macdonald's point of view, the more important aspects of the affair were showing the flag of British authority and proving that the railway had transformed Canada into a country capable of suppressing challenges to its sovereignty in the most remote sections of habitable territory. To be sure, the Opposition made searing accusations of mismanagement, but Macdonald met their charges that the war could have been avoided with counter-charges that his own "half breed" policy had been far more liberal than his opponents.[86]

Indeed, on native affairs in general he claimed to be the epitome of enlightened and progressive action, and he moved to substantiate his claim in April with a diversionary franchise bill that included proposals for nearly universal suffrage for white men and extension of the vote to certain single women and the Six Nations of Loyalist Indians in Ontario.[87]

The Liberals were triply embarrassed. Having denounced Macdonald's handling of North West matters, they seemed sympathetic to natives; then, having posed as friends of the Indians and the Métis, they were embarrassed by their own vehement opposition to the inclusion of certain loyal native people in the national franchise because David Mills said they were "savages." Thus, they were set up to be embarrassed the third time when they fought the aid for the railway that had saved the nation from a prolonged war with Canada's native peoples.

The CPR did receive its aid package in July. In the same month, Louis Riel stood trial at Regina where he was held accountable for treason and sentenced to hang. Riel dropped to the end of the hangman's rope in Regina on November 16. The railway reached its official completion almost at the same time in a last-spike ceremony on November 7. Still jubilant over the success of his railway, Stephen wrote Macdonald just before Riel's execution to inform the Prime Minister of his pleasure with the rising value of CPR stock over the preceding week and to tell Sir John how "glad" he was that the "mischievous crank Riel is going to have justice meted out to him."[88] No other correspondent with Macdonald was as quick to link the two events so directly, but few people other than Stephen knew how closely the Métis loss had been joined to the railway's gain.

Notes

1. See Mailhot and Sprague, "Persistent Settlers."
2. There were no "Class 16" claims (land disputes) in the detailed report upon St Laurent submitted by the Lands Board to headquarters in the autumn of 1884. See University of Alberta Archives. William Pearce Papers, MG 9/2/4-4, vol. 4, pp. 224-275.
3. For the system of sectional survey adopted by Canada see Chester Martin. *"Dominion Lands" Policy.*
4. Flanagan, *Riel and the Rebellion,* pp. 30-33, 37-40.
5. PAC, RG 15, vol. 277, file 44447, p. 19; and House of Commons Debates, speech by Edward Blake, 6 July 1885, p. 3100.
6. The report of William Pearce, "All Claims to land ... on the South Saskatchewan" (University of Alberta Archives, Pearce Papers, MG 9/2, series 5, vol. 1, file 6 and series 4, vol. 4, pp. 888-901) states that some of the land was open for entry as early as 1881. But in response to a question on the subject in the House of Commons on

June 8, 1885, Macdonald admitted that much of the district was not open for home-stead entry until February 15, 1884 (House of Commons Debates, 8 June 1885, p. 2358).

7. PAC, Records of the Department of the Interior, RG 15, vol. 336, file 84478, George Duck to Commissioner of Dominion Lands, 15 June 1884.

8. Flanagan, *Riel Reconsidered,* p. 33.

9. Pearce, "All Claims to Land," p. 6-8.

10. PAC, Macdonald Papers, Incoming Correspondence, pp. 42053-42056 42067-42070.

11. Ibid., pp. 42048-42050, Mills to Laird, 18 March 1878. Later, Macdonald told the House of Commons that Mills had given the appropriate response. See House of Commons Debates, 6 July 1885, p. 3112.

12. PAC, Macdonald Papers, Incoming Correspondence, pp. 42067-42070, Minutes of the Council of the North West Territories, 2 August 1878.

13. Ibid., pp. 138984-138987, "Confidential Memorandum: Remarks on the Condition of the Half Breeds of the North West Territories, 20 December 1878."

14. See Macdonald's sketch of the history of Manitoba land claims reported to the Governor General in August 1884 (ibid., Transcripts, vol. 585, Macdonald to Lansdowne, 5 August 1884).

15. Ibid., Incoming Correspondence, pp. 42072-42083, Bishop Grandin to Dennis, 18 January 1879.

16. Ibid., pp. 42084-42091, Bishop Machray to Dennis, 15 February 1879.

17. Statutes of Canada (1879), Chapter 31: "An Act to amend and consolidate the several Acts respecting the Public lands of the Dominion," section 125(e).

18. Pearce, "All Claims to Land," p. 6.

19. PAC, Macdonald Papers, Incoming Correspondence, pp. 42244-42250, Clarke to Grahame, 20 May 1884.

20. Ibid., pp. 42242-42243, Grahame to Macdonald, 29 May 1884.

21. Ibid., pp. 42767-42778, Dewdney to Macdonald, 14 June 1884.

22. Ibid., pp. 42251-42253, White to Irvine, 10 June 1884.

23. Ibid., pp. 42254-42255, White to Crozier, 10 June 1884.

24. See, for example, the letter from André to Dewdney, 7 July 1884, that the Governor forwarded to Macdonald (ibid., pp. 42277-42280).

25. Ibid., pp. 134906-134916, White to Macdonald, 7 July 1884.

26. Other sources tend to corroborate the police report. See "Supplement 2: The Settlers of the Colony of St Laurent," in Mailhot and Sprague, "Persistent Settlers," pp. 18-26.

27. PAC, Macdonald Papers, Incoming Correspondence, p. 148567, "Estimated Number of Half Breeds."

28. Ibid., Transcripts, vol. 585, Macdonald to Lansdowne, 10 July 1884.

29. Ibid., Macdonald to Lansdowne, 5 August 1884.

30. Ibid., Incoming Correspondence, pp. 32872-32879, Lansdowne to Macdonald, 5 August 1884.

31. Ibid., Transcripts, vol. 585, Macdonald to Lansdowne, 12 August 1884.

32. Ibid.

33. Ibid., Incoming Correspondence, pp. 32884-32887, Lansdowne to Macdonald, 13 August 1884.

34. Ibid.

35. Ibid., pp. 32893-32895, Lansdowne to Macdonald, 23 August 1884.

36. Ibid., Letter Books, vol. 23, pp. 33-34, Macdonald to J.C. Aikins, 28 July 1884.

37. Ibid., Transcripts, vol. 585, Macdonald to Lansdowne, 12 August 1884; and Letter Book, vol. 23, pp. 56-57, Macdonald to Donald A. Smith, 5 September 1884.

38. Ibid., Incoming Correspondence, pp. 32872-32879, Lansdowne to Macdonald, 5 August 1884.

39. Why Langevin failed to fulfill the mission is a problem of considerable complexity. The conventional explanation (See Stanley, *Riel,* p. 285; and Bob Beal and Rod Macleod, *Prairie Fire: The 1885 North-West Rebellion* [Edmonton, 1984], pp. 117-118) is that Langevin's change of itinerary represented his own independent alteration of plans. Having arrived at Regina in the last week of August, he is supposed to have been so fatigued by the earlier part of his journey that he could not face travelling 200 miles over muddy cart trails to St Laurent just to suffer the harangues of political malcontents. Thus he cancelled the trip despite the consequences. Langevin proved later that he was indeed capable of foolish initiatives. But the cancellation of the Riel mission was more than foolhardy. Once Riel had been informed that Langevin was visiting in 1884—in the role Smith had played in 1869-70—and once it became known that Riel regarded the meeting as "marked proof of good will towards the North West" (Riel quoted in Beal and Macleod, *Prairie Fire,* p. 118), cancellation without justification or notification of regret was equivalent to provocation.

    The difficulty with assigning sole responsibility to Langevin is evidence of earlier communication with Macdonald. The day of Langevin's departure from his home, August 18, Sir Hector sent a brief note to the Prime Minister inviting last-minute instructions (PAC, Macdonald Papers, Incoming Correspondence, pp. 97438-9743). There is no record of Macdonald's response, but on August 19 a telegram went from Langevin to Judge Rouleau at Battleford informing him that Sir Hector would not be making the digression to Batoche (Stanley, *Riel,* p. 285). Subsequently, Rouleau either forgot or was instructed not to report the news to Riel, with the result that the Métis continued an unsatisfying vigil, constantly watching the roadways to Batoche for some face resembling Langevin's.

    If the change was Langevin's mistake, Macdonald had an opportunity to correct it on August 29 when his good-will ambassador sent him a message before leaving Manitoba for Regina (PAC, Macdonald Papers, Incoming Correspondence, pp. 97441-97442). Langevin reported that the train had taken him as far as Brandon. After a brief visit with Dewdney he expected to continue on to the end of the railway: "In a week I will have reached the end of the road and be on the return." Obviously, that itinerary precluded the errand to Batoche. If Macdonald's previous plans were still in effect, it was important to intercept Langevin before his return. No record of attempted interception has been found. Nor did Macdonald complain later about a unilateral upset of his conciliation scheme.

40. PAC, Macdonald Papers, Incoming Correspondence, pp. 122328-122331, Stephen to Macdonald, 17 July 1884.

41. Ibid., Transcripts, vol. 585, Macdonald to Stephen, 18 July 1884.

42. Ibid., Incoming Correspondence, pp. 122340-122347, Stephen to Macdonald, 22 July 1884.

43. Macdonald's letters to Stephen were dated 24 and 30 July 1884 (both in ibid., Transcripts, vol. 585). Stephen's to Macdonald were 27 July, 2 August (two letters), and 13, 16, 19 August (all in ibid., Incoming Correspondence, pp. 122353-122419).

44. Ibid., Transcripts, vol. 585, Macdonald to Stephen, 30 July 1884.

45. Ibid., Letter Book, vol. 23, pp. 59-60, Macdonald to Baring Brothers, 6 September 1884.

46. Ibid., Incoming Correspondence, pp. 112802-112805, Macpherson to Macdonald, 31 December 1884.

47. Ibid., pp. 97452-97456, Langevin to Macdonald, 6 November 1884.

48. Ibid., pp. 112802-112805, Macpherson to Macdonald, 31 December 1884.

49. Ibid., Letter Book, vol. 23, p. 101, Macdonald cypher telegram to Stephen, 20 January 1885.

50. Ibid., Incoming Correspondence, p. 122608, Stephen cypher telegram to Macdonald, 20 January 1885.

51. Ibid., pp. 122818-122821, Stephen to Macdonald, 15 April 1885.

52. See Stephen's letters of 3, 8, 9, 12, 13, 19 February and 2 March in ibid., Incoming Correspondence, pp. 122643-122704.

53. Ibid., Transcripts, vol. 585, Macdonald to Tupper, 24 January 1885.

54. Ibid.

55. Ibid., Incoming Correspondence, pp. 42935-42937, Riel to Bishop Grandin, 7 September 1884.

56. See PAM, Riel Papers, item 414, Tach_ to Riel, 4 October 1884.

57. Lansdowne did not forward the petition as requested. See Lansdowne to Derby, the Colonial Secretary, 21 April 1885 (PAC, Records of the Governor General, RG 7 G 10, vol. 8).

58. PAC, Macdonald Papers, Incoming Correspondence, pp. 42977-42983, quoted by Dewdney to Macdonald in reply, 4 February 1885.

59. Ibid., p. 148567, "Estimated Number of Half Breeds." Although the document is undated, contextual evidence makes clear that the numbers were determined in the summer of 1884. See also the Governor General's recital of the same figures in PAC, RG 7, G 10 (Drafts to Colonial Secretary, Secret and Confidential), vol. 8, Lansdowne to Derby, 21 April 1885.

60. Ibid., pp. 42977-42983, Dewdney to Macdonald, 4 February 1885.

61. PAC, RG 15, vol. 336, file 84478, A.M. Burgess to Duck, 6 February 1885.

62. See University of Alberta, William Pearce Papers, MG 9/2/4-4, vol. 4, pp. 224-275, 961-962 in relation to Pearce's published report of "All Claims to Land."

63. Their claims were taken up in the autumn of 1885, and accorded the same entry privilege as the others. See University of Alberta Archives, William Pearce Papers, MG 9/2/4-4, vol. 4, pp. 961-962.

64. PAC, Glenbow Dewdney Papers, p. 545, Macdonald to Dewdney, 20 February 1885.

65. PAC, Macdonald Papers, Incoming Correspondence, pp. 43010-43013, Dewdney to Macdonald, 11 March 1885.

66. Ibid., pp. 122735-122742, Stephen to Macdonald, 11 March 1885.

67. See, for example, Macdonald to T. Robertson, in ibid., Letter Book, vol. 23, pp. 85-86.

68. Ibid., Transcripts, vol. 585, Macdonald to Tupper, 17 March 1885.

69. Hudson's Bay Company Archives (hereafter cited as HBCA), D.20/33, fo. 67-74, Lawrence Clarke to Joseph Wrigley, 14 March 1885.

70. HBCA, B332/b/1, vol. 1, fo. 96-121, Clarke to Wrigley, 6 July 1885.

71. Ibid., fo. 87, Clarke cypher telegram to Dewdney, 17 March 1885.

72. Ibid., fo. 82, Dewdney cypher telegram to Clarke, 17 March 1885.

73. Ibid., fo. 81, Dewdney cypher telegram to Clarke, 17 March 1885.

74. Ibid., fo. 44, Wrigley cypher telegram to Clarke, 17 March 1885.

75. Ibid., fo. 96-121, Clarke to Wrigley, 6 July 1885.

76. N.F. Black, *History of Saskatchewan and the Old North West* (Regina, 1913), p. 267. The same story appeared in a contemporary account of Clarke's role by James Isbister. See clipping from Winnipeg *Sun,* 19 June 1885, in PAC, Macdonald Papers, Incoming Correspondence, p. 43861.

77. The opponents of Riel are named in Pearce's manuscript copy of "All Claims to Land" (University of Alberta Archives, Pearce Papers, MG 9/2, series 4, vol. 4, pp. 888-901.

78. PAC, Macdonald Papers, Transcripts, vol. 585, Macdonald to Caron, 23 March 1885.

79. Ibid., Incoming Correspondence, pp. 43020-43023, Dewdney to Macdonald, 23 March 1885.

80. "Speedy" and "gallant" were Macdonald's adjectives in Parliament. See House of Commons Debates, 6 July 1885, p. 3117.

81. A detailed, sensational account of the conflict appears in Beal and Macleod, *Prairie Fire,* pp. 151-159.

82. PAC, Macdonald Papers, Letter Books, vol. 23, p. 140, Macdonald to Dewdney, 29 March 1885.

83. See Blake's questions on the matter, House of Commons Debates, 31 March 1885, p. 838, and 1 April 1885, p. 872.

84. Desmond Morton, *The Last War Drum* (Toronto, 1972), pp. 40-44.

85. On the final siege, in particular, see Walter Hildebrandt, *The Battle of Batoche: British Small Warfare and the Entrenched Métis* (Ottawa, 1985).

86. See Blake's seven-hour speech and Macdonald's shorter reply in the House of Commons Debates, 6 July 1885, pp. 3075-3117.

87. See Malcolm Montgomery, "The Six Nations and the Macdonald Franchise," *Ontario History* 57 (1967), pp. 13-25.

88. PAC, Macdonald Papers, Incoming Correspondence, pp. 123001-123008. Stephen to Macdonald, 14 November 1885.

CHAPTER

3 CANADIAN SOCIETY: OLD AND NEW DEFINITIONS

Dissatisfaction with accounts of Canada's past dominated by political and economic factors led to the reorientation of Canadian historical studies in the decades following World War II, though it was only in the 1970s that new methodologies, different approaches and alternate subject matter became prominent. Nowhere was the impact greater than in the study of Canadian society. In 1958 few argued with A.R.M. Lower's *Canadians in the Making: A Social History of Canada* which characterized the later nineteenth century as the "horse and buggy" age. Though a distinguished historian, Lower romanticized the "sturdy yeomanry" and spun yarns about "the tinkle of the bells on the ' cutter' as it rolled along in the moonlight over the snow, with plenty of ' buffalo robes', a good horse, and, if you were lucky, your best girl beside you." The first selection in this unit is a chapter from his book.

This anecdotal approach was on open invitation to critics who asked other questions of different sources and from different perspectives. Sociologist S.D. Clark had been the trailblazer with his *Social Development of Canada* (1942), a structural/functionalist examination of emerging frontier societies. He drew heavily on court records and provided a narrative of deviant behaviour during times of unnatural stress. His *Church and Sect in Canada* (1948) was both more specialized and satisfactory. Other scholars were at work on classes and class relations, elites and the working class, the family, leisure, mobility, immigration, religion and education, though there was little cohesion among these disparate activities. After a very difficult start, *Histoire sociale / Social History*, a journal co-sponsored by the University of Ottawa and Carleton University in 1968, provided the focus for this "New Social History." The celebrated *Annales* approach was the inspiration, and while the tradition had many disciples among French-Canadians it was not easily transported to English Canada, which was more influenced by American sociology and the Marxist perspective.

In the 1970s and 1980s studies appeared on subjects such as literacy, demography, standards of living, housing, social mobility and class structure, with quantification a favoured methodology. The overall result was the creation of a very different society from Lower's "horse and buggy" world.

The second selection in this chapter, by Colin Howell, from *Histoire sociale/Social History*, used sport as a vehicle to look at social structure and society. In "Baseball, Class and Community in the Maritime Provinces, 1870-1910" Howell appears to be recounting the growth of organized sport, but in reality is examining the manner in which "reformers, entrepreneurs, gamblers, working people, athletes and spectators used unpredictable ways to shape the game to meet their own needs."

While it is not included in this unit, the article by Michéle Martin in Chapter 5 on the "Feminization of the Labour Process in the Communication Industry: The Case of the Telephone Operators, 1876-1904" offers a feminist perspective on the role of women in society. For them there were no moonlit nights in the "cutter."

Suggestions for Further Reading

Abbott, Frank, "Cold Cash and Ice Palaces: The Quebec Winter Carnival of 1894," *Canadian Historical Review*, LXIX, no. 2 (June 1988), 167-202.

Backhouse, Constance B., "Nineteenth-Century Prostitution Law: Reflections of a Discriminating Society," *Histoire sociale/Social History*, XVIII, no. 36 (November 1985), 387-423.

Benson, John, "Hawking and Peddling in Canada, 1867-1914," *Histoire sociale/Social History*, XVIII, no. 35 (May 1985), 75-83.

_____, *Petticoats and Prejudice: Women and Law in Nineteenth Century Canada*. Toronto: The Osgoode Society, 1991.

Bradbury, Bettina, "Pigs, Cows, and Boarders: Non-Wage Forms of Survival among Montreal Families, 1861-91," *Labour/Le Travail* XIV (Fall 1984), 9-46.

_____, "The Fragmented Family: Family Strategies in the Face of Death, Illness, and Poverty, Montreal, 1860-1885," in *Childhood and Family in Canadian History*, ed. Joy Parr. Toronto: McClelland and Stewart, 1982, 109-128.

_____, "Women and Wage Labour in a Period of Transition: Montreal, 1861-1881," in *Histoire sociale/Social History*, XVII, no. 33 (May 1984), 115-31.

Cohen, Marjorie Griffin, "The Decline of Women in Canadian Dairying," *Histoire sociale/Social History*, XVIII, no. 34, (November 1984), 307-334.

Delottinville, Peter, "Joe Beef of Montreal: Working Class Culture and the Tavern, 1869-1889," *Labour/Le Travailleur*, VIII/IX (Autumn 1981/Apring 1982), 9-40.

Gagan, David, and Rosemary Gagan, "Working Class Standards of Living in Late-Victorian Ontario: A Review of Miscellaneous Evidence on the Quality of Material Life," *Journal of the Canadian Historical Association*, New Series, I, no. I (1990), 171-193.

Harvey, Kathryn, "To Love, Honour and Obey: Wife-battering in Working-Class Montreal, 1969-79," *Urban History Review*, XIX, no. 2 (October 1990), 128-140.

Kealey, Linda, ed., *A Not Unreasonable Claim: Women and Reform in Canada, 1880s-1920s*. Toronto: Women's Press, 1979.

Lenskyj, Helen, *Out of Bounds: Women, Sport, and Sexuality*. Toronto: Women's Press, 1986.

Metcalfe, Alan, *Canada Learns to Play: The Emergence of Organized Sport, 1807-1914*. Toronto, 1987.

Palmer, Bryan D., "Discordant Music: Charivaris and Whitecapping in Nineteenth-Century North America," *Labour / Le Travailleur*, III, (1978), 5-62.

Prentice, Alison, and Susan Mann Trofimenkoff, eds., *The Neglected Majority: Essays in Canadian Women's History*, Vol. 11. Toronto: McClelland and Stewart, 1985.

Ward, Peter, "Courtship and Social Space in Nineteenth-Century English Canada" *Canadian Historical Review*, LXVIII, no. 1, (March 1987), 35-62.

_____, *Courtship, Love, and Marriage in Nineteenth-Century English Canada*. Montreal: McGill-Queen's University Press, 1990.

A STURDY YEOMANRY: CANADA IN THE 'HORSE AND BUGGY' AGE

A.R.M. Lower

'The Horse and Buggy Age' is a belittling phrase. To the smart modern city dweller, it conjures up a picture of old men with beards poking along country roads and using queer words, which they enunciate (over the radio) in still queerer voices. It is especially hard for the modern city dweller, with his ant-like ways, to imagine another mode of life, different from his own and with different values. It always has been hard for the city dweller to appreciate rural values (especially when so many city dwellers are escapees from the country). During most of history the countryman's fortunes have answered to the derisive terms the city dweller applies to him, for he usually gets the worst of it, and sooner or later is depressed to the level of either a peasant, a serf, or a slave. More rarely, he is elevated to that of gentleman or feudal nobleman—in which case he earns the citizens' equally hearty contempt for different reasons.

There have been, however, rare periods when the country has provided a way of life that was good and neither depressed nor elevated, whereby large numbers

Lower, A.R.M., "A Sturdy Yeomanry: Canada in the 'Horse and Buggy' Age" from *Canadians in the Making: A Social History of Canada* (Toronto: Longmans, 1958), 327–344. Reprinted with the permission of A.R.M. Lower's Literary Executor.

of men attained to substantial heights of well-being. These have been the 'yeoman' periods, when sturdy, independent men owned their own land and lived their own lives, with no consciousness of inferiority to others. The 'franklin' of the English Danelagh appears to have been such a man, as was the English yeoman of the seventeenth century and early eighteenth century—the man who took the measure of Charles I and his cavaliers. We read of the same type in more distant times, in both Greece and Rome, and we also read sad poetry about their decline.—

"But a bold peasantry, their country's pride
When once destroyed, can never be supplied...."

It has been North America's boast that her soils could provide the foundation for such a yeomanry as no other land in the world had ever previously been blessed with. The boast has not been idle, for if there has been anything more distinctive about the continent than its millions of 'sturdy yeomen' who called no man master, it is hard to say what it has been.

To-day our 'bold peasantry', assailed by the machine, by over-supply and by the impossibility of getting help, is changing its nature. Some of it is turning itself into a cross between capitalist *entrepreneur* and country gentleman. Some of it is sinking into 'small-peasant' status. It is leaving the land in increasing numbers and experts tell us that the exodus will have to go on, the farm people's proportion to the whole of the population steadily declining. The situation has gone farthest in the United States, but Canada must follow the same path. This chapter, therefore, is concerned with an era that probably has already passed.

What era? That era before the opening of the West had introduced pure commercial agriculture, before modern power had been applied directly to the farm, before the process of sub-urbanization had begun, but after the hardships and the crudities of the pioneering age had been overcome. That era of hearty work in the fields, man with man, of simple yet abundant fare, of good housing and substantial comfort, which was briefly interposed between the days of settlement and the sweeping over the countryside of the industrial revolution and its urban values. The era when the countryside was following its own way of life, and not looking over its shoulder on the fashionable pace-setting of the city. It was the era which in New England claimed its poetic voices to preserve it for posterity: the era of 'The One-Horse Shay,' of "The Barefoot Boy" and the smithie standing "Under the Spreading Chestnut Tree." In English Canada, it found few poetic voices to sound its praises but to-day many are the retrospective testimonies which appear to its excellence.[1] As befits Canadian reticence, all of these are in prose and most of them hide their sentiment behind a bantering humour.

Such an era, thanks to the mobility of things in Canada, was necessarily fleeting. A solid, settled rural life had no sooner emerged than it began to be eroded. No social situation is ever completely neat, so that different regions meet their fate at different times, but a rough average would give us the first generation after Confederation, down to the first decade of the new century, for the period wherein 'the horse and buggy age' reached its characteristic expression, its high point. The age, it is now clear, was in itself an aspect of the industrial revolution of the nineteenth century, for it depended upon gravel roads, machine craftsmanship in conveyances and field implements, and to some degree on long-distance haulage by railroads. It is the equivalent of the 'coaching era' in Great Britain, or of the clipper ship, which latter was in itself perfection but the kind of perfection that has to be pushed aside when entirely new conceptions come in to play, as they did with steam power. The 'horse and buggy age' is merely an interval, a delicious hesitation or hovering, between the old saddle-horse and ox-cart era, civilized man's best previous effort, and the high-speed technique of our own times.

The Canadian Countryside

In the eighteen-seventies all over Ontario, the fine commodious brick houses were rising that still dot the countryside. In most other provinces, building was in frame, and in the better parts, such as the Annapolis Valley, the frame house, like its prototype in New England, got some paint. Big barns were going up too but these rarely got paint, whatever province they were in. About 1878, there appeared that series of *County Atlases* of Ontario which depicted the houses and farms by name, both in drawings and on maps. They add vastly to our knowledge of the countryside at that time. While presumably only the best places are shown in the cuts, enough are shown to convince us that the older districts were becoming not only comfortable but wealthy. Inside those houses, there was plenty of furniture—of varying excellence—plenty of warmth and food. Warmth came from stoves, the fireplaces having been either closed up or not having been installed in the newer houses, and from wood cut on the occupants' own farm by their own hands, with no obligations to a power saw: it "warmed them twice'. Goldwin Smith, in his astringent way, bade the people of the day remember that 'the stove is as debilitating as the tropics'. He was wrong: it did not carry tropical diseases and it was a good ventilator. Nothing more cheery than a good maple fire in a big iron stove, with the men sitting about it smoking their pipes and telling tales of winters that really had been winters! Nothing, except the tinkle of the bells on the 'cutter' as it rolled along in the moonlight over the snow, with plenty of 'buffalo robes', a good horse, and, if you were lucky, your best girl beside you. It is distressing to reflect that the children of to-day have never heard the most distinctive of all Canadian sounds—the merry jingle of the sleigh-bells!

At every farmhouse in those days, winter and summer, there was hospitality and seldom was the stranger turned away. On every table there was plenty, sometimes "a rude plenty," which is what Lord Durham alleged the

French-Canadian peasantry possessed, sometimes a well-served plenty. And if a countryside was anywhere near average, cleanliness could be depended on—the women saw to that. If a family fell below the line, it soon got a reputation. There had been plenty of filth among the immigrants; where had it gone to? That is hard to say, but in thirty or forty years, gone, for the most part, it had.

The country-side had become not only clean but, with exceptions, godfearing and law-abiding. When one man, in too much of a hurry, attempted to take in his grain of a fine Sunday, "the neighbours soon stopped that,' an old lady who had been one of them exclaimed. Church-going became the rule and in most districts those not associated with a church would have been regarded as 'queer'. It was around Confederation that the innumerable little brick churches which dot the countryside of Ontario began to appear: the brave days of the circuit rider were already far away. Nearly all those country churches were plain, and. many of them ugly, though to this statement Anglican churches were sometimes an exception, and these latter often attempted to keep their grounds attractive, a sin against Puritan unworldliness which Methodists and Presbyterians rarely committed. Whatever the denomination, when the community turned out on some public occasion, such as a local funeral, everyone participated. In some districts children were given half holidays for funerals (theoretically, to enable them to attend), and at the service 'the connection' sat in the centre of the church. But already, so intricate were blood ties becoming that at most funerals approximately the same people—that is, most of the district—sat in the centre.

Except in certain 'hard-rock' areas, denomination—within Protestantism—was already becoming of secondary importance. It was the local community and the blood group which counted. Differences remained, of course. Methodists maintained and extended their formidable list of taboos—taboos against alcohol and tobacco, against the theatre and cardplaying, against dancing, against all sin whatsoever. Their 'camp-meetings' had pretty well disappeared, but they still carried on their 'love-feasts' and revival meetings. Such practices staid Scottish Presbyterians could not abide. When a Glengarry Scot paused awhile to hear a Methodist revivalist exhorting, his comment was "Yon man talks to God as if he were a sma' boy, and he was telling him to come down out of his apple tree!" Methodists were themselves to become decreasingly effervescent as the century were on, so that less and less was to separate them and the Presbyterians. The years after church union (1925)—mooted for long before—were to make it clear, indeed, that it was not Methodists who had swallowed Presbyterians, but Presbyterians who had swallowed Methodists.[2]

Not every countryside was idyllic: frontier roughness struck through many of them, and in some, cases of severe disorder have been recorded. There was what has been pictured as the reign of terror conducted about 1875 by the 'Black Donnellys' in the township of Biddulph, Ontario. The story has it that for years the Donnelly pair and their seven sons terrorized the countryside, carrying highway robbery, arson, assault, destruction of property and even murder to all who opposed their will.[3] If half the legend they left behind is true, some modifications need to be made in the traditional picture of British law and order. Transfer this story of local bad men to another age and put in a public authority much weaker than the weak authority of the law in the countryside of 1875, and you get an explanation of medieval feudalism. Centuries before, the terrorizing Donnellys could have defied authority and, by building castles, could have turned themselves into feudal barons.

Ontario in 1875 was, however, not Europe in 1075. With little towns and villages springing up everywhere, authority was never far away and there was not opportunity for many Black Donnellys. Disorder in town and village rapidly came down into one of two forms, either local rowdiness interspersed with the occasional but not frequent crime of violence, or the scrimmages conducted by the rank and file of the Orange lodges.

"In Coldwater, there is neither law nor order. The place has a number of toughs, and people are afraid to come to town at night for fear of being pounced upon by some of these night owls. People have had their horses beaten and their rigs overturned or broken."[4] Coldwater, a little village near Midland, Ontario, was at that time a frontier sawmill town, and the situation described, which is much the same as in the contemporary 'wild west' (except for the absence of six-shooters) may be considered normal for a frontier community of the time. In the neighbouring settlement of Orillia, which was a little larger, matters did not go quite as far, and the case of the half-drunk lumberjack whose arrest was attempted (unsuccessfully) by the wholly drunk constable[5] suggests one stage away from frontier conditions: there was at least a constable present on the streets of Orillia in 1875, even if a drunken one.

Rural disorder was still annually translated into urban by the Irish, either as migrants from the country-side or direct. The only recorded reading of the Riot Act in the city of Toronto occurred on July 23rd, 1874, when a Roman Catholic procession began moving down Church Street. "Crowds of anti-Catholics began stoning it. The procession, which was going to a service at St. Mary's Church at Bathurst and Adelaide Streets, kept moving. When it reached Bay Street, Mayor Francis H. Medcalf appeared to read the Riot Act...."[6] But as compared with the conditions of a generation before, already referred to, those of the post-Confederation period were tapering off into their subsequent peacefulness. Rural disorder in Canada has been a wave following the frontier.

The Typical Canadian Farmer

Just after Confederation, if we may judge by statistics,[7] the typical Canadian farmer was the owner of between fifty and one hundred acres. In Ontario, he had some twenty-two acres under crop and in Quebec, about seventeen. In the upper province the typical farmer grew some seventy-two bushels of wheat, for this was the great wheat period, and in the lower, twenty. In Ontario, he possessed about eight head of cattle and in Quebec, just over six. His farm had two or three horses in Ontario and one or two in Quebec. The Quebec discrepancy in horses was made up in oxen, of which there were about two to every five farms.

In both provinces the average family was large, though it was getting smaller. In 1851 it had been between six and seven persons, but by 1871, it had come down to under six in Ontario and about six and a half in Quebec. In both, each farm family apparently possessed one or two 'light carriages' (though the average was higher in Ontario than in Quebec). 'Light carriage' may have been the general term for the various passenger 'rigs' that had been coming in since the eighteen-fifties, of which the buggy was the most important, numerically and socially, with the democrat (a 'rig' with two or three cross benches accommodating the entire family) not far behind.

The average farm already had a fair amount of machinery on it. In each case, the Ontario farm was more fully mechanized than was that of Quebec.[8] But it also still produced many of the traditional commodities whose manufacture has long since been transferred to factories. Thus the Ontario farmers each made twenty pounds of home-made cheese. Even in homespun cloth, the Ontario farm women turned in a respectable total, only a fraction of a square yard of homespun linen each, it is true (though cumulatively this mounted up to a good deal), but over ten square yards each of homespun cloth. In Quebec, these figures were far exceeded, there being ten square yards of linen made on every farm and twenty-eight square yards of cloth. The Ontario farm was already a snug place, for it had enough garden and orchard to give every occupant the proportion of an acre per farm and he grew, according to the census, twelve bushels of apples on it, to say nothing of other fruits. No wonder the Canadian farm wife's cellar shelves have traditionally groaned with the weight of their long rows of preserves, all put down against the winter that was just round the corner.

If these dry facts are for the 'average' farmer, then among a large number of persons, some must have been high above the average, while others would be far below it. That is, in this most democratic of occupations and this most democratic of countries, there must already have been a rural class line in the making: this, however, would correspond with the distribution of soils by districts, leaving members of any single rural community on a footing of relative equality. The soil itself sorted out our farmers into groups all the way from big men at the top to a class at the bottom which had all the ear-marks of a peasantry except a peasantry's stability and tradition. It was a class found everywhere in Canada, one grading down to a 'poor white' status, and uncomfortably numerous.

The 'sturdy yeoman' of this chapter is the 'average farmer' whom our statistics depict. He is the fortunate person on reasonably good soil who can win a modest and independent competence. By Confederation it was evident that he was flourishing and after Confederation the marks of his success became more and more evident in good houses, large barns, the improvement of roads, new school buildings—not that formal education was making much of a showing— and the adoption of mechanical improvements as they came along. Yet, in human affairs, as in the sea, the big fish swallow the little ones. If this goes on long enough, the families at the top draw away from the yeoman class, educate their children, become superior to manual work and turn themselves into 'gentlemen farmers'. A further stage is reached when urban wealth begins to buy land and set up plaything farms with employees to run them.

In a new country such as ours, the social processes, as compared with those of the old world, are rapid. In the spoil of North America, land was the most desirable booty from the first and it was secured in every conceivable way, direct and indirect, honest and dishonest; mostly, it might seem, dishonest. But apparently few of the land speculators retained their holdings as family estates: their object was simply resale at a higher price. The home farm of the famous Colonel Talbot, who, with all his faults, was not exactly a land speculator, consisted of about six hundred acres, and it is still intact.[9] Here was 'gentleman farming' continuously from the beginning. There has not been much of it in Canada and of what there has been, not much has been successful. One instance from a later period and province is perhaps illustrative. In the early eighteen-nineties, an English immigrant of the 'gentleman' class bought land in south-western Manitoba and began to farm it: his employees were other young Englishmen of similar type. These young men were required to dress for dinner every night. Hunters were kept. The experiment did not last long. Similar stories are told of the fruit ranchers in the interior of British Columbia.

This mention of British Columbia brings us to a still later period in time, but not in social development. Among the fruit ranchers of the Okanagan there have been many attempts to transfer the 'gentleman farmer' concept to Canada, but few of them have been successful. If this social type is to emerge among us, it will be through evolution from the ranks, and so far, the conditions of our life have made against that occurring. Thus the writer knows two good Ontario farms each of which produced a minister of the crown, but both these men were accustomed to pitch hay and feed the cattle with the rest of the farmers about them.[10] In the same region there formerly were a number of 'gentlemen' (all English) farmers, but gradually they gave way to 'yeomen': nowhere were farms consolidated into 'estates' with rent-paying tenantry.

There have been many instances of urban wealth buying into the land for 'plaything' purposes. One of the earliest of these was that of the Honourable George Brown, who early in the eighteen-sixties acquired 'Bow Park Farm', in a loop of the Grand River near Brantford. Here he raised pure-bred cattle and set up as a country gentleman. A fine residence was built (which is still in use) but eventually Brown's toy ceased to have its original interest and he made it into a limited company. It is still a farm, well managed by a graduate of the Ontario Agricultural College, and producing an immense amount of food every year, but it did not descend to the second generation of Browns. Since 1911, it has been owned and operated by Canadian Canners, Ltd., which company is now as Canadian as the old McLaughlin Motor Car Co., in that it has become a subsidiary of an American firm.[11]

Most cities of any size have had rural retreats on their edges which have been owned by wealthy men and have been used as farms. These 'farms' have been good speculations but they have necessarily been transient. This is especially noticeable around Toronto, where the rapid advance of the city has raised land values astronomically.

On a beautiful autumn day during his first year in the University of Toronto, the writer remembers taking a walk up Spadina Road, over the hill, where 'Pellatt's Castle' now stands, and on to St. Clair Avenue. There at the corner of St. Clair and Spadina Road, were open fields and a farmer with his team working in them. But even by that time, the plaything farms were out beyond this genuine farm, far to the north-east of the city.

In the eighteen-forties there arrived in Upper Canada from northern Ireland a young man named William Tyrrell. He became a successful builder, and an interesting group of houses on King Street in Kingston, still first-class residential property, is his work. In the eighteen-fifties he built a big house in Weston, Ontario. His sons went to the university and both became well known. One of them lived to become the grand old man of Canadian geology, Dr. J. B. Tyrrell, the hero of the epic trip of exploration across the Barren Lands of the Canadian Arctic (1893-1894). Dr. Tyrrell, after making a fortune in northern Ontario gold mining, settled down in his sixties on a farm at the edge of Toronto. He planted an orchard of Northern Spy apples, and lived to harvest many thousands of bushels of apples from it. He had neighbouring farms literally pushed on him by their owners, who seemed to wish nothing so much as escape into a job from the responsibilities of yeoman status. Now his splendid orchards seem about to be engulfed by an advancing city. His heirs will reap the financial gains, but a beautiful and productive bit of countryside will have been turned into dull city streets and a distinguished Canadian name disappear into the relative anonymity of city life.

Ontario has so little good farm land that probably all of it will be suburbanized sooner or later and taken out of production, but it is Ontario which, because of its rapid development, best illustrates the social evolution of the country-side. And, of course, in the post-Confederation period, the Ontario farm was the representative Canadian farm. Rural Ontario was a northern projection of American rural society and most of the points that could be made about the one could be made about the other. In both it was the average man who counted. That average man might be a relative new-comer, as he usually was in Ontario, or he might be of some ten generations on this continent: whichever he was, he followed just about the same way of life, for new-comers rapidly fitted themselves into the prevailing pattern. In this way, the Canadian country-side represents the migration of the country-side of New England and New York, with its customs and attitudes not greatly changed.

The statement would not be valid for French Canada, which has its own way of life, but even there, the environment being similar, relatively the same responses were produced. The major difference would be that the French-Canadian farmer has always had that family attitude towards his farm which has been weak in English Canada. In French Canada, the family farm is an ancestral possession, handed down from father to son (by a peculiar system of inheritance which does not involve the rank in the family of the heir so much as his fitness to carry on). In English Canada, it is much closer to a piece of real estate, and few farmers have ever hesitated to sell out when offered a good enough price. Even so, there are plenty of farms in English Canada on which the family that received the original grant from the Crown still resides. English Canada's system of inheritance is also its own: it seems to consist mainly, though there are no rules, in leaving the farm to a son and requiring him to give mortgages to the other children, share and share alike. During the depression of the nineteen-thirties, the interest payment on these mortgages (which rapidly got out to nephews, nieces and more distant relatives) often became so onerous, that the occupant of the farm simply surrendered it and moved away. In French Canada, one son seems to expect, and to be expected, to stay on the farm: he may marry and bring his wife home. In English Canada this has never been more than exceptional, and since the father was often quite capable of carrying on for years after his boys grew up, more often than not they struck out for themselves. Then, at the father's death or retirement, the farm would be sold. For reasons such as these there has always been a rapid flux in the English-Canadian ownership of land as compared with French Canada. A comparison of names, farm by farm, as given in the atlases of 1870, with the present occupancy of farms shows huge changes, but in French Canada it is almost normal for the same family to have been on the same farm since the beginning, in some cases three centuries ago.

The consequences of rapid change in ownership have often been disastrous to the land. If a man expects to leave to his son the farm he has himself inherited, then he will probably take care of the soil, the trees and the property. The English-Canadian farmer, necessarily with exceptions, has had little of this respect for the land: he has looked on his farm not altogether as a mine but as something from which he expected to extract the utmost in terms of production. This does not mean that he has invariably been a bad and careless farmer, for where the soil is good enough to withstand his assaults, he is quite likely to have co-operated with it, if only because good farming pays. But poor land makes the owner ruthless. He will overgraze, and cut the trees, squeezing the last ounce of raw material out of his property. The evidences of this are spread all over Canada in the form of eroded hill-sides, filled with great gullies or desolate square miles of bare rocks, and here and there the skeletons of dead trees. A few generations of 'farming' have reduced districts in the Caledon Hills or the Kingston-Belleville neighbourhood to desert. There is not much point of talking about 'sturdy yeomen' in these districts, for the people in them go down with the land.

The Clash between Rural and Urban Values

Whether the soil be poor or good, whether the farmer foolish or wise, the temptations of a commercial way of life such as ours must, except in infrequent cases, drive the occupant to forcing his land. It sometimes seems as if the most dangerous man to have on the farm is the farmer. The aristocratic system of the old world at least had the merit, through its tenant farming, of making the farmer behave himself. In Canada tenancy has made things worse, for then neither owner nor tenant has had a full sense of responsibility. Nor does family pride of possession often come to the soil's rescue, for in English Canada the farmer who would count on his son to succeed him would as likely as not get fooled by the son moving off to the nearest town, out West, or over to the States (later to come back, horribly patronizing, as a visitor, to show the old folk 'how well he had done').

Added to all this heavy discount on 'a sturdy yeomanry' was (and is) the endemic 'slap-dashery' of the frontier—the readiness to make do, the shiftlessness, the fixed notion that no job is worth doing really well (after all, the aim is the barn door) and that precision is almost reprehensible: this fumbling carelessness, invariably accompanied by a narrow pride in the values it is supposed to represent as opposed to those of a more advanced external world, has often marked the Canadian farmer. "I don't need no men in books to tell me how to run my farm," said an old farmer to the present writer in his youth.

It is the rapid change in the ownership of land which, among other things, requires us to consider the period after Confederation as not permanent: there can be nothing permanent about the country-side of English America, for it reflects the speed of change that marks our civilization as a whole. The 'sturdy yeoman', therefore, no sooner emerged than he began to change into something else. By modern times he seems to have become either the owner of a machine shop for extracting food values from the soil, a man chained to a herd of cows and the city dairies, a fairly large-scale capitalist, with a capitalist's attitude towards the land—the land as a factory; or at the other end of the scale, a poor white skulking on the margins of the better farming districts. Or it would be fairer to say he is becoming such things, for there are still sturdy farmers left, and there will be until they are submerged by city values.

That is just the point: "submerged by city values!" Country communities to have built up their own way of life must have had long periods of relative isolation. This has produced local customs, dress, dialects. A remote and isolated island would exemplify the extreme case. We have plenty of remote islands in Canada, but few genuinely isolated ones: even the Magdalens have had cable and steamer connection for a century. Nevertheless it is such spots which have built up their own way of life and have been least overwhelmed by city values. The more extensive and richer rural districts have been exposed to these from their first day of settlement, and it is only because cities were themselves weak that a distinctive rural way of life could get established. As we have seen, even so it has been more or less transitory.

The settler no sooner got on the land than he began to leave it, as his descendants still do. For this there are many reasons, the most direct of which is the end of available land, the next, dislike of the drudgery which farm life entailed. Most men who stuck it out through pioneer conditions and raised a family on their holding were anxious to see their sons settled around them, and often by watching their opportunities, they were able to get neighbouring farms, either from the Crown or from other holders. In this way family settlements sometimes expanded over a considerable area. But the process could not go on indefinitely and when virgin land was gone, a man with a number of sons had to have a long purse and buy out his neighbours, if he wished to keep his boys about him. In the process, someone had to go away: talk about keeping youth on the farm has always been nonsense. The only way of keeping youth on the farm would be to subdivide the farm until eventually it would come down to Oriental conditions, with one farmer on an acre. Under Canadian circumstances, the resulting standard of living can be imagined. Youth has always had to leave the farm and always will. Where love of the ancestral acres is strongest—in Quebec—young people leave the farm in greater numbers than they do elsewhere, there being more of them to leave.

A charming account of a youth spent on a farm well past the pioneering stage, yet presenting just the set of conditions whose description has been attempted here, is the semi-autobiographical book *The Master's Wife,* by the late Sir Andrew Macphail, a Prince Edward Islander. Shy, proud, stiff Highlanders fill the pages, transplanted Highlanders whose life revolves around religion, the Scottish psalms, the Scottish Sabbath and work, work, work. They reflect plain living and high thinking, natural delicacy, poise and manners, all the pride of the tribesman. "The truth is, the Highlanders were the last community of gentlemen...." Hence, Macphail says, when great men came among them, there was no sense of inferiority, and no failure of courtesy: there were no rude assertions of equality, just the tribesman's natural assumption of it. But surely here was an attitude which marked many other Canadian country dwellers: there were few among them to pull a subservient forelock, like English labourers in the romantic-novel tradition. And few, too, to play the gentleman. If

English people of 'the classes' always received such objectionable demonstrations of equalitarianism in Canada, was it probably not their own fault? The writer once happened to blunder into a log hut where a simple French-speaking Canadian was making maple syrup. While he was there, no less a personage than the Governor General, the late Lord Byng, happened to come in. The syrup-maker received him without the slightest trace of embarrassment, without truckling, without coldness, without fuss! It was Lord Byng who appeared not quite at his ease.

One of Macphail's chapters is entitled "The Escape". What is the escape? It is the escape from the land, from drudgery. And what is the escape route? It is schooling; not education, but schooling, which if it led to the right kind of escape might incidentally, as in the case of the Macphails, become education. One wintry day in Kingston, Sir Andrew's brother, Alexander, was seated before his comfortable fire with a couple of younger men. A workman was visible through the window, shovelling the snow as it fell. 'Sandy' turned to the young men, indicated the contrast presented by the two sides of the window and said one word: "Latin!"

Sir Andrew himself was largely self-educated, with the assistance of his father, a sort of bush-school inspector. He won a scholarship which took him to Prince of Wales College, Charlottetown, for a couple of years and then, aged eighteen, became a school teacher, salary $380.00 a year. But that was riches in 1886! From country school teacher, he went on to McGill and later, a large reputation. How many have followed that escape route from the farm! And how few among them have, incidental to their schooling, found an education! It is no wonder that cultural standards in Canada remain at a low level, when education has had to begin anew at the beginning with each generation and has also so often been regarded merely as a vocational can-opener.

Macphail was entirely frank about it. No Macphail had ever 'worked'—that is, sunk to the status of manual employee (they all 'toiled' hard enough on their farm)—therefore stick to your books! Master the Latin declensions and the mathematical formulae, not for themselves but as keys—keys to the prison that held you. The irony of it is that it probably all came out just as well as the helping-lame-dogs-over-stiles type of thing: "The masters in that Orwell school felt that their whole business was done when they had kept order, so that those who desired to learn were left free in silence ... no boy was compelled to attend school; he was not inveigled into a scholarly course which he was too feeble-minded to pursue.... Best of all, he returned to the land, or to a trade, before he was rendered incapable of dealing with them...."

The Presbyterian Scot has been notorious for following this escape route of education, or rather, schooling. "Father" (in E. A. Corbett's *Father, God Bless Him*[12]) was typical "in never dreaming that any of his children would not go on to the highest type of education attainable." "Father" in this case was a minister, and his sights were raised higher. But every farm, whatever the racial or religious background of the occupants, had to serve as an escape route of some kind, for it was from the farms that virtually the whole population of the country was recruited.[13]

The Dispersion of the Farm Boys

The farm boy came to town and he might end up anywhere from a day labourer to an intellectual, from a pauper to a millionaire. It was largely his energy that lent such a mighty sweep to North American civilization. The Canadian farm not only furnished the recruits for our growing cities, but sent its sons far afield and into every calling: in the eighteen-seventies and eighties, they migrated by the tens of thousands to the American West, where such states as North Dakota became almost more Canadian than anything else. About the same time in our own North West Territories, they were sending that wedge of Anglo-Saxon Protestantism westward along the Canadian Pacific Railway from the Red River to the mountains, and this region to this day remains most faithfully a reflection of eastern Canada.

The farm boys found all the frontiers there were to find. They went into the bush and became lumbermen and river drivers.[14] As river drivers, they developed that pride in their dangerous calling which has spilled over into many a native ballad:—

> O ye maidens of Ontario, give ear to what I write,
> In driving down these rapid streams where raftsmen take delight,
> In driving down these rapid streams as raftsmen they must do,
> While these low and loafing farmer boys they stay at home with you.
>
> Oh, these low and loafing farmer boys they tell the girls great tales.
> They'll tell them of great dangers in crossing o'er the fields,
> While the cutting of the grass and weeds is all that they can do,
> While we poor jolly raftsmen are running the Long Soo.
>
> And when the sun is going down, their plows they'll cast aside.
> They'll jump upon their horse's back and homeward they will ride.
> And when the clock strikes eight or nine, then into bed they'll crawl,
> While down on Lake St. Peter we stand many a bitter squall.

In all probability, the writer of that ballad—*Ye Maidens of Ontario*—was himself an Ontario farm boy who had escaped into the larger, more exciting world of the river driver.

Just as farm boys from the Maritimes in preceding generations had taken to that most extensive of all frontiers, the sea, so in central Canada, they took to the lakes. To the lakes they carried their farm nomenclature, so that a shackle is not a shackle to the lake sailor but a clavis. And in one other way, at least, they carried their folk instinct abroad with them. If they made ballads in the bush and on the river, they made them on the lakes:—

Come all ye young men listen
While a warning I'll give you,
Pray never go a-sailing
To plough those waters blue;
Oh never go a-sailing,
No matter what they pay—
Think of those poor dear fellows
Drowned on the last of May.

The Steamer "D. D. Calvin"
The "Bavaria" in tow
Loaded timber at St. Eguss (*sic*)[15]
And for Garden Isle did go,
All started on her homeward trip
With spirits light and high,
Never dreaming that so soon
On the bottom some would lie.

John Marshal was her master,
A man we all know well,
For courage as a seaman
Few could as well excel.
He leaves a wife and a family
To mourn his dreadful fate.
And likewise Felix Compeau,
Who acted as first mate.

And as for Sandy Berry—
I pen this with regret—
His tall and manly figure
We cannot easily forget.
But the strongest and the bravest
When called upon must go—
We hope to meet in Heaven,
Where high winds never blow.

But there were other victims,
Whose names we only know
But none the less our sympathy
Out to their friends shall go.
For the Lord who reigns above us
And doeth all things well
Has taken them from a troubled earth
And gone with them to dwell![16]

As the farms prospered or became overcrowded, as farmers educated their children or simply were compelled to find room for them somewhere else, the farm boy spread out further and further into the life of the country. He secured his share of places in the professions. He made his contribution to public life. In the United States it used to be thought necessary to believe that presidential candidates had been born in log houses (though few of them had been). In Canada, such a birthplace would have been no demerit for high office, though here again, relatively few could boast it: of the prime ministers of Canada only Arthur Meighen seems to have been a farm boy. But the farms furnished many of the secondary figures, and numbers of the rank and file.

Most fundamental of all, perhaps, the patterns of life worked out in the country-side have gone deep into our outlook. Canada is no longer predominantly a rural country, but a high proportion of its people are still close to their rural origins; their family memories go back to the farm, and a good many of their values. The latter may be simple, but they have nearly always been wholesome. Since there are few really large cities in Canada, these standards have a good chance for survival, through association and renewal. In this way, the era of 'the sturdy yeomen', gone though its finest expression may be, remains a continuing force.

Notes

1. Witness such books as K. C. Cragg, *Father on the Farm* (Toronto, 1947), John Coburn, *I Kept My Powder Dry* (Toronto, 1950), Sir Andrew Macphail, *The Master's Wife* (Montreal, 1939), E. A. Corbett, *Father, God Bless Him* (Toronto, 1953), R. S. McLaughlin, *My Eighty Years on Wheels,* as told to Eric Hutton (Maclean's Magazine, Sept. 15th, Oct. 1st, Oct. 15th, 1954), C. L. Burton, *A Sense of Urgency* (Toronto, 1952), Luella Creighton, *High Bright Buggy Wheels* (Toronto, 1951), and many others.

2. The *religion* of the country-side, as contrasted with its denominationalism, is not here discussed. For the most part, under whatever forms it expressed itself, it partook of the semi-pantheism, that regard for the eternal Great Mother, which comes naturally to country people everywhere. Upon this foundation was erected the framework of Christian belief and virtue.

3. See *Weekend Magazine,* Vol. 4, No. 46, 1954. The present writer does not vouch for the details.

4. From an Orillia newspaper of about 1875.

5. Ibid.

6. Toronto *Globe and Mail,* Saturday, May 30th, 1953, in an article by Robert Fulford.

7. These are drawn from the census of 1871.

8. Reapers and mowers, Ontario .21 per farm; Quebec, .04. Horse rakes, Ontario .29; Quebec, .08.

9. And to-day (typically) in the hands of a family living in the United States.

10. But with the introduction of certain new crops the situation is changing. On the good lands of Elgin County there are a number of large farms, whose owners are not only prosperous but wealthy. These men are reported as identifying themselves with the upper *bourgeoisie* of the neighbouring towns and cities.

11. *Globe and Mail,* Nov. 9th, 1956.
12. Toronto, 1953.
13. The statistics show a large immigration between 1871 and 1891, but on looking at the figures for native-born and foreign-born in the two periods, it is impossible to find the immigrants. The returns themselves make it clear that the country in the period grew from itself, that is, mainly from its country-side.
14. See, for example, Ralph Connor, *The Man from Glengarry, Glengarry School Days,* etc., etc.
15. Sandusky? Oak timber used to be brought from such ports for export.
16. Courtesy of Elizabeth Harrison, Kingston, who collected this ballad on Garden Island, Ont.

BASEBALL, CLASS AND COMMUNITY IN THE MARITIME PROVINCES, 1870-1910

Colin D. Howell

In the past few years, historical writing on the history of sport has concentrated upon the relationship of sport to society, rather than merely chronicling the accomplishments of great athletes or celebrating sport as a form of character building. Serious academic work, such as Tony Mason's history of Association Football, Wray Vamplew's analysis of professional sport in Victorian Britain, or Alan Metcalfe's study of the emergence of a disciplined and organized sporting culture in Canada, has drawn widely upon the insights of the "new" social history to understand how sport shaped community identities and, yet, was shaped itself by class, ethnic and gender rivalries.[1] This analysis of the early history of baseball in the Maritime Provinces and New England looks at how the development of the game was linked to Victorian notions of respectability and to the growing discourse that emerged with respect to the public organization of play and leisure.[2] In so doing, it investigates the subtle and often unpredictable ways in which reformers, entrepreneurs, gamblers, working people, athletes and spectators shaped the game to meet their own needs. Seen in this light, the history of baseball involves what Raymond Williams refers to as the "social relations of cultural production", social processes actively shaped by human agents, neither fully determined by nor independent of the capitalist mode of production.[3]

The study of baseball provides a useful window into the continuing redefinition of class relations, gender roles and community identity that accompanied

From *Histoire sociale / Social History,* XXII, no. 44 (November 1989), 265-286. Reprinted by permission of *Histoire sociale / Social History.*

the industrial transformation of the Maritimes in the last third of the nineteenth century.[4] Baseball's early development was closely linked to the expansion of urban centers in the region in the industrial age. Some historians have suggested that the game's appeal lay in its ability to evoke images of rural simplicity in an age of industrial dislocation;[5] others argue that the game replicated the attitudes of the industrial workplace in its emphasis on organization, precision and discipline.[6] Whatever its appeal, baseball originated and flourished in urban centers and small towns. Promoted by a group of middle and upper-class reformers who regarded sport as a powerful antidote to crime, rowdiness and class hatred, the game was played primarily by adolescents and young men who had only recently entered the world of work. But the interests of reformers and players did not always coincide. If reformers prized baseball for its blending of teamwork and individual initiative, its cultivation of the "manly virtues" and its uplifting character, they also remained suspicious of the way in which players, spectators and speculators approached the sport.

Baseball first came to the Maritimes during the 1860's and, over the next two decades, grew rapidly in popularity, spreading from the larger metropolitan centers such as Saint John, Halifax and Moncton to smaller communities like Woodstock, St. Stephen, Fredericton, New Glasgow, Westville and Kentville. Although a number of Saint John residents had earlier played pick-up games of "rounders"—a precursor of the modern game of baseball—it was not until 1869 that Mr. P.A. Melville, a prominent newspaperman, introduced baseball to Saint John. Within five years, a number of local club teams, including the Invincibles, the Mutuals, the St. Johns, the Shamrocks, the Athletes and the Royals, were playing each other and occasionally challenging teams from St. Croix, Fredericton and Bangor, Maine. Organized largely along occupational, ethnic and religious lines, the teams were still exclusively amateur. As of yet, the promoters of the game thought more of its civilizing influence than its profit potential. There was little gate money, and given the limited provision for field security, spectators often crawled over and under fences to escape admission.[7]

Baseball came to Halifax at about the same time it originated in Saint John. In May 1868, the Halifax *Reporter* announced a meeting of the Halifax Baseball Club at Doran's Hotel, followed a few days later by an announcement of an organizational meeting at the Masonic Hall of another independent club and the election of the team's officers.[8] The Halifax club's first president was Dr. A.C. Cogswell, a long-time proponent of organized recreation in Halifax. Like many of his contemporaries, Cogswell saw sport as a remedy to youthful idleness and indolence, and a force contributing to mental well-being and physical health. A few years earlier, Cogswell had led a campaign for a public gymnasium, which, the *Acadian Recorder* predicted, would rescue Halifax youth from "gawking lazily at street corners to stare at passers-by, lounging about drinking saloons, smoking and guzzling" and partaking of "other irrational modes of getting over life."[9] Another of Cogswell's contemporaries, Superintendent John

Grierson of the Halifax Protestant Boy's Industrial School, shared this faith in the uplifting character of organized recreation. "The necessity of providing recreation for lads of this class", wrote Grierson about the boys in his charge, "is now universally admitted."[10] The Industrial School sported a gymnasium and playing ground for cricket and baseball, and the boys played challenge matches against the Young Atlantas and Young Oxfords of Halifax.[11]

Baseball was particularly attractive to reformers because it brought into play the so-called "manly virtues": courage, strength, agility, teamwork, decision-making and foresight. It was inexpensive and took little time to play or witness, so that a busy man can gain in two hours on the ball field rest and relaxation that elsewhere he would seek in vain."[12] Another virtue, from the reformer's perspective, was that it appealed in particular to working-class youth. A sample of players whose names appeared in newspaper box-scores in Halifax, between 1874 and 1888, makes this clear. Of the 133 players whose occupation can be traced through census records and city directories, the vast majority came from working-class backgrounds. Clerks, labourers and unskilled workers made up 45.8 percent of the sample: tradesmen such as cabinet-makers, carpenters, tailors, blacksmiths, machinists, brass-finishers, gasfitters, printers, bakers, plumbers, coopers and bricklayers comprised another 31.5 percent; and merchants, students and professionals made up the remaining 22.7 percent. (*See* table 1).

TABLE 1   Occupation of Halifax Baseball Players, 1874–1888

	Number	*%*
Clerks (including bookkeepers and accountants)	29	21.8
Labourers (including teamsters, janitors, messengers, seamen, porters and stable boys)	32	24.0
Tradesmen	42	31.5
Students, merchants and professionals	30	22.7

If baseball was basically a working man's sport, it was also a young man's game. The ages of those who appeared in box-scores for the first time ranged from a 12 year old student to a 46 year old physician, Chandler Crane. Most players, however, began their careers in their late teens or early twenties and few continued to play into their thirties. The average age of those appearing in box-scores for the first time was 22.6 years. Given that some continued to play after that, it is reasonable to assume that the average age of those who played the sport was somewhat higher, but did not exceed twenty-five years.

Data available with respect to the ethnic origin and religious preference of 153 players also reveals a heavy concentration of Irish Catholics on Halifax's ball diamonds. Irish and black players made up 59.4 percent of the sample; those of English origin 20.9 percent; Scots and Germans 7.8 percent each. With respect to religious denominations, Catholics comprised 60.7 percent of players (compared to slightly more than 40 percent of the total population), Anglicans 15.7 percent, Baptists (including African Baptists) 11.1 percent and Presbyterians 7.8 percent.

Working men also made up a substantial portion of the audience for baseball games. At the end of the 1877 season in Halifax, for example, Thomas Lambert, a well-known labour leader and employee at Taylor's Boot and Shoe Factory, presented a silver ball and bat to the city champion, Atlantas, on behalf of the mechanics of Halifax. (The *Acadian Recorder* reported that the prize was offered by the mechanics of the city alone, in recognition of their dedication to the game.)[13] Lambert's involvement in baseball is intriguing. A major figure in the working-class movement, he had come to Halifax in 1865 with the 2nd Battalion of the Leicestershire regiment.[14] Soon after, he took up employment at Taylor's factory and became one of the first trade unionists in Halifax to attain international prominence. In 1869, he was elected an international officer of the Knights of St. Crispin and he became First Grand Trustee of the International Lodge in 1872.[15] Although there is no evidence that Lambert ever played baseball, he was instrumental in organizing a team at Taylor's after the company defeated the shoemakers in a bitter strike at the factory. Subsequently, in September 1877, Lambert appears as scorekeeper in a game between the Crispin Club of Taylor & Company and a team representing W.C. Brennan & Co. Later in the same month, two teams from Taylor's—``Lambert's Nine" and "Baldwin's Nine"—squared off, with the Lambert's playing to a 28-18 victory.[16]

Workers, then, were involved in the game as organizers, players and spectators. As spectators, they seemed more than willing to pay the standard 25 cents admission fee for competitive club or inter-city matches. Although not much is yet known about the impact of industrialization on the real wages of working men and women in the urban centers of the Maritimes, or upon the family wage, it is likely that factory workers such as Lambert were enjoying an increasing real income, similar to workers elsewhere in Britain and North America at this time.[17] The gradual tightening of workplace discipline, the growing separation of work and leisure and the concomitant shortening of the workday, moreover, nurtured an increased demand for organized leisure by working people and bourgeois proponents of rational recreation alike.[18] The movement of women into industrial and clerical work also led them to seek out ways to fill their leisure time, one of which was attendance at sporting events.[19] In the last quarter of the 19th century, therefore, the changes wrought by industrialization had engineered the basic prerequisite for the commercialization of baseball—the creation of an audience.

For spectators and players alike, class, ethnic and community identities, and rivalries provided an important impetus to the game. In Halifax, for example, challenge matches between the "Mechanics" and the "Laborers", the "Barkers" and the "Growlers", the "Southends" and the "Northends", the "Young Atlantas" and the "Young Oxfords", the "True Blues" and the "Greenstockings" involved rivalries based upon occupation, location, ethnicity and age. In addition, teams representing various employers such as the "Heralds", the "Recorders", the "Chronicles", the "Dolphins" (for Dolphin's Factory) and Taylor's Factory, sometimes served to secure an identity to the firm and, in other cases, encouraged worker solidarity. While the Taylor Factory teams seem to have been made up exclusively of working men, the Dolphins had a lineup which in addition to factory hands included manager K.J. Dolphin.[20] Now and then, novelty games attracted sizeable crowds, as was true of the match in July 1878 between the Fat-Men—Dolphin was suited up here as well—and the Atlantas, a competitive team who agreed to pitch, bat and throw left-handed in order to give their obese opponents a chance at victory. "The match ... was a complete success", reported the *Acadian Recorder,* "and the crowd assembled, numbering nearly 500 persons, was kept in continual roars of laughter by the blunders and exertions of the Fat Men."[21]

The rivalries that attracted the greatest spectator interest were those between teams representing various towns and cities throughout the Maritimes and New England. Particularly significant here was the impetus to the game provided by the completion of the Intercolonial Railway to Halifax in 1876. The Intercolonial linked the major urban centers of the region and allowed for dependability in the scheduling of challenge matches. Railway service made it possible for barnstorming New England club and college teams to tour the region during the summer, while telegraph communication allowed promoters to schedule games with touring teams in return for expenses and a guaranteed portion of the gate. By the last half of the 1870's, regional championships were being held annually. In 1875, for example, the Halifax Atlantas travelled to Saint John and defeated the Mutuals and Shamrocks of that city and, in the following year, the Moncton Invincibles travelled to Halifax to play the Atlantas and Resolutes to determine the Maritime champion. The Atlantas prepared for the match by enclosing their grounds and charging an admission fee, and before a large crowd, defeated Moncton 15 to 12.

By the 1880s, inter-urban contests had become regular fare. Indeed, when pioneer baseball player James Pender announced his retirement in 1888, after fourteen years on the most competitive Halifax teams, he could count among his appearances victories over the Saint John Mutuals and Shamrocks, the Moncton Redstockings and various other teams from Londonderry, Fredericton, Houlton,

St. Stephen, Bangor and Boston.[22] By this time, too, the baseball culture of the Maritimes was becoming more intimately linked with that of New England, a hardly surprising development considering the significant exodus of young Maritimers during the seventies and eighties to the "Boston States".[23]

The gradual integration of Maritime and New England baseball during the 1880's brought a number of changes in the nature of the sport in this region. During the 1885 season, baseball promoters in Saint John contracted with the Queen City team of Bangor, Maine, to play a challenge match in Saint John. Although this was an error-filled match (17 errors on one side and 28 on the other), the lopsided 17-5 victory for Bangor provided an impetus for Maritime teams to import coaches and players from the United States. During the 1888 season, the Saint John Nationals imported two college ball players, Wagg and Larabee, from Colby College, and in so doing, ushered in an era of professional baseball. The following year, three more imports, Small, Rogerse and Parsons were added to the team and the Shamrocks secured the services of Edward Kelly of Portland, Maine, and William Donovan of Bangor. In 1890, Fredericton and Moncton established professional teams, and a four-team New Brunswick professional league was established relying heavily upon imported players. The Nationals (now called the Saint John Athletic Association) discarded Rogers and signed Jack Priest, Billy Pushor, Billy Merritt and pitcher "Harvard" Howe. The Shamrocks cut Kelly and added Jim and Joe Sullivan, Abel Lezotte, Jack Griffin and John "Chewing Gum" O'Brien.[24]

The development of professional baseball during the late 1880's contributed to the sharpening of metropolitan rivalries that accompanied the coming of industrial capitalism to the region. This was particularly true of the region's two largest urban centers, Saint John and Halifax, neither of which could establish a commercial or industrial hegemony over the entire region. Whenever it could, the Saint John press contrasted the bustling exuberance of the New Brunswick centre to that of somnolent Halifax. A dispatch from the Saint John *Telegraph,* carried in Halifax newspapers on 31 July 1888, described games between the Nationals of Saint John and the Atlantas of Halifax as a "very easy contract" and suggested that if Halifax remained uncompetitive, the Nats would have to go south of the border to find better competition. "The Atlantas play good ball in the quiet town of Halifax", the *Telegraph* concluded, "but when they come to a great city like Saint John, the noise and bustle and excitement seem to unnerve them."[25] In the following year, when the Socials travelled to Saint John to play a challenge match during the Saint John city carnival, they were treated to a city parade which routinely burlesqued Halifax. One float was a replica of the mail steamer *Atlas* detained in fog eighty hours outside Halifax Harbour. Another was adorned with a banner "Little Sister Halifax. Haligonian Specialties. Fog in summer, harbour skating in Winter." When the Socials were subsequently defeated by the Saint John Club, one newspaper wrote that "bright, active, energetic Saint John scored one against her old and unprogressive rival yesterday, and she did not require the assistance of ... (the umpire) to make that score either."[26]

Halifax held its own summer carnival in early August 1889. The roster of activities included a match between a New York cricket team and the Garrison team, single scull races, a Labrador whaler boat challenge, fencing and gymnastic displays, wrestling and even a mock military battle at Point Pleasant Park. The highlight of the carnival, however, was a series of baseball games between the Halifax Socials and the John P. Lovell Arms Company and Woven Hose teams of Boston. These teams were made up of players signed and paid to advertise the companies' wares, and were probably the strongest teams in the United States outside of organized baseball. The Socials fared well against high calibre competition such as this. During the 1889 season, the Socials played twenty-one matches against teams from other cities, winning eleven. In addition to the two teams from Boston, their opponents, in 1889, included Portland, Bath, Gardner and Bangor, Maine; Bates College—as "gentlemanly a set of fellows as ever graced a diamond"—and the Boston St. Stephens. In the following season, the Holy Cross Collegians, the Worcester professionals and a regular assortment of teams from Maritime centres provided Halifax with stiff competition.[27]

Although the establishment of professional baseball enhanced the calibre of competition in the Maritimes, it also raised questions about the essential purpose of sport itself. Initially, sport advocates hoped that baseball would serve, as cricket and rugby had done, to enhance "gentlemanly" values.[28] Bedecked in uniforms that occasionally included high sneakers and bow-ties, players were often admonished against uttering derogatory remarks about their opponents and the umpire. Newspaper accounts of games regularly criticized the practice of "kicking", or disputing an umpire's decision, and derided those players who would not accede to the arbiter's authority. Protests of calls were seen to be the responsibility of the team captain, and individual players were urged to defer to the captain's authority. The extent to which "kicking" was criticized, however, reveals that the players themselves did not conform easily to the "gentlemanly code" that others wished to bring to the game.

Nor were umpires always the neutral officials that they were supposed to be. Poorly trained and often not completely cognizant of the rules, umpires were frequently biased in favour of their home teams during inter-urban matches. After a game between the Saint John Nationals and the Halifax Socials in 1888, for example, the Saint John press charged umpire William Pickering, who regularly played second base with the Socials, with "bare-faced cheating", and also alleged that a Mr. F. Robinson of Halifax had bribed the umpire. Robinson admitted boasting to friends in a local hotel that he had bought Pickering, but denied actually having done so.[29] In the following year,

Pickering was again the subject of criticism for his partisanship during a dou-ble-header between the Socials and a team from South Portland, Maine. Both games, said the Halifax *Acadian Recorder,* featured obviously partisan umpir-ing and, in the second, Pickering was calling strikes against Portland batters that were nowhere near the plate.[30]

Despite these instances of favouritism, it was generally conceded that the authority of the umpire was an essential component of the game. This was a com-mon theme in the columns of F.J. Power, sporting editor for both the *Acadian Recorder* and the Halifax *Daily Echo,* and a well-respected umpire whose career behind the plate spanned four decades. Power's career began during the 1870's as a player for the Atlantas, but he soon turned to umpiring on a regular basis. As an umpire, Power was an authoritarian figure, respected for his integrity and decisiveness in dealing both with players and unruly fans. Even spectators came to recognize his authority. At one point, for example, Power demanded the ejection of a spectator for joking that the umpire had a glass eye. "He sim-ply raised his arm", said the *Acadian Recorder,* "and a big policeman escorted ... [the fan] out."[31]

Incidents such as these reveal the hope of many sports reformers that base-ball would encourage cultivated behaviour and respect for authority. Players were expected to approach the game in a mannerly and respectable fashion, playing for the love of the sport and avoiding disparaging remarks about their opponents. But the importation of professional players from the United States during the late 1880's raised doubts that these goals could be achieved. In July 1888, a crowd of 1,200 Haligonians, including a "large gathering of the fair sex,"[32] turned out to see the Saint John Nationals and their star import player named Wagg. A pitcher from Colby College, playing under an assumed name in order to maintain his eligibility for college baseball, Wagg struck one newspa-perman as resembling "the lecturer outside a side-show at the circus". In the sixth inning, a number of "hoodlums" tried to stop Wagg's "continual prattle by endeavouring to irritate him ..., but it was useless." The same reporter crit-icized William Pickering, the second baseman and notorious umpire, for loud and uncontrolled language and chided Fitzgerald of the Atlantas for talking too much while guarding his base.[33]

Now and then, games degenerated into actual violence. During one game in-volving two Saint John teams in September 1901, pitcher Webber of the Alerts was "grossly insulted" by first baseman Friars of the Roses, caught hold of him by the neck and shook him. There was immediate confusion, the bleacherites swarmed on the field, and fisticuffs broke out between Protestant and Catholic spectators. The second baseman, Bill O'Neil called for the cops. "It was not nice for the people present, especially the ladies, and players should restrain them-selves no matter how great the insult", said the Saint John *Globe.* "... If a player makes a habit of using nasty, insulting epithets to opposing players, he should certainly be suppressed. There is some excuse for a man who in the heat of passion shows a disposition to administer bodily punishment, but nothing but contemptuous loathing for one who prefers to waggle an unguarded and insulting tongue."[34]

The concern of most sports reformers was that undisciplined behaviour by the players would encourage similar rowdiness amongst the audience. Promoters of the game especially feared the effect of unruly behaviour and "bad manners" upon women spectators. Women, of course, were important to the future of the game, not only as patrons, but also as symbols of respectability; their attendance provided the game with the hallmark of gentility that reformers wished to establish. Boorish behaviour by male spectators, of course, undermined the quest for respectability. Aware of this, the Saint John *Progress* of 11 August 1888 apologized for the behaviour of a few boors who crowded in the press box and smoked persistently, even though ladies were present. The columnist took further pains to assure female spectators that the perpetrators of this "crudeness" were not pressmen.[35] The *Acadian Recorder* was equally concerned about "hoodlums", "toughs" and "persons of a similar character", many of whom snuck into the grandstands and took the seats of paying patrons.[36] Soldiers from the Garrison at Halifax were another source of displeasure. During a game between Saint Mary's and the Garrison, before a crowd of 1,200 spectators, about a hundred men of the ranks "shouted, jeered, hooted and made all sorts of remarks about the opposing players". Noting a similar occurrence in a recent match in the United States, the columnist judged the incident in Halifax to be particularly unsavoury. In the American game, "the language was of a more humorous nature, and there were no remarks unfit for ladies to hear as in this instance. It is said that such actions take place in Montreal, the reporter concluded, but he found no reason for them to occur in Halifax.[37]

Unruly crowd behaviour obviously contradicted the conception of baseball as a "gentleman's game" played before a respectable audience. Bourgeois sport reformers, many of them medical doctors, educators, ministers, or journalists, hoped that the extension of organized sport to working people would help create a common culture that transcended class interest, and dreamt of a world of play where class distinctions would be eradicated. The editor of the Sydney *Record,* for example, believed that sport and physical exercise would help empty prisons, asylums, workhouses and relieve unemployment. With more recreation, he concluded "a good half of our social problems might disappear."[38] When the reality fell short of the ideal, these bourgeois sportsmen blamed the subversion of the game upon professionalism. The commercialization and professionalization of team sport, they argued, attracted less dignified members of the working class who put financial reward above the values of self-discipline, self-sacrifice and teamwork, and who indulged in various forms of desultory and unsavoury behaviour. These attitudes were no doubt confirmed when the off-field activities of two of the early imports to Saint John, James Guthrie and Edward Kelly, blossomed into a public scandal in September 1889. These two Irish-American ball players had arrived in Saint John from Maine, in the summer of 1889, accompanied by a number of young girls destined for employment in a bordello run by Mattie Perry, sometimes known as "French Mattie". One of the girls was a young teenager from Bangor named Annie Tuttle who had been recruited by Guthrie's companion Lizzie Duffy. When Annie Tuttle's mother travelled to Saint John in search of her daughter and reported her disappearance to the authorities, the police raided Mattie's Brittain Street house and found the young girl there. Mattie was told to leave the city at once and accompanied by Kelly, "one of her boon companions in Saint John for some weeks", left that night on the American Express for Presque Isle, Maine. Guthrie, also "well known in baseball circles" in both Bangor and Saint John, left on the same train with Lizzie Duffy.[39]

Of greater concern to reformers than this connection between the world's oldest and youngest profession was the increasing influence that betting men seemed to exercise upon the sport. Critics of professionalism noted the greater likelihood of corruption, gambling and match-fixing among professional players, no doubt sympathizing with the Toronto *Mail*'s description of a professional as a "double cross athlete who would cut his throat to keep his reputation as crooked if he thought that anyone was betting that he would live."[40] Indeed, gambling was widespread and substantial sums of money changed hands, particularly in matches involving urban rivals or barnstorming clubs from the United States. Players were by no means immune from the lure of quick money and when the odds warranted, occasionally had friends place bets against them. One such incident took place in Halifax in September 1890, when a number of Saint John players threw a game against the Halifax Socials. Beginning in the third inning, a number of curious incidents raised the suspicion of many in the crowd of over 1,000. It was in that inning that a Saint John man whose money was being wagered on the Socials walked across the field to the Saint John players' bench. Shortly thereafter, the umpire, himself from Saint John, began to make calls that favoured Halifax, giving bases on balls to the Socials on obvious strikes. For Saint John, Priest the pitcher struck out by swing at balls nowhere near the plate, and third-baseman Parsons, after hitting safely, removed his hand from the base and allowed a Socials player to tag him out.[41] This transparently fixed match, said the *Daily Echo,* provided an indication of the depth that professional players could sink to when betting men were interested.[42]

A number of reasons were given to explain the fix. In the first place, the Socials were going to Saint John the following week and a victory for the Halifax team would ensure Saint John promoters a big crowd. It was also widely believed that revenge was the motive, because the better who had fixed the match had been taken advantage of by a Halifax gambler who bet $300 on the Saint John team at two-one odds during the first game of the series. Haligonians were further outraged when a correspondent of the Moncton *Times* reported that upon returning home, a banquet was held for the Saint John players, despite their acknowledged throwing of the game. Seven of the nine men, the *Times* correspondent reported, were involved in the fix and they "openly avow and boast of it". At the dinner, an MPP from Saint John chaired the festivities which included a succession of speeches glorifying the players. "This barefaced outrage on public morals", the correspondent concluded, "will perhaps bring a gulled public to some sense of the honour involved in professional baseball."[43]

The thrown match at the end of the 1890 season had a devastating impact upon professional baseball in the region. Prior to that time, the elevated standard of play that accompanied the importation and payment of athletes had attracted a growing clientele. Players were performing before crowds that averaged about 1,200 in Halifax and Moncton, and about three times that number in Saint John. In the latter city, fan interest was so great that the King Street merchants installed a telephone at the baseball grounds, in August 1888, so that after each inning, the score of the game in progress could be telephoned to the DeForest and March store, at the corner of King and Germane Streets, and placed on a large blackboard which could be seen from a considerable distance.[44] This enthusiasm for the game attracted sports entrepreneurs, who with admission prices of 25 cents and an extra 10 cents for admission to the grandstand and prize purses that sometimes were as high as $500, could bring in as much as $1,500 for a single match in Saint John, or $1,000 in Halifax or Moncton.

During the 1890s, fan interest waned. In the wake of the discrediting of the game's integrity, the Halifax Socials disbanded and, through the 1890s, baseball in Halifax was played on a decidedly amateur level. Rivalries between employees at manufacturing or commercial establishments, or between ethnic groups, or recreational clubs provided the community with interesting but not outstanding baseball. Matches with other city clubs or touring teams were rare, and although there were sporadic attempts to revive competitive baseball in the city, there was little enthusiasm for the professional game. In Saint John, the nineties saw the emergence of a great rivalry between two city teams, the Alerts and the Roses, the former supported largely by the Irish Catholic community and the latter appealing to an Anglo-Protestant constituency.

The collapse of professional baseball in the 1890s accompanied the diffusion of the amateur game throughout the Maritimes. In Pictou County, Nova Scotia, baseball originated as a result of the efforts of newspaperman R.S. Theakston.[45] The nineties also saw the flourishing of the game in the coal-towns of Joggins, Westville and Springhill, where baseball was an important cultural component of worker solidarity, and in "busy Amherst", one of the most rapidly growing industrial towns in the region. "The baseball craze has struck Springhill", said the

Springhill News and Advertiser of 13 August 1896, "there are about three teams at Miller's Corner ranging from 6 years of age to 60, also two teams on Herritt Road and two or three in town."[46] Springhill was by no means unique. Rivalries based both upon propinquity and shared occupational and cultural identities, invigorated matches between Joggins, Springhill and Westville. Before long, towns from Truro to Annapolis were playing each other and accepting American challenges. Similar rivalries emerged in the western counties of Nova Scotia between Windsor, Kentville and Middleton; further south in Digby and Yarmouth; across the Bay of Fundy in Macadam and Woodstock; and in a number of border towns in Maine.

If the 1890s witnessed the diffusion of the sport beyond the large metropolitan centers to the smaller towns of the region, the absence of high level inter-urban competition in Halifax, Moncton and Saint John provided a boon to the development of baseball for women and racial minorities during the 1890s. In 1891, a touring ladies team from the United States caused great excitement, playing in a number of towns in the region. In Nova Scotia, the women defeated all-male clubs in Amherst, Annapolis and Middleton and before a crowd of 3,000, beat a Halifax amateur club by an 18-15 score. Tours of this sort helped secure the legitimacy of female participation in organized team sport, much to the delight of feminists such as Grace Ritchie of Halifax who regularly advocated women's greater involvement in sporting activity. The reaction to the entrance of women into baseball's male domain, however, was mixed. Those who feared the emergence of the "new woman" were concerned that participation in sports such as baseball contradicted the ideal feminine personality, while others regarded physical training for women an antidote to nervous exhaustion or "neurasthenia". Prevailing notions of biology emphasized woman's nurturing character, her physical frailty and her nervous irritability, and suggested that women were particularly susceptible to an imbalance of physical and mental faculties.[47] Involvement in competitive sport and physical exercise still had its critics, but by the 1890s, there was a growing acceptance of female athleticism because it compensated for nervous debilitation.[48]

The tour of the "Chicago Ladies", in 1891, brought the debate over women and sport to center stage. The Truro *Daily News* reported that a clergyman in New Glasgow had spoken strongly against the tour at a local prayer meeting, while in Truro, a delegation of citizens unsuccessfully lobbied the Mayor to prevent the team from playing.[49] On the day of the game, the Truro newspaper noted that "many people, doubtless, will be there to witness the antics of the girls, but if all reports be true, the propriety of attending is very questionable."[50] After the games in Truro and New Glasgow, the local press criticized the women as frauds who could not compete on equal terms with men although they presumed to do so. "They are nothing better than a lot of hoodlums from a crowded city", said the New Glasgow *Eastern Chronicle,* "... they are frauds of the first order."[51]

Despite these criticisms, a few days later, a crowd of 3,000 assembled at the Wanders Grounds, in Halifax, to watch the women. In addition to the paying patrons, boys climbed electric light poles and trees outside the grounds and a crowd "containing people of all classes of life" assembled on Citadel Hill, overlooking the field.[52] In Halifax, there was little of the hostility that accompanied the team's visit to New Glasgow and Truro. The women were popular as well in Amherst, where the victory of the girls over the local boys' team was "both interesting and exciting". In the opinion of the Amherst *Evening News,* there was "nothing, whatever, here which would warrant their being refused the privilege or opportunity of playing."[53] The Moncton *Transcript* agreed and announced the intention of local officials to invite the women to play another match in the city on their return from Nova Scotia.[54]

The tour of the Chicago team provided an important impetus to the organization of women's baseball teams throughout the region. Women were playing baseball in most of the major urban centers before 1900 and even in smaller communities such as Bocabec, New Brunswick, and Oxford, Nova Scotia, teams of women baseballists risked the wrath of the churches as they pushed forward into a formerly male sporting domain. This activity seems to suggest that the idea of maternal feminism and the doctrine of "separate spheres" were by no means universally accepted by turn of the century Maritime women.[55]

Black teams also flourished in a number of Maritime communities during the 1890s. The most powerful of these was the Halifax based Eurekas who during the 1890s lost only one match, that to the Amherst Royals in 1897. Other black teams active in this period were the Fredericton Celestials, the Truro Victorians, the Dartmouth Stanleys and Seasides and the Independent Stars and North Ends of Halifax. For the black minority in the region, baseball and other sports provided an avenue to respectability and relative acceptance by the white majority. Involvement in athletics created local heroes and encouraged black pride, but also offered a chance for black athletes to visit other communities in the region and demonstrate their skills. While black teams rarely played against their white counterparts, they nonetheless contributed to the more organized character of 19th-century sporting life, establishing regional championships and attracting sizeable paid gates. Although the press was inclined to emphasize the "ludicrous incidents" that took place in black baseball, it is fair to say that the coverage of black sporting activity was one of the more positive elements in the press's treatment of the black community in the 19th-century Maritimes.[56]

If the 1890s saw the diffusion of the sport throughout the region and the emergence of women and blacks on the baseball diamond, the opening of the new century witnessed the renewed ascendancy of professional baseball in the Maritimes. Professional teams once again graced the diamonds of Halifax, Fredericton, Saint John and Moncton, and smaller communities also began importing players. Many of these imports were college students from American universities such as "Colby Jack" Coombs, a Moncton pitcher who would later star in the major leagues and ultimately be inducted into the Hall of Fame. Others, who would play or had at one time played in the big leagues, were Bill O'Neill the Saint John native and starting leftfielder for the Chicago White Sox in the 1906 World Series, Larry McLean of the Halifax Resolutes and Bill Hallman, a former second-baseman for the Philadelphia Athletics turned thespian, who played on the touring Volunteer-Organist baseball and theatre company team.[57]

The opening decade of the 20th century also witnessed the first connections between organized baseball activity on the mainland and on Cape Breton Island. Baseball was slow to arrive in Cape Breton, but by 1905, teams in Sydney, Sydney Mines, Reserve Mines and Glace Bay were importing players. The Sydney *Record* of 21 August 1905 reported that better baseball than had ever been witnessed on the Island was now being played, "though the results are getting to depend too much on which team can import the most and best men."[58] The Dominion No. 1 team was the only team in this colliery district league that chose not to import men. Crowds of 800 per game were common in Cape Breton during the 1905 season, and seeing the potential for lucrative gates, sports promoters like M.J. Dryden of Sydney began to call for a strictly professional baseball operation for the 1906 season.

Although there were those who regarded the provision of recreation to the colliers of Cape Breton as a valuable antidote to class antagonism, not everyone supported the introduction of professional baseball. The editor of the Sydney *Record* regarded it warily, thinking it a scheme of unscrupulous promoters who, in preying upon the mining districts, would encourage idle habits amongst the working class. The summer months, the editor continued, were already busy with sports, picnics, excursions and holidays which took people away from the workplace. "We should be the last to deny to anybody a reasonable amount of recreation and a reasonable amount of holidays", the editor wrote, "but this taking a day or a half day off at frequent intervals disorganizes the working man. England today is suffering from an excess of the sporting and holidaying spirit and she is in consequence feeling the competition of the steadier and more industrious continental nations."[59] In taking this stand, the newspaper was echoing the position of the operators of the Dominion Coal Company who complained that the scheduling of games before 5 o'clock resulted in "a considerable number leaving work early in the day, three or four times a week."[60]

Another concern was that the commercialization of baseball undermined respect for the sancity of contract. Contract jumping was widespread in the early years of baseball, and without a rigorous governing body for the sport, there were few prohibitions against athletes selling their services to teams on a game-by-game basis. In a game between the Saint John Roses and Fredericton Tartars, in August 1890, for example, the Roses were without four of their players. Friars and Shannon abandoned the club to play a game for Eastport against

Calais, Maine. Cunningham was in Houlton playing for the Alerts, while Bill O'Neil was at Black River training for a race for a money purse.[61]

During the same season, the Halifax Resolutes offered a sizeable sum to Fredericton's pitcher "Harvard" Howe to pitch a single challenge match against Moncton. Due to the expense, ladies, who had earlier been admitted free, now were required to pay a fee of 15 cents.[62] The Resolutes followed a similar course later in the 1900 season, securing a pitcher by the name of Holland from the Saint John Roses to pitch against the Alerts.[63] The inability or unwillingness of clubs to enforce player contracts encouraged widespread player raiding between teams. During the 1901 season, for example, trainer John J. Mack, a professional athletic coach of the Wanderer's Amateur Athletic Club in Halifax, was implicated in an attempt to induce the star battery of the Alerts (Webber and Dolan) to jump the club and sign with the Halifax Resolutes. The Saint John *Globe* noted that Mack and Mr. Nevill, who was attached to the Resolutes club, offered the players salaries higher than those presently offered in the fast New England League. "All this goes to show", said the *Globe,* "how the baseball craze is taking hold of Halifax; how the ring of sporting men, whose sole idea of sport is to gamble on it, are getting in their fine work and are turning the game into a money making speculation, robbing it of all that is genuine and lowering its standard to those of cock-fighting or pugilism."[64] Without an effective regulatory body that could tighten up these loopholes, there was little hope of overcoming the problems of contract jumping. If clubs tried to enforce their contracts, the players would simply play for a release. League officials also found that the lax administration of contracts left them unable to discipline players who broke league regulations. They could only shake their heads in annoyance when players like first baseman Joe Donnelly, suspended from the Maine-New Brunswick League one week, became a regular in the lineup of the Halifax Socials the next.[65]

By the middle of the first decade of this century, then, the contradictions professional baseball presented to the dream of recreational respectability were abundantly clear. Rather than encouraging a oneness of sentiment that transcended class lines, the development of baseball seemed to reveal the worst influences of commercialism, a flagrant disrespect for the sanctity of contract, an encouragement of reckless gambling and unruly crowd activity. Competitive baseball also undermined the participatory character of amateur athletics. Rather than playing themselves, spectators preferred "to watch a few experts whose business it is to play for the public amusement", and, in turn, while neighbouring provinces were scoured for ball players in return for "a good salary, a lazy time and the small boys idol", local amateur sport withered.[66]

There were other problems. On the field of play, the working men who played alongside college students seemed not to be uplifted to respectability, but in the eyes of sports reformers, posed a threat to the respectable character of young college men. This concern was by no means confined to critics of professionalism in the Maritimes. Dr. E.H. Nichols of Harvard University opposed college students playing alongside professionals in summer leagues and voiced the increasingly widespread belief that the longer a person stays in pro-ball "the worse he becomes".[67] Between the turn of the century and World War One, therefore, reformers made a concerted effort to separate amateur and professional sport and to define new standards of play that would distinguish professional baseball from the "gentlemanly amateurism" of the college game. In the United States, the NCAA took steps towards this end, striking a Committee, in 1913, to rid college baseball of objectionable practises. Reporting in the following year, the Committee made a number of suggestions for changes in the game. The Committee recommended:

1. strict adherence to base-coaching rules, especially those prohibiting coaches from inciting or gesticulating to the crowd or using defamatory language;

2. enforcement of rules against blocking the runner, prying runners off base or other forms of trickery, in order to bring a decorum to the game;

3. prohibition of verbal coaching from the bench;

4. prohibition of encouragement of the pitcher from outfielders. "Remarks of endless iteration" were deemed disagreeable to spectators, thus, encouragement should only come from the infield;

5. prohibition of catchers talking to batters;

6. restriction of indecorous or unseemly behaviour.

The report concluded that "a college baseball game is a splendid contest of skill between two opposing nines before an academic throng of spectators. It is not a contest between a visiting team and a local team assisted by a disorderly rabble."[68]

The debate over amateurism was equally energetic in the Maritimes by 1910. In that year, the Halifax *Herald* ran a series of fifty columns on amateurism and professionalism in regional sporting life. Much of the debate centered upon the rapid growth of professionalism in hockey, but baseball was also a matter of lively concern. The *Herald's* position was clear. The main evil was not payment, but the system of amateurs and professionals playing alongside each other. What justification was there for promoters paying one athlete while exploiting another? This inequality of treatment encouraged amateurs to turn professional, many of whom would still be playing for the love of the game, except that someone was "getting the green on the side".[69] At the same time, the *Herald* admitted that working-class athletes needed compensation for lost wages and the sacrifice of time, noting the argument of a well-known Maritime catcher who pointed out that he could not afford to play ball on a Saturday afternoon without compensation for docked wages. But the same player's suggestion that the Maritime Provinces Amateur Athletic Association (MPAAA) give up its jurisdiction over baseball and let amateurs and pros play side by side was given a hasty rejection. "Amateurs and Pros Mix", said a head-line of 25 February, "No! No! Say All in chorus!"[70]

The growing support for a clearer demarcation of amateur and professional sport led the Maritime Provinces Amateur Athletic Association to tighten its reg-ulations with respect to amateur standing. Critical here was the resignation of James G. Lithgow as President of the MPAAA and his replacement, in 1909, by a new president Dr. H.D. Johnson of Charlottetown. Lithgow, actively in-volved in sporting organizations in the region and at one time president of the Nova Scotia Amateur Hockey league, had often turned a blind eye to violations of amateur standing. He must have been naive, the Halifax *Herald* concluded, not to know that professionalism was widespread, particularly after a lawsuit involving a Fredericton hockey club revealed that all its players, in the 1908 sea-son, were under salary and that many of them were playing in Nova Scotia during the 1909-1910 season.[71] As incoming president of the MPAAA, Johnson took immediate steps to separate amateur and professional play and instituted a tighter transfer rule to discourage player raiding in both hockey and base-ball. Johnson's position on amateurism was to let bygones be bygones; subsequent violations of amateur standing, however would be severely dealt with. In the future, Johnson declared, there would be no reprieve. "Once a pro-fessional, always a professional" now served as the ruling maxim of the MPAAA.[72]

Ironically, these new regulations tended not to encourage the development of competitive amateur baseball in the region, but led to a more thorough-going system of importing professionals, some of whom were on option from major league teams, others who continued to play ball in the summer, while attend-ing American universities in the off-season. In 1911, a professional New Brunswick-Maine baseball league was formed which, though not formally part of organized baseball, relied heavily on players from major league organiza-tions. A four-team professional league followed in Nova Scotia, in 1912, with teams in Stellarton, Westville and Halifax. Other independent professional teams operated in Cape Breton, Yarmouth and in the coal mining town of Springhill. The success of these leagues—in August 1912, over 8,000 specta-tors attended a game between the Saint John Marathons and Houlton, Maine—quickly attracted American promoters such as Frank J. Leonard of the Lynn Baseball Club of the New England league who envisaged a prosper-ous new league in Maine and the Maritimes.[73]

Although Leonard's initial attempt to create a regional professional league ended in failure, it was taken up once again in the spring of 1914. The new or-ganizer was Montrealer Joe Page, sports agent for the Canadian Pacific Railway. Operating on behalf of officials of the Saint John baseball teams, Page hoped to spearhead a new professional league in the Maritimes. This league, slated to op-erate as a Class "D" circuit within organized baseball, was to include teams in Halifax, Saint John, Moncton, Stellarton and New Glasgow. Page, who also envisaged his trains transporting players and fans to and from matches, helped secure a number of name players for the new circuit, including former Boston, Detroit and Cleveland player Cy Ferry. Unfortunately for Page, when Moncton and New Glasgow demanded guarantees of $2,745 for thirty-eight appearances in Halifax and an equal amount from Saint John, yet offered none in return to the other clubs, the scheme was scuttled.[74] With the coming of the war in Europe, the prospects of reviving the experiment were permanently dashed. In future years, the distinctions between amateur and professional were strictly maintained. The Depression of the twenties and thirties ensured that professional play would no longer be the widespread phenomenon that it had been before 1914.

Between the origins of Maritime baseball in the late 1860s and the outbreak of World War One, then, life on the region's sandlots changed drastically. Emerging out of the transformation of the region that accompanied the development of industrial capitalism in the 1870s and 1880s, baseball appealed initially to bourgeois reformers intent upon establishing appropriate standards of respectability and gentlemanly play. But the gamblers, promoters, players, spectators, ethnic groups and women athletes who also played a role in shaping the game brought their own needs to the sport. By the turn of the century, therefore, most reformers recognized their inability to use baseball as a means of social control, and were beginning to demand the separation of amateur and professional play.

The results of the drive to separate amateurism and professionalism were somewhat ironic. Although successful in encouraging a clearer demarcation between amateur and professional sport, reformers such as Dr. Johnson and F.J. Power were faced with the growing public acceptance of professional athletics. Yet, in the longer run, the triumph of professionalism over amateurism served the interests of the bourgeoisie just as well.[75] The period between 1870 and 1914 was one in which baseball was transformed from a cultural struggle involving reformers and "rowdies" to a more manageable form of organized mass leisure. And, if the transformation of baseball from an instrument of socialization to that of a marketable spectacle failed to eradicate class conflict as reformers had hoped, baseball gradually became one of the unifying enthusiasms that bridged class divisions and encouraged community solidarity.[76] The roots that baseball sank in the towns and cities of the region prior to World War One, in fact, were so deep that they would nurture the sport for another half century. Only in recent years, with the coming of television and the increasing sophistication of the consumer marketplace, has baseball become essentially commodified and detached from its community roots. The result has been the withering of community baseball in the Maritimes and the incorporation of the region into a modern baseball culture of mass-produced Toronto Blue Jay caps and Montreal Expos sweatshirts. That, however, is another story altogether.

Notes

The author wishes to thank Ian MacKay, Keith Walden, Gerald Redmond, John Thompson, David Bercuson and members of the Halifax History Seminar for their helpful suggestions in the development of this paper.

1. Tony Mason, *Association Football and English Society, 1863-1915,* Brighton, 1980; Alan Metcalfe, *Canada Learns to Play. The Emergence of Organized Sport, 1807-1914,* Toronto, 1987: Wray Vamplew, *Pay Up and Play the Game. Professional Sport in Britain, 1875-1914,* Cambridge, England, 1988. *See* also James Walvin, *The People's Game: A Social History of British Football,* Bristol, 1975.

2. On the centrality of the idea of respectability in Victorian thought, *see* F.M.L. Thompson, *The Rise of Respectable Society. A Social History of Victorian Britain, 1830-1900,* Cambridge, Mass., 1988. For an appreciation of the relationship of respectability to the reform of leisure and recreation, *see* Peter Bailey, *Leisure and Class in Victorian England. Rational Recreation and the Contest for Control,* London, 1978; Eileen Yeo and Stephen Yeo, *Popular Culture and Class Conflict: Explorations in the History of Labour and Leisure,* Sussex, 1981.

3. Raymond Williams, *Culture,* Glasgow, 1981, p. 67.

4. The literature on the industrialization of the Maritimes is extensive. *See* in particular T.W. Acheson, "The National Policy and the Industrialization of the Maritimes, 1880-1910", *Acadiensis,* vol. 1, n° 2. Spring 1972, pp. 3-28; L.D. McCann, "The Mercantile-Industrial Transition in the Metal Towns of Pictou County, 1857-1931", *Acadiensis,* vol. 10, n° 2, Spring 1981, pp. 29-64.

5. Allan Guttmann, *From Ritual to Record: The Nature of Modern Sports,* New York, 1978, pp. 100-108.

6. Steven M. Gelber, "Working at Playing: The Culture of the Workplace and the Rise of Baseball," *Journal of Social History,* vol. 16, n°. 4, Summer 1983, pp. 3-22.

7. Saint John, *The Globe,* 14 December 1901, section 4, p. 7.

8. Halifax *Reporter,* 9, 12 May 1868.

9. *Acadian Recorder,* 18 July 1857.

10. First *Annual Report,* Halifax Industrial Boy's School, 1864. *See* in particular the section entitled "Amusements".

11. *See,* for example, *Acadian Recorder,* 15 October 1877.

12. *Acadian Recorder,* 11 August 1888.

13. *Acadian Recorder,* 11 September 1877.

14. *Ibid.,* 7 March 1891.

15. Knights of St. Crispin. "Proceedings of the 5th Annual Meeting of Grand Lodge, April 1872", New York: Journeymen Printer's Cooperative Association, 1872.

16. *Acadian Recorder,* 6, 18 September 1877.

17. For Great Britain, *see* E. Hopkins. "Working Hours and Conditions During the Industrial Revolution: A Reappraisal", *Economic History Review,* vol. XXXV. 1982. For the United States, *see* John Modell, "Patterns of Consumption, Acculturation and

Family Income Strategy in Late Nineteenth Century America" in Tamara K. Hareven and Maris Vinovskis, eds., *Family and Population in Nineteenth Century America*, Princeton, 1978: Clarence Long, *Wages and Earnings in the United States, 1860-1890.* Princeton, 1960.

18. Ray Rosenzweig, *Eight Hours for What We Will. Workers and Leisure in an Industrial City.* London, 1983. The development of organized sport, amateur athletic associations and the YMCA also provided alternatives to the tavern as the focus of leisure activity. *See,* for example, Peter Delottinville. "Joe Beef of Montreal: Working Class Culture and the Tavern, 1869-1889", *Labour Le Travailleur,* vol. 8, 1981, pp. 34-35.

19. Kathy Peiss, *Cheap Amusements: Working Women and Leisure in Turn-of-the-Century New York,* Philadelphia, 1986.

20. *Acadian Recorder,* 8 July 1881.

21. *Ibid.,* 11 July 1878.

22. *Ibid.,* 27 September 1888.

23. Alan A. Brookes, "Outmigration from the Maritime Provinces, 1860-1900: Some Preliminary Considerations", *Acadiensis,* vol. 5, no 2, Spring 1976, pp. 26-55.

24. Saint John *Globe,* 14 December 1901.

25. Quoted in *Acadian Recorder,* 27 July 1889. *See* also *ibid.,* 3 October 1889.

26. *Ibid.,* 27 July 1889.

27. *Ibid.,* 5 August 1889. On the Bates College nine, see *ibid.,* 8 June 1889.

28. On the relationship between team sport and Victorian notions of manliness and the inculcation of ideals of teamwork, patriotism, courage and respectability, *see* Morris Mott, "The British Protestant Pioneers and the Establishment of Manly Sports in Manitoba", *Journal of Sport History,* vol. 7, n° 3, Winter 1980, pp. 25-26; "One Solution to the Urban Crisis: Manly Sports and Winnipegers, 1890-1914", *Urban History Review,* vol. XXII, n° 2, October 1983, pp. 57-70; Norman Vance, *The Sinews of the Spirit: The Ideal of Manliness in Victorian Literature and Religious Thought,* Cambridge, 1985; Brian Dobbs, *Edwardians at Play,* London, 1973; S.F. Wise, "Sport and Class Values in Old Ontario and Quebec", in W. Heick and R. Graham, eds., *His Own Man Essays in Honour of A.R.M. Lower,* Montreal, 1974. For a contemporary view, *see* J. Castell Hopkins, "Youthful Canada and the Boys' Brigade", *Canadian Magazine,* vol. IV, n° 6, pp. 551-566. On working-class opposition to bourgeois reformism, *see* Joe Maguire, "Images of Manliness and Competing Ways of Living in Late Edwardian Britain", *British Journal of Sports History,* vol. 3, December 1986, pp. 256-287.

29. *Acadian Recorder,* 20, 21 September 1888.

30. *Ibid.,* 30 May 1889.

31. *Acadian Recorder,* 24 July 1900. During the 1870's Power had played and umpired games for money, but this was "when the distinction between amateur and professional athletics was unknown in this city." Despite subsequent protests that his earlier actions violated his amateur standing, Power was reinstated as an amateur by the Maritime Provinces Amateur Athletic Association's Executive Committee in 1888. *Ibid.,* 23 May 1888.

32. *Ibid.*, 3 July 1888.
33. *Ibid.*
34. Saint John *Globe,* 12 September 1901.
35. Saint John *Progress,* 11 August 1888.
36. *Acadian Recorder,* 25 May 1900.
37. *Ibid.*
38. Sydney *Record,* 19 July 1905.
39. *Acadian Recorder,* 18 September 1889.
40. Quoted in Frank Cosentino, "Ned Hanlan—Canada' Premier Oarsman—A Case Study in 19th Century Professionalism", *Canadian Journal of the History of Sport and Physical Education,* December 1974, vol. V, n° 2, p. 7.
41. Acadian Recorder, 8 September 1890.
42. Halifax *Daily Echo,* 11 September 1890.
43. *Acadian Recorder,* 8 September 1890.
44. *Ibid.*, 4 August 1888.
45. Halifax *Chronicle Herald,* 16 August 1951.
46. Springhill *News and Advertiser,* 13 August 1896.
47. Carole Smith Rosenberg and Charles Rosenberg, "The Female Animal: Medical and Biological Views of Women and Her Role in Nineteenth Century America", *Journal of American History,* vol. 60, September 1973, pp. 332-356.
48. Michael J.E. Smith, "Graceful Athleticism or Robust Womanhood: The Sporting Culture of Women in Victorian Nova Scotia, 1870-1914", *Journal of Canadian Studies,* vol. 23, n°s 1-2, Spring-Summer 1988, pp. 120-137; Helen Lensky, *Out of Bounds, Women, Sport, and Sexuality,* Toronto, 1986; Kathleen E. McCrone, *Playing the Game, Sport and the Physical Emancipation of English Women, 1870-1914,* Lexington, Kentucky, 1988.
49. Truro *Daily News,* 18 August 1891.
50. *Ibid.*, 19 August 1891.
51. New Glasgow *Eastern Chronicle,* 21 August 1891.
52. *Acadian Recorder,* 24 August 1891.
53. Amherst, *The Evening News,* 20 August 1891.
54. Quoted in the *Acadian Recorder,* 20 August 1891.
55. *Cf.* Michael J.E. Smith, "Female Reformers in Victorian Nova Scotia: Architects of a New Womanhood", M.A. thesis, Saint Mary's University, 1984.
56. On the propensity to comment upon ludicrous incidents, *see* the *Acadian Recorder,* 14 August 1900, for a game between the Eurekas and Seasides before an audience of 250. Black baseball originated in the 1880s and by the end of the century, there was an annual regional championship, *Ibid.*, 28 August, 11 September, 18 September 1900.
57. Joseph Reischler, *The Encyclopedia of Baseball,* 5th edition, New York, 1983; Sydney *Record,* 8 August 1906.

58. Syney *Record,* 30 July, 21 August 1906.

59. *Ibid.,* 2 August 1906.

60. *Acadian Recorder,* 4 August 1906. The coal operators argued that the scheduling of baseball before 5 o'clock seriously embarrassed the company and diminished output. "Picnics have also contributed their share of adverse influence", said the *Recorder,* "but baseball is the principal sinner." The company prevailed upon the league to move the starting time to 5 o'clock from 3:30 p.m., but this proved inconvenient. The company also proposed that all games be held on Sunday, but the miners refused this interference in their leisure and opposed Sunday baseball on religious grounds. *See* also Sydney *Record,* 23 July 1906.

61. *Acadian Recorder,* 27 August 1900.

62. *Ibid.,* 18 July 1900.

63. *Ibid.,* 24 July 1900.

64. Saint John *Globe,* 25 June 1901. Born in 1870 in Chelsea, England, Mack was an accomplished coach, athletic director at Columbia College, New York, in the 1899-1900 term and trainer for the Wanderer's Amateur Athletic Club in the summer season for a number of years. Mack denied allegations of unfair practise, but admitted writing to Webber who was "under his care in the University of Maine all last winter and spring" and who contacted Mack expressing his desire to play in Halifax. Halifax *Herald,* 26 June 1901. In 1905, Mack was hired as Yale's athletic director. *Acadiensis Recorder,* 15 August 1905.

65. Saint John *Globe,* 11 August 1911.

66. Sydney *Record,* 23 July 1906.

67. Dr. E.H. Nichols, "Discussion of Summer Baseball", *American Physical Education Review,* vol XIX, n° 4, April 1914, pp. 292-300.

68. "Committee on Ridding College Baseball of Its Objectionable Features", *American Physical Education Review,* vol. XIX, n° 4, April 1904, pp. 313-314.

69. Halifax *Herald,* 11, 14 January 1910.

70. *Ibid.,* 25 February 1910.

71. *Ibid.,* 11, 22 January 1910.

72. *Ibid.,* 6, 7 January 1910.

73. *Acadian Recorder,* 14, 30 August 1912.

74. *Ibid.,* 18 April, 6, 15 May.

75. The separation of amateurism and professionalism in athletics may be seen as part of a broader sorting out of high-brow and low-brow culture at the end of the 19th century. In this regard, *see* Lawrence W. Levine, *Highbrow / Lowbrow: The Emergence of Cultural Hierarchy in America,* Cambridge, Mass., 1988.

76. Ian Gordon McKay, "Industry, Work, and Community in the Cumberland Coalfields, 1848-1927", pt. 1, Ph.D. thesis, Dalhousie University, 1983, pp. 370-373. McKay makes a similar argument with respect to baseball in the town of Springhill.

CHAPTER
4 JOHN A. MACDONALD — THE NATURE OF POLITICAL LEADERSHIP

It has been a favourite observation of political commentators that "Canada is a difficult country to govern." Leaders, confronted with the task of creating national political parties, have had to find integrating policies which would counteract the country's geographical, economic, linguistic, and cultural diversity. It has frequently been argued that this dynamic has put a premium on compromise, forcing political leaders to abandon principles as they sought policies which would appeal to diverse regions and interest groups.

In the generation after Confederation, John A. Macdonald created the first successful "national" party, and in doing so established the model which other political leaders would emulate. Peter Waite, in his study of "The Political Ideas of John. A. Macdonald," delivered as a lecture in 1968, while recognizing Macdonald's superb qualities as a political tactician and strategist, nevertheless concluded that "Macdonald's political principles were unformulated and inchoate." The Canadian parliamentary system, he suggested, by its very nature "puts a premium upon techniques rather than upon ideas."

In the second article in this chapter, Gordon Stewart, approaching the political system from an entirely different perspective, draws attention to the extraordinary importance which patronage assumed very early in the Canadian political system, and concludes that the patronage system was independent of party in the sense that it was virtually identical under both Conservative and

Liberal governments in the period before World War I. The very effectiveness of the patronage system in cementing political loyalties and creating stable political parties, he argues, had the unfortunate result of allowing political parties to ignore "the need to think about genuine accommodation" on issues of major national importance, thus reinforcing the inherent parochialism of Canadian politics.

Suggestions for Further Reading

Carty, R. Kenneth and W. Peter Wards, eds., *National Politics and Community in Canada*. Vancouver: University of British Columbia Press, 1986.

Creighton, Donald, *John A. Macdonald*. 2 volumes. Toronto: Macmillan, 1952, 1955.

Christian, W. and C. Campbell, *Political Parties and Ideologies in Canada*. Toronto, 1974.

Preece, Rod, "The Political Wisdom of Sir John A. Macdonald," *The Canadian Journal of Political Science*, XVII, no. 3 (September 1984), 459-486.

Roberts, Barbara, "'They Drove him to Drink': Donald Creighton's Macdonald and his Wives," *Canada: An Historical Magazine*, III, no. 2 (December 1975), 50-64.

Stevens, Paul, "Wilfrid Laurier: Politician," in *The Political Ideas of the Prime Ministers of Canada*, ed. Marcel Hamelin. Ottawa: University of Ottawa Press, 1969.

Stewart, Gordon T., *The Origins of Canadian Politics: A Comparative Approach*. Vancouver: University of British Columbia Press, 1986.

THE POLITICAL IDEAS OF JOHN A. MACDONALD

P.B. Waite

The origins of this paper help to explain its argument. When I was first asked by the University of Ottawa, the proposed title was, "The political ideas of John A. Macdonald." I thought I would have a try at this, but I soon ran into logical difficulties. Two weeks later a letter came from M. Hamelim which neatly resolved the difficulties. In that letter the title for the lecture was put as, "The political *beliefs* of John A. Macdonald." This suited me much better, and for three halcyon weeks I laboured happily on that subject. Then the blow fell. The printed pamphlet formally announcing the series arrived. The title read, "The political ideas of John A. Macdonald." So I was back with my problem unresolved. Broadly speaking, it is unresolved still.

In 1933, T. W. L. MacDermott published a paper in *CHR* called "The political ideas of John A. Macdonald." MacDermott concluded that Macdonald was not a man of ideas at all; indeed, that the principal deficiency in Macdonald's political thinking was "its essentially unreflective character." It was a good paper, based

From Marcel Hamelim (ed.), *The Political Ideas of the Prime Ministers of Canada* (Ottawa: University of Ottawa Press, 1969), 51-68. Reprinted by permission of the University of Ottawa Press.

on some study of the great collection of Macdonald papers, and it generated several other essays of the same type, mainly from political scientists the aridity of whose normal work made them turn to the luxuries of history.

Clearly MacDermott's argument needed some re-examination, perhaps to refute it, perhaps more thoroughly to substantiate it, perhaps to amend it. Had I been A. J. P. Taylor, I should have stood MacDermott's argument on its head, and argued cogently, firmly, and with the greatest relish, that Macdonald was positively full of political ideas. Such an attack on MacDermott's views would have brought out a number of spectators, and would doubtless have appeared in one of those slim and often incomprehensible books of readings published by our busy Canadian publishers, entitled, *Was Macdonald a man of ideas?*

I regret I cannot do that. Broadly, I agree with MacDermott, and the purpose of this paper tonight is to elucidate the argument; what will emerge from this unlovely approach will I hope be an attempt at an assessment of Macdonald's political beliefs. So that M. Hamelin was right after all.

For if by political ideas is meant a systematic corpus of political principles, a body of doctrine that can be said to represent a solid core of thought in a man's political life, then we shall look in vain for it in Sir John A. Macdonald. Macdonald was a lawyer; training in the common law might almost be said to inhibit the formation of political principles. Every common law case is, in the nature of things, different; a body of principles can be extracted from the common law only by a complex and painful process of induction. The common law is, in its very nature, an empirical subject: each case is, so to speak, *sui generis,* and the successful prosecution of it demands not so much the application of principle as the use of ingenuity. It seems to me that the political ideas of Sir John Macdonald owe much to his experience of the law. His mind was too flexible, his antennae too sensitive to allow him to be very comfortable with principles, away from what he seems to have felt were the realities of political life. He seems always to have had an inherent distrust of political principles—he would probably have called them nostrums—that were sometimes articulated by others. In his view there seems to have been a crudeness, an arbitrariness, in the application of political ideas to such a delicate and complex business as parliamentary government. In his view parliamentary government could not be worked, nor its political parties formed, if politicians eternally sat upon their principles. T. W. L. MacDermott called Macdonald an empiricist through and through: we should be more inclined to add the word pragmatic. For Macdonald the supreme test of any policy was in the results. He would adjust his views and policies to the temper of the time, abandoning cheerfully, though cautiously, any policy that seemed outdated or impossible to work. No Canadian politician, except perhaps M. King, ever had such a grasp of the art of the possible. At its best this adjustability was admirable: at its worst it was timidity, and where parliamentary votes were concerned Macdonald could be timid indeed. Many successful politicians are.

Thus Macdonald's political principles were unformulated and inchoate. If you had asked him what they were he would have passed you off with a story about those unfortunate politicians who stuck to their principles and sank with them. Yet, behind his empirical *modus operandi,* Macdonald seems to have followed certain innate, though largely unarticulated, precepts. He could, of course, believe, as many of his contemporaries believed, in the greatest good for the greatest number. That view of Bentham's was consistent either with an aristocratic *or* a socialist view of society. Macdonald seems to have been not far at times from the views of John Austin. Like Austin, he was probably a good Benthamite. Austin, it may be remembered, published in 1859, the year of his death, *A Plea for the Constitution,* a criticism of Lord Grey's easy assumptions of freedom broadening down by parliamentary reform. Austin denied that parliamentary reform had anything to do with improving the lot of the poor. Extension of the franchise might make things much worse for everyone. Austin believed indeed that if the poorer classes were given political power they would use it only to plunder the rich. Macdonald seems to have had some Austinian leanings; he was not, however, so naive as to believe that aristocracy was invariably well-intentioned. He seems to have felt, however, that political reforms did not reform much; they were simply changes, for better or for worse, and one made one's accommodations as best one could.

Thus for Macdonald the word "reform" was largely devoid of positive significance. The nearest we get to Macdonald's own dialectic is his willingness to tidy up issues, or institutions, which have become the object of strong public criticism. Such is the provenance of his University Bill of 1847, or his support of the Clergy Reserves Act of 1854-1855. He would come to such a position slowly, even reluctantly, as if instinctively averse to changing institutions unless pressure for their being changed was overwhelming. Then he would take the matter in hand, usually with a shrewd eye for the practical core of it; and usually his legislative dispositions were made with a certain tenderness toward well-established interests and customs, as if he were making a compromise between the past and the present. He distrusted the reforming temperament; he distrusted that view of society which sees in changes of institutions or of laws the panacea for the problems of human society.

The reason for that assumption was his view of human nature. Human beings do not change, and since they do not, the root character of life cannot change much either. Reform this, or reform that: but human beings will find holes in any system. So Macdonald took men as they were. Unlike Mackenzie, he did not pitch his standards high; he never shared that sublime belief in the perfectibility of man which was the great inheritance of the dissenting churches. This scepticism, if that is the word, about human beings, laid Macdonald open to the charge of playing men from their wickedness; that is, by expecting men to be depraved, he depraved them. This was a Cartwright charge, and unfair, but in the stresses of politics, it was too much always to expect Macdonald to resist using those vulnerabilities of human nature that were the most conducive to political success. To be realistic about men thus led insensibly to exploiting them. "A good carpenter," he wrote T. C. Patteson in 1874, "can work with indifferent tools." So, he went on, stop attacking F. W. Cumberland, the Managing Director of the Northern Railway; "we may want to use him hereafter."

Undoubtedly Macdonald felt, as did many others of his time and since, that political stability depended upon political power being in the hands of those who had the most stake in the country; that property and power belonged naturally together. Intelligence and knowledge were all very well, but they could not always be trusted to act in the best interest of society. They were not stable enough; there was no fly-wheel, even with intelligence: only the commitment to society that property inevitably entailed could give that.

But the moment one says this, one hesitates. Macdonald was too shrewd and changeable to be fastened down quite so neatly. In that uncanny way of his, he could sense a change in the public view about society. Just when one would have expected him to be thoroughly settled, even reactionary, about the rights of property, he has established another new position. We find him writing to Sir John Rose, in 1880, when Macdonald was 65, that the Canadian public seemed "more and more inclined toward the idea that vested rights must yield to the general good." A cynic might say that this only illustrated how little vested rights, or property, Macdonald had. And that he had little property was perfectly true. And of course it is uncertain whether Macdonald himself actually subscribed to that view, that vested rights must yield to the general good. He only said that he felt the public did. One has always to remember with Macdonald that he was perfectly capable of assuming a position for the benefit of the person he was addressing. Writing to Rose, a London financier of considerable means, he speaks of property yielding to the general good: writing to W. R. Meredith, the leader of the Ontario Conservatives, he spoke, just two years later, of the paramount importance of the rights of property. What Macdonald said was not always what he thought. This is elementary; but historians, who deal in documents, tend to put too much weight on the evidence documents provide. Macdonald was perfectly capable of putting on a bit of blarney, in talk or in letters, to influence someone.

Macdonald was quite ready to use whatever means at his disposal to influence that great unknown, public opinion. Perhaps that is the reason he had not much respect for newspapers. He believed, perhaps rightly, that they were engines for the formation, maintenance or alteration of public opinion. He never *under*-estimated their value: he certainly never *over*-estimated their significance. "Mere newspaper articles," he would say, as if half-contemptuous of the means used to hoodwink the gullible public. His scorn for newspaper opinion was especially noticeable if he could carry his party with him. The Riel agitation, more especially since it had originated with the newspapers, would, he believed, blow itself out, the way all popular storms would; so indeed it did, but not before it had further undermined the already shaky foundations of the Conservative party in Quebec. If a statesman should follow public opinion, Macdonald said, he should follow it only in the way a coachman follows his horses, guiding and directing with a firm hand.

But when all that be said, I think one can discern that Macdonald knew that if he were not prepared to change his views, the world would change without him. And he never liked that prospect. He was always rather uncomfortable too far away from the ideas of his time. This indeed raises a problem with any discussion of the political beliefs of Macdonald: his political career began in 1844 and ended in 1891. It is impossible to assume that the views he held in 1844 would survive unchanged through half a century of Canadian politics and social changes. So the title, and this whole paper, does some violence to the way a man and his ideas change, especially a man with such a sensitive seismograph as Macdonald.

In one sense, however, he remained very much the same all his life: he believed profoundly in the laws and observances of society. He had a lawyer's respect for the law, and a great distaste for breaking it; for all his remarkable agility, he was always careful of his legal ground. He once explained the famous "double shuffle" of 1858 on the ground that he did not want to break the law. If he disliked lawlessness, that is not to say he opposed violence. He was a product of his time, and his time knew many forms of violence, private and public, that were ignored by the law or even accepted by society. Macdonald himself had a blaze of blue eyes and a temper to go with it. He was beside himself at Donald Smith in 1878 and roared at him, "I can lick you quicker than hell can scorch a feather." Only the intervention of men of both parties prevented violence. That was the way of the world then: a school of hard knocks for a world of hard knocks. Everyone knew it and everyone accepted it. So did Macdonald, the way he accepted much in the Canadian society of his time. He moved effortlessly through all ranks of society; he had the easy grace of a man well-attuned to the manners and mores of society. And he believed in them. Society had evolved certain conventions and ways of doing things that ought to be observed. He could, when he had a mind to, assume a dignity which it was dangerous to cross. Edgar Dewdney, Indian Commissioner of the Northwest Territories, made so bold as to address Macdonald, the Cabinet Minister directly. Macdonald told Dewdney that on official matters he must address himself to Macdonald through the Deputy Minister. "Forms," Macdonald said firmly in a PS, "are things." Forms were real; they were indispensable in a civilized society. In this sense he was an arrant conservative, and his sense of social conventions amounted at times to timidity at flaunting them.

At times, and in other shapes, this attitude became political timidity. Macdonald was as susceptible in this respect as other Canadian prime ministers, Mackenzie King being the most obvious example. In Macdonald's later years political timidity—that is, political timidity where there was no immediate party advantage involved—became a positive weakness. It was owing in part to the difficulty of recruiting and keeping able new men, which was itself partly due to Macdonald's instinct for tried and true friends; it was also owing in part to the sheer difficulty of governing Canada. As every Canadian prime minister has had to learn, Canada is a hard country to govern. In 1885 the Cabinet was a mess; Macdonald admitted that himself. He got his old friend Alexander Campbell to stay on, but in agreeing to do so, Campbell wrote: "... let me say how much I hope we may get on without this eternal yielding to everyone, who has, or thinks he has, control of a few votes ... The constant giving way to truculent demands and our delays and the irritation and mischief which they produce are in everybody's mouth...." Of course this was easy counsel from a Senator.

It was this kind of philosophy that made Macdonald a good party man. Much of Macdonald's conception of politics turned upon party and what it meant to him. Party was a nexus of power, loyalty and rewards. Independence of mind was all very well, and Macdonald would go a long way to accommodate a talented but refractory follower: but what he could not forgive was disloyalty in the face of the enemy. Once battle lines were drawn in the House he expected his followers to follow, and through thick and thin. It was easy to be loyal when things were going well; that sort of loyalty was agreeable, but it did not count. What mattered was loyalty when the going got rough. He never really forgave Donald Smith for what Macdonald regarded as his apostasy that terrible night on November 4, 1873 when Smith's speech really destroyed whatever hope the Conservative government had left. That was unforgivable. For a Conservative to bring down a Conservative government on a mere issue of principle was wicked. To him it was a kind of treason not to stick to the party. Take the problem of the Lieutenant-Governor of Ontario in 1887. John Beverly Robinson had been Lieutenant-Governor of Ontario since 1879, and was very anxious to stay on, but was already two years and eight months over his five-year term. There was to be an election in 1887, in June, and it was certain that if the Liberals (Macdonald called them Grits) won, they would immediately install one of their friends as Lieutenant-Governor of Ontario. It was too big a plum to lose this way. Macdonald wrote that, much as he would like to leave Robinson in his office, he could not; there was that election, and if the Conservative party were to lose it, "it would have been treason to my party if I had left your important office to the chance of being filled by the Grits."

Equally, he expected his appointees to behave as Conservatives. George Kirkpatrick in 1888 wanted a cabinet post. Macdonald said no: "You are not strong enough in the House, when you were Speaker of the Commons you were afraid of Blake, and decided Parliamentary questions against your Conservative friends." This would not do. It was the same with CPR. No doubt there were Grits employed on the CPR, but the Government did not expect them to have important jobs, or to last long if they did. This was made so completely clear to Stephen and Van Horne that by 1884 Macdonald was able to assert that the CPR had no one working on the line who was not—he used Van Horne's pithy phrase—a fully circumcized Conservative. Thus when in power he could be—and was—quite unscrupulous about using it for party advantage. Of course Macdonald would never willingly do violence to what Canadian political society would accept. But they had learned to accept much. Governor-Generals were apt to be intractable at times—Lord Lorne was not ready to dismiss Lieutenant-Governor Letellier—but even Governor-Generals could be got round. So Macdonald would often have his way. His political power he used to back the CPR to the hilt; he also used it to gerrymander Ontario in the Conservative interest in 1882, a process he seems thoroughly to have enjoyed; he also used his power more roughly in the Franchise Act of 1885.

A Franchise bill had been hovering about Parliament Hill since Confederation. Macdonald had talked of it in 1867. It was read a first time in 1869; it got a second reading and committee in 1870; it was announced twice in 1873; it then dropped out of sight for ten years, appearing again in 1883 when it was read a first time. So too in 1884. In 1885 it was read again. There was very little agitation for the change. It had elicited little comment in the past. Few believed it would be enacted in 1885. But the Riel rebellion made it seem much more important to secure the right kind of electorate for that next election.

The ostensible purpose of the bill was to establish Dominion qualifications for elections to the Dominion Parliament. Up to 1885 the right to vote had been determined by each of the provinces. Those who voted in provincial elections voted in the federal. The idea of a Dominion franchise was on the face of it reasonable; but it looked more reasonable than it was. Canadian society, just 18 years after Confederation, was still highly diverse. A 20 acre farm in P.E.I. might have a radically different valuation than one the same size in Ontario. A property franchise imposed by the Dominion was thus basically inequitable. The Franchise bill might be said to illustrate Macdonald's determination to broaden the franchise. It was nothing of the kind. As the bill was first presented it restricted the franchise. Macdonald did not believe, any more than Austin believed, in broadening the franchise. To Macdonald, as to most Canadians, democracy was a word with pejorative significance. Democracy meant a rabble, with its unblushing insistence on the most blatant elements of political life—the election of judges in the U.S. being just one example.

But in the Franchise bill there was a clear party advantage to be gained, too. The bill was handled with such extraordinary ineptitude that the impression is left that it was deliberately designed to provoke the Opposition. Macdonald introduced it for second reading on April 16, 1885 with a speech occupying exactly one page of Hansard. He seemed utterly to have failed to master the details. Richard Cartwright was indignant:

> The First Minister deliberately precipitated a measure on this House which he knew would meet with the most intense opposition, which he knew involved an almost interminable discussion, and he did that mainly for the reason that

he desired [...] to deprive my hon. friends [...] of the opportunity of calling him and his government to account for that misgovernment which has set this country in a flame.

After the bill passed second reading, it was at once bogged down in Committee of the Whole where it remained for six mortal weeks, to the exclusion of nearly everything else, punctuated only now and then with telegrams from the North-West that Caron or Macdonald would obligingly read to the House. Eventually even Macdonald was fed up. The day before the bill finally passed third reading—that was only on June 10th—he found J.D. Edgar, Liberal MP for West Ontario waiting outside the House while prayers finished, and told Edgar of a painter who once had painted a picture of a barnyard, and took months to paint in the straw; and when the painting was finished, there could be seen painted in one corner, "No more damned barnyard paintings for me." Macdonald then added to Edgar, "No more damned Franchise bills for me."

Even more remarkable was Macdonald's attitude to patronage. Here he was consistent. In 1849 Robert Baldwin had asked his advice about an appointment in Hastings County; Macdonald replied that he could not conscientiously give such advice since he did not support the Lafontaine-Baldwin government. In 1878, in opposition again, he asserted that if a man had no confidence in a government he could not expect to receive any benefits from it. He said the same thing in 1890: "A member of Parliament in opposition, having no confidence in the Government is [in respect of recommendations for patronage] in the position of any other Canadian." Mackenzie Bowell was rather more explicit:

Everything in the whole system of Government, in connection with patronage, is carried on upon this principle: You consult your friends when anything is to be done in a constituency, and it is the merest hypocrisy to preach or lay down any other doctrine as being practiced by any political party in this country.

Macdonald would not have said that, but he would have agreed with it. Thus Macdonald was always quite ready to make the most of party advantage; and far from weakening him with his own followers, this made him the more admired and liked. In some things it is a tragedy for Canadian politics that Macdonald was often admired by his followers for the wrong reasons.

He would support his own followers as they supported him. When one of his own backbenchers addressed the House, even if the speech were bad, the struggling speaker was sure of Macdonald's attention. Not for Macdonald that happy oblivion of Blake's, sleeping at his desk, his head across his folded arms. Macdonald would listen, even turn in his seat and interject "Hear, hear!" to some awful platitude when the rest of the House was waiting impatiently for the speech to end. In 1879, Arthur McQuade, MP South Victoria, was on the floor late at night discussing some exhausted aspect of the National Policy. McQuade was neither a frequent speaker nor a good one, and after his speech, when the

House broke up for the night, McQuade happened to go out just in front of Macdonald. Macdonald put his arm around McQuade's shoulders and said, not too quietly, "McQuade, you spoke like an angel. I am proud of you."

Macdonald was also friendly with opponents. G. W. Ross, Liberal from West Middlesex, tells how in 1883 he got into a hot argument with D. B. Woodworth (MP Kings, N.S.) during Estimates. About midnight Ross went down to the restaurant for tea (he was a prohibitionist) and Sir John came in, sat down with Ross and ordered whisky and sherry. After some agreeable talk, Macdonald got up and said to some Conservatives nearby, "Come, boys, hurry up. Doug Woodworth and Ross have been into a devil of a row for the last hour, and I am going to take a hand in the sport." A few minutes later Ross was sitting in the House while Macdonald sternly castigated him for his remarks against Woodworth but half an hour before. Macdonald could utterly disarm opponents outside the House, and a Liberal at loose ends might find, if he were not careful, that he was tied to the old man's train.

It is a comment on Macdonald's political principles that he did not really believe that men were moved by political principles at all. Greed, love, friendship, he understood. He seems to have distrusted people like Blake, who could apparently allow political principles to stand in the way of political advantage. Blake's hedging on the tariff, most dramatically in the Malvern speech of 1886, was the result of Blake's having carefully thought through what he believed was the real position of Canada: but to Macdonald it was inexplicable. It was just handing the Conservatives a gift on a platter. Blake's policies were, in Macdonald's view, bad for Blake's own party. This illustrated to Macdonald not Blake's principles but his ineptitude.

This seems to suggest that in the parliamentary system of government where executive and legislature are mutually dependent, the practice of government can become nearly an end in itself. In other words, that the Cabinet system puts a premium upon techniques rather than upon ideas. Who in the parliamentary system can afford the luxury of abstract principles devoid of practical content? The answer is: the Opposition, of course. Opposition tended to make Macdonald, as most parliamentarians, much more willing to accept substantial changes in ideas and policies. Macdonald, though never very long in opposition (1848-54, 1862-4, 1873-8) took up at least one of his policies while in opposition, the protective tariff, in 1876. Macdonald had never had strong views about free trade one way or the other. In this, as in so many other issues, he was quite eclectic, leaving the impression that when the right time came he would make up his mind and not before. It was extraordinarily difficult, on many major issues of his day, to fasten him down. "John A. is *such* a dodger," wrote one exasperated observer. Macdonald picked up the protective tariff when, rather to his surprise, he found considerable opposition developing to the draft reciprocity treaty that George Brown brought back from Washington in 1874. And when the Liberals failed to raise the tariff in 1876—even for much needed revenue—Macdonald had a clear and, as it turned out, powerful issue. He made still more of it by calling it—this was a masterpiece (and not his invention either)—the National Policy.

Moreover, Confederation, it will be recalled, he accepted completely only after having been defeated in the House in 1864 and was thus faced with the disagreeable prospect of opposition. Macdonald's view of Confederation is so well known it hardly needs repeating here. He was firmly convinced that the centrifugal weight inherent in the conjuncture of the four disparate provinces of 1867 required as offset a large measure of centralization. He was quite willing that Confederation be called "federal" ; he really did not care what it was called. And "federal" was a word that had political conveniences in Canada East. But in his view if Canada was to be put together in any effective way a strong and heavy governor had to be placed in the centre against the mass that regional, centrifugal interests of the provinces carried.

This centralization was achieved, as everyone knows, by a variety of devices, but especially by the fullest and most sweeping grant of power known to British constitutional usage: the power to legislate for the peace, order and good government of Canada. Once that was secured all Macdonald needed then was room for manoeuvre. Hence, the less written down the better. Macdonald disliked written axioms. "Peace, order and good government" was thus a generous, general, umbrella-like grant of power that suited him perfectly. Given that, he could say, as he did say at the Quebec Conference in 1864, that the British North American constitution should be "a mere skeleton and framework that would not bind us down. We have now all the elasticity which has kept England together." Skeleton, framework, elasticity: these are Macdonald's ideas about the BNA Act. How Macdonald proposed to use this elasticity is well illustrated in his memorandum on disallowance of June, 1868, where he made it abundantly clear that the Dominion government was going to use it more often in the future than the Colonial office had used it in the past.

Behind Macdonald's distrust of written constitutions lay his conviction that no written instrument can avoid the effects of change, and the more that is written down the more difficult these effects will be. The Manitoba school question, arising in 1890, was difficult intrinsically, but it was difficult politically not only because of what it was, but because of the constitutional safeguards that had been thrown around education, at the insistence of Galt and others, in the BNA Act, and later in the Manitoba Act. (And the fact, incidentally, that there was an important conflict between the former and the latter.)

A question arises why, given Macdonald's recognition of the necessity of change, did he omit, or allow to be omitted, any machinery for amending the BNA Act? It is difficult to believe that it was oversight. The alternative, that it was deliberate, makes more sense. Any problem that required a real constitutional amendment could indeed be solved by a recommendation to the British Parliament by the Canadian government of the day. But a more effective changing of the constitution could be managed—provided it did not stretch the letter too far—through the unobtrusive means of constitutional practice. Given some degree of party unity, the Conservative party could, with its control of the Quebec legislature, and for a time the Ontario, and later the B.C. and Manitoba legislatures, make constitutional prescriptions within the elastic structures of the BNA Act. That this design was frustrated is well known, and the means by which it was done forms one of the interesting chapters in Canadian political history after 1867, associated with the Privy Council rather than with the Supreme Court. Macdonald supported the creation of the Supreme Court of Canada in 1875; but he opposed the attempt, unsuccessful as that attempt was in the 1870's, to abolish appeals to the Privy Council, that golden chain, as he described it, of Imperial power that he did not want to break. Yet too much weight should not be put on this metaphor. Macdonald even here could shift. The inconvenience of appeals to the Privy Council in criminal cases was shown by Riel's appeal in 1885. In 1887, quietly, with a minimum of fuss (as an amendment to the Criminal Procedure Act) abolition of appeals to the Privy Council in criminal cases was put through Parliament.

It is easy to label Macdonald as an imperialist; easy and wrong. He was not, not in any of the usual connotations of the word. Everyone remembers, of course, "A British subject I was born and a British subject I will die." But this expression has to be read in its context, which was the election of 1891, one of those traumatic Canadian elections, like 1911, and perhaps 1958, where Canadians were asked to vote on whether they wanted to be Americans or remain Canadians. Besides, British subject meant at that time a subject of the Queen, which all Canadians were. In 1891 Macdonald was asserting his Canadian allegiance; whether subsumed within that was any particular loyalty to Great Britain as such is quite another matter.

In a broad sense it can be said that he was loyal to the Imperial idea because he could not conceive of any form, any practical form, of Canadian independence without imperialism. Canada without some form of British commitment behind her would simply become American, since Americans had never really given up the hope of acquiring Canada, and were not to do so for many a year yet. (Perhaps they haven't even now; but it can at least be said it has taken much quieter forms. Buying us out is a very unobtrusive process.) So Macdonald was bound realistically to support the Imperial idea. But having said that, we must at once put severe limitations on how far Macdonald would take that idea. It was not far. He was never, for example, an Imperial federationist. He was indeed contemptuous of Imperial federation, as he was of all empty theorizing. Nor was he ever a believer in Britain, right or wrong. He had no interest in helping bail out Gladstone and Company from their mess in the Sudan in 1885. He refused categorically to have anything to do with it. Nor was he prepared to accept the Imperial prescription for Canada at Washington in 1870 and fought a long and skillful rear-guard action to preserve as much of Canadian rights as he could.

No, Macdonald was not an imperialist; he was a Canadian; doubtless a central Canadian, and doubtless with some Ontario biases though they were not the obvious ones; his attitude to Great Britain was a compound of respect for her political system, her system of laws, and his delight in her history and literature; but he had been too long in Canada—since 1820—to have any real loyalties to Great Britain as a political unit. His loyalty was to British political traditions and all they meant.

He was indeed a good House of Commons man. In the House he had a careless nonchalance of manner, would lean his head on the desk behind him and pull his knees up against the edge of his own; or he would twist his limber legs under his seat; or he would turn to listen to the speakers of his party behind, or exchange glances and witticisms with the men around him. On his feet he was not a great debater, not at least in the conventional sense of that word; he had little oratorical skill: his technique was more subtle. As Rodolphe Lemieux recalled him, "... nul ne pouvait commander l'attention de la chambre d'une manière plus absolue, plus magnétique. Nature prime-sautière, esprit vif, sa verve et son humour captivaient l'auditoire."[a] He would parry attacks with some wry caricature of what his opponents had meant, some happy exaggeration of their position, then cap it with a story drawn from his years with sherry and books, from Dickens, Sheridan, Disraeli, or from his lore of British or Canadian Parliamentary history. "There he would stand," writes Sir John Willison, "with his back to the Speaker, while the Opposition chafed at the cool but skillful exaggeration ... and the Conservatives cheered with delight, and wagged their heads and shrugged their shoulders in sympathy with the old man's bantering humour." Macdonald was also good at clearing away underbrush; he would step into a debate bogged down in details and acrimony, set a problem in perspective, warm it with a bit of laughter and common sense, and not infrequently restore the House to good humour and purpose.

Macdonald had a marvellous memory for names and faces, a knack only Lord Dufferin could match. The stories are still legion; and whatever may be said about them, they were the stuff that made and kept Macdonald's great following loyal to the end. Macdonald cultivated his talent: he used it; he never forgot that popularity was power; but his liking for human beings was genuine. He was not naive or unrealistic; "there is no gratitude to be expected from the public," he wrote Stephen in 1888, "I have found that out years ago."

Macdonald was in fact a shrewd judge of people. After Joseph Pope became Macdonald's private secretary, in 1882, Pope remarked of J. J. C. Abbott that he had an agreeable nature and a sweet smile. "Yes, a sweet smile," said Macdonald, "but it is all from the teeth outwards." When John S. D. Thompson of Nova Scotia was being solicited through Charles Hibbert Tupper for the post

---

[a] ...no one else could catch the attention of the House so completely and magnetically. His lively nature, quick spirit, energy and humour entranced his audience.

of Minister of Justice, a letter arrived from Thompson that seemed to young Tupper a definitive no. Macdonald looked at the letter, looked at young Tupper, and quietly said, " 'whispering she would ne'er consent, consented'. He is our man when we want him." He was.

Macdonald was not to be pushed too far too often. Votes were one thing, and he was apt to be excessively flexible in yielding to votes; but importunities within the Cabinet he was apt to be impatient with. Macdonald could be very sharp defending his deputy-minister against a tough-minded MP or a member of the Cabinet on the prowl for patronage. Few were more importunate in this respect than the Tuppers, both father and son. In 1878 old Charles Tupper insisted that the Winnipeg law firm of Stewart Tupper and Hugh John Macdonald be given the government business to handle there. Macdonald disliked the idea; Tupper insisted; the upshot was that though Macdonald and Tupper sat side by side, in Parliament, and political platforms, they exchanged not a word nor wrote each other a line other than on business for two years, between the end of 1878 and 1881. As for young Tupper, a chip off the old block: "Dear Charlie," Macdonald scribbled cheerfully on one of Charles Hibbert Tupper's impertinent letters, "skin your own skunks. Yours always JAMD."

However, Macdonald did not, as a rule, nurse his resentments. "A public man," he told Chapleau in 1885, "can have no resentments." When something unfortunate, but irreparable, had happened, he would say, "What's done is done. There's no use crying over spilt milk." Forget, and keep going. This was easier because misadventures did not surprise him. He was not easily surprised at anything. The world did not run smoothly: it hadn't and it wouldn't. His advice to T. C. Patteson was, "Take things pleasantly and when fortune empties her chamber pot on your head—smile and say, 'We are going to have a summer shower.' "

This resilience in Macdonald was a product of that profoundly empirical sense of relevance that informed his whole political thinking. The expression "political ideas" connotes abstraction, or at least a systematic body of political principles. Macdonald never delighted in abstractions or in systems. They never touched his nature. One cannot really say that Macdonald did not have a speculative mind; he was too intelligent thus to be labelled. His mind simply rejected, though perhaps only temporarily, ideas that seemed to him incapable of practical application. If a belief or an idea became politically powerful he would tend to reach for it, and if possible appropriate it, as he did with Confederation. Indeed Macdonald's own comment on his own inveterate practicality comes in the Confederation Debates, in a reply to Luther Holton, MPP for Chateauguay:

> Well, Sir, I am satisfied to confine myself to practical things—to the securing of such practical measures as the country really wants. I am satisfied not to have a reputation for indulging in imaginary schemes and harboring visionary ideas that may end sometimes in an annexation movement, sometimes in Federation,

and sometimes in a legislature union, but always utopian and never practical. I am satisfied to leave the imaginary, the poetic and the impossible to the hon. member for Chateauguay.

The stability of complicated natures, Talleyrand once wrote, comes from their infinite flexibility. There was always this catlike resilience in Macdonald. Although after the great *débâcle* of 1873, gloomy about his party's future, and doubtless about his own political career, he went home to Earnscliffe that brisk cold afternoon of Wednesday, November 5, 1873, and said to Agnes, his wife, "Well, that's done. It's a relief to be out of it." And so saying, put on his dressing gown, gathered his decanter of sherry, two or three books, and went to bed to read. That was that.[b]

POLITICAL PATRONAGE UNDER MACDONALD AND LAURIER

Gordon Stewart

It is standard knowledge that patronage was endemic to Canadian politics in the 1867-1911 period. Source-books for undergraduate students contain sections on patronage and the major historians who have written about these years refer to the ubiquitous nature of patronage, describing it as the natural currency of public life.[1] Professor W. L. Morton has pointed out that the cabinet minister of the time, "a beneficiary of patronage himself ... was well disposed towards being a dispenser of patronage. Indeed it was the power to distribute patronage that in the main gave his office meaning and substance."[2] In his authoritative account of this period Professor Peter B. Waite remarks of Mackenzie Bowell, minister of customs throughout the entire span of Macdonald's administrations from 1878 to 1891, that his "principal pre-occupation was patronage."[3] As well as these reminders from respected modern scholars, the official records of the period offer testimony to the pervasiveness of patronage. Commissions to investigate the civil service were established in 1880-81, 1891-92, 1907-08, and 1911-12 and all drew attention to the "patronage evil."[4] In 1909 the Department of Marine and Fisheries had the doubtful honor of being the object of a separate investigation and it failed to disappoint its critics, revealing widespread practices not only of patronage but also of cor-

---

From *The American Review of Canadian Studies,* X, no. 1 (Spring 1980), 3-26. Reprinted by permission of the Association for Canadian Studies in the United States.

[b] The main sources for this paper are the Macdonald Papers, Pope Papers, and Thompson Papers in the Public Archives of Canada; the Alexander Campbell and T. C. Patteson Papers in the Public Archives of Ontario; and the House of Commons *Debates,* 1875-1891.

ruption.[5] Newspapers, periodicals and parliamentary debates are full of dramatic stories, charges and counter-charges concerning patronage. Major political scandals of the time, involving national figures such as Charles Rykert and Hector-Louis Langevin, revolved round issues of patronage.[6] Because of this kind of evidence it is now common knowledge that patronage was of central importance to Canadian political life. Yet there has been no study made of the workings and significance of patronage. Professor Hodgetts has noted this odd gap in Canadian historical studies. "It is somewhat curious," he writes, "that the practice of patronage has never been the subject of sustained analysis on the part of Canadian social scientists and historians." [7] This article is an attempt at such an analysis.

I

A useful and informative starting point for examining the mechanics of the patronage system is to look at John A. Macdonald's own constituency of Kingston. The picture that emerges from the Kingston patronage evidence shows that patronage was distributed by the party on a bureaucratic-like basis. Appointments and contracts were not distributed hurriedly but invariably followed discussion between local party leaders in Kingston and the Member of Parliament (in this case Macdonald) in Ottawa. Those party activists seeking posts in the public service or public contracts made application, usually in writing, to the executive committee of the local Conservative Association. The committee considered all the applications, weighed the contributions of each applicant to the party's electoral campaigns and then passed on a recommendation to Macdonald who in turn would pass on the name to the appropriate cabinet minister for formal action. In no case in the correspondence was consideration given to the applicants' qualifications—the sole criterion was service to the party.[8]

Within the executive committee there was formal discussion over each piece of patronage. The local party, through its executive committee, functioned almost as an employment agency for party workers. In 1889, for example, Edward Smythe, a barrister and president of the Liberal-Conservative Association, discussed with Macdonald various jobs in the Kingston Post Office. Smythe informed Macdonald that the committee had now filled all but one of the current vacancies. "That will leave," he noted, "a vacancy among the letter carriers that we will subsequently fill up." [9] Two months earlier Macdonald had written to the executive committee to inform the local party leaders of changes in the Kingston post office that would open up new jobs. These developments, Smythe replied, "received the hearty recommendation of our Executive Committee." [10] When the committee discussed the distribution of such posts, the merits of the candidates were discussed exclusively in terms of their work in the local party organization. Writing in January 1891 in connection with the application of William A. Newlands for a clerkship in the post office, J. A. Metcalfe explained that "his [Newland's] father and brother are active workers in the Conservative interest and William A. is a good Conservative." Metcalfe added that Newlands had followed the proper procedure, having "applied through the Executive Committee." [11] Once Macdonald received the recommendation from the committee, he passed it on to the cabinet minister in charge of the appropriate department. In response to one such recommendation to the Customs Department, the minister, Mackenzie Bowell, sent a note to Macdonald explaining he had signed the necessary papers implementing the requested appointments. Mackenzie Bowell pointed out that neither of the two individuals recommended had "passed the 'qualifying' examinations" and therefore could not be employed as landing-waiters or clerks. But they still received posts in the customs service.[12] Local party considerations took precedence over questions of qualifications.

Because party considerations were paramount it was essential for any applicant to show a solid record of work in local electoral campaigns. An example of these values occurred over the position of second engineer at the federal dry dock facility in Kingston. Thomas McGuire, a local party notable, had been told "the Conservative Association have recommended" Joseph Levitt for the post. McGuire wrote in support of Levitt and warned Macdonald about two other aspirants for the job who should be rejected because they had made contract with the Liberal "enemy." Those other two, wrote McGuire, "are Heretics while Levitt is one of the Faithful as that term is understood by the archbishop." [13] In another case the importance of long, faithful and uncontaminated party service was emphasized. In this instance the record of the family as a whole was considered. A "claim of patronage has been brought before the Executive Committee," wrote J. H. Metcalfe to Macdonald. "I do not admire the tone of the letter yet as the old man and his sons have never gone grit I feel kindly disposed toward them." [14] During the winter of 1890-91 similar considerations dominated discussion of a vacancy for a staff officer in the militia. In December 1890 S. M. Conger, president of the Prince Edward County Liberal-Conservative Association, pressed the claims of his candidate, Colonel Graveley. Conger wrote of Graveley that he was not only "a most efficient military officer ... he is more ... he is a staunch Conservative and has made many sacrifices for the party." [15] Another endorsement of Graveley came from R. R. Pringle of Cobourg who reminded Macdonald that "as far as this riding is concerned he [Graveley] has always worked well and he certainly sacrificed himself when he ran for the local [elections] when nothing but defeat stared him in the face." [16] Writing from Port Hope another correspondent addressed himself to the essential point—Graveley deserved the appointment because of "his service to the party." [17]

The fact that service to the party was the most important element in appointments did not make Macdonald's or the committee's task any easier for in many cases there were several suitable party workers seeking a post. In such cases it was difficult to make a recommendation without causing dissent and factionalism in the local organization. In other cases local party notables might either try to dominate the executive committee or try to by-pass the committee and deal directly with Macdonald on patronage issues. All these factors appeared over the appointments of a landing-waiter in the customs service at Kingston, a case that well illustrates some of the local complexities involved in distribution of patronage. In this instance John Gaskill of the Montreal Transport Company and a prominent local Conservative had ignored the work of the executive committee and had pressed his own candidate on Macdonald. On January 8, 1891 Macdonald was warned by George Fitzpatrick of the consequent trouble—"Gaskill is raising a row and I hear that the Executive Committee had a real lively time yesterday. The Kilkenny Election was nothing to it."[18] Fitzpatrick sent a telegram to Macdonald asking that the appointment be held up until a local solution to the conflict was found. The situation was more tangled because Gaskill's candidate had been "insulting" to the executive committee. The committee's viewpoint was put by John McIntyre who explained to the Prime Minister that "we are all anxious to do what we can for the party ... but I know the majority of the Committee will feel greatly humiliated if Gaskill is allowed to reverse every recommendation that is made."[19]

The Kingston patronage letters also reveal that Macdonald and local party leaders did not deal simply with appointments but also were actively involved in promotions within the public service and even in the creation of new posts to satisfy the patronage demands within the party. In September 1889, for example, John Haggart, Postmaster General in Ottawa, replied to the Prime Minister concerning the promotion of a clerk within the postal service. Macdonald himself had requested the promotion after hearing from the executive committee and Haggart was willing to comply except there was no vacancy to which the clerk could be promoted. Haggart, however, went on to suggest a solution. He could do what Macdonald requested by "providing in the Estimates for the coming year a first-class clerkship in the Inspectors office at Kingston."[20] There was no discussion about the necessity of a clerkship; it was simply to be created in the interests of the local party.

From this Kingston evidence we begin to get an idea of the workings of patronage, particularly the relationship between Ottawa and the localities. The Member of Parliament, in this case Macdonald, made the formal and final decision about appointments from the Kingston area as he passed on names to other cabinet ministers. Usually the MP received the nomination from the local executive committee. It was assumed that the local party organization, by its executive committee, was the normal channel through which patronage business flowed. When acting on patronage matters the committee did so in a formal way, receiving and reviewing applications, weighing credentials, passing resolutions and forwarding the recommendation to the MP at Ottawa. One final point to emerge is that the structure of the patronage system, as revealed in the Kingston evidence, excluded outsiders from sharing in contracts and appointments. The patronage was given only to local figures who could prove their loyalty to the local party organization.

II

The Kingston evidence while informative may not be typical because of Macdonald's position as Prime Minister. This may have led him to leave much of the daily patronage business in the hands of the local leaders. It is therefore essential to examine other evidence to assess whether this pattern was representative.

One report during the period revealed a good deal about the day-to-day workings of the patronage system. This was the investigation in 1909 by Judge Cassels into the Department of Marine and Fisheries. A basic point made in the report was that since 1867 the department had been used by both the Conservatives and Liberals, when they were in power, for partisan purposes. Positions and contracts were given to reward party activists. Regular "patronage lists" drawn up by the MP and local party leaders were kept on file so business could be directed to party faithful. "The system," noted the report,

> seems to have been handed down from one administration to another since Confederation.... It is apparently based on the old maxim of 'to the victor belong the spoils' utterly ignoring the fact that the money to be disbursed is mainly contributed by the people generally and not the money of the political followers of the party at the time being in power.[21]

During the course of the investigation the activities of the department's office in Halifax provided detailed evidence on how the system worked. In the case of Halifax the MPs were active in the regular distribution of jobs and contracts. The report explained that

> patronage in Halifax extended beyond the mere naming of the merchants and others who should comprise the patronage list. It extended to the nomination by the Members of Parliament representing the constituency of individuals or an individual to whom orders were to be given.[22]

The questioning of witnesses showed the way things were managed. When work needed to be done or supplies furnished "then the members would recommend ... that the orders should be given to A, B, C, or D as the case may be." Mr. Jonathan Parsons, the Department's chief agent in Halifax, explained that this was done "under the rules of patronage." He further explained that these rules applied "from year to year and from month to month every year." On every occasion a contract was to be placed the MPs "would designate ... which merchant or manufacturer or dealer particular orders should be given to." The questioning concluded:

Q: That has been the cause?

A: Yes

Q: Each time?

A: Yes

Q: So it is not your independent judgment that was exercised from time to time as to where the work should be done or by whom material should be furnished; that was done upon the recommendations?

A: By the member of parliament having the patronage.[23]

The evidence also showed that aside from this regular management of patronage the MPs authorized "taking on an employee" because they "had the patronage." [24]

The 1909 Report on the Department of Marine and Fisheries confirmed the assessment made the previous year by a civil service inquiry that the organization of the department, comprehensively influenced by patronage, had "few redeeming features." The Commission of 1908 had made a broad investigation of the public service outside the home departments in Ottawa and had concluded that these outside agencies were entirely at the disposal of the party in power. "As a rule," the commissioners explained,

> in the outside service ... politics enter into every appointment and politicians on the spot interest themselves not only in the appointments but in the subsequent promotion of the officers ... in the outside service the politics of the party is of greater importance in making appointments and promotions than the public interests of the Dominion.[25]

In each locality the MP and the party leaders regarded appointments and contracts as their exclusive right to be used to reward local party workers. "In practically no case," the commissioners discovered, "is it possible to fill a vacancy in one locality by a transfer from another." [26] In the Inland Revenue Department, for example, "political appointments as in other branches of the public service, prevail and as a rule the officers in one district are confined to that one district." In Montreal all the appointments in the customs service were made "at the insistance of the members of parliament for the district." Indeed throughout the entire customs service the commissioners concluded that each riding was "looked upon as local patronage" and that posts were awarded to local people only.[27] In his evidence Dr. Barrett, inspector of Inland Revenue at Winnipeg, explained the active role MPs took in preserving local patronage exclusively for local party use. Barrett described how when a post became available "the member for the constituency says, 'No, I will not allow any one outside my constituency to go in there.' " In Winnipeg as in Kingston, the names for appointments were "generally given by the Liberal Association of Winnipeg." Barrett emphasized that "when the Conservatives were in power they did the same thing." [28] In their general observations on this kind of evidence, the commissioners concluded that "each locality was separately guarded."[29] Even the national party leader could not interfere with this local exclusivity. Writing to a party worker who had asked for a position outside his own constituency, Wildred Laurier pointed out how hard this would be to arrange. "I need not tell you," wrote the Prime Minister, "that it is always difficult to bring an outsider into a locality." [30]

It is important to note that this type of patronage distribution exclusively to party activists was not confined to minor posts in the customs or postal services and other such branches of the federal bureaucracy but operated at all levels. This can be demonstrated by looking at Macdonald's policies in making appointments to the bench and the bar. County judgeships and the earning of the title of Queens Counsel (QC) were sought-after plums in the legal profession and were at the disposal of the party in power. As with the customs service workers and post office employees the positions in the judiciary were given by the party in power primarily on the basis of the candidate's service to the party. An example of the essential relationship between party service and advancement in the legal profession is contained in correspondence from 1887 between John Small and John A. Macdonald. Small wrote a confidential memorandum to the Prime Minister with a list of barristers eligible for a QC and set out against each name the reasons for his recommendation:

> Michael Murphy: defeated candidate 1882 ... attended meetings in recent elections ... Roman Catholic;
>
> Daniel Defoe: strong supporter, always took a prominent part in political movements;
>
> James Reeve: did good work in the last election;
>
> James Fullerton: takes the platform in the interests of the party;
>
> George Blackstock: has contested elections;
>
> Emerson Coalsworth: rising young barrister, pillar of the Methodist Church, a strong Temperance advocate, President of the Liberal Conservative Association for his ward, was my agent in the last election.[31]

These candidates for QC had varied characteristics—some Roman Catholic, others Methodist, some with long legal experience, others just beginning to become noted in the profession—yet each shared one necessary qualification without which any other would be useless. In one way or another all had worked for their local Conservative parties either by running as candidates, being speakers or canvassers, or drawing up and scrutinizing the voters lists. It was this kind of information on good hard party work that Macdonald looked for when creating a new batch of QC's. And these criteria were well understood throughout the party. In October 1889 Robert Birmingham, the Secretary-Treasurer of the Liberal Conservative Union of Ontario, sent Macdonald "the names of a few legal friends who rendered us special service in the recent campaign in the hope that you might be able to repay them with the much sought after QC." [32]

The next step up beyond QC were county judgeships and these too were distributed with the party's interest in mind. The context in which the awarding of judgeship was discussed can be seen from a case involving the Prime Minister, Frank Smith, the Senator who was the most important Ontario Catholic in the party, and B. L. Doyle, a party worker seeking a promotion to the bench. Doyle set forth his qualifications which rested on the premise that his "services to the Party for the last 15 years entitled me to something." He then proceeded to recount the details of this party work, emphasizing that he had "stood by the party in the darkest hours of its severest trials [and] fought for it when it was down and persevered in the desperate struggle on behalf of our principles till the victory again crowned our efforts." Doyle then went on to describe the election campaigns, particularly the one of 1878, in which he had done a great deal to get out the Catholic vote. He concluded his letter with the blunt request—"I want a County Judgeship." [33] This request was endorsed by Senator Frank Smith, who confirmed that Doyle had indeed done all the party work he claimed to have done over the years. Smith wrote of Doyle that he was "a plucky, active man whom I know to have worked hard for his party." Therefore, concluded the Senator, "he deserves to get what he asks." [34] Macdonald was unable to satisfy Doyle immediately because of some rival candidates but he did promise to do what he could and in January 1880 Doyle was appointed junior judge of Huron county. [35]

Other evidence from the Macdonald papers confirms this pattern of judicial appointments being related to partisan activity. In November 1883 Robert Smith QC was recommended for a vacant judgeship in Huron. He was considered deserving of such honor because he was "ever willing to go where duty to his party called him." In April 1885 H. C. Gwyn applied to the Prime Minister for a vacant judgeship on the grounds that he had been:

> actively identified with the party ... and up to a year ago and for seven or eight years previously [was] the Secretary of the Liberal-Conservative Association of North Wentworth ...[36]

In May 1884 a Conservative MP recommended J. M. Hamilton of Sault Saint Marie for a judgeship, explaining that Hamilton was "very much esteemed throughout Algoma and it is of some political importance that he should be appointed." [37] About a year later another conservative MP, N. C. Wallace, in recommending Edward Morgan, a barrister for a junior county judgeship in York, explained that Morgan had "fought, bled and almost died for the Party and has very much stronger claims than anyone else that has been proposed for the position." [38] In the summer of 1887 A. M. Boswell, a party leader in Toronto, after reporting to Macdonald about party fund raising turned to judicial patronage and recommended N. C. Stewart for a junior judgeship in that city. Stewart, explained Boswell, was "an out and out Conservative and as steady as a rock. At one time he was not a cold water man but now he is all right." [39]

This evidence concerning the legal profession confirms that at all levels of public employment, from judgeships down to landing-waiters in the customs service, the party in power distributed patronage only to those who had worked for the party. It was not enough simply to be a contributer to party funds or an occasional canvasser but necessary to prove a long period of active, dedicated work in the ridings. The immutability of this standard was well illustrated by a case from London, Ontario that developed in that spring of 1900. It concerned the family of John A. Donegan who had volunteered to fight in the Canadian contingent in the Boer War. Donegan had been killed in South Africa, leaving a widow and two sons in London. There were some efforts to find jobs for the two boys to help support the family and James Sutherland, a Liberal MP, had written to local party leaders in London asking their views of the proposal to find posts for the Donegan boys. It might be expected that in this part of Ontario the sons of war-dead in South Africa would receive sympathetic treatment but the local party balked and refused to consider them for any posts. In response to Sutherland's inquiries, George Reid, a local party leader, explained that

> as for making a position for either of the Donegans in this locality, it would be very unpopular, they have never been Friends of ours in any particular and [it] would never do to appoint any one who has not been identified with the work of the party.... To appoint him for any position purely [and] simply because his father was killed in Africa would be to my mind very absurd.[40]

Reid also pointed out that the man who was doing most to find jobs for the Donegans was not a party supporter. If he had been, that might have been a reason to give the Donegans something to reward a party worker but, warned Reid, there was no point in helping the Donegans' backer for "he is a strong supporter of the enemy and of no use to us whatsoever." [41]

A comprehensive example of the normalcy of these expectations is contained in some private correspondence between Laurier and Roy Choquette concerning the Liberal party in the district of Quebec. Following the Liberal victory in 1896 Laurier had asked Choquette to report on the patronage requirements of the local party in the Quebec area. Choquette was to sound out party notables and send Laurier "une liste des nominations ... sur lesquels nos amis insistent le plus pour le moment."[c] On September 12 Choquette sent Laurier a detailed list of demands by Quebec Liberals:

> Voici ce qui en est: L'Hon. M. Joly [controller of Inland Revenue] devrait immédiatement remplacer le Dr. Fiset de St. Sauveur par le Dr. Coté, et ce, pour faire plaisir à nos jeunes amis de Québec M. l'Orateur, devrait remercier de ses services M. Fournier, pour satisfaire M. Talbot, et en même temps le Ministre des Chemins de fer devrait faire l'échange des stations du l'Intercolonial entre

---

[c] a list of nominations...that our friends insist upon most at present

Castonguay de St. Charles et M. Roy de St. Moise. M. l'Orateur devrait encore destituer un nommé Gagnon, messager sessional pour donner satisfaction à M. LaForest, notre candidat contre Costigan. M. Paterson [minister of customs] ou Joly devrait remplacer Philéas Dubé, de Fraserville, officier du Douane, part M. Amédé Gagan de St. Arseire, comte de Temiscouta....[d] [42]

Choquette then continued, in the same matter-of-fact manner, to list further patronage requirements of other important local Liberals, each of whom, typically enough, had specific rewards in mind for himself and his fellow-workers:

Pour faire plaisir à l'ami Lemieux, un nommé Baudin, gardien de phare de la Grande Rivière, et qui a voulu le battre à son arrivée à cet endroit, devrait être remercié de ses services et remplacé par M. William Bisson.

L'ami Fisset attend avec impatience ce qui lui est promis depuis longtemps, la nomination du Dr. Ross de Ste. Flavie, à la place du Dr. Gauvreau, partisan bleu enragé, comme médecin du port à la Pointe au Père; et la nomination du Dr. Boullion, de Matane, à la place du Dr. Pelletier comme médecin du port à cet endroit.

L'ami Angers aimerait avoir la reinstallation immédiate de M. Joseph Gaudreau, comme maître de poste à Grands Fonds, Malbaie.[e] [43]

Choquette ended this list of patronage requirements by briskly noting his own demands, "Quant à moi," he wrote, "si l'ami Fisher [minister of Agriculture] pouvait me nommer Desiré Vezina à la place de Zephiron Danceuse comme homme de police à la Grosse Ile, et l'ami Mulock [postmaster-general] me nommer M. Georges Gagné, maître de poste à Ste. Pierre, à la place de madame C. Dienne, j'en serais bien content." [f] [44]

The working of the patronage system as revealed by these examples continued right down to the eve of World War I. The Royal Commission that

---

[d] Here is what they are: the Honourable Mr. Joly (controller at Inland Revenue) should immediately replace Dr. Fiset of St. Saveur with Dr. Coté in order to please our young friends in Quebec City. Mr. Speaker should thank Mr. Fournier for his services and thus satisfy Mr. Talbot, and at the same time, the Minister of Railways should switch Castonguay from St. Charles and Mr. Roy from St. Moïse in their positions on the Intercolonial. In order to please Mr. LaForest, our candidate running against Costigan, Mr. Speaker should also let go a certain Gagnon who was a messenger during the session. Mr. Paterson (Minister of Customs) or Joly should replace Philéas Dubé from Fraserville as the customs officer with Mr. Amédé Gagan from St. Arseire in the riding of Temiscouta..."

[e] To please our friend Lemieux, a certain Baudin, who is lighthouse keeper on the Grand River and who wished to fight with him when he arrived there should be thanked for his services and replaced by Mr. Willaim Bisson. Our friend Fisset is still waiting impatiently for what he was promised long ago: the appointment of Dr. Ross of Ste. Flavie to the post of harbour doctor at Pointe au Père instead of Dr. Gauvreau, who is a strong Conservative supporter; and the nomination of Dr. Bouillon of Matane instead of Dr. Pelletier as harbour doctor at this location.

[f] As for me, if our friend Fisher (Minister of Agriculture) could appoint Desiré Vezina as head of police on Grosse Île to replace Zephiron Danceuse, and if our friend Mulock (Postmaster General) would appoint Mr. Georges Gagné as postmaster at St. Pierre to replace Mrs. C. Dienne, I would be very happy.

investigated the civil service in 1911-1912 uncovered the same practices that their predecessors have [sic] described in the 1880's and 1890's. One particular interchange between the commissioners and a witness laid out clearly the mechanics of the patronage system. The witness was Robert G. MacPherson, post-master at Vancouver. He was asked how appointments were made to the staff and the following exchange took place:

A: Appointments are made through recommendations by the patronage committee or the members supporting the government
Q: Do they communicate directly with you when vacancies occur
A: No. I will apply for one or two men to the department at Ottawa who authorize the appointment of men who shall be recommended by the member of parliament or the patronage committee as the case may be.[45]

From the other side of Canada, on Prince Edward Island, came evidence of how the system worked there. Thomas Mann, agent at Charlottetown for the Department of Marine and Fisheries, explained that appointment and purchasing worked "by patronage." If a position fell vacant, "the members supply a list of men they want put on and if they are suitable I put them on...." In the matter of buying supplies these were purchased "from the patronage people." The questioning continued:

Q: You have a list
A: It is not a list from the government, just from the local members. They do the same as when the other government was in power. They have their friends to go and so have these
Q: You have a patronage list
A: A patronage list of friends to go to the same as before.[46]

The evidence in this section has provided an overview of the workings of the patronage system in the years between 1878 and 1911. There emerges a remarkable similarity in how the system worked under Macdonald and Laurier and a remarkable stability in a system that had the same structure in 1912 as it did in the 1880's. From Vancouver to Halifax, from London to Quebec, from Winnipeg to Prince Edward Island, Conservative and Liberal administrations of the period used their power in the same way. Federal posts and contracts were given to local party activists in a regular, time-honored manner. Although the actual decisions on patronage were made by the cabinet ministers in Ottawa, the evidence shows that much of the work in terms of identifying applicants and proposing candidates was done by the local party organization, usually working through a committee. It is also clear that the patronage system applied to all levels of the public service from judgeships down to temporary positions in the post office. The system had become so rooted a part of Canadian political culture that it was considered legitimate and normal. It was only late in the period with the Royal Commission of 1911-1912 that serious questions were raised about the impact of so extensive a system of patronage on Canadian governments and their effectiveness in dealing with the needs of society.[47]

III

To understand all the ramifications of the patronage system it is essential to re-late it to the structure of Canadian society during this period. The first and most fundamental point to make here is that Canada was a small-town, rural society which was only beginning to be changed by the consequences of indus-trialization and urbanization. Professor Waite has reminded us of this basic fact in his authoritative study of the period between 1873 and 1896. The rural nature of Canada, he writes, "must be kept continually in mind when considering the character and setting of Canadian life. The conservativeness of the French-Canadian countryside is well known, its resistance to social change is as strong as its political allegiances, but so much of Canada was similar ... Canada was rural." [48] In 1881 the census classified 81% of the population as rural. By 1911 it was down to 56%, still over half the population. But even that figure does not tell the whole story. The census for 1911 shows that out of a total popula-tion of 7,206,643 there were 5,507,214 Canadians living in rural areas or in towns with less than 30,000. As late as 1911 about 76% of the Canadian popu-lation was living in small-town or rural conditions.[49]

One characteristic related to these conditions is that Canadian society was localistic. Professor Gibson has remarked on this quality of Canadian society, pointing out that "at Confederation and for many years afterwards, the Canadian people, a small and widely dispersed population, formed a simple and individ-ualistic society, exhibiting strong local loyalties." [50] The evidence on patronage cited above shows again and again how social and political leaders in each lo-cality were anxious to keep "outsiders" from moving in to their traditional sphere of influence. An insight into the isolation and localism of Canadian so-ciety in this period is provided by the memoirs of the historian A. R. M. Lower. He was born and raised in Barrie, Ontario, and recalled that in 1907 when he was eighteen years old he "had not been more than sixty or seventy miles away from home." Lower wondered whether he was "exceptional" in being thus rooted. "It is remarkable," he then added, "how local everyone was in those days." [51]

Another basically important fact to be borne in mind was that there was lim-ited economic growth during this period and that in contrast to the United States, for example, there was no dramatic advance of industrial capitalism. Even the Laurier "boom years" after 1900 rested on the development of agri-culture in the West and well into the first decade of the twentieth century contemporaries still regarded Canada's economy as essentially an agricultural one.[52] In 1896 Bryon Walker wrote in the *Monetary Times* that agriculture was "the substratum of our well-being." [53] Two years later D. R. Wilkie in a speech before the Canadian Bankers Association explained that Canada "was essentially an agricultural country" [54] and in 1907 this characteristic was again referred to, that "the real backbone of Canada is its agricultural and its dairy and pastoral interests." [55] A 1906 piece in *Industrial Canada* pointed out that "Canada is and always will be a great agricultural country ... [the farmer] is the very foundation stone of our social economy." [56]

A natural consequence of this reality was the relative insignificance of the industrial, manufacturing sector of the Canadian economy in moulding the social structure and value system of Canada. Some caution is required in broaching this topic for there is some disagreement among scholars about the nature and performance of the Canadian economy during this period. It used to be a conventional enough statement that there was little economic development between 1867 and 1900, at which point there was a take-off based on the wheat boom in the West. The picture of unrelieved gloom for the pre-1896 years can no longer be sustained, as Professor Waite has recently explained in his assessment of the new evidence.[57] There was steady growth in some manufactures; the GNP rose from $710,000,000 in 1873 to $1,800,000,000 in 1896. Clearly the economy did grow and the transportation and banking structures developed before 1900 proved a solid base from which the more rapid, diversified growth of the twentieth century could develop. Yet while acknowledging the reality of this economic growth its limitations must be kept in mind. The manufacturing firms in Canada were small, employed tiny work forces and had a very restricted impact on the social structure.[58] In 1870 the average number of persons employed in each manufacturing establishment was 4.6; in 1890 it had risen to only 5.5.[59] Manufacturing was still small-scale, decentralized and geographically dispersed.

These economic circumstances were important for sustaining such a flourishing patronage system. The key point is that there were limited job opportunities available in the private manufacturing sector and that as a consequence federal contracts and positions in the federal public service were important areas of career opportunities.[60] In a system in which there was dynamic capitalist growth as in the United States, employment opportunities at the disposal of the federal government assumed a minor place but in the case of Canada such opportunities were a foremost feature in the job market. The way in which the Donegan family immediately turned to political patronage for jobs is a good example of the role federal posts played in this respect. When it is further remembered that the major capitalist activity of the period—the Canadian Pacific Railroad—was also controlled by the state, it is clear that federal patronage played a dominant role in job distribution in post-Confederation Canada. It is revealing to note that patronage started to decline once the economy began to develop and diversify. There were several reasons for the decline of patronage after the 1914-18 war but one of the basic ones was that the advance of manufacturing reduced the heavy dependence on the federal government (and therefore the federal political parties) for jobs and contracts.[61]

The slow development of industry in Canada had another social consequence that intensified the central significance of the patronage system. Again
in contrast to contemporary United States, where capitalists and businessmen
formed he dominant social class, these groups were numerically small and socially insignificant in Canada. In a society where industrial development was
in its infancy and where manufacturing was small-scale, the professional middle classes flourished.[62] The prestige occupations in Canada lay in this
area—barristers, solicitors, clergy, civil servants. In the case of Quebec the pre-
eminence of these groups is accepted readily enough. Jean-Charles Falardeau
has provided a good summary of the situation in Quebec, pointing out that by
the mid-nineteenth century the professional middle-classes had succeeded the
traditional elites. "La noblesse professionelle," Falardeau notes, "constituent
effectivement, jusqu'à l'époque contemporaine, l'élite Canadienne-Française—
c'est cette élite que l'on est tenté d'appeler et que l'on appelle souvent notre
bourgeoisie." [g][63] But while this social phenomenon of a "bourgeois" class composed mostly of professionals rather than businessmen is normally associated
with Quebec, it was equally a hallmark of English-Canadian society before the
industrialization of the twentieth-century. Because there was no rapid capitalist and industrial development in Canada, there failed to develop a large
and powerful middle class whose members could earn a living in ways that
were open to trained and educated men in the United States and Britain.
Opportunities for upward mobility through business corporations or by selling
technical skills were very limited in Canada. This weakened "the development
within Canadian society of capitalist, urban middle-class social values and
forms of social structure." [64] In these circumstances there was little choice for
each generation between 1867 and 1911 but to earn a living and gain social
status by entering the legal profession or gaining a position in the public service.

A nice example of the social prestige a professional man could achieve in this
small-town society was given by the Civil Service Commission in their 1908
report. Looking back to the 1880's for an overview of the reasons why public
service was so attractive to Canadians the commissioners pointed out the advantages:

> Owing to the small mileage of railways and to the lack of communications most
> of the necessities of life raised in the different localities were consumed locally.
> Butter, eggs, meats, foodstuffs and articles entering into daily consumption
> were produced in the locality in which they were consumed. The same charac-
> teristic feature was applicable to domestic servants employed in the households
> of officials in the public service. A generation ago there was no means by which
> the farmers' daughters could remove easily from the locality in which they were

---

[g] Up to the present time, the professional elite basically made up the French-Canadian elite and it
is to this elite that we tend to and indeed often do refer to as our middle class.

born, and as the supply of domestic servants was greater than the demand the wages were comparatively small.... The civil servant in these days, although not in receipt of a large income, had his wants satisfied cheaply and without stint.[65]

Not all public employees could afford servants. Nevertheless it is a valid proposition that for most of the 1867-1911 period, bearing in mind prevailing economic conditions, the public service was the biggest single area of attractive, secure and prestigious employment. Even as late as 1911 employees in the public service still talked in terms of the "dignity" and "respectability" of their position in society.[66] The only way to get one of these jobs was to have some claim on one of the two political parties. It was these basic social and economic realities that enabled the political parties to make the patronage system such a powerful organizing force in Canadian society and politics.

IV

These final two sections will put forward some general conclusions about the significance of the patronage system and its long-term consequences in Canadian political development. The first point to make is that the pervasive patronage system that lasted throughout these years confirmed the power and prestige of professional middle classes who ran the two federal parties. In Canada these middle class groups—barristers, solicitors, doctors, notaries—which controlled the political parties did not, as in Europe, face serious social or economic competition. There was no aristocratic or traditional landed class that still had an influence in public affairs; there was no lingering peasant presence upon which a political movement could be based; there was no rapidly expanding capitalist class deriving wealth and power from industrialization; there was no mass labor movement seeking to form its own party. In these conditions the federal political parties, representing the dominant middle class and particularly the professionals, were extraordinarily influential in Canadian society. To understand the ramifications of these circumstances it is useful to consider the observations made by Hans Daalder in his analysis of political development in Western Europe.[67] Daalder, in tackling the question of how political elites relate to other elite groups in society, has suggested that one method of assessing the relative power of elites is to gauge the extent to which important positions within society could be obtained without reference to the political elite, without going through party channels.[68] In Canada nearly every important position in society was available only through the two political parties. Judges were appointed on the basis of partisan loyalty; QC's were distributed to lawyers who had been active in party work; senators were purely political appointments; posts throughout the public service, from the most senior down to the temporary and from Halifax to Vancouver, were disposed of by the parties to those who had worked for them. Even men with technical qualifications, such as civil engineers seeking work on the railroads, thought it wise to let their party credentials be known.[69] And in filling these positions the party leaders were approached in a supplicating manner by archbishops, bishops, deacons, priests, ministers, university principals, manufacturers and individuals from their prominent social groups. In Daalder's terms the political elite in Canada was the top power elite, no other group approaching it in terms of power and influence.[70]

The course of Canada's economy during these years helped sustain the dominant role of the parties and their patronage system. Again it is helpful to compare Canada with Europe and the United States. Jacques Ellul has written that "the nation-state is the most important reality of our days.... Nowadays it is the state that directs the economy.... The state is not just a superstructure. Marxist analysis is only valid in the nineteenth century when the emergence of uncontrolled, explosive economic power relegated a weak, liberal and unclearly delineated state to the shadows and subjugated it." [71] In Canada things did not happen this way. There was no explosive economic growth and the state was not relegated to a position of insignificance by the powerful forces of industrial capitalism. On the contrary, the state in Canada, the federal government, was the single most important energizing agency as it took the lead in stimulating economic growth, protecting infant industries, building a national transportation network as well as constructing its own physical presence in hundreds of public work projects across the country in the form of harbours, bridges, railways, post offices, customs houses and other buildings to house its bureaucracy. Upon entering office, each political party fell heir to this extensive sphere of government activity. In the United States the party in power had similar room for maneuver but in that country the party's scope for activity was circumscribed by other powerful interests in the expanding capitalist economy whereas in Canada the parties faced no rivals. Quite simply in Canada the parties were dominant and pervasive. A contemporary observer in the 1880's caught this development in the new Confederation. There was in Canada, he wrote, "an overgrowth of partyism." [72] In these circumstances the patronage system was like water finding its own level as it permeated post-Confederation Canadian society.

Another important point to emerge from the ramifications of the patronage system is that in the 1867 to 1911 period English- and French-Canadians were more alike in their social and political behavior than has commonly been accepted. Scholars have drawn attention to the fact that a major reason for the French-Canadian attachment to the Union (1840-1867) was that the Qu_b_cois professional middle class received, through patronage, opportunities for social advancement. Jacques Monet has well described this phenomenon in the twenty years before Confederation. "For two generations since 1800," explains Monet,

> The Canadian professional class had been struggling to secure an outlet for its ambitions: so now with a kind of bacterial thoroughness it began to invade

every vital organ of government, and divide up among its members hundreds of posts as Judges, Queen's Counsels, Justices of the Peace, Medical Examiners, school inspectors, militia captains, postal clerks, mail conductors, census commissioners. And as the flatteries and salaries of office percolated down to other classes of society—from merchants who wanted seats on the Legislative Council down to impoverished habitants on the crowded seigneuries—the Canadians came to realize how parliamentary democracy could be more than a lovely ideal. It was also a profitable fact. And henceforth ... there could be guaranteed for all French-Canadians the possibility of room at the top.[73]

This process continued after 1867. Jean-Charles Bonenfant has described a typical pattern of upward mobility through politics—"l'homme politique était bourgeois d'une certaine aisance, ayant de préférence une formation juridique, se faisant élire à la chambre basse pour mourir plus tard conseiller legislatif, senateur ou juge." [h][74] Jean Falardeau in his analysis of nineteenth century Quebec society also draws attention to the relationships among politics, patronage and social status. Falardeau makes distinctions between professionals and politicians, suggesting that the political bourgeoisie represented by such leaders as La Fontaine and Laurier and the members elected to Ottawa were more susceptible to English values, while within the localities of Quebec the "pure" professionals such as doctors, advocates, notaries, derived office and rewards from political patronage but remained rooted in Quebec language and culture. By the middle of the nineteenth century these professional and political elements, flourishing off the patronage system and all its ramifications, had replaced the ailing seigneurs as "la class dirigeante" in Quebec. Falardeau describes them in that perceptive phrase already noted as "la noblesse professionelle." [i][75]

All this may be familiar enough but such historical social analysis should not stop short at the Ottawa river. Most of the preceding observations about the mobility patterns, values and social aspirations of the Quebec middle classes apply almost as well to English Canada between 1867 and 1911. Of course conditions were not identical in English Canada and Quebec. In the English provinces there were more varied responses to business, finance and commerce; there were more opportunities in these fields and more social credit attached to them. Also in English-Canada there was no one dominant church to which all successful men had to defer or relate in some manner. Yet recent research has downplayed some of these conventional distinctions and shown that Quebec's response to economic change was not as reactionary as was once supposed.[76] Whatever the final verdict of scholars on these distinctions it is essential to point out the similarities that did exist. Before industrialization developed in a

---

[h] the man of politics was from the middle class and possessed some personal fortune, preferably had some legal background and got himself elected to the lower house in order to later die as a legislative assistant, senator or judge.

[i] the ruling class...the professional class

dynamic manner in the decade after 1900, English-Canada was a rural, small-town and churched society with limited contacts with the secular and transforming world of industrial capitalism. The opportunities for posts and social advancement through businesses and companies were restricted. It was a society in which the most prestigious and important groups were the professional middle classes; a society in which patronage was normal, legitimate and pervasive; a society in which patronage was the single most important route of upward mobility to sought-after positions that gave security and status. English-speaking Canadians like their counterparts in Quebec turned to the patronage of the parties to become judges, senators, QC's, post office officials, customs service officials, collectors of inland revenue, medical examiners and a multitude of other positions in the public service. The operation of these social processes in English-Canada may have been less intense than in Quebec, more directly linked to business and commercial goals, but the profound similarities between French- and English-Canadians remain. There was then a fundamental convergence in how English- and French-Canadians regarded politics and political parties and the social ramifications of politics. In particular both major ethnic groups in Canada shared the same expectations and derived the same kind of rewards from the system of political patronage. On patronage English- and French-Canadians spoke the same language.

V

In the turning to the long-term consequences of the patronage system a paradox appears. On the one hand patronage helped to create and maintain political stability, an essential condition if Confederation were to succeed, but on the other hand it helped to entrench a political culture which because of its nature pushed problems concerning the nature of Confederation to the background. On the positive side the ability of the parties to utilize patronage on so grand a scale over so long a period helped them to attract and retain supporters and thereby establish a solid base in the population. The process of establishing political stability has been analyzed by many scholars studying new nations in the modern world and one conclusion they have come to is that political stability usually requires political parties to have an extensive and influential reach in society. The political parties must be able to show that they can effectively reward supporters and so encourage loyalty to the party. Often some form of patronage or corruption is the means by which a party establishes its position. As Joseph Palombara puts it, "corruption or its functional equivalent may be critically important to a developing nation." [77] For example, in such a new nation if merit alone were the criterion for appointment to the public service then there would be a growth of bureaucratic power which would push the parties to the sidelines and thus lead to political instability as the parties became unable to attract and reward supporters. In the Canadian case patronage functioned in this manner. Patronage cemented the support of both federal parties, enabled them to exert extensive influence throughout society, and thus helped create a stable party system.

Such an achievement should not be underestimated in a country as fragmented ethnically and regionally as Canada. But for the achievement of political stability there was a price to pay. One of the adverse consequences of the patronage system was that it encouraged the persistence of localism in Canadian politics. The way in which patronage was dispersed made every local party organization across Canada jealous of its own territory and suspicious of outsiders. Local exclusivity was sanctioned by the national party leaders. Indeed, this was a deliberate object of policy in order to create strong local organizations to fight election campaigns. This tendency must be kept in perspective. Localism, given the social, economic and geographic setting of Canada at the time, was bound to be a natural characteristic of Canadian politics.[78] The parties were moulded by the type of society in which they functioned. It is therefore a question of degree. Localism was bound to exist and the parties could either simply live with this reality or try to lessen its impact or encourage its persistence. They did the last. The patronage system of the two parties encouraged Canadian political culture to remain localized. From a party viewpoint this was a good thing since it created strong, loyal, hard-working local associations that could be managed by skilled leadership in Ottawa from the center of the patronage web. But it also restricted the vision of those in politics: MPs and local party notables were not encouraged by the system to interest themselves in affairs outside their own areas. The system worked in the direction of local inwardness. Because of this the Canadian House of Commons was in a metaphorical sense "la maison sans fenêtres." [j] [79] The MP's vision was narrowly focussed back into his locality and the windows on national issues were closed or obscured. The long reign of the patronage system contributed to a persistent parochialism in Canadian politics.

The great paradox lying at the center of Canadian political culture in this period was that this emphasis on localism and avoidance of debate on the relationships between the two racial groups were the very reasons for the success of the party system in maintaining stability prior to 1911. To explain this paradox it is useful to relate the case advanced in this article to recent work done by Arend Lijphart on elite accommodation and consociational democracy.[80] Lijphart's model seems a fruitful one to apply to Canada. He argues that European countries which have an ethnically segmented population have developed a peculiar form of democracy. In these systems each major ethnic group supports its own political party and the leaders of these parties, the represen-

---

[j] the house with no windows

tative elites, negotiate and mediate to form governments and maintain stability without sacrificing the interests of one particular group. Thus while there may be little communication and even great tension between the various linguistic blocs the elites of each group compromise in an attempt to reach solutions to national problems. The system then is characterized by elite accommodation. In a stimulating and thoughtful study Kenneth McCrea has applied the consociational democracy model to the Canadian case.[81] McCrea points out that the model can be useful for Canada only if it is modified to account for the fact that the two major ethnic blocs have never been represented by separate political parties at the national level. If accommodation does take place between the elites of each society, it must take place within the parties rather than between ethnically based parties. Having made this adjustment to the model McCrea analyzed how the system has worked in Canada and concluded that "even by the most charitable interpretation, the political system's capacity to learn and adapt to linguistic-cultural diversity has not been high." [82] The federal parties have not been able to work out solutions to national problems but have instead created a situation of "immobilism and stalemate" in which the federal government seems weak and ineffective. Accommodation within the parties which should have been going on since 1867 has not taken place. On the contrary the gulf between English- and French-Canadians has widened to the point where the continued survival of the nation is in doubt. McCrea concludes that the Canadian political system has a low learning capacity.[83]

This is a complex topic which requires multi-factor analysis. Yet one of the principal reasons for the apparent ineffectiveness of the federal party system lies in the structure of parties as they developed between 1878 and 1911. The cardinal point here is that both parties relied on patronage so heavily that they reduced the need for any genuine accommodation on such issues, for example, as language in the public service. As Brown and Cook have recently pointed out, communication between the two races hardly existed except in the realm of politics. In 1902 Lord Minto remarked that he found "the leaders of society of both races unacquainted with each other. " [84] In these conditions much depended on the intercourse among the politicians of each race within the two federal parties and they found it easier and more congenial to deal with patronage and localized politics rather than "questions of race." [85]

The impact of patronage limited accommodation in the whole system of appointments and promotions in the public service. As far back as 1877 William Le Sueur drew attention to the fact that in the Canadian public service no heed was paid to whether or not an employee or candidate was bilingual and no recognition or reward was given to those who happened to be bilingual. Le Sueur pointed out that:

> in a service where two languages are used it is obviously unfair that a man who brings to the Service a knowledge of both, and whose knowledge of both is made use of by the Department in which he serves, should derive no advan-

tage whatever from the fact. Such, however, is the fact. In the Department in which I serve a man who knows both French and English is made to do work requiring a knowledge of both those languages and to do it for his seniors. A senior clerk may send to a junior clerk that portion of his work which requires knowledge of a second language and the junior gets nothing at all in the way of promotion for this special qualification.[86]

It is important to emphasize that both English- and French-speaking politicians were responsible for this non-recognition of the value of two-language people in the public service—it was not a policy concocted by bigoted Anglo-Canadian politicians. The fact that a contemporary like Le Sueur could put his finger on a fundamental issue like this shows that it is not anachronistic to suggest that more could have been done by the parties to incorporate linguistic duality more securely and formally into the structure of the federal administration. The parties did not do so because it did not occur to them to do so. Whether they came from the Gaspé or western Ontario or Halifax or Vancouver the politicians of the day were interested in the public service from the viewpoint, above all, of patronage. Their interest lay in placing party workers in the service, not trying to make the civil service a setting for reasonable accommodation of French- and English-Canadian interests.[87] In such ways the patronage system, while satisfying the immediate needs of local party associations in Quebec and the rest of Canada, constricted any incipient structural accommodation between the two racial blocs.

Canadians of the twentieth century are reaping the harvest of patronage politics during the 1867 to 1911 period. Parties relied heavily on patronage to satisfy ethnic groups within each party and so avoided the need to think about genuine accommodation in terms of the relationship of English- and French-Canadians in Confederation. Patronage was a great strength yet also a great weakness in the Canadian party system. It enabled the parties to flourish and maintain political stability as long as social and economic conditions were fertile ground for patronage and as long as society placed no major demands upon the parties. But once conditions changed, as Canada became an industrialized, urbanized society, as the provinces became more powerful and, above all, as Quebec modernized and began demanding that attention be paid to the basic meaning and structure of Confederation, then the parties which had been successful before 1911 began to become less effective. Their historical development had not prepared them for finding solutions to national problems.[88]

Notes

1. W.L. Morton, "The Cabinet of 1867," in F. W. Gibson, ed., *Cabinet Formation and Bicultural Relations* (Ottawa, 1970), p. 3; an example of a source book treatment of the topic is J. H. Stewart Reid, Kenneth McNaught, Harry S. Crowe, *A Source book of Canadian History* (Toronto, 1964), pp. 331-346.

2. Morton, "The Cabinet of 1867," p. 2. Political reminiscences of the period are full of references, charges and counter-charges to patronage and corruption. Richard Cartwright, *Reminiscences* (Toronto, 1912), is particularly rich in this regard. So too is W.T.R. Preston, *My Generation of Politics and Politicians* (Toronto, 1927).

3. Peter B. Waite, *Canada 1874-1896* (Toronto, 1971), p. 96.

4. Commission to Inquire into the Present State and Probable Requirements of the Civil Service (1868-1870), 1st and 2nd Reports in Sessional Papers, #19 (1869), 3rd Report in Sessional Papers, #64 (1870); Royal Commission to Inquire into the Organization of the Civil Service Commission (1880-81), 1st Report in Sessional Papers, #113 (1 80-81), 2nd Report in Sessional Papers #32 (1882); Royal Commission to Inquire into the Present State of the Civil Service at Ottawa (1891-92), Report in Sessional Papers, #16C (1892); Report of the Civil Service Commission (1907-08), Sessional Papers, #29A (1907-08); Commission to Inquire into the Public Service (1911-12), Sessional Papers, #57 (1913).

5. Report of Investigation into the Department of Marine and Fisheries, Sessional Papers, #38 (1909).

6. Waite, *Canada 1874-1896,* pp. 218-221, 230.

7. J.E. Hodgetts, William McClockey, Reginald Whitaker, V. Seymour Wilson, *The Biography of an Institution. The Civil Service Commission of Canada 1908-1967* (Montreal, 1972), p. 8.

8. The evidence is taken from the John A. Macdonald Papers, Public Archives of Canada [hereafter P.A.C.], Vol. 14, Kingston Patronage. On the formalities of the process see John McIntyre to John A. Macdonald, October 11, 1891.

9. Edward Smythe to John A. Macdonald, Kingston, November 13, 1889, Private, Macdonald Papers, Vol. 14, P.A.C

10. Smythe to Macdonald, Kingston, September 17, 1889, Private, Macdonald Papers, Vol. 14, P.A.C.

11. J.A. Metcalfe to John A. Macdonald, Kingston, January 18, 1890, Macdonald Papers, Vol. 14, P.A.C.

12. Mackenzie Bowell to John A. Macdonald, Ottawa, January 8, 1891, Macdonald Papers, Vol. 14, P.A.C.

13. Thomas H. McGuire to John A. Macdonald, Kingston, January 9, 1891, Macdonald Papers, Vol. 14, P.A.C.

14. J.A. Metcalfe to John A. Macdonald, Kingston, November 29, 1890, Private Macdonald Papers, Vol. 14, P.A.C.

15. M. Conger to John A. Macdonald, Picton, December 26, 1890, Macdonald Papers, Vol. 14, P.A.C. The militia appointment involved the interests of several ridings in southeast Ontario.

16. R.R. Pringle to John A. Macdonald, Cobourg, December 28, 1890, Macdonald Papers, Vol. 14, P.A.C.

17. H. Ward to John A. Macdonald, Port Hope, December 23, 1890, Private. On the relationship of this piece of patronage to local party "strength" see also Sam Hughes to Charles Tupper, Jr., Lindsay, Ontario, December 25, 1890, Macdonald Papers, Vol. 14, P.A.C.

18. George Fitzpatrick to John A. Macdonald, Kingston, January 8, 1891, Private, Macdonald Papers, Vol. 14, P.A.C.

19. John McIntyre to John A. Macdonald, January 10, 1891, Private.

20. John Haggart to John A. Macdonald, Ottawa, September 19, 1889. In another case Edward Smythe discussed with the Prime Minister the plight of "our old friend B. McConville," a party activist who had been given a contract for carrying the mail and now wished the amount to be increased. See Smythe to Macdonald, Kingston, September 17, 1889. Private, Macdonald Papers, Vol. 14, P.A.C.

21. Report of Investigation into Department of Marine and Fisheries (1909), P. 10.

22. *Ibid.,* p. 41.

23. *Ibid.,* p. 44.

24. *Ibid.,* p. 42-43.

25. Report of the Civil Service Commission (1907-08), pps. 37, 27.

26. *Ibid.,* p. 28.

27. *Ibid.,* p. 89-90.

28. *Ibid.,* pps. 7, 28, 440-443.

29. *Ibid.,* p. 28.

30. Hugh Falconer to Wilfred Laurier, Shelbourne, Ontario, January 13, 1908; Laurier to Falconer, Ottawa, January 15, 1908, Private Laurier Papers, P.A.C. Vol. 950.

31. John Small to John A. Macdonald, Toronto, April 5, 1887, Confidential, Macdonald Papers, P.A.C., Vol. 24.

32. Robert Birmingham to John A. Macdonald, Toronto, October 10, 1889, Macdonald Papers, P.A.C., Vol. 24. Macdonald kept a list of all the barristers in Toronto and noted opposite each name the party affiliation. He also estimated the composition of the Ontario bar as a whole according to party membership. The Toronto bar had 150 barristers eligible for the QC—95 were Conservatives, 55 were "Reformers." See List of in Toronto, Macdonald Papers, P.A.C., Vol. 24.

33. B.L. Doyle to Frank Smith, Goderich, November 28, 1879, Private, Macdonald Papers, P.A.C., Vol. 25 II.

34. Frank Smith to John A. Macdonald, [?], December 1, 1879, Macdonald Papers, P.A.C., Vol. 25 II.

35. N.O. Cote, *Political Appointments, Parliaments and the Judicial Bench in Canada 890-1903* (Ottawa, 1903), pp. 571-72.

36. H.C. Gwyn to John A. Macdonald, Dundas, April 22, 1885, Macdonald Papers, P.A.C., Vol. 26.

37. S. Dawson to John A. Macdonald, Ottawa, May 13, 1884, Macdonald Papers, P.A.C., Vol. 26.

38. N.C. Wallace to John A. Macdonald, Ottawa, July 15, 1885, Private, Macdonald Papers, P.A.C., Vol. 26.

39. A.M. Boswell to John A. Macdonald, Toronto, July 7, 1887, Macdonald Papers, P.A.C., Vol. 27 II.

40. George Reid to James Sutherland, London, May 4, 1900, Laurier Papers, P.A.C., Vol. 873.

41. *Ibid.*

42. Roy Choquette to Wilfred Laurier, Ottawa, September 12, 1896, Personelle, Laurier Papers, P.A.C., Vol. 833.

43. *Ibid.*

44. *Ibid.* Laurier himself would act on these patronage requests, even down to the most minor, by notifying (as Macdonald had done) the appropriate minister of the necessary appointments. For example, in response to one request for Liberal appointees to the International railroad Laurier made out a memorandum naming those employees to be dismissed and indicating their replacements. See H.G. Carroll to Wilfred Laurier, Quebec, December 29, 1896; Memorandum by Laurier in Reply, n.d., Laurier Papers, P.A.C., Vol. 833.

45. Royal Commission on the Public Service (1911-12), p. 1292. Macpherson's evidence was given on July 30 and 31, 1912.

46. *Ibid.*, pp. 1416-1417.

47. With the changes wrought by industrialization and urbanization the Canadian government was forced to acknowledge that the patronage-ridden public service system was inefficient and ineffective in the new conditions. This was a basic factor pushing for change. Public opinion was also increasingly critical of patronage after 1900, and an increasing sense of professionalism within the service were additional factors. Public employees in the western provinces were particularly critical in their appearance and representation to the Royal Commission of 1911-12. See R.C. Brown and R. Cook, *Canada 1896-1921. A Nation Transformed* (Toronto, 1974), pp. 192-194, 321; Norman Ward, *The Canadian House of Commons* (Toronto, 1950), pp. 275-281; Royal Commission on the Public Service (1911-1912), pp. 16-20, 337-338; Civil Service Commission (1908-09). p. 13. The latter report noted that "it was the universal feeling amongst the officials who gave evidence ... that this patronage evil was the curse of the public service."

48. P.B. White, *Canada 1873-1896* (Toronto, 1971), pp. 8-9.

49. M.C. Urquhart and K.A.H. Buckley, eds., *Historical Statistics of Canada* (Toronto, 1965), pp. 5, 14-15, Series A 15-19 and A 20-24. On pp. 5-7 Urquhart and Buckley discuss the problems of "urban" and "rural" classification in this period.

50. F. Gibson, ed., *Cabinet Formation and Bicultural Relations* (Ottawa, 1970), p. 171.

51. A.R.M. Lower, *My First Seventy-five Years* (Toronto, 1967), p. 33. Some examples of suspicion of "outsiders" appear in this article. The patronage papers of both Macdonald and Laurier are full of other instances. For example a lawyer looking for work in London, Ontario was regarded with deep antipathy because he had no roots in the area. Another individual who was not known locally was described as an "unscrupulous professional man" —i.e., with no base in the local church or community, simply interested in pursuing a career wherever he could get a job. See John Barwick to John A. Macdonald, Woodstock, February 10, 1879, Macdonald

Papers, P.A.C., Vol. 251; A. McKean to John A Macdonald, Bothwell, Ontario, September 19, 1887, Macdonald Papers, P.A.C., Vol. 271. Also see note 30 above for an example in the Laurier Papers.

52. Michael Bliss, "A Living Profit: Studies in the Social History of Canadian Business 1883-1911," Ph.D. Thesis, University of Toronto, p. 331.

53. *Monetary Times,* June 21, 1896, quoted in Bliss, "A Living Profit," p. 331.

54. *Journal of Commerce,* November 4, 1898, pp. 634-635; Byron Walker to G.F. Little, October 10, 1907, both quoted in Bliss, "A Living Profit," p. 331.

55. Byron Walker to G.F. Little, October 10, 1907, quoted in Bliss, "A Living Profit," p. 331.

56. *Industrial Canada,* March 1906, p. 484, quoted in Bliss, "A Living Profit," p. 332.

57. Waite, *Canada 1893-1896,* pp. 74-78.

58. S. D. Clark, "The Canadian Manufacturers Association," *Canadian Journal of Economics and Political Science,* Vol. IV (1938), pp. 506-508. R. T. Naylor, *The History of Canadian Business 1867-1914,* 2 Vols., Toronto, 1975), Vol. 2, pp. 276-284 argues Canadian industrial development was stultified during these decades.

59. Urquhart and Buckley, eds., *Canadian Historical Statistics,* p. 463, Series Q 1-11.

60. Naylor, *History of Canadian Business 1867-1914,* Vol. 2, pp. 276-284. Contemporaries talked of the very recent growth of industrial capitalism in Canada and referred to the fact that there was not as yet a class of entrepreneurs who could sit back and enjoy their profits. W. T. R. Preston in *My Generation of Politics* (Toronto, 1927), pp. 204, 487 described the 1880's and 1890's as "the twenty years [which witnessed] the creation and establishment of a capitalist system." Robert Laird Borden in his *Memoirs* (Toronto, 1938), p. 151, pointed out that "we have no men of leisure or of means." Goldwin Smith in his *Reminiscences* (New York, 1910) pp. 456-457, 487 remarked that "Toronto wealth is not munificent. It certainly is not compared with the United States." All these points reflect the fact that Canadian industry was as yet only a struggling part of the social and economic structure.

61. The Report of the Civil Service Commission (1907-08), pp. 14, 17, pointed out that public service positions while still sought after were becoming less attractive as opportunities expanded in the economy. They pointed to the significance of the fact that the lower levels of the public service were being increasingly filled by women. Norman Ward in his study of Canadian MPs emphasizes that many of them went on to important patronage positions. "The evidence is fairly strong," he writes, "that politics in Canada is by no means the precarious occupation it is often assumed to be. Until very recently, only a small number of private businesses were in a position to provide positions for 30% of their employees." See Ward, *Hourse of Commons,* p. 98-101, 103, 146.

62. Bliss, "A Living Profit," pp. 1, 321, 341; S. D. Clark, *The Developing Canadian Community* (Toronto, 1968), pp. 227, 234. Clark argued that "in a way scarcely true of any other Western nation, the middle class in Canada has been the Establishment."

63. J. C. Falardeau, "Evolution des structures sociales et des élites au Canada francais Quebec," 1960), pp. 10-11.

64. Clark, *The Developing Canadian Community,* pp. 243-252.

65. Report of the Civil Service Commission (1907-08), pp. 14-17.

66. Royal Commission on the Public Service (1911-12), p. 1213.

67. Hans Daalder, "Parties, Elites and Political Development in Western Europe," in Joseph Palombara and Myron Weiner, eds., *Political Parties and Political Revolution* (Princeton, 1966).

68. *Ibid.,* p. 75. Daalder talks of the "reach" or "permeation" in society of political parties.

69. For example, George Grant to John A. Macdonald, Kingston, November 26, 1883, Macdonald Papers, P.A.C., Vol. 26, Bishop of Hamilton to Macdonald, Hamilton, October 15, 1880, Macdonald Papers, P.A.C., Vol. 25 II, Bishop of Peterborough to Macdonald, Peterborough, November 23, 1887, Macdonald Papers, P.A.C., Vol. 27 I, Reverend A. McKean to Macdonald, Bothwell, September 19, 1887, Macdonald Papers, P.A.C., Vol 27 I, Byron Nicholson to William Gibson, Quebec, November 28, 1908 (Nicholson was a newspaper editor and "literateur"), Laurier Papers, P.A.C., Vol. 950, Thomas Swan to John A. Macdonald, Mount Forest, Ontario, March 17, 1883, Macdonald Papers, P.A.C., Vol. 5 (Swan owned a carriage works business), R. McKechnie to Macdonald, Dundas, March 11, 1891, Macdonald Papers, P.A.C., Vol. 22 (McKechnie was head of a manufacturing company and former President of the Canadian Manufacturers Association). On railroad patronage see N. A. Belcourt to Laurier, Ottawa. August 31, 1904, Laurier Papers P.A.C., Vol. 950. Also, Waite, *Canada 1873-96,* pp. 136-137, Brown and Cook, *Canada 1896-1921,* pp. 147-153.

70. Alexander Tillock Galt caught the essence of this condition in the new confederation when he wrote that "politics form the only short cut from the middle to the upper ranks." See O. D. Skelton, *The Life and Times of Alexander Tillock Galt* (Toronto, 1920), pp. 377-379. In 1880 an observer noted the dominance of fashionable society in Ottawa by politicians, civil servants and associated professionals. See J. E. Collins, *Canada Under Lord Lorne,* p. 309. See also Lady Aberdeen's comments in Saywell, ed., *The Canadian Journal of Lady Aberdeen* (Toronto, 1960), p. 42. J. W. Dafoe, "Canadian Problems of Government," *CJEPS,* Vol. V (1939), p. 288, pointed out that a career in politics in pre-1914 Canada carried more "personal distinction" than since that time and that to be an MP "meant a good deal more than it does now; and to be a member was a very general, if not all but universal desire among ambitious men."

71. Jacques Ellul, *The Political Illusion* (New York, 1967), p. 9.

72. Hans Muller, *Canada. Past, Present and Future* (Montreal, 1880), p. 7. J. D. McClokie back in 1948 described a new state form, "the party state" in which the political party was the most dominant power. See McClokie, "The Modern Party State," *CJEPS,* vol. XIV (1948), p. 143.

73. Jacques Monet, "Les Idées politiques de Baldwin and LaFontaine," in Hamelin, ed., *The Political Ideas of the Prime Ministers of Canada* (Ottawa, 1969), pp. 16-17. See also l'Hon. Charles Langelier, *Souvenirs Politiques* (Quebec, 1912), pp. 25-26.

74. Jean-Charles Bonenfant, "L'evolution du statut de l'homme politique Canadien-Français," in Fernand Dumont et Jean-Paul Montmigny, eds., *Le Pouvoir dans la société Canadienne-Française* (Quebec, 1966), pp. 117-118.

75. Falardeau, "Evolution des structures," op. cit., p. 11. The phrase "La noblesse professionelle" comes from P. J. O. Chauveau, *Charles Guerin. Roman de moeurs canadiennes* (Montreal, 1853), pp. 55-56.

76. For example, William F. Ryan, *The Clergy and Economic Growth in Quebec 1896-1914* (Quebec, 1966). Two other studies put Quebec economic development in a much clearer light than traditional works. See Albert Faucher, *Quebec en Amérique au XIX siècle* (Montreal, 1973) and Jean Hamelin and Yves Roby, *Histoire Economique du Québec 1851-1896* (Montreal, 1971). Faucher, for example, deals with the economic divergence between Quebec and Ontario in terms of technical development, regional pulls and so on rather than in terms of differences in value systems. See too the assessment in Brown and Cook, *Canada 1896-1921*, pp. 127-143.

77. Joseph Palombara, ed., *Bureaucracy and Political Development* (Princeton, 1963), p. 11; Hodgetts, et al., *Biography of an Institution*, pp. 14-16.

78. Gibson, ed., *Cabinet Formation*, p. 171. See note 51.

79. Daalder, "Parties, Elites and Political Development," op. cit., pp. 64-65.

80. Arend Lijphart, *The Politics of Accommodation. Pluralism and Democracy in the Netherlands* (Berkeley, 1968). "Typologies of Democratic Systems, *Comparative Political Studies,*" Vol. I (1968), pp. 17-35, "Consociational Democracy," *World Politics,* Vol. 21 (1969), pp. 207-225.

81. Kenneth D. McRae, *Consociational Democracy. Political Accommodation in Segmented Societies* (Toronto, 1974).

82. *Ibid.,* pp. 250, 259-260.

83. *Ibid.,* pp. 254, 261.

84. Brown and Cook, *Canada 1896-1921,* pp. 164-165.

85. In a letter written shortly before his death Macdonald complained, almost in a tone of surprise, that such issues should arise in Canada, that it was "a great pity that these questions of race should arise so frequently." John A. Macdonald to Alphonse Desjardins, Ottawa, January 6, 1891, Alphonse Desjardins Papers, P.A.C., MG 271, E22.

86. Notes on Civil Service Reform by William D. LeSueur Select Committee on Present Conditions of the Civil Service (1877), p. 106.

87. McRae's comments are pertinent here. "In retrospect," he writes, "the quest to accommodate linguistic diversity in Canada may be viewed as a series of lost opportunities ... and it seems likely that this low capacity of the system to devise effective solutions has helped to increase the intensity of linguistic and cultural cleavage in recent decades." McRae, *Consociational Democracy,* p. 259.

88. It is necessary not to press this case too far lest the tone become anachronistic. Professor Creighton has warned against placing politicians of post-Confederation Canada in an alien context. They were not eighteenth century politicians inter-

ested in ethnic and cultural issues. They were Victorian politicians who were successful in building a viable Canada in arduous circumstances. D. G. Creighton, *Canada's First Century 1867-1967* (Toronto, 1970), p. 8. These are weighty reminders of the dangers of anachronistic analysis. Yet, as the 1877 evidence of LeSueur shows, there were alternatives even in the context of the times. Macdonald and Laurier then can be characterized as limited in their responses to the basic problem of Confederation—and these limitations took root and flourished because the patronage system enabled the political leaders to close their minds to structural responses to the "question of race."

CHAPTER
5 WOMEN AND WORK

The virtue of hard work traditionally was taken for granted in our society, and a body of homilies justified it. For example, there was "pride in one's work," all work was "noble," "work is love made visible," and, above all, "a woman's work is never done." These pre-industrial ideas were carried into the modern period when the idealization of the solitary artisan completing his task became even more powerful when placed in relief against those in mindless factory jobs. As the twentieth century wore on laments over the "tyranny of work" replaced the hymns celebrating its virtue. Historians of the "New Left," in particular, have raged against the indecency of the workplace and the inevitable class conflict starkly manifest in industrial strikes. They reinvented the history of the early industrial era, making the working class and its culture the centrepiece, not only of their studies, but of Canadian history as well. The journal *Labour / Le Travailleur*, which was begun by the Committee on Canadian Labour History in 1976, became the catalyst for many innovative studies, though it stumbled at the beginning. The title *Le Travailleur* and the very first article "Most Uncommon Common Men" were inadvertent indications of a male world view of work. The title was changed to *Labour / Le Travail* with issue number 13 in 1983. Numberous articles on women and work, the subject of this chapter, appeared in the journal, including one of the readings reprinted here.

The reformulation of Canadian history from a woman's perspective has been extensive, with the nature of both paid and unpaid work being of special interest. During the past twenty years studies have ranged widely, including house and farm work, industrial and clerical employment, teaching, the sweat shops, and the streets. In the process the nature of analysis has diverged as well, from maternal feminist views which sought a place for women in the past, through marxist and radical views with agendas, to an emphasis on gender itself. The readings offered here represent three different views from that literature. The first, by Sara Brooks Sundberg, on "Farm Women on the Canadian Prairie Frontier: The Helpmate Image" is the more traditional and

places women solidly within the farm structure "as homemakers, home manufacturers, field hands and wage earners" as well as nurses. From her analysis
of reminiscences Sunberg concludes: "Although women's responsibilities on the
farm meant hard work, prairie women did not unanimously agree that their
work on the farm was drudgery."

In the second reading in this chapter, Star Rosenthal's "Union Maids:
Organized Women Workers in Vancouver 1900-1915," the relationship of women
and work is placed within the union structure in which women faced injustice
not just from employers but from male unionists, who practised "overt discrimination" against both non-white and female workers. While the prejudice
against non-whites has been acknowledged, trade unions today "refuse by and
large to see the parallels to their attitudes towards women workers." Rosenthal's
"union maids" struggled in a hostile environment. The third selection,
"Feminization of the Labour Process in the Communication Industry: The Case
of the Telephone Operators, 1876-1904" by Michèle Martin, is solidly within
the "New Social History" with its emphasis on concepts and methodology.
Martin reviews the evolution of studies on women's work and offers her analysis of a "female job ghetto" with low pay based on "sexually stereotyped
requirements."

Suggestions for Further Reading

Acton, Janice, Penny Goldsmith and Bonnie Shepard eds., *Women at Work. Ontario,*
1850-1930. Toronto: Canadian Women's Educational Press, 1974.

Bourne, Paula, *Women's Paid and Unpaid Work: Historical and Contemporary*
Perspectives. Toronto: New Hogtown Press, 1985.

Bradbury, Bettina, "Women's History and Working Class History," *Labour/Le Travail,*
19 (Spring 1987), 23-43.

Briskin, Linda and Lynda Yanz, eds., *Union Sisters: Women in the Labour Movement.*
Toronto: The Woman's Press, 1983.

Carroll, William K. and Rennie Warburton, "Feminism, Class Consciousness and
Household-Work Linkages among Registered Nurses in Victoria," *Labour/Le Travail,*
24 (Fall l989), 131-145.

Kealey, Linda, "Canadian Socialism and the Woman Question, 1900-1914," *Labour/Le*
Travail, 13 (Fall 1984), 77-100.

Kinnear, Mary, " 'Do you Want your Daughter to Marry a Farmer?': Women's Work on
the Farm, 1922," in *Canadian Papers in Rural History,* ed. Donald H. Akenson.
Vol. VI. Gananoque: Langdale Press, 1988, 137-153.

Lindstron-Best, Varpu, "'I Won't be a Slave!' - Finnish Domestics in Canada, 1911-30,"
in *Looking into My Sister's Eyes: An Exploration in Women's History,* ed. Jean
Burnet. Toronto: Multicultural History Society of Ontario, 1986, 33-53.

Parr, Joy, *The Gender of Bread Winners: Women, Men, and Change in Two Industrial*
Towns 1880-1950. Toronto: University of Toronto Press, 1990.

Roberts, Wayne, *Honest Womanhood: Feminism, Femininity and Class Consciousness*
Among Toronto Working Women, 1893 to 1914. Toronto: New Hogtown Press, 1976.

Sangster, Joan, "The 1907 Bell Telephone Strike: Organizing Women Workers," *Labour/Le Travailleur*, 3 (1978), 109-130.

Strong-Boag, Veronica, "Keeping House in God's Country: Canadian Women at Work in the Home," in *On the Job: Confronting the Labour Process in Canada*, ed. Craig Heron and Robert Storey. Montreal: McGill-Queen's, 1986, 124-151.

_____, "Pulling in Double Harness or Hauling a Double Load: Women, Work and Feminism on the Canadian Prairie," *Journal of Canadian Studies*, XXI, no. 3 (Fall 1986), 32-52.

Tillotson, Shirley, "'We May all Soon be "First-Class Men': Gender and Skill in Canada's Early Twentieth Century Urban Telegraph Industry," *Labour/Le Travail*, 27 (Spring 1991), 97-125.

Trofimenkoff, Susan, "One Hundred and Two Muffled Voices: Canada's Industrial Women in the 1880s," *Atlantis*, III, no. 1 (Fall 1977), 66-82.

FARM WOMEN ON THE CANADIAN FRONTIER: THE HELPMATE IMAGE

Sara Brooks Sundberg

'Poor girl!' say the kind friends. 'She went West and married a farmer'—and forthwith a picture of the farmer's wife rises up before their eyes; the poor, faded woman ... hair the color of last year's grass, and teeth gone in front.[1]

In the case of farm life on the grassland frontiers of western Canada there is little argument that life was difficult for women. Nevertheless, women were part of the earliest efforts to establish agricultural settlements on the prairie and plains of the western interior of Canada. What were the experiences of these women, and how did they respond to pioneer life in the grasslands?

Previous attempts to answer these questions have not revealed women's experiences in all their variety. Instead what has emerged are images that obscure differences between individual women's experiences. Responding to these images, this study examines, from the perspective of women themselves, one image of pioneer farm women on the Canadian prairies—that of pioneer farm women as helpmates.

In her analysis of the helpmate image for frontiers-women in the United States, Beverly Stoeltje writes, "the primary defining feature of [helpmates] was their ability to fulfill their duties which enabled their men to succeed, and to handle crises with competence and without complaint."[2] Carl Dawson and Eva R. Younge, in *Pioneering in the Prairie Provinces: The Social Side of the Settlement Process,* expresses this image when they use this description to depict the experiences of pioneer farm women in Canada:

As for the pioneer woman, what shall we say? When her man was at home she stood shoulder to shoulder with him in the conduct of the day's affairs. When he was absent ... she cared for the family, she looked after the stock, she took upon her lone shoulders burdens which were none too light for husband and wife to bear.[3]

Because a pioneer woman's experiences were tied to the needs of her husband and family she, as June Sochen explains in her study of frontier women, "is not the prime mover in her life. She does not determine her own individual destiny."[4] This image is taken to its gloomy extreme in the following interpretation of prairie women's lives:

A prairie woman's life was defined by the needs of her family. When her children left, the habit of working remained. Tasks which once were necessary for survival now had no point, yet they had become so much a part of her that only death could bring release.[5]

Another dimension of the image of pioneer women as helpmates is the notion that farm work for pioneer women was drudgery. A recent study of Canadian prairie women describes farm life for pioneer women in dreary terms:

For the typical pioneer woman, life was a hectic chorus of mend, weed, pump, chop, churn, bake and scrub. If she had children—and families tended to be large in those days—they added their giggles and howls.[6]

The monotony of pioneer life was intensified by the isolation of the prairie frontier. Women stoically endured these hardships because, as prairie pioneer Nellie McClung explained, they were just too busy to complain.[7]

But Nellie McClung also observed "that people love to generalize; to fit cases to their theory, they love to find ... farmers' wives shabby, discouraged and sad."[8] Women's writings challenge these images and generalizations. Autobiographies, letters, journals, and reminiscences recount the experiences of women as wives, mothers, daughters, and single women on the frontier. They are some of the sources used in this essay. These women are not representative of pioneer farm woman as a whole. Instead they are a small group of women who had the ability and the inclination to record their experiences and attitudes. In some cases women wrote contemporary accounts, in others they relied upon memory. Regardless of these distinctions and limitations, women's writing still clearly reveal a rich variety of experiences which are useful in examining images of pioneer farm women in the grasslands.

Most Canadian pioneer women came to the grasslands in one of two migrations. The first wave began about 1870 and lasted until the late 1890s. Prior to 1870 the grasslands were part of Rupert's Land, a broad expanse of territory, controlled by the Hudson Bay Company. Its boundaries lay between the Red River in the east and the Rocky Mountains in the west. In 1870, the Canadian government acquired Rupert's Land from the Hudson Bay Company and the grasslands began to be recognized for its agricultural potential. Settlers from various parts of Ontario, the United States, and Europe trickled into the grasslands.

By the late 1890s, a second, larger migration began. Promising free homesteads and assisted passages, the Canadian government and the Canadian Pacific Railway launched vigorous advertising campaigns to encourage agricultural settlement within the grasslands. Partially as a result of these campaigns, significant numbers of settlers from the United States, Great Britain, the Balkans, the Ukraine, and Russia immigrated to the grasslands of Canada. The rapid influx of settlers during this second migration lasted until about World War I. The pioneer experiences of most women cited in this study fall between 1870 and 1914.

The beginnings of the first migration to Canada coincided with the passage of Homestead legislation in 1872, which provided settlers with 160 acres of land for a ten dollar fee, providing they plowed the land, built a shelter, and lived on the property for six months out of a year for three years. The lure of cheap land, the chance for economic independence, captured the imaginations of women as well as men. Sarah Roberts, an early twentieth-century Alberta pioneer, remembered that land was a major factor influencing her family's decision to move from Illinois to Canada, "We had lived for years in Illinois where land is priced at one hundred dollars per acre. No doubt the thought of receiving 480 acres 'free' made more of an appeal to us than was justified."[9] It is important to note that Sarah Roberts included herself as part of the decision-making process to move west. Her participation in this process is contrary to the notion that women did not affect decisions concerning their futures and the futures of their families.

In fact, women were sometimes the first to recognize the opportunities inherent in western land. In 1880 Letitia McCurdy Mooney persuaded her husband that the future of their children depended upon their opportunity to acquire fertile land. Letitia's daughter, Nellie Mooney McClung, recalled her mother's persuasive argument to move west:

> "We'll have to go some place, John," she said one night to my father. "There's nothing here for our three boys. What can we do with one-hundred-and-fifty stony acres? The boys will be hired-men all their lives, or clerks in a store. That's not good enough!"
>
> Father was fearful! There were Indians to consider, not only Indians, but mosquitoes. He had seen on the Ottawa what mosquitoes could do to horses; and to people too. No! It was better to leave well enough alone.[10]

Clara Goodwin, another late nineteenth-century Manitoba pioneer, remembered "my mother had visited Winnipeg the year before and was very much taken with the West. I remember quite distinctly her saying to my father, 'Richard, you MUST go to that country! That's the place to live!'"[11]

Sometimes it was not just the economic opportunities that persuaded women to suggest moving their families to the west. Letters from friends and family exerted a strong influence. Lulu Beatrice Wilken recalled that her mother was persuaded to go west to Saskatchewan by her brother Edward:

> So he wrote to her to try to persuade Father to move his family West and to take up land also.
>
> I am sure that it did not take long to convince Father of the advantages to be obtained in such a move, and, in the spring of 1891, Mother took her three small children and joined her brother.[12]

For Muriel Parsloe it was not enticements from family members, but a sense of adventure that caused her to initiate her family's move to Swan Lake, Manitoba. After reading an advertisement for western Canadian land she said, "We've tried Australia, let's take a trip to Canada and see how we get on there."[13]

A more conventional reason brought Kathleen Strange to the grasslands. It was because of their doctor's recommendation that Kathleen Strange and her husband purchased a farm in the remote area of Fenn, Alberta, in 1920. The active outdoor life of a farm in the west was their doctor's prescription for an injury received by Kathleen's husband in World War I.[14]

Unmarried women also came to farms in the grasslands. Western farmland offered these women a means for achieving economic independence. Land was not "free" for these women. Women could not obtain "free" homesteads unless they were the sole support for their families. Qualified women took advantage of this opportunity. A women's column in a 1914 issue of the *Grain Grower's Guide* carried this appeal:

> Dear Miss Beynon: I am writing to ask for a great favor for a very deserving widow with children. She wants to homestead and has not the wherewithal to look about.... perhaps some of the kind sisters know of one suitable for mixed farming....[Intending Homesteader][15]

A notable example of a successful woman homesteader during this period is Georgina Binnie-Clark. For a period of about five years between 1909 and 1914, Binnie-Clark owned and operated her own wheat farm in the Qu'Appelle Valley in Saskatchewan. In her book *Wheat and Woman,* Binnie-Clark detailed her farming experiences and argued the case for farming as a means of achieving economic independence for women.[16]

Unmarried women came to farms in the grasslands for other purposes as well. In 1886 the Canadian Pacific Railway issued a questionnaire asking women about their lives in the Northwest Territories. One of the questions read, "Can hard-working honest girls easily obtain situations at good wages on farms or [in] households in the North-West...." A concise reply came from Mrs. T. D. Elliott in Alexandria. She answers, "1. Good girls can get plenty of good places at good wages then marry good young men with good farms."[17] Opportunities for women in farm homes as domestics or home-helps promised gains for women in other ways besides wages. The shortage of females on the frontier was a prominent theme in appeals for female immigrants to the west. This theme was evident in the *MacLeod Gazette* of May 15, 1896:

> "Do you know" remarked W. D. Scott to a Toronto newspaper reporter, "one of the greatest needs in the North West at the present time? It is women, simply women. Married men with their wives are contented enough out there, but single men on farms are apt to get lonely. If girls could only be persuaded to go out there they would be sure of good situations, and I tell you it would not be long before they would get married."[18]

Educated middle-class women from the British Isles were prime targets for these appeals. At the turn-of-the-century the British Isles found itself saddled with an over-supply of single, middle-class women unable to find suitable jobs. Employment and marriage opportunities in the Canadian west offered relief to these women. In her book *West-Nor'-West,* published in 1890, Jessie Saxby, herself a middle-class British widow, expressed this concern:

> In Britain one of the most urgent social difficulties is what to do with our surplus women—how to provide for them, how to find remunerative employment for them. In Canada one of the most urgent social difficulties is how to persuade women to come there.... In Quebec, in Winnipeg, in Regina, everywhere, I was told the same thing. "Oh, if respectable women from the old country would come out West!"[19]

To assure the successful adaptation of British emigrant gentlewomen to the west, emigration societies and training schools were established to provide information about the west and to instruct women in necessary domestic skills.

Women did not always have a choice of whether to stay in their present circumstances or to take a chance in a new land. Edna Jaques' family migrated from Ontario to Moose Jaw, Saskatchewan, in 1902. She remembered her father announcing they would leave for Moose Jaw:

> His name was Robert Jaques. He came to visit dad one day in January 1902. They were in the parlor talking and laughing together.... Suddenly the folding doors between the two rooms opened and dad stood in the doorway (I can see him yet) and loudly announced to my mother, "We're leaving Collingwood." Taking a long breath he said, "We're going homesteading in the Northwest Territories...."
> My mother fainted.[20]

Nevertheless, after the initial shock some women adapted to the idea, as did Jessie Raber's mother. Jessie Raber remembered that even though it was her father's idea to take up a homestead near Lacombe, Alberta, in 1895, her mother soon recognized the economic and social advantages of the move.

Mother said perhaps she had been selfish in not being anxious to move to a farm in Canada before, for she knew that a growing family did need plenty of room. The milk, fresh eggs and the wonderful vegetables one could grow in Canada: for she did want us all to grow up into strong and healthy men and women, with good educations.[21]

Other women remained unconvinced of the advantages of a westward move. Clara Middleton "had no urge to go adventuring," but went along because "Homer was bent on it [and] that was enough for me."[22] Laura Salverson simply resigned herself to the inevitable, "And now George had the grand vision of the independent life of a landowner.... There was nothing to be done about it, except to let the disease run a swift unhindered course."[23]

Without the satisfaction that comes from participation in an important decision and without the confidence that comes from belief in the promise of a new land, women's journeys to Canada could be painful experiences. Maria Adamowska's family emigrated from the Ukraine to Alberta in 1899. She recalled her mother's sad experience:

Mother, on the other hand, was tenderhearted. Of all the trials that had been her lot in life, this one was the most bitter. Whenever father had mentioned going to Canada, she had started to cry. And she cried all the way on the train and missed seeing the lovely sights in God's good world.[24]

The experience of this unhappy emigrant woman fits one aspect of the helpmate image. That is, in this instance, Maria Adamowska's mother did not determine her own future. However, clearly this is not true for all women on the frontier. Women came to the grassland frontiers for themselves, as well as for others, and when they did come for others, they were energetic, as well as reluctant, pioneers.

Whatever their reasons for coming to the grasslands, women worked when they arrived. As prairie homesteader Georginia Binnie-Clark observed "On a prairie settlement the women work ... I owe one debt to my life on the prairie and that is a fair appreciation of my own sex."[25] For married women, the home was the hub of pioneer farm women's work. In her study of frontier women's work, Susan Armitage identifies two categories of household work. The first category, household maintenance, involves routine activities, such as cooking and cleaning.[26] The lack of mechanical aids made their chores time consuming. The experience of Laura Salverson's mother, an Icelandic immigrant, illustrated this fact, "Mama was forever busy. She had a passion for keeping things scoured and scrubbed.... When you carried water from a pump half a block away or melted snow after the winter set in, all this washing and cleaning consumed a lot of time."[27] In another example, Kathleen Strange remembered a dreaded chore, wash day:

Washing! What a job that always was. Usually it took me the entire day. In summer I washed outside; in winter, down in the basement. The boiling, sudsy water had to be carried in pails from the stove to wherever my tubs were set. More than once I burned myself severely, spilling water on unprotected hands and legs.[28]

Nevertheless, some women found satisfaction in these routine chores. Edna Jaques recalled the "glow" on her mother's face as the wash emerged "whiter than white."[29] Lulu Beatrice Wilken remembered the pride her mother felt in the polished appearance of the floor in their sod shack. Years of washing with hot sudsy water made it smooth and white.[30]

It was not just the lack of conveniences that made chores time consuming. It was also the number of people requiring women's care. Because children were potential laborers, large families were an asset. Women often had several children to tend, in addition to housekeeping chores. Jessie Raber, daughter of immigrant parents who homesteaded in Alberta during the early 1900s, remarked on her mother's experience, "Mother often wished she could bundle us all off to school or somewhere. Just think, seven [children] under her feet all day and every day. Such patience she must have had."[31]

The number of people in a household was enlarged in other ways as well. Hospitality was an integral part of frontier life and an important social custom. Saskatchewan pioneer Harriet Neville remembered "No stranger was ever refused meals or shelter night or day at our home."[32] Sometimes women turned this custom to profit by taking boarders and earning a wage.

It should be noted here that daughters, like their mothers, worked on the family farm. Often they assumed their mother's chores, thereby reducing their mother's overall workload. For example, as a teenager, Jessie Raber assumed responsibility for much of the cooking and for care of the younger children.[33] In some cases daughters' chores as surrogate mothers came at an early age. Because both her parents worked outside the home, Veronica Kokotailo, even though she was only five years old at the time, took care of the younger children![34] Daughters also worked as field hands. Nellie McClung recalled overseeing the cattle rather than going to school.[35]

Daughters contributed to the family's economic well-being in other ways. In some cases they worked as home-helps, a term applied to domestic help, to earn wages to assist their parents. Ukrainian immigrant Anna Farion remembered her work as a home-help. "My work was harder than the year before as there were four children, and four or five hired men to look after. But I stuck it out, as I wanted to help my parents as much as I could."[36] In another way Anna's experience illustrates the hardships some immigrant girls and women experienced. Earning only a few dollars a month, Anna requested a raise. Her employer "brushed me off with the rejoinder that she had trained me for the job and, besides, she had paid Kolessar $5.00 for me. Her words hurt me deeply. Evidently, I had been sold...."[37]

Not all immigrant girls and women working as home-helps encountered discriminatory treatment of this kind. In an effort to evaluate employment opportunities for British women, Elizabeth Keith Morris travelled throughout western Canada during the early part of the twentieth century. She considered the position of home-help suitable employment for capable British women:

> The position of home help is a safe, cheap and sure way of earning capital to start in other work, of learning Canadian methods and requirements, and of feeling one's feet in a new country; but the work is hard and heavy including washing, ironing, baking, scrubbing, ... therefore, only to be undertaken by the robust.[38]

The second category of frontier women's work was household sustenance. Armitage defines household sustenance as "work which contributed directly to family economy by making cash expenditure unnecessary."[39] Farm women were manufacturers in their own homes. Harriet Neville used skins to make "hoods, mittens, muffs and necks" as well as spinning wool to make clothing, bed mattresses and quilts.[40] The daily entries of Mrs. Seward St. John revealed she made butter and raised chickens to use in trade for other goods.[41] Lulu Wilken remembered "Soap making is an art, ... The fat and lye water had to be boiled to the right stage, and the proper proportions of water and grease maintained or they would separate and it became a failure."[42] Mrs. Emma Phair remembered that her mother manufactured the fuel necessary for their cooking stove. "She knew just how many twists of straw it took to heat the oven for baking.... It took one hundred and twenty five twists to heat the oven; four bags altogether to heat the oven and bake the bread."[43]

Women's contributions to sustenance reached beyond the domestic sphere. They worked as field hands. Late nineteenth-century homesteader Harriet Neville drove the oxen while her husband pitched hay.[44] Another Saskatchewan pioneer, Mrs. Edward Watson, noted that she and her children built their sod barn,[45] and Sarah Roberts helped to brand cattle.[46] Some women, like Georgina Binnie-Clark preferred outdoor work. She wrote:

> I worked hard through June at the stoning, and started to harrow ... From the beginning I was perfectly happy working on the land, only I wished it was someone else's turn to get those tiresome three meals a day.[47]

Sarah Roberts, on the other hand, said of her branding job: "I stayed with my job until it was done, and I am glad that I never had to do it again. I think that it is not a woman's work except that it is everyone's work to do the thing he needs to do."[48] Veronica Kokotailo's mother must have agreed. For two weeks she worked for a neighbor plastering his barn. Her payment was a pail of potatoes.[49]

Aside from their responsibilities as homemakers, home manufacturers, field hands, and wage earners, women performed other important functions. They were nurses and doctors for their families and neighbors. In a letter written to her grandmother from her family's Saskatchewan homestead, Maryanne

Caswell described picking herbs for medicinal purposes.[50] Ukrainian immigrant, Maria Adamowska remembered, "As I was reaping with a sickle, I cut my finger. The gash was so deep that the finger dangled, just barely held on by the skin. Mother managed to splice it somehow, and the wound healed."[51] Even in the prairie town a woman's medical skills were relied upon. As late as 1930, Fredelle Maynard, a young resident of the town of Birch Hills, Saskatchewan, recalled that a doctor's responsibilities were limited to declaring quarantine and delivering babies.[52] In more isolated areas women acted as midwives, even if they were inexperienced. Clara Middleton described such an experience:

> We got home about midnight and at one o'clock came Mr. Barnes. His wife was in labour, and would I come? I protested that I wouldn't be any good, that I knew nothing.... No; his wife wanted me.
> "It's up to you," said my husband, but I knew by his tone that he had no doubts. I could almost hear him thinking, "You're a woman and you're needed."[53]

The thoughts of Clara's husband are a fitting description of women's work on the prairie. Women performed whatever work was needed. Regardless of training or experience women were expected to be self-reliant. Sometimes the responsibilities of self-reliance could soften women's adjustment to the isolation of the frontier. For example, Clara Middleton remembered that women acted as morticians as well as doctors. The ritual of preparing a body for burial provided women the opportunity to support and comfort one another.[54] In another example, Harriet Neville, finding herself isolated from nearby schools during the winter of 1884-1885, ordered textbooks from Toronto and kept regular school hours for her children. Of this experience she said, "One thing these things did for me. I never had a moment to be lonely to feel the lack of neighbors. I slept well and did not dream so much about old friends."[55]

Nevertheless, the challenge of self reliance proved too great for some women. On their way to their homestead in Manitoba, Nellie McClung remembered encountering a family returning from the prairie. The wife, dressed in a silk dress and flimsy shoes, was sobbing. She tearfully explained, "She hated the country ... it was only fit for Indians and squaws...." In an effort to comfort the woman, Nellie's mother suggested that perhaps the woman would be more comfortable travelling in simple clothes. The roads were muddy, sturdy shoes and gingham dresses were more practical. The woman did not sew, her mother had always done her sewing. "Mother's zeal began to flag, 'Take her back,' she said to Willard, 'she's not the type that makes a pioneer.' "[56]

The confining nature of women's work was a different source of discontent for women. Peace River pioneer Ida Scharf Hopkins articulated this frustration:

> Much as the woman becomes completely involved in the homestead life many of the challenges become repetitive....

We women were never unhappy, but sometimes life was a bit dull. There was so little variety in the day-by-day routine. So much necessary work to be done there was little time or energy left for anything else. We had to keep the homefires burning.[57]

But women did appreciate their vigorous lives on the frontier prairie. Saskatchewan pioneer Alice Rendell illustrated this when she wrote to a friend in 1904:

I would never advise anyone to come out here who is the least afraid of work. They are better off at home. There is plenty of room to breathe in this country and if the work is hard the freedom, which is the indispensable attribute of life here, makes one far less susceptible to physical fatigue.... Here one feels that each week's work is a step onward whilst in the old country oftentimes a year's toil brought nothing but disappointment and additional anxiety.[58]

Kathleen Strange, like Alice Rendell, appreciated freedom. For Kathleen, pioneer life offered a new opportunity to work as a full partner with her husband. She missed this partnership in her later, less rigorous role of a city wife:

My own life, on the other hand, is almost completely changed. And, most important of all, I am deprived of one particularly vital thing. On the farm I was a *real* partner with my husband, sharing with him in almost every detail of his daily work. Now his work is carried on in a downtown office, with professional help. There is little I can do to assist him.[59]

Prairie farm women like Kathleen Strange were, indeed partners with their husbands, not only because they shared in their husbands' day-to-day work, but also because of their own day-to-day responsibilities. Farm women's roles as homemakers, home manufacturers, field hands, wage earners, doctors, morticians, and teachers meant that women made substantial contributions to the business of farming. These contributions receive inadequate recognition when interpreted from the perspective of women as helpmates. Viewed as ancillary to the work of farm men, our conception of prairie farm women's work loses equality within the economic structure of the farm, an equality which is justified given women's roles as providers of valuable goods and services.

In a similar way the diversity of prairie farm women's experiences is lost when they are assigned the blanket role of helpmate. Women in this study reveal that it is a mistake to assume that all women on farms were wives and mothers. Single women were farmers in their own right, and they worked on farms as home-helps or domestics. Women's experiences also reveal that contrary to the image of women as obedient helpmates, some women did affect the decision-making process which led to their pioneer experiences in the grasslands. Some women actively participated in the decision-making process, others made the decision solely on their own.

Women's experiences differed in other important ways as well. Although women's responsibilities on the farm meant hard work, prairie women did not unanimously agree that their work on the farm was drudgery. The notion of universal drudgery, more than any other aspect of the helpmate image, deprives women of any possibility of joy or fulfillment in the process of pioneering. Prairie women's experiences reveal that although some women found their chores monotonous and confining, others felt obvious pride in their accomplishments. Some even found their responsibilities to be useful buffers between themselves and the loneliness of the frontier. Others appreciated the freedom and opportunity resulting from their work. As Kathleen Strange perceptively observed, "Drudgery! That is a word with many connotations. What is drudgery to one person may not be drudgery at all to another."[60]

The image of the stoic, hardworking helpmate not only homogenizes prairie women's experiences, it leaves some experiences out altogether. What about the women who could not cope with frontier life on the prairie? What factors made the difference between success and failure? We lose part of the story of women who stayed, when we ignore those who left.

The experiences of women in this study raise more questions than they provide answers. Yet the diversity of experiences revealed in women's writings admonish us to look more closely at our images of pioneer farm women on the Canadian prairie.

Notes

1. Nellie McClung, *In Times Like These* (1915; reprint ed. Toronto: University of Toronto Press, 1972), p. 109.

2. Beverly Stoeltje, " 'A Helpmate for Man Indeed': The Image of the Frontier Woman," *Journal of American Folklore* 88 (January-March 1975): 32.

3. Gerald Willoughby, *Retracing the Old Trail* (Saskatoon, 1933) quoted in C. Dawson and E. R. Younge, *Pioneering in the Prairie Provinces: The Social Side of the Settlement Process,* Canadian Frontiers of Settlement Series, Vol. 8 (Toronto: The Macmillan Co. of Canada Ltd., 1934), p. 19.

4. June Sochen, "Frontier Women: A Model for All Women?" *South Dakota History* 7 (1), 1976: 36.

5. The Corrective Collective, *Never Done: Three Centuries of Women's Work in Canada* (Toronto: Canadian Women's Educational Press, 1974), p. 54.

6. Linda Rasmussen, et al., *A Harvest Yet to Reap: A History of Prairie Women* (Toronto: The Women's Press, 1976), p. 42.

7. Ibid., pp. 42-43.

8. McClung, p. 109.

9. Sarah Ellen Roberts, *Alberta Homestead: Chronicle of a Pioneer Family,* Lathrope E. Roberts, ed. (Austin: University of Texas Press, 1971), p. 4.

10. Nellie McClung, *Clearing in the West* (New York: Fleming H. Revell Company, 1936), p. 32.

11. Audrey Peterkin and Margaret Shaw, *Mrs. Doctor: Reminiscences of Manitoba Doctors' Wives* (Winnipeg: The Prairie Publishing Company, 1976), p. 2.

12. Lulu Beatrice Wilken, "Homesteading in Saskatchewan," *Canada West Magazine* 7 (Spring 1977): 27.

13. Muriel Jardine Parsloe, *A Parson's Daughter* (London: Faber and Faber Ltd., 1935), p. 220.

14. Kathleen Strange, *With the West in Her Eyes* (Toronto: George J. McLeod, Ltd., 1937), p. 8.

15. "Sunshine," *The Grain Grower's Guide,* 11 March 1914, p. 20.

16. Georgina Binnie-Clark, *Wheat and Woman* (1914; reprint ed. Toronto: University of Toronto Press, 1979).

17. Canadian Pacific Railway, *What Women Say of the Canadian Northwest* (n.p. 1886), p. 32.

18. *MacLeod Gazette,* 15 May 1896 quoted in Rasmussen, et al., p. 14.

19. Jessie M. E. Saxby, *West-Nor'-West* (London: James Nisbet and Company, 1890), p. 100.

20. Edna Jaques, *Uphill All the Way: The Autobiography of Edna Jaques* (Saskatoon, Saskatchewan: Western Producer Prairie Books, 1977), p. 14.

21. Jessie Browne Raber, *Pioneering in Alberta* (New York: Exposition Press, Inc., 1951), p. 10.

22. Clara and J. E. Middleton, *Green Fields Afar* (Toronto: The Ryerson Press, 1947), p. 12.

23. Laura Salverson, *Confessions of an Immigrant's Daughter* (London: Faber and Faber Ltd., 1939), p. 480.

24. Maria Adamowska, "Beginnings in Canada," in *Land of Pain; Land of Promise: First Person Accounts by Ukrainian Pioneers 1891-1914* trans. Harry Piniuta (Saskatoon, Saskatchewan: Western Producer Prairie Books, 1978), p. 54.

25. Georgina Binnie-Clark, *A Summer on the Canadian Prairie* (London: Edward Arnold, 1910), p. 278.

26. Susan Armitage, "Household Work and Childrearing on the Frontier: The Oral History Record," *Sociology and Social Research* 63 (3): 469.

27. Salverson, p. 37.

28. Strange, p. 220.

29. Jaques, p. 105.

30. Wilken, p. 28.

31. Raber, p. 67.

32. Harriet Johnson Neville, "Pioneering in the North-West Territories," Harriet Purdy and David Gagan, eds. *Canada: An Historical Magazine* 2 (June 1975): 42.

33. Raber, pp. 136-137 and 140-141.

34. Anne B. Woywitka, "A Roumanian Pioneer," *Alberta History* 21 (4) 1973: 22-23.

35. McClung, *Clearing in the West*, p. 116.

36. Anna Farion, "Homestead Girlhood," in *Land of Pain; Land of Promise*, p. 92.

37. Ibid., p. 91.

38. Elizabeth Keith Morris, *An Englishwoman in the Canadian West* (Bristol: J. W. Arrowsmith or London: Simpkin Marshall, 1913), p. 188.

39. Armitage, p. 469.

40. Neville, pp. 48-51.

41. Seward T. St. John, "Mrs. St. John's Diary," *Saskatchewan History* 2 (Autumn 1949): 25 and 29.

42. Wilken, p. 29.

43. Isabel M. Reekie, *Along the Old Melita Trail* (Saskatoon, Saskatchewan: Modern Press, 1965), p. 49.

44. Neville, p. 20.

45. Mrs. Edward Watson, "Reminiscences of Mrs. Edward Watson," *Saskatchewan History* 5 (Spring 1952): 67.

46. Roberts, p. 226.

47. Binnie-Clark, *Wheat and Woman*, p. 151.

48. Roberts, p. 226.

49. Woywitka, p. 22.

50. Maryanne Caswell, *Pioneer Girl* (McGraw-Hill Co. of Canada Ltd., 1964), 10th letter.

51. Adamowska, p. 67.

52. Fredelle Bruser Maynard, *Raisins and Almonds* (Toronto: Doubleday Canada, Ltd., 1972), p. 16.

53. Middleton, p. 48.

54. Ibid., p. 51.

55. Neville, p. 30.

56. McClung, *Clearing in the West*, p. 58.

57. Ida Scharf Hopkins, *To the Peace River Country and On* (Richmond, British Columbia: The Author, 1973), pp. 118-119.

58. Alice Rendell, "Letters from a Barr Colonist," *Alberta Historical Review* (Winter 1963): 24-25.

59. Strange, p. 292.

60. Ibid., p. 276.

UNION MAIDS: ORGANIZED WOMEN WORKERS IN VANCOUVER 1900-1915

Star Rosenthal

The history of women in the labour force is by and large a neglected area of study, especially with regard to trade unionism. For British Columbia in the early years of this century, while there are various accounts of men's union struggles, there does not exist at present any published secondary material on the union activity of women. This article will attempt to give a preliminary account of the organization of some women workers in Vancouver during the period from 1900 to 1915.

Research on such a topic is full of problems. Women's organizing efforts are recorded in scattered fashion throughout old labour newspapers and minutes of meetings, but the records are fragmentary and often ambiguous. It is extremely rare to find accounts by the women themselves, so their motivations are often a matter of speculation. The failure of historians and trade unionists of the time to record women's activities has contributed to a present lack of knowledge of this area. The main chronicles of labour history in B.C. and Canada ignore the very existence of women workers, let alone their union activity.[1] The earlier failure to record information probably stemmed from a belief that women's struggles were unimportant or insignificant in a historical context. The failure of later historians to retrieve what data exist seems to reflect this same belief.

As a consequence of this ignorance of the role of women in the labour movement, various myths have arisen. One, of course, is that women have not attempted to organize in the past. Another, which was also prevalent in the earlier period, is that women are in fact unorganizable. This latter myth was in the past based simply on prejudice against women, but nowadays uses the erroneous historical myth as a rationale.

The trade union movement has both shared in and propagated these assumptions. Then and now a male-dominated movement, it has a tendency to view women as reactionary, materialistic and non-class-conscious. Their supposed nonparticipation in trade unionism is blamed on "false consciousness" and "femininity," and because of this, female workers, especially in white-collar occupations, tend to be ignored when unions conduct organizing drives. Thus the myth of unorganizability is perpetuated. For example, until very recently mainstream trade unions did not make any significant effort to organize bank workers, who are mostly female. It took a small, independent and feminist union in B.C., the Service, Office and Retail Workers' Union of Canada, to change this situation. They conducted a drive to organize these workers, re-

From *BC Studies*, no.41 (Spring 1979), 36-55. Reprinted by permission of *BC Studies*.

ceived a good response, took their case to the Labour Relations Board, and won the right for bank workers to be unionized. As soon as SORWUC's success became apparent, the labour movement jumped on the bandwagon and allocated funds and a female organizer to start its own drive for a bank workers' union.

The labour movement in the early part of this century had much the same attitude towards women as the modern trade unionists. Women were often seen as a threat to male job security, and instead of the unions trying to organize them, the response to this "threat" was to admonish women to remain in the home. Also, the medical misconceptions of the day led people to believe, for example, that work in factories wasn't healthy for women specifically, rather than leading them to push for improved health and safety standards for all workers. These factors contributed to resolutions such as the following put forward by the Dominion Trades and Labor Council in their 1903 platform of principles. They called for "abolition of child labor by children under 14 years of age; and of female labor in all branches of industrial life, such as mines, workshops, factories, etc."[2]

Ten years later attitudes had not changed. At a meeting of the Vancouver Trades and Labor Council (VTLC) in 1913, a delegate from the Moulders' Union presented a motion that women not be employed in foundries, as "we consider such labor for women is physically, mentally and in every way detrimental to the sex and consequently to the race."[3] This motion was endorsed by the Council.

By 1915, however, some change was made in official policy, at least. The annual convention of the Trades and Labour Congress of Canada discussed amending the 1903 principle cited above to read: "Abolition of child labour by children under sixteen years of age and the establishing of the principle of equal pay for equal work for men and women."[4] It is unclear if this amendment passed.

In looking at the history of women in the labour movement, it is interesting to note that there are some obvious parallels to the history of non-white workers. Overt discrimination was practised especially against Chinese, Japanese and East Indians by the society at large, and this was reflected in the union movement. The same kinds of myths grew up about these workers as grew up about female workers, that they were potential scabs rather than potential union comrades.

In every labour newspaper of the period, there are repeated calls for bans on immigration, boycotts of businesses owned by Asian people or businesses which employed them, and general racist comments, such as by the Press Agent for the Waiters and Waitresses Union, who termed Orientals "yellow objects."[5] Instead of trying to establish a feeling of solidarity with immigrant and female workers, the labour movement fell back on the rhetoric of "unorganizability," and its solution to all of these low-wage workers was to send them back where they came from, either across the seas or to the kitchen. The outstanding exception appears to have been the Industrial Workers of the World, who interestingly enough advocated both the organization of Asiatics[6] and the active participation of women (such as Elizabeth Gurley Flynn) as leaders and members.

Both Japanese and native Indian workers attempted to organize at times during these years, but were subject to sabotage by the racist attitudes of the other workers. In 1893, for example, Japanese fishermen were asked to support a strike by the Fraser River Fishermen's Protective and Benevolent Association, but were turned down when they wanted to join the Association. An offer of $500 to the Association, to help them set up their own Japanese Fishermen's union, was also rejected. In 1900 they did set up their own Japanese Fishermen's Benevolent Society, with 1,250 members, which took a leading part in the strike of Fraser River Fishermen in 1900. Native Indians took part in this, as they had in the 1893 strike. Native Indians were also organizing in the lumber industry, and formed the main part of the IWW Lumber Handlers' Union, around 1906.[7]

Nowadays, trade unions have changed their line on the unorganizability of non-white workers, and generally look back on this period of their history with shame. They acknowledge that their past attitudes and policies in this respect stemmed from prejudice.[8] Strangely, though, they refuse by and large to see the parallels to their attitudes towards women workers.

Women, however, *did* organize, despite the lack of support from their union brothers. They joined male unions, formed their own locals, and even their own separate unions in many of the main occupations in which they were employed. In addition to this, they gave active support to men's union struggles, and organized campaigns to buy only union-made goods in what they called "Label" campaigns. Their organizations during this period were generally short-lived, but their failure seems to be due more to objective conditions such as economic depression, lack of labour movement support, lack of legislative protection and political power, than to what historian Wayne Roberts, criticizing recent historical studies, refers to as the "allegedly warped personality structure of their femininity."[9]

This article aims, through a compilation of primary source materials, to recover for the reader a general outline of Vancouver women's early trade union activities. Hopefully, with the presentation of factual data, it will be seen that, just as the history of non-white workers has been distorted by prejudice, so has the history of women workers.

At the turn of the century, women's place in the labour force was changing. While the majority of wage-earning female workers remained in such occupations as domestic service, positions such as sales clerk were becoming "women's work" and still others, such as telephone operators, used female labour more or less from their inception. Between 1891 and 1911, the percentage of working women in Canada engaged in domestic and personal service work dropped from 51.9 percent to 38.1 percent. The percentage of women in trade and merchandising rose from 4 percent to 11.6 percent, and the percentage of professional women rose from 10.2 percent in 1891 to 16.1 percent in 1901, and then dropped slightly to 15.9 percent in 1911. The percentage of women in manufacturing remained steady throughout these years, at around 25 to 27 percent of all women in the labour force.[10]

In 1911, women made up only 13.4 percent of the total workforce in Canada, and of these women 23.8 percent were immigrants.[11] The highest proportion of immigrant women were in domestic and personal service (55.2 percent), with manufacturing claiming almost 20 percent of the immigrant women. For women born in Canada the situation was different. Only 32.7 percent of them were in domestic and personal service, and 29.23 percent were in manufacturing.[12] The statistics for domestic service are easily explainable by the fact that many women were imported specifically to be domestic servants by organizations such as the Salvation Army.

One of the most interesting statistics is that of the ages of workers. In 1911 51.5 percent of female workers were under the age of 25. Approximately 49 percent of these were from 15 to 24 years old, and 2 percent were between 10 and 14 years old. Most of the female children under 15 in the workforce were in domestic and personal service (56 percent) or manufacturing (35.5 percent).[13]

Between 1891 and 1911, B.C.'s workforce underwent a significant change. The percentage of workers who were female went from 4.4 percent in 1891 to 5.86 percent in 1901, and had almost doubled the 1891 figure by 1911, when 8.07 percent of the workforce was female. These figures are much below the Canadian average, which went from 12.2 percent in 1891 to 13.39 percent in 1911. Alberta and Saskatchewan had even lower percentages of women workers in 1911 than did B.C. The Canada Census Report attributes these low rates to the pioneer nature of the western provinces at this time, and the fact that there were simply more men than women living there.[14]

In B.C. in 1911, the occupational distribution was somewhat different from the national averages, although the same general trends are shown. Forty-two percent of B.C. working women were domestic and personal service workers, slightly higher than the national figure; manufacturing claimed 19.6 percent, lower than nationally; and professionals comprised 19.5 percent of the female workforce, higher than the national average.[15]

To narrow it down even further, in Vancouver women were 14.6 percent of the workforce, about one percentage point more than nationally. In actual numbers, this meant that in 1911 there were only 6,452 women (and 44,176 men) employed in the city of Vancouver. Of this number (6,452), the largest group were in domestic service (2,720 women), followed by 1,484 in the professions and 1,075 in trade and merchandising. Here, however, the census figures become clearer. Of "professional" women, 604 turn out to be stenographers and typists, 357 teachers (a very low-paid, low-status job at this time), and 242 nurses. In trade and merchandising 548 were saleswomen and 292 were office employees.[16]

In looking at these figures, Wayne Roberts' statement that working women before 1914 were "politically and socially isolated"[17] takes on a new dimension. In Vancouver, at least, they were also numerically isolated. Not only were there very few of them, but the nature of their occupations meant that they were scattered and fragmented, in offices, stores and homes all over the city. Their hours of work were long, and they did not have access to the resources of middle- and upper-class women, such as club rooms and adequate, affordable transportation, not to mention childcare and servants.

Given all this, it is not hard to see the difficulties which women and girls faced in trying to unionize. That women did organize argues either a large degree of class-consciousness, or a large degree of desperation, or both. Union activity took place in many of the main occupations in which women were engaged. Only some of these occupations will be touched on here, and it must be emphasized that the accounts that will be given by no means pretend to be definitive.

One of the better known, if only recently, of the organizing efforts of women of this period is that of the female telephone operators. Employees of what was originally the New Westminster and Burrard Inlet Telephone Company, later B.C. Telephone Company, organized a Vancouver local, No. 213, of the International Brotherhood of Electrical Workers (IBEW), in October 1901. (The parent body had been formed in 1891.)[18] They held two major strikes, one in 1902 and one in 1906.

On 26 November 1902 telephone operators, and male linemen, inspectors, trouble men and repairers all went out on strike for higher pay, shorter hours, and recognition of the union. The operators were asking for a wage increase of $2.50 per month, and the male employees wanted increases of from $5.00 to $10.00 per month. Two days after the start of the strike, on November 28, New Westminster employees went out in sympathy, as did Victoria employees on November 29.[19]

The strike lasted until 12 December 1902.[20] The telephone company was forced to suspend service temporarily, and the general Vancouver business community went up in arms against the phone company, supporting the strikers and offering to send volunteers to run the service. The telephone company then, as now, was not a popular institution in the city, as they tended to behave as a law unto themselves, and of course had a monopoly on an essential (for businesses) service. One incident serves to illustrate this: in June of 1905 a B.C. Telephone superintendent and five workmen were arrested for destroying public property—they had been tearing up a city street, presumably to lay cables, without city permission.[21]

Either during or just after the strike, the telephone operators decided to form their own organization, a branch of the local called Auxiliary #1 of Local 213. They had their own officers: Miss J. Hunter of 812 Homer St., president; Miss F. Livingstone, 660 Granville St., vice-president; Miss J. Browne, 827 Richards St., recording secretary; and Miss E. Bentley, 1121 Seymour Street, treasurer.[22] A local labour newspaper reported of Auxiliary #1 that they "control their own business, local 213 being represented by two delegates at their meetings."[23]

The Telephone Company appears to have given in to all of the strikers' demands. IBEW Local 213 was recognized, and the eight-hour day granted to the operators, although the company reserved the right to request that they work Sundays. A half-holiday every sixth Saturday was given, and three days per month sick leave. An immediate advance of $2.50 per month was to be given every operator who had been six months in receipt of her present salary, and scheduled increases every six months after until the top limit was reached. For city operators this meant a ten-day probationary period at the start, then $20 per month for the first six months, increasing to $30 per month after two and a half years. For long distance operators and "assistant chiefs," $32.50 per month was to be paid the first year and $35.00 per month thereafter. In contrast the linemen were to receive a new starting salary of $3 per day, approximately $66 per month for a five and a half day work week, assistant foremen $3.25 per day, and so on.[24]

A month and a half after the conclusion of the strike the operators celebrated by getting together a committee of five women and five men to organize a dance at the O'Brien Hall, which was frequently used for various union social events. Eighty couples came and appeared to enjoy themselves; according to *The Independent,* "One of these affairs which go to make life worth the living was held Wednesday night in the O'Brien Hall. The telephone operators entertained themselves and their friends at dancing, games, luncheon, etc."[25]

The gaiety had totally died down, however, by 1906. On February 22, the telephone operators struck to protest the company's refusal to hire only members of what the *Labour Gazette* called the "Telephone Operators Union," the auxiliary branch of Local 213. The next morning, all the IBEW members employed there also walked off the job. Thirty-four female operators and twenty male workers were involved. This time, though, there was no service interruption, as by a day after the start of the strike, the company had twenty-one operators working.

The operators said that the cause of the strike was

> that the officers of their union had been discriminated against, and an attempt had been made by the management of the company to induce them to disband. It was on this account that the operators asked for recognition of their auxiliary, in the form in which the men's union was recognized.[26]

The company claimed that their agreement to give hiring preference to IBEW members was made only with the men, and that the female operators had expressed no desire for such an agreement. They also said that on 9 January 1906 thirty-one out of thirty-seven operators had signed a declaration that they did not wish to belong to the union. Since then many had joined it (possibly out of indignation at being coerced to sign the declaration!) and had asked that only members of the union should be employed. The company said they could not grant this demand, as it would mean dismissing the other operators. They also used a technicality to claim that the men had broken their agreement by striking. Finally, the dispute was referred to the Vice-President of the International.[27]

The strike dragged on for months, with claims and counter-claims being made by the company and the strikers. Finally, in May, B.C. Telephone broke off all negotiations. No settlement was made, and the places of all the strikers were filled.[28] Local 213 of the IBEW still exists in Vancouver today, but the power of the Telephone Operators Union appears to have been permanently broken by their defeat in this strike.

Various other unions had women among their membership, where women were a small or large part of the industry. One of these was the Retail Clerks International Protective Association, which was formed in August 1899 and chartered in January 1900. The Vancouver union was apparently the first of its kind in Canada. It tried to affiliate with the American National Association of Retail Clerks, which became the International so as to include "Canadian subordinates."[29]

Female clerks are mentioned as active members as early as 1902, when they were reported as attending a meeting in Victoria. By mid-1903, the total membership was seventy-two and enlarging. They campaigned for shorter hours, closing on Sundays and legal holidays, and met with some success in getting stores that stayed open until 9 or 10 o'clock at night to close earlier. They also asked union members and the public to demand to see a clerk's union card, and if it could not be produced, not to buy from that clerk.[30]

By late 1904 or 1905 the union had disbanded.[31] In May 1913 reorganizing had started, with women and men joining together to form a union.[32] In February 1914 the VTLC received a communication from the Retail Clerks Protective Association about organizing a local of the union in Vancouver.[33] In April 1913 it was reported that women clerks made from $3 to $25 per week, the average wage being $10 per week. At the same time, the local Women's Council estimated that the bare minimum for survival for a woman was $7.50 per week: $5 for room and board (a very conservative estimate); $.50 for carfare: $.50 for laundry; $1.50 for all clothing necessary. Girls of fourteen and under were employed by the stores at $3 a week, working for at least two years before gradually rising to a living wage.[34]

Other unions with female workers in them included the Bookbinders' and the Tailors' unions. The Bookbinders Union was established about 1901, as Local 105 of the International Bookbinders Union. In 1903 they are reported as having a full membership of "workmen," and no mention is made of female members at this time, although they could well have been there.[35] In Toronto, women had formed the Women's Bindery Union in 1901, and by 1902 had 350 members.[36] By 1913, there must have been a significant female membership in Local 105, as it is one of the few unions mentioned, in the monthly report of the Vancouver Women's Correspondent to the *Labour Gazette,* as having women members.[37] In 1914 the total membership of the union was thirty-one.[38]

Data on tailoresses are somewhat more accessible, as prominent trade unionist and suffragist Helena Gutteridge was a member of the Tailors' Union.

She represented the union as a delegate to the VTLC, became the recording secretary of the council, led the British Columbia Women's Suffrage Society, and later became a Vancouver alderwoman.[39] The Tailors' Union began in the early 1890s, but dissolved in the depression of 1893-5. In 1898 it was reorganized, with a Miss McRae serving as the treasurer.[40] She was still active in the union in late 1913, when she is mentioned as attending VTLC meetings to report on garment workers.[41] Sometime during these years, the union became the United Garment Workers of America (UGWA).

The 1911 census lists 86 tailoresses and 484 tailors in the city of Vancouver. There were also 388 dressmakers, all female, 7 male milliners, plus 26 female and 46 male "other clothing makers." These women workers appear to have been older than in many other trades—424 of them were in the 25-65 years old bracket, and only 248 were under 25.[42]

Although there were obviously women in the union from its 1898 inception, reports on the extent of early female participation could not be found for this study. In April 1913, however, it was reported that tailors were trying to organize tailoresses, despite "opposition" from the IWW.[43] In June of that year, tailoresses in conjunction with tailors decided to organize to get the forty-eight hour week, and in August there was a strike of twenty garment workers, ten men and ten women, in a joint effort to reduce the work week from fifty-four hours to forty-eight. It had been estimated that garment workers received from $6 to $15 a week on a nine-hour day basis.[44]

The UGWA and the IWW appear to have had a jurisdictional dispute in B.C. as well as in other places in North America. In November 1913 Miss McRae brought to the attention of the VTLC meeting the fact that at Turner Beeton Company in Victoria an IWW label was being used. In March 1914 a warning was given at another meeting that the Turner Beeton Company label was "not that of a bona fide international union. It was known as a Pacific Coast union, using a yellow label, and was only a local organization." Later in the year the UGWA sent circulars to the VTLC explaining the dispute between them and the Industrial Tailors Union International (formerly Journeymen Tailors International). Apparently delegates from the latter union had been attending VTLC meetings.[45]

The Shirt, Waist and Laundry Workers International Union established a local in Vancouver on 12 March 1902. Local 105 originally included among its officers three women: vice-president Mrs. Henderson, financial secretary Miss M. Whitmar, and treasurer Miss Jealouse. A year and a half later, Miss Whitmar (or Whitmore) was listed as the vice-president, and the other women were no longer officers. A Miss Lomie had replaced Miss Jealouse as the treasurer.[46]

Laundry Workers in Vancouver struck at least once or twice around 1902-1903, but the data on this are rather confusing, and the extent of women's participation not clear. One strike is reported to have occurred when the Excelsior Laundry declined to put work schedules into effect.[47] A benefit was given for striking laundry workers on 30 April 1903 in the form of a dance and social at O'Brien Hall.[48] The *Labour Gazette* mentions another strike on 12 June 1903 that lasted until June 29. It involved fifteen workers at two laundries who struck in a refusal to work with non-unionists, and was settled by arbitration. A slight increase in wages is the only reported outcome.[49]

The SWLWIU established a local in Victoria as well, in November 1903.[50] On 19 June 1905 a strike was held by thirty employees, of whom twenty-two were girls and women, to recover back wages owed them. They were not paid as usual on Saturday night, and some of the women did not have enough money to last until Monday, so were given assistance by the other workers. One woman with three small children was evicted by her landlord, and the children's breakfast on Monday "came from the lunchpails of the striking laundrymen and laundrywomen."[51]

By the end of 1902, the Vancouver local had 70 members,[52] but in 1904 the union sent a letter to the VTLC expressing their intention to withdraw delegates from the Council.[53] Sometime after this they disbanded. In early 1914 they re-formed as Local 37 of the Laundry Workers and re-affiliated with the VTLC.[54] By April they had one place willing to sign up with them, and were working on two others. One business, Pioneer Laundry, responded by firing four or five employees who joined the union.

Over 700 women were said to be working in laundries in Vancouver in 1914, and women on heavy machines received only $9 a week.[55] The report of the first female inspector for the Civic Health Department stated that the work in laundries was done standing, in buildings which were generally hot, and about three days of the week the women worked nine-hour days.[56]

An early women's union to which only one reference was found was the Factory Workers Union, in existence in 1903. It was composed of women who worked in candy factories and confectionery shops, and had, according to *The Independent,* "a fair membership." The paper also reported that "J. B. Williams enjoys the proud distinction of being the only male member of this progressive union. And the girls [sic] have made him president."[57] In 1911 there were only thirty-one female workers in biscuit and confectionery making.[58] Figures could not be found for the earlier period.

One union in which women first formed part of the membership, and later launched their own autonomous local, was the union which incorporated hotel and restaurant employees. It was called, variously, Local 28 of the Waiters and Cooks Union, the Waiters and Waitresses, the Cooks, Waiters and Bartenders, and so on. The women's local suffered from the same confusion when established, being termed usually the Waitresses Union, but also the Waitresses and Lady Cooks Union, or the Hotel and Restaurant Employees Union, Local 766.

The original union started as a Knights of Labour local in 1898 or earlier.[59] Women were probably involved in it from the beginning. Waitresses are mentioned frequently in reports of the union's activities, and in 1903 at least one of the officers was female, a Miss A. Scuitto, the recording secretary.[60] The union was rabidly anti-Oriental, and one of its main concerns during this whole period was lobbying for restrictions on immigration, asking union members and the public not to patronize establishments owned by or employing Orientals, and trying to prevent white women from being employed by Orientals or even working along-side them.

This bias was present in the Waitresses Union as well, which was organized in June or July 1910, with thirteen women present at the meeting. They sent delegates to the VTLC regular meetings, and seem to have maintained an active presence there. An estimate at this time shows 300 women employed in hotels and restaurants in the city.[61] This appears to have been fairly accurate, as in 1911 the census lists 232 female restaurant employees and 155 female hotel and boarding house employees.[62]

By August 1910 five hotels and cafes employed union waitresses. Mrs. Rose Gardiner, who reported this fact to a VTLC meeting, also "discussed the proposition confronting the waitresses and the necessity of doing something to assist the girls in their battle to improve conditions."[63] In September an agreement for hotel and restaurant owners to sign was drawn up and sanctioned by the VTLC. It read:

> We, the undersigned, do hereby agree to employ union waitresses and to apply to the secretary of the waitresses' union when there is a vacancy in my place ... [to take effect] for a term of one year, from September 1, 1910. The waitresses' union, in consideration of the signature herein contained, do promise the support of the local unions and the central bodies in Vancouver to support houses displaying the card of the Waitresses Union, Local 766, Vancouver.[64]

By October membership was increasing, but the demand by employers had outstripped the supply of union waitresses. Delegate Gardiner told the VTLC that the union was going to hold a dance at German Hall, on the corner of Robson and Granville, and a note of annoyance can be heard as she continued "that they would expect the delegates to the council and the members of organized labour generally to assist them as they had promised repeatedly to." At subsequent meetings she took the floor to make racist comments on Chinese cooks, and she specifically complained about one restaurant where the Chinese owner had a white wife who waited on the tables.[65]

In 1913 the Women's Correspondent of the *Labour Gazette* reported that waitresses received $10 per week for an eight-hour day, and $12 per week for a ten-hour day with board. The Waitresses Union was still going strong and maintaining their close relationship with the mainstream trade union movement. Their headquarters was located in the Labour Temple,[66] and their delegate to the VTLC, Miss Polly Brisbane, was elected Statistician of that body, a position she held until her resignation in May 1914. In 1913, when Helena Gutteridge asked the VTLC to appoint a female delegate to appear before the Minister of Labour (along with delegates from women's societies), Polly Brisbane was chosen, and accepted.[67]

In January 1914 Miss Brisbane reported the membership of her union as thirty-five, with two members being unemployed. But in June of that year her report to the VTLC was that the charter of the Waitresses Union had been sent back. The waitresses were merging back with the men, into one union. Miss Brisbane continued to attend meetings as a delegate for a while, and filled in as Statistician occasionally, but eventually dropped out of sight.[68]

Possibly the most interesting union of the period was the Home and Domestic Employees Union of British Columbia. This organization was made up entirely of women and was not connected with any male union. The aims and policies of the union were expressly radical and feminist, and the president of the HDEU wrote shortly after its formation that "[the HDEU] bids fair to be one of the most important organizations of women ever formed."[69]

The HDEU was started on 19 March 1913 at a meeting at the Labor Temple to which about thirty-five women came. They were governesses, housemaids, nursemaids, cooks and other domestic workers. Their aims were ambitious. Aside from the three main objectives of the union—the nine-hour day, a minimum wage, and recognition as a body of industrial workers—they hoped eventually to establish a union hiring hall where employers would directly contract workers, to keep records on every place where members had worked or were at present employed, and to someday lease a building for a co-operative rooming house where they could live in healthy surroundings and enjoy a social life.[70]

Within a month they had fifty members,[71] and by August 1913 there were sixty-five women in the union.[72] At this point they applied for affiliation with the VTLC, and were accepted. Two delegates were sent to the VTLC meetings, a Miss K. McCall and a Miss M. E. Priest. Later a Miss A. M. Evans and the president of the union, Lillian L. M. Coote, also attended these meetings.[73] Applications for membership were to be sent to the union secretary, Miss E. Plaister, at 1537 Fifth Avenue East. Their office was in the Labor Temple, where the reading room had been divided in half and rented to them.[74]

Like the Waitresses Union, and possibly despite their belief in industrial unionism, they appear to have had a close relationship with the main labour movement. At one VTLC meeting, Miss Evans "requested the delegates to do all they could to make known the objects of her organization, and asked union men to urge women to join." Miss Evans also joined an organizing committee, together with Miss Coote, Helena Gutteridge and a male business agent, to look into organizing laundry workers in December 1913.[75] In January 1914, the B.C. Federation of Labour held its Fourth Annual Convention, and resolutions passed included one "Endorsing the Domestic Employees Union, pledging hearty co-operation and demanding that any eight-hour law enacted shall include domestic employees in its scope."[76]

The union was sensitive to the problems of organizing women in domestic service. The long hours worked and the tiring nature of the work meant that it was difficult for women to attend meetings or even to go to the office to register. To deal with this, the HDEU planned to establish what they called a "walking bureau,"[77] presumably to go house-to-house as had been done earlier by a woman in Toronto.[78] They also dealt with the fear that single women might get married and leave the union by pointing out that many married women continued to do domestic work in the daytime, and left their children at the city creche. When this question arose at their first meeting, the reply was that "no woman of the working classes who gets married need be afraid that she may have to leave the union because she is not out working. And anyhow, does a woman work less hours, or get more wages, when she gets married than she did before? Well then."[79]

The HDEU rejected the low status of their work, and the idea that they were "service" workers. They saw themselves, according to Miss Coote, as industrial workers under the capitalist system. Their Membership Creed, a copy of which was framed to hang on the wall of their club room in the Labor Temple, stated: "Believing that the home has a greater influence on the community than the community has on the home, we pledge ourselves as members of the union, to do all in our power to dignify the labour pertaining thereto."[80]

President Lillian Coote wrote a series of articles for the *B.C. Federationist* on the theories of the union and their goals. These form some of the only documents written by the women workers themselves that exist from this period, and in them she dealt with a variety of topics.

On working conditions for domestic employees, she stated that fourteen-hour days were common, and that even when not working, the women were almost totally at the disposal of their employers. Although the women came from differing social stations, their position in society was "a relic of feudalism."[81]

Upper- and middle-class women came in for some heavy criticism. On the same day that the HDEU was formed, 200 club women sold a women's edition of a daily paper on Vancouver streets, to raise money for a Women's Building. Miss Coote commented sarcastically that "they were filled with enthusiasm at what they appeared to think was their own original idea, namely the *awakening of women to the power of combination*" (her emphasis).[82] In a later article she went on to say:

> One cannot help wondering whether the many philanthropically inclined women of this province have seen fit to practically ignore the domestic problem question owing to the fact that the remedy would affect them—that they ... fall short when it is a problem of touching their own pockets.... [83]

But she also understood the nature of these women's position and the nature of women's work:

> Work must be clearly defined. Some women call afternoon teas, entertaining their husbands' friends, dressing to pay calls, etc., work and to a certain extent they are justified, because their object is mental and social advancement, which cannot be obtained without work of some sort or other. But after all, they have a free will in regard to their affairs, and if in the pursuit of their own advancement they work, it is they who reap the benefits of so doing.
>
> There is another class of women, namely, the wives of working men.... Their husbands take it for granted that their wives work because they like it. Some men are foolish enough to say that it is not really work—it is just "keeping at it." These women, however, do not need our sympathy—the remedy is in their own hands.[84]

Lillian Coote was certainly not a revolutionary, although she talked about the employees' "relationship with labor and capital,"[85] and the "degradation of a system which bartered for practically the ownership of an individual." She, and the union, hoped to force legislation to be enacted to carry out their main objects. To this end, they determined to hold public meetings once a month "to show to the public the necessity of what they are asking."[86] In 1914, a bill was introduced in the provincial legislature, an "Act Relating to the Employment of Domestic Employees." It contained provisions for a nine-hour day and a fifty-four-hour week; it would have ended wage deductions for breakage of goods; and it stated that "wages" should mean lawful money of Canada, and should not include recompense by way of room and/or board. I: did not get past committee.[87]

At the time of the union's formation in 1913, it was reported that the average wage for domestics was $30 per month with room and board. By the end of 1915 this had fallen to from $10 to $15 per month.[88] Vancouver was in a deep depression and unemployment was extremely high. Women who lost their jobs in other trades turned to domestic service in large numbers, which further contributed to the lowering of wages. Skilled domestic workers apparently were continually leaving the city, some to go south, in search of better wages and conditions. In 1915, the Home and Domestic Employees Union, faced with such heavy odds against them, appears to have dissolved.[89]

By now it should have become clear that, far from showing a "lack of interest in her economic future ... [and] lack of interest in trade unions,"[90] women attempted to organize persistently in most of the major occupations they were engaged in, during the 1900-1915 period. Although the forms of this organization varied, and women were not necessarily interested in forming their own autonomous or semi-autonomous unions, their belief in trade unionism was clearly demonstrated.

Since statistics on the make-up of union membership, in unions composed of both men and women, probably do not exist, it is even possible that unions thought of as mostly male may have been largely female in composition. Though the leadership of these unions tended to be largely male, this does not necessarily reflect the proportions of the membership. In turn, the male domination of leadership positions does not mean that women were not interested in or did not have a permanent commitment to trade unions. Many other factors could have been responsible for the largely male leadership, not the least of which would have been children, for married women, and the burden of housework for all women, cares which would have reduced to almost nothing the time available to them for attending meetings and conventions. Another factor was probably the negative attitudes of many male unionists towards women working for wages at all, let alone their holding leadership positions in trade unions.

The problem remains of how many women participated in these unions; in other words, were they only a small percentage of working women and, if so, why? The first question may be unanswerable, although further enquiry may turn up more data. At this point, though, it appears that their numbers were indeed small in relation to the total female working population.

This leaves the second question, of why this was so. When the nature of women's work and of their lives at this period in time is looked at, it is not justifiable to assume simply that their own psychology was to blame. Undoubtedly psychology had something to do with it—most women at this time probably assumed that they would at some point marry; and given the kind of work available to women—work performed for long hours, under oppressive and unhealthy conditions, at incredibly low wages, they also probably hoped not to have to work outside their homes as well as in them. Given this hope of temporary status as a worker, and the economic marginality of many women's survival (and therefore the need to cling to what jobs they had), some women would not have been willing to risk joining or starting a union in an age where no protective legislation existed ensuring union rights.

The objective difficulties surrounding unionization must have been enormous for them, in any case. Most women were separated from each other both at their workplace and when they returned home; they lacked places to meet each other where they could realize their common problems; and they did not have media avenues wherein to discuss their grievances. Their long hours of work, combined with the housework they returned to, meant not only that it would have been hard to find time to meet, but also indicates that many women must have spent their lives in a state of mental and physical exhaustion. Lillian Coote stated one of the objectives of the Home and Domestic Employees Union to be "help other women to realize that there is something more in life than work and sleep."[91]

The fact that the unions formed did not last for long can be partly attributed to just such difficulties. The lack of permanent and measurable improvements in wages and working conditions, due to employer intransigence and the anti-union policies of government, must also have been a discouraging factor. In the later years from 1911 on, and especially from 1913 to 1915, Vancouver, in common with the rest of the country, was suffering from a severe economic depression. Under these conditions, resulting in an employer's labour market, the situation for trade unions and workers in general was hardly favourable.

In sum, it seems rather amazing that women were able to organize at all. But organize they did, despite the overwhelming odds against them, and in large enough numbers to justify re-evaluating their place in the history books.

Notes

1. To test the truth of this assertion, see for example: Paul Phillips, *No Power Greater;* Ross McCormack, *Reformers, Rebels and Revolutionaries;* Charles Lipton, *The Trade Union Movement of Canada 1827-1959;* Stuart Jamieson, *Times of Trouble: Labour Unrest and Industrial Conflict in Canada 1906-1966.*

2. *The Independent,* 29 August 1903.

3. *Vancouver Trades and Labour Council,* General Meetings minute (hereinafter *VTLCg*), 21 August 1913.

4. *Labour Gazette,* (hereinafter *LG*), Ottawa, Canada, Vol. XVI, October 1915, p. 405.

5. *Independent,* 3 January 1903.

6. A. Ross McCormack, *Reformers, Rebels and Revolutionaries: The Western Canadian Radical Movement 1899-1919* (Toronto and Buffalo: University of Toronto Press, 1977), p. 102.

7. Paul Phillips, *No Power Greater: A Century of Labour in British Columbia* (Vancouver: B.C. Federation of Labour and Boag Foundation, 1967), pp. 25, 35-37, and 46.

8. See, for example, Edward S. Seymour, *An Illustrated History of Canadian Labour 1800-1974* Ottawa: Canadian Labour Congress, 1976, p. 10, where he calls a 1906 resolution to stop the immigration of Asiatics and East Indians "a tragic testimony in labour history by trade unionists."

9. Wayne Roberts, *Honest Womanhood: Feminism, Femininity, and Class Consciousness Among Toronto Working Women 1893 to 1914* Toronto: New Hogtown

10. *Census of Canada,* 1911, Vol. VI, Table 11, p. xx.

11. *Ibid.,* Table 13, p. xxi.

12. *Ibid.,* Table 14, p. xxii.

13. *Ibid.,* Tables 20 and 21, pp. xxvii, xxviii.

14. *Ibid.,* Table 7, p. xvii.

15. *Ibid.,* Table 15, p. xxiii.

16. *Ibid.,* Table VI, pp. 286-96.

17. Roberts, *Honest Womanhood,* pp. 10-11.

18. *Independent,* 5 September 1903.

19. *LG,* Vol. III, December 1902, pp. 477 and 479.

20. *Ibid.,* Vol. III, January 1903, p. 566.

21. *Victoria Daily Times,* 23 June 1905 and 26 June 1905.

22. *Independent,* 31 January 1903. Directory of Unions.

23. *Ibid.,* 31 January 1903.

24. *LG,* Vol. III, January 1903, p. 517.

25. *Independent,* 31 January 1903.

26. *LG,* Vol. VI, March 1906, pp. 1030-31.

27. *Loc. cit.*

28. *LG,* Vol. VI, April 1906, p. 1153, and June 1906, p. 1383.

29. *Ibid.,* 5 September 1903.

30. *Ibid.,* 17 May 1902; 5 September 1903; 27 December 1902.

31. *B.C. Federationist,* 27 December 1912, p. 25.

32. *LG,* Vol. XIII, June 1913, p. 1380.

33. *VTLCg,* 19 February 1914.

34. *LG,* Vol. XIII, April 1913, p. 1080.

35. *Independent,* 5 September 1903.

36. Roberts, *Honest Womanhood,* p. 23.

37. *LG,* Vol. XIII, April 1913, p. 1079.

38. *VTLCg,* 15 January 1914. Report by the delegate of the union named Mowatt, to the VTLC.

39. Doreen Madge Weppler, *Early Forms of Political Activity Among White Women in British Columbia 1880-1925* (Burnaby, B.C.: Simon Fraser University, unpublished M.A. Thesis, 1971), pp. 33 and 84, footnotes.

40. *Independent,* 5 September 1903.

41. *VTLCg,* 16 October 1913 and 6 November 1913.

42. *Census of Canada,* 1911, Vol. VI, Table VI, pp. 288-89.

43. *VTLCg,* 17 April 1913.

44. *LG,* Vol. XIV, July 1913, p. 42, and September 1913, p. 266: Vol. XIII, April 1913, p. 1080.

45. *VTLCg,* 6 November 1913; 5 March and 19 November 1914.

46. *Ibid.,* 5 September and 7 November 1903.

47. Weppler, *Political Activity,* pp. 32-33.

48. *B.C. Federationist,* 27 December 1912, p. 19.

49. *LG,* Vol. IV, July 1903, p. 88.

50 *Ibid.,* Vol. IV, December 1903, pp. 591 and 679.

51. *Victoria Daily Times,* 19 June 1915, p. 4.

52. Weppler, *Political Activity,* p. 32.

53. *VTLCg,* 18 November 1904.

54. *Ibid.,* 5 February 1914.

55. *Ibid.,* 2 April 1914.

56. *LG,* Vol. XV, August 1914, pp. 189-90.

57. *Independent,* 5 September 1903.

58. *Census of Canada,* 1911. Vol. VI, Table VI, p. 288.

59. Weppler, *Political Activity,* p. 35.

60. *Independent,* 5 September 1903.

61. *Western Wage Earner,* July 1910, p. 11.

62. *Census of Canada,* 1911, Vol. VI, pp. 286-88.

63. *VTLCg,* 18 August 1910.

64. *LG,* Vol. XI, October 1910, p. 421.

65. *VTLCg,* 6 October 1910; 3 November 1910; 17 November 1910.

66. *LG,* Vol. XIII, April 1913, pp. 1079-80.

67. *VTLCg,* 21 May 1914; 3 July 1913.

68. *Ibid.,* 15 January 1914; 4 June 1914, and various dates to end of 1914.

69. *B.C. Federationist,* 28 March 1913, p. 3.

70. *Ibid.,* 28 March 1913, pp. 1 and 4.

71. *Ibid.,* 18 April 1913, p. 1.

72. *LG,* Vol. XIV, August 1913, p. 152.

73. *VTLCg,* 7 August and 21 August 1913; 6 November 1913; 8 January 1914.

74. *B.C. Federationist,* 28 March 1913, p. 4; *VTLC,* Board of Directors, meetings minutes, 11 July 1913.

75. *VTLCg,* 20 November and 18 December 1913.

76. *LG,* Vol. XIV, February 1914, p. 954.

77. *B.C. Federationist,* 18 April 1913, p. 1.

78. Roberts, *Honest Womanhood,* p. 15.

79. *B.C. Federationist,* 28 March 1913, p. 4.

80. *LG,* Vol. XIV, September 1913, p. 266.

81. *B.C. Federationist,* 28 March 1913, p. 3.

82. *Loc. cit.*

83. *Ibid.,* 11 April 1913, p. 2.

84. *Ibid.,* 4 April 1913, p. 2.

85. *Loc. cit.*

86. *Ibid.,* 28 March 1913, p. 3; 18 April 1913, p. 1.

87. *LG,* Vol. XIV, April 1914, p. 1163.

88. *Ibid.,* Vol. XIII, April 1913, p. 1079; Vol. XVI, November 1915, pp. 569-70.

89. Genevieve Leslie. "Domestic Service in Canada, 1880-1920." in *Women at Work: Ontario 1850-1930* (Toronto: Canadian Women's Educational Press, 1974), p. 123.

90. *LG,* Vol. XIII, April 1913, p. 1079.

91. *B.C. Federationist,* 11 April 1913, p. 2.

FEMINIZATION OF THE LABOUR PROCESS IN THE COMMUNICATION INDUSTRY: THE CASE OF THE TELEPHONE OPERATORS, 1876-1904

Michèle Martin

In early 1880, the first woman was hired by Bell Telephone Co. as an operator in the Main Exchange in Montreal, and soon after the company's managers in Toronto also hired a woman. Thus began the replacement of an all male operating labour force by one that was entirely female. At the time, the use of "boys" as operators was said to be a total failure. A Bell Telephone Company manager stated that if the company continued with boys as operators, "it was virtually facing bankruptcy."[1]

This article examines the process of feminisation in the telephone industry. It especially focuses on the Bell Telephone Company[2] in Ontario and Quebec, with particular emphasis on Montreal and Toronto.

I

During the last decade, the issue of feminisation has occasioned a growing debate among social scientists, especially feminist writers. Much has been said, about the feminisation of teaching,[3] of office work,[4] and of domestic labour.[5]

Prentice's "The Feminisation of Teaching in British North America and Canada, 1845-1875," presents a largely economic analysis of the phenomenon. She argues that the creation of a public school system promoting the grading of school children "led to the feminisation of the teaching labour force." The feminisation of teaching brought cheap and effective teachers to a section of the system which was considered unattractive by men. Low wages for women allowed school boards to give higher wages to male, career-oriented teachers. However, the social acceptance of women as teachers was essential,[6] and contemporary beliefs such as the degrading of the profession by its feminisation, the ineptitude of women at discipline, and the identification of women with truncated

From *Labour/Le Travail,* XXII (Fall 1988), 139-162. Reprinted by permission of the Canadian Committee on Labour History.

career paths had to be overcome.[7] Moreover, the willingness of women to take badly paid teaching jobs with difficult working conditions, where they were in a position of subordination, was due, according to Prentice, to a crowded female labour market coupled with women's personal choice to work outside the home.[8] In short, Prentice argues that a change in educational organisation due to the building of a public school system, the existence of a large female reserve army of labour, and the changing social role of women are the main factors which influenced the feminisation of teaching in the mid-nineteenth century.

Danylewycz, *et al.,* also recognised economic factors as central in the feminisation of teaching. Yet, in "The Evolution of the Sexual Division of Labour in Teaching: A Nineteenth Ontario and Quebec Case Study," they suggest that other elements have also influenced the evolution of the feminisation of teaching, especially in Ontario and Quebec. In Ontario, for instance, age structure, ethnicity, and the household status of teachers were also responsible for the change in elementary school teaching, while in Quebec alternatives in terms of job openings for men, and male under-schooling in comparison to women, encouraged the feminisation of teaching in elementary school.[9]

Lowe's "Women, Work and the Office" supports these arguments as well. Lowe argues that the transition from small entrepreneurial capitalism to corporate capitalism led to the feminisation of office work. He identifies four models used to account for feminisation: the "consumer choice" model; the "reserve army of labour" model; the "demand" model; and the "segmentation" model.[10] However, none of these presents a satisfactory explanation for the feminisation of telephone operators.

The "consumer" choice model is "based on the concept of rational economic choice" made subjectively upon a family consensus in view of economic necessities of the household. Women are assumed to exercise free choice and the model explains work rates in terms of subjective processes rather than socio-economic variables.[11] The second model uses the Marxist concept of "reserve army of labour" to explain the place of women in the labour force. This model, developed by Braverman, emphasizes the ways in which capital has created a supply of cheap female labour related to the decreasing or increasing demand on the labour market made by the requirements of capitalists.[12] It is helpful in explaining the position of women after they have been integrated into the labour market, and in shedding light on the process of their exploitation by capitalist industry. The "demand" model is concerned with the occupational segregation of women through the manipulation of job requirements. This model argues that an increased supply of female labour is caused by the growing demand for women in certain occupations. Gender discrimination in terms of specific occupations is "reinforced by the process of sex-labelling." The labour supply is manipulated by capital in terms of job requirements and wages.[13] Finally, the "segmentation" model, proposed by Edwards, gives the "structural properties" as the basic elements of the process of feminisation of an occupation. It suggests that sex-based dimensions of power and inequality can be related to the fragmentation of the labour force in the labour process developed by corporate capitalism. Sex differentiation would be due to changes in productive process, mostly brought about by the technologisation of the work place. This would create "sub-markets" constituted of new occupations with different characteristics and working conditions.[14]

While each model identifies some factors influencing the process of the feminisation of occupations, none of them furnishes an adequate explanation. While the "consumer choice" model suggests a weak concept of rational and conscious choice subjectively made by women, the "reserve army of labour market" model, although it explains women's inferior position within the labour force in capitalist production, does not give the essential elements to understand the process through which women are hired in the first place. The "demand" and the "segmentation" models furnish more concrete conceptions. For the case with which I am concerned—telephone operating—the former model suggests that operating work became a female occupation because of changes made by the telephone industry in terms of job requirements. Sexually stereotyped requirements were assigned to the occupation, and with these came low wages. On the other hand, the "segmentation" model would emphasize that this new assignment of requirements was due to the fact that operator's work was segmented from other occupations and did not require high skills. Moreover, the level of stability did not have to be high because it was easy to train new operators. Training time for that occupation correspond to the time necessary to subject the operators to the switchboard.

However, according to Lowe, the segmentation model largely explains the feminisation of office work. Fragmentation of the work rendered the job unattractive to skilled workers. This opened the occupation to women through a "secondary labour market of female clerks."[15] In effect the manipulation of sex-labelled job characteristics by the employers resulted in the appropriation by men of the most interesting and rewarding positions in the office and left the "minor tasks" to women. Those were at the bottom of the hierarchy of occupations in bureaucratic organisations and required qualifications usually attributed to women in a patriarchal society: obedience and submissiveness.[16]

Finally, another debate on the process of feminisation is concerned with domestic work. In "Capital, the State and the Origins of the Working-Class Household," B. Curtis investigates how domestic labour became women's work. This is a result, he says, of the separation of household and industry under capitalism, and was sustained by state activity. "It is the state that reproduces labour power in the commodity form and that reproduces the oppression [or subordination] to which the unemployed domestic worker is subject."[17] From the struggle of the working-class against exploitative working conditions, and for a domestic life, emerged the working-class household with women in the subordinated position of full-time houseworkers without economic power[18]: in periods of high labour demand, women participated in certain sectors of the labour market, and when unemployed, they were dependent on their husbands. "Their condition as housewives structure[d] their participation in production in capitalist industries [and] ... *discipline[d] them in relations of subordination and dependence* ..."[19] Thus, women's subordination was not simply the result of sexist attitudes, says L. Briskin in "Domestic Labour," "rather, it [was] *firmly rooted in the material conditions of women's lives,* primarily in the institution of the family."[20] A definite split occurred between domestic labour and capitalist production which forced women into labour consisting mainly of the reproduction of the labour force.

In their respective analyses of the feminisation of the domestic labour, Briskin and Curtis argue the centrality of women's subordination for understanding the expansion of the capitalist economy. It is an essential element of the manipulation of women as domestic workers and as wage labourers. Indeed, the concept of subordination, which is also discussed in Luxton's *More than a Labour of Love,*[21] but which is absent from the previously reviewed studies, is indispensible to understanding not only women's acceptance of second rate and low waged jobs, but their willingness to take occupations whose demands include patience, obedience and submissiveness. Women's subordination, institutionalized in the family and the workplace, is central to the moral regulation of women in the public realm. Here it works to incite women to consider their work as a "labour of love." Telephone operating had many of the characteristics of a labour of love.

The degree of feminisation of an occupation is affected by the state of the labour market, and the financial structure of the organisation within which the process occurs. Moreover, the traditional attitudes towards women in the society in which the process occurs influence the characteristics attached to the job.[22] Other factors such as age structure, ethnicity, household status, job openings, and level of education have also to be taken into consideration to account for the timing of the phenomenon. Finally, there seems to be a general consensus among researchers that the feminisation of an occupation results in a decrease of its social status and in a reduction in its pay.

These assumptions suggested in the debate on job feminisation do not satisfactorily explain the process of feminisation of the operating labour force in the telephone industry. Indeed, although the latter passed from an entirely male to an entirely female force, the telephone company's administrators who organized the hiring of women seemed to imply that the job had never been suitable to the male personality, although the work was directly related to the handling and repairing of technical apparatuses, a domain commonly reserved to men.[23] Moreover, the feminisation of the operating occupation did not undermine its economic status and was not due to a new fragmentation of work within the operating workplace. Rather, it appears that the job of operator acquired a higher social status after its feminisation and, although the job was low-waged, the wages did not decrease, at least in absolute terms, after the feminisation of the labour force. Wages for female workers stayed relatively the same as for male workers. Finally, unlike the case of teaching and office work, operators were not confined to inferior position, but had access to the highest degrees of a hierarchical scale, created within the operating labour force.[24]

This article investigates how the occupation of telephone operator came to be a female job ghetto. Its main theme is that the process of feminisation of operating work was central to the rapid development of the telephone industry in late nineteenth and early twentieth centuries. The particular characteristics of the women operators facilitated the telephone industry's transition from a small-scale enterprise to a modern corporate capitalist monopoly. In effect, the telephone system represented a general, public system producing individual, private telephone calls. The work of the operators as mediators in the production of telephone calls placed them in a paradoxical situation in which their intervention was essential in the connection of subscribers on telephone lines and, at the same time, was resented as an obstruction to the privacy of these calls. This situation in which the operators were a necessity and a nuisance at the same time created contradictions which the telephone business attempted to resolve in developing a set of moral regulations to be applied to the female operators. In fact, the feminisation of the operating work occurred during the mid-Victorian period, in a context of intense moral regulation for those women working in the public sphere. As mediators between subscribers, the operators had to imitate the "moral values" conveyed by those with whom they were regularly in contact. Rules and regulations coming from the company gradually covered not only the technical aspects of their formation but their "moral education" as well. Thus, feminisation brought no decline to the job's social status, that is, honour, but rather created some moral barriers intended to improve the public "image" of the telephone system and, thus to activate the development of the enterprise. The features of the female operating labour force in question were its adaptability first to the "military" discipline necessary to work on increasingly mechanized switchboards in huge central offices, then to the growing administrative control and moral regulation, finally to the wide variety of customers' demands. The definition of the operating work was dramatically altered during the period from its creation in 1876 to its near elimination in the early 1920s, with the coming of automatic switchboards.

This study is concerned with the characteristics of the operating work which were used in its definition as "women's work." What factors motivated the telephone industry to shift very early towards women operators, despite the technical nature of the job, the "risky" night shifts, and patriarchal attitudes about women's work outside the home?

II

The development of the telephone system coincided with a wave of capitalist concentration in Canadian industry. Small entrepreneurial businesses were becoming large capitalist firms. In this competition, the development of technical means of communication, through which capitalists could rapidly get relevant information on national and international markets, played a central role.[25] A network of telegraphic communication already existed which had considerably shortened the circulation time of invested capital. However, the telegraph was relatively slow and access to it was limited by the mastery of specific skills. When the telephone came on the market, it represented the "ideal" means through which business transactions could be made from person to person. Bell Telephone Company's management was quick to understand the utility of the telephone for businessmen and oriented its development from the outset to please that group of subscribers. Before direct-dial systems, telephone operators mediated between subscribers.

In order to understand the extension of the telephone system (with particular attention to the Bell Company's development in the provinces of Quebec and Ontario), it is useful to divide its expansion into two stages based partly on the improvement of the technical means, partly on the economic and political climate. The first period, 1876 to 1889, was that of the establishment of Bell Telephone Company. During the first years, from 1876 to 1880, a certain number of independent companies had started in the business, some using A.G. Bell's invention, others employing Edison's. However, in 1880 Bell's company, represented by C.F. Sise, an American businessman, bought most of these businesses in Montreal and Toronto, as well as in the other towns and cities of Quebec and Ontario. Bell's company began to feel its way towards the realisation of what would become one of the biggest private monopolies in Canada. The technical means of the telephone were still in an experimental stage and their performance, although advertised as "wonderful" in the newspapers of that time, created much frustration and despair for both management and subscribers. The switchboards had a capacity of fifty lines and were operated manually. When there were more than fifty subscribers in an exchange, two or more sections of the switchboard, which were interconnected by conducting strips known as "trunk," were necessary. If a subscriber was calling someone on a different section of the switchboard, the two sections had to be plugged or switched together. This job was done by "switch-boys" under the operators' command. Unlike the operators, the switch-boys did not have any direct contact with the subscribers.[26] In this type of telephone system, the operating work actually constituted the most reliable part of the telephone business.

The second stage, from 1890 to 1904, was the period of confirmation. It involved some major developments of the technical means of telephoning which attracted a larger number of subscribers. One major development was the enlargement of the switchboards and the elimination of the switch-boy's job. Operators could then carry out the whole process of connecting two subscribers' calls. This was a period of continual, although not spectacular growth, which was accompanied by a more formal organization of the operating labour force. The company began to impose a hierarchical structure on operators based on formal rules and regulations. In this period women replaced men as operators.[27]

At the beginning of its expansion, the telephone system was operated by a male labour force. As the telephone industry developed, however, the telephone companies started to hire women for the operating work, asserting that their personalities were "better suited" to the work. By the end of the 1880s, almost all telephone operators were women. Indeed, the job of operator became a prototypical job ghetto from which the male labour force was almost entirely barred. Nonetheless, during the first years of the telephone's development, telephone companies, including Bell Exchange, had hired "boys" as operators. According to a manager who worked as a male operator in 1878, "it was most natural to use boys as operators in the first telephone exchanges. Boys and young men had served as telegraph operators from the beginning. Then, too, it was unthinkable in the early eighties that a girl should be out after 10 o'clock so that the operating staff on the night shift was of necessity male."[28]

In the mid-Victorian era, the period of the early development of the telephone, official discourse presented men as assertive and aggressive and women as submissive and passive. A woman was expected to be patient, tactful, prudent, as well as forceful and courageous within her family in order to "use to the advantage the limitless and indivisible affection she *owe[d]* her husband." At the same time, she was required to be intelligent, discerning, firm, and energetic with her children to "properly direct their education." This difference in social expectations for men and women was based on the distinct role to which each gender was subordinated:

> A young lady, unlike a young man, is not in the least required to be present in the public sphere; on the contrary, it is in the interior of the family, under the eyes of her parents, that she ought to reveal all the treasures of purity, modesty, humility, and piety, which her heart possesses. These are the best qualities, the most beautiful ornaments of the young girl.[29]

This image of modest, pure and submissive women was particularly widespread in the dominant and middle classes which attempted to convey their "ideal" moral virtues to the other classes through magazines and newspapers. An article entitled "The Family," in *Le monde illustré,* a newspaper written by philanthropically minded bourgeois and middle class ladies but intended for lower-middle and working classes,[30] made it clear that a woman

> ... ought never to seek other than the pure pleasures which the interior of the family offers to her. Woman's life, that life full of love, self-denial, and sacrifice, should only be lived there; so that the obscurity of her surroundings might make her virtues shine forth more brightly.[31]

Furthermore, since woman's place was in the interior of her family, she was not allowed to go outside of it alone, particularly not in the evening. According to the Catholic church, these "feeble creatures ought never to be left ... without effective control and supervision."[32] This constant supervision was to be performed by their husbands, parents or by a responsible person, approved by the parents, to protect women against "a liberal current of ideas" and against "pronounced tendencies towards excessive liberty."[33] This protective attitude towards women's "fragility" and "vulnerability" applied to their social rights as well. Because women had to be protected, their guardians needed the power necessary to subdue the "dangers." In as much as men were to be the protectors, they required control of the means of protection. Since one of them was the material means provided by labour, men's power was extended to women's right to have a job as well. Hence, women's work was socially ill-regarded, and that which was available usually was in the form of low-status and low-paid jobs. As the Archbishop of Montreal stated,

> The ignorance of some and the ill-will of others work to produce an unfortunate situation in which people come to believe that equality [between men and women] involves identical rights, and women are urged to enter into a ridiculous and odious revolt with men on a field of combat where neither the conditions of the struggle nor the chances of success could possibly be equal. The realisation of such theories would be obnoxious to women and the family, and would shortly lead to the fall of one and the ruin of the other.[34]

Equal opportunity at work would cause family breakdown and women's "fall." This was a common patriarchal discourse during the first periods of development of the telephone industry and one which guided its employment policies. Joan Sangster stresses that Mackenzie King's "perceptions of the operators reflect[ed] a Victorian image of woman," and that the Ontario press sustained that view as well. In the press reports of the 1907 telephone operators' strike, "it was the moral, rather than the economic, question of woman labour which was emphasized." This Victorian view of woman was not restricted to the dominant class, however. According to Sangster, trade unionists held similar opinions. "The views of many craft unionists were dominated by their belief that woman's role was primarily a maternal and domestic one." Moreover, "it was woman's contribution to the home rather than her status as a worker, which was most often stressed in the labour press. In fact, concern that woman's wage labour would destroy the family was very strong."[35] This concern was general. The telephone industry recruited its first operators among a group of "boys" who were already employed as telegraph messengers and who knew a little about electrical communication, although they were by no means skilled labourers. Besides, young men were "cheaper" than mature and married men.[36] These young telegraph messengers were paid only by the message, and very poorly so.

The Operators' Work

In the early 1880s, when the telephone industry started hiring operators, the labour process was largely unstructured. It consisted mainly of improvised work on an unsophisticated technical instrument which provided an irregular production in quality and quantity. No specific conditions were required. In fact, the only requirements attached to the job of operator were to be male and young: "They were boys 16 or 17 years old, and young imps, immune to all discipline."[37] Nevertheless, the telephone company pioneers and managers had not "envisioned the fact, later proved by experience, that *men and boys were temperamentally unsuited* to the exacting duties of switchboard operation, and that this work was *destined to be performed by members of the opposite sex*."[38] The larger the operating rooms, the more undisciplined were the "boys." John J. Carty, an operator during this period, remembered that male operators were very "wild." William J. Clarke related the "fondness for clowning and practical jokes of the boys and young men employed in the operating room" when he was one of them. These jokes were "often at the expense of the subscriber." Moreover, male operators were not submissive and when "subscribers were rude the boys did not always turn the other cheek but matched insult for insult and curse for curse." Furthermore, according to Clarke, the boys were inclined to "wrestling on the floor," failing to answer incoming calls. Their training was very casual. They would "drop into the office during a slack period on Saturday and Sunday to learn how to operate the switchboard at which [they were] to start on Monday." The majority of the male operators were doing operating work on a part-time basis and were employed for other work either within the telephone companies or for other industries. In spite of that, some men who were operating asserted that there was the prospect of advancement within the telephone business, especially with Bell Telephone Company after its incorporation in 1880, and that since "most of them were ambitious," this "tended to keep them trying to do a good job in spite of the natural tendencies."[39]

Even after Bell Telephone Company started to hire women as day operators,[40] men continued to be hired during the day in order "to connect the calling lines with the trunk line to office called," or, in other words, to do the technical work necessary within the exchange. Besides, male operators continued to work on the evening and night shifts, some starting at 6:00 p.m., others at 10:00 p.m., according to the size of the exchange in which they were working. In big and busy offices, male operators were used as little as possible, and only during the period of the day where the business was quiet. However, company managers concluded that "... boys as operators were proved complete and consistent failures. They were noisy, rude, impatient and talked back to subscribers, played tricks with wires, and on one another."[41] The company's response to such undisciplined behaviour was an attempt to enforce control over the male operators in order to meet the subscribers' complaints. In a letter to the local managers in Montreal, in response to a complaint he received against a male operator, L.B. McFarlane assessed Bell Telephone Company's expectations towards the operators' attitude with the subscribers: "He as well as other operators should know they have no business to talk back to a subscriber, and you can inform him that if we have any further complaint of this nature his services will be dispenses with."[42] Nonetheless, disciplining male operators did not transform their "unsuitable characteristics" into suitable qualities for the operation of the telephone system.

The operator's work did not represent a sub-market created by the telephone industry for women, however. The particularity of that job was that it involved both "masculine" and "feminine" tasks. It implied a technical knowledge of electricity to cope with frequent repairs; as a mediating job, it entailed a direct contact with subscribers, a sort of "labour of love."[43] It seems that, in 1876, the telephone business gave more importance to the technical aspect, and hired young men for the work. Undoubtedly, patriarchal attitudes were mainly responsible for that first decision. However, bad experiences with men made Bell Telephone Company managers realise that, to keep their few customers, they had to emphasize the characteristics attached to the mediating aspect of the occupation. The position of operator came to be seen as "naturally" women's work.

In 1880, Bell Telephone Company hired the first female operator to work in the Main Exchange in Montreal.[44] The early experience of the industry had already pointed to a few specific requirements for the operator's work which appeared essential to the expansion of the telephone system. The telephone company concentrated on matching poor wages with adequate characteristics for its operators. The particularity of the product—an instantaneous telephone call—and the essential role of the operators as mediators to produce it, created a situation in which users and operators were constantly interacting. Since the subscribers were mostly businessmen from the dominant and middle classes, the company's managers decided that "courtesy" and "discipline" were the most important qualities to "perform successfully the duties of ... [such] subordinate places" as telephone operators.[45] K.J. Dunstan, general manager for the Ontario district, insisted that "rules and discipline" were to be "strictly enforced" to insure operators' courtesy with users: "Mistakes may be overlooked, but lack of courtesy is an unpardonable offence. Subscribers will forgive a great deal if the operator is invariably pleasant and polite [and submissive], and the necessity of only employing educated and refined operators is very apparent."[46] The solution to that problem appeared to be hiring women as operators: "A woman would give better service and be a better agent," said C.F. Sise, general-manager of Bell Telephone Company.[47] It was suggested to employ "young women at salary not greater than commission amounts to commission men," the telegraph messengers, who treated the telephone as secondary to their own business, and acted very independently. "The young women would be *directly under the company's control,* would attend promptly to calls and are as a rule more honest and careful than men."[48] Hence, the company's attempt at structuring the labour force by starting a process of subjection of its male operators through enforcement of control and work discipline led to a process of feminisation of the occupation. The unresponsive behaviour of the male operators to the process of subjection forced the company's management to adopt a policy of hiring female operators.

The first woman was hired soon after "a conference between Mr. Forbes, president of the American company, Mr. Sise, Mr. Baker and myself [K.J. Dunstan] re. girls as telephone operators. Mr. Forbes said he believed they were used somewhere, did not know where and had heard nothing against them."[49] Sometime later, Mr. Dunstan in the Toronto exchange hired the "Misses Howell" as telephone operators.[50] These women and most female operators were mainly coming from lower-middle and respectable working classes. They were "girls"[51] who needed to earn some money and, at the same time, could meet the moral standard of subscribers coming from the dominant and upper-middle classes. On the other hand, subscribers had also some duties vis-à-vis the female operators, as a message in the telephone directories indicated: "Ladies are employed as operators; we ask for their courteous treatment."[52] The occupation of telephone operator was a new opening for the large female reserve army of labour. An operator described the place of women on the labour market at that time: "Few jobs were open to women then; even most stenographers were male."[53] Another operator of the 1880s reinforced that statement: "Employment for women back in the 80's was limited to teaching school, factory work, restaurant and domestic work."[54] Some women preferred telephone operating to teaching: "Teaching was prosaic, poorly paid and the profession was overcrowded."[55] It appears, though, that female teachers and telephone operators were from the same classes. Moreover, some of the requirements for getting the jobs were similar. For instance, for both occupations, women had to present recommendations from three persons, including their clergymen.[56] Age limits were also imposed, and although Bell Telephone Company accepted women as young as fourteen years old as operators in the 1880s,[57] when the schools for operators started in 1900, the age limit increased to seventeen. Finally, women needed to have "good memories," "be tall enough so that their arms would reach all lines on the switchboard and be slim enough so that they could fit into the narrow spaces allotted to the #1 standard switchboard positions."[58] L.B. McFarlane, Bell Telephone Company's manager for Canada East, declared in the *Daily Witness* that "in their selection the greatest care is exercised. They must be girls of irreproachable character, recommended by their clergymen."[59] With such requirements as recommendations from a clergyman, doctor and property owner, it is clear that these women could only be from "respectable" backgrounds.

However, the feminisation of the occupation of operator entailed some difficulties for the company. Indeed, although the telephone operating work required no particular skills, some technical knowledge in the field of electricity was useful. The telephone system in its early development constantly required minor repairs and adjustments which were effected by the "boys."[60] Since Bell Company's managers thought women incapable of doing electrical work, for a few years after the hiring of the first woman as operator, boys continued to be hired to do the technical aspect of the job. While women answered the subscribers, the young men were connecting the busy lines with the trunk. However, this was inconvenient, said a female operator at that time, as the boys were playing tricks on the female operators whom they did not like.[61] The problem was resolved by the company's managers who provided all female operators with a "small book on telephone troubles and how to remove them," a book which helped the female operators to be "more self-reliant and to fix small troubles that will come up."[62] Thus, for equal wages, women provided the telephone industry with new labour power, furnishing not only the "feminine" qualities of submission and courtesy, but the "masculine" characteristics of technical and mechanical skills as well. In spite of changes applied to the job definition and its labelling as a "female" occupation, some essential aspects of the work remained traditional male domains to which the hired women had to adapt, at least until the end of the 1890s, when the improved technology eliminated the need for such interventions. It seems, then, that women had succeeded in adapting to the "male" characteristics of the work, while men had failed to adjust to its "female" features. For the telephone company, this represented a value which even its most chauvinist managers could not ignore.[63]

Yet, the process of feminisation of the operator's occupation did not happen instantly. As an operator remarked: "Elimination of the masculine touch ... was not made with one gesture. It covered a long period of years."[64] On the one hand, in that mid-Victorian society so very protective of "ladies' virtues," "some people thought that it was pretty hazardous to allow women to be at work at night alone."[65] Since the "traffic load" was much lighter at night than during the day, the company continued to hire male operators for the evening and night duties for many years after women had started as day operators. The first hiring of a woman as night operator occurred in 1888.[66] On the other hand, even male day operators were not eliminated all at once. Rather, women gradually replaced the "boys" as they were promoted to higher wage jobs, as they quit, as they were dismissed for bad conduct, or as jobs were opened.

Still, the job, by then, was seen as a female occupation which, as B. Lalonde, a female operator in Ottawa put it: "requires a lot of *devotion* and brings very little gratitude from the public." The operators were "women who have *put their femininity to the service of the community*. Very few men would be patient enough to perform the duties of a telephone operator."[67] An Ontario newspaper, *The Watchman,* gave a very accurate summary of the sex-labelled characteristics defining the operator work as a female job:

> In the first place the clear feminine quality of voice suits best the delicate instrument. Then girls are usually more alert than boys, and always more patient. Women are more sensitive, *more amendable to discipline,* far gentler and more forebearing then men.... Boys and men are less patient. They have always an element of fight in them. When spoken to roughly and rudely they are not going to give the soft answer. Not they. And every man is a crank when he gets on a phone. The personal equation stands for naught. He is looking into the blank wooden receiver and it doesn't inspire him with respectful politeness.[68]

Apparently, then, woman's upbringing in Victorian society gave her all the necessary qualities to be a perfect operator. She was said to be "gifted" with "courtesy," "patience," "skillful hands." In addition, she possessed a "good voice" and a "quick ear," and was "alert," "active," "even-tempered," "adaptable," and "amendable."[69] As such, the female operator was considered "the heart of the place,"[70] "the most valuable asset that a telephone company possesses," "the stock in trade" of that company.[71] One of her major assets was her "voice." The "feminine" voice was considered "limitless" in terms of possibilities in the operation of the telephone.[72] The perfect operator had a "gentle voice; musical as the woodsy voices of a summer day," "sweetly distinct to the subscribers ... yet ... carefully articulated."[73] This voice was supposed to play "a big part in moulding the temper of the time. Irascible, petulant, hurried, the subscriber cannot help but feel the influence of that something which appeals to him as quiet, dignified, soothing, until his temper melts away as the mountain snows before the compelling chinook of the south west."[74] The operator's voice was transforming the technical work into a "labour of love."

Thus, the female operator was a great asset to the telephone business. Telephone companies's managers did not hesitate to say that she was instrumental in the growth of the telephone industry. As L.I. McMahon, a Bell Telephone Company's official, pointed out: "If ever the rush of girls into the business world was a blessing it was when they took possession of the telephone exchanges."[75] Yet, she was very poorly paid, and her working conditions were difficult, in spite of the improvement of her physical environment by Bell Telephone Company, with the addition of rest rooms, comfortable cafeterias, modern bathrooms, etc.[76] For that reason, this soothing effect that the operators exerted on the subscribers (who were still mostly male) and which was considered a "feminine" quality, was not to be found in all of them. Indeed, with the technical improvement of the telephone system, the task of operating was becoming increasingly exacting and the subscribers more and more demanding, so that only "girls with steady nerves and a phlegmatic constitution" could stand the constant pressure. Moreover, a hierarchy had been created within the operating labour force. In 1884, a female chief-operator had been appointed in Montreal, creating the first rank in a hierarchy that was to grow over the years, with the addition of female supervisors and assistant chief-operators. In fact, all these appointments were given to women, although men were still working as night operators.[77] These women's task was to exercise a tight control over the regular operators. The discipline imposed on the operators for the subscribers' satisfaction and the company's development was "unfriendly to relaxation." "You can't make an operator out of a nervous girl. That has been tried ... she produces a species of emotion which borders on hysteria," said McFarlane.[78] Hence, since the work was so demanding and nerve racking, the operators occasionally would loose their tempers and surprise the subscribers who were used to more consideration, especially from women. An operator describes some ways of dealing with "arrogant" subscribers: "There are plenty of ways one finds to avenge one's self upon the telephone bogs. You can give them the click of the 'busy back,' you can ring the bell in their ears, or you can simply let them wait and rattle their hooks."[79]

In general, however, the operator's job was seen as a "respectable" occupation for women. Mary Rosetta Warren, an operator in Montreal from 1880 to 1891, clearly summarizes the "spirit" of the operators of that period: "I doubt whether the modern operator ever felt the *thrill and glamour* that we did in being part of the early telephone development ... It was a daily occurrence to be asked by a subscriber to say a few words to a gentleman who had never used a telephone before—*which made me feel very important.*"[80] In short, the company's decision to sex-label telephone operating as a female position did not, as generally suggested in the literature on feminisation, decrease its economic and social status but, rather, increased the qualitative requirements of the job, and made it possible for the company to obtain better educated and better qualified applicants. The feminisation of the operating work transformed a job which was considered at the outset as a part-time occupation of male operators into a "labour of love" for female operators. Although the female operators doing such work were considered to be finding their reward more in the "love" they received from the subscribers than in the wages they were given by the company, it gave women opportunities to be upwardly mobile, within the operator force. In fact, while the true operator was invaluable to the company, the occupation offered by the telephone industry constituted one of the few opportunities of "decent" job for young women despite low wages attached to it.

IV

It is impossible to find a pay-roll book for the first period of expansion of the telephone business, as wages were based on arbitrary criteria such as age, discipline, quality of voice, etc., which manager McFarlane called the operator's "ability and experience."[81] However, operators' life stories give a fair account of the wages they earned when working for Bell Telephone Company. For example, during the 1880s, an operator earned $8.00 per month for 12 hours—and sometimes 16 hours—of work per day.[82] Overtime was not paid and, often, operators worked two or three years without an increase. In addition, night operators, who were men, were better paid than day operators. Frank A. Field, for instance, who was a night operator in 1889 was paid $25 per month.[83] L.I. McMahon stated that "girls came in not because they were cheaper, but because they were better."[84] In a way, he was right. A male day operator was paid $8 per month in 1879, the same as a female operator in 1880. The difference, however, lay in the fact that the occupation of operator represented, for men, a job "secondary to their own business"[85] while, for women, it constituted a fulltime job. It seems that operators' wages varied according to other obscure criteria as well. For example, in 1880, Lillian W. Camp earned $12 per month (soon raised to $17.50) in Montreal while eleven years later, in the same city, Florence Hendry earned $12 per month.[86] Moreover, Margaret E. Helsby, who was also working in the Montreal Exchange, earned $20 per month in 1889, while Ethel V. Hannaford earned $12 per month in 1908 in Hamilton, both working nine hours per day.[87] These few examples show the arbitrariness of the operators' wages during the period studied. The common denominator, however, was that most of them were paid very little. Indeed, in a sample of seven operators working during the period from 1880 to 1902, five earned $12 or less per month[88,] which certainly did not constitute living wages. As an operator pointed out: "We were just unsophisticated school girls who lived at home with our parents—but where else could we live on ten dollars a month?"[89] Even L.B. McFarlane said, in 1905, during hearings of the Select Committee on the Telephone, that operators' wages "were probably insufficient to get along with respectability."[90] Yet, the job was considered "steady work ... which [gave] one a sense of security in case of illness ... and [provided] pension plans."[91] Besides, other female jobs were not much better paid. For instance, in 1901, in the clothing industry, female factory workers earned about $16 per month while female workers in the book binding and publishing industry earned between $15 and $18 per month.[92] On the other hand, a 1879 *Montreal Daily Witness* reported that "the girls who can use the new typewriter machine ... are earning from $10.00 to $36.00 a week."[93] As for teachers, their wages varied greatly according to their classification and the place where they were teaching. In 1870, a third class female teacher earned between $13 and $20 per month while a first class teacher could earn as much as $34 per month.[94] Finally, in 1889, women caretakers in school institutions earned around $30 per month.[95] Perhaps women did not engage in the operator occupation for the pay alone which compared unfavourably with other jobs, but rather for the job status. The direct contact with the subscribers and the role of community agent rendered their job "glamorous" in comparison with teaching in obscure places or cleaning a building. Moreover, because of the "spirit

of family" developed by Bell Telephone Company's patriarchal attitude, operators stated that they were "proud" to work for the telephone industry "which has
contributed so much to the needs and comfort and convenience of civilization."[96]
The telephone company seemed to be, for the young women, "a new door ... toward the economic independence for which they were striving,"[97] and a way to
obtain some social recognition as useful members of the society. This seems to
support Prentice's claim that women accepted poorly paid job outside the household in order to be provided with "respectable independence,"[98] even if the
wages would not support them independently.

V

The feminisation of the occupation of operator in the telephone industry brought
new opportunities to women on the labour market. However, although this
gave Bell Telephone Company the appearance of being a progressive employer,
it is clear that the company started the process of feminisation of its operating labour force as a response to an acute problem of production which it had
encountered with its male operators. After a few years of craftwork development, the telephone business started to expand more systematically, especially
after the Bell Telephone Company was chartered in 1880. It is not a coincidence that the feminisation of the operator's occupation started with the
incorporation of Bell Company. The high quality work produced by women contributed to the expansion of the telephone industry. Finally, the feminisation of
the job of operator constituted, for the telephone industry, more efficient exploitation of its employees as it was paying equal wages for higher and better
quality production by female operators. The process of feminisation of the operator's occupation supports some of the assumptions suggested in the different
perspectives attempting to explain the process of feminisation of the labour
force. The telephone industry manipulated the job requirements and applied
stereotyped female qualities to the job of operator. Moreover, due to the technical
segmentation of the labour process, the job was a low-skill occupation requiring
low level of stability which corresponded to the sex-labelling assignation of low
stability given to women. As it was, the level of turnover at the switchboard
was very high as most operators left after one or two years either to marry, or
because of physical or nervous breakdown due to the constant pressure exercised
on them. Finally, women were forced, in some ways, to take that low-paid job,
as the female reserve army of labour was large and the jobs open to women
were few.

    The operator occupation, however, did not represent a sub-market job in-
volving a low social status. The job was a very important part of the production
process of the telephone industry, and acquired a higher social status after
being labelled as a "female" occupation, although its wages did not improve.

This higher status was partly due to the fact that barriers of "respectability" were placed before prospective employers, and because certain behavioural demands were imposed on actual employees. Moreover, when the process of feminisation began, the job was not entirely defined as a female occupation. Some of its characteristics (for example, repairing electrical breakdown) were "male," and women had to adapt their socially recognised skills to these job demands. Thus, although the case of the telephone operators supports several conceptions of the reviewed researches on feminisation, there exist some differences at the level of its location in the structure of the organisation, as well as in term of social status and social mobility.

Notes

I would like to thank Bruce Curtis and anonymous readers for their helpful comments on a first draft of this article. This study would not have been possible without the generous access to the archives of Bell Canada and the Archdiocese of Montreal which I was allowed. Of course, all errors are my own responsibility.

1. Early operators' file, Bell Company's Historical Collection (hereafter called BCHC).
2. This decision is based on the fact that most data are from Bell Telephone Co. However, some data from other telephone companies in the United States and Canada show that competitive businesses were using more or less identical hiring policies. Hence, examples from other companies will also be employed when relevant.
3. See, for example, Alison Prentice, "The Feminisation of Teaching in British North America and Canada, 1845-1875," *Social History,* 3(1975), 5-20; and M. Danylewycz and A. Prentice, "Teachers' Work," *Labour/Le Travail,* 17 (1986), 58-80; M. Grumet, "Pedagogy for Patriarchy: The Feminisation of Teaching," *Interchange,* 12 (1981), 165-84.
4. See G.B. Lowe, "Women, Work and the Office: The Feminisation of Clerical Occupations in Canada, 1901-1931," *Canadian Journal of Sociology,* 5 (1980), 361-81; "Class, Job and Gender in the Canadian Office," *Labour/Le Travail* 10 (1982), 11-37.
5. See B. Curtis, "Capital, the State, and the Origins of the Working-Class Household" and L. Briskin, "Domestic Labour: A Methodological Discussion," in B. Fox, ed., *Hidden in the Household* (Toronto 1980), 101-34, 135-72.
6. Prentice, "Feminisation," 6-7.
7. *Ibid.,* 19.
8. *Ibid.,* 16-7.
9. M. Danylewycz, *et al.,* "The Evolution of the Sexual Division of Labour in Teaching: A Nineteenth Century Ontario and Quebec Case Study," *Social History,* 16 (1983), 81-109.
10. Lowe, "Women, Work, and the Office."

11. *Ibid.,* 367.

12. H. Braverman, *Labor and Monopoly Capitalism* (New York 1974), 385.

13. Lowe, "Women, Work, and the Office," 368.

14. *Ibid.,* 369-70.

15. *Ibid.,* 371.

16. *Ibid.,* 375-6.

17. B. Curtis, "Capital," 131. Note that B. Fox shows that women are not simply a labour reserve as Curtis implies, but continually occupy certain sectors of the paid labour force. See Fox, *Hidden in the Household.* On the debate on domestic labour, see also M. Barrett and R. Hamilton, eds., *Politics of Diversity* (London 1986). B. Taylor's *Eve and the New Jerusalem,* (New York 1983) outlines changing domestic politics in nineteenth-century England.

18. *Ibid.,* 121.

19. *Ibid.,* 113-4, emphasis added.

20. L. Briskin, "Domestic Labour," 137, emphasis added.

21. M. Luxton, *More than a Labour of Love* (Toronto 1980).

22. Women's subordination resulting from economic structures caused them to accept occupations characterised by low-wages, low-status jobs, and requiring such characteristics as obedience and submissiveness.

23. Although a few occupations needing some technical skill, for example bookbinders, were given to women, it is a fact that these jobs were mainly attributed to men.

24. Here the phenomenon may be compared to that examined by R. Edwards in *Contested Terrain* (London 1979). In "bureaucratic control," Edwards points out, a hierarchy is created within each occupation, giving the illusion of advancement in the general hierarchy of the enterprise. However, although it is relatively easy to climb the hierarchical scale within a specific occupation, it is very difficult to have access to other "job families" rated at a higher level of the general hierarchy of the enterprise. For the operators, for instance, it was near to impossible to become local managers, except in very small rural exchanges and, then, they were paid as supervisors.

25. I analyze the role of communication in the process of accumulation in "Communication as Circulation: A Political Economic Analysis," paper presented at the meeting of the International Association of Communication Studies, Montreal, 25 May 1987. See also my "Communication and Social Forms: A Historical Study of the Development of the Telephone, 1876-1920," unpublished Ph.D. thesis, University of Toronto, 1987.

26. " 'Bread Toaster' to Common Battery: Mostly about Boy Telephone Operators and Operating Conditions in the Nineteenth-Century," unpublished manuscript, 1943, Operators-Boy file, BCHC.

27. The job of operator was labelled "female only" long before it actually became an entirely female job. Indeed, it had been recognized as a woman's occupation while there are still male operators working on the night shifts. This will be discussed later.

28. " 'Bread Toaster' to Common Battery," Operators-Boy file, BCHC.

29. *Mandements, lettres pastorales, circulaires, et autres documents,* 9 (1882), 439, Diocese of Montreal Historical Collection (hereafter DMHC).

30. The periodical gave advices on how to economise, low budget recipes, etc.

31. "The Family," *Le Monde Illustré,* 1884. This is not to say that all working-class women followed this advice.

32. *Mandements, Lettres Pastorales, Circulaires et autres Documents,* 13 (1901), 453, DMHC.

33. *Ibid.,* 9 (1887), 66.

34. *Ibid.,* 14 (1909), 577.

35. Joan Sangster, "The 1907 Bell Telephone Strike: Organizing workers," *Labour / Le Travail* 3 (Fall 1978), 122-3, 126-7. Although Sangster's study is concerned with a period not covered by this paper, it is safe to state that these social prejudices expressed in 1907 must have been even stronger earlier.

36. This was also true for other occupations. See Danylewycz, "Evolution," 101.

37. K.M. Schmith, "I Was Your Old 'Hello Girl'," *The Saturday Post,* 12 July 1930.

38. F.B. Jewett, "The Social Implication of Scientific Research in Electrical Communication," *Bell Telephone Quarterly,* 14 (1936), 205-18. Emphasis added.

39. " 'Bread Toasters' to Common Battery," 2, 3, 4, BCHC. In contrast to female operators, the prospect of advancement for male operators was not limited to that occupation. It involved other job families such as technicians and, even, managers.

40. Shortly after Bell Telephone Co. started to hire women as operators, other independent telephone companies followed their example.

41. K.M. Schmitt, "I was." These "unsuitable" characteristics, however, might have been intensified by the poor wages given to the operators. According to C.F. Sise, males would apply as operators only "as spare-time job as the income was too low." (C.F. Sise's Letter, 21 February 1887, BCHC). Since males had other possibilities of income—even within the telephone industry—they were not particularly attracted by the operator's work.

42. Letter from L.B. McFarlane to C.E. Cutz, 7 July 1887, document #27144-44, BCHC. This worker was probably a night operator as the day operators were already women, especially in big cities.

43. Other occupations involved one or the other of these two characteristics. However, the case of the operators was unique in that the job become a female occupation *uniting* those two aspects.

44. "Telephone History—Montreal," no date, BCHC.

45. H.S. Coyle, "The Operating Forces of Modern Telephone Exchange," Telephony, 2 (1901), 218.

46. K.J. Dunstan, "Office Management," no date, BCHC.

47. Report of Meeting of C.F. Sise with Local-managers, 16-17 May 1887, document #26606, BCHC, 9.

48. Questionnaire from C.F. Sise to Local-managers, 16 May 1887, document #27344, BCHC, 3, emphasis added.

49. K.J. Dunstan's Life Story, BCHC. Mrs. Dunstan and Baker were local-managers respectively in Toronto and Hamilton, and Mr. Sise was general manager of Bell Telephone Co.

50. K.J. Dunstan's payroll, October 1880, document #2405b, BCHC.

51. I use the word "girl" despite its sexist connotation, because it was the way the female operators were referred to by most people, including themselves.

52. Telephone Directory, Halifax, N.S., March 1886, BCHC.

53. K.M. Schmitt, 1930, *op. cit.*

54. "60 Years at the Switchboard," *Michigan Bell Magazine,* October 1940, BCHC. At that period, women could also be hired to work on typewriter machines, taking the place of male copyists and shorthand writers. See "New Industry," *Montreal Daily Witness,* 4 January 1879.

55. K.M. Schmitt, "I was."

56. Later, Bell Telephone Co. required five letters of recommendation. In addition to the three formers, one letter was required from a physician and one from a property owner.

57. "60 Years at the Switchboard."

58. Quotations and Anecdotes file, BCHC.

59. "Across the Wires," *The Daily Witness,* 21 March, no date, in *McFarlane's Scrapbook,* document #12016, BCHC. Although there is no date on the article, the clipping was glued in McFarlane's scrapbook among other newspaper clippings dated of the end of the 1890s.

60. Actually, several of these young men later became technicians, linemen, and, even, managers for Bell Telephone Co.

61. K.M. Schmitt, "I was."

62. Document #27344, BCHC, 7.

63. Since women were considered useless and inefficient in technical and mechanical work, some companies's managers had serious reservations. (Document 27344, BCHC, 5) These, however, faded when confronted with some female operators, especially in small towns, who had effected—with the aid of the instructions in the small book—all the work necessary to maintain the telephone exchange in working condition.

64. K.M. Schmitt, "I was."

65. "Use of Women Operators at Night," *Quebec City Letters,* 1888, BCHC.

66. K.M. Schmitt, "I was."

67. B. Lalonde's Life Story, 1906, BCHC. Emphasis added.

68. "Who Wouldn't Be a Telephone Girl?" *Watchman,* 12 June 1898.

69. *Ibid.*

70. "Héros inconnus et méconnus: la téléphoniste," *La Patrie,* 14 July 1908.

71. "Treatment of Telephone Operators," *Telephony,* 8 (August 1904), 124-5.

72. "Voice Culture," *Mail,* 2 August 1916.

73. "A Study of the Telephone Girl," *Telephony,* 9 (1905), 388-90.

74. *Ibid.*

75. "Girls Were Never Greater Blessing than When They Entered Phone Exchanges," *News,* 4 November 1916.

76. Here I do not completely agree with Sangster who stated that the 1907 strike of the operators in Toronto was the significant event which brought more comfortable surroundings to the operators. (Sangster, "1907.") Indeed, already in 1896, the biggest exchanges were provided with an "early form of air conditioning, recreational and lunch rooms, steel locker for each worker, drying room (even for clothing), bathrooms where last fashion baths were available for operators if necessary." (H.G. Owen, *One Hundred Years,* Bell Canada Publication, 1980, BCHC, 12.) A telephone company's manager stressed that these improvements in the physical environment were not primarily for the operator's well being, but "I suppose the plan has its humanitarian side, but it is also a good business investment. Give your employees a pleasant and comfortable place in which to work, treat them with consideration and the results will more than repay for the trouble." ("Treatment of Telephone Operators.") This shows that many years before the Toronto strike, telephone companies had already understood some psychological principles at the basis of the employees' productivity.

77. However, there were no opportunities for women to get a promotion outside the operating labour force. They could not, for instance, be appointed as local-managers, the most lucrative position. Actually, the promotion of women as chief-operators and supervisors was due to patriarchal attitudes, since the managers felt that women would be more protective towards the young operators, like good mothers!

78. "Across the Wires."

79. "The Diary of a Telephone Girl," *The Saturday Evening Post,* 19 October 1907.

80. M.R. Warren's Life Story, 1880-1891. Emphasis added. The story was told in 1937, which sheds more light on what she meant by "modern operator."

81. "Across the Wires."

82. Mary Ann Burnett's Life Story, 1887, BCHC.

83. F.A. Field's Life Story, 1889, BCHC.

84. "Girls Were Never Greater Blessing...."

85. Document #27344, 3.

86. L.W. Camp's Life Story, 1880-95; F. Hendry's Life Story, 1891-1931, BCHC.

87. M.E. Helsby's Life Story, 1888-96; E.V. Hannaford's Life Story, 1908-17, BCHC.

88. Life Stories of M. Hill, 1900; F. Hendry, 1891-1931; M.E. Helsby, 1888-96; M.A. Burnett, 1887-1916; M.I. Phillips, 1889-93; W. Chevalier, 1896.

89. K.M. Schmitt, "I was."

90. "Telephone Inquiry on Wages and Living Expenses," *Montreal Gazette,* 11 February 1906. Another inquiry occurred, started by the 1907 Bell Telephone strike. However, it does not contain relevant data related to the subject of this article, as its target was limited to the Toronto operators working in 1907.

91. C.M. Cline's Life Story, 1907, BCHC.

92. *Census of Canada,* III (Ottawa 1901).

93. "A New Industry," *Montreal Daily Witness,* 4 January 1879.

94. Prentice, "Feminisation," 14.

95. Danylewycz and Prentice, "Teachers' Work," 75.

96. Olive Geach's Life Story, 1918-20, BCHC.

97. "60 Years at the Switchboard," 1940.

98. Prentice, "Feminisation," 17.

CHAPTER

6 RADICALISM AND THE CANADIAN WORKING CLASS, 1900-1919

In the course of the 1980s, the study of the history of Canadian workers came to be dominated by a generation of self-styled "New Left" historians such as Greg Kealey and Brian Palmer, to name only the two most prominent. Ideologically committed and intellectually indebted to the revisionist Marxist analyses of men such as E.P. Thompson of Great Britain and the American Herbert Gutman, this school set out in the early 1970s to cast what until then had been known in Canada as "labour history" in a new mould, "working class history."

For New Left historians, the concept of working-class history was an urgently needed new departure in Canadian historiography, for in their view the old labour history left much to be desired. The traditional, pre- and immediate post-World War II institutional studies by trail-blazers such as Harold A. Logan, which focussed on formal trade union organizational structures, were considered too elitist and too consensus-oriented. The latter criticism was levelled as well against the more modern "social democratic scholars" of the 1950s to the 1970s such as Eugene Forsey, Stuart Jamieson and Ken McNaught. The "Old Left" tradition in Canada, as represented by Charles Lipton, was also deemed unsatisfactory. It was not so much rejected by the New Left as dismissed as feeble and unsophisticated in its application of Marxist principles to the study of the Canadian working class.

The main wrath of the New Left, however, was reserved for another group of Canadian historians, the product of the expanding university world of the 1960s, which eschewed Marxist theory for a supposedly non-ideological, realist approach to the study of working-class history. The leading spokesman for this group, which came to the fore in the 1970s, was David Bercuson, but it also included individuals such as Irving Abella and Ross McCormack. For New Leftists, the deliberate rejection of Marxist theory meant this group could never come to a genuine understanding of the history of Canadian workers.

In particular, New Left historians stressed that the study of working class history must explain the development in Canada of what it called a "working class culture." The imperatives of the capitalist system, they argued, had elicited a common response from workers across the country, both in the workplace and in their everyday lives, and thereby produced a distinct and identifiable class culture. The Bercuson approach disputed the very existence of such a culture, arguing that the history of Canadian workers was marked more by factors which divided them—region, ethnicity, gender—than by those which united them.

The essence of the debate between these two poles of interpretation is to be found in the two articles presented here with respect to the development of radicalism within the Canadian labour movement in the first two decades of the twentieth century, culminating in the year of labour revolt, 1919. David Bercuson's "Labour Radicalism and the Western Industrial Frontier, 1897-1919" presents the view that western Canadian workers were more radical than their eastern Canadian and Maritime counterparts, a fact attributable in large part to their immigrant origins. In "1919: The Canadian Labour Revolt," on the other hand, Greg Kealey rejects the west/east distinction, arguing that by 1919 labour revolt was endemic across Canada and not limited by regional or other boundaries. Students should also carefully assess the implications for the Bercuson/Kealey debate of recent feminist articles such as Mary Horodyski's "Women and the Winnipeg General Strike of 1919."

Suggestions for Further Reading

Abella, Irving, *Nationalism, Communism and Canadian Labour: The CIO, the Communist Party and the Canadian Congress of Labour, 1935-1956*. Toronto: University of Toronto Press, 1973.

Bercuson, David. J., "Through the Looking Glass of Culture: An Essay on the New Labour History and Working-Class Culture in Recent Canadian Historical Writing," *Labour/Le Travail*, VII (Spring, 1981), 95-112.

Bradbury, Bettina, "Women's History and Working-Class History," *Labour/Le Travail*, XIX (Spring, 1987), 23-43.

Conley, J.R., "Frontier Labourers, Crafts in Crisis and the Western Labour Revolt," *Labour/Le Travail*, 23 (Spring 1989), 9-37.

Forsey, Eugene, *The Canadian Labour Movement, 1812-1902*. Ottawa: The Canadian Historical Association, 1974.

Horodyski, Mary, "Women and the Winnipeg General Strike of 1919," *Manitoba History* (Spring, 1986), 28-37.

Jamieson, S., *Times of Trouble: Labour Unrest and Industrial Conflict in Canada, 1900-1966*. Ottawa: Privy Council Office, 1971.

Kealey, Greg, "Labour and Working-Class History in Canada: Prospects in the 1980s," *Labour/Le Travail*, VII (Spring, 1981), 67-94.

Lipton, Charles, *The Trade Union Movement in Canada*. (3rd ed.), Toronto: NC Press, 1967.

Logan, Harold, *Trade Unions in Canada*. Toronto: Macmillan, 1948.

McCormack, A.R., *Reformers, Rebels, and Revolutionaries: The Western Canadian Radical Movement, 1899-1919*. Toronto: University of Toronto Press, 1977.

McInnis, Peter, "All Solid Along the Line: The Reid Newfoundland Strike of 1918," *Labour/Le Travail*, XXVI (Fall, 1990), 61-84.

McNaught, Kenneth, *A Prophet in Politics*. Toronto: University of Toronto Press, 1959.

Naylor, J., "Toronto 1919," Canadian Historical Association, *Historical Papers*, 1986, 33-55.

Palmer, B., *A Culture in Conflict: Skilled Workers and Industrial Capitalism in Hamilton, Ontario, 1860-1914*. Montreal: McGill-Queen's University Press, 1979.

Reilly, N., "The General Strike in Amherst, Nova Scotia, 1919," *Acadiensis*, IX, (1980), 56-77.

LABOUR RADICALISM AND THE WESTERN INDUSTRIAL FRONTIER, 1897-1919

David Bercuson

The rapid growth of the Canadian west from the mid-1890s to the start of World War I was based upon the arrival and settlement of millions of immigrants. [Throughout this essay the term is applied generally to all those who migrated to the frontier including central and eastern Canadians.] The agricultural frontier attracted prospective farmers from every corner of the globe and their settlement saga has held the attention of a generation of Canadians. The frontier has been called a great leveller which broke down class distinctions because men were equal, free and far from the traditional bonds and constraints of civilization.[1] On the frontier every 'Jack' was as good as his master. But the settlement of the agricultural frontier was only part of the total picture of western development. An urban-industrial and a hinterland-extractive frontier was being opened at the same time which underwent spectacular productive ex-

From *The Canadian Historical Review*, LVIII, no. 2 (June 1977), 154-175. Reprinted by permission of the University of Toronto Press.

pansion and attracted many thousands of pioneer workers. Most of these men had gone to the frontier pushed by the same ambitions and seeking the same opportunities as other immigrants. But once in western Canada most entered into closed and polarized communities and were forced to work in dangerous or unrewarding occupations. For these men there was little upward mobility, little opportunity for improvement. They were not free and were not as good as their masters.

The pioneer workers had come a long way to improve themselves. Most lost the inhibitions and inertia which usually characterized those who stayed behind. They were ready to work hard and live frugally, to sacrifice, to do what was necessary to win the rewards they had come to seek.[2] But their way was usually blocked, their efforts thwarted not because of their failures but by a system. They usually faced a big difference between what they had sought and what could be achieved. Some immigrants came from such poverty and desperation that anything was an improvement and they were satisfied. But most eventually decided to break out of the closed systems which bound them or, if they could not break out, to smash them. The system thus lost its claim to their hearts and minds and labour radicalism emerged.

Were western workers really more radical than those in central Canada and the maritime provinces? The answer depends upon the definition of radicalism because major, prolonged, and violent strikes, as well as political insurgency, can be found in all regions of Canada during this period.[3] The dictionary is precise: Radicalism is 'the quality or state of being radical' while radical is 'favoring fundamental or extreme change: specifically, favoring such change of the social structure; very leftist.' Militancy is 'the state or quality of being militant' while militant is 'ready and willing to fight; warlike; combative.'[4] These definitions allow the conclusion that up to 1919 western workers were more radical than those of other regions though they were, perhaps, no more militant. Their radicalism emerged in several ways, which involved efforts to effect radical change. For example, the Socialist Party of Canada, which called for the elimination of capitalism and its replacement by the dictatorship of the proletariat, had its headquarters in Vancouver, the bulk of its membership in the west, and, after 1914, the official endorsation of District 18 of the United Mine Workers of America. Major Socialist party supporters could be found in the leading ranks of western unions—George Armstrong, Robert B. Russell, Richard Johns in Winnipeg, Joseph Sanbrooke in Regina, Joseph Knight and Carl Berg in Edmonton, William Pritchard, Jack Kavanagh, Victor Midgley, A.S. Wells in Vancouver. Support for other left-wing socialist parties, such as the Social Democratic party, was also centred primarily in western Canada. Though union members in other parts of the country engaged in independent political action, only in the west was their politics so definitely and unmistakable Marxian. Radical industrial unionism and syndicalism also flourished in the west. The Industrial Workers of the World [IWW], the United

Brotherhood of Railway Employees, the American Labour Union, and the One Big Union all attained varying degrees of success in western Canada but almost none in Ontario, Quebec, or the maritimes. The west's attraction to these forms of unionism was also reflected in its experiments with general strikes.[5]

Western radicalism reached the peak of its influence in 1919. Conventions of the British Columbia Federation of Labor, the Alberta Federation of Labor, and District 18 of the United Mine Workers passed resolutions advocating worker control of industry, the formation of syndicalist-oriented unions, and general strikes to achieve political change. The workers pointedly expressed sympathy and support for Russian and German revolutionaries.[6] These three gatherings were prelude to the now famous Western Labor Conference held in March 1919 at Calgary and to the emergence of the One Big Union.[7] In each case large and representative bodies of western workers declared that their unions must be instruments for social change. This was the essence of western labour radicalism.

There were, to be sure, radicals in central Canada and the maritimes. The coal miners of Cape Breton were susceptible to radical ideas, particularly after 1917 when the Provincial Workmen's Association [PWA] was disbanded. In 1919 there was some experimentation with general strikes on a limited scale and some scattered sympathy for the One Big Union idea.[8] But, for the most part, Nova Scotia miners responded to the exigencies of militancy, not political radicalism. Syndicalism, with its rejection of electoral politics, went against the grain of a group of workers 'content to remain within the rules.'[9] When the Nova Scotia Independent Labour party was formed in 1919, it advocated traditional progressive reform such as the initiative, referendum, recall, and proportional representation.[10] J.B. McLachlan, a radical Scottish miner who led the drive to destroy the PWA in the coal fields, tried to lead District 26 of the United Mine Workers into the Red International of Labor Unions in the early twenties.[11] He was personally popular but stood outside the mainstream and his views alienated others and eventually undermined his own support.[12] There was a tradition of independent political activism amongst island miners but it tended towards labour-oriented reform, not socialist or marxist radicalism. Outside the coal fields even this tradition was almost non-existent.

In a 1966 article, and later in his history of the IWW, Melvyn Dubofsky sought to explain labour radicalism in the American west particularly amongst miners. He asserted that rapid industrialization, the introduction of technological innovations, ethnic homogeneity of the workforce, and other factors created class polarization in the mining industry. Polarization led to class war which, in turn, led to the development of class ideology. Dubofsky did not agree with the idea that western American radicalism was 'the response of pioneer individualists to frontier conditions.'[13]

The validity of this argument is something which American labour historians are more competent to judge but its applicability to Canada should be seriously questioned. There was certainly rapid industrialization in the Canadian west but there was no technological revolution in mining because most coal and hardrock mining began *after* the major technological changes in the western United States had occurred. Americans were mining for metals on a large scale in the 1870s and when Canadian hardrock mining did begin in the 1890s it was initially financed and directed largely by Americans who generally applied what they had already learned.[14] Most western Canadian coal mines were too small to benefit from the major advances of the day and mechanization was not widespread prior to 1919. The ethnic homogeneity pointed to by Dubofsky did not exist in western Canada. In the Kootenay region, for example, 34 per cent of the male population in 1911 were Canadian, 24 per cent British, 25 per cent European, 10 per cent American, and 4 per cent Asian.[15] In Vancouver 28 per cent were Canadian, 33 per cent British, 9 per cent European, 7 per cent Asian, and 9 per cent American. If Dubofsky's ideas are to be applied to the Canadian west, they will have to be significantly altered because the opening of the western Canadian mining frontier and the settlement, growth, and industrialization of western Canadian cities occurred at least two decades later than in the United States.

Paul Phillips has put forward arguments rooted in Canadian experience. He asserted that the character of western labour developed in response to the nature of the resource-based economy.[16] The National Policy of tariff protection to manufacturers raised the costs of primary production, encouraged investment in commerce and transportation but provided 'little or no scope for industrial expansion in the west ...' Employers developed 'a short-term rather than a long-term view toward labour issues' and were not greatly interested in 'developing a permanent and peaceful relation with the labour force.' Phillips believed these factors, combined with regional isolation, created 'greater insecurity of employment and wages ...' primarily because 'frontier employers ... wanted to shift as much of the entrepreneurial risk onto the employees as possible.' In this way the resource-based economic structure of the region created 'a very much more militant and class-conscious type of union.'

If Phillips' thesis is to hold it must apply to the miners because they were clearly the vanguard of radicalism. The National Policy may have forced an inordinate concentration on resource extraction in the west and pressured employers into 'short-term' attitudes but resource extraction was also significant in Nova Scotia which, in this period, produced more coal than Alberta and British Columbia combined.[17] The mine workforce in Nova Scotia in 1910 was slightly more than 17,000 out of a total labour force of just over 173,000. This was a far larger proportion of the workforce than in either Alberta or British Columbia or even the two together.[18] The miners of Nova Scotia should have been under the same constraints and difficulties as those of the west because if the National Policy put difficulties in the path of western resource extraction industries, it also created problems for maritime resource extraction industries. Indeed, Nova Scotia coal operators, even the giant Dominion Coal (and British

Empire Steel and Coal which succeeded it), could not compete in the lucrative markets of Ontario against Pennsylvania and West Virginia coal because of insufficient tariff protection.[19] If the National Policy was responsible for labour radicalism in western Canada, why not Nova Scotia? Nova Scotia miners were often very militant but prior to 1919 showed little radicalism.

The capital structure of mining in western Canada was actually far from being unsophisticated or 'frontier-like.' Andy den Otter observed that 'although Alberta's coal deposits were vast, mining ventures did not realize quick, high returns but required very careful planning and large scale, long-term financing.' Thus the federal government granted Sir Alexander Tilloch Galt large tracts of land to subsidize his combined railway and coal mining operations in the Coal Banks (Lethbridge) area and enabled him to attract the British investment capital needed for expansion in the 1890s.[20] Investors such as Barings and Glyn and Company, the Grand Trunk Railroad, the Industrial and General Trust, and other like concerns could hardly have held short-term, quick return, expectations. Similarly, railway companies such as the CPR could not have acted the role of 'frontier employers' in their ownership of, or investment in, large mining properties. Canadian Pacific took over F. Augustus Heinze's smelter at Trail (and the railways and land grants that went with them) in 1897.[21] This was the beginning of Consolidated Mining and Smelting (Cominco), which combined Heinze's operation with large Canadian Pacific investments and acquired valuable properties such as the Sullivan mine at Kimberly, British Columbia.[22] Cominco soon became the largest employer of miners and smeltermen in the region and was clearly intended to be a long-term capital venture. The Crows Nest Pass Coal Company, with a capitalization in 1911 of $3.5 million, had an agreement with Canadian Pacific, concluded in 1897, to provide coal for smelting and other purposes.[23] This mining concern earned large profits[24] selling coal and coke to smelters in the west Kootenay and Boundary regions and was typical of many mines in the area.

The mineral economy of the British Columbia interior quickly developed a complex inter-related structure. Coal mines supplied coal and coke to the smelters while hardrock mines supplied ores.[25] As long as the smelters operated profits were made. The smelter concerns may have had to sell their products in an unprotected world market but there were few uncertainties associated with this phenomenon in the period under examination. The mines in the region were prosperous and went through phenomenal growth up to the end of World War I. New smelters were opened, rail lines laid, mines dug, and camps, towns, and cities expanded.[26] The key to the region's success was the low cost of extraction and the high grades of ore. Even world depressions had little impact in the region's hot house economic atmosphere. One observer commented: 'During the past summer [1897] the rapid decline in the value of silver, that proved so disastrous to other silver countries, had little effect on our silver mines, other than to check investment, as the ores were usually of such high grade, as to leave, even at the lowest price, a good margin of profit.'[27] What was true of silver was also true of copper. The size of the deposits and the heavily mechanized nature of the industry, combined with cheap railway charges, kept profits high. Another observer claimed that 'nowhere on the continent can smelting be carried on more cheaply given fair railroad rates and fuel at a reasonable cost.'[28] Both conditions existed and business boomed except for a brief period just after the turn of the century. Some of the mine owners blamed the downturn on restrictive mining legislation and labour agitators (there was a major strike at Rossland that year) but the *British Columbia Mining Record,* leading journal of the industry, attributed the condition to swindling, mismanagement, and over-taxation.[29] Stagnation there was—for a few years—but the factor which most often closed down the smelters and caused a back-up of ore and production cuts in the hardrock mines was strikes in the coal fields supplying fuel to the area.[30]

The collieries of Vancouver Island do not easily fit a general picture of struggling and uncertain resource extractors. The largest operator was the Dunsmuir family who sold out to Canadian Collieries in 1911. The Dunsmuirs enjoyed steady markets in the United States at the turn of the century and were able to sell as much as 75 per cent of their production in San Francisco. This was true for all the collieries on the island.[31] During these years 30 to 40 per cent of the coal consumed in California was mined in British Columbia—the largest amount from any one source.[32] Profits to the Dunsmuirs from coal were enhanced by land grants and subsidies acquired from the British Columbia government to build the Esquimalt and Nanaimo Railway.[33] When the Dunsmuirs sold out to a syndicate headed by Sir William Mackenzie, co-owner of the Canadian Northern Railway, the new company, Canadian Collieries (Dunsmuir) Limited, was capitalized at $15 million.[34] Mackenzie's interest in coal was not confined to Canadian Collieries. He and Sir Donald Mann, his partner in the Canadian Northern, provided half the capital to develop the Nordegg Field in Alberta through Mackenzie, Mann and Company Limited. The other half of the money came from the German Development Company, which was sole owner of the Brazeau Collieries in the same area.[35] These mines, like many that were opened in western Canada, were 'steam' coal operations which sold everything they could produce to the railways. The greatest market problem facing most of these mines prior to World War I was the increased use, particularly in California but also in Canadian coastal areas, of California fuel oil to replace coal.[36] This problem was, however, seriously aggravated by the serious production cuts in the island collieries resulting from the 1913 coal strike.[37] Up to this point island coal production showed a slow but steady increase.[38]

The mining industry may not have been protected by National Policy tariffs but it was frequently given generous subsidies by provincial and federal governments. It also had little trouble attracting capital from Britain and the United States as well as major Canadian companies such as Canadian Pacific. Some of the region's most intransigent employers were the largest. Canadian Collieries and Granby Consolidated Mining and Smelting were probably the most 'hard nosed' operators in western Canada and yet were large, heavily capitalized, and secure. Their attitude to industrial relations may have been short-sighted but could hardly have been prompted by insecurity. They shifted risks to their workers because they, like most employers, wanted to and, unlike some employers, were able to. The National Policy had little to do with it.

The argument could be made that the National Policy was the culprit behind most labour problems in the area because it had produced a resource-based economy in the west and such economies are riddled with labour problems. This is clearly so simplified that it explains nothing. Industry in the west was primarily resource-based because that was where the resources were (and still are). In this period there had been no appreciable industry established in urban areas but the west was still very young and industrial output was expanding at tremendous rates.[39] It is an interesting but fruitless exercise to speculate if, in this period, the economy would have been resource-based anyway or whether the National Policy was already suppressing the growth of secondary industry. The key problem here is whether western manufacturing had yet reached the point where it was large enough to be restricted by the National Policy. So far, there is no answer to the question.

What about the 'domestic' coal operators—those smaller mines producing coal for heating purposes? These mines in the east Kootenays and Alberta had more limited markets.[40] They could not compete with Pennsylvania anthracite in Winnipeg or points east because American coal, though usually slightly higher in price, was better quality.[41] They were also unable to compete in the coastal trade, in Canada or the United States, and had no entry to the northern California market. The prairies, northern Idaho, and eastern Washington were their domain. These operators sold in a less certain market than the steam coal producers or the Vancouver Island collieries and their uncertainty *was* at least partly due to the absence of sufficient tariff protection. However, they were the most reasonable for their employees to deal with and were less reluctant to sign agreements recognizing unions.[42] Perhaps the very uncertainty of their markets prompted them to avoid serious labour troubles, unlike a powerful giant such as Canadian Collieries.

Phillips asserts that western employers tended to take short-run, commercial views of their relations with their workers primarily because they purchased capital goods in a high-priced, protected market and sold their raw materials in unprotected world markets,[43] like the prairie grain farmers. But the parallel was superficial in reality whatever it may be in theory. Perhaps Phillips has explained why there were some uncertainties amongst western resource extraction employers at certain times, but even this tells little. There was no necessary connection between these uncertainties (when they did occur) and the rise of labour radicalism. There is, in fact, no real evidence that mine owners or smelter operators, with large capital investments in their enterprises, acted any differently from industrial capitalists anywhere. Conversely, there is no evidence that manufacturers in central Canada, when faced with the inevitable uncertainties of business, acted any differently from the resource extractors. Unions were fought and demands resisted by most businessmen when the cost of the struggle fell within economically acceptable limits. Unions were tolerated and their demands considered when the cost of resisting was greater than the price of capitulation. When mine owners in the Crowsnest Pass area faced a strong union (organized before the scattered operators had a chance to unite against it) in the reality of a limited labour supply and uncertain markets, they chose to deal with their workers. But the large operators of Vancouver Island, with a ready surplus of Chinese labour, assured markets, and facing a struggling union, dug in their heels.

The men who worked the mines of western Canada were mostly immigrants. This is in sharp contrast to the mine workforce in Canada's other major mining area—Nova Scotia. The 1911 federal census revealed that almost three-quarters of the mine employees in Nova Scotia were Canadian born compared to 12 per cent in Alberta and 16 per cent in British Columbia mine workers.[44] This picture is reflected in the male population of two Nova Scotia coal counties, Cumberland and Inverness. Eighty-one per cent of Cumberland men and 92 per cent of Inverness men were Nova Scotia born. In British Columbia 22 per cent of the men in Nanaimo District and 11 per cent in Kootenay District were native to the province. Conversely, only 19 per cent of Cumberland and 8 per cent of Inverness men were immigrants, while immigrants accounted for 78 per cent of the males of Nanaimo District and 89 per cent in Kootenay District. The western mines and mining communities were almost exactly opposite in composition to the mines and mining communities of the east. In addition, as Donald MacGillivray has pointed out, the strong presence of the Roman Catholic church in Cape Breton, with its belief in an organic, structured society, was important. Conservative religious traditions added to the influence of conservative metropolitan centres such as Halifax and Antigonish. His picture is one of an essentially conservative community with a 'thread of radicalism.'[45]

The pioneer immigrant nature of western mining society is reflected in other statistics. In the two Nova Scotia counties the ratio of men to women was 1.04:1. In Nanaimo District the ratio was 1.7:1 and in Kootenay District 1.9:1 The average age of mine employees in the west was higher than in Nova Scotia. Eighty per cent of British Columbia mine employees were between twenty-five and sixty-four years of age, while 70 per cent of Alberta and 65 per cent of Nova Scotia mine employees were in the same range. Literacy rates were also higher in the western mining regions for Canadian- and British-born miners. A composite emerges: in Nova Scotia young men born in the mining communities, or living in towns or on farms close by, went into the collieries at the earliest opportunity. They had travelled little, were younger, and less educated than western miners. They probably worked for the company their fathers had served before them and had few expectations about improving their immediate environment. In western Canada the miners had come from Ontario or Idaho or Wales or Italy or Austria to make their fortune. Perhaps they simply sought more cash to send back to the village. Troper and Harney have pointed to a crisis in rural village life in late nineteenth-century Europe as a factor causing young men to seek opportunities elsewhere[46] and many were clearly refugees from economic hardship.[47]

The British and Americans who came to the mining communities were usually skilled miners as were some Canadians from Nova Scotia.[48] The vast majority of European miners had been peasants and had no experience in mining. One result was that better paying jobs—miners in the hardrock mining industry, contract miners in the coal fields—usually went to Anglo-Saxons while the lower paying positions—muckers (ore loaders) in hardrock mining and 'day men' in the collieries—were taken up by the Europeans.[49] Contract mining was an especially skilled occupation in the coal fields since a miner had to know the best way to work a seam, shoring and bucking, safety techniques, coal quality, and other factors in order to earn an above standard wage. In hardrock mining the use of machinery such as air drills rendered many old skills unnecessary but certain semi-skilled procedures and techniques were still required for the use of air drills, blasting, and other jobs.

The urban workforce was also mostly immigrant during this period. The composition of western cities contrasted sharply with those of the east and more closely reflected the ethnic and demographic profile of the western mining regions. The 1911 census showed that only slightly more than 12 per cent of Vancouver men and 18 per cent of the women were British Columbians.[50] In Halifax about 88 per cent of the men and 89 per cent of the women were born in Nova Scotia. Hamilton, one of the county's most heavily industrialized cities, contained a larger proportion of immigrants than Halifax—about 41 per cent of the men and 33 per cent of the women (primarily from the British Isles), but most of the population was born in Ontario. Calgary closely matched Vancouver in that 90 per cent of the men and 84 per cent of the women were immigrants, most from Great Britain but with a very large number of Canadians. Here, about 12 per cent of the men and 14 per cent of the women were from the United States and approximately 12 per cent of the men and 8 per cent of the women were from Europe. Though Winnipeg was the oldest, largest, and most industrialized western city its profile closely followed the other western urban areas. Seventy-nine per cent of the men and 73 per cent of the women were immigrants. The British were the largest group—32 per cent of the men, 26 per cent of the women—followed by Canadians and Europeans. The ratio of men to women was also disproportionately high in the two most western cities, reflecting their frontier character: 1.5:1 in Vancouver, 1.6:1 in Calgary. In Winnipeg the ratio was 1.2:1. The ratios were more normal in the east: 1.1:1 in Hamilton, 1:1 in Halifax.

Immigrants responded differently to the industrial frontier. Those who came from deplorable conditions of poverty, powerlessness, and oppression sometimes found the new cities and mining communities of the west considerably better than whatever they had left behind. Most of the Italians in British Columbia were from southern Italy, an area of grinding rural poverty.[51] They probably felt a distinct improvement in their situation simply because of the steady wages. Many never intended to remain in Canada and only stayed as long as necessary to earn cash to bring home. Donald Avery has called them sojourners.[52] They constituted a conservative element: in the radical and tumultuous environment of the Kootenay country, Trail, with a heavy Italian immigrant population, was an island of labour tranquillity.[53] Managers welcomed Italians to the mining communities because of their excellent (or infamous?) reputation as strikebreakers.[54] The Chinese were in much the same position. They too found Canada to be a heaven compared to what they had left. It is impossible to tell whether their strikebreaking activities resulted from exclusion from unions by white workers or vice versa but their conservative temper and exclusiveness mirrored the attitudes of many Italians.

At the other end of the scale were the British, Canadians, and Americans who had been reared in liberal democratic societies, were used to a democratic franchise, and might well have been involved in trade union or radical activities. These workers enjoyed an additional advantage over Europeans since they knew English and were familiar with the methods and mores of the political system. They were usually the most radical in their response to hardships and inequities and always provided the leadership for the socialist and syndicalist movements that vied for the allegiance of western workers. When the Social Democratic party was formed in 1911 a large majority of its membership was European but every one of its public leaders was Anglo-Saxon.[55]

British and American workers brought well-developed traditions of trade unionism and radicalism to western Canada. The British labour movement had been undergoing continuous change, growth, and increased militancy and radicalism since the London dock strike of 1889. Amalgamation and industrial unionism vied with socialism, syndicalism, and anarchism as theories and ideas were adopted, discarded, re-examined and adopted again. Leaders such as Keir Hardie, Tom Mann, James Connolly, and other worker-philosophers kept British labour in ideological turmoil.[56] The British labour movement, from which thousands of western workers had graduated, was in constant search for new directions and more effective means of bringing the organized power of the workers to bear.

Much the same sort of thing was happening in the United States, particularly the western mining states which sent the bulk of the American hardrock miners to the British Columbia interior. These men had no use for the business unionism and conservative moderation of Samuel Gompers and formed radical industrial unions such as the Western Federation of Miners and the United Brotherhood of Railway Employees. They founded the American Labor Union to challenge the AFL and supported socialist and syndicalist causes.[57]

These British and American workers drew on a rich heritage of trade unionism and radicalism developed in industrial and/or urban contexts. When they found themselves closed in by their adopted society, their unions beset upon by courts and governments, their employers using police, spies, dismissals, evictions from company towns, and alliances with governments against most efforts to organize, they responded with all the fury of the militancy and the radicalism they brought with them.

The new societies of the western mining camps were totally polarized as were the economic regions in which mining was carried out. Company towns were a feature of the region because most of the coal and ore deposits were far from normal settlement areas. It was not possible for miners to live in Lethbridge or Victoria and work in the collieries nearby, even when they were close. The company camps grew immediately adjacent to the collieries and the miners were forced to spend most of their lives in these controlled towns. The company town could be a wretched place, with stinking outhouses, no fresh water supply, dilapidated shacks, and cold, damp bunkhouses. There may have been no medical facilities, no schools, bad food, lice-ridden blankets, and frequent attacks of typhoid.[58] Or a company town could have been the epitome of paternalism. Nordegg, in the Coal Branch area of Alberta, was planned as 'a modern and pretty town' with the best equipped hospital west of Edmonton, bathrooms in the larger cottages, a poolroom, a miners club, and several company stores.[59] Martin Nordegg, who laid out the town, decided to paint the miners' cottages in different pastel shades.[60] In the British Columbia interior the Granby Consolidated Mining and Smelting Company offered cottages with electric lights, running water, and sanitary facilities. Their town had a recreation hall, meeting hall, tennis court, reading room, baseball diamond, and moving pictures.[61] All the towns and camps scattered throughout Alberta and British Columbia had one thing in common—they were closed societies, highly polarized, which isolated the workers and made them as dependent on each other above the ground as they were below. In Nordegg, for example, it was not long before company officials and their families occupied the cottages on the heights and refused to mix with the miners.[62] In the Granby camp the velvet glove concealed a company policy of ejecting 'agitators.'[63] On Vancouver Island the Dunsmuirs' favourite tactic for dealing with labour unrest was to eject miners from the company towns.[64] There was never any question about who owned and controlled. The miners faced this reality every time they went to the company store, used company scrip (which was still circulating in Nordegg as late as 1915), or availed themselves of any company facility.

The polarization of the camps was enhanced by the newness of society on the mining frontiers. The only important social institutions were the companies and the unions. That which the company did not provide the union did. The unions built their own halls, which served as the major recreation area for the men—a place where they could bitch and drink away from company ears. The union provided compensation, helped with legal fees in suits brought by accident victims, or provided burial funds. In the BC interior the only hospital for miles was apt to be owned and financed by the union as was the case in Sandon.[65] The unions, whether the Western Federation of Miners or the United Mine Workers, were organized on the basis of a lodge for each colliery, mine, or smelter. The lodge was, therefore, locally organized and supported. The men were the local and the local was the men-identification was complete. When the United Mine Workers fought wage reductions in Alberta and the Crowsnest Pass in the years 1924-5, the miners who disagreed with this policy did not leave their unions, they withdrew their locals and established 'home locals'[66] which survived to be reunited in a rejuvenated District 18 in the early 1930s.

Mining society was raw. There was no established tradition of servitude or corporate paternalism handed from generation to generation such as existed in many Nova Scotia coal communities. In most company-owned towns and camps the presence of church and other moderating social institutions was weak while the class structure of the community reflected its totally mine-oriented existence. There were miners and their families and the managers. There were no teachers, clerks, merchants, priests, salesmen, artisans, doctors, or other professionals. And if there were they too were company employees. Mining was the only industry and the entire social and economic structure of the region depended upon the labour of the miners or the smeltermen. In southern Alberta mining communities were often located near agricultural districts but this did not lessen the polarity of the camps because the professional miners resented the farmers who came looking for work after the harvest, found employment in the mine, and undercut the earnings of the permanent miners.[67] Some mining towns—Rossland and Sandon in the British Columbia interior, Drumheller in south central Alberta—were open communities not under direct company control. A handful of tailors, drygoods merchants, tobacconists, hoteliers, barmen, and preachers set up shop to service the miners' needs. Well-stocked bars in small frame hotels and enterprising prostitutes provided 'recreation'[68] as did miners' day parades and, in the hardrock country, July Fourth celebrations. Relay races, rock drilling contests, and union band concerts drew large crowds and eager participants. These towns offered more individual freedom— the men could come and go if they were single and debt-free—and more class diversity than closed company camps. But they were always isolated, by miles of open prairie or by the high mountains and thick forests of the rainy Kootenays. And though not owned, they were dominated by the mining companies whose managers formed a close bond with the handful of local independent businessmen. Costs to the miners in these towns were high—for room, board, or recreation[69]—and the everpresent closeness and isolation helped make them pressure-cookers of discontent.

The polarization of these communities was also reflected in the limited opportunities for improvement available to the workers. Day men (paid a flat daily wage) might become contract miners (paid by the amount of coal dug, graded as suitable and weighed at the pit head) but this was as far as they could go. In the hardrock mines a mucker might become a miner, an even less important promotion that that from day man to contract miner in the coal fields.

Working conditions were uniformly poor. Death rates in western coal mines were more than twice those of Nova Scotia (see Table I). The mines were newer than those in Nova Scotia and the men and their managers had less expertise in how to extract the mineral.[70] It was not discovered until after several major disasters, in which hundreds of miners were killed, that the coal of the east Kootenay region was fifteen times more gaseous and therefore much more likely to cause explosions than comparably-graded bituminous in Pennsylvania.[71] In the hardrock mines heat, unstable explosives, faulty machinery, unguarded shafts, flooded sumps, cave-ins, and mining related diseases took a constant toll of lives.[72] Here conditions were about the same as those of the American hardrock mines.

TABLE 1   Fatalities per Million Tons of Coal Mined over One Decade

	1907	1908	1909	1910	1911	1912	1913	1914	1915	1916	Avg
BC	13.96	8.53	23.75	8.92	7.30	9.25	10.5	9.39	26.36	11.26	12.92
ALTA	10.35	5.96	4.14	20.08	4.13	6.09	6.50	54.68	5.24	4.30	12.15
NS	5.61	6.09	5.82	5.05	5.18	4.46	5.95	4.72	5.74	3.99	5.26
US	na	5.97	5.73	5.62	5.35	4.53	4.89	4.78	4.27	3.77	4.99

SOURCES: Nova Scotia, *Annual Report on Mines 1940* (Halifax 1941), 114; ibid. (1944), 186); Alberta, *Annual Report of the Department of Public Works of Alberta 1916* (Edmonton 1917), 110; British Columbia, *Annual Report of the Bureau of Mines 1910* (Victoria 1911), 230; ibid. (1920), 358

When conditions in mining camps and in the mines themselves were intolerable, there were few places to escape. The skilled miners were tied to their occupations (if not to the company store) and faced lower wages as unskilled workers in cities or as agricultural labour. American hardrock miners could always migrate back across the border, and many appear to have done so, but mines there were just as dangerous and the communities just as polarized as in Canada. Those miners with families had little mobility to begin with. The unskilled single miners did have options, but very restricted ones.

Southern Alberta coal mines were located near agricultural areas and even those not so near were a short train ride away. But agricultural labour, when available, was twenty-four hour a day work at low wages. Farmers gained unsavoury reputations amongst migratory agricultural workers from both sides of the border because of the treatment meted out to their employees. Added to this was competition from small farmers needing additional cash[73] and immigrants who wanted to learn homesteading before filing on a piece of their own land.[74] Every fall thousands of men were brought west by the railways to help bring in the harvest. Even if work was available under decent circumstances it would rarely be steady since farms were still small and extra labour requirements were seasonal. For the single miners of the BC interior or Vancouver Island, however, even this was not an option.

The other escapes were railway construction work and migration to the cities. Railway construction workers—navvies or 'bunkhousemen'—were just above slaves in the general scheme of things. Under the direction of brutish foremen, navvies worked from dawn past dusk clearing rights of way, laying track, hauling rock and gravel. The work was gruelling and the pay negligible. The food was usually bad—though a charge was always deducted for it, the sleeping conditions fit for animals: bunks rigged up in old box cars with almost no heat, proper ventilation, or space to move. Sanitary facilities were nonexistent. The workers on these construction jobs were closely watched to assure that 'agitators' would not get close to them.[75] It was a wise policy. When the IWW managed to get a foothold in the construction camps in the Fraser River canyon in 1912 two long strikes of navvies, one on the Grand Trunk Pacific, the other on the Canadian Northern, gave these wretched men an opportunity to protest their deplorably bad working and living conditions.[76]

The cities offered the greatest chance to escape. Here, at least, there was recreation, companionship, freedom to roam about, and, during this period, usually plentiful work. But if the city offered good opportunities for advancement and the chance to forge a decent life for the skilled worker, it offered barely enough to get by for the unskilled. Urban slums blighted the new cities of the west and in times of depression, when there was no work to be had, primitive and patchwork welfare schemes offered little hope.[77] In truth, western cities were also closed and polarized societies for many thousands of industrial workers.

Every western city had an 'across the tracks.' In Calgary there were tent towns in Hillhurst or near the Centre Street Bridge. In Edmonton frame shacks were thrown up along the Grand Trunk Pacific main line, near the Calder Yards, or east of Mill Creek. In Vancouver tenements scarred the urban landscape along the waterfront to the southeast of Stanley Park. In Winnipeg there were the tenements and broken down hovels of the 'North End' where over-crowding, lack of sanitary facilities, and a near absence of fresh water created one of the highest infant mortality and death rates per thousand persons on the continent.[78] For the unskilled these slums were a dead end.

The skilled fared better. They built modest homes in Calgary's Mount Pleasant or Winnipeg's Ward 4 near the Point Douglas Yards. Many eventually went into business on their own and started printing shops, contracting firms, and other small enterprises. A few became successful in politics. The skilled workers quickly formed themselves into an aristocracy of labour, their exclusive and conservative craft unions presiding over respectable Trades and Labor Councils.

For the unskilled there were no unions since the crafts would not stoop to attempting mass organization. They had no political voice because of restrictive franchises. Many of the Europeans sought out ethnic-based socialist clubs and in Winnipeg Jews and Ukrainians organized vigorous and active left-wing par-ties[79] but they had no real power. This was a common frustration which affected both the skilled and the unskilled: the cities of western Canada were tightly controlled by commercial élites who ran them like closed corporations.[80] Winnipeg offers the best though certainly not the only example and this was re-flected in the restricted franchise, based upon property qualification. In 1906, when Winnipeg contained over 100,000 persons, only 7784 were listed as mu-nicipal voters.[81]

This situation was particularly hard for workers. The city government was reluctant to spend money to improve facilities in the North End. It provided little impetus for the privately owned but municipally chartered street railway system to operate adequate services in working-class areas. It was not receptive to requests for improved health and building bylaws or minimum wage sched-ules from the local labour movement. The imbalance of electoral power also assured the election to office of men such as Thomas Russell Deacon who, in the midst of the depression of 1913-15, opposed giving his policemen a day's rest in seven and told his city's unemployed to 'hit the trail' but struggled hard to ob-tain a municipal vote for property-owning corporations.[82] Men like Deacon were representative of and supported by a commercial élite which constantly stymied and frustrated the working people's attempts to make their jobs safer, their homes more secure, their lives better.

Nevertheless, the cities were clearly the best places to be on the industrial frontier, especially for skilled workers. They could find the jobs and build the homes and families they had come to the west for. Unless and until they were thwarted in their own drives for improvement they remained moderate, though reform minded. The unskilled were better off in the cities but just barely. They were still powerless, living in bad conditions, earning low wages, and living in fear of unemployment. The cities were significantly different from the mining communities in that they offered some middle ground between polarized extremes. Here there were churches, religious and social clubs, city missions, ethnic self help societies, socialist and free thought clubs, and libraries.[83] Here, also, there appeared to be a middle class—clerks, salesmen, priests, professionals—lacking in the mining communities. The mix was not as volatile, the chances for improvement better, the edges not so rough. Perhaps this is why radicalism took longer to dominate the cities.

All western workers were not radicals. Those who were did not become radical at once. The coal miners of Vancouver Island, the Crowsnest Pass, and Alberta and the hardrock miners of the British Columbia interior were the vanguard of radicalism in the west, founding it, nurturing it, and lending its spirit of revolt to other western workers. These miners early rejected reformism and swung behind marxist political organizations, particularly the Socialist Party of Canada. They also provided the most fertile ground in the west for doctrines of radical industrial unionism and syndicalism and were amongst the strongest supporters of the Industrial Workers of the World. The miners formed a large and cohesive group in British Columbia and they quickly overwhelmed, dominated, and greatly influenced the urban crafts and railroad lodges. Radicals were more influential in Vancouver prior to 1914 than other western urban centres. In Alberta the urban crafts formed the Alberta Federation of Labor partly to offset the radical influence of the coal miners who dominated the labour movement in the south,[84] but by 1918 the miners had become undisputed masters of the provincial labour movement. Radicalism, therefore, emerged first and was strongest in the highly polarized and closed mining communities. In these camps workers with a common employer and common interests were grouped into a single community. Their struggle with their bosses did not begin with the morning whistle and end when the shift was over because the entire area was controlled by their employer and they were forced to cope with the company on a twenty-four hour basis. Since they were grouped into one place a little radical propaganda went a long way.

The situation in the cities was, as we have seen, different and radicalism took much longer to dominate, even though it was always present. Prior to the war urban workers were ready to defend the rights of groups such as the IWW but, for the most part, refused to endorse their aims. Urban workers even elected radicals to important positions, particularly in Vancouver, but would not support radical objectives. Though a socialist such as R.P. Pettipiece was editor of the *B.C. Federationist,* a moderate such as W.R. Trotter (a trades congress organizer), was a regular contributor. In part this was the result of indecisiveness and ideological uncertainty. Christian Sivertz, socialist and a leader of the British Columbia Federation of Labor, demonstrated this lack of clarity when he wrote that a general strike (contemplated to support the Vancouver Island coal miners in 1913) would make employers aware that such a weapon existed and they would then be 'more amenable to reasonable consideration of the demands of organized labor.'[85] This one radical leader only supported a general strike to force the bosses to be more reasonable. Clearly the pressures of polarization and limited opportunities were not yet great enough or had not yet been perceived by enough workers to have thoroughly radicalized the Vancouver labour movement. Radical strength existed in that radicals had achieved important positions, but there was no concerted radical purpose. In the other major urban centres—Calgary, Edmonton, and Winnipeg—radicals played second fiddle to men such as Alex Ross, Alfred Farmilo, and Arthur W. Puttee. All this changed after 1914.

The emergence of radicalism as the dominant factor in the urban labour movement was primarily due to the war. The domestic industrial and political situation convinced many urban workers that opportunity and mobility were illusions. Inflation and manpower shortages prompted moves to increased organization, union recognition, and higher wages but these drives were usually stymied by court injunctions, federal orders in council, and the indifference or hostility of the Imperial Munitions Board. Many otherwise economic and industrial issues, such as higher wages for railway shopcraft workers, became politicized as worker hostility towards the war itself became the major issue. Western urban labour turned increasingly against the war and, conversely, more supportive of radical alternatives.[86] Urban labour leaders were also immigrants and now reacted in a fashion similar to their brothers in the mines. By September 1918 the urban-industrial and the extractive-hinterland labour movement was united behind radical leadership.

Western labour radicalism was born when immigrant industrial pioneers entered into the closed, polarized societies of the mining communities and the western cities. Once settled there was little chance for improvement. Many of these individuals could not accept their change in status from free immigrants, some of them from a rural background, to regulated and enclosed industrial workers.[87] In Nova Scotia and in central Canada, by contrast, radicalism was slow to develop. Its signs were not apparent in Nova Scotia until sixty years after mining began in earnest and at least two generations had worked in the mines. Young men growing up in the closed communities of the Nova Scotia coal towns knew little else and expected little better. They too would go down in the mines and would live in the company towns as did their fathers before them. If not, they would themselves emigrate. In central Canadian cities radicalism was never a dominant factor though it was always present. But in the west most workers did expect better. Those who had worked the land in Europe, who had survived the mining wars of the American frontier, who escaped the turbulence, insecurity, restrictiveness, and polarization of British society, or the falling wages and lower productivity of the Welsh coal fields, had come to the Canadian frontier for a new start and better opportunities. But they soon found themselves victims of a new oppression. This was the frontier; but the mining communities were pockets of industrial feudalism denying the opportunity of the frontier to those who sought it while the cities were only slightly better. This deep frustration provided fertile soil for the socialists and syndicalists who offered radical change and abolition of 'wage slavery.' The freedom which was sought, but not found, could be found yet in the commonwealth of toil. It became apparent to those with little patience that the traditional methods of business unionism—organization, negotiation, strike, arbitration, and so on—won no battles. Even the few victories that were achieved changed little; perhaps a slightly higher wage or shorter hours, but the company town, the slum, the whole polarized and closed environment continued to exist. In one sense the entire labour system in the west was a closed environment. Thus the one apparent hope—the unions—offered little real hope.

For many who sought improvement the only answer lay with those who attacked the basic structure of the system that held immigrant workers in thrall: the political socialists who preached the dictatorship of the proletariat and scorned reformism; the syndicalists who advocated use of the trade unions as instruments for radical change; the radical industrial unionists who advocated general strikes to overcome the combined power of employers and state. These solutions offered hope to men who refused to wait for gradual, evolutionary improvement. Far from becoming a leveler, the Canadian industrial frontier was the chief stimulus to the development of class consciousness and radical working-class attitudes in the Canadian west.

Notes

1. The classic statement is 'The Significance of the Frontier in American History' in Frederick Jackson Turner, *The Frontier in American History* (New York 1920). A Canadian discussion is included in M.S. Cross, ed., *The Frontier Thesis in the Canadas: The Debate on the Impact of the Canadian Environment* (Toronto 1970), 104-25.

2. Some immigrant attitudes can be found in H. Palmer, ed., *Immigration and the Rise of Multiculturalism* (Toronto 1975), 82-111. A good account of a Ukrainian pioneer worker is A.B. Woywitka, 'Recollections of a Union Man,' *Alberta History*, autumn 1975, 6-20.

3. See S.M. Jamieson, *Times of Trouble: Labour Unrest and Industrial Conflict, 1900-1966* (Ottawa 1968), 62-151.

4. Taken from *Webster's New World Dictionary of the American Language, College Edition* (Cleveland and New York 1968)

5. For examples see P. Phillips, *No Power Greater* (Vancouver 1967), 60, 72-3: M. Robin, *Radical Politics and Canadian Labour* (Kingston 1968), 127-32: E. Taraska, 'The Calgary Craft Union Movement, 1900-1920' (unpublished MA thesis, University of Calgary, 1975), 69-70; D.J. Bercuson, *Confrontation at Winnipeg* (Montreal 1974), 58-65, 83.

6. See British Columbia Federation of Labour, *Proceedings of the Ninth Annual Convention* (Calgary 1919), 2, 4, 5, 7; Alberta Federation of Labor, *Proceedings of the Sixth Annual Convention* (Medicine Hat 1919), 41; 'Sixteenth Annual Convention District 18 United Mine Workers of America' (typewritten), 133.

7. One Big Union, *The Origin of the One Big Union: A Verbatim Report of the Calgary Conference, 1919* (Winnipeg nd), 10-12

8. I am grateful to E.R. Forbes for bringing these events to my attention. See his 'The Maritime Rights Movement, 1919-1927: A Study in Canadian Regionalism' (unpublished PH D thesis, Queen's University, 1975), 88-9.

9. D. MacGillivray, 'Industrial Unrest in Cape Breton 1919-1925' (unpublished MA thesis. University of New Brunswick, 1971), 35, 44

10. Ibid., 33

11. H.A. Logan, *Trade Unions in Canada* (Toronto 1948), 334-5

12. MacGillivray, 'Industrial Unrest,' 226

13. M. Dubofsky, 'The Origins of Western Working Class Radicalism, 1890-1905,' *Labor History,* spring 1966, 131-54

14. R.M. Longo, ed., *Historical Highlights of Canadian Mining* (Toronto 1973), 21-3; M. Robin, *The Rush for Spoils* (Toronto 1972), 25-6

15. Canada, *Census of Canada* 1911, II. 377-8 [hereafter *Census*]

16. P. Phillips, 'The National Policy and the Development of the Western Canadian Labour Movement,' in A.W. Rasporich and H.C. Klassen, eds., *Prairie Perspectives 2* (Toronto 1973), 41-61

17. *Census,* v, 106-9, 118-19

18. Ibid., 10-11

19. E.S. Moore, *The Mineral Resources of Canada* (Toronto 1933), 188-92

20. A.A. den Otter, 'Sir Alexander Tilloch Galt, the Canadian Government and Alberta's Coal,' *Historical Papers* 1973, 38

21. R. Chodos, *The CPR: A Century of Corporate Welfare* (Toronto 1973), 63-5

22. J.L. McDougall, *Canadian Pacific* (Montreal 1968), 143-8

23. Chodos, *The CPR,* 63-4

24. Public Archives of Canada, Sir Thomas Shaughnessy Papers, Canadian Pacific Railway Letterbooks, Shaughnessy to Elias Rogers, 4 March 1903. I am grateful to Donald Avery for bringing this source to my attention.

25. Ibid., Shaughnessy to W. Whyte, 27 March 1907

26. H.A. Innis, *Settlement and the Mining Frontier* (Toronto 1936), 282-320, contains the best description of the region's growth.

27. Ibid., 280

28. Ibid., 284

29. Robin, *Spoils,* 76

30. This emerges constantly in Innis. See, for example, pages 284, 285, 288, 289. He notes that the 1911 Crowsnest Pass coal strike necessitated the importation of 41,000 tons of coke from Pennsylvania (285).

31. British Columbia, *Annual Report of the Minister of Mines* (for the year ending 31 December 1914) (Victoria 1915), 333 [hereafter *Mines Reports*)

32. *Mines Reports* 1902, 1202

33. Robin, *Spoils,* 79-80

34. *Mines Reports* 1915, 348

35. A.A. Den Otter, 'Railways and Alberta's Coal Problem, 1880-1960,' in A.W. Rasporich, ed., *Western Canada Past and Present* (Calgary 1975), 89-90

36. C.J. McMillan, 'Trade Unionism in District 18, 1900-1925: A Case Study' (unpublished MA thesis, University of Alberta, 1968), 23

37. *Mines Report* 1914, 329

38. Ibid., 1915, 426

39. *Census,* III, XI-XIII

40. den Otter, 'Railways,' 84

41. Canada, 'Evidence Presented to the Royal Commission on Industrial Relations, 1919' (typewritten). Testimony of Jesse Gough, 690-2, and C.G. Sheldon, 1003-6 [hereafter 'Royal Commission Evidence']

42. Jamieson, *Times of Trouble,* 99, 126-32

43. Phillips, 'National Policy,' especially 41-3

44. *Census,* II. All these statistics were compiled from Table xv. Literacy rates were obtained from Table xxxv.

45. MacGillivray, 'Industrial Unrest,' 23-4

46. H. Troper and R. Harney, *Immigrants* (Toronto 1975), 8

47. See, for example, H. Palmer, *Land of the Second Chance* (Lethbridge 1972), 29-30, 71-2, 194; Woywitka, 'Recollections,' 6

48. For American examples see A.R. McCormack, 'The Emergence of the Socialist Movement in British Columbia,' *B.C. Studies,* spring 1974, 6; A.R. McCormack, 'The Origins and Extent of Western Labour Radicalism: 1896-1919' (unpublished PH D thesis, University of Western Ontario, 1973), 24, 104.

49. D. Avery, 'Foreign Workers and Labour Radicalism in the Western Canadian Mining Industry, 1900-1919' (paper presented to the Western Canadian Urban History Conference, Winnipeg, October 1974), 4-5, 8-9

50. *Census,* II, Table xv

51. Palmer, *Chance,* 174; J.S. Woodsworth, *Strangers within our Gates* (Rep. ed., Toronto 1972), 133

52. Avery, 'Foreign Workers,' 7, discusses this and the 'padrone' system.

53. I am grateful to Professor S.H. Scott for his impressions of the role of the immigrants in the Trail labour movement.

54. Avery, 'Foreign Workers,' 8

55. Robin, *Radical Politics,* 104-15, tells of the birth of the SDP.

56. H. Pelling, *A History of British Trade Unionism* (London 1963), 94-100; McCormack, 'Emergence,' 6

57. V.H. Jensen, *Heritage of Conflict: Labor Relations in the Non Ferrous Metals Industry up to 1930* (New York 1950), 61-2, 64-70

58. Glenbow Alberta Institute [GAI], United Mine Workers of America, District 18 Papers. 'Report of Alberta Coal Mining Industry Commission, Dec. 23, 1919' contains valuable information concerning the state of Alberta coal towns.

59. M. Nordegg, *The Possibilities of Canada are Truly Great* (Rep. ed., Toronto 1971), 176-7

60. Ibid., 184

61. 'Royal Commission Evidence,' 393-5, 405-7

62. Nordegg, *Possibilities,* 196-8

63. 'Royal Commission Evidence,' 396-7

64. Phillips *No Power,* 5-9

65. University of British Columbia Special Collections [UBC], *By Laws and Sketch of Sandon Miners' Union Hospital* (Sandon, nd)

66. F.P. Karas, 'Labour and Coal in the Crowsnest Pass' (unpublished MA thesis, University of Calgary, 1972), 36-51, 129-33

67. GAI, United Mine Workers of America, District 18 Papers, 'Special Convention held at Calgary, June 14-16, 1921' 101-5, 108

68. James Gray discusses prostitution in Drumheller in *Red Lights on the Prairies* (Toronto 1971). See also Provincial Archives of British Columbia, Cominco Papers, Add. MS 15/8/3, 'St. Eugene Arbitration.'

69. For Kootenay town living costs see 'St. Eugene Arbitration,' and Cominco Papers, Add. MS 15 9/2.

70. McMillan, 78-82, summarizes some of the dangers and the evolution of safety legislation.

71. British Columbia, *Special Report on Coal Mine Explosions, 1918* (Victoria 1918), 529-30

72. R.E. Lingenfelter, *The Hardrock Miners* (Los Angeles 1974), 12-26, tells of conditions in American hardrock mines in the period prior to 1896. For evidence that many of these conditions existed in British Columbia mines see UBC, Orchard Interviews. Interview of William Byers, 7-10. Byers worked in the Phoenix and Rossland area. See also *By Laws and Sketch of Sandon Miners' Union Hospital.*

73. D.P. McGinnis, 'Labour in Transition: Occupational Structure and Economic Dependency in Alberta, 1921-1951' (paper read to the Western Canadian Studies Conference, Calgary, Alberta, March 1975), 4-6

74. This was a close to universal experience. See G. Shepherd, *West of Yesterday* (Toronto 1965), 17-18, for one example.

75. E. Bradwin, *The Bunkhouse Man* (Rep. ed., Toronto 1972), 63-90

76. Jamieson, *Times of Trouble,* 143-6

77. J. Taylor, 'The Urban West: Public Welfare and a Theory of Urban Development,' in A.R. McCormack and I. Macpherson, eds., *Cities in the West* (Ottawa 1975), 298-301

78. A.F.J. Arbitise, *Winnipeg: A Social History of Urban Growth, 1874-1914* (Montreal 1975), 223-45

79. Ibid., 163-5

80. J.M.S. Careless, 'Aspects of Urban Life in the West, 1870-1914,' in A.W. Rasporich and H.C. Klassen, eds., *Prairie Perspectives* 2, 32-5

81. Artibise, *Winnipeg,* 38

82. *The Voice* (Winnipeg), 9 and 16 Jan. and 9 Oct. 1914

83. Artibise, *Winnipeg,* 113-65

84. Taraska, 'Calgary Craft Union Movement,' 38-40

85. *B.C. Federationist,* 'Wage Workers' Forum,' 12 Sept. 1913

86. See Phillips, *No Power,* 61-77; Bercuson, *Confrontation,* 32-77.

87. This phenomenon has been explored in Herbert G. Gutman, 'Work, Culture, and Society in Industrializing America, 1815-1919,' *American Historical Review,* June 1973, 531-87.

1919: THE CANADIAN LABOUR REVOLT

Gregory Kealey

In late March 1919 a worried Union government appointed a Royal Commission to "enquire into Industrial Relations in Canada." From 26 April to 13 June, the Commissioners toured industrial Canada visiting 28 cities from Victoria to Sydney and examining a total of 486 witnesses. Their travels coincided with the greatest period of industrial unrest in Canadian history. Their report, published in July 1919, and the subsequent September National Industrial Conference held to discuss their recommendations, appear now only as minor footnotes to the turbulence of the year. Like many Royal Commissions, the Mathers investigation proved far more important than the lack of tangible results.

The Royal Commission on Industrial Relations had two recent and prominent predecessors in its field of inquiry: the 1914 United States Commission on Industrial Relations and the 1917 British Whitley Committee on Industrial Conciliation. It also had one earlier Canadian predecessor, although one suspects

From *Labour/Le Travail,* XIII (Spring 1984), 90-114. Reprinted by permission of the Canadian Committee on Labour History.

it was but dimly remembered in 1919. The Royal Commission on the Relations of Capital and Labor had been appointed by a previous Conservative prime minister, Sir John A. Macdonald, at a similar moment of crisis in class relations in 1886. That inquiry had also included trade unionists as commissioners, had toured the industrial sections of the nation, and had interviewed hundreds of Canadian workers. Its report also received little attention and resulted only in the establishment of Labour Day as a national holiday—a considerable accomplishment compared to the complete legislative failure of the Mathers Commission.

The Royal Commission on the Relations of Capital and Labor, a testament to the turmoil of the "Great Upheaval," has been extensively studied by historians interested in the social history of Canadian workers in the late nineteenth century. The Industrial Relations Commission, however, has received far less attention. Yet the evidence it heard is an equally rich source for the post-war upsurge of working-class militancy. The very titles of the two Royal Commissions convey much about the transformation which had taken place in Canadian industrial capitalist society in the approximately thirty intervening years. The rather quaint, Victorian "Relations between Labor and Capital" with its echo of classical political economy gives way to the modern sounding "Industrial Relations," hinting now not at conflicting classes but at a system of mutual interests. If the titles suggest something of transformed bourgeois and state attitudes, then the contents of the two collections of testimony tell us much about the development of the Canadian working class. The specific material complaints enumerated by Canadian workers vary little from 1886 to 1919—unemployment, low wages, high prices, long hours, unsafe and unsanitary working conditions, abysmal housing, the super-exploitation of women workers, employer blacklists, non-recognition of unions, refusal of collective bargaining—all remain a constant in the working-class bill of grievances. What differs, however, is the workers' attitude. The cautious note of respectability and, in some cases, of near deference present in 1886 was transformed into a clarion cry for change. From Victoria to Sydney, Canadian workers appeared before the 1919 Commission and defiantly challenged it. From Socialist Party of Canada (SPC) soap-boxer Charles Lestor in Vancouver to the Nova Scotia leaders of newly-organized District 26, United Mine Workers of America (UMWA), the message the Commission received was the same across the country. The capitalist system could not be reformed, it must be transformed. Production for profit must cease; production for use must begin.

British Columbia MLA J.H. Hawthornthwaite, a former SPC stalwart and then Federated Labour Party leader, asserted in his appearance before the Commission:

> Working men today understand these matters ... and if you go into any socialistic bodies and listen to the discussion you would understand the grasp that these men have. I do not know any college man or university man who can for ten minutes hold their own in an argument among these people.[1]

Workers across the country more than lived up to Hawthorthwaite's boast. In city after city, the Commissioners were regaled with Marxist-influenced histories of the development of industrial capitalism. A few of these lectures came from middle-class proponents of the workers' movement such as Edmonton Mayor Joseph Clarke or social gospel ministers William Irvine, A.E. Smith, William Ivens, Ernest Thomas, and Salem Bland. But more impressive were the many workers—some well-known leaders, but many not—who appeared to explain patiently to the Commissioners, in the words of Edmonton Grand Trunk Railway machinist E.J. Thompson, "We are the producers and we are not getting what we produce." Like most other workers who appeared, Thompson was uninterested in the Commission's extensive plans for Industrial Councils; only "complete ownership of the machines of production by the working class" would suffice, he asserted. When pushed by hostile Commissioners who claimed that the new Canadian National Railway represented the nationalization he sought, Thompson responded in kind, reminding the Commissioners that workers saw their investigation as nothing but "a talkfest" and as "camouflage" for the anti-labour Union government.[2]

Thompson's evidence is of interest for two reasons: first, he was not a front-line leader of western labour; second, he came directly out of the railway machine shops. In city after city, metal trades workers from the shipyards, from the railway shops, and from the more diversified contract shops came forward and talked socialism. Even James Somerville, the International Association of Machinists' (IAM) Western representative, who predictably chose to distinguish himself from the radicals in his testimony, and who worried about the workers having "gone so far that they do not recognize the authority even in their own organization," explained:

> One of the things they want first is nothing short of a transfer of the means of production, wealth production, from that of private control to that of collective ownership, for they know that is the only solution.[3]

Lest there be any notion that this was a regional manifestation of class unrest, let us travel east to Sudbury, Ontario. There Frederick Eldridge, a machinist and secretary of the local Trades and Labour Council, received "considerable handclapping, stamping of feet, and vocal enthusiasm" from the Commission's working-class audience, when he asserted:

> The workers do not get enough of that which they produce.... I advocate government ownership of everything: mills, mines, factories, smelters, railroads, etc. That is the only solution of the problem and I am only one of hundreds of workmen in Sudbury that think the same thing.[4]

In Toronto, machinist James Ballantyne called for the nationalization of all industry.[5] In Hamilton, IAM District 24 representative Richard Riley more cautiously noted that "although a great many workers have not given the matter much thought, they are beginning to think that there must be a change of the system, that is to say the present competitive system."[6] When the Commission reached Montreal, John D. Houston of IAM District 82 presented a prepared brief on the economic system, arguing in part:

> I believe that in the system of ownership lies all our social problems.... For 300 years or over, while the businessman was consolidating his position as captain of industry, the institutions of autocracy provided, through the law, the machinery of force and fraud which was rigorously applied, to make the worker a proletarian with no means of livelihood except to work for wages or a salary....

He closed with the familiar call for production for use, not for profit.[7]

By the time the Commission arrived in the Maritimes, the Commissioners' impatience was showing, no doubt increased by the mounting industrial crisis which was sweeping the nation. While the evidence of their sessions in Amherst, Nova Scotia, at the height of the General Strike there, has unfortunately been lost, evidence from New Glasgow and Sydney demonstrates the eastern manifestation of the workers' revolt.[8] While UMWA District 26 leaders such as Dan Livingstone, Robert Baxter, and Silby Barrett provided much of the fire, Alex T. Mackay, representing carmen and steelworkers, infuriated the Commissioners by warning of an intensification of the struggle:

> The way the fight in Winnipeg will be terminated, will very largely influence the attitude throughout Canada. I think if matters are allowed to run their course there will be no interference in this part of Canada, but if there is any attempt at coercion, the first shot fired in Winnipeg, will hit every labouring man in eastern and western Canada, and the result will be confusion from the Atlantic to the Pacific.[9]

A day earlier, in Halifax, Nova Scotia Federation of Labour organizer C.C. Dane had threatened a province-wide General Strike for the eight-hour day and had added almost gratuitously: "Industrial unrest? Why, gentlemen, we have none to what we are going to have. I am a Bolshevist and I will warn these two governments that trouble is coming and the men will have what belongs to them."[10] Dane, a boilermaker from Australia, had played a major role in the March 1919 establishment of the Federation.

Machinists were not the only group of workers who testified in these terms. Indeed most workers who appeared made similar points, although not always couched in a socialist framework. An additional important group of witnesses who echoed much of the above but who also added a new dimension to the workers' revolt were women witnesses. Unlike the young women workers paraded before the 1886 Commission, who testified only to oppressive conditions and often answering in monosyllables, the women appearing in 1919 included representatives of retail clerks' unions, women's labour leagues, local councils of women, and consumer groups. Among them were then-prominent figures such as Montreal's Rose Henderson or later leading Communist militant Bella Hall, but also many women who enjoy no such historical fame. These women universally complained of bad housing, runaway inflation, high food prices, and the low wages paid to working women. Calgary's Mrs. Jean MacWilliams, who had organized laundry workers, asked rhetorically, "Are we in favour of a bloody revolution?" and answered, "Why any kind of revolution would be better than conditions as they are now."[11] In Saskatoon, Miss Francis, representing the local TLC, demanded that "plundering must cease, profiteering must go, commercialized industries and institutions must give way to the larger hopes of the people" and "production for use" must replace "production for profit."[12] Mrs. Resina Asals of the Regina Women's Labour League told the Commission:

There is only one thing that the workers have to thank the capitalists for, and that is that they have tightened the screw up so much that they are awakening the worker up to the fact that he is the most important factor and that until we produce for use instead of profit this unrest will still prevail. Let the workingman, the one who produced, have control and then we shall see the light of a new dawn.[13]

Rose Henderson simply advanced the proposition that "the real revolutionist is the mother—not the man. She says openly that there is nothing but Revolution."[14] Working-class women, both wage workers and unpaid domestic workers, also had started to view the world in new ways in 1919.

These examples are intended simply to demonstrate that the revolt was national in character and that its seeds were not rooted in any unique regional fermentation. The "radical" west and the conservative east have become sorry shibboleths of Canadian historiography. The foundations of our understanding of 1919 must be built on national and international conjunctures. While the local and regional pictures are not identical, as we come to know the history of eastern and central Canadian workers as well as we know that of western workers, the similarities of struggle begin to outweigh the initial impression of regional particularism. World War I, a profoundly national experience for Canadians, helped provide part of the cement for this nascent national working-class response.[15] Moreover, we should also remind ourselves at the outset that, as David Montgomery has argued, "Strikes can only be understood in the context of the changing totality of class conflicts, of which they are a part."[16] In 1919 Canada, that totality was increasingly national in scope.

Yet World War I, while providing specific sparks to light the flame of working-class struggle in 1919, should not be viewed as its cause. Underlying structural changes in capitalist organization, both on a national and international scale, must be viewed as providing the necessary fuel for this fire.

TABLE I   **Strike Activity in Canada, 1912-1922**

Year	Number of Strikes	Number of Workers Involved	Striker Days Lost
1912	242	43 104	1 136 345
1913	234	41 004	1 037 254
1914	99	9 911	491 358
1915	86	11 480	95 242
1916	168	26 971	241 306
1917	222	50 327	1 123 916
1918	305	82 573	657 152
1919	428	149 309	3 401 843
1920	459	76 624	814 457
1921	208	28 398	1 049 719

Indeed, although the early war years 1914 to 1916 had seen little overt class conflict in Canada, the changes in the capitalist organization of production and the consequent "remaking" or reconstitution of the working class was well advanced before the outbreak of war. The years 1912 and 1913 should be seen as a prelude to the 1917 to 1920 conflagration. Table I demonstrates this continuity with pre-war class conflict.[17] This argument is not unique to this paper as various community studies, including Bercuson's on Winnipeg and Reilly's on Amherst, have perceived the continuity of class struggle between the pre- and post-war period.[18] This continuity extended, however, throughout the entire country. Craig Heron and Bryan Palmer's perceptive study of strikes in southern Ontario from 1901 to 1914 demonstrates a pattern that held for the other cities whose labour history has been chronicled, including Winnipeg.[19] Lest there be any doubt about this, note the provincial distribution figures in Table II for the pre- and post-war peak strike years. The one striking anomaly on Table II, namely the especially high British Columbia figures, are largely accounted for by loggers' strikes as shown in Table III. When we turn from regional variation to the industrial pattern for these years, some other important common ingredients emerge, especially the ongoing importance of mining and the metal trades. Yet our attention is also drawn to new developments apparent only in the later period such as the importance of wartime shipbuilding, and the rise of logging and "service strikes."

A more specific look at 1919 and especially at the months of May, June, and July helps to clarify some of these points. While these months generally figure high in the calendar of industrial conflict, clearly summer 1919 was not

TABLE II Number of Disputes by Province

	1912	1913	1917	1918	1919	1920
N.S.	9	12	8	18	19	39
P.E.I.	1	–	2	–	–	1
N.B.	21	20	5	11	19	15
Que.	32	31	31	28	100	79
Ont.	100	114	68	112	158	122
Man.	13	6	18	20	16	5
Sask.	19	10	6	10	13	4
Alta.	23	15	24	53	29	39
B.C.	22	25	55	46	73	124
Interprov.	2	1	5	7	2	1
Total	242	234	222	305	428	459

TABLE III Number of Disputes by Selected Industry

	1912	1913	1917	1918	1919	1920
Logging	1	–	1	–	32	66
Coal Mining	6	5	22	49	22	48
Other Mining	6	6	6	3	10	14
Metal Mfrg.	27	30	44	43	46	61
Shipbuilding	2	3	13	16	25	12
Steam Railway	16	8	12	16	6	2
Electric Railway	2	7	5	11	12	5
Service	12	18	11	30	39	38
General	–	–	–	1	12	–
Total	72	77	114	169	204	246
N	242	234	222	305	428	459
% Total	29.8	32.9	51.4	55.4	47.7	53.4

simply any year. Table IV shows both the geographic and industrial range of the strikes and Table V highlights the central role of coal, the metal trades, shipbuilding, and, of course, the general strikes themselves in the wave of unrest.

The summer strike wave consisted of three main types of strikes: first, local strikes contesting the normal range of issues; second, general strikes called in support of such local strikes as in Winnipeg, Amherst, and Toronto; and, third, general sympathy strikes called either in support of the Winnipeg General Strike or to protest its repression. Variants two and three have received some attention, although even here the focus on Winnipeg has tended to obscure these less well-known struggles. Local strikes, however, have received little study.

FIGURE 1   Striker Days: May, June, July 1919

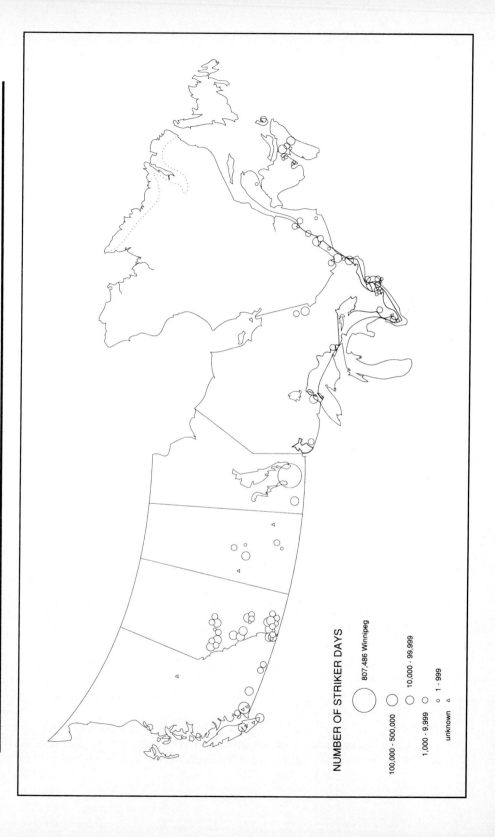

NUMBER OF STRIKER DAYS

807,486 Winnipeg

100,000 - 500,000

10,000 - 99,999

1,000 - 9,999

1 - 999

unknown

TABLE IV Strikes: May, June, and July 1919[1]

A. By Month:	Number of Strikes (total)	Number of Strikes (complete data)	Number of Workers Involved[2]	Duration in Worker Days[3]
May	110	96	68 606	742 506
June	101	89	84 054	1 274 998
July	84	75	71 121	555 802
Total	210[4]	178[4]	114 423[4]	2 573 306
B. By Province:				
Nova Scotia	11	9	3 461	85 135
New Brunswick	6	6	128	631
Quebec	57	50	25 988	395 285
Ontario	90	78	34 544	632 409
Manitoba	6	5	21,756	817 686
Saskatchewan	9	7	2 041	31,833
Alberta	9	8	9 271[5]	304 967[5]
British Columbia	23	16	17 234[5]	305 360[5]
Total	210[6]	178[6]	114 423	2 573 306

[1] Strikes in progress.

[2] Figures for strikes beginning before May or extending beyond the end of a month are not adjusted to account for strikers returning to work.

[3] Figures are adjusted to account for strikers returning to work.

[4] Totals are for strikes in progress over the three month period.

[5] Includes provincial estimates for the District 18 coal mining strike.

[6] District 18, UMWA strike counted once.

Table V, while describing all industrial action in these three months of 1919, suggests how important the local or category one conflicts were to the strike wave. Clearly these strikes cannot be described in this paper in any detail but I will highlight a few to suggest the range of activity. Let us reverse the historiographic trend and travel across the country from east to west.[20] In Moncton, N.B., and Amherst, N.S., moulders won victories over iron founders. A lockout of 350 quarry workers in Sweet's Corner, N.S., lasted 55 working days and resulted in higher wages. Brief walkouts on the street railway systems in Halifax and Moncton also occurred. The most significant story in the Maritimes, however, focused on Amherst and we will return to it in our discussion of general strikes.

Quebec's 57 strikes were highly concentrated in Montreal which accounted for 47 of them (82 per cent). Outside Montreal, the major strikes occurred in the shipbuilding industry at Lauzon and Trois Rivières, and in the metal trades

FIGURE 2   General Strikes, 1919

FIGURE 2   GENERAL STRIKES, 1919

TABLE V   **Strikes: May–July 1919, by Industry**

	Number	%	Number of Workers Involved	%	Duration in Strikes Days	%
Mining	11	5.2	10 216	8.9	340 216	13.2
Manufacturing Total	101	48.1	43 495	38.0	922 117	35.8
Mfrg. Leather & Textile	(20)	(9.5)	(9 505)	(8.3)	(204 897)	(8.0)
Mfrg. Metal & Shipbldg.	(43)	(20.5)	(24 590)	(21.5)	(623 577)	(24.2)
Construction	32	15.2	9 829	8.6	185 488	7.2
Transportation & Public Utilities	21	10.0	4 772	4.2	68 964	2.7
Service & Public Administration	19	9.1	1 137	1.0	4 799	.2
Other Industries	14	6.7	607	5	18 036	.7
General	12	5.7	44 367	38.8	1 033 686	40.2
Total	210	100.0	114 423	100.0	2 573 306	100.0

at Lachine and Sherbrooke. The brief metal strikes were both successful for the workers, and the Trois Rivières shipyard strike won union recognition for the strikers. Montreal, however, was the centre of activity in Quebec. Indeed, the Borden government was sufficiently alarmed about the conflicts in Montreal that the city was included on their emergency daily briefing list. Over 22,000 workers in Montreal struck during the three-month period, logging nearly 380,000 striker days lost. Again the metal trades and shipbuilding figured prominently. A metal trades strike at Canadian Car and Foundry in early May involving 4,000 workers ended in victory after only three days. In the ship-yards, however, it took a one-day strike to force negotiations and then a five-week strike before the employers conceded to some of the demands of their 3,500 workers. This strike was led by a General Strike Committee, not by the union officials of the Marine Trades Federation. A major strike of 2,000 wire workers failed after three weeks. A series of skirmishes in the garment trades led to a number of worker victories, and a major battle involving over 3,500 workers at Dominion Textiles gained some employer concessions after nearly three months of struggle. This strike was marked by a successful sympathetic strike at Montmorency Falls where 1,100 workers stayed out for ten days in support of their Montreal comrades and returned to work with a wage increase. Other industrial workers showed a new ability to organize as well. Over 1,400 rubber workers, for example, won a compromise settlement after a strike of three weeks, as did 350 sugar refinery employees, while 700 meat packers won a quick victory to match a settlement won earlier by Toronto workers. This militant activity on the part of industrial workers represented a new departure for Montreal's working class, as did the willingness of Montmorency textile workers to resort to a sympathy strike.[21] While the majority of the Montreal Trades and Labour Council (MTLC) opposed a general sympathetic strike, the tactic had proponents in Montreal. The machinists (IAM) and the engineers (ASE), true to national form, held a massive support rally in late May which was addressed by Winnipeg strike leader R.J. Johns, who was in Montreal representing Division #4, railroad shop craft workers, at Railroad Board arbitration meetings. Those attending, identified as workers from the Canadian Vickers Shipyard, heard speeches from A.H. McNamee, president of the ASE, and radical machinists Richard Kerrigan and William Turnbull, as well as from Montreal "reds" such as Beckie Buhay and Albert St. Martin.[22] In early June the MTLC endorsed the 44-hour week and called for the reinstatement of the postal workers who had been dismissed in Winnipeg.[23] At their subsequent meeting in mid-June the arrests of the Winnipeg strike leaders were roundly condemned and Richard Kerrigan led a debate in which the Canadian Vickers General Strike Committee sought to gain the endorsation of the Council for a general sympathetic strike. In this, they failed.[24]

Ontario's 90 strikes involving 34,122 workers were not as concentrated as Quebec's, although Toronto did account for 22 (24 per cent) in addition to its General Sympathetic Strike, which I will deal with later. Ottawa had eleven strikes, London seven, Hamilton six, St. Catharines and Windsor, five each. Major mining strikes took place in Cobalt and Kirkland Lake where 2,200 and 525 miners respectively struck for eight and 21 weeks. In both cases the miners were defeated by intransigent mining companies, although not before there had been discussions of a Northern Ontario-wide general strike.[25]

In Toronto, newly-organized workers in the meat packing industry, organized on an industrial basis, took on the giants of the industry, including Swift Canada, as over 3,000 workers struck in the stockyards area after the companies refused to negotiate with the union. In addition to union recognition, they sought the eight-hour day and 44-hour week, and guaranteed minimum levels of employment. After just over a week on the picket line in early May, an IDIA board was agreed to by both sides and reported unanimously on 29 May mainly in favour of the workers, granting a 48-hour week, a weekly guarantee of 40 hours, overtime pay, a formal grievance procedure, and seniority provisions. This settlement became the model for the industry and workers in Montreal, Ottawa, Hamilton, and Peterborough fought for it in summer 1919 and spring 1920.[26] Beginning in July almost 2,000 Toronto garment workers led by the International Ladies Garment Workers Union (ILGWU) struck over 40 shops for twelve weeks before winning wage and hour concessions. Both of these industries involved high proportions of ethnic workers and their successful strikes suggest the expansion of both trade union organization and class struggle to new and difficult terrain.

Ontario's shipyard workers, who in 1918 had organized a Marine Trades and Labour Federation of Canada, engaged in a series of seven strikes covering almost all the province's shipbuilding centres. Bridgeburg, Collingwood, Fort William-Port Arthur, Midland, Welland, and Toronto each witnessed strikes involving workforces ranging from 100 to 1,300. Most of these strikes were fought for wage increases and the 44-hour week, and resulted in significant worker gains. In Collingwood, however, 900 workers failed in a three-week strike in July demanding the rehiring of Orange fellow-workers who had been fired for refusing to work on the glorious twelfth.

In the metal trades, which included many of the same trades as shipbuilding, 1919 saw the machinists attempt to gain Ontario-wide uniformity of wages and conditions. The first provincial convention of Ontario machinists held in Toronto in July 1918 had decided to force this issue. Their major aim was to gain the eight-hour day and 44-hour week and in spring 1919 metal trades meetings were organized province-wide to prepare for that struggle. IAM Vice-President John McClelland reported that "the largest halls in many of the towns" were "too small to accommodate the crowds." Moving beyond IAM exclusivism, McLelland worked for "complete affiliation of the metal trades," and "in the meantime" organized metal trades councils as the basis for a strike which would "completely close down the industry until a settlement is reached."

The Toronto campaign became the central battle for the war for recognition of the metal trades councils as bargaining agents and for the eight-hour day. The demands were sent to the employers on 1 April and tools were dropped on 1 May by some 5,000 metal trades workers. Meanwhile in Peterborough, approximately 100 moulders struck on 1 May and were followed by their fellow workers in Brampton (thirty) and Hamilton (250) on 5 May. Four days later the Kingston Metal Trades Council struck the Canadian Locomotive Company, pulling out 650 workers. On 12 May the Ottawa Metal Trades Council called some 200 machinists and patternmakers out of fifteen small shops. The following day Brantford moulders struck. St. Catharines moulders and machinists left work on 23 May.[27]

The results of these strikes varied but by and large they were defeated. In Toronto the metal trades council ended its strike on 28 July, although 750 moulders refused to end their strike which was still continuing at year's end. In Peterborough the moulders won a victory after a 22-week strike. Their fellow craftsworkers in Brampton returned after eight weeks but 250 striking moulders in Hamilton remained out for the rest of the year. In Kingston a compromise ended the metal trades strike after almost 26 weeks, while Ottawa machinists and patternmakers admitted defeat after almost thirteen weeks on the lines.

Brantford moulders remained out the entire year. Clearly the metal trades workers' optimism as they approached May Day 1919 had turned out to be illusory.

In the west, Manitoba's strikes revolved totally around the epic struggle in Winnipeg and the General Sympathy Strike in Brandon which we will turn to later. In Saskatchewan, the pattern was similar involving primarily sympathetic strikes. In Alberta, however, a successful Calgary metal trades strike in April and May won shorter hours and higher wages for machinists, moulders, and other metal workers. In addition, UMWA District 18's over 6,200 coal miners left the pits at the end of May and stayed out until 1 September when they returned on the advice of OBU leaders.[28] This General Strike was exceptional in that as a "100 per cent" strike involving the maintenance people, it transgressed UMWA custom and in the fact that some of the firebosses, the foremen in the mines, also took part. By July what had started partially as a sympathy strike with Winnipeg had been transformed into a major struggle for recognition of the OBU which would play itself out over the next few years.

In British Columbia the District 18 strike spread into the southeastern coal field and a series of small logging strikes under the leadership of the new, later OBU, B.C. Loggers Union took place. The major activity in B.C., however, also revolved around the June sympathy strikes.

The three General Sympathetic Strikes generated by local industrial struggles were in Amherst, N.S., Toronto. and Winnipeg. The sensitive work of Nolan Reilly has provided us with a model study of the community background to the Amherst General Strike, an event which had gone almost unnoticed. In Amherst, the local Federation of Labour, under the rubric of One Big Union, led a general strike which spread out from the Canadian Car and Foundry workers' demands that they receive pay equal to that which their 4,000 Montreal co-workers had won in a three-day strike in early May. The company's intransigence led to a city-wide walkout involving all of Amherst's major employers. While proceeding from local causes and representing the culmination of a decade of industrial conflict in Amherst, the strikers identified themselves with the national struggle, as their enthusiastic correspondence with the OBU suggests.[29]

Events in Toronto in 1919, while less dramatic than those in Amherst, nevertheless caused Prime Minister Borden and his government considerable consternation.[30] As elsewhere, the metal trades were central in the crisis. Toronto's extensive foundries, machine shops, and metal factories had been at the core of war production. The city's metal trades workers, who had organized a joint council in 1901 and who had endorsed a call for industrial unionism in 1913, led the battle to enforce collective bargaining and a "fair-wage schedule" on the Imperial Munitions Board (IMB).[31] This struggle first came to a head in spring 1916 when Toronto machinists tried to extend gains they had made in some shops in December 1915 to the entire city. In addition, Hamilton machinists also demanded parity with their Toronto comrades. The joint threat of a general metal trades strike in Toronto issued by IAM District 46 in March, and a machinists' strike in Hamilton, combined with McClelland's public worry that he could no longer retain control of his people, led to the appointment of a three-member government commission to investigate the munitions plants in Toronto and Hamilton and the general extension of the Industrial Disputes Investigation Act (IDIA) to all war industry. This commission, however, which the Trades and Labour Congress (TLC) regarded as a victory, eventually proved meaningless when Hamilton employers refused to abide by its recommendation of the nine-hour day and wage increases. The subsequent Hamilton-wide strike of some 2,000 workers which included a coalition of machinists (IAM), engineers (ASE), and unorganized, unskilled workers ended in a major defeat for Hamilton workers at the hands of Canadian Westinghouse, National Steel Car, the Steel Company of Canada, Otis Elevators, and Dominion Steel Foundry. Although Toronto IAM members, for the second time in only a few months, threatened a general strike in sympathy with the Hamilton workers, the IAM international leadership managed to prevent it. The Metal Trades Council did manage, however, to help move the Toronto Trades and Labour Council (TTLC) significantly to the left during these developments. In March and April TTLC condemnation of the Borden government and of the IMB for failure to implement a fair-wage schedule had been shelved by a worried TLC executive in Ottawa. Both Secretary Draper and President Watters apparently hoped their cap-in-hand lobbying would result in a breakthrough. In this they were to be sadly disappointed. The late March extension of the IDIA to cover shipbuilding and munitions led to a furious response from the TTLC which "emphatically denounced this uncalled for and unwarranted action" and accused the TLC executive "of not fulfilling their obligation to the workers of Canada."[32] Thus Toronto and Hamilton metal trades workers as early as summer 1916 found themselves moving in opposition to state labour policy and already identifying their differences with both the TLC leadership and to some degree with their own international officers such as McClelland and James Somerville, all of whom were continually promoting patience and industrial peace. These latter strategies looked increasingly problematic. Thus, as Myer Siemiatycki has noted with considerable irony, "the war-induced epidemic of general strikes, which one prominent unionist subsequently dubbed 'Winnipegitis,' found its earliest germination in Toronto."[33]

By the time of the next major metal trades struggle which came in May 1919, the metal workers exercised considerable control over the TTLC. In a May Day meeting, the TTLC voted to contact all Canadian Trades and Labour Councils to get support for the metal trades fight for the eight-hour day. Moreover, they "requested sympathetic action to bring about the result desired." A 13 May meeting demanded that metal trades employers negotiate and then issued a call for a general strike convention for one week hence. While this motion noted western strikes in Winnipeg and Calgary and other Ontario strikes, its major interest was in the Toronto Strike.[34]

The vote in favour of a general strike by 44 unions representing 12,000 workers led to hurried correspondence between Toronto politicians and Ottawa. Newton Rowell, president of the Privy Council, sought permission from his cabinet colleagues to pressure the employers to concede to the demand for collective bargaining. If they refused, he proposed to embarrass them publicly. Not surprisingly, a hurried negative response came from Minister of Finance Thomas White who had consulted Minister of Labour Gideon Robertson.[35] The following day Toronto Mayor Tommy Church wrote directly to Prime Minister Borden seeking government legislation on shorter hours, explaining that his offer of mediation had won a brief delay in the planned walkout, and seeking Borden's personal intervention in the talks if necessary. Borden's agreement provided Church with an important talking point in a 27 May conference at City Hall which brought together the strike leaders and some of the major metal employers such as Findlay of Massey-Harris and White of Canadian Allis-Chalmers. Although the employers made no major concessions, the workers were placed in an embarrassing situation and finally agreed to Church's proposal that a joint delegation visit Ottawa and talk to Borden. Subsequently the union "convention" authorized this trip, while reaffirming that the General Strike would commence on Friday, 30 May, unless the right of collective bargaining and the 44-hour week were granted to the Metal Trades Council.[36]

Borden's intervention led only to an offer of arbitration, which the workers scornfully declined, but again the employers scored a minor publicity coup by offering a compromise 48-hour week, although not agreeing to Metal Trades Council recognition.[37]

The sympathetic strike commenced on 30 May and from 5-15,000 workers left their jobs. The strike's strength predictably lay in the metal trades, in shipbuilding, among some groups of building trades workers, especially carpenters, and among garment workers. Its major failing was the decision by civic employees and especially the street railway workers to stay on the job until their contract expired on 16 June. The strike lasted until 4 June when it was called off by the Central Strike Committee at the request of the Metal Trades Council. The Committee of fifteen which ran the strike included nine metal trades workers, four building trades workers, and two garment trades workers.[38]

Although the left in Toronto had suffered a defeat in this struggle, they were not repudiated. Instead they took control of the TTLC in its subsequent July election. Left-wing revelations that prominent right-wingers on the Council's executive had received $5,000 from the Toronto Employers' Association to support a new labour paper in Toronto which had worked to divide metal trades workers during the strike, helped them gain control. These charges were sustained by a Council investigation.[39]

The Winnipeg General Strike we will simply pass over in order to discuss the rather less well-known wave of general sympathy strikes. Compilation of these is somewhat risky since the Department of Labour's official version and even their manuscript materials do not necessarily conform to all strikes mentioned in the labour press or even in the various security reports which crop up in the Borden Papers and elsewhere. Table VI lists those identified in Department of Labour data (A) and then adds a list compiled from other sources (B).[40]

TABLE VI General Strikes in Sympathy with Winnipeg, May-July 1919

Location	Dates	Number of Workers Involved	Duration in Strike Days
A. Brandon	20 May–2 July	450	10 200
Calgary	26 May–25 June	1 500	31 700
Edmonton	26 May–25 June	2 000	24 000
Saskatoon	27 May–26 June	1 200	24 000
Prince Albert	28 May–23 June	300	5 000
Regina	29 May–26 June	350	1 500
Vancouver	3 June–4 July	8 000	160 000
New Westminster	13 June–23 June	537	3 400
Victoria	23 June–7 July	5 000	28 000

B. Atikokan, Ont.	Neepawa, Man.	Melville, Sask.
Fort Frances, Ont.	Souris, Man.	Moose Jaw. Sask.
Rainy River, Ont.	Battleford, Sask.	Radville, Sask.
Redditt, Ont.	Biggar, Sask.	Yorkton, Sask.
Sioux Lookout, Ont.	Hudson Bay Jct., Sask.	Prince Rupert, B.C.
Dauphin, Man.	Humboldt, Sask.	McBride, B.C.
Minnedosa, Man.	Kamsack, Sask.	Fernie, B.C.

In Manitoba many small railroad junction towns such as Dauphin supported Winnipeg as did workers in Brandon. The strike in Brandon, the longest of all the sympathy strikes, was extremely solid and orderly. It eventually involved civic workers who had fought and won their own strike in April but who still came out in solidarity as repression mounted in Winnipeg. Controlled throughout by the Brandon Trades and Labor Council, the strike extended to unorganized workers who were guaranteed "full protection" from the labour council.[41]

The list of small Saskatchewan railway junction towns makes clear the support of railroad shop workers and of some running trades workers, although the Brotherhoods exerted all the pressure they were capable of to prevent this. Prince Albert's sympathy strike involved mainly Canadian Northern workers.[42] In Saskatchewan's larger urban centres a similar pattern prevailed. Regina workers initially supported a general strike but only a minority eventually struck, mainly from the railroad shops. In Moose Jaw, shopcraft workers, street railway workers, civic employees, and some building trades workers provided the strike's backbone. Saskatoon's sympathy strike was the most successful in the province and included the Sutherland CPR shop workers, street railway workers, freight handlers, postal workers, teamsters, and at least eleven other local unions.

In Alberta, as elsewhere in the west, both Edmonton and Calgary workers had flirted with general strikes earlier. In Edmonton, the Trades and Labour Council had endorsed a general sympathy strike in October 1918 to aid the Canadian Brotherhood of Railway Employees. Events in 1919 led to a vigorous left-right struggle for control of the Edmonton TLC which culminated in late April in the expulsion of the Carpenters, led by SPC militant Joe Knight, Federated Labour Union, No. 49, which included Carl Berg and Sarah Johnson Knight, and the UMWA, Local 4070. As a result of the expulsions, the machinists and street railway workers also left the council. Despite this serious split, a successful sympathy strike was organized. The Federated Railway Trades (shop workers) introduced a motion in the ETLC calling for a meeting of all Edmonton trade unionists to plan for a strike. At that meeting the machinists successfully moved for a strike vote of all unions to report to a Central Strike Committee composed of representatives from both sides of the previous split. This vote resulted in a 1,676-506 vote for a strike with 34 of the 38 unions voting casting pro-strike ballots; eleven locals, however, failed to vote. Major strike support came from railway carmen, machinists, railroad shop workers, street railway workers, coal miners, building trades workers, and civic employees. The strike held until the Committee called it off and was marked by a minimum of disorder of any kind. This partially resulted from the tacit support the strike received from pro-labour Edmonton Mayor Joe Clarke, who RCMP security regarded as less than trustworthy.[43]

In Calgary the huge CPR shops were central both to the city's economy and to its trade union movement. Carmen, machinists, and all the other Railroad Shops Federated Trades exercised a considerable thrust for and experience of amalgamation. During the war years, the machinists came to dominate the CTLC and, as Taraska has argued, forged "a new working-class solidarity which led to class conscious action."[44] Militance and political lobbying on the part of munitions workers led to a Provincial Munitions Commission ruling that war contracts should go only to union shops. Thus by the end of 1915 the war shops were fully unionized. Skilled machinists' leaders such as Socialist and Labour Alderman A. Broach, R.J. Tallon, and H.H. Sharples came to dominate the local council and to push it successfully into local politics. Tallon became president of Division 4 of the Railway Employees Department of the American Federation of Labor in 1917 which represented over 50,000 shopcraft workers on the Canadian railways. The Division, created to negotiate directly with the Railway War Board, entered negotiations with the CPR in April 1918. After heated negotiations the Board offered parity with the United States McAdoo Award which was rejected by an overwhelming Division 4 vote. Armed with this rejection, Division 4 leaders threatened a nation-wide rail strike. A series of walkouts led to dire threats from the government and the active intervention of the AFL which ordered Division 4 to accept the Board's offer. In September reluctant railway shop workers did so but in Calgary trouble flared up quickly when the CPR victimized some freight handlers who had not been formally allowed to enter Division 4. The freight handlers struck demanding the McAdoo Award. Calgary Labour Council unions voted in favour of a general strike in support of the freight handlers and a shopcraft workers' strike began on 11 October 1918. Street railway workers and civic employees also struck in sympathy. The threat to prosecute under Privy Council Order 2525 banning all strikes proved futile when Alberta courts refused to uphold it. A compromise, arranged by Senator Gideon Robertson, ended the affair in late October but general strike tactics had definitely been sustained. This set the scene for the following year's city-wide metal trades strike in April and the subsequent sympathy strike in May and June. Predictably the major support during the general strike came from the CPR Ogden shops and the Metal Trades Council. One outstanding feature of this strike was the creation of an extremely active Women's Labor Council.[45]

In British Columbia, the SPC-controlled Vancouver Trades and Labour Council (VTLC) responded more slowly and deliberately to events in Winnipeg. In mid-May VTLC President Harold Winch of the longshoremen and Secretary Victor Midgley wired Winnipeg congratulating the workers for their "cohesion" which "augured well for the future."[46] The following week they warned the Borden government that any military interference in Winnipeg would force them to call a general strike and simultaneously requested that all Vancouver trade unions take a vote on the question.[47] One week later they issued the following demands:

> Realizing that while there are many problems that face the workers that cannot be solved under capitalism, and that the end of the system is not yet: also realizing that the present situation is a political one, due to the action of the Dominion Government in the Winnipeg strike, and that as taking care of the soldiers ... are working class problems, the majority of the soldiers being members of the working class, therefore be it resolved that the following be the policy of the workers in Canada now on strike, or about to come on strike in support of the Winnipeg workers:

1. The reinstatement of the postal workers....
2. The immediate settlement of the postal workers' grievances.
3. The right of collective bargaining through any organization that the workers deem most suited to their needs.
4. Pensions for soldiers and their dependents.
5. A $2,000 gratuity for all those who served overseas.
6. Nationalization of all cold storage plants, abbatoirs, elevators....
7. A six-hour day.

They closed by calling for the strike to continue until either the demands were granted or the government resigned and called new elections.[48]

The strike, which commenced on 3 June, initially saw 37 unions out but this actually increased in the first few days of the strike. As elsewhere, it found its major support among the metal trades, in the shipyards, and on the street railway. Unique to Vancouver as a major port, however, was the militant support of longshoremen, sailors, and other marine workers. As in Calgary, a series of women's meetings met with enthusiastic support.[49]

While the SPC provided leadership and intellectual sustenance, their reluctance and fears were manifest. Even at the final preparation meeting on 2 June, William Pritchard posed the question less than enthusiastically:

> Their comrades were in the fight, and it was now a question of standing by them, and, if necessary, going down with them—or, later, going down by themselves. His advice was: "If you are going to drown—drown splashing!"[50]

Two weeks later at an SPC educational, W.W. Lefeaux explained that party policy did not include promoting strikes, only analyzing and explaining them.[51]

The strike ended in confusion a week after Winnipeg's return to work. A recommendation from the strike committee to go back earlier had been voted down by rank-and-file militants.[52] The strike committee's final report to the VTLC indicated that 45 unions had struck over the course of the strike, but admitted the initial vote had been a narrow 3,305-2,499 victory. Although 57 per cent of those voting favoured the strike, the under 6,000 votes represented only 40 per cent of VTLC members.[53]

In Prince Rupert a sympathy strike had commenced earlier on 29 May when railroad workers left their jobs, while in Victoria the sympathy strike developed very slowly with considerable reluctance being shown by Victoria TLC leaders. Nevertheless almost 5,000 workers left their jobs on 23 June, following the lead of the Metal Trades Council, and remained out until early July.[54] A smaller sympathy strike also took place in New Westminster.

These Canadian events captured the attention of European militants. On 14 June 1919, in Turin, Italy, Antonio Gramsci described "The Revolutionary Tide" which had brought "the struggle on a world scale." "The revolution can no longer be exorcized by democratic swindlers, nor crushed by mercenaries without a conscience," the Italian revolutionary argued. Gramsci's youthful optimism stemmed partially from his view of current world struggles and specifically of those in Canada where, he argued, "industrial strikes have taken on the overt character of a bid to install a soviet regime." Meanwhile, in Glasgow, John MacLean enthused about "the great Canadian strike," which, he argued, had stimulated American labour's "general rank-and-file strike which terrorized the union leaders."[55] While these claims appear exaggerated in retrospect, the important point here is that 1919 was an international event, or as MacLean termed it: "class war on an international scale." It was no more limited to Canada than it was to Winnipeg within Canada. In the years from 1917 to 1920, a working-class movement whose internationalism had been destroyed in 1914, ironically responded with an international surge of class militancy which knew no national limits and few, if any, historical precedents.

One little-known example of the international nature of the uprising can be drawn from Newfoundland, then a self-governing British colony in the North Atlantic. The story of Newfoundland's working class largely remains to be written but in the years 1917 to 1920 at least it resembled closely the Canadian and international pattern of revolt. In the immediate pre-war years Newfoundland fishermen and loggers had commenced to organize. The meteoric rise of the Fishermen's Protective Union, representing both groups of workers, led not only to industrial gains but to great political success and legislative reforms. In the later war years, an economic crisis which revolved around profiteering and rampant inflation led to an investigation which found that the St. John's merchants had indeed engaged in rapacious price gouging. In 1917, St. John's workers created the Newfoundland Industrial Workers' Association (NIWA), an avowedly industrial unionist organization which immediately proceeded to organize workers across the island. Thus, Newfoundland workers conformed to the international wave of industrial unionist unrest. Equally the NIWA found its leadership in the railway shops of the Reid Newfoundland Company and among local socialists and drew its membership from St. John's metal shops and the foundry. Its major industrial battle against Reid Newfoundland involved a three-week strike of 500 railway workers in spring 1918 which involved threats of an island-wide walkout and extensive sympathetic activities in St. John's.[56]

The international literature on the post-war upsurge has blossomed of late and important articles by Larry Peterson and James Cronin have chronicled these red years in rich international comparison.[57] As has often been the case, the comparative insights offered by international labour and working-class history open some interesting avenues for investigation. First, however, let us eliminate a few dead ends of previous Canadian investigation. In the aftermath of the strike, the *B.C. Federationist* concluded: "The first lesson that workers must learn is that only by organization and cohesion, not only in each centre, but throughout the country, can they resist the encroachments of capital."[58] Similar statements have often been used to buttress a "western revolt" notion of 1919, arguing that only workers west of the Lakehead behaved "radically." The lesson, however, surely lay not in a regional understanding of the revolt but rather in the reverse—namely, the necessity of perfecting nation-wide organization. The defection of the AFL, the TLC, and much of the international union leadership had left the working-class movement fragmented and, although the SPC leadership tried valiantly to fill the gap, the consequent breakdown in communications and lack of a national focus proved costly. While the established weekly labour press and the emergent daily strike bulletins were remarkably vibrant and blanketed the country with an extraordinary and rich range of labour opinion, they carried little national coverage. Thus workers in Vancouver knew little of Amherst, and District 18 miners lacked direct contact with their Nova Scotia District 26 comrades. The revolt was not western, however, it was national; but the size and regional fragmentation of the country proved a major impediment to systematic national organization and co-ordination.

Second, there is no doubt that the AFL and TLC leadership, not to speak of the railroad running trades leadership, played reprehensible roles. They undoubtedly exploited their image as respectable labour leaders who believed in the sanctity of contracts. We must add, however, that this ideological and political battleground existed within the North American labour movement everywhere, not only on both sides of the border but also at both ends of each country. The struggle within the TLC so often depicted as east/west was not so simple. At the 1917 TLC convention in Ottawa the debate on the executive's collapse on the issue of conscription and their decision not to resist the law once enacted revealed no simple regional vote. In a lengthy debate 28 delegates spoke with only nine fully supporting the executive of which only two actually supported conscription. The nineteen speakers who opposed the executive included eleven eastern delegates and eight westerners.[59] Eastern opponents included moderate Toronto socialists John Bruce and Jimmy Simpson and Montreal radical machinists Tom Cassidy and Dick Kerrigan. Cassidy engaged in the debate's major rhetorical flight, albeit prescient in light of events in 1919:

> When the machine guns are placed on the streets of Winnipeg to shoot down strikers, also in Montreal, Vancouver Island, and other places, it shows that these organized soldiers are willing to shoot their fellow workingmen. I am not afraid to die.... The masters of the world must be whipped.... We have only one enemy and that is the international capitalist class.

When the vote finally came the major amendment, introduced by Alberta leaders Farmilo and Ross, failed narrowly 101 to 111. Since there were only 44 western delegates present, it should be clear that there was considerable eastern opposition to conscription as well. Indeed when a conciliatory division on conscription itself was taken only ten delegates voted in favour of the calling-up of manpower.

At the 1918 TLC convention in Quebec where seething western discontent eventually led to plans for the Calgary Conference of March 1919 similar non-regional divisions were evident. Westerners represented only 45 of 440 delegates. While radical motions were consistently lost and elections to executive positions saw moderates emerge victorious, nevertheless there were far more votes for radical positions than simply those of the west. For example, the one roll call vote on a Winnipeg motion to release all conscientious objectors from prison was narrowly defeated 99 to 90. The minority radical vote was composed of 58 eastern delegates and 32 western, while the conservative vote included two westerners and 97 easterners. The clear lesson to be learned was that the west should send more delegates.[60]

When the TLC met in Hamilton in fall 1919 the battle between craft unionism and the OBU for control of the labour movement was raging. In that context and with OBU members and sympathizers either departed or expelled, it should not surprise us that the Convention witnessed much red-bashing. Yet there was also an undercurrent of support for industrial unionism and disgust for the TLC's failure to support Winnipeg workers. There was vociferous eastern criticism of the TLC leadership. Toronto delegate Birks denounced "organized officialdom within the trade union movement as something opposed to the spirit and mind of the rank and file."[61] District 26 leader J.B. McLachlan introduced a motion for a general strike demanding the restoration of freedom of speech and of the press and the repeal of the Criminal Code amendments passed during the Winnipeg General Strike.[62] Toronto carpenter McCallum, speaking "as a member of the working-class movement," argued that craft unions were outmoded and asked "Why ban men who demand change?"[63] St. Catharines' delegate Grant "advocated the adoption of the shop steward as the most effective form of organization."[64] Later Ottawa stonecutters introduced a motion for broad joint strikes and denounced their international for ordering them back to work during a general building trades strike in May 1919. As one delegate argued, "the boss beat us because we were divided into small locals." Winnipeg's George Armstrong availed himself of this opportunity to condemn "the machinery of the AFL which made massed action impossible."[65]

Similar battles went on within the international unions as well. For example, the 1920 convention of the IAM saw bitter debate about the expulsion of OBU supporters. Montreal and Toronto machinists led a losing but fiery effort to defend their comrades.[66]

The fight in the Canadian labour movement thus rested on different views of labour's future organization. The western SPC leaders looked to the OBU as the way forward. Despite much historical debate about the intellectual orientation of the OBU, which I will not detail here, the OBU was certainly not syndicalist. An organization led by the SPC could never have been anti-political and thus the supposed "turn" to politics after Winnipeg is nonsense. The political aims of the SPC never varied.[67]

The strike wave, of course, gained SPC leadership only begrudgingly for that very reason. The SPC doubted the wisdom of the industrial actions but had no choice but to lend its leadership skills to the working-class militancy which engulfed the nation. They never, however, viewed 1919 as a nascent revolution. They were politically too experienced for that. While Joe Knight and Carl Berg in Edmonton allowed their rhetoric to exceed the SPC line in the heady days of June 1919, the leading Vancouver comrades never lost sight of the limitations of the situation. Thus, *The Soviet* could argue, displaying the syndicalist tendencies of Knight and Berg:

> In Winnipeg and Toronto today the same condition is observable. The General Strike by paralyzing industry, paralyzes government. The Strike Committees are forced to rule the cities, to "exempt" certain industries and services in order to provide for elementary human needs; they must police the cities themselves. Willy-nilly "this production for use and not for profit" is undertaken for the benefit of the workers. It displaces the capitalist government which operated for the benefit of the bourgeoisie....[68]

Vancouver's *Red Flag,* on the other hand, was consistent and cautious. The OBU, it noted, simply represented:

> ... a decided urge towards industrial unionism which has lately become very insistent. We have referred to this movement several times and have criticized it and analyzed it. That is our function. We don't initiate movements, we seek to understand them. We realize that beyond a very transitory influence, great movements are not caused by individuals, they are the result of conditions.[69]

Later, after the Winnipeg General Strike has commenced, they warned:

> It may be that some half-baked socialist is voicing Revolutionary phrases in Winnipeg. We doubt it. We know that a bunch of workers who are able to keep their heads in spite of the extreme provocation to which they are being subjected will not allow any muddle head from their own ranks to precipitate trouble.[70]

Simultaneously, the *B.C. Federationist* editorialized:

> Neither the Seattle nor the Winnipeg strikes were revolutionary upheavals. They were strikes in the one instance for higher wages, and in the later case, for the recognition of the right to collective bargaining. Is that a revolutionary strike?

In that same editorial they cautioned against violence and promoted discipline "because the ruling class have the guns, and if blood is shed, it will be the blood of the working class." In a revolution, they continued, it was necessary to "control the means of coercion," and there was no such opportunity in Canada.[71] A week later they again emphasized. "The strike is not a revolutionary strike," and argued instead: "The issue is political. The workers must take the matter up on those lines, and wring political concessions from the master class, and beat them at their own game."[72] All of this fits well with William Pritchard's now famous aphorism: "Only fools try to make revolutions, wise men conform to them."[73]

Ironically, Aaron Mosher, the president of the Canadian Brotherhood of Railroad Employees, shared the SPC perspective to the degree that he recognized that radical leaders could not be held responsible for the labour revolt. In a letter volunteering his services to Prime Minister Borden, he noted:

> Numerous telegrams we are receiving from our local branches throughout the entire west asking authority to strike and the fact that some of our members have gone on strike after authorization was denied them, leads me to believe that it is not just a few labour agitators at Winnipeg who are causing the unrest. In most cases, I am sure the rank and file in the labour movement are forcing the leaders to take the stand they have taken, and it would be well to look into this phase of the situation.[74]

Commissioner Perry of the Royal North West Mounted Police argued similarly in his "Memorandum on Revolutionary Tendencies in Western Canada:"

> At the foundation of all this agitation is the general restlessness and dissatisfaction. The greater number of labour men, and probably of the community as a whole, are in an uncertain, apprehensive, nervous and irritable temper. Perhaps these agitators are but the foam on the wave.[75]

Let us take Mosher's advice and Perry's metaphor and close this paper with a consideration of the causes of the "wave" of unrest.

Eric Hobsbawm, some 20 years ago, suggested that:

> The habit of industrial solidarity must be learned ... so must the common sense of demanding concessions when conditions are favourable, not when hunger suggests it. There is thus a natural time lag, before workers become an "effective labour movement."[76]

Writing ten years later, Michelle Perrot argued: "The strike is a weapon of conquest, the major instrument of a working class more and more desirous and capable of improving its lot, more and more fascinated by the possibilities of the strike."[77] By 1919, Canadian workers had certainly become an "effective labour movement" and they also had developed in wartime conditions a considerable fascination with "the possibilities of the strike." Indeed, as this paper argued earlier, the 1919 revolt represents a return, albeit at a higher level of intensity, to the pre-war pattern of conflict. This intensification was fueled by the addition of new groups of workers to the struggle. These new groups included public service workers, west coast loggers, and previously unorganized or at best partially organized groups of industrial workers such as those in Toronto's and Montreal's packing houses and garment shops. Among these last groups of workers, as also in Winnipeg and certainly as in the coal mines of

District 18, another crucial new ingredient was present—ethnic solidarity. In 1919, momentarily at least, the divisiveness of ethnicity was surpassed in the struggle. A Canadian working-class movement which had been swamped with new immigrants from eastern and southern Europe in the pre-war years had matured, coalesced, and to some degree at least, commenced the process of incorporating the new workers into the movement. These "new" Canadian workers, as we are only now coming to realize, often were not "new" to the working class. Indeed Finns, Jews, and Ukrainians often arrived with a more extensive socialist background than their much celebrated English and Scot immigrant comrades. A brief Winnipeg example demonstrates this point poignantly. In the aftermath of the strike a number of "aliens" were transported to Kapuskasing, Ontario to await deportation. All had been arrested in the riot on Bloody Saturday. The *Strikers' Defense Bulletin* provided short biographies of thirteen ethnic workers. One German sheet metal worker joined twelve east Europeans hailing from Galicia (seven), Bukovina (two), "Austrian Poland," the Ukraine, and Russia. Occupationally, they included two boilermakers' helpers, a carpenter, a teamster, and eight labourers. Of the labourers, three were unemployed and the others worked for the city, on the railroad, in a restaurant, in the railway shops, and for Swift's. This state-selected group of foreign-born Winnipeg workers demonstrates graphically the ethnic presence in the Winnipeg strike. This presence was not unique to Winnipeg.[78]

In addition to the new ethnic component of the labour movement there was also a more pronounced presence of women workers. The new involvement of public sector workers brought groups of telephone operators and civic employees, while organization also spread to department store clerks and waitresses, and, of course, into the heavily female garment trades. In Winnipeg, Toronto, Calgary, Vancouver, and elsewhere women workers played important roles in the 1919 strikes, both as strikers and as members of Women's Labour Leagues and Councils which, in some cases, emerged during the general strikes.[79]

Thus the structural transformation of the working class generated by the Second Industrial Revolution and by the ongoing process of the concentration and centralization of capital, which on some levels weakened the working-class movement, simultaneously stimulated an enhanced capacity for collective resistance at the workplace. Thus, scientific management and other managerial innovations, which attacked what Robert Morris has usefully termed the "moral economy of the skilled man," began the process of generating an industrial union response.[80]

The rapid urban expansion generated by monopoly capitalist growth also played its role in the revolt. The working-class neighbourhoods of Toronto's and Montreal's garment districts or those associated with the huge metal plants and railroad shops in those cities and in the west became centres of workers' lives and slowly began to generate working-class community institutions. North-end Winnipeg is perhaps the most celebrated example, but all Canadian cities developed equivalent districts. While sometimes ethnically segregated, these areas often took on instead occupational associations as in Toronto's stockyard area or even Toronto's Junction district. In this period before the automobile's dispersal of the working class, a relationship continued to exist between domicile and workplace. We need to know much more about these communities and their role in sustaining working-class opposition. Neighbourhood may have played another role as well. Witness after witness before the Mathers Commission complained of poor and expensive housing in Canadian towns and cities. This near-universal complaint also undoubtedly contributed to the working-class revolt of 1919 and helped to widen it beyond simple workplace issues. Thus the general and sympathetic strikes extended beyond organized workers to embrace many workers outside the unions.

Also helping to widen the conflict in a similar fashion were the inter-related issues of inflation, the cost of living, and war profiteering. Recent econometric work on real wages in the first three decades of the twentieth century confirms that "real wage rates declined significantly during the First World War."[81] The new national index compiled by Bertram and Percy shows a low of 85.5 in 1917 (1913 equals 100), while Eleanor Bartlett's work on Vancouver shows the low point as either 1917 or 1918, depending on the choice of indices. What is clear in these studies and in earlier studies of Montreal, Toronto, and Winnipeg is that workers suffered a real decline on a national basis during the second half of the war. These econometric data provide the hard confirmation, for those who still need it, of the testimony of hundreds of workers before the Mathers Commission. They complained continuously of high food prices, of blatant profiteering, and of bureaucratic ineptitude, as well as of inflationary rents and inadequate housing. These complaints united all workers in ways that the more limited workplace battles sometimes failed to. Moreover the political dynamite in this situation was the clear dichotomy between a government which refused "fair wages" and conscripted manpower, and a government which allowed blatant profiteering and refused to conscript wealth. The transparency of the relationship between capital and the state in the war years allowed socialist propaganda to reach a growing and increasingly sympathetic audience. Demands for nationalization of abbatoirs, cold storage plants, and elevators, which might at first seem surprising, must be viewed in this context. As Cronin has argued in the European context, the coincidence of these consumer demands with intense struggles at the point of production helped to deepen class conflict into something approaching conscious class struggle.[82]

The violent repression in Winnipeg, the strike trials and the martyrdom of the leaders, the creation of the Royal Canadian Mounted Police, the conscious victimization of thousands of strikers, the TLC's retreat into craft exclusivism, all suggest a bleak aftermath and a story of defeat.[83] Yet as late as September 1919, Commissioner A.B. Perry of the new RCMP, an acute observer of labour radicalism, warned of the continuing "general state of unrest" which he found "far from satisfactory." Further, he cautioned:

> The leaders of the recent movement are determined, resourceful men; that their aims and objects are revolutionary in character has been clearly established. They have sustained a temporary setback, but to think we have heard the last of them is only resting in a false sense of security.[84]

The war on the labour left did continue and proved successful in the short term.

Yet the seeds of industrial unionism would survive to sprout later. Moreover, if the 1920s and early 1930s appear as a period of relative national labour quiescence, the phenomenon is far from unique. The working-class movement in other advanced industrial countries also slipped into what Yves Lequin has recently termed "the great silence," a period which stretched from the end of the great revolt until the resurgence of industrial unionism in the mid to late Depression years.[85] The fascination with industrial councils and various other welfare capitalist schemes which was so evident in the Mathers Commission and in the National Industrial Conference also had ambiguous results. The seemingly tame industrial councils often provided the basis for the new thrust to real industrial unions when the time was again propitious for working-class struggle.[86]

Defeats should not be confused with failure and perhaps the SPC leaders should be allowed to write their own epitaph. In Winnipeg, F.W. derived the following "Lessons of the Strike:"

> This is only a local momentary defeat on a world-wide battle front. Remember that permanently we cannot lose. Every struggle ... a lesson in class solidarity. Every brutal act of suppression brings capitalism nearer to its inevitable doom.... Courage, fellow workers. Study your class position and you cannot lose.[87]

Meanwhile in Vancouver, Comrade C.K. addressed "The Burning Question of Trade Unionism," echoing a Daniel DeLeon pamphlet title. Developing a "dialectical" position against the old "philosophy of misery" school, he argued that trade unions must be viewed not simply as they are but rather as they might develop. The events of 1919, he wrote, led inexorably to the workers' recognition of the need for political action. He closed on an optimistic note which, although too reminiscent of Second International evolutionism, nevertheless might be a message for all of us in this period of renewed attacks on labour:

> There is a benevolent appearing old gentleman wearing long white whiskers clad in a nightshirt and carrying a scythe. He is known as "father time." The fact is not generally known but he is a socialist of the most pronounced revolutionary type. He is very busy among the trade unions these days. He is working for us.[88]

Notes

1. Royal Commission on Industrial Relations, Evidence, Victoria, B.C., 26 April 1919, 242-3. (Henceforth cited as Mathers Commission.) One SPC view of the Commission is *Causes of Industrial Unrest* (Winnipeg 1919), a pamphlet published by SPC Local No. 3.

2. Mathers Commission, Evidence, Edmonton, Alta., 6 May 1919, 987-90.

3. *Ibid.,* Moose Jaw, Sask., 9 May 1919, 1330-42.

4. *Ibid.,* Sudbury, Ont., 17 May 1919, 1968-72.

5. *Ibid.,* Toronto, Ont., 28 May 1919, 2940-4.

6. *Ibid.,* Hamilton, Ont., 21 May 1919, 2261-81.

7. *Ibid.,* Montreal, Que., 29 May 1919, 3255-60.

8. For a partial reconstruction of this evidence from newspaper sources, see Nolan Reilly, "The General Strike in Amherst, Nova Scotia, 1919," *Acadiensis,* 9 (1980), 56-77; see also *Eastern Federationist,* 14 June 1919.

9. Mathers Commission, Evidence, New Glasgow, N.S., 5 June 1919, 3533-55.

10. *Ibid.,* Halifax, 4 June 1919, 4355-9. On Dane, see Clifford Rose, *Four Years with the Demon Rum* (Fredericton 1980), 5-9, 83.

11. *Ibid.,* Calgary, Alta., 3 May 1919, 786.

12. *Ibid.,* Saskatoon, Sask., 7 May 1919, 1036.

13. *Ibid.,* Regina, Sask., 8 May 1919, 1191.

14. *Ibid.,* Montreal, Que., 29 May 1919, 3163.

15. See Russell Hann's excellent introduction to Daphne Read, comp., *The Great War and Canadian Society* (Toronto 1978), 9-38.

16. David Montgomery, "Strikes in Nineteenth-Century America," *Social Science History,* 4 (1980), 100.

17. All strike data in this paper are drawn from recalculations for the Historical Atlas of Canada, volume III. These recalculations are based on the addition of Maritime provinces material compiled from local sources by Ian McKay of Dalhousie University and on a careful re-examination of all the "incomplete" files available in the PAC, Department of Labour, Strikes and Lockouts files. This work commenced by Peter DeLottinville has been carried through to completion by Douglas Cruikshank. These data currently being compiled for publication in the Atlas provides an entirely new data series for Canadian strike activity. For a report on McKay's work, see his "Strikes in the Maritimes, 1900-1914," *Acadiensis,* 13 (1983), 3-46.

18. David Bercuson, *Confrontation at Winnipeg: Labour Industrial Relations, and the General Strike* (Montreal 1974) and Reilly, "The General Strike."

19. Craig Heron and Bryan D. Palmer, "Through the Prism of the Strike: Industrial Conflict in Southern Ontario, 1901-14," *Canadian Historical Review,* 58 (1977), 423-58.

20. Unless other sources are cited this account draws on PAC, Department of Labour, Strikes and Lockouts files as well as on the original published version, *Labour Gazette,* 20 (1920), 267-94.

21. For a brief account, see Terry Copp, *Anatomy of Poverty* (Toronto 1974), 134-5.

22. *Gazette* (Montreal), 28 May 1919.

23. *Ibid.,* 6 June 1919.

24. *Ibid.,* 20 June 1919. For a brief reminiscence of the emerging Montreal red world, see Catherine Vance, *Not by Gods, But by People: The Story of Bella Hall Gauld* (Toronto 1968), 19-44. On the Vickers strike see. *Ontario Labor News.* (Toronto), 1 July 1919.

25. On Cobalt, see Brian F. Hogan, *Cobalt: Year of the Strike, 1919* (Cobalt 1978); on Kirkland Lake, see Laurel Sefton MacDowell, *'Remember Kirkland Lake': The Gold Miners' Strike of 1941-42* (Toronto 1983). 58-60, and Wayne Roberts, ed., *Miner's Life: Bob Miner and Union Organizing in Timmins, Kirkland Lake and Sudbury* (Hamilton 1979), 1-2.

26. J.T. Montague, "Trade Unionism in the Canadian Meat Packing Industry," unpublished Ph.D. thesis, University of Toronto, 1950, 31-8 and George Sayers Bain, "The United Packinghouse, Food and Allied Workers," M.A. thesis, University of Manitoba, 1964, 35-67.

27. *Machinists Monthly Journal,* 31 (April 1919), 330, cited in Donald Wright, "Belshazzar, the Medes, and the Persians: The Rise and Fall of the Metal Trades Strike in Toronto, 1919," unpublished paper, Dalhousie University, 1979. Planning for 1919 took place at the second Provincial Convention of the IAM in late November 1918. See *Labour Gazette,* 19 (1919), 51-2. See also *Ontario Labor News,* 1 May-1 July 1919.

28. For details see David Jay Bercuson, ed., *Alberta's Coal Industry 1919* (Calgary 1978); Bercuson, *Fools and Wise Men: The Rise and Fall of the One Big Union* (Toronto 1978), 196-214; Allen Seager, "Socialists and Workingmen: The Western Canadian Coal Miners' Movement, 1900-1920," paper presented at American Historical Association Meetings, December 1982.

29. Nolan Reilly, "The General Strike," his "Notes on the Amherst General Strike and the One Big Union," *Bulletin of the Committee on Canadian Labour History,* 3 (Spring 1977), 5-8, and his "The Emergence of Class Consciousness in Industrial Nova Scotia: A Study of Amherst, 1891-1925," Ph.D. thesis, Dalhousie University, 1982. See also *Eastern Federationist,* 24 May-21 June 1919.

30. Borden Papers, PAC, MG 26 H vol. 113 pt. 1 and pt. 2, file OC 564 (henceforth Borden Papers.) See, for example, N.W. Rowell to White, Toronto. 26 May 1919; White to Rowell, Ottawa, 26 May 1919; T.L. Church to Borden. Toronto, 27 May 1919; Church to Borden, 31 May 1919; Church to Borden, 2 June 1919.

31. The literature on the munitions industry, the IMB, and labour unrest is growing, but for contrasting views, see: D.J. Bercuson, "Organized Labour and the Imperial Munitions Board." *Relations Industrielles,* 28 (1974), 602-16; Peter Rider. "The Imperial Munitions Board and its Relationship to Government, Business, and Labour, 1914-1920," Ph.D. thesis, University of Toronto, 1974, esp. ch. 9: Michael Bliss, *A Canadian Millionaire: The Life and Business Times of Sir Joseph Flavelle, Bart., 1858-1939* (Toronto 1978), esp. 270-2, 280-4, 320-5, 378-81; Myer Siemiatycki, "Munitions and Labour Militancy: The 1916 Hamilton Machinists' Strike," *Labour/Le Travailleur,* 3 (1978), 131-51; Craig Heron, "The Crisis of the Craftsman: Hamilton's

Metal Workers in the Early Twentieth Century," *Labour/Le Travailleur,* 6 (1980), 7-48; and, for Toronto metal trades background, Wayne Roberts, "Toronto Metal Workers and the Second Industrial Revolution, 1889-1914," *Labour/Le Travailleur,* 6 (1980), 49-72.

32. TTLC, *Minutes,* 2. 16 March, 6, 20 April 1916, including correspondence from Draper and Watters of the TLC.

33. Siemiatycki, "Munitions and Labour Militancy," 141.

34. TTLC, *Minutes,* 1. 13, 15 May 1919; *Ontario Labor News,* 15 May 1919.

35. Borden Papers, Rowell to White, 26 May 1919 and White to Rowell, 26 May 1919. Statistics from *Ontario Labor News,* 1 June 1919.

36. *Ibid.,* Church to Borden, 27 May 1919 and "Minutes of Toronto Meeting."

37. *Ibid.,* Borden to R.O. Hawtrey, 2 June 1919.

38. Low estimate is Department of Labour; high estimate is given by Mayor Church in letter to Borden, 2 June 1919. The *Globe* decided on 8000. See *Globe,* 30 May-7 June 1919.

39. TTLC, *Minutes,* 7, 21 August, 3 October, 6 November, 4, 18 December 1919, 22 January, 19 February 1920; Michael J. Piva, "The Toronto District Labour Council and Independent Political Action, 1900-21," *Labour/Le Travailleur,* 4 (1979), 126-8. See also *The New Democracy* (Hamilton), 31 July, 7 August 1919.

40. Data on additional Saskatchewan locations from W.J.C. Cherwinski, "Organized Labour in Saskatchewan: The TLC Years, 1905-45," unpublished Ph.D. thesis, University of Alberta, 1972, chapter 2, and his "Saskatchewan Organized Labour and the Winnipeg General Strike, 1919," unpublished paper, Memorial University of Newfoundland, 1976; for Prince Rupert, see *B.C. Federationist,* 30 May 1919; for Radville through Souris, see Walter Scott Ryder, "Canada's Industrial Crisis of 1919," unpublished M.A. thesis, University of British Columbia, 1920, 36. How reliable this last list of whistle stops (literally) is, isn't clear. Ryder, however, was writing in the immediate aftermath of the event and most of these are railway junction towns where there were probably significant groups of shopcraft workers.

41. On Brandon, see A.E. Smith, *All My Life* (Toronto 1949), ch. 3-6: Kathleen O'Gorman Wormsbecker, "The Rise and Fall of the Labour Political Movement in Manitoba, 1919-1927," M.A. thesis, Queen's University, 1977, esp. ch. 2: Brandon Trades and Labor Council, *Strike Bulletin,* 21-31 May 1919; *Western Labor News* (Winnipeg), 7, 9 June 1919. On the earlier Brandon strike, see *Confederate* (Brandon). 4 April 1919 and *Western Labor News,* 25 April, 7 May 1919.

42. On Saskatchewan see Cherwinski, "Organized Labour," ch. 2 and his "Organized Labour and the Winnipeg General Strike."

43. For the Edmonton strike, see William R. Askin, "Labour Unrest in Edmonton and District and its Coverage by the Edmonton Press, 1918-19," unpublished M.A. thesis, University of Alberta, 1973 and Carl Betke, "Influence and Community: The Ambiguity of Labour Organization in Edmonton, 1906-1921," unpublished paper presented at the Canadian-American Urban Development Conference. University of Guelph, August 1982. See also *The One Big Union Bulletin* (Edmonton), 25 March

1919; *Edmonton Strike Bulletin,* 5, 11 June 1919; and *Edmonton Free Press.* 12 April-12 July 1919.

44. For Calgary, see Elizabeth Ann Taraska, "The Calgary Craft Union Movement, 1900-20," unpublished M.A. thesis, University of Calgary, 1975, quotation at 46 and *Calgary Strike Bulletin,* 30 May-24 June 1919.

45. *Ibid.,* ch. 5 and *Labour Gazette,* 18 (1918), 615, 759, 857, 1005 and 820, 974-5.

46. *B.C. Federationist,* 16 May 1919 and Vancouver Trades and Labor Council, Executive Minutes, 15 May 1919. See also Paul Phillips, *No Power Greater* (Vancouver 1967), 80-1; *Strike Bulletin* (Vancouver), 9-26 June 1919; *The Camp Worker* (Vancouver), 2 June 1919; *The Vancouver Citizen,* 16 June-3 July 1919; and *The Critic,* 26 April-12 July 1919.

47. *Ibid.,* 23 May 1919; Borden Papers, G.H. Deane to Borden, Vancouver, 27 May 1919, J. Kavanagh, Secretary VTLC, to Borden, 27 May 1919; and VTLC, Executive Minutes, 22, 27, 28 May 1919.

48. *B.C. Federationist,* 30 May 1919.

49. For list of unions supporting the strike, see *Ibid.,* 6 June 1919. On women, see *Strike Bulletin,* 16 June 1919. It is worth noting the *Citizen,* the viciously anti-union publication of the Citizens' Committee, propagandized actively for women's support. See, for only two examples, "To the Women," 20 June 1919 and "Women! With Whom?" 21 June 1919.

50. *B.C. Federationist,* 6 June 1919.

51. *Ibid.,* 20 June 1919.

52. *Ibid.,* 27 June, 4 July 1919.

53. *Ibid.,* 4 July 1919. For another brief account of the Vancouver Strike, see Elaine Bernard, "Vancouver 1919," *Democrat* 20 (June-July 1980).

54. Phillips, *No Power Greater,* 80-1. See also the short memoir by machinist Arthur J. Turner, *Somewhere—A Perfect Place* (Vancouver 1981), 22-6, for a brief memory of the Victoria Sympathy Strike. See also *Semi-Weekly Tribune* (Victoria), 14 April-30 June 1919 and Victoria Trades and Labor Council, Minutes, esp. 9 June 1919.

55. Antonio Gramsci, *Selections from Political Writings (1910-1920)* (New York 1977). 61; Nan Milton, ed., *John MacLean: In the Rapids of Revolution* (London 1978), 190, 137.

56. On Newfoundland, see Melvin Baker, Robert Cuff, Bill Gillespie, *Workingmen's St. John's: Aspects of Social History in the Early 1900s* (St. John's 1982). Also Robert Cuff, "The Quill and the Hammer: Labour Activism in Newfoundland and Nova Scotia. 1917-1925," Honours B.A. thesis, Department of History, Memorial University of Newfoundland, 1980; Bill Gillespie, "A History of the Newfoundland Federation of Labour, 1936-63," unpublished M.A. thesis, Memorial University of Newfoundland. 1980; John Joy, "The Growth and Development of Trades and Manufacturing in St. John's, 1870-1914," unpublished M.A. thesis, Memorial University of Newfoundland, 1977; and Ian McDonald, "W.F. Coaker and the Fishermen's Protective Union in Newfoundland Politics, 1909-1925," unpublished Ph.D. thesis, University of London, 1971.

57. Larry Peterson, "The One Big Union in International Perspective: Revolutionary Industrial Unionism 1900-1925," *Labour/Le Travailleur,* 7 (1981), 41-66; James E. Cronin, "Labor Insurgency and Class Formation: Comparative Perspectives on the Crisis of 1917-1920 in Europe," *Social Science History,* 4 (1980), 125-152.

58. *B.C. Federationist,* 4 July 1919.

59. Trades and Labour Congress of Canada, *Proceedings,* 1917, 141-55. For a good example of similar fights in the U.S., see Cecelia F. Bucki, "Dilution and Craft Tradition: Bridgeport, Connecticut, Munition Workers, 1915-1919," *Social Science History,* 4 (1980), 105-124. Also see John Laslett. *Labor and the Left* (New York 1970), *passim.*

60. *Ibid.,* 1918, 138-9. Note that my count is slightly at variance with Gerald Friesen, 'Yours in Revolt': Regionalism, Socialism, and the Western Canadian Labour Movement," *Labour/Le Travailleur,* 1 (1976), 141. The point, of course, remains the same. His count, however, is 29 west and 51 east vs. 3 west and 81 east.

61. *Ibid.,* 1919, 165.

62. TLC, *Proceedings,* 1919, 156-7. See David Frank, "The Cape Breton Coal Miners, 1917-1926," unpublished Ph.D. thesis, Dalhousie University, 1979, 315-19.

63. *Ibid.,* 166.

64. *Ibid.*

65. *Ibid.,* 190-2.

66. On the IAM, see *Proceedings,* 1920, especially 129-40, 559-62, 248-56, 187-98, 380. See also *Bulletin* (Winnipeg), April-August 1919.

67. The syndicalist "accusation" has come ironically from both ends of the ideological spectrum over time. Gideon Robertson, for example, simply, and I believe sincerely, equated the OBU with the IWW. Later communist historians, refusing to forgive Bob Russell's refusal to join the CPC, have made the same charge. More recently some historians have repeated the error, while not necessarily sharing either Robertson's or the CPC's political position. See, for example, *Canada's Party of Socialism* (Toronto: Progress, 1982), 32-3; James Foy, "Gideon Robertson: Conservative Minister of Labour, 1917-1921," unpublished M.A. thesis, University of Ottawa, 1972; Bercuson, *Confrontation at Winnipeg,* 89; Bercuson, *Fools and Wise Men, passim;* A. Ross McCormack, *Reformers, Rebels, and Revolutionaries: The Western Canadian Radical Movement 1899-1919* (Toronto 1977), 98, 112-3, 143 ff: Martin Robin, *Radical Politics and Canadian Labour 1880-1930* (Kingston 1968), 150-1, 171-7, 275. This argument is not unique to this paper, of course. See Peterson, "One Big Union," 53-8 and Friesen, 'Yours in Revolt,'," 139-40 for similar interpretations.

68. *The Soviet* (Edmonton), 1, 13 (20 June 1919).

69. *Red Flag* (Vancouver), 1, 9 (22 March 1919).

70. *Ibid.,* 1, 18 (24 May 1919).

71. *B.C. Federationist,* 23 May 1919.

72. *Ibid.,* 30 May 1919.

73. Gloria Montero, *We Stood Together: First Hand Accounts of Dramatic Events in Canada's Labour Past* (Toronto 1979), 14. Also, of course, the source of Bercuson's title.

74. Borden Papers, A.R. Mosher to Borden, 29 May 1919.

75. Department of National Defence, RG 24, vol. 3985, N-S-C 1055-2-21, *Secret.* "Memorandum on Revolutionary Tendencies in Western Canada," prepared by Assistant Comptroller, RNWMP.

76. E.J. Hobsbawm, *Labouring Men* (London 1964), 144.

77. Michelle Perrot, *Les Ouvriers en grève, France 1871-90*, Tome I (Paris 1974), 64.

78. The new literature on ethnic workers is already too voluminous to list, but note especially Varpu Lindstrom-Best's work on the Finns and Orest T. Martynowych's essays on Ukrainian socialism. See, also, the special issue of *Canadian Ethnic Studies,* 10 (1978) on ethnic radicalism. For the Winnipeg data, see *Strikers' Defense Bulletin,* 1, 4 (27 August 1919). For additional Winnipeg evidence see Donald Avery, "The Radical Alien and the Winnipeg General Strike of 1919," in Carl Berger and Ramsay Cook, eds., *The West and the Nation* (Toronto 1976), 209-31 and his "Ethnic Loyalties and the Proletarian Revolution," in Jorgen Dahlie and Tissa Fernando, eds., *Ethnicity, Power, and Politics in Canada* (Toronto 1981), 68-93.

79. On Vancouver telephone operators and the General Strike see Elaine Bernard. *The Long Distance Feeling: A History of the Telecommunications Workers Union* (Vancouver 1982), 50-65.

80. Robert Morris, "Skilled Workers and the Politics of the 'Red' Clyde," unpublished paper, University of Edinburgh, 1981. As Morris notes, his echo of Edward Thompson's "moral economy" is intentional.

81. On the war economy in general see R.T. Naylor, "The Canadian State, the Accumulation of Capital, and the Great War," *Revue d'études canadiennes,* 16, 3 and 4 (1981), 26-55. On inflation specifically see: Terry Copp, *Anatomy of Poverty,* for Montreal, Michael J. Piva, *The Condition of the Working Class in Toronto;* Harry Sutcliffe and Paul Phillips, "Real Wages and the Winnipeg General Strike: An Empirical Investigation," unpublished paper, University of Manitoba, 1973; Gordon Bertram and Michael Percy, "Real Wage Trends in Canada 1900-26," *Canadian Journal of Economics,* 12 (1979), 299-312; and Eleanor Bartlett, "Real Wages and the Standard of Living in Vancouver, 1901-1929," *B.C. Studies,* 51 (1981), 3-62. For a slightly later period, see Michael J. Piva, "Urban Working-Class Incomes and Real Incomes in 1921: A Comparative Analysis," *Histoire sociale/Social History,* 31 (1983), 143-65. See also for a U.S. comparison, Frank Stricker, "The Wages of Inflation: Workers' Earnings in the World War One Era," *Mid-America,* 63 (1981), 93-105. For the general U.S. economic context, see David M. Gordon, Richard Edwards, Michael Reich, *Segmented Work, Divided Workers: The Historical Transformation of Labor in the United States* (New York 1982), 127-64.

82. Cronin, "Labour Insurgency and Class Conflict," *passim.* See also his *Industrial Conflict in Modern Britain* (London 1979), 109-20.

83. Much of this has been chronicled elsewhere. For an apologetic but detailed description of the creation of the RCMP see S.W. Horrall, "The Royal North-West Mounted Police and Labour Unrest in Western Canada, 1919," *Canadian Historical Review,* 61 (1980), 169-90. On victimization, especially of postal workers, see Borden Papers, various letters June to September 1919, pp. 62179-257. On one particularly unseemly aspect of TLC behaviour, see Tom Traves, 'The Story that Couldn't be Told': Big Business Buys the TLC," *Ontario Report,* 1, 6 (September 1976), 27-9.

84. A.B. Perry, "Draft Memorandum," 1 September 1919. Royal Canadian Mounted Police Papers, volume 1003, PAC.

85. Yves Lequin, "Social Structures and Shared Beliefs: Four Worker Communities in the Second Industrialization," *International Labor and Working Class History,* 22 (1982), 1-17.

86. On Councils in Canada, see Bruce Scott, 'A Place in the Sun': The Industrial Council at Massey-Harris, 1919-1929," *Labour/Le Travailleur,* 1 (1976), 158-92; Tom Traves. *The State and Enterprise: Canadian Manufacturers and the Federal Government 1917-1931* (Toronto 1979), 86-94; and Foy, "Gideon Robertson." For U.S. comparisons see Stuart D. Brandes, *American Welfare Capitalism, 1880-1940* (Chicago 1976), *passim,* but esp. 119-48.

87. *Socialist Bulletin* (Winnipeg), 1, 7 (July 1919).

88. *Red Flag,* 1, 22 (21 June 1919). For an academic echo of labour's educational gains from the strike, see D.G. Cook, "Western Radicalism and the Winnipeg Strike," M.A. thesis, McMaster University, 1921, which argues, on the basis of interviews with Winnipeg strikers, that: "The gains of the strike were many for the labour group. The six-week's strike was like a college course in Economics. Papers were read, issues discussed, and many addresses were given by the leaders. Many of the labour men became enlightened as to the real struggle. There grew a strong spirit of solidarity in the rank and file of labour." (62).

CHAPTER
7 THE GREAT WAR

Although Canada entered the war enthusiastically in August 1914 at Britain's side, the experience proved to be traumatic, both because of the nature of the war and because of the divisions within Canadian society which the war exposed. The fervour at the outbreak of war masked the fact that Canada entered the war without any clear understanding or definition of the role which the country was to play. Was she, for example, simply a colony giving loyal support to the Mother Country? Or was she a nation fighting in defence of freedom as one of the Allies? The contribution expected of a dependent colony would be far different than that from a country which considered itself on a par with the other Allies.

As the war progressed, it became clear that Canadians were divided on these issues. Had the war ended quickly, as virtually everyone assumed it would, these divisions would probably not even have become apparent. This particular war, however, because of its nature, dragged on endlessly without any visible results and put an enormous strain on the resources of all the belligerents, including Canada.

The first reading in this unit examines some of the strains within Canadian society caused by the war. It is usually assumed that the major division caused by the war was between French and English Canada, and in this reading Susan Mann Trofimenkoff describes the impact of the war on Quebec, arguing that it created or exacerbated divisions not only between French and English, but also within the French community itself.

In the second reading, Stuart Robson turns the question around and assesses the impact of Canada on the war. This is an important question, since many commentators, both at the time and later, accused the government of Sir Robert Borden of imposing unnecessary strains on Canadian society, given Canada's role as a very junior partner in the war effort. Robson suggests that, on the contrary, the Canadian contribution to the Allied victory was not only substantial; it may even have been decisive.

Suggestions for Further Reading

Armstrong, Elizabeth, *The Crisis of Quebec, 1914-1918*. New York: Columbia University Press, 1937. Reprinted Toronto: McClelland and Stewart, 1974.

Berger, Carl, ed., *Conscription 1917*. Toronto: University of Toronto Press, 1969.

Berton, Pierre, *Vimy*. Toronto: McClelland and Stewart, 1986.

Bray,R.M. "'Fighting as an Ally': The English-Canadian Patriotic Response to the Great War," *Canadian Historical Review*, LXI, no. 2 (June 1980), 141-168.

English, John, *The Decline of Politics: The Conservatives and the Party System, 1901-20*. Toronto: University of Toronto Press, 1977.

Graham, Roger, "Through the First World War," in *The Canadians, 1867-1967*, ed. J.M.S. Careless and R.C. Brown. Toronto: Macmillan, 1968.

Granatstein, J.L. and J.M. Hitsman, *Broken Promises: A History of Conscription in Canada*. Toronto: Oxford University Press, 1977.

Nicholson, G.W.L., *Canadian Expeditionary Force*, 1914-1919. Ottawa: Queen's Printer, 1962.

Ramkhalawansingh, Ceta, "Women during the Great War," in *Women At Work: Ontario, 1850-1930*, ed. Janice Acton, *et al*. Toronto: Canadian Women's Educational Press, 1974.

Socknat, Thomas, "Canada's Liberal Pacifists and the Great War," *Journal of Canadian Studies*, VIII, no. 4 (Winter 1983-84), 30-44.

_____, *Witness Against War: Pacifism in Canada, 1900-1945*. Toronto: University of Toronto Press, 1987.

Wilson, Barbara, M., ed., *Ontario and the First World War, 1914-1918: A Collection of Documents*. Toronto: The Champlain Society, 1977.

THE PRUSSIANS ARE NEXT DOOR

Susan Mann Trofimenkoff

Nationalists in Quebec have never forgotten the First World War and Liberal politicians have been a close second in reminding voters of its political ravages. For many nationalists the war years turned French Canada into Quebec. For many Liberals the blunders of federal Conservatives during the same years provided electoral ammunition for generations to come. To some French Canadians, the war revealed the basic incompatibility of Canada's two people: alien cultures finally exposed, in total disagreement over the demands of imperialism, the force of nationalism, and the logic of feminism. For other French Canadians, the crises of the war years—from Ontario schools to conscription to votes for women—were just that, temporary aberrations from the Canadian norm of compromise and forbearance. The difference of opinion within French Canada troubled the nationalists as much as English Canadian hostility although no one seemed unhappy to see the momentary reference to separatism disappear from the headlines as quickly as it appeared late in 1917.

From *The Dream of Nation: A Social and Intellectual History of Quebec* (Toronto: Gage Publishing, 1983), 201-216. Reprinted by permission of Gage Educational Publishing Company.

Certainly separatist thoughts were far from anyone's mind in the summer of 1914. Even the vaguely voiced notion of Canadian autonomy from Britain was swept aside in a wave of enthusiasm for European military adventures. The British declaration of war on Germany in early August bound the entire empire, if not to actual participation, then to a legal state of war. In fact no one lingered over legal niceties: there was no questioning of Canadian support for and participation in the British war effort. Crowds in the cities of Quebec vied with those in other Canadian centres to express their emotion. The Quebec government was as generous as that of the other provinces in offering an assortment of Canadian agricultural products freely to Britain. Four million tons of Quebec cheese thus made its way across the Atlantic accompanied by the salmon, hay, cattle, apples, and potatoes of the Canadian cornucopia. Only Henri Bourassa wryly commented upon the supplementary freight trains required to haul all the generosity to Canadian ports and the likelihood of much of it rotting on the quays of Liverpool before it could be distributed and consumed. But even he, although acknowledging no constitutional obligation to be involved in Britain's wars, admitted to a moral interest in the outcome for the two European countries with which Canadians had historical and emotional ties.

Canadian assistance and support was easy enough to offer when no one knew the extent or the demands of the war. Wilfrid Laurier, leader of the Liberal opposition in the House of Commons, offered his entire support to the Conservative government of Robert Borden. From the Liberals would come no questioning, not a word of reproach, as long as there was danger on the European front; the friends and foes of Great Britain should know that Canadian hearts and minds were united. Such magnanimity was as shortly lived as it was eloquently expressed. But in the spirited summer days of 1914, this political co-operation enabled the Canadian government to pass the War Measures Act which sanctioned extensive controls over the lives and economic activities of Canadians. In Quebec the lieutenant-governor offered all the resources of the province for the defence of Canada; Sir Lomer Gouin, the premier, indicated that Quebec government employees could enlist and continue to receive full salary. The archbishops of Quebec and Montreal spoke of the sacred duty of Canadians to aid Great Britain. Only later in the war were appeals made in the name of Canada's two "mother countries"; in the early months some French Canadians seriously wondered whether the war was not divine retribution for a France that had strayed from the path of true religion. The mayors of Quebec City and Montreal joined the chorus of assistance to Great Britain and the popular press followed suit. After all, the war was only supposed to last a few months; those few Canadian soldiers who were likely even to go overseas—as volunteers, the prime minister carefully assured the country—would be home for Christmas after a pleasant European tour.

The recruiting stations were barely open when some French Canadians began wondering just where the real battle was. Indeed, a number of nationalist leaders were being recruited, not to the Canadian Expeditionary Force—although there were some there such as Olivar Asselin, a military enthusiast ever since his participation in the Spanish American war at the end of the nineteenth century—but rather to assist their French-speaking compatriots in Ontario. There, the Prussians were not across the Atlantic but across the street, the trenches held not by allied forces but by mothers armed with hatpins. The military analogies in the exaggerated language of Ottawa's *Le Droit,* a paper begun in 1913 to speak for the growing number of French Canadians in eastern Ontario, revealed both an ignorance of the horror of European trench warfare and the depth of the hurt occasioned by the Ontario school question. The intermingling of the war's demands with English Ontario's implacable hostility to all things French dampened French Canadian enthusiasm for the war effort and created a new breed of nationalist.

The increasing number of French Canadians in Ontario seems to have been at the origin of the dispute over bilingual schools that began in 1912. By that date, one-tenth of Ontario's population was French-speaking as newcomers moved in from Quebec to join well-established communities in southwestern Ontario, to add to the newer settlers in the north along the lines of the National Transcontinental, or to swell the French presence in Ottawa and the counties of eastern Ontario. Their arrival complicated the lives of English-speaking Catholics, particularly in the schools, and raised fears among English-speaking Protestants, always suspicious of Catholicism and even more so when it was linked to the French language. Moreover the concentrated presence of French Canadians in three distinct areas of the province also had political implications for the Conservative provincial government. When many of them also showed signs of imitating their Quebec relatives by organizing formal interest groups, English-speaking Ontarians became distinctly hostile. In 1910, for example, the *Association canadienne-française d'éducation d'Ontario* held its first conference in Ottawa. Twelve hundred delegates from French-speaking areas of the province voiced their concern for the twenty-five thousand youngsters attending bilingual primary schools in the province: they wanted their children properly taught by competent teachers with legislative grants for their schools.

Other Ontarians had similar worries but for quite different reasons. Bilingual schools had no legal existence in the province; they had simply developed along with the French-speaking population, usually as part of the Catholic separate school system constitutionally guaranteed since 1867, but sometimes, if a given district had no separate school, within the public school system. Administrators in the ministry of education had nightmares about the complexities and the very thought of a third school system with multiple demands for classrooms, teachers, inspectors, and programs. Where would one find competent seventeen-year-olds able to teach the entire primary program in both languages and frequently in a single classroom for the scant hundred dollars annual salary offered by most school boards? Should French be encouraged at all when Ontario's industrial future, and the youngsters' place in it, was assuredly English? Like Manitobans of the late nineteenth century, English-speaking Ontarians could only measure progress in English terms.

Quebec nationalists always had difficulty with the fact that the school question surfaced because of the complaints of a Catholic bishop. The ideological connection that had been developing since the late nineteenth century, thanks largely to ultramontane logic, between language, religion, and nationality could not quite hold in the face of bitter Irish-French disputes in Ontario. The villain was supposed to be clad as an Orangeman; instead, in his first appearance, he wore the cassock of a priest. Monseigneur Fallon, the bishop of London, complained to the Ontario government and the press that the bilingual schools in his diocese were producing poorly trained children, inferior to those in the English language separate schools. The public controversy that swirled around Fallon's remarks induced the provincial government to investigate the bilingual schools of the province and, once the investigation confirmed the accusations, to pass regulatory measures. On the assumption that a single language would cure all the practical problems which the investigator, Dr. Merchant, spotted in certain of the bilingual schools, the ministry of education added Regulation XVII to its decrees for elementary schools. Beginning as a mere directive in 1912, the regulation, slightly modified in the face of Franco-Ontarian opposition, became law in 1915. By then its purpose was hopelessly enmeshed with the Canadian war effort, as nationalists from Quebec fanned the flames of resentment between English- and French-speaking Ontarians.

To both Quebecois and Franco-Ontarians, Regulation XVII implied the end of French language teaching in Ontario. Its stipulation that French could be used as a language of instruction only in the first two years of the primary program, after which pupils were expected to know enough English to continue their schooling in that language, and that French as a subject of study should be limited to one hour a day, raised all the old fears of assimilation. In vain, and indeed not very loudly, did the Ontario government protest that the regulation only applied to an annually construed list of bilingual schools where English was inadequately taught or where the teachers lacked the proper qualifications. In vain did it tinker with the inspection system of the regulation: no one within the ministry of education or outside knew precisely how the regulation was to work or just what it intended. French Canadians, ever fearful, and increasingly sensitive to the question of language as the early twentieth century tumbled people together, believed the regulation meant their demise.

Little during the war years was to relieve their anxiety. While the Ontario government threatened to cut off provincial funds from schools that did not obey Regulation XVII, fanatical Protestants in the province urged even more severe restrictions. The Orange Order, claiming to defend British principles and therefore the English language, urged the abolition of all bilingual schools since they were agents of French Canadian infiltration into the province. Worse still for the Orangemen was that those French Canadians were probably disloyal, given their poor showing in the enlistment figures for the war. Just as unsettling for French Canadians was the feud with their fellow Catholics. Prompted by Monseigneur Fallon, English-speaking Catholics, with a population three times that of the French in Ontario, argued that the senseless struggle over language risked endangering the much greater principle of Catholic education. If the French Canadians annoyed the Ontario government to such an extent that it decided to turn on separate schooling itself, where would Catholics be then? The two groups of Catholics came to legal blows in Ottawa when the English and French sections of the Ottawa separate school board disputed the majority French section's defiance of Regulation XVII. While lawyers contested the validity of the regulation and of the government's means of enforcing it, French-speaking children and their mothers defended the schools and the teachers of their choice. A Laval University student newspaper cheekily remarked that the real threat to French civilization in the world was no longer in Flanders but in the schools of Ottawa.

Although the school question was to assist them in doing so, French Canadians had not yet drawn a frontier along the provincial boundary. Those in Quebec gladly lent their ideological and financial support to *Le Droit* and the *Association canadienne-française d'éducation d'Ontario*. The Franco-Ontarian leaders were all relative newcomers and they called upon intellectual and nationalist sustenance from their home province. Nationalist spokesmen from Quebec visited Ontario and reported on the struggle to their colleagues in Montreal and Quebec. Henri Bourassa was a favourite guest at Ontario gatherings; his powers of logic and persuasion were solace to the embattled minority. Bourassa in fact saw the French-speaking minorities in the rest of Canada as the outposts of Quebec: their defence against the attacks of a bigoted majority assured Quebec's own survival; if they succumbed, Quebec would be next. Bourassa's paper *Le Devoir* thus gave full coverage of the events in Ontario. Nationalist associations in Quebec held fund raising campaigns to assist the Ontarians in their educational and legal defiance of Regulation XVII. Quebec bishops encouraged the campaigns and approved clerical ones launched from the pulpits of parish churches. The Catholic school commission of Montreal voted funds to assist the bilingual campaign in Ontario. Even the Quebec government, gingerly stepping on the mine field of interference in another province's affairs, passed a motion regretting the divisions over the bilingual school question in Ontario. It also permitted municipalities in the province to make financial contributions to patriotic, national, or educational causes, the latter intended to cover the Franco-Ontarian situation. Businesses even began to register the cost of French Canadian unhappiness as Quebec clients refused to place orders with Toronto firms. Through it all, the force of numbers became increasingly obvious, although seldom openly admitted. French Canadians were only safe in numbers and only in Quebec did they have the numbers.

Quebec's federal politicians would never make such an admission, but they too had to swallow much of the bitterness of the school question. Indeed, with some of the more dramatic episodes of the struggle taking place within shouting distance of Parliament Hill, they could hardly avoid the issue even if they had wanted to stay on the neutral terrain of education being a provincial matter. The tattered remains of the nationalist alliance with the Conservatives in 1911 rallied sufficiently to have cabinet ministers Pierre-Edouard Blondin, Thomas-Chase Casgrain, and Esioff-Léon Patenaude request that prime minister Borden refer the entire question of the status of the French language in Canada to the Privy Council for clarification. Borden refused on the grounds that the British North America Act was perfectly clear: French had a legal existence in the debates and recordings of the federal parliament, in those of the Quebec provincial legislature, and before the federal and Quebec courts. He refrained from adding "and no further" that many Conservatives then and since have muttered. Nor would he, along with most English Canadians, accept an argument for French based on natural right or even on the legally imaginative grounds that French Canadians, in Saskatchewan for example, required education in French in order to be able to take a case to a federal court in that province in their own language. In fact none of the defenders of bilingual schools in Ontario denied the necessity of learning English; they simply wanted their children taught in French as well.

But when such views were expressed in the federal parliament, they encountered a blank and sometimes hostile wall. Borden refused a petition from senator Philippe Landry and most of the Quebec bishops requesting federal disallowance of Regulation XVII; in the background some of his Conservative colleagues began to grumble about French Canadian participation in the war effort. In May 1916, the MPs voted down an intricately worded resolution from Ernest Lapointe, Liberal member for Kamouraska, requesting that the Ontario government not infringe upon the linguistic privileges of French-speaking school children. The Liberal leader, Laurier, barely kept his Ontario members in line for the vote as westeners openly balked and voted with the Conservative majority. Behind the defeat, legitimate enough on the grounds of federal non-interference in provincial matters, was also the grim sentiment expressed by the former western Liberal MP, Clifford Sifton: the Franco-Ontarian agitation was criminal and unpatriotic at a time of national crisis. For Sifton and many English Canadians the real national crisis was on the European battlefield; for many French Canadians it was in the linguistic heart of Canada. When Abbé Lionel Groulx, six years later, placed the federal debate over the school question at the centre of his novel *L'Appel de la race,* he barely mentioned the war. But he did sanction the dissolution of a marriage—a personified Confederation—on the grounds of linguistic and racial incompatibility.

In 1916, however, the war could not be forgotten. Canadian involvement was about to produce a clash between French and English that would make the Ontario schools question pale in comparison. Rumours of compulsory military service were already touring the country when some of the signs of appeasement appeared in the bilingual schools dispute. The courts left no doubt that Regulation XVII was quite within the power of the Ontario government although the learned law lords in London confessed to finding the language obscure, the effect difficult to ascertain, and some of the methods of enforcement dubious. But they also decreed that the Ottawa separate school board was overstepping its jurisdiction by defying the regulation. The pope also had a word to say on the matter. Responding to the appeal of different groups of Canadian Catholics, he advised moderation and tolerance. The unity of the Canadian Catholic church was essential and he was not at all sure that Quebec clerical involvement on behalf of the Franco-Ontarians was serving that cause. While a few French Canadian priests wondered privately about the power of the Irish in Rome and Henri Bourassa pointedly refrained from any comment in *Le Devoir,* the papal directive did in fact carry some weight in calming emotions. Among English-speaking Ontarians, some soothing voices began to be heard as Liberals and businessmen invented *bonne entente*[a] in an effort to repair the broken bridges of politics and commerce. Meanwhile the Ontario government found its regulation increasingly difficult to enforce and ultimately abandoned it in 1927. Only the Orange Order was left to fulminate against separate schools themselves, but even its fury abated when conscription offered a more exciting battleground for denouncing French Canadians. Although the schools question trailed off somewhat ignominiously, its stark lesson of numbers, reinforced by the implication of brute force in the conscription issue, was not forgotten.

By late 1916 the war that had been expected to be brief had become an endless bloodbath. It sucked up men, munitions, and supplies and buried them all in the trenches and then the mud of western Europe. Ever since the initial heroic send-off of one hundred thousand Canadians in the early autumn of 1914 from the final training camp at Valcartier near Quebec City, the numbers of enthusiastic recruits had steadily declined. There were only so many able-bodied recent British immigrants in the western provinces; they had been the first to respond to the imperial summons. In contrast, native born Canadians held back, their tie to empire easily calculated by the number of generations their families had been in the country. The appeal of patriotism and religion, used effectively in both French and English Canada, began to wear thin as God appeared quite indifferent to the slaughter. Moreover the war was economically beneficial to Canada: western farms and eastern industries competed much more effectively for man and woman power than did the Canadian

---

[a] good feelings

Expeditionary Force. But as the number of casualties rose and the number of recruits declined, the murmurings began. Population figures alone meant that English Canadian families were receiving more of the dreaded beige telegrams announcing death; the lists of wounded, missing, and demised were automatically longer in the English language newspapers. But when the murmurings turned into a slogan—"equalization of sacrifice"—then people began watching the enlistment figures and pointing to that part of the country producing the fewest recruits.

Naturally, Quebec was at the bottom of the list. As the oldest Canadians, Quebecois had the least interest in the war; no emotional tie pulled them to Britain or France. Besides, they had never found a comfortable place in the Canadian military service. Even the frequent presence of a French Canadian as minister or deputy minister of the department of the militia could not camouflage the essentially alien character of the institution for French Canadians. Few of the higher officers were French-speaking. Only a tiny fraction of the cadets at the Royal Military College in Kingston, the training school for military officers, was French Canadian and all the instruction was in English. Being an officer meant being or becoming English. The senior officers of the permanent, as distinct from voluntary, militia tended in fact to be British and they shared imperial enthusiasms. They had neither time nor patience for developing military attachments among French Canadians. The suggestion that a distinctive uniform, modelled on that of the *Zouaves,* might add to the attractiveness of the military for young French Canadians was vetoed at the very time when some English Canadian regiments were permitted to don the equally foreign and much less practical kilt. Not surprisingly, by 1912, there were only twenty-seven French Canadian compared to two hundred and twenty-seven English Canadian permanent officers in the Canadian militia.

Furthermore, nothing during the war years made French Canadians any more welcome in Canadian military ranks. The language of instruction and command remained English. The difficulty of raising and maintaining French-speaking units without having them dispersed to reinforce others was obvious in the amount of political pressure required to form and sustain the French Canadian Royal 22nd Battalion. There at least French Canadians were able to develop an outstanding military force of their own, envied indeed by English Canadians. But elsewhere, appointments or promotions of French Canadians to the higher ranks of the military were few and far between. Even the minister of the militia during the early years of the war, Sam Hughes, could not hide his hostility: he particularly did not wish to have French-speaking military units accompany Catholic popular processions. And he was careful to keep the one French Canadian general, Francois-Louis Lessard, busy in Canada instead of sending him overseas. Also, his own department established crude enlistment quotas based on a simple proportion of the total Canadian population. With twenty-eight percent of the population, Quebec should be producing twenty-eight percent of the recruits. Proportionately to the other regions of the country, however, Quebec had fewer men of military age, fewer bachelors, fewer casual labourers, and fewer British born, all of whom tended to be first in line at the recruiting stations. No statistics measured the impact of the Ontario school question or of Henri Bourassa's increasingly virulent anti-war tirades in *Le Devoir*. Although dead silence greeted Armand Lavergne's outburst in the Quebec legislature early in 1916 that every penny spent on recruitment in Quebec was money stolen from the Ontario minority, the mass circulation *La Presse* placed the controversy over bilingual schools in Ontario at the head of its list of reasons why French Canadians did not rush to enlist. Given so little encouragement to do so, it is perhaps surprising that as many as thirty-five thousand French Canadians found their way into Canada's armed forces by 1918 at all (approximately half of them before conscription and half after).

By early 1917 conscription was more than just a rumour. Prime minister Borden was determined to raise the number of Canada's soldiers to half a million, a figure he had set a year earlier. But the task became all the more difficult as the number of recruits no longer kept pace with the increasing casualties. The war itself was particularly bleak, the outcome no longer sure, and the end nowhere in sight. Russia withdrew from the allied cause into revolution and civil war; the United States had not yet rallied its forces; the French army was fed up and mutinous; successful submarine warfare sapped the strength and morale of Britain. All of that Borden absorbed in a visit to England in the spring of 1917. At the same time he admitted that volunteers were no longer forthcoming in Canada. Neither national registration nor the idea of a home defence force early in 1917 succeeded in producing new recruits. National registration in fact raised more suspicion than enthusiasm. This country-wide registration of talent and availability for various wartime jobs also recorded the number of military prospects and French Canadians were not alone in suspecting a trap. Both the Liberal press and labour organizations across the country joined them in wondering about the political motives of the enquiry. At the same time, employers and unions alike resisted the government's suggestion that more female labour be hired in order to release men for military service. In last minute efforts to attract men, the military itself consented to lowering its medical standards while recruiting agents took to haranguing crowds lined up for Saturday night entertainment. French Canada's one general attempted his own campaign for volunteers in Quebec. But the indifference was constant and it was all across the country. The people who were by then shouting so loudly for conscription clearly were not the same people as those who were supposed to sign up.

One of the first victims of conscription may have been in the House of Commons itself where the Military Service Bill proposing conscription was introduced in June 1917. Sir Wilfrid Laurier, far too old for military service, may yet have felt most severely the brunt of compulsion in the bill. During the debate over the government proposal to raise one hundred thousand recruits from various categories of male British subjects aged between twenty and forty-five, Laurier was forced to preside over the disintegration of the Liberal party. His westerners had already balked over the Lapointe resolution a year earlier; now they were adamant supporters of the government's conscription bill. Some of them were already dickering with the Conservatives about a possible "Union" government that would unite all right-thinking Canadians in a thorough prosecution of the war effort. Laurier himself wavered just long enough to sense that any co-operation on his part in imposing conscription would send Quebec voters in droves into the nationalist embrace of Henri Bourassa. He therefore drew back from the temptation to join a Union government. But the various votes on the conscription bill carried off many of Laurier's followers from Ontario and the Maritimes, voting with their western colleagues in favour of conscription. To his remnant of French Canadian Liberals from Quebec was added a handful of one-time nationalists from the Conservative benches. Laurier was thus forced to abandon his concept of national unity and to take on the leadership of one group only, a group primarily defined by language and race. In opposing conscription Laurier was also forced to discard his own promise of 1914 of a united war effort; Canadian hearts and minds were far from united on this question and he could not pretend otherwise. Given that stand, Laurier was then forced to pursue his opposition to conscription all the way to a federal election. No unanimous consent was forthcoming to prolong the life of parliament as had happened in 1916 to avoid the disruptions of a wartime election. Unanimity no longer existed and the disruptions would have to take their course. That they did, and very bitterly too, in the federal election of December 1917.

Laurier's reasoned parliamentary opposition to conscription was a careful translation of the emotional opposition seething in Quebec. Laurier argued from law and precedent and politics: none of them sanctioned conscription. The government had no mandate to impose compulsory military service on the country. Some Liberals even accused the Conservatives of digging up conscription as a popular cause to cover up a moribund government. Certainly the measure was part of an increasing number of controls exercised by the federal government over the lives of ordinary Canadians. Justified by the war and facilitated by the War Measures Act, various controls from rationing to price fixing, from decrees against hoarding to those against loitering, probably overwhelmed the civil service more than anyone else, but they did indicate the state's willingness to go beyond persuasion to actual coercion in directing the activities of its citizens. Provincial governments—all except Quebec's—had also imposed restrictions, most notably in supervising the drinking habits of people by means of prohibition; the federal government would follow suit in 1918, although none of the laws lasted very long. Even the votes and incomes of Canadians came under close scrutiny by the federal government. By means of the Wartime Elections Act in 1917, the Conservatives carefully disenfranchised certain Canadians of European background and just as carefully enfranchised the female relatives of soldiers. And in the same year the government introduced the income tax, thereby controlling the revenues of all Canadians, supposedly as a temporary measure to meet the mounting costs of the war effort. In such a context conscription was hardly an unusual idea. To Laurier, however, the setting could be no excuse: conscription was an illegitimate ploy on the part of a flagging government. The least it could do was hold a referendum on the question. Laurier may have expected the government to lose such a referendum, given the opposition of the working classes and of French Canadians to conscription. And if it won, well there would at least be some democratic justification for the measure.

The difficulty was that the democratic numbers game on such an issue was racially fixed. On the whole, English Canadians supported conscription and were easily able to silence the protests of farmers and workers in western Canada; French Canadians virtually unanimously opposed it. It was all very well for French Canadian Liberal politicians in Ottawa or Quebec to follow Laurier's lead and claim that Quebec would accept a Canadian verdict in a referendum; they really could not be sure. The issue cut too close to the bone: it was a majority of a different language and culture imposing military service for a foreign war upon a minority. In that light democracy could be an instrument of force. No one spoke of rape, Canadians of the time being much too prudish; but many people did recall the Conquest. No one in the eighteenth century had asked permission for that use of force; no one was likely to do so in twentieth. Laurier's amendment to the Military Service Bill, that it be submitted to a popular referendum, was soundly defeated.

With the passage of the Military Service Bill, popular passions over conscription intensified throughout the summer and early autumn of 1917. While Henri Bourassa wrote in *Le Devoir* of national suicide for a foreign cause, the *Globe* in Toronto referred to conscription as fresh dedication to the cause of liberty. Mass meetings in Quebec filled the Sunday air with protest. Some federal Conservatives from Quebec hastily resigned from the government; others, remaining and even voting for conscription, knew that their political days were numbered. Young men took off for the woods, preferring to camp out in hiding rather than risk the legal intricacies of the exemption process. Senior students in classical colleges suddenly sported clerical garb and earnestly declared their intention to become priests, an occupation exempt from conscription. A last minute attempt at voluntary recruiting netted a grand total of ninety young men in the province. In some minds, the possibility of civil war loomed as a logical, perhaps even a deserved, consequence of the government's insensitivity. The Ontario schools question surfaced again, tangled with the conscription debate in the Commons, and left French Canadians profoundly uneasy about their place in Confederation. Attacks on their language and their faith were crystallizing in the imposition of military service. Henri Bourassa claimed that the conscription law, enacted early in August 1917, was an open invitation for a popular uprising.

The uprising, such as it was, occurred in the form of a federal election. The Conservatives took no chances on the outcome. They lured conscriptionist Liberals from the west into a Union government and ensured even more western backing by exempting twenty year old farm workers from their military obligations. They even wooed the women with the strange beginnings of federal woman suffrage in Canada. Assuming that the wives, daughters, and sisters of Canadian soldiers would vote Conservative in order to bring their men home sooner, the government accorded them the vote. It also organized the overseas military vote in such a way as to favour Conservative candidates. The government hardly needed the popular press to fan passions and prejudices, but that was precisely what the elections of 1917 did. Of the many issues confronting the country from profiteering and the cost of living to immigration and the nationalization of the railways, the press preferred the sensationalism of Quebec's opposition to conscription and English Canada's reaction to it. The English language press quoted Henri Bourassa's arguments against the war and treated him, and by extension all French Canadians, as a traitor. A vote for Laurier would be a vote for Bourassa, for Quebec control of the entire country, for withdrawal from the war, and for the imposition of bilingual schools throughout the land. Quebec was the spoiled child of Confederation and should be compelled to do its share for the war effort. A map of Canada depicted Quebec in black, the "foul blot" on the country. Surrounded by such images, Unionist candidates in Quebec could hardly open their mouths. They were heckled, shouted down, pelted with rotten eggs, and threatened with revolver shots. No paper would carry their message to French-speaking voters. The nationalists, less of an organized political force than in 1911 but holding a much more volatile issue, urged support for Laurier, a mere six years after they had turned on him as a traitor. They insisted upon the suspension of the Military Service Act while Laurier stated more vaguely the Liberal policy of maintaining Canada's war effort by voluntary means. The result was predictable: all the ridings but three in Quebec voted Liberal; all the ridings but twenty in the rest of the country returned Unionist candidates. No one took heart in the mere three hundred thousand popular vote difference between Unionists and Liberals since the parliamentary composition was much more striking: Quebec in opposition and English Canada in power.

The first response came from the Quebec legislature. A rather sorrowful motion, introduced by Joseph-Napoléon Francoeur, raised the question of separatism. If Quebec was so despised, perhaps it should opt out. Although a few students and an obscure clerical paper trumpeted the power of an independent Quebec with its control of rail and shipping routes, Francoeur was much more despondent and the assembly greeted his motion in the same way. A rather desultory debate never even came to a vote on the dreary proposition that:

> This House is of the opinion that the province of Quebec would be disposed to accept the breaking of the Confederation pact of 1867 if, in the other provinces, it is believed that she is an obstacle to the union, progress and development of Canada.

With the onus put upon the rest of Canada, few Quebecois presumed to read the minds of their English-speaking compatriots, minds that had spoken all too clearly in the recent elections.

Neither the election nor the hint of separatism put a stop to French Canadian opposition to conscription nor even to government blundering in its relations with Quebec. Only in January 1918 were the first men requested to report for military induction and most of them successfully claimed exemptions. Conscription ultimately produced some eighty thousand soldiers in Canada, about a quarter of whom were from Quebec but not all French Canadians. Few of them went overseas, let alone to the battlefront, before the end of the war in November 1918. The numbers were minimal for the hostility aroused and the symbolism created. Few French Canadian families would forget English-speaking agents ferreting out their young men. Few young men would forget the months in hiding to escape the law or, for those enrolled, the low status of a conscript especially if he spoke French. More dramatic, because more public, were the anti-conscription riots in Quebec City in the early spring of 1918. Sparked by mounted police rounding up presumed defaulters and fed by popular discontent over wartime prices and rationing, the unrest boiled around the provincial capital for three days. True to form and no doubt fearing complicity between rioters and French Canadian troops, Borden had English-speaking soldiers from Toronto sent to assist in quelling the disturbances. Well might some Quebecois wonder just where the war was being fought.

For other French Canadians an even greater threat to the social order was issuing from Ottawa. Relegating *Le Devoir's* commentary on the Quebec City riots to his second-in-command, Henri Bourassa took on what he obviously considered a much more serious problem, that of suffrage for women. By 1917 all of the provinces west of Quebec had introduced the suffrage and the women involved had no intention of limiting their voting to the provincial sphere. They argued their special interest in matters of social reform, from prohibition to public health. They pointed to their wartime activities in fund raising, support to the troops, and actual military service as nurses. Speaking through the National Council of Women, various women's associations convinced prime minister Borden to enlarge his peculiar precedent of 1917 and introduce total woman suffrage for federal elections. The bill was progressing through its various stages in the Commons at the very time of the anti-conscription riots in Quebec City. Meanwhile, Bourassa was exposing in *Le Devoir* all the ill effects of woman suffrage. Once women had the vote they would no longer marry since they would be engaged in fearsome competition with men. The family would thereby disintegrate, the education of children would be abandoned, and the privileged position that women now merited because of their maternal functions would disappear. Social degradation would follow woman's degradation.

For Bourassa, the suffrage, like feminism, was one more foreign import threatening the social structure of French Canada. It was a direct consequence of the individualism of Protestant religions; perhaps it suited Anglo-Saxon women who had long since lost their ability to influence society by feminine charm and natural means, but it was quite alien to French and Catholic women. The latter, Bourassa was convinced, did not want the vote; they were surely glad to be free of the civil and military duties that accompany a say in public affairs. Nor would they wish to take part in the cabals and base intrigue of political warfare. Their place was quite literally in the home; only by staying there could they aspire to any social role at all let alone one claiming superiority. To step into the public sphere was to defy their sex, to deny the family as the basic social unit, to disrupt all notion of hierarchy and authority, to destroy the subordination of rights to duties. In spite of the feminist argument that the vote was a mere means of bringing women's moral and social concerns to bear more directly on society, Bourassa spotted the radicalism of the measure. Once women had the vote they would be in a position of equality with men in terms of their relationship to the state. That relationship would no longer be mediated by men and who knew what the social consequences of that challenge to the natural order might be? Expressing what the Montreal *Gazette* termed "mouldy ideas," Bourassa and some of the French Canadian opponents of the woman suffrage bill in the House of Commons—none of whom was able to stop the bill's passage—thought they knew what suffrage would lead to and they did not like the prospect at all. French Canada would be irretrievably changed, and for the worse.

A number of clerics added their amen to the views of Bourassa and the politicians. The theologian Louis-Adolphe Paquet, surveying the world from within the walls of the Quebec seminary where he taught candidates for the priesthood, also foresaw the evil of women in competition with men as a result of the suffrage. With Saint Paul, Saint Thomas, and the current pope, Benedict XV, on his side, Paquet could safely condemn the challenge to authority, the family, and society that lay behind feminist demands. But he was not as sure as Bourassa that the demands were foreign. Rather he feared that much in contemporary French Canadian society actually spawned feminism: the education of young girls was much too similar to that of boys; too many young women defied parental authority in their clothing and their behaviour; the economic necessity of jobs in industry and commerce, which Paquet acknowledged, took women out of their homes, tossed them together, and facilitated their developing new aspirations. Paquet would have girls carefully educated for their maternal and religious role, differentiating their training not by talent but by class. No matter whom they married, all young women would have the same basic function—to develop the virtue of their sons and sustain the faith of their husbands, although depending on whether their husband was a farmer or a judge, their station in life would be different and would require special training. The cardinal archbishop of Quebec, Monseigneur Bégin, echoed Paquet's views by carefully culling papal antipathy to woman suffrage and passing it on to his priests. In their teaching and preaching, they were to keep in mind that neither the interests of society nor natural law justified votes for women. The Catholic press dutifully followed suit in opposing suffrage for women.

The major feminist organization in Quebec, the *Fédération nationale Saint-Jean-Baptiste,* also followed the clerical directive and subordinated its early interest in the suffrage. Instead it concentrated on preparing women for the proper exercising of the vote. Working as closely as it did with clerical groups, the *Fédération* perhaps could not avoid the intense hostility the male hierarchy of the church evinced towards the idea of legal equality for women. Sharing similar views about the roles of women in the family, in society, and in the preservation of French Canadian culture, the women of the *Fédération* may have been just as sensitive to the enormous wounds the war years delivered to French Canada. Those wounds in turn may have reinforced the feminists' compulsion to soothe rather than disrupt. Certainly the journalist Fadette, writing in *Le Devoir,* thought Quebec women would exercise their new found and unasked for federal political right with more moderation than English Canadian women: she was half-pleased and half-alarmed to see the Montreal Women's Club, a member of the local branch of the National Council of Women, split over the issue of conscription. Once women entered politics, she surmised, all their endeavours would be contaminated.

The fear of contamination coloured many French Canadian reactions during the years of the First World War. The English Canadian association of imperialism and nationalism was fraught with dangers (notably that of fighting in distant wars) for French Canadians who associated nationalism with anti-imperialism. The French Canadian link between language, religion, and nationality had proven to be tenuous when confronted with co-religionists who spoke another language and compatriots who professed another religion, all of whom tied the future of a quite different Canadian nation to the English language. And in the face of a determined majority on the conscription issue, an equally determined minority could only succumb: conscription does not permit compromise. When that same majority went beyond trampling on the national sensitivities of French Canadians to threaten a fundamental notion of social order in the family by granting women the vote in 1918, the minority could only withdraw into self-protection, nursing its differences in an alien world. With Prussians in various guises on all the frontiers, it was time to shore up the defences.

TIPPING THE BALANCE: THE CANADIAN CORPS IN 1918

Stuart Robson

In recent years, historians have examined the impact the Great War of 1914-1918 had on Canada. But what about the reciprocal of this? What impact did Canada have on the war? With so much attention devoted to the attack on Vimy Ridge in April 1917, its sequel, the remarkable achievement of the Canadian Corps in the climax of the war, has been overlooked, aside from Daniel Dancocks' valuable recent book, *Spearhead to Victory: Canada and the Great War.* This omission in the literature leaves the impression that Canada was a spear-carrier rather than a spearhead. Of course, in a broad sense, such a modest view seems sensible. No matter how well led or highly motivated, four divisions cannot possibly tip the balance in a war on the grand scale.

Or can they? Canadian accounts of the war tend to take the overall patterns of the war for granted, and in particular to pass lightly over what was happening in Germany, especially in the final months of the war. This reflects the more general unwillingness to look closely at the history of 1918, a year considered best forgotten even at the time. Because the details of the shocking German plunge from near-victory to catastrophic defeat have either been misconstrued or ignored, the connection between the military situation and the German decision to call for a cease-fire has not been drawn adequately. In other words, to assess the role Canada played in the outcome of the war, we must know something about why the war began, why it continued as it did and especially how and why it ended as it did.

The war did not begin by accident. It began because the major powers in Europe consciously chose violence rather than negotiation to maintain their interests. Because no one goes to war to lose, each power believed that, either on its own or in coalition, it was stronger than its rivals, or at least strong enough to achieve through war what it no longer believed it could obtain through negotiation. In short, each power had a different estimate of the distribution of power. Until they once again agreed on who was strong and who weak, they continued to prefer violence. The failure of all the military plans in 1914 encouraged this preference because it left the situation ambiguous, with Germany too strong to consider a negotiated peace and the Entente powers (Britain, France and Russia) for the moment too weak. Germany had won the initial round, but only in a limited way. She still could not persuade France, Britain and Russia that time was not on their side. They in turn had good reason to think that it was.

From *The Beaver*, LXIX, no. 5 (October-November 1989), 17-28. Reprinted by permission of *The Beaver*.

As it happened, the head of the German High Command in 1914, Erich von Falkenhayn, agreed that time favoured the Allies. He wanted to force a decision as soon as possible. Tactical victories over Russia were easy to come by, but Russia could always trade space for time and wait for her Western allies to win. So Falkenhayn turned to the Western Front. Although he saw Britain as the main enemy, he could not get at British seapower, although he reserved unlimited submarine warfare as a trump card, nor could he reach the British Army, which had yet to arrive in force and was holding the line in Flanders, impossible ground for a major attack. That left France. Falkenhayn decided to attack Verdun, not necessarily to take the complex of fortresses there, but to draw France into its defence, after which German guns would pound the French Army to death. Thus began the longest unbroken battle in history, from February to November 1916. At first, Falkenhayn's strategy worked to perfection. The French lost their great outlying fortresses at Douaumont and Vaux, and, as Falkenhayn hoped, staked everything on defending what they still held on the right bank of the Meuse River, including Verdun itself. But gradually, the same process that bedevilled the Allied commanders overwhelmed Falkenhayn. In his own mind he might have fixed limits to his attack, but set-piece battles on such a colossal scale were beyond finely-tuned control. As the German Army strained to take Verdun, it came in range of French guns on the left bank of the river. To clear away harassing fire from the flanks of their main attacks, the Germans had to broaden these attacks, and the greater their effort, the more the battle degenerated into mutual attrition. Britain complicated Falkenhayn's calculations by launching her own massive attack at the Somme, starting on 1 July 1916. To be sure, the first day at the Somme was a well-planned disaster in which almost 20,000 British soldiers died. But when the Russians broke through Austrian lines in late June, Germany faced cruel pressure on three fronts. With Falkenhayn's original idea of an artfully limited attack in ruins, he was forced to resign. In his place came the winning team from the Eastern Front, Hindenburg and Ludendorff.

Field Marshal Paul von Hindenburg was not a simple, elderly figurehead. He possessed a measure of shrewdness and *gravitas* that steadied the German Empire in the perilous years after September 1916. Above all, he stabilized his partner, the brilliant, volatile Erich Ludendorff, whose nominal title was First Quarter-Master General but who in fact became the real head of the Imperial German Army and the dominant force in the state. Ludendorff's fanatical pursuit of total victory and an empire in the east gave his ambitions a distinct resemblance to those of Hitler two decades later. Given the similar result, a total defeat, one might think he was as unbalanced a military leader as Hitler would prove to be. Yet *hubris* did not affect the two men the same way. It was part of Hitler's personality from the start, the gleam to the dark star he followed. It only overtook Ludendorff at the peak of his mercurial career, after diligence and intelligent staff work had raised him from humble origins. So when he took over, his problem was not yet overweening pride, but the refusal of the enemy to concede it was losing. As long as the Allies held on, Germany was back to the dilemma Falkenhayn had seen so clearly: she could not win a long war on two fronts, but she could not force the enemy to concede that she had already won a short war on both fronts.

Ludendorff's first move was to wind down the futile battle of Verdun. He then had the Siegfried complex built, an immense system of concrete pillboxes, interlocking fire and barbed wire cutting off the bulge in the Somme front. Known to the Allies as the Hindenburg Line, "Siegfried" reduced the manpower needed to hold the central part of the Western Front and allowed Ludendorff to plan a major offensive in the East. To weaken Russia further, he contrived to import the "bacillus of revolution", Lenin, in a sealed train. Finally, to break the Western allies, he played the trump card Falkenhayn had considered, unlimited submarine warfare. Although this would probably bring America into the war, the German Navy insisted that Britain would capitulate before America could make her power felt.

Just as the war in 1916 had almost conformed to Falkenhayn's stratagems, 1917 went virtually as Ludendorff hoped. Russia succumbed to liberal revolution in February and to Lenin in October; Lenin then bowed to a renewed German offensive and agreed to the punitive Treaty of Brest-Litovsk early in 1918. After Germany renewed unlimited submarine warfare, America declared war in April 1917, but by the end of the year, her change to belligerent status had if anything weakened the Entente powers by siphoning off supplies they would otherwise have received. Colonel Potter of M*A*S*H might remember being in a chateau under fire in 1917, but the record suggests he was a year out. In the spring of 1917, the great French offensive devised by General Robert Nivelle fell on the empty wasteland the Germans had left behind after their stealthy withdrawal to the Hindenburg Line. When the French reached the main German positions, their losses were severe enough to trigger a mutiny among most of the divisions in the zone of war. Ostensibly to relieve pressure on the French, but probably to force a British-made decision, Field Marshal Sir Douglas Haig launched the Third Battle of Ypres at the end of July—literally launched it too, because of the torrential rains at the start, which swamped a battlefield already turned into a morass by heavy shelling. The ensuing ordeal, summed up in the ominous word "Passchendaele", might have had a point had the Australian-led attacks of its middle phase been its terminus. Ludendorff reacted to the massive artillery shoots and sophisticated infantry attacks of General Sir Herbert Plumer's Third Army with almost visceral pain. But the rains returned in October and, against the advice of his field commanders, Haig decided to push on to higher ground. With the Australian Corps exhausted, he gave the leading role to his other shock troops, the Canadians. Somehow they succeeded in taking Passchendaele. How they did it beggars belief; why they had to is even harder to fathom. By the time 1918 dawned, the only limit to the apparently endless war of attrition that most observers could see was the finite reserve of able-bodied manpower. With America mobilizing faster than the Germans expected but slower than the Allies hoped, time still ran against Germany. In the short run, however, Ludendorff had one great advantage. He now faced only one important front, and he had the added manpower and new techniques to end the stalemate in the trenches and force the enemy to capitulate.

Ludendorff launched Operation Michael on 21 March 1918, sending 76 divisions mainly against the understrength British Fifth Army, which was in the St. Quentin area recovering from Passchendaele. First in March and again in April, he ruptured the first and second zones and broke into the British rear. Preceded by precise artillery fire and led by storm troopers trained to flow around pockets of resistance, the Germans brought back open warfare for the first time since late 1914.

Ludendorff's plan was to split the British from the French and force them to fold back to the Channel coast, like a giant door hinging on Flanders. When instead the British shoulder held north of the main German attack, Ludendorff switched to Flanders. Again the attack began well, but again it bogged down. Ludendorff had the idea of deep penetration, but in 1918 he did not have the means to achieve it. His flowing attack depended entirely on foot soldiers and artillery to sustain its momentum. He could break in and through, but not out.

By July, Ludendorff was winning his way to defeat. His attacks devoured the best of his troops, especially those in the almost suicidal storm troop battalions. Unrest bordering on revolution was stirring in Austria-Hungary and even in Germany, where munition workers had staged a general strike in January. The bacillus of revolution he had planted in Russia was beginning to infect Germany as surely as the Spanish flu virus was starting to devastate the entire world. Ideology in turn paled beside hunger as an incentive to protest, and by 1918, the collapse of the German railway system, the inability of her political system to ration food equitably, and the British blockade were together reducing the war economy to a shambles.

In German war diaries, we can follow the gradual withering of Ludendorff's great offensives, even while the German Army was advancing. Like the nation as a whole, the Army was starving; the advance at times halted when even the elite storm troopers looted British supplies of food and liquor. As the Germans went forward, they moved into the Somme battlefields of 1916, devastated ground that favoured the defence and prevented supplies from keeping up with the advance. Moreover, the regular line troops were now moving in the open. After adapting to trench war, they felt vulnerable and tended to dig in just out of habit. But often they had a good reason to take cover, because moving out of the trenches exposed them to a danger they had hitherto been able to ignore: attacks from the air. The Allied air forces flew strafing runs and contact patrols around the clock, and along with isolated gun batteries, had a field day. Above all, as the battle wore on, the Germans finally used up the cream of the Imperial Army, the NCO's and experienced rankers who had survived the Allied offensives because of their inimitable professional skill.

Throughout the late spring and early summer, Ludendorff kept launching fresh attacks in his desperate effort to bring the enemy to terms, but even though the goal of each new attack was defined more precisely and realistically, he could not regain the initiative. Thrashing about for the enemy weak-point, he attacked the French at Rheims. Pétain however parried the Rheims attack easily, without calling for reserves as Ludendorff hoped. Confused about what to do next, Ludendorff decided to attack in Flanders as a diversion. Before he could try another expedient, the French clarified the situation. On 18 July fifteen French and four American divisions, with 500 tanks, broke through the German line at Villers-Cotterets and pushed the Germans back almost ten kilometres.

When Ludendorff realized that the Franco-American victory jeopardized all the territory in the Marne salient that Germany had won since March, he asked the Flanders Army Group to send its Chief of Staff, General Fritz von Lossberg, along for a conference. Lossberg was a legend to veterans of the Western Front because of his inspired handling of the defence at the Somme. He had been sceptical about the March offensive from the moment it had first been proposed. In virtually unnoticed memoirs that appeared in 1941, Lossberg recalled that Ludendorff seemed overwrought and *"frontfremd"* or estranged from the front. He admitted to Lossberg that a strategic retreat to the Hindenburg Line would have made sense, but was impossible for "political reasons", which turned out to mean his own prestige and that of the Army. In summing up his experience with High Command, Lossberg placed the blame for Germany's military catastrophe squarely on Ludendorff.

Colonel Mertz von Quirnheim, attached to the Bavarian General Staff and a close colleague of Ludendorff, recorded a bizarre conversation around this time. Ludendorff told him that the Marne Salient could not be held, and went on to say:

> "I am not superstitious, or well, maybe I am. Look, on July 15 I had no confidence [in the attack on Rheims]". With that he opened the right drawer on his desk and took out a rather battered prayer-book of the [Moravian] Brotherhood. He read me the Scripture given in it for July 15. He contrasted it to the passages on our other days of attack ... We spoke seriously for quite a while. I was really very moved. Excellency took leave with the words "I hope the Good God will not desert us"; I answered that He surely would not. Excellency quite broken.

It ill behooves fellow countrymen of Mackenzie King to sneer about superstition in high places. Self-confidence, however, is especially important in questions of command, and realizing that Ludendorff was deriving his self-confidence from the German equivalent of bird entrails must have had a devastating impact on the officers at headquarters. Mertz worried that Ludendorff was afraid people would say he had lost his nerve. Because of this fear, he might be prone to expose the Army to fatal risks. By 29-31 July, Mertz noted in his diary that Ludendorff had gradually calmed down, putting Villers-Cotterets behind him, but "the collapse of nerve even so has not been exactly glorious".

The worst was yet to come. The British had their own elite storm troopers, the Australians and Canadians. The Canadian Corps was relatively untouched by the German onslaught in the spring and so was fresh and fully-manned. Moreover, its four divisions had grown used to working together, so that it had the flexibility of a division but the size of a corps—in effect, it was a super-division. Led by the two Dominion Corps, on 8 August General Rawlinson's Fourth Army crashed through the depleted German Second Army near Amiens. The panic among German troops that had dismayed Ludendorff on 18 July was repeated on a more alarming scale, with retiring troops accusing reinforcements of strike-breaking and prolonging the war. To Ludendorff, 8 August was "the black day of the German Army in the history of this war".

When Ludendorff met the Kaiser on 13 August, he admitted the war was lost and offered his resignation. The Kaiser rejected the offer. Privately, Ludendorff told the new Foreign Secretary, Admiral Paul von Hintze, that his earlier assurances of victory no longer applied and that he was unsure of what was coming. Hintze thought that even this belated and humbling admission was too optimistic, especially when to military adversity was added the news that Austria-Hungary was about to sue for peace.

Ludendorff was on a rack. Professionalism and success had brought him far beyond his bourgeois origins, but one sign of fallibility would send him back to obscurity. He had staked everything on his spring offensive. When tactical success did not translate into strategic advantage and the enemy was no closer to submission, he sensed that fortune had deserted him. Commanders are under intense stress at the best of times. Haig coped with the pressure by placing everything in the hands of his Presbyterian God, keeping the obscenity of war well clear of his headquarters, and blaming Lloyd George and the politicians, or "the frocks", for anything that went wrong. Ludendorff had his prayer book but no equivalent to Lloyd George. The victory that had beckoned would have been in his name alone; the defeat that now loomed would also be his. Rather than admit that he and Germany were cornered, he kept up the habits that had brought success: prodigious working hours, an obsession with detail and a rigid, impassive exterior. But with all his will turned to the effort of keeping up a bold front. Ludendorff was unable to carry out his main duty. He could not face the situation he had created. The civilian government, and Hintze in particular, pleaded for a straight report on the military situation. But how could Ludendorff tell mere civilians what he almost refused to admit to himself? At most, he would concede that the chance of military victory was now uncertain. That much was obvious to everyone. What the government needed to know was how well a defensive struggle might go, but that was the sort of losing game that Ludendorff would not play. So, as he stayed locked in the prison of his own mind, Germany lost whatever slim chance she might have had to organize a firm defence along the Hindenburg Line and put out careful feelers for a negotiated peace. Hintze in August thought that Ludendorff's private remark had authorized him to sound out the Queen of the Netherlands to serve as an intermediary, but, lacking any clear appreciation of the military picture, he did not want to let a pre-mature request for good offices inspire rumours that Germany was finished. Such rumours would only inflame enemy hopes and destroy German morale. So Hintze waited. With a whole world waiting too, he was not alone.

From the point when the twin disasters of 18 July and 8 August revealed both the probability of defeat and Ludendorff's nervous exhaustion, factions began to form among the staff officers at General Headquarters. Ludendorff's protege, Colonel Bauer, saw that his boss was cracking up under the pressure and brought in a young officer to take over some of the paper work. The new assistant, Colonel Heye, turned out to be more than a clerk; in fact, he soon became the key man in the effort to get rid of Ludendorff and put the Kaiser and the government fully in touch with the military situation. Early in September, Heye took over the Operations Division from Colonel Wetzell, but not before Wetzell heard Ludendorff blandly insist that the Foreign Office and Hintze must be deceived about the military crisis or else they would become too anxious. Horrified at the implications of such a cover-up, Wetzell brought in an Army psychiatrist, Dr. Hochheimer, hoping that the doctor would find reasons of health to ease Ludendorff out of command. According to the diary of Colonel Mertz, Dr. Hochheimer diagnosed overwork, loss of buoyancy and enervation. Ludendorff took this miracle of scientific diagnosis in good stride, saying that he had reached the same conclusions himself. Dr. Hochheimer prescribed a regime of breathing exercises, walks, massages, shorter hours, longer sleeps and singing German folk-songs upon rising. He also suggested that headquarters be shifted to the aptly-named Belgian town of Spa. Later he even threw in a spot of hypnosis. Wetzell's ploy had failed and he was on his way out.

Heye drew together a group of dissident officers that used private contacts with the Kaiser's entourage and the Foreign Office to undermine Ludendorff. On 25 September, when he ordered all Army Groups not to retreat an inch, Heye simply discontinued the order. He urged Ludendorff to go to Berlin, tell the Kaiser and Hintze just how dangerous the situation really was and have them request negotiations for an armistice. Ludendorff refused, but later that day, in conversation with the Surgeon General, Dr. Schjerning, he learned that what he had believed to be an outbreak of pulmonary plague in the French Army was in fact the Spanish influenza that had hit Central Europe earlier. "I clung to this news [of the plague] like a drowning man to a straw", the distraught Ludendorff told Schjerning, who was so alarmed by such irrationality that he reported the conversation to Heye and Mertz. These two called a meeting of the Heye group for the following morning. At it, they decided to summon the Foreign Secretary to Spa. One of the officers present, Lersner, was delegated to telephone Hintze and tell him that the military situation was critical.

Hintze did not need Lersner's message to guess what was happening. He had written off Ludendorff as an incurable optimist since August and had been relying since then on his own sources of information. He and the officials in the Foreign Office had prepared the machinery for cautious peace feelers, but the whole plan waited upon the frank admission by the Army that the military situation was grave. To act in advance of such an admission might shatter the morale of the Army: to act too late, to wait until the chance of collapse became a reality, would open the way to anarchy and revolution.

Lersner's message thus conveyed to Hintze something other than what the Heye group intended. They thought he was entirely in the dark and should know that a military collapse was a possibility in the long run. He *knew* what 8 August had meant and assumed that the telephone call from the staff officers was hinting about some specific military reverse that had just occurred or soon would. Hintze hurried along to see the ancient Chancellor, Count Hertling, and begged him to go to Spa to find out what on earth was happening. Hertling refused, and so, early on 28 September, Hintze decided to go himself to bring the situation to a head. Then Hertling told him that they would both go. Hertling had changed his mind because he had spoken to the Vice-Chancellor, Friedrich von Payer. Payer in turn had just learned from his close friend, the Progressive Reichstag deputy Conrad Haussmann, that the co-ordinating committee of the left-wing majority in the Reichstag had decided that Hertling must be replaced by a government enjoying the confidence of the Reichstag, a government pledged to peace and reform. But just when Hertling decided to bow to the Reichstag majority and resign, word arrived from Spa that Hindenburg and Ludendorff wanted to talk to him about forming a new government. Unknown to anyone in Berlin, Ludendorff had decided that the game was over, and that the parliamentary politicians would be just the people to take all the blame for losing.

What then had happened on or about 28 September to change Ludendorff's mind and admit openly what he had privately conceded for six weeks? A Franco-American attack had gone well in the Argonne on 26 September; on the 28th, Bulgaria sued for peace, opening the way for the Allied forces in Salonika to move up the Danubian basin. Above all, on 27 September General Sir Arthur Currie's Canadian Corps, working as part of the British First Army under General Sir Henry Horne, forced the Canal du Nord. The brilliant set-piece attack was the only real success on the day, proving the formidable threat German defences still posed, especially the machine-gunners. But it also showed that the entire line was vulnerable, a verdict confirmed on 28 September when the British Second Army and the Belgians attacked around Ypres. Ludendorff was caught between the rampaging Canadians and the British advance in Flanders. He did not have the manpower to stop both. To be sure, Germany still occupied more territory than she had the year before, still had a solid and seasoned army of two and a half million men, still enjoyed powerful defensive positions, and still faced an enemy that had only begun to operate mass armies offensively and was almost as exhausted as Germany. There was no general Allied advance in the Great War. If victory was out of the question for Germany, the alternative to victory, even at this late hour, need not have been total defeat. A negotiated peace, reflecting the stalemate still prevailing, if barely, was still possible. It required a defensive military strategy and canny diplomacy. Both these requirements, however, depended on the mind and nerve of the commander. But on 28 September, Ludendorff simply broke down.

After Heye had begun the process of calling in the politicians by putting Lersner in touch with Hintze, he told Ludendorff that the Foreign Secretary would be coming to Spa. Heye and his supporters then set to work convincing Hindenburg that the Army must finally ask the government to open negotiations. Realizing he was without supporters, feeling the panic of July and August return, despite massage, folk songs and hypnosis, Ludendorff lashed out at his subordinates. He screamed that the Kaiser was a weakling, that the Navy was to blame, that he was beset by treachery and deception. His voice shrill and hoarse, his fists clenched, he let hysteria wash over him; around 4:00 in the afternoon, literally foaming at the mouth, he collapsed. To be sure, reports of his paralysis and collapse were later denied, but all the reports came from eyewitnesses and the denials from Ludendorff partisans who were not present.

By 6:00 p.m., Ludendorff had recovered sufficiently to make his way to Hindenburg's room. He told Hindenburg that the collapse of the Balkan Front had convinced him that the defence of Germany was about to unravel. The government must therefore offer peace and request an armistice. Apparently shaken by Ludendorff's earlier behaviour, Hindenburg agreed. We will never know for certain what was actually the last straw for Ludendorff, but the timing of events and the secondary importance of the Bulgarian collapse makes it more likely that the combined victories of the Canadians at the Canal du Nord and the British in Flanders were the key blows, and of these two, it was the compact and inexorable advance of the Canadians that was the more intimidating.

Starting on 8 August, the Canadian Corps met and defeated 47 divisions, a quarter of the German Army. Currie later took this as proof that the Germans acted as if stopping the Canadians meant stopping everything. If so, we can see why the Canadian success at the Canal du Nord on 27 September might have loomed so large in the mind of Ludendorff. In playing such a disproportionate role in the defeat of Germany, the Corps necessarily ran up a sobering rate of casualties, almost 46,000 dead, wounded and missing between 8 August and 11 November, or 20 percent of the total Canadian losses in the war. In cit-ing these figures, Daniel Dancocks has rightly insisted that the Canadians took a decisive part in the victorious campaign of the British Army. In the first instance, however, it is the losers who decide who wins a war, and in coming to a decision that the power of the enemy is greater than their own, they are the ones who must assess what is the most effective threat they face.

Examining what Ludendorff made of the situation and how he reacted does not tell us whether it was the Canadians in particular who broke his will to carry on. Given the complexity of a total war lasting well over four years, such a bold claim would be simplistic. Nor can it be verified; Ludendorff began the notorious "stab in the back" legend at the very moment he demanded a new government that could obtain a ceasefire. As he told his intimate staff, "Those who prepared the soup should eat it". His malign effort to evade responsibility not only weakened the later German Republic, but muddied the waters sufficiently to prevent historians from penetrating the fog of war around his headquarters. Still, when one puts the achievements of the Canadian Corps in the last hundred days beside Ludendorff's increasingly desperate reactions, one can make at least a circumstantial claim that the Canadians tipped the balance.

CHAPTER
8 AGRARIAN REVOLT IN THE 1920s

From the time of Confederation to the Great War, the two party system inherited from Great Britain prevailed on the national political scene in Canada, although, by the turn of the twentieth century the capacity of the old-line parties to accommodate the divergent interests of region and class in Canada was beginning to be strained. The appearance of a loosely knit group of Québécois *Autonomistes* under the direction of Henri Bourassa in the election of 1911 was, in retrospect, one sign of the break-down of the traditional two party system, although their absorption by Sir Robert Borden's Conservative party in the immediate post-election years seemed then to belie any long-term problems with the system itself. Another was the rumblings of discontent from the farmers of Western Canada just prior to and during that same election. Here again, however, the fact that Sir Wilfrid Laurier's Liberal government went down to defeat embracing the platform of reciprocity with the United States so dear to the hearts of Western Canadian farmers suggested that the traditional system remained strong.

World War I threw a wild-card into the political game, particularly from the Western Canadian perspective. Answering the calls of patriotism and duty, prairie farmers by and large set aside their partisan interests and dedicated themselves to winning the war by whatever means necessary. Many whole-heartedly supported Sir Robert Borden's adoption of conscription for overseas service in the spring of 1917 (though not for their sons, needed at home on the farm), and were horrified at the failure of their leader, Sir Wilfrid Laurier, and their party, the Liberal Party, to enter into a coalition government in support of the measure. Forced to choose Borden's Union government over the Laurier Liberals in the December, 1917 election, farmers were uprooted from their traditional political homeland.

In post-war Canada, farmers and their leaders such as Thomas A. Crerar found themselves in the political wilderness, unable to continue supporting the increasingly conservative and reactionary Union administration, but equally unable to return to the Liberal fold, led after the fall of 1919 by the Laurier protege, William Lyon Mackenzie King. The result was the formation of the Progressive Party of Canada, the subject of the readings here. As the first of the "third" parties to occupy the Canadian landscape, the factors which brought the Progressive Party into existence are vital to an understanding of a critical era of Canadian political history.

Ably presenting a traditional view is the now classic work of W.L.Morton, the long-time dean of Western Canadian historians in general, and of the Progressive Party in particular. In "The Western Progressive Movement, 1919-1921," Morton examined the political and economic underpinnings of what he considered essentially to be a sectional protest movement. The second and more recent selection is taken from Gerald Friesen's *The Canadian Prairies: A History*. Friesen notes, as have others, that the Progressive movement drew support from areas well beyond the Canadian West, and should, therefore, be understood as more than simply an expression of a particular regional discontent.

Suggestions for Further Reading

Allen, Richard, "The Social Gospel as the Religion of the Agrarian Revolt," in *The West and the Nation: Essays in Honour of W.L. Morton*, ed. Carl Berger and Ramsay Cook. Toronto: McClelland and Stewart, 1976, 174-186.

Griezic, F., "The Hon. Thomas Alexendar Crerar: The Political Career of a Western Liberal Progressive in the 1920s," in *The Twenties In Western Canada*, ed. S.M. Trofimenkoff. Ottawa: National Museum of Man, 1972, 107-137.

Kechnie, Margaret, "The United Farm Women of Ontario: Developing a Political Consciousness," *Ontario History*, LXXVII, no. 4 (December, 1985), 267-280.

Kinnear, Mary, "'Do you Want your Daughter to Marry a Farmer?': Women's Work on the Farm, 1922," in *Canadian Papers In Rural History*, Vol.VI, ed. D.H. Akenson. Ganonoque, Ontario: Langdale Press, 1988, 137-153.

Laycock, David, *Populism and Democratic Thought in the Canadian Prairies, 1910 to 1945*. Toronto: University of Toronto Press, 1990.

Morton, W.L., *The Progressive Party in Canada*. Toronto: University of Toronto Press, 1950.

Rolph, W.K., *Henry Wise Wood of Alberta*. Toronto: University of Toronto Press, 1950.

Sharp, Paul F., *The Agrarian Revolt in Western Canada*. Minneapolis: University of Minnesota Press, 1948.

Thompson, J.H., "'The Beginning of our Regeneration': The Great War and Western Canadian Reform Movements," Canadian Historical Association *Historical Papers*, 1972, 227-245.

THE WESTERN PROGRESSIVE MOVEMENT, 1919-1921

W.L. *Morton*

The Progressive Movement in the West was dual in origin and nature. In one aspect it was an economic protest; in another it was a political revolt. A phase of agrarian resistance to the National Policy of 1878, it was also, and equally, an attempt to destroy the old national parties. The two aspects unite in the be-lief of all Progressives, both moderate and extreme, that the old parties were equally committed to maintaining the National Policy and indifferent to the ways in which the "big interests" of protection and monopoly used government for their own ends.

At the root of the sectional conflict, from which the Progressive Movement in part sprang, was the National Policy of 1878. Such conflict is partly the re-sult of the hardships and imperfect adaptations of the frontier, but it also arises from the incidence of national policies.[1] The sectional corn develops where the national shoe pinches. The National Policy, that brilliant improvisation of Sir John A. Macdonald, had grown under the master politician's hand, under the stimulus of depression and under the promptings of political appetite, until it had become a veritable Canadian System Henry Clay might have envied. Explicit in it was the promise that everybody should have something from its op-eration; implicit in it—its inarticulate major premise indeed—was the promise that when the infant industries it fostered had reached maturity, protection would be needed no more.

This, however, was but a graceful tribute to the laissez-faire doctrine of the day. This same doctrine it was which prevented the western wheat grower from demanding that he, too, should benefit directly from the operation of the National Policy. That he did benefit from the system as a whole, a complex of land settlement, railway construction, and moderate tariff protection, is not to be denied. But the wheat grower, building the wheat economy from homestead to terminal elevator in a few swift years, was caught in a complex of production and marketing costs, land values, railway rates, elevator charges, and inter-est rates. He fought to lower all these costs by economic organization and by political pressure. He saw them all as parts of a system which exploited him. He was prevented, by his direct experience of it, and by the prevailing doctrine of laissez-faire, from perceiving that the system might confer reciprocal benefits on him. Accordingly, he hated and fought it as a whole. Of the National Policy, however, the tariff was politically the most conspicuous element. Hence the

From The Canadian Historical Association *Annual Report* (1946), 41-55. Reprinted by permission of the Canadian Historical Association.

political battle was fought around the tariff; it became the symbol of the wheat growers' exploitation and frustration, alleged and actual. Like all symbols, it over-simplified the complexities it symbolized.

This clash of interest had, of course, to be taken into account by the national political parties. The Liberal-Conservatives, as creators of the National Policy, had little choice but to extol its merits even in regions where they seemed somewhat dim. They could stress its promise that a good time was coming for all, they could add that meanwhile the Yankees must be held at bay. When the Liberals quietly appropriated the National Policy after attaining national power in 1896, the task of the Conservatives became much easier. Not only could the Liberals be accused of having abandoned their principles; they could even be accused of unduly prolonging the adolescence of infant industries. A western Conservative, Mr. Arthur Meighen, could indict the Laurier administration on the charge of being maintained in power "behind ramparts of gold"[2] erected by the "interests." This echo of the "cross of gold" was not ineffective in the West, where the charge that there was no real difference between the parties on the tariff not only promoted the growth of third party sentiment, but also prolonged the life of western conservatism.

The Liberals, for their part, had not only abandoned "continentalism" in the Convention of 1893, but with the possession of power had developed that moderation without which a nation-wide majority may not be won or kept in a country of sectional interests.[3] Liberal speakers might proclaim that the party was the low tariff party; Fielding might make the master stroke of the British preferential tariff; certain items might be put on the free list here, the rates might be lowered on certain others there; but the Liberal party had become a national party, with all the powers and responsibilities of government, among them the maintenance and elaboration of the now historic National Policy. In consequence each national party began to appear more and more in the eyes of the wheat grower as an "organized hypocrisy dedicated to getting and holding office,"[4] and the conditions were created for a third party movement in the West.

The tariff, then, was a major predisposing cause of a third party movement in the West. Down to 1906 the British preference and other concessions of the Fielding tariff, together with reiterated promises of further reductions, kept the western Liberals within the fold. The completion in that year, however, of the three-decker tariff marked the beginning of more serious discontent. It grew with the offer of reciprocity in the Payne-Aldrich tariff of 1909. With the increase of agricultural indebtedness, concomitant with the settlement of the West, and the disappearance of the advantageous price differential between agricultural prices and those of manufactured goods, on which the wheat boom had taken its rise, the discontent deepened. It found expression through the grain growers' organizations, those "impressive foci of progressive ideas."[5] In 1909 came the organization of the Canadian Council of Agriculture, in 1910 Laurier's tour of the West,[6] and the Siege of Ottawa by the organized farmers. Plainly, the West was demanding its due at last. The Liberal party, which had lost support in Ontario in every election since 1896, which saw its hold in Quebec threatened by the Nationalists under Bourassa, could not afford to lose the support of a new and rapidly growing section. In 1911 the helm was put hard over for reciprocity, and Liberal prospects brightened in the West.[7] But this partial return to continentalism in economic policy was too severe a strain for a party which had become committed as deeply as its rival to the National Policy. The "Eighteen Liberals" of Toronto, among them Sir Clifford Sifton, broke with the party, and it went down to defeat under a Nationalist and a National Policy cross-fire. At the same time the Conservative party in the West, particularly in Saskatchewan and Alberta, suffered strains and defections which were to show in a lowered vitality in succeeding elections. But the offer of reciprocity remained on the statute books of the United States for another decade, and year by year the grain growers in convention demanded that the offer be taken up.

The demand of the western agrarians for the lowering of the tariff, however, was by no means an only factor in the rise of the third party. Into the West after 1896 poured immigrants from the United States and Great Britain. Most of the Americans came from the Middle West and the trans-Mississippi region. Many brought with them the experience and the political philosophy of the farmers' organizations and the third parties of those regions. Perhaps the clearest manifestation of their influence on the political development of the West was the demand for direct legislation which found expression in those forums of agrarian opinions, the grain growers' conventions, and which also found its way to the statute books of the three Western Provinces. From the British Isles came labour and socialist influences, felt rather in labour and urban circles, but not without effect among the farmers. These populist and socialist influences were mild; their exponents were in a minority. Nonetheless, they did much to give western discontent a vocabulary of grievance. Above all, they combined to repudiate the politics of expediency practised by the national parties, to denounce those parties as indifferently the tools of the "big interests," and to demand that the farmer free himself from the toils of the old parties and set up a third party, democratic, doctrinaire, and occupational.[8]

In the Canadian West this teaching fell on a soil made favourable not only by a growing disbelief in the likelihood of either of the national parties lowering the tariff, but also by a political temper different from that of Eastern Canada. (One exception must be made to this statement, namely, the old Canadian West in peninsular Ontario, from which, indeed, the original settlement of the West had been largely drawn.) This difference may be broadly expressed by saying that the political temper of the eastern provinces, both

French and English, is whiggish. Government there rests on compact, the vested and legal rights of provinces, of minorities, of corporations.[9] The political temper of the West, on the other hand, is democratic; government there rests on the will of the sovereign people, a will direct, simple, and no respector of rights except those demonstrably and momentarily popular. Of this Jacksonian, Clear Grit democracy, reinforced by American populism and English radicalism, the Progressive Movement was an authentic expression.

No better example of this difference of temper exists, of course, than the Manitoba school question. Manitoba was founded on a balance of French and English elements; this balance was expressed in the compact of the original Manitoba Act, the essential point in which was the guarantee of the educational privileges of the two language and religious groups. The balance was destroyed by the Ontario immigration of the eighteen-seventies and eighties; in 1890 Manitoba liberalism swept away the educational privileges of the French minority and introduced the "national" school, the chief agency of equalitarian democracy. This set in train a series of repercussions which, through the struggle over the Autonomy Bills in 1905, the introduction of compulsory education by the Liberal party in Manitoba in 1916, and the friction caused by Regulation 17 in Ontario, led up to the split in the Liberal party between the western and the Quebec Liberals on the Lapointe resolution in the federal Parliament in 1916. This split not only foreshadowed and prepared the way for that on conscription; it also contributed to the break-up of the old parties which opened the way to the rise of the Progressive party after 1919.[10] The western Liberals, that is to say, were turning against Laurier because they feared Nationalist domination of the party.

Thus it was that the ground was prepared for the West to throw its weight behind Union Government, first suggested as a war measure, then persisted in to prevent a Liberal victory under Laurier. Western Liberals and radicals did so with much reluctance and many misgivings. An independent movement was already taking root.[11] For the Liberal party, an electoral victory was in sight, following a succession of provincial victories and the discontent with the Borden Government's conduct of the war.[12]

This probable Liberal victory, to be based on anti-conscription sentiment in Quebec and low tariff sentiment in the West, was averted by the formation of the Union Government. The issue in that political transformation was whether the three western Liberal governments could be detached from the federal party. But the attempt made at the Winnipeg convention in August, 1917, to prepare the way for this change was defeated by the official Liberals.[13] The insurgents refused to accept the verdict of the convention; and by negotiations, the course of which is by no means clear, the support of the three western administrations and of the farmers' organizations was won for Union Government. Thus the leadership of the West was captured, and assurance was made doubly sure by the Wartime Elections Act. At the same time, the nascent third party movement was absorbed by the Union Government, and the Liberal party in the West was wrecked by the issue of conscription, as the Conservative party had been mortally wounded by reciprocity.

Though the Union Government was constituted as a "win the war" administration, which should still partisan and sectional strife, other hopes had gone to [sic] its making. It was thought that a non-partisan administration might also be an opportunity to carry certain reforms, such as that of civil service recruitment, that it would be difficult, if not impossible, for a partisan government to carry. There was also, and inevitably, the tariff. The Union Government was not publicly pledged to tariff reform, but there can be no doubt that western sentiment had forced Unionist candidates to declare themselves on the tariff; indeed many western Unionists were low tariff Liberals, or even outright independents. The eastern industrialists, on the other hand, were alert to see that the weighty western wing of the Cabinet should not induce the government to make concessions to the West. Thus there was an uneasy truce on the tariff question during the remainder of the war, the issue lying dormant but menacing the unity of the Government and its majority once the pressure of war should be removed. The test was to come with the first peace budget, that of 1919.

These, then, were the underlying causes of the rise of the western Progressive Movement. In 1919 they came to the surface, unchanged in themselves but now operating in a heated and surcharged atmosphere. That there would have been a Progressive Movement in any event is not to be doubted; the war and the events of the post-war years served to give it explosive force.

Certain elements in this surcharged atmosphere were general, others peculiar to the farmer, in effect. Chief of the general elements was the fact that the War of 1914-18 had been fought without economic controls of any significance. The result was inflation with all the stresses and strains inflation sets up in the body economic and social. The high cost of living, as it was called, was an invariable theme of speakers of the day, particularly of spokesmen of labour and the farmer. The farmer was quite prepared to believe that he, as usual, was especially the victim of these circumstances, and would point to the "pork profiteers," to clinch his contention. Inflation was at the root of the general unrest of the day, and the influence of the Russian Revolution, the radical tone of many organizations and individuals, the Winnipeg strike, and the growth of the labour movement are to be ascribed to inflation rather than to any native predisposition to radical courses.

Among the farmers' special grievances was the conscription of farmers' sons in 1918. The farming population of English Canada, on the whole had supported conscription, but with two qualifications. One was that there should also be "conscription of wealth," by which a progressive income tax was meant. The other was that the farms should not be stripped of their supply of labour, a not unreasonable condition in view of the urgent need of producing food. But the military situation in the spring of 1918 led to the revocation of the order-in-council exempting farmers' sons from military service. The result was a bitter outcry from the farmers, the great delegation to Ottawa in May, 1918, and an abiding resentment against the Union Government and all its works, especially in Ontario.

In the West itself, drouth, especially in southern Alberta, had come to harass a farm population already sorely tried. Suffice it to indicate that in the Lethbridge area of southern Alberta, the average yield of wheat between 1908 and 1921 ranged from sixty-three bushels to the acre in 1915 to two in 1918, and eight in 1921.[14] This was the extreme, but the whole West in varying degrees suffered a similar fluctuation in yield. It was a rehearsal of the disaster of the nineteen-thirties.

To the hazards of nature were to be added the hazards of the market. In 1917 the government had fixed the price of wheat to keep it from going higher, and had established a Wheat Board to market the crops of the war years. Now that peace had come, was wheat once more to be sold on the open market, or would the government fix the price and continue to market the crops through the Wheat Board, at least until the transition from war to peace was accomplished? Here was a chance to make the National Policy a matter of immediate benefit and concern to the western farmer, a chance not undiscerned by shrewd defenders of the National Policy.[15] Here also, under the stimulus of war, was the beginning of the transition from the old Jeffersonian and laissez-faire tradition of the frontier West, to the new West of wheat pools, floor prices, and the Cooperative Commonwealth Federation. The point of principle was clearly grasped by the farmers, but their response was confused. The Manitoba Grain Growers and the United Farmers of Alberta declined in annual convention to ask the government to continue the Wheat Board, but this decision was severely criticized, one might almost say, was repudiated, by the rank and file of the membership. The Saskatchewan Grain Growers, who met later, emphatically demanded that the Wheat Board be continued. In the upshot it was, but only for the crop yield of 1919, and in 1920 it was liquidated. From this action came much of the drive, indeed the final impetus, of the Progressive Movement.[16] Thereafter the western farmer was caught between fixed debt charges and high costs on one hand and falling prices on the other; his position seemed to him desperate. From his despair came first, the Progressive electoral sweep in the West, and then the economic action which created the wheat pools.

Finally, there was the question of tariff revision. It was, however, no longer the simple clash of sectional interests it had been. The customs tariff had been increased to help finance the war. Any revision now would affect governmental financing of the war debt, and also the financial resources of private individuals and corporations in the post-war period. In short, the question had now become, what place should tariff revision have in reconstruction?

It was to this question that the Union Government had to address itself, while preparing the budget of 1919 under the vigilant eyes of the farmers' organizations on the one side and of the Canadian Manufacturers' Association on the other. The decision was, in effect, to postpone the issue, on the ground that 1919 was, to all intents and purposes, a war year and that only a very moderate revision should be attempted. The decision was not unreasonable, and was clearly intended to be a compromise between eastern and western views on the tariff.[17] But western supporters of the Union Government were in a very vulnerable position, as the McMaster amendment to the motion to go into Committee of Supply was to show.[18] The pressure from the West for a major lowering of the tariff was mounting and becoming intense. In the outcome, the Honourable Thomas A. Crerar, Minister of Agriculture, resigned on the ground that the revision undertaken in the budget was insufficient. In the vote on the budget he was joined by nine western Unionists. This was the beginning of the parliamentary Progressive party.

The position of the remaining western Unionists became increasingly difficult, though also their pressure contributed to the moderate revision of 1919.[19] The fate of R. C. Henders is very much in point. Henders had been, as President of the Manitoba Grain Growers, an ardent and outspoken agrarian. In 1916 he had been nominated as an independent candidate for Macdonald. In 1917 he accepted nomination as Unionist candidate and was elected. In 1919 he voted with the Government on the budget, on the ground that this was in effect a war budget, and the time premature for a revision of the tariff. In 1920 the United Farmers of Manitoba, following the action of their executive, "repudiated his stand, accepted his resignation, and re-affirmed [their] confidence in the principles of the Farmers' Platform."[20] In 1921 he vanished from political ken. An honest man had taken a politically mistaken line and was mercilessly held to account. Such was the fate of western Unionists who did not cross the floor or find refuge in the Senate. Western low tariff sentiment would admit of no equivocation.

The third party movement, stirring in the West before 1917 but absorbed and over-ridden by the Unionist Government, was now free to resume its course with a favourable wind fanned by inflation, short crops, and post-war discontent. A chart had already been provided. The Canadian Council of Agriculture had in 1916 taken cognizance of the mounting demand that political action be taken by the farmers. Without committing the Council itself, it prepared the Farmers' Platform as a programme which the farmers' organizations might endorse and which they might press upon the government. The events of 1917 diverted attention from it, but in 1918 it was revised and enlarged, and in 1919 was adopted by the farmers' organizations. In substance, the platform called for a League of Nations, dominion autonomy, free trade with Great Britain, reciprocity with the United States, a lowering of the general tariff, graduated income, inheritance, and corporation taxes, public ownership of a wide range of utilities, and certain reforms designed to bring about a greater measure of democracy, such as reform of the senate, abolition of titles, and the institution of direct legislation and proportional representation.[21] The platform gave the incoherent western discontent a rallying point and a programme, and was the occasion for the organized farmers entering federal politics. Its title, "The New National Policy," was a gage of battle thrown down before the defenders of the old National Policy, a challenge, direct and explicit, to make that policy national indeed.

This decision to enter federal politics was opportune beyond the dream of seasoned politicians. The prairie was afire in a rising wind, and soon the flames were flaring from one end of the country to the other. In October, 1919, the United Farmers of Ontario carried forty-six seats in a house of 111, and formed an administration. Later in the same month O. R. Gould, farmers' candidate in the federal seat of Assiniboia, defeated W. R. Motherwell, Liberal stalwart and a founder of the Grain Growers' Association, by a majority of 5,224.[22] A few days later Alex Moore carried Cochrane in a provincial by-election for the United Farmers of Alberta. In 1920 the organized farmers carried nine seats in Manitoba, seven in Nova Scotia, and ten in New Brunswick.[23] By-election after by-election went against the Government, usually to farmer candidates, until the smashing climax of the Medicine Hat by-election of June, 1921, when Robert Gardiner of the U.F.A. defeated a popular Unionist candidate by a majority of 9,764.[24] Even the Liberals' tariff plank of 1919 did little to check the sweep of the flames. The political prophets were estimating that of the forty-three seats west of the lakes, the Progressives would carry from thirty-five to forty.[25]

All was propitious, then, for the entry of the Progressives into federal politics. There they might hope to hold the balance of power, or even emerge as the largest group. The work of organization was pushed steadily. In December, 1920, the Canadian Council of Agriculture recognized the third party in the House of Commons as the exponent of the new national policy and endorsed the members' choice of the Honourable T. A. Crerar as leader.[26] During 1920 and 1921 Progressive candidates were nominated by local conventions in all federal constituencies in the West.

Two major difficulties, however, were arising to embarrass the Progressives in their bid for national power. The first was the charge that they were a class party. The second was the demand that political action be taken in the provincial as well as the federal field.[27] These embarrassments were eventually to split the Movement, defeat its bid for national power, and reduce it to the status of a sectional party.

The origin of these divisions in the Movement may best be examined by turning to provincial politics in the West. That the entrance into federal politics could not be kept separate from a demand that political action be taken in the provinces, arose in part from the federal composition of national parties. Any fed-

eral political movement is driven to attempt the capture of provincial governments, in order to acquire the means, that is to say, the patronage, whereby
to build an effective political organization. It is not to be supposed that this political maxim was unknown to the leaders of the Progressive Movement. They
hoped, however, that national success would be followed by a voluntary adherence of the western governments, which would render capture by storm
unnecessary.

The Progressive Movement, at the same time, was a genuine attempt to
destroy machine politics, and there was in its leadership a sincere reluctance to
accept the facts of political life. They hoped to lead a popular movement, to
which the farmers' economic organizations would furnish whatever direction was
necessary. It was the zeal of their followers, eager to destroy the old parties
wherever they existed, that carried the Progressive Movement into provincial
politics.

Province by province, the leaders were compelled to bow to the pressure of
the rank and file, and allow the organized farmers to enter the provincial are-
nas. The methods and the results, however, were by no means identical, for
they were conditioned by the different political histories of the three provinces.

In Manitoba the dominating fact was that from 1899 until 1915 the province
had been governed by the Conservative Roblin administration. The sheer power
and efficiency of the Roblin-Rogers organization, perhaps the classic example of
the political machine in Canadian history, accounts in great part for the victory
of the anti-reciprocity campaign in Manitoba in 1911. Its spectacular demise in
the odour of scandal in 1915 left the provincial Conservative party badly shat-
tered. Henceforth there were many loose Conservative votes in the most
conservative of the Prairie Provinces, a province a whole generation older than
the other two, and during that generation the very image and transcript of
Ontario. But the succeeding Liberal Government, that of the Honourable T. C.
Norris, was reformist and progressive. There was little the Grain Growers could
ask of the provincial administration that it was not prepared to grant. Why
then should the organized farmers oppose the Norris Government? The answer
was that the Progressive Movement was, for many Progressives, a revolt against
the old party system, and the provincial Liberal organization had been affiliated
with the federal Liberals. It might, indeed, become a major buttress of liberalism as the breach between the Laurier and the Unionist Liberal closed. If the
old parties were to be defeated at Ottawa, they must be rooted out at the source
of their strength in the provinces. Out of this conflict, largely one between leaders and rank and file, came the decision of the new United Farmers of Manitoba
in 1920 that the organization as such should not enter provincial politics, but
that in the constituencies the locals might hold conventions, nominate candidates, and organize. If a majority of constituencies should prove to be in favour
of political action, then the executive of the United Farmers would call a provincial convention to draft a platform.[28] As a result, political action was taken

locally, and nine farmer representatives were elected to the Manitoba legislature in 1920.[29] As a result of this success, the U.F.M. placed the resources of the organization behind the farmers' political action,[30] and in the election of 1922 the farmers won a plurality of seats in the legislature. The suspected *rapprochement* of the Norris Government with the federal Liberals may have contributed to its defeat.[31]

In Saskatchewan and Alberta the dominating factor was that at the creation of the two provinces in 1905 the federal Liberal government used its influence to establish Liberal administrations. In Canada the possession of power is all but decisive. Governments fall not so much by the assaults of their enemies as through their own internal decay. From 1905 until 1921 the Liberals ruled in Alberta; from 1905 until 1929 they were in power in Saskatchewan. Moreover, in both, the Conservative party was cut off from patronage and unnaturally compelled to be a party of provincial rights. Both provincial Conservative parties declined from 1911 on, and rapidly after the provincial elections of 1917. In these provinces too, the administrations were careful to govern in harmony with the wishes of the organized farmers. Why then should the farmers enter provincial politics against the Liberal government? Again the answer is that the provincial Liberal parties were affiliated with the federal party, and were examples of the machine politics which Progressives hoped to destroy, politics rendered noisome by the corruption arising from the scramble for the resources of the West, and the political ruthlessness of the professional politicians of the day.

Down to 1917 the political developments of the two provinces were alike, but a remarkable diversion occurs thereafter. In Saskatchewan the Liberal party enjoyed shrewd leadership, considerable administrative ability, and a fine political organization. Threatened by scandal in 1917, it made a remarkable recovery under Premier William Martin. In that almost wholly rural province, the Liberal government was a government of the grain growers. Leadership, as in the instance of the Honourable Charles A. Dunning, graduated from the Association to the government. The slightest wish of the Saskatchewan Grain Growers became law with as much dispatch as the conventions of government allow.[32] When the demand for provincial political action arose, Premier Martin met it, in the Preeceville speech of May, 1920, by dissociating the provincial from the federal party. At the same time the weight of the executive of the Grain Growers was thrown against intervention as a separate party in provincial politics. As in Manitoba, when the demand, partly under pressure from the Non-Partisan League, became irresistible, it was referred to the locals.[33] The locals gave little response during 1920-1, and an attempt of third party men in 1921 to commit the central organization to political action was foiled.[34] As a result, the provincial Progressive Movement in Saskatchewan became largely an attempt at organization by independents, under the leadership of Harris Turner of Saskatoon.[35] Before organization could be well begun, Premier Martin dissolved the legislature and headed off the movement by a snap election. This was decisive. Only thirteen independents were returned, to a great extent, it would seem, by Conservative votes, for the provincial Conservative party simply did not contest the election. Thus the Liberal administration in Saskatchewan survived the Progressive rising, but at the price of severing temporarily its ties with the federal party.

In Alberta the same story was to have a very different outcome. Not only was the Liberal party of that province less fortunate in its leadership, though no less realistic in its tactics, not only did it suffer division by the quarrel over the Alberta Great Waterways Railway scandal, which created a weakness in the party that the division into Laurier and Unionist Liberals did nothing to mend;[36] but the farmer organization of that province was separate in its leadership from the government, and that leadership was from 1915 the leadership of Henry Wise Wood. In Alberta, the forceful personalities were outside the government; in Saskatchewan, they were, on the whole, in the government or close to it. Alberta lost the brilliant A. L. Sifton to the Union Government in 1917, and Alberta alone possessed a Henry Wise Wood. Wood and the executive of the United Farmers of Alberta were no more anxious than other leaders of the farm organizations to go into provincial politics. He, indeed, was on principle opposed to going into politics at all. The drive for a third, independent, farmer party, however, developed much greater force in Alberta than elsewhere. This was partly because the decline of the Conservative party was even more pronounced in Alberta than in Saskatchewan. It was also because the Non-Partisan League became more powerful in that province than in Saskatchewan. American populism and British radicalism had freer play in frontier Alberta than in older Saskatchewan. The Non-Partisan League, for example, captured two provincial seats in Alberta in 1917, whereas it had captured only one in Saskatchewan in the same year, and that by a fluke. The League went on to threaten to capture the locals of the U.F.A. by conversion and infiltration. This was a threat that could not be ignored, because it was in and through the locals that the farmers' organizations lived. Wood and the U.F.A. leaderships were therefore caught on the horns of a dilemma. They knew that political action had invariably ruined farm organizations in the past, as the Farmers' Alliance in the United States had gone to wreck in the Populist party. They knew also that they might lose control of the U.F.A. if the Non-Partisan League obtained control of a majority of locals and assumed leadership of the drive for political action. Wood solved the dilemma by his concept of "group government", and in doing so crystallized the strong tendency of the Progressive Movement, a tendency which owed much to the Non-Partisan League, to become a class movement, deeply averse to lawyers, bankers, and politicians. The U.F.A. would take political action, but it would take it as an organization. It would admit only farmers to its ranks; it would nominate only farmers for election; its representation in the legislature would constitute a separate group, co-operating with other groups but not combining with any to constitute a political party. Guided by this concept, the U.F.A. in 1919 entered politics, both federal and provincial.[37] In 1921 it won a majority of the seats in the Alberta legislature.

These varying fortunes of the Progressive Movement in the three provinces were significant for the character of the federal Progressive party. Broadly speaking, two concepts of the character and future of the party prevailed among its members. One, which may be termed the Manitoba view, was that the Progressive Movement was one of insurgent liberalism, which might have the happy result of recapturing the federal Liberal party from the control of the conservative and protectionist Liberals of the East. This was the view, for example, of J. W. Dafoe, a mentor of Progressivism. It aimed at building up a national, popular movement by "broadening out," by "opening the door" to all sympathizers. The Saskatchewan federal Progressives also accepted this view, the more so as the provincial movement had been headed off for a decade. The other concept may be called the Alberta concept. It was that the Progressive Movement was an occupational or class movement, capable of extension by group organization to other economic classes, but not itself concerned with bringing about such extension. Farmer must represent farmer, the group must act as a group.

It may be noted in passing that neither view of the Progressive Movement demands an explicit farmer-labour alliance. Why Progressivism did not develop this characteristic of the earlier Populist party and the later Cooperative Commonwealth Federation cannot be explained here, but it may be said that the leadership of both wings of the Movement was averse to an open alliance with labour.

Here again is the two-fold character of the Progressive Movement postulated in the opening paragraph. Progressivism which was an economic protest, seeking a natural remedy by political action little more unconventional than a revolt-from caucus rule, is here termed Manitoban. Progressivism which was doctrinaire, class conscious, and heterodox, is here called Albertan. The former assumed that exploitation would cease in a society made competitive by the abolition of protection; the latter proposed to produce a harmony of interests by putting an end to competition by means of the co-operation of organized groups. Both tendencies, of course, existed all across the Movement. Each was personified and had as respective protagonists the Honourable T. A. Crerar and Henry Wise Wood.

The extremes, however, were fundamental and irreconcilable. Manitoban Progressivism sought economic ends through conventional political means and admitted of compromise with the old parties. Albertan Progressivism sought much the same economic ends, but also sought to transform the conditions of politics. In this it was closer to the essential nature of Progressivism, with its innate distrust of elected representatives and of party organization.[38] Its pledging of candidates, its frequent use of the signed recall, its levy on members for campaign funds, its predilection for direct legislation and for proportional representation, establish its fundamental character. That in so conducting itself it was to give rise to forms of political organization which old line politicians were to envy, is one of those little ironies which delight the sardonic observer.

An examination of the course of the general election of 1921 adds little to the exposition of the theme. As revealed in the campaign literature, it turned on the issues of protection and of the class doctrines of Henry Wise Wood. Prime Minister Meighen, first of those western men with eastern principles to be called to head the Conservative party, put on the full armour of protection, and fought the western revolt in defence of the National Policy. It was courageous, it was magnificent, but it was not successful. His party attacked the Progressives as free traders seeking to destroy the National Policy for selfish class advantage. Mr. W. L. Mackenzie King stood firmly on the Liberal platform of 1919, which, marvelously contrived, faced squarely all points of the political compass at once. Liberal strategy was to avoid a sharp stand, to pose as the farmers' friend—"There never was a Farmers' Party while the Liberals were in power"[39]— and to denounce the class character of Progressivism. Mr. Crerar was in the embarrassing position of a leader whose followers persist in treading on his heels, but he fought the good fight with dignity and moderation, protesting that his was not a class movement.

In the upshot, the Progressives carried sixty-five seats, and emerged as the second largest group in the House. Coalition with the Liberals was seriously considered and was rejected only at the last moment, presumably because Messrs. Crerar and Drury could not obtain from Mr. King those pledges which would have ensured the identity of the group and the curbing of the protectionist elements in the Liberal Cabinet. This decision marked the beginning of the disintegration of the Movement, for the Progressives neither imposed their policies on the Liberals nor definitely became a parliamentary party seeking office. With that fatal tendency of third parties to avoid responsibility, of which George Langley had warned a decade before,[40] they declined to become even the official opposition.

Thereafter Manitoban Progressivism lost its bright speed amid the sands and shallows of official Liberalism. Albertan Progressivism, represented by the Ginger Group, the federal U.F.A. members and a few others, alone survived the decay of Progressive zeal, and remained for fourteen years to lend distinction to the national councils, and to bear in its organization the seeds at once of Social Credit and the Co-operative Commonwealth Federation.

Notes

1. *Cf.* Frederick Jackson Turner, *The Significance of Sections in American History* (New York, 1932), 314.

2. *Hansard,* 1910-11, I, 1918.

3. Wilfred E. Binkley, *American Political Parties* (New York, 1944)—"... Madison's principle that a nation wide majority can agree only on a moderate program," 87; also 17-18.

4. Dafoe Library of the *Winnipeg Free Press,* Dafoe Papers, Dafoe to Sir Clifford Sifton, July 21, 1919; on the prospects of re-organizing the Liberal party.

5. *Manitoba Free Press,* April 10, 1917, 9.

6. *Grain Growers' Guide,* September 14, 1910, 13. Fred Kirkham, advocate of a third party, wrote to the editor from Saltcoats, Saskatchewan: "If the memorials presented to Sir Wilfrid Laurier have failed to imbue him with the determination to battle with the vested interests of the East to grant our just requests, we have no alternative but to become democratic insurgents, and form a new party and find a new general to fight under. We must be courageous in politics before Laurier will treat with us as a big community of votes to be reckoned with."

7. Public Archives of Canada, Laurier Papers, 3089, J. W. Dafoe to Laurier, April 28, 1911. "In my judgment reciprocity has changed the whole political situation in the West. Until it was announced the drift out West was undoubtedly against the government; but now it is just other way about."

8. *United Farmers of Alberta, Annual Report,* 1910, 43. "Moved by the Vermilion Union: Resolved, that ten farmers, as members of Parliament with votes would have more weight in shaping the laws and influencing government than one thousand delegates as petitioners:

Therefore be it further resolved that the farmers, to secure this end, should vote for farmers only to represent them in Parliament and vote as a unit and cease dividing their voting power. Carried."

9. I am indebted to Professor J. R. Mallory of Brandon College, now of McGill, for a discussion clarifying this point.

10. *Manitoba Free Press,* May 13, 1916. Editorial, "Consequences." "Whatever may be the political consequences of this blunder to Liberalism in Canada at large, Western Liberalism will not suffer if it adheres to the independence which its representatives have displayed at Ottawa this week. These developments at the capital must tend to strengthen the feeling which has been growing steadily for years that Western Liberals need not look to the East, at present, for effective and progressive leadership .... Canadian public life will thus be given what it sorely needs, ... a group of convinced radicals ... To your tents, O Israel!"

11. *Ibid.,* June 28, 1917, 9. "The Saskatchewan Victory." "The Canadian West is in the mood to break away from past affiliations and traditions and inaugurate a new political era of sturdy support for an advanced and radical programme. The break-up of parties has given the West its opportunity; and there is no doubt it will take advantage of it." At least four independent candidates had been nominated in the West before June, 1917, in provincial and federal seats. In December, 1916, the Canadian Council of Agriculture had issued the first Farmers' Platform.

12. Henry Borden (ed.), *Robert Laird Borden: His Memoirs* (Toronto, 1938) II, 749-50, J. W. Dafoe to Borden, September 29, 1917.

13. Dafoe Papers. Dafoe to Augustus Bridle, June 14, 1921. "The Western Liberal Convention was a bomb which went off in the hands of its makers. It was decided

upon at Ottawa by a group of conscription Liberals; the intention was to bring into existence a Western Liberal group free from Laurier's control who would be prepared to consider coalition with Borden on its merits, but the Liberal machine in the West went out and captured the delegates with the result that the convention was strongly pro-Laurier."

14. *Report of the Survey Board for Southern Alberta*, January, 1922.

15. *Hansard*, 1919, 1, 558. Colonel J. A. Currie (Simcoe) "I am quite in agreement with the hon. member for Maple Creek (J. A. Maharg) when he says we should fix a price for the wheat of the West. That is in line with the National Policy." See also the Right Honourable Arthur Meighen's proposal for a modified Wheat Board in his speech at Pottage la Prairie during the campaign of 1921. *Canadian Annual Review*, 1921, 449-50.

16. *Cf.* Vernon C. Fowke, *Canadian Agricultural Policy* (Toronto, 1946), 268.

17. The changes were as follows: the 7 1/2 per cent increase for war purposes was removed from agricultural implements and certain necessities of life; the 5 per cent war duty was modified; an income tax was levied.

18. Fourteen western Unionists voted for the amendment. *Hansard,* 1919, IV, 3,678.

19. *Hansard,* 1919, IV, 3475. W. D. Cowan, Unionist (Regina). "I believe that the changes which have been made in the tariff have been made entirely because of the agitation which has been carried on by the West. We have had, for the first time, I fancy, in the history of Parliament, a western caucus and in that we have been united. Old time Liberals united with old time Conservatives. On the one point that they should try to get substantial reductions in the tariffs...."

20. *Canadian Annual Review,* 1920, 741.

21. See *ibid.,* 1919, for text, 365-8.

22. *Parliamentary Companion,* 1921, 196.

23. *Manitoba Free Press,* February 25, 1921; *Grain Growers' Guide,* August 4, 1920, 4, and October 27, 1920, 5.

24. *Parliamentary Companion,* 1922, 247.

25. Dafoe Papers, Dafoe to Sir Clifford Sifton, January 20, 1920.

26. *Grain Growers' Guide,* December 15, 1920, 3. Resolution of executive of the Canadian Council of Agriculture in meeting of December 7-9, 1920.

27. Dafoe Papers, Dafoe to Sir Clifford Sifton, January 26, 1921. "Crerar's only troubles out here arise from the ardor with which certain elements in his following insist upon organizing a purely class movement against the three local governments, thereby tending to antagonize the very elements which Crerar is trying, by broadening its basis, to add to his party."

28. *United Farmers of Manitoba Year Book,* 1920, 67.

29. *Grain Growers' Guide,* July 7, 1920, 6. Editorial, "The Manitoba Election." "The United Farmers of Manitoba, as an organization, took no part in the election, and each constituency where farmer candidates were nominated and elected acted entirely on its own initiative."

30. *Ibid.,* January 19, 1921, 3.

31. *Manitoba Free Press,* April 28, 1922. Dafoe Papers, Dafoe to Sir Clifford Sifton, July 7, 1922.

32. *Minutes of the Annual Convention of the Saskatchewan Grain Growers' Association,* February 18-21, 1919, 4. Report of Premier Wm. Martin's address. "There are questions now coming before you affecting the welfare of the whole community of the Province. It is the policy of the present government and will continue to be the policy of the present government to carry out these suggestions."

33. *Ibid.,* February 9-13, 1920, 114-19.

34. *Ibid.,* January 31-February 4, 1921. The debate on provincial political action was involved; a motion to enter provincial politics as an organization was defeated (118) and a motion to support action by constituencies was, it would seem, shelved (93).

35. *Saskatoon Daily Star,* June 1, 1921. Report of the convention of independents at Saskatoon, May 31, 1921.

36. John Blue, *Alberta Past and Present* (Chicago, 1924), 125. "The session of 1910 witnessed a perturbation and upheaval that split the Liberal party into two factions, which more than a decade afterwards regarded each other with some jealousy and distrust."

37. *United Farmers of Alberta, Annual Report,* 1919, 52-3.

38. *Grain Growers' Guide,* March 5, 1919, 26. Article by Roderick McKenzie on "Political Action." "The purpose of the movement inaugurated by the farmers is that whenever the time comes to make a choice of representation to parliament, the electors get together to make their selection."

39. P.A.C., Pamphlet no. 5081, *Group Government Compared with Responsible Government.*

40. *Grain Growers' Guide,* September 21, 1910, 13-14. "It may be urged that a separate farmers' party might influence the government even if it did not become strong enough to take on itself the actual work of governing. The answer to that is this. The legitimate objective of a political party is to control the legislative and administrative functions. Without [that] objective it cannot exist for any length of time...."

POLITICS AND CULTURE

Gerald Friesen

The flowering of revolutionary socialism was a significant event in the history of western Canadian politics, but, having withered so quickly, it was quickly forgotten in the wider community. Other more moderate solutions to social injustice soon competed for public attention and, within months, seemed to be the only viable alternatives to the established order. Revolution was then left behind, and

From *The Canadian Prairies: A History* (Toronto: University of Toronto Press, 1986), 364-74. Reprinted by permission of the University of Toronto Press.

reform became the dominant concern of the dissatisfied. Throughout the 1920s, reformist amelioration of the Canadian capitalist system was discussed in church, union, and farm meetings. The central topics in most debates were the 'progressive movement' and its kin, the 'farmers' political parties,' but many allied themes, including co-operatives, the United Church, and labourism, were also touched on.

One reason for the preoccupation with reform lay in the changed social structure of western Canada in the decades after 1900. Whereas the radical industrial and mine workers organized in a constituency of perhaps 250,000, the moderates of the prairies could expect support from 2 million citizens—at least four of five in the regional population. Farmers and professionals were fundamental to the new reform movement. The 'professionals'—teachers, ministers, newspaper men and women, health and social workers, government employees—had become much more numerous and, because of their education and skills, more important as commentators on and participants in public affairs, and their rise to prominence was one reason for significant new departures in the reform camp. The background of these individuals was often rural, one suspects, because most Canadians lived in rural communities before 1900, but they became city or town dwellers when they pursued advanced education and they remained in the city or maintained their contact with 'urban' life when they took up full-time jobs. They were mostly Protestant, English-speaking, and Canadian or British-born, though there were significant exceptions, and they were attuned to the language of urban social reform that was so prominent in the early twentieth century. They were the heart of the 'middle' group, between business leaders and labourers, in city and town. Some of them would have claimed to be Social Gospellers, others evangelical Christians, but almost all would have acknowledged the power of religion in their lives. Moreover, they were infected by the contagion of the 'western myth': they believed that they lived in a democratic malleable community and thus could effect significant social change. These reformers of the 'middle' class allied with the farm men and women of the prairies to create powerful social reform movements in the 1920s.

If the urban professional group seemed a new factor in the prairie political community, the farmers' world had changed to such a degree that it, too, could be described as substantially different in character from its pre-1900 equivalent. The place of farm dwellers in the prairie social order has not been established satisfactorily by students of prairie history. Some farmers were only a short step from the illiteracy and poverty of the most primitive Old Country peasant or slum conditions, but many others were just as literate as their counterparts in the offices and professions of the Atlantic world's urban centres. They had been raised in the era of the educational reforms of Victorian England and Canada; their generation shared an unusually rich, unusually democratic introduction to the entire history of English culture. These farmers, men and women, should be viewed in the context suggested by Paul Fussell's survey of English literature in the First World War:

By 1914, it was possible for soldiers to be not merely literate but vigorously literary, for the Great War occurred at a special historical moment when two 'liberal' forces were powerfully coinciding in England. On the one hand, the belief in the educative powers of classical and English literature was still extremely strong. On the other, the appeal of popular education and 'self-improvement' was at its peak, and such education was still conceived largely in humanistic terms. It was imagined that the study of literature at Workmen's Institutes and through such schemes as the National Home Reading Union would actively assist those of modest origins to rise in the class system ... The intersection of these two forces, the one 'aristocratic,' the other 'democratic,' established an atmosphere of public respect for literature unique in modern times ... In 1914 there was virtually no cinema; there was no radio at all; and there was certainly no television. Except for sex and drinking, amusement was largely found in language formally arranged, either in books and periodicals or at the theater and music hall, or in one's friends' anecdotes, rumors, or clever structuring of words.[1]

Studies of Canadian society may eventually demonstrate that this same literary and scientific sophistication was present in a significant proportion of prairie farm families.[2] Many farmers, like many of their city cousins, were literate and forceful. They were able to think their way through tracts of agrarian reformism and selections of Victorian poetry and to reach conclusions concerning political change.

If one thing was soon apparent to western Canadian activists, urban and rural, in the anxious years of 1918 and 1919, it was the uselessness of the Union government. For a group that had been elected with such widespread support on the prairies in the late autumn of 1917, the Borden Unionists had frittered away their advantage with remarkable dispatch. The budget of 1918 brought little relief to the west and, if anything, only made more evident how different were the economic interests of central and prairie Canada. The Unionist transportation policy included nationalization of the Canadian Northern Railway, which was welcomed, but the Crow's Nest rates were still suspended. Moreover, as a result of wartime inflation, freight rates were increased as soon as the new administration thought it feasible—that is, a week after the 1917 election. The rising cost of living was a matter of concern to every citizen, and, in the prairie west in particular, the rulings of both the food controller and the fuel controller were subject to harsh criticism because they did not take into account the special circumstances of life on the prairies, especially on the prairie farm. Perhaps the failure of the Union government was due to errors not of policy but of communication; certainly, prairie dwellers took strong exception to its secrecy, its rule by order-in-council, and its refusal to explain its course. But, whether the problem had several explanations or very few, the Unionists were a disappointment.[3]

Where to turn? The customary answer in Canadian politics was the Liberal party, but the events of the war had made that an unlikely alternative for most westerners. Laurier's defence of French-Canadian language rights had displeased many prominent prairie Liberals in 1916, and such influential party members as John Dafoe, editor of the *Manitoba Free Press,* now advocated the creation of a separate western Liberal party: 'These developments at the capital must tend to strengthen the feeling which has been growing steadily for years that Western Liberals need not look to the East, at present, for effective and progressive leadership. The time is ripe for Western Liberals to decide that they will rely upon themselves—and thus do their own thinking, formulate their own policies and provide their own leaders. Canadian public life will thus be given what it sorely needs—a group of convinced radicals who will be far more interested in the furthering of their programme than in office-holding ... "To your tents, O Israel.' "[4] In this statement, one sees both the regional sentiment and the desire for reform that characterized so much western political rhetoric in this era.

Many Canadians who wished to reform their nation turned to another political force, the Progressive movement, as the vehicle to implement their ideals. The Progressive uprising was a complex phenomenon. It has been described as a farm movement, a sectional protest, a vehicle for the social gospel, and a quest for cheaper government; it was all of these things and more. In its name, 'third party' provincial governments were elected in Ontario (1919), Alberta (1921), and Manitoba (1922), and significant movements under similar titles influenced the course of politics in all the other provinces; 65 members of the federal Parliament were elected under its banner in 1921, and 12 remained under variants of that name after the 1930 federal election. It was the most important departure from the two-party system since the consolidation of the Liberals and Conservatives in the 1870s and can be seen as the forerunner of the 'protest' parties of the 1930s. The Progressive movement was, for most of the 1920s, the focus of prairie reform activity and ideological debate.[5]

Western farmers provided one bulwark of the Progressive campaign. They had borne the costs of the settlement experiment and had had to struggle for every dollar. They had campaigned for branch lines, for regulation of grain grading and weighing practices, and for competitive elevator and grain buying systems. They had risked heavy investments, including years of their own labour, in the dangerous gamble on weather and price that was the eternal lot of the farmer. Thus they knew the benefits of organization and lobbying campaigns and had sufficient reasons—tariff reform, restoration of the Crow's Nest freight rates, completion of the Hudson Bay railway, and a revised grain marketing system—to want to continue their political activities. The war slowed their campaign, but during 1919 the farmers made important strides.

Two components of this 'agrarian revolt' made it much larger than merely a prairie phenomenon. The first, which prairie farmers shared to some extent with farmers across the nation and across the continent, was rooted in the consciousness of their distinctiveness as an occupational group. To be a farmer was to be a unique and valuable contributor to the social and economic fabric of the nation, in this perspective, and to have special interests in common that were not acknowledged by governments in power. This agrarian mystique drew strength from ideas as old as western civilization and from relatively recent insights. On the one hand, agriculture was a way of life: Virgil's honest yeoman celebrated life on the soil and the physiocrats of the French Enlightenment claimed that agriculture was the foundation of all wealth; the Romantics and the modern apostles who advocated a 'return to the land' seemed to provide proof that rural life created purer character. But, beside these nostalgic and essentially undemonstrable—however popular—notions, there was a sense that modern farmers were also 'professionals.' They were scientists, insofar as they had to understand and implement the findings of entomologists and plant breeders and soil surveyors; they were engineers when they repaired equipment; they were accountants when they balanced revenues against expenditures; they were 'modern'—for which one should read 'educated and respectable'—in the increasingly urban-determined definition of society and culture. And like businessmen and manufacturers, they recognized that modern times required the organization of an economic interest group if their viewpoint was to be presented forcefully to public and government alike. In the identity created by occupational and romantic definitions of their life, all Canadian farmers could find common ground. Such views lay behind the foundation of the Canadian Council of Agriculture in 1909, a national institution in which farmers could lament the continued evil of the tariff and warn of the dangers of rural depopulation. Such campaigns sustained farmers' self-esteem in the face of fashionable literary denunciations of rural life and demonstrated that they were an occupational group distinct from all others. Indeed, in the rhetoric of some, they were a 'class.'

Canadian farmers, like other occupational groups, did not have a complete identity of interests. Though they were united by their anger against the growing urban derision directed at rural life, for example, they found that BC fruit growers, Quebec dairy farmers, and Saskatchewan grain exporters did not have a common perspective on government policies that affected agriculture. Where a Nova Scotia farmer was moved by his concern for the Intercolonial, his Manitoban counterpart was anxious about the Crow's Nest rate and the Hudson Bay or Peace River rail outlets. In this sense, farm protests were marked by a second significant defining characteristic—they were provoked by a regional as well as an occupational consciousness. Thus, where traditional prairie grievances about central Canadian politicians, manufacturers, and bankers fed the prairie farm revolt, other grievances fuelled similar farm revolts in other regions.

Another element in the post-war movement can best be described as a product of the 'middle group'—neither radical labourer nor business leader—that had become a force in prairie society. These people have not often figured in accounts of the Progressive movement, and yet they must have been central to it. Protestant ministers, for example, helped to develop reform ideas because they were often present at farm meetings, delivering the prayers and brief biblical illustrations that provided a convincing religious interpretation of the otherwise unconventional talk about a new party. It is reasonable to assume, too, that where regional and occupational interests coincided with Progressive platform planks, as was the case for prairie elevator agents or maritime fishermen, there would Progressive supporters be found. But, as we learn more about this unusual protest movement, we learn that its support was even more widespread and diverse. In Nova Scotia and New Brunswick, the Progressives were briefly the vehicle of the broadly based Maritime Rights activists in 1919-20. In Ontario, the United Farmers joined with the labour movement to form a provincial government in 1919; surely, the 'Progressive' reform platform had a wide economic and occupational appeal in that province. And, on the prairies, town dwellers as well as farmers voted for Progressive candidates in the 1921 federal election; they also voted for UFA candidates in Alberta in 1921 when farmers formed the provincial government, for UFM candidates in 1922 when they formed the Manitoba government, and for the Progressives who ran in Saskatchewan provincial contests, with less success, in 1921 and 1925. As was the case for farmers, so with non-farmers, the appeal of the Progressives varied with the region and the riding. Thus, on the prairies, traditional regional stereotypes and economic interests may have created the impression that the Progressives were the party of regional and farmers' occupational protest, but they were more.

As many observers recognized, and as the support of teachers, elevator agents, and shopkeepers made evident, the Progressives were seeking significant social and economic change. In part, theirs was a campaign for regional justice because it called for the redistribution of wealth from the urban heartland to the periphery. In addition, though the analysis was rudimentary and the term was not used in today's sense, it was a campaign for 'class' justice. The Progressives recognized the growing danger of the concentration of capital in fewer and fewer hands; they feared the emergence in Canada of an aristocracy of wealth that would be every bit as oppressive as the entrenched oligarchies in European societies; and they were determined to ensure that democracy in politics and just rewards in income would be the lot of every Canadian. Their stand on the tariff was not just an expression of the farmers' interest in cheaper imported implements but was a defence of 'the people of Canada' against the 'protected interests'; the 'privileged class' must not be permitted to become richer at the expense of the 'poor' or 'the masses'; and these privileged citizens should not continue to subvert the old-line parties by contributing 'lavishly' to campaign funds, thus lowering 'the standard of public morality.' These quotations, taken from the Progressive platforms prepared by the Canadian Council of Agriculture in 1916 and 1918, demonstrated the movement's awareness of the divergence of class interests in Canada. And the Progressive solution for the revenue shortfalls entailed by tariff reform—to tax the value of unimproved land and to employ graduated taxes on personal income, large estates, and corporation profits—also constituted an attack on concentrations of wealth and power.[6]

Progressivism appealed to a wide range of voters. It represented an inchoate movement for 'betterment' that could be depicted as cheaper government in Manitoba, cleaner government in Saskatchewan, regionally and occupationally fairer government in Nova Scotia or Ottawa, and, in every venue, democratic and godly government. William Irvine, the Alberta minister and farm-labour MP, wrote at this time: 'The line between the sacred and the secular is being rubbed out' because 'everything is becoming sacred.' The ideals of the social gospel became, for many, the ideals of the political movement. Salvation was thus transformed into a matter of concern to legislatures.[7]

Despite their apparent consensus on the nation's ills, Progressives never did agree on a diagnosis or a remedy. Two schools of Progressive thought can be distinguished for purposes of discussion. The dominant perspective in the early 1920s, led by T.A. Crerar, president of the United Grain Growers and cabinet minister in the Union government, was strongest in Manitoba and Saskatchewan and most complacent about the achievements of prairie society. As represented by Crerar and his two allies, George Chipman of the *Grain Growers' Guide* and John Dafoe of the *Manitoba Free Press,* these 'Manitoba' Progressives believed that a few changes in federal policy would effect vast improvements in the nation. Most important, they believed that these changes could be achieved within the existing political system. If the Liberal party would adopt a low-tariff plank and shed its big business ties in eastern Canada, the transformation of the party system would be complete. Crerar and Dafoe were the foremost exponents of the western mission to the nation. The democracy and opportunity of the region had permitted them and, in their observation, hundreds of thousands of others to get a new start and to establish a secure existence. If only these principles could be communicated to the rest of Canada, they believed, it would become one of the world's finest societies.[8]

The second perspective was expressed by H.W. Wood, president of the United Farmers of Alberta, and was strongest in that province and among some Ontario farmers.[9] These 'Albertans' shared neither Crerar's satisfaction with the contemporary west nor Dafoe's confidence in the two-party parliamentary system. They argued that Canada's political institutions must be scrapped because big business, by means of its control of secret well-disciplined party caucuses, subverted the will of the people. The Albertans asserted that a new world order was just around the corner: individual and social perfectibility could be achieved when, as appeared likely, the growing hostility of industries, classes, and nations finally drove the competitors to acknowledge that 'co-operation' alone would save them from extinction. The victory of this superior principle—that is, recognition that co-operation arose from and superseded 'competition' as the fundamental organizing principle in society—would be achieved in the domestic political arena when the futile wars of the obsolete party system were replaced by the harmony of 'group government.'[10]

Though never entirely explained, group government depended on an assumption that economic interests provided individuals with their primary identity. Thus the inevitable emergence of economic organizations based on the division of labour, in the Albertan perspective, would intensify the conflict among labourers, capitalists, and farmers until they agreed to co-operate for the good of all. Achievement of group government and of 'co-operation,' an extraordinary departure for any society, was the Albertan equivalent of the syndicalists' general strike or the revolutionary socialists' day of proletarian revolution. According to Calgary's philosopher-politician William Irvine, group government would be the farmers' great contribution to social harmony—because farmers, of all the occupational groups, realized the virtues of co-operation: 'Although fathered by oppression, the farmers' movement has escaped that bitterness of feeling against capital, and that extreme rashness both of expression and action, so characteristic of labor. The farmer, in reality, combines in his own profession, the two antagonists. He is both capitalist and laborer. He knows that production is not furthered when war is going on between the two. He sees, also the hopeless deadlock between organized capital and organized labor in the world of industry and commerce, and is thus led to the discovery of co-operation as the synthesis without which progress cannot be made.'[11] Here was an alternate vision of the world and an alternate version of the reform mission. Rooted in the western Canadian preference for non-partisan politics and also in the national demand for reform, it was also a rejection—at least in part—of the Marxists' insistence on the primacy of property relations. Instead, the Albertans added a form of British guild socialism—an evolutionary rather than a revolutionary outlook—to reform Darwinism and co-operativism.[12] And they insisted that the very process of farming created a 'class' or occupational identity.

Manitoban and Albertan Progressives shared aspects of an outlook. Both were reformist in comparison to the revolutionary socialists of the labour movement because they accepted then-current relations of property. Both believed the old-line political parties were corrupt tools of the Big Vested Interests (so-called, according to farmer-philosopher E.A. Partridge, because of the size of the owners' vests). But the Albertans were more radical than the Manitobans and, in their way, as radical as any member of the One Big Union, because they believed that a change in the political system could transform power and status relations in an entire society. Marxists would condemn as naive the Albertans' refusal to tinker with the ownership of property; conservatives would smile at their ideal of individual and social perfectibility; but the Albertans did make an important contribution to the shaping of Canadian political institutions.

At first glance, Progressivism must seem an utter failure. It collapsed quickly in the Maritimes, was merely a one-term administration in Ontario, and never did achieve power in Saskatchewan. The farm governments in Manitoba and even in Alberta, despite the professed ideology of the 'Albertan' camp, accepted the conventions and customs of the parliamentary system, including the leading role of the cabinet, caucus discipline, and advisory but not authoritative party meetings. Both prairie farmer governments were noted for responsible, cautious, even conservative legislation and administration in the 1920s. There was nothing in the provincial record, it might appear, that suggested long-term significance for this reform outburst.

The federal Progressives seemed to be even less effective. Though they briefly controlled the balance of power in the House of Commons, and were sufficiently numerous to be offered the leadership of His Majesty's Opposition, they were caught between the Manitobans' desire for rapid reform of the party system and the Albertans' determination to create a new governmental structure.[13] In the end, dread of caucus discipline led them to reject both coalition with the Liberals and the leadership of the opposition. Instead, they sat as a third force in the House of Commons, voted as individuals rather than a party, and gradually lost their force and their purpose. Crerar resigned as their leader in 1922, to be replaced by the mild Robert Forke, and, by the time of the budget debate in 1924, when they suffered a serious split, their effectiveness had ended. They elected only 24 MPS in the 1925 general election and 20 in 1926, by which time they were obviously a spent force on the national scene. The fall of the Progressive party was as abrupt as its rise.

The collapse of the Progressive movement in national electoral politics and its apparent conservatism in prairie provincial politics should not be construed as proof of its futility. Rather, as the experienced journalist, John Dafoe commented, progressivism remained a vital force in public life: 'The Progressives represented a western outlook, which has not vanished by any means. If it does not present itself through the media of Progressives it will appear in some other form. That point should not be lost sight of.'[14] Its ideals underlay the organization of the wheat pools and the consumer co-operatives. Its successes included partial restoration of the Crow rate. Its sense of mission was an important influence in the creation in 1925 of a new national Protestant church, the United Church of Canada, from the Methodist, Presbyterian, and Congregational churches. And its determination to counteract the rise of powerful industrial and merchant capitalists found an outlet in other better-organized, better-based political movements. Of these, the most important in the long run, though only a splinter in the 1920s, was the labour group. Thus progressivism should be seen as a step in the development of a Canadian critique of monopoly capitalism. It collapsed because its tactics and leadership were insufficient to meet the challenges of the time.

Notes

1. Paul Fussell *The Great War and Modern Memory* (New York 1977) 157-8

2. Sarah Carter 'Material Culture and the W.R. Motherwell Home' *Prairie Forum* 8 no 1 (1983) 99-111; Ian Clarke, Lyle Dick, Sarah Carter *Motherwell Historic Park* History and Archaeology no 66 (Ottawa 1983)

3. Thompson *Harvests* 153-61; Robert Craig Brown *Robert Laird Borden: A Biography* II 1914-1937 (Toronto 1980)

4. *Manitoba Free Press* 13 May 1916

5. W.L. Morton *The Progressive Party in Canada* (Toronto 1950)

6. The platforms are reprinted in ibid 300-5. As T.A. Crerar, soon to be the leader of the movement, explained to Alberta farm leader H.W. Wood, the Progressives 'must proceed on broad, sane lines of policy, and not from a sectional or class point of view'; Crerar to Wood, 15 March 1918, in George Chipman Papers, Queen's University.

7. Richard Allen 'The Social Gospel as the Religion of the Agrarian Revolt' in Carl Berger and Ramsay Cook eds *The West and the Nation: Essays in Honour of W.L. Morton* (Toronto 1976) 181-4, 185

8. Morton *The Progressive Party* 106-19, 160-4; Ramsay Cook *The Politics of John W. Dafoe and the Free Press* (Toronto 1963); Ian MacPherson 'George Chipman and the Institutionalization of a Reform Movement' Historical and Scientific Society of Manitoba *Transactions* series III no 32 (1975-6) 53-65

9. C.B. Macpherson *Democracy in Alberta: Social Credit and the Party System* (Toronto 1953); W.L. Morton 'The Social Philosophy of Henry Wise Wood' in A.B. McKillop ed *Contexts of Canada's Past: Selected Essays of W.L. Morton* (Toronto 1980)

10. Reginald Whittaker, Introduction to the Carleton Library Edition, in William Irvine *The Farmers in Politics* first pub 1920 (Toronto 1976) XV-XXV

11. Irvine *Farmers* 101-2

12. Ian MacPherson 'Selected Borrowings: The American Impact upon the Prairie Co-operative Movement, 1920-39' *Canadian Review of American Studies* 10 no 2 (fall 1979)

13. The party standings after the 1921 elections were Liberals 116, Progressives 65, Conservatives 50, Labour 2, other 2.

14. *Manitoba Free Press* 30 October 1925

CHAPTER

9 THE GREAT DEPRESSION AND UNEMPLOYMENT POLICIES

The "Great Depression" of the 1930s almost haunts Canada. Fear of a similar catastrophe and comparisons with current difficulties pervaded both academic and non-academic literature as well as political programmes for fifty years afterwards. The economists dominated the early studies on the 1930s, followed closely by political apologists for one or the other of the Bennett Conservatives or the King Liberals. Some of the best studies concentrated on the third parties, especially the Cooperative Commonwealth Federation, the *Union Nationale* and Social Credit, and their impact on political culture. There was also a significant body of Marxist literature, which stressed the failures of the system, but which also emphasized the conditions of the destitute, primarily the single males. While all of these works made token reference to the pain and suffering during the 1930s, especially in the West, most were concerned with political, ideological or developmental agendas of one sort or another. To the economists, for example, the depression provided the justification for their Keynesian and post-Keynesian models.

By the 1970s a more dispassionate examination of the 1930s began to take place, although the political aspects continued to dominate. In the first selection, "Canadian Unemployment Policy in the 1930s," James Struthers offers a revisionist view of the convoluted positions taken by federal leaders, though his content remains traditional and his essential concern is with politics. His final comment demonstrates his cynicism about the leadership: "By 1945, then, Canadians were finally ready to fight the Great Depression of the 1930s."

The depression they planned to avoid was the one with long lines of destitute men at soup kitchens, with crowds of men in relief camps or riding the rails, and with threatening masses of men on picket lines. Rarely did images of women enter the picture, yet women were perhaps even greater victims in the 1930s than men. It was women who were left behind to make do when the men hit the rails. It was women who had to raise the children, often without any assistance. It was women who had to serve potatoes three times a day, if they had them, and it was women who had to lay the dead when the men were away. While the plight of women has been graphically recorded in books like *The Wretched of Canada* (1972), edited by L.M. Grayson and Michael Bliss, and Barry Broadfoot's *Ten Lost Years, 1929-1939: Memories of Canadians Who Survived the Depression* (1973), some suspect a conspiracy of silence over their condition in that decade. After all, there were hundreds of thousands of unemployed women, and where are their pictures? They are the subject of Ruth Roach Pierson's "Gender and the Unemployment Insurance Debates in Canada, 1934-1940." If Pierson is correct it was not an oversight that women were excluded both from images of the Depression and the beneficence of the government. "Masculine independence and feminine dependence" were consciously legislated by a patriarchal system that discriminated on the basis of gender.

Suggestions for Further Reading

Bird Patricia, "Hamilton Working Women in the Period of the Great Depression," *Atlantis*, VIII, no. 2 (Spring 1983), 125-136.

Broadfoot, Barry, *Ten Lost Years, 1929-1939: Memories of Canadians Who Survived the Depression*. Toronto: Doubleday, 1973.

Coulter, Rebecca, "Young Women and Unemployment in the 1930s: The Home Service Solution," *Canadian Women Studies*, VII, no. 4 (Winter 1986), 77-80.

Dumas, Evelyn, *The Bitter Thirties in Quebec*, trans. Arnold Bennett. Montreal: Black Rose Books, 1975.

Grayson, L.M., and Michael Bliss, eds., *The Wretched of Canada: Letters to R.B. Bennett, 1930-1935*. Toronto: University of Toronto Press, 1972.

Horn, Michiel, ed., *The Dirty Thirties: Canadians in the Great Depression*. Toronto: Copp Clark, 1972.

Struthers, James, *No Fault of Their Own: Unemployment and the Canadian Welfare State, 1914-1941*. Toronto: University of Toronto Press, 1983.

CANADIAN UNEMPLOYMENT POLICY IN THE 1930s

James Struthers

I

One of the problems of discussing unemployment during the Great Depression is the danger of becoming overcome by a sense of déja vu. Today unemployment officially stands at over 12% of the workforce; perhaps as many as 2,000,000 Canadians are without work and according to the Economic Council of Canada the jobless total is unlikely to drop below 10% until 1987. Yet despite these appalling figures, our government, as in the 1930s, tells us it cannot act to create jobs because its first priority must be to reduce the deficit in order to restore business confidence.

Although the arguments behind today's economic policies are certainly different from those of the 1930s, many of the essential moral homilies remain unchanged. Canadians in the 1980s, like their parents and grandparents of the 1930s, are being told they can't expect to hope for recovery without practising severe restraint, self-discipline, hard work, and much tightening of belts. Despite these frightening parallels, however, we haven't yet been surrounded by soup kitchens, relief camps, food vouchers, bankrupt provincial governments, and trainloads of hungry single men 'riding the rods' in search of work or relief. Yet all these sights and problems were characteristic of the failure of governments to respond to unemployment during the 1930s. Why this was so I'll attempt to explain in this paper.

To a large extent the unemployment policies pursued by R.B. Bennett and Mackenzie King in the 1930s were continuations of approaches and attitudes towards joblessness that had been widespread in Canada before 1930. Canadians had become well acquainted with cyclical unemployment—or trade depressions as they were then called—well before the 'dirty thirties.' The 1870s, the early 1890s, and the years 1907-08, 1913-15, and 1920-25, were all periods of heavy unemployment in this country. From this perspective it's best to think of the Great Depression as simply the most intense and long-lasting of a series of "waves" of unemployment which battered all western industrial economies during the last half of the 19th and first third of the 20th centuries.

Because of our climate we were also quite familiar with seasonal unemployment. Canada is infamous for being an 'eight months country.' Each winter tens of thousands of Canadians working in the country's great outdoors industries—construction, agriculture, forestry, fishing, and transportation—routinely lost their jobs, often for up to six months of the year due to bad

From *Windy Pine Occasional Paper No. 2* (Peterborough: Canadian Studies Programme, Trent University, 1984). Reprinted by permission of Trent University.

weather. Even in the boom years of the so-called 'roaring twenties' (1926-29), winter unemployment rates averaged well over 10% of the workforce. So the sight of hungry, jobless men walking the streets in search of work or relief was quite familiar to most urban-dwellers in Canada.

Why, then, did the Great Depression take us so much by surprise? Why, for example, didn't Canada follow Great Britain's lead in 1911 by devising new institutions and policies, such as a national system of unemployment insurance and a state employment service, to cope with the problem of joblessness? There were a number of reasons for our unpreparedness but three were particularly important. In the first place, seasonal unemployment was predictable. Winter was a fact of Canadian life; therefore, newspapers, politicians, businessmen, and others argued that workingmen should save up enough money during the summer to tide themselves and their families over the winter. Moreover, it was simply assumed (without any evidence) that wages for seasonal labour were high enough to allow them to do so. To provide the seasonally unemployed with relief, it was argued, would discourage habits of thrift, frugality, and self-reliance.

As for cyclical unemployment, attitudes towards this problem were shaped by two factors. First, recovery in the past had always occurred eventually. The market did correct itself. Therefore, all a country could do was to 'tough it out' by practising restraint and doing nothing to discourage business confidence, especially on the part of foreign investors. Secondly, Canada was a New World society with a developing farm frontier. It was also a country which, in the three decades before 1930, had become increasingly preoccupied with rural depopulation. And it was a country in which farmers were still politically powerful and were continually complaining about the shortage of farm help at affordable wages. For these reasons, legislation such as unemployment insurance, which might be appropriate in more crowded, congested, and highly urbanized societies such as Great Britain, was deemed by business and farm leaders to be inappropriate for Canada. There was always work for the unemployed, even if only for room and board and little more, they argued, on the nation's farms during the winter. If life in the city was made too easy through doles and unemployment insurance for the idle, might not even more men and women be encouraged to leave the land altogether?

Finally, working-class political pressure, in the form of strong trade unions and labour parties, was extremely weak in Canada before World War II. Farmers and businessmen, on the other hand, were politically powerful. Hence governments responded to their views on the unemployment question and not to the views of those who were most likely to become unemployed.

As a result of these attitudes, Canadian governments, although well acquainted with unemployment before 1930, were hopelessly ill-equipped for dealing with it. No one kept unemployment statistics; there was no efficient state employment service; no public welfare departments existed at the federal or provincial level and there were only four at the municipal level. In all of Canada before 1930 there were less than 400 trained social workers. Relief, where available, was granted by private religious charities or by 19th century poor law "Houses of Industry," both of which operated at the local level. In Toronto as late as 1932, jobless men still had to line up at the local House of Industry, first built in the 1830s, to get a bag of groceries or a basket of coal and were expected to saw wood or break rocks in exchange for this miserly relief. Moreover, with the brief exception of the years 1920-21, when the threat of unemployed World War I veterans loomed large throughout Canada, provincial governments along with Ottawa denied any responsibility for coming to the aid of the jobless. Public relief where given was an exclusively local matter financed solely out of local taxes, chiefly on property. One of the sad ironies of the "dirty thirties" was that although no other country, except perhaps the United States, was more economically devastated by the Great Depression than Canada, no other country was as ill-prepared for dealing with its consequences. On the eve of 1930 we lacked even the bare bones of a permanent welfare structure for relieving those in need.

II

The origins of Canadian unemployment policy in the Depression lie within the 1930 federal election. On the one hand Mackenzie King went into the election—at a time when unemployment was about 12%—denying that there was a jobless problem and bragging that he would not give a 'five cent piece' to any Tory provincial government for unemployment relief. King also claimed that the whole idea of an unemployment crisis was simply a Conservative pre-election plot.

Bennett, on the other hand, made what from our perspective today seem like recklessly extravagant promises. He claimed he would 'end unemployment,' 'abolish the dole,' and provide 'work and wages for all who wanted it.' Not surprisingly, Bennett won the election, largely on the strength of his promises to do something about the unemployment crisis.

Despite the boldness of his rhetoric, however, (which reflected his egotism, arrogance, and over-confidence in his own abilities) Bennett really had very traditional ideas about how to deal with unemployment. Like King, he believed the problem in 1930 was largely a seasonal and temporary phenomenon which would quickly right itself. Unlike King, Bennett as a good Tory, also believed that sharply boosting the protective tariff would stimulate investor confidence, create jobs by reducing reliance upon imports, and ultimately force other nations to lower their trading barriers against Canadian exports. It was through these tariff hikes that Bennett hoped to 'end unemployment.'

But these hikes would take time to produce results. Since Bennett had promised to provide jobs immediately, he also introduced a $20,000,000 emergency relief act in the summer of 1930 to tide people over with what was expected to be a difficult winter. $16,000,000 was to be spent on public works and, most significantly, the projects were to be administered by local and provincial governments who together were expected to contribute 75% of their cost. Unemployment relief, Bennett insisted like King before him, was primarily a local responsibility. Ottawa's help was on a temporary, emergency basis only, and would last only until the effects of his tariff hike were felt.

Through providing money for relief projects such as provincial road-building Bennett also hoped to deal with another pressing problem. Transient, unemployed single men, largely immigrants, were trapped in Canadian cities because the lumber, construction, and agricultural industries which normally drew them out of cities were closed down. Such men, cut off from family ties, coming from different cultural backgrounds, and with nothing to lose, were considered to be a serious menace to law and order. Bennett's relief projects would draw them out of the cities and put money into their pockets for the winter months ahead.

Between the fall of 1930, when he first took office, and the spring of 1932, Bennett adhered to this policy of using public works or relief works as they were called, to fight unemployment. Indeed, throughout the fiscal year 1931-32 his government spent almost $50,000,000 or more than twice as much as it had the previous year on this approach. Nevertheless, by the spring of 1932 unemployment stood above 20% of the workforce and the federal deficit was over $151,000,000, almost half of total government revenue for that year. As a result, Bennett quickly became disillusioned with public works as a means of relieving unemployment.

In the first place, he had used this approach only as a temporary stop-gap expedient. Neither he nor anyone in his government were believers in Keynesian deficit-spending as a way out of depression; therefore there was no expectation that public employment could be used in itself as a recovery strategy. Moreover, by 1932 it had become obvious that the Depression was more than a 'temporary' problem. Secondly, by 1932, local and provincial governments, especially in the west, could no longer afford to pay their 75% share of the cost of these increasingly expensive relief works and Bennett had no intention of assuming a larger share of the cost. Finally, Bennett and Canadian businessmen were increasingly alarmed at the size of the federal deficit and the level of taxation which in themselves appeared to be a threat to investor confidence, and hence a barrier to recovery.

For all these reasons, then, Bennett reversed his unemployment policy in the spring of 1932 virtually abandoning reliance on public works and instead depended almost solely upon direct relief or the provision of a 'dole' to tide the unemployed over the worst of the Depression until recovery began. His chief unemployment policy, now that tariffs and public works had failed, was to attempt to eliminate the deficit and to balance the federal budget. This meant keeping expenditure on the jobless down to the lowest level consistent with their physical survival. At the same time, Bennett also refused to modify his policy that unemployment relief was primarily a provincial and local responsibility. His government would pay only one-third the cost of direct relief in any town or city and would contribute nothing to the costs of its administration.

III

Once Bennett opted for a policy of direct relief as his sole remaining means of dealing with unemployment, he entered into a nightmare of contradictions, ironies, and paradoxes which he had never anticipated and which would ultimately destroy his administration. Five such anomalies were of particular importance. The first was the paradox of residency requirements for relief. Since local governments, under Bennett's policy, had to assume anywhere from one-third to one-half the cost of relief on a rapidly diminishing and highly regressive property tax base, they attempted to limit their own relief costs in the only way possible, namely by restricting eligibility for relief to their own municipal residents. Only those who could prove anywhere from six months to, in some cases, three years continuous residence in a city before applying for the dole were deemed eligible to receive it. In a country like Canada with a geographically diverse and highly mobile labour market, many of the unemployed who had been on the road looking for work could not qualify for relief when they needed it. To get the dole they had to return to their home town which they had left in the first place because there was no work. Bennett's policy, then, discouraged the unemployed from looking for work outside their town or city for fear of becoming ineligible for relief.

Transients also posed a contradiction. Tens of thousands of Canada's unemployed were immigrant, seasonal workers—bunkhouse men—who by the very nature of their work on the frontier could not qualify for relief in any city. Bennett's earlier public works policy had, in part, been intended once again to get them out of urban areas. Now, without public works, they had no choice but to drift back into Canadian cites where they could find neither relief nor work. As a result, transient single men 'riding the rods' from town to town were quickly recognized as a serious menace to law and order. Since the cities refused to assume responsibility for them, and since Bennett refused to assume responsibility for relief, he decided upon another alternative suggested to him by General Andrew McNaughton of the Canadian army—relief camps, run by the Defense Department. Here the men could be kept out of the cities, provided with room, board, and clothing and put to work on useful projects to preserve their morale. There was only one hitch. Since Bennett had already abandoned public works as a relief policy, the men couldn't be paid a wage, not without arousing serious unrest from married unemployed men on direct relief. Instead they were paid a 20¢ daily 'allowance' in return for their labour in the camps.

Why would single men go into such camps for 20¢ a day? Cut off from direct relief in the cities, they had no choice except starvation, which is why the 20,000 men in the camps after 1933 quickly referred to them as 'slave camps' and ultimately organized the relief camp strike and 'On to Ottawa Trek' of 1935, which ended in a bloody two hour riot with the RCMP in Regina. As one camp inhabitant cynically put it in 1933, 'You come in broke, work all winter and still you are broke. It looks like they want to keep us bums all our lives.'

Relief standards posed a third source of contention. By insisting on primary local and provincial responsibility for the financing of relief, and by assuming no share in the cost of administering relief, Bennett's government ensured that relief scales—that is, how much money or its equivalent in food vouchers a family would receive—varied dramatically from city to city, depending upon the health of local economies and the political complexion of local city councils. A survey by the Canadian Welfare Council of relief standards in 50 Canadian cities during September 1936 showed just how far such scales of aid could differ. In London, Ontario, a family of five could receive no more than $40.39 a month for food, fuel, and shelter costs. That same family in Toronto could get $58.87; in Hamilton $34.40; in Ottawa $45.32; in Quebec City $26.66; in Calgary $60.00; and in Halifax a mere $18.86. Such gross variations in support within cities of comparable living costs was, of course, morally indefensible. Within Ontario, the Canadian Association of Social Workers discovered, in a survey of 107 municipalities, that not one provided the food allowance recommended by the Ontario Medical Association as the minimum necessary to maintain nutritional health. Food allowances in Toronto alone were 40% below the minimum standard which the League of Nations defined as necessary to maintain health. Since Bennett had promised, when elected in 1930, to 'abolish the dole,' such gross variations and substandard levels of support in a policy of direct relief which his administration had initiated, was political catastrophe.

The bankruptcy of first local and then provincial governments was the fourth disastrous consequence of Bennett's relief policy. By insisting that local and provincial governments were to be held primarily responsible for the cost of relief, Bennett's unemployment policy concentrated the fiscal cost of the Depression where its impact was greatest—that is, in western Canada. By 1932, all four western provinces were technically bankrupt because of the cost of paying their two-thirds share of direct relief and were only kept solvent by continual federal loans and grants. By 1937 Ottawa would be paying 85% of all relief costs in Saskatchewan; 71% in Alberta; 69% in British Columbia; and 68% in Manitoba; while still insisting that relief was a local responsibility. In Ontario and Quebec, in contrast, Ottawa paid only 29% and 32% respectively of relief costs.

To give an equally paradoxical example of the contradictions of this policy, in Forest Hill, a very wealthy area of Toronto with few unemployed, per capita relief costs to taxpayers averaged only $4.00 a month in 1934. In East York, a working-class borough only a few miles away, with almost 50% of its population on relief, the cost of the dole averaged $25.00 a month per taxpayer. Yet the people of Forest Hill, in many cases, were the employers of those living in East York. By drawing municipal boundary lines around themselves, they could enjoy the lowest relief taxes in Canada and shove the burden of the Depression onto their unfortunate employees.

The final irony of direct relief was the fact that you had to be totally destitute to receive it. Insurance policies, bank savings, home equity, automobiles, everything of value had to be liquidated in many municipalities before a family could become eligible for the dole. Hence, what was the point of saving for a rainy day if you knew beforehand that all your assets would be confiscated before you could become eligible for aid? Far better to spend your money while you had it, since if you lost your job you would soon be just as badly off as the man down the road who had saved nothing.

IV

Because of contradictions such as these, by 1933-34 Bennett was desperately looking for alternatives to his relief policy. There were two directions he could go. The first, urged increasingly by the provinces, the municipalities, organized labour, some social workers, and the unemployed, was to take over total responsibility for unemployment relief instead of continuing to contribute on a one-third basis. Had Bennett followed this option, residency requirements for relief could have been abolished; the provinces, particularly in the west, and the municipalities would once again have been fiscally solvent; and most importantly the levels of assistance for families on the dole across Canada could have been raised to a national minimum standard sufficient to ensure that everyone received at least enough food, shelter, and clothing to remain healthy and to enjoy reasonably decent living standards.

Bennett had absolutely no interest in taking this route, however. In the first place, it would have cost far more to the federal government, already concerned primarily in reducing, not increasing, its deficit. Secondly, it would have necessitated the creation of a permanent federal welfare bureaucracy at a time when Bennett was still convinced that the unemployment crisis was temporary. Finally, and most importantly, Bennett and his advisors believed that a national minimum standard of relief would increase the numbers of those unemployed. Why? Because wage rates for those already working in Canada, particularly unskilled labourers, had been so lowered by the Depression (clothing workers in Montreal and Toronto, for example, often made only $10.00 for a 60 hour work week) that for a large segment of Canada's working-class a dole which provided healthy and decent living standards would be preferable to work.

This was certainly the conclusion of Charlotte Whitton, Canada's most well-known social worker, an arch social conservative, and Bennett's key advisor on relief policy in the 1930s. In a 1932 report to the government on relief in western Canada, Whitton told Bennett that 40% of those living off the dole on the prairies didn't really need it; that the very existence of direct relief in the west was drawing tens of thousands of farm families into the western cities during the winter, thus artificially boosting the unemployment rate; and that by contributing to local and provincial relief efforts, Bennett's government had only succeeded in making thousands of immigrant and poor rural families "permanently dependent at a scale of living which they never had and never will be able to provide for themselves."

With this kind of advice coming from the chief executive of the Canadian Welfare Council it was small wonder that Bennett himself concluded in 1934 that the people had become "more or less relief-conscious and were determined to get out of the Government, whether it be municipal, provincial, or federal, all they could." Instead of opting to take over total responsibility for unemployment relief, Bennett decided over the winter of 1934 to move in exactly the opposite direction: to sever all of Ottawa's ties with the dole and turn the whole ugly, embarrassing business completely back to the provinces and municipalities.

From this perspective, unemployment insurance, which the British had pioneered in 1911, began to appear more and more attractive as a policy alternative for the Bennett government. In the first place, at a time when unemployment still hovered at 20% of the workforce, Bennett simply could not withdraw from direct relief and abdicate all responsibility for the jobless. He had to have some political alternative to put in its place. Unemployment insurance fit the bill nicely for a number of reasons. Businessmen, particularly bankers and insurance company and real estate executives, favoured such a measure by 1934. These financial organizations now held many worthless municipal and provincial bonds and had become convinced that direct municipal relief was a highly inefficient way to finance the costs of unemployment. Far better, such businessmen argued, to build up an unemployment fund in good times through insurance premiums which could be used to aid the jobless during depressions. Better yet, unemployment insurance seemed to reinforce thrift. Since the premiums were compulsory, it forced workers to defer part of their incomes for a rainy day. Thus, unlike the dole, it didn't reduce everyone to complete and utter destitution before they could become eligible for aid. Moreover, because 80% of the cost of unemployment insurance could be financed by compulsory premiums paid by workers and employers, it would cost the federal government only a fraction of what was presently being spent on relief. As a result, unlike the dole, unemployment insurance would not interfere as directly with the widely shared desire among businessmen to see a balanced federal budget.

Finally, precisely because it was called unemployment "insurance," actuarial science, not nutritional standards of human need, could provide an arbitrary ceiling on benefits which in any case would always be kept to a fixed percentage of existing wage rates. In this way unemployment insurance seemed to pose no threat to the market-determined distribution of income. Under the legislation Bennett eventually introduced in the early months of 1935, Canadians had to work a minimum of forty weeks over two years to be eligible for any benefits whatsoever, which in any case were set at a maximum of $11.40 a week for a family of five, almost 40% below the $17.30 a week which the Montreal Council of Social Agencies recommended as the minimum amount necessary to maintain health.

Under Bennett's unemployment insurance act, then, only those workers who were most regularly employed could qualify for benefits and the levels were set low enough to ensure that in no case would life on unemployment insurance be preferable to any form of work offered by Canadian employers anywhere in the country. In other words, unemployment insurance, as drafted by Bennett's advisors, was designed to reinforce the work ethic and to provide a perfect political cover for a federal withdrawal from relief. It was not designed to reduce poverty or to provide unemployed Canadians with a level of support adequate to maintain health and decency.

Most importantly, unemployment insurance offered nothing to the 1.2 million Canadians who were already on relief in 1935. Since their family breadwinners were obviously not working, they could not pay any premiums or qualify for benefits. It was a good idea for future depressions, but unemployment insurance really provided no solution to the problems of the 1930s.

Nevertheless, Bennett proceeded with his strategy. In June 1934, he told the premiers that all federal support for relief would be cut off on August 1st. After tremendous political pressure, he subsequently modified this policy to a 22% federal cut-back in relief spending. Then, in September, Bennett asked the provinces whether they would be willing to surrender their exclusive jurisdiction over unemployment insurance to Ottawa. Outraged by his high-handed pressure tactics and unilateral cut-backs, the premiers understandably refused. As a result, faced with an election and almost certain defeat in 1935, Bennett simply introduced his unemployment insurance bill in Parliament as part of his package of New Deal reforms, knowing full well that without provincial agreement the bill was probably unconstitutional and hence useless, as indeed it turned out to be.

After five years in office, Bennett went down to spectacular defeat in the 1935 election, his party losing all but 39 seats. He also left a very meagre legacy for his successor, the Liberal leader Mackenzie King. The attempt to provide work for the jobless had been abandoned after 1932; relief standards across Canada were grossly inadequate everywhere; four provincial governments were technically bankrupt; single unemployed men in the relief camps had walked out and rioted in their attempt to reach Ottawa; and unemployment insurance, the only creative piece of legislation on the jobless crisis to emerge from Bennett's administration, was clearly unconstitutional.

V

In what ways, if any, did Mackenzie King pursue different policies for the remainder of the Depression? Unlike Bennett in 1930, King made no promises in the 1935 election beyond pledging to provide sober, orderly government. As a result, he had no political I.O.U.'s to redeem. In fact, the most striking aspect of King's unemployment policy is that from December 1935 until the spring of 1938 it was virtually a carbon copy of Bennett's. In the first place, he continued to insist that the jobless were primarily a local and provincial responsibility. Secondly, after a quick hike in federal relief contributions immediately after the election, King began systematically to cut back on Ottawa's support of the dole to such an extent that by 1937, in cities such as Winnipeg, Ottawa was paying only 20% of relief costs and on a national basis, only 30%, compared to the one-third share Bennett had paid throughout most years of his administration. Like the Tory prime minister, King's first priority was to balance the budget.

King's administration also refused to define any national minimum standard of relief, based on medical or nutritional standards. Instead, his government defined a national *maximum*. In October 1937 King's minister of labour, Norman Rogers, announced that Ottawa would in no province pay more than 30% of the dole's cost, and in every city the standard of living on relief had to be kept below the average going rate for unskilled labour in the surrounding area, in order that "work incentives" could be enforced. This policy was adopted at a time when most provinces had no minimum wage for men.

Although King did abolish Bennett's hated relief camps for single men in 1936, the alternative he put in their place was, in many ways, much worse. This was a farm placement scheme which paid about 45,000 of Canada's single unemployed $5.00 a month to work on farms across the country. This was less than the infamous 20¢ daily "allowance" the men had received in the camps, and there was no guarantee that food, clothing, shelter, and medical care provided by individual impoverished farmers across Canada would be comparable to what the army had offered in the relief camps. As one army commander pointed out when the camps were shut down in 1936 and many men refused to leave, "the men prefer to stay where they have 'regular hours' and good food, rather than leave for farms, where they have to work harder, longer hours, and for lower wages, with a possibility that they may not collect their wages in the fall." Although cynical in its conception, King's farm placement scheme nonetheless did solve the problem of chronic unrest among transients. Spread out individually across Canada rather than concentrated in the camps, single men proved almost impossible to organize politically after 1936.

King's overall unemployment strategy duplicated Bennett's in two other ways. As Bennett had done after 1932, until the severe recession of 1938, King rejected public works as an antidote to unemployment, in marked contrast to the massive works schemes pioneered by Franklin Roosevelt's New Deal south of the border. Instead, King relied totally on direct relief as a means of caring for the jobless. King also refused to enact an unemployment insurance plan, claiming that the political opposition to the measure by New Brunswick, Quebec, and Alberta made impossible the unanimous consent which he claimed was necessary for a constitutional amendment.

In only two areas did King take actions significantly different from Bennett's. In April 1936 he appointed a National Employment Commission, chaired by Montreal industrialist Arthur Purvis, to investigate the unemployment and relief situation and to come up with recommendations for reform. Secondly, in August 1937, he appointed a Royal Commission on Dominion-Provincial Relations, chaired by Supreme Court justice Newton Rowell, to investigate and attempt to straighten out the tangled web of federal-provincial financial relations, particularly the continuing inability of the western provinces to stay fiscally solvent without federal loans and grants.

The most significant result of both these commissions is that they ended up saying the same thing. The NEC, which reported in January 1938, and the Rowell-Sirois Commission, as it came to be called, which reported in May 1940, both argued that the first step in combatting unemployment and restoring fiscal solvency to the provinces and local governments was for Ottawa to put in place immediately a national employment service and system of unemployment insurance, and to assume total financial and administrative responsibility for unemployment relief. In short, both commissions argued that Ottawa should take the route both Bennett and King had rejected throughout the entire depression, namely to accept primary responsibility for unemployment. The jobless crisis, both commissions argued, was a *national* problem, reflecting Canada's national economy; consequently, relief to those without work should be first and foremost a national responsibility. Only Ottawa through its unlimited taxing power, they argued further, possessed the fiscal strength to pay for these relief costs. Finally, reflecting the new Keynesian sophistication being developed within the department of finance, both commissions concluded that only Ottawa could inject enough purchasing power into the economy through insurance and relief payments and public works to push levels of demand up high enough to stimulate economic growth and thus ultimately to eliminate unemployment.

It would be pleasant to report that after receiving this sensible advice, King realized the error of his ways and reversed his economic policies. In fact, he did no such thing. When he discovered that the NEC was about to recommend federal control of relief, King pulled out every stop he could to kill the Commission's final report. When that proved impossible, thanks to Arthur Purvis' integrity, King simply ignored it. Why? The reason was best expressed by Mary Sutherland, King's closest confidant on the NEC and the author of a dissenting minority report. In it, Sutherland articulated the basis for Ottawa's continued resistance throughout the 1930s to accepting primary responsibility for the jobless. "No matter which government is responsible for and administers relief ...," Sutherland wrote, "there will be constant pressure to increase the benefits and to enlarge the base of admittance to benefits. If responsibility is centralized in the Dominion government, the counter-pressure from local taxpayers will be eased. The irksome, unwelcome, and hard check provided by necessity, by municipal officials, harassed by mounting demands on diminishing revenues, will be removed."

In short, Sutherland, like King and R.B. Bennett, believed that national responsibility for relief would cost too much and would erode the work ethic. If Ottawa controlled relief, it would have to define a national minimum standard of support, or in effect a national poverty line, across the country. In a country like Canada with widely diverse regional wage rates and living standards, such a national minimum would inevitably be higher than existing wage rates for many of the working poor. The result would be to attract this class out of work and onto relief, thus increasing unemployment. Sutherland's argument was, in this sense, almost identical to the one first put forward by Charlotte Whitton in her 1932 report on relief in western Canada. Only by keeping relief a local responsibility and local governments on the edge of bankruptcy could relief costs and benefit levels be kept to the barest minimum.

Ironically, putting more purchasing power directly into the hands of the jobless and their families in the form of higher relief benefits was exactly what *was* needed in order to push up consumption and effective demand to levels that would in turn encourage investment and employment. But as long as the Bennett and King administrations continued to approach the relief question from the angle of its effects upon the work ethic of individuals rather than upon the purchasing power of all the unemployed, they simply could not see this. As a result, in their relief policy, as in their wider economic policies of balanced budgets, a sound dollar, and regressive taxation, Bennett and King inhibited the chances of recovery.

VI

In 1940, after World War II had begun, Canadians finally did see enacted a constitutionally valid scheme of unemployment insurance. The pressures of war and the need for national unity had dissolved the political objections of the three dissenting provinces. More importantly, King's own fear of post-war unemployment, and of how jobless veterans would respond to relief of the 1930s variety, now galvanized him into making unemployment insurance a first priority of the government, particularly with an election looming on the horizon in 1940. Wartime mobilization and the potential labour shortage also gave the federal government a vital need for creating a national employment service, motive which had not been present during the heavy labour surplus of the

1930s. Finally, the necessity for massive war expenditures gave Ottawa an overpowering political argument for trying out new Keynesian ideas such as deliberately incurring large deficits, a policy which would have left most Canadian businessmen aghast in the Depression.

The tragedy of unemployment policy in the 1930s is that strategies for dealing with joblessness which *were* politically possible, indeed essential in the context of the war, were not deemed possible, given Canada's political landscape in the Depression. The essential continuity and the essential failure of the policies pursued by both R.B. Bennett and Mackenzie King lay in their refusal to accept that the unemployed were a national responsibility. This refusal, in turn, was rooted in what might be termed the dilemma of 'less eligibility' in a market economy. In a private enterprise system, business and the market set wage levels and living standards. During the 1930s, for many *working* Canadians, these standards and wages were below what was necessary to ensure a decent and healthy standard of living. As a result, both the Bennett and King governments believed they could not provide higher relief benefits for the jobless without attracting many of the working population onto the dole. Without direct state intervention or trade union pressure to improve working conditions and living standards for low income Canadians, or in other words, without massive intervention into the marketplace, the government felt limited in the benefits it could provide for the unemployed. And in the political context of the 1930s, given the absence of a serious political threat from the left or a strong labour movement, the pressure simply was not there for either Bennett or King to move in a direction that would have been regarded by Canadian businessmen as serious meddling in their affairs.

Only war, with the full employment it would bring and the strong labour union organization it would permit, could create a political climate in which it would be possible to effect these kinds of permanent structural reforms to underpin working-class incomes. By 1945, then, Canadians were finally ready to fight the Great Depression of the 1930s.

GENDER AND THE UNEMPLOYMENT INSURANCE DEBATES IN CANADA, 1934-1940

Ruth Roach Pierson

On 22 January 1935, in a House of Commons debate on the extent of unemployment in Canada, J.S. Woodsworth cited an account of murder and suicide from the *Winnipeg Free Press* of 18 December 1934. A Valour Road man had re-

From *Labour/Le Travail*, XXV (Spring 1990), 77-103. Reprinted by permission of the Canadian Committee on Labour History.

turned to his home to find his baby boy aged 18 months drowned in the bathtub, his five year-old daughter strangled, and his wife poisoned. The wife had come to Canada from England four years previously. The husband had not been able to find steady work for some time. The family had been trying to survive on relief, but, according to the *Free Press,* "there had not even been enough money in the house to buy the poison," a germicide, that the wife had ingested. In the note she had left on the kitchen table, she wrote " 'I owe the drug store 44 cents: farewell.' "[1]

In the narrative of the Great Depression, both as told at the time, and in the main by historians after the fact,[2] it is men who fill the ranks of the unemployed—men who ride the rails, men who stand in the bread-lines, men who sell apples on street corners. Single unemployed women have a shadowy presence at best.[3] The married woman appears not as a person in her own right. If she was employed, she was seen as a symbol of the cause of unemployment among men and, if dependent, as a symbol of the high cost of male unemployment to society.[4] The Great Depression was construed as a period of gender crisis. The focus of concern at the time, however, was masculinity in crisis, for the perception of crisis was framed by the belief that the position of head of household and family provider was an essential property of masculinity, a position that male unemployment undermined. While female unemployment was trivialized, male unemployment was seen not as undermining but rather as intensifying what was believed to be woman's complementary and natural role as nurturant wife and mother.[5]

Given the near invisibility of the army of unemployed women in the perceptions of politicians then,[6] and of mainstream historians more recently, it is not surprising that the subject of the female worker rarely surfaced in the unemployment insurance debates of the 1930s; nor is it surprising that gender issues, and the implications of legislation and policies for women, are not central to James Struthers' classic account of the emergence of Unemployment Insurance in Canada.[7] But if we understand gender to be a fundamental social category, we are justified in asking where and how concern for women fits into the Depression-era discussion of unemployment insurance. And if we further understand gender to be relational, to be a category comprising all that which shapes social relations between the sexes,[8] then we are justified in examining the gender implications for women of the silences regarding them: that is, of the measures that made no mention of them, of the concepts into which they were invisibly enfolded, and of the assumptions through which masculine priority was inscribed.

Unemployment insurance (UI) legislation was introduced and passed in the Commons only once during the Great Depression, in 1935, although a further bill was drafted in 1938. The initial UI legislation appeared as the only developed part of the omnibus Employment and Social Insurance bill which passed third reading in March 1935. But after the election in October resoundingly defeated R.B. Bennett's Conservative government and returned the

Mackenzie King Liberals, the bill was never implemented. Although the bill's easy passage had testified to broad public support,[9] Bennett had not sought the consent of the provincial premiers to the idea of federal jurisdiction over unemployment insurance and other essential social services. When, in 1937-8, King considered introducing an Unemployment Insurance bill similar in basic outline to the UI provisions of the 1935 Act, his fear of effecting Ottawa's jurisdiction over unemployment relief far outweighed his commitment to a federal UI scheme. Because he was also wary of triggering a dominion-provincial jurisdictional row, and knew that the Judicial Committee of the Privy Council of Great Britain had, in December 1936, declared the Employment and Social Insurance Act of 1935 *ultra vires,* King sought the provincial premiers' support for amending the British North America Act to grant constitutionality to federal unemployment insurance legislation. But once it was clear that only six of the nine premiers were prepared to offer unreserved support, King used this lack of unanimity to justify postponing introduction of the UI bill, pending the report of the Royal Commission on Dominion-Provincial Relations. The Rowell-Sirois Commission Report eventually concluded, in February 1940, "that the care of employables who are unemployed should be a Dominion function."[10] But it was the outbreak of war in September 1939 that, as Struthers notes, "created the compelling new reason for unemployment insurance,"[11] namely, the perceived need to safeguard veterans and the enlarged war-time civilian labour force against the widespread unemployment expected in the wake of demobilization and the return to peace-time production. On 18 June 1940, King could tell the Commons that all provinces now agreed to an enabling amendment to allow for the introduction of the UI bill. And on 11 July 1940, he announced British Parliamentary approval of a constitutional amendment giving the federal government power over unemployment insurance.[12] In the first days of August, the legislation quickly passed both houses of the Canadian Parliament and became law.

The debate on unemployment insurance in Canada revolved around these three pieces of legislation: the UI provisions of the Employment and Social Insurance Act of 1935, the Unemployment Insurance Bill of 1938, and the UI Act of 1940. Participants in the debate were many and included Members of Parliament, the ministers of labour, finance, and insurance and their top civil servants, trade union leaders, spokesmen for associations of manufacturers and financial institutions, members of governmental commissions, members of women's organizations, and academic social investigators. Of great influence behind the scenes were A.D. Watson,[13] Chief Actuary, Department of Insurance, and Hugh Wolfenden, his actuarial associate and consultant on contract until their falling out over the 1940 legislation. Also influential was the British expert D. Christie Tait of the International Labour Organization, who was brought in to review the 1938 draft bill and whose views helped shape the

1940 Act. It is in the vision of unemployment insurance articulated in the proposals for, the drafts of, and the responses to UI legislation that we shall search not only for the positioning of women in the scheme but also for the gender assumptions implicitly embedded in the entire discourse. In particular, we want to examine how a sex/gender system was inscribed in the overall conceptualization of unemployment insurance as well as in the paragraphs of draft and enacted legislation and in the administrative structure created for its implementation.[14]

Sex Distinctions in Contribution and Benefit Rates

We can isolate seven components of the legislation that were crucial in determining coverage: the method of calculating amount of contribution and amount of benefit; the provision of dependants' allowances; the setting of an income ceiling; the naming of categories of uninsurable employment (that is, the exception of certain occupations); the imposition of statutory conditions of eligibility for benefit; the qualification period; and the method of calculating the benefit period. In only one of these components was the female sex mentioned explicitly. This was in the 1935 Act's provisions for calculating contributions and benefits. (Married women received explicit mention in the 1935 schedule governing "special cases," and wives in the discussion of and clauses covering dependants' allowances, as we shall see.) The 1935 Act divided all insured persons into four major groups by age, and then further subdivided each group by sex. A flat rate of contribution was set for each sex (always higher for males) within each major age group. Accordingly, in all age categories, girls paid a lower contribution than boys, and women a lower one than men. As benefits were related in part to contributions, it followed that girls would receive lower benefits than boys, and women lower benefits than men of the same age.[15] The flat-rate system and the graduation of the rate according to distinctions of age and sex derived from British unemployment insurance legislation, the general model for the Canadian UI legislation until 1940.[16]

The 1938 draft bill, however, while retaining the four major groups based on age distinctions, eliminated sex distinctions entirely.[17] As Chief Actuary Watson noted in March 1938, the new UI bill was marked by an "absence of any distinction in benefits or contributions as between men and women, or as between boys and girls."[18] Given, as already mentioned, that unemployment in Canada in the 1930s was largely regarded in political and academic circles as a male problem and unemployed women as a consequence received little official concern, and given that the discourse at every level of the society from radio drama to university lecture castigated married women in paid employment for taking jobs from men,[19] how can we account for the 1938 draft bill's elimination of the distinction based on sex?

Insofar as policy analysts, legislators, and political and labour activists thought about women during the Great Depression, they tended to divide them into two categories, that of female worker and that of wife/mother.[20] It was, by and large, ideologically anathema for a woman to combine these two categories in herself.[21] Those who did risked putting themselves outside the solicitous embrace of public policy. Let us consider, for instance, the unwed mother who, by necessity, combined motherhood with work for pay because she was ineligible for a mother's allowance (only one of the provinces with such legislation—British Columbia—provided allowances for unmarried mothers, and then only under exceptional circumstances).[22] Bearing the stigma of having transgressed patriarchal morality and largely bereft of child care facilities,[23] the single mother had to scrounge in the dregs of the job market for employment. A second type of woman who violated the female worker/wife and mother dichotomy was the employed married woman. Even before the Depression, women with paying jobs who married were forced to resign from federal and provincial civil service posts, and from teaching positions and other white-collar jobs.[24] During the Depression, as already has been noted, social censure directed at married women for causing male unemployment intensified.[25] As the Depression worsened, married women's right to employment became an increasingly divisive issue among members of the National Council of Women of Canada as local Councils of Women, and even some Business and Professional Women's Clubs, went on record as opposed to married women working for pay.[26]

Of the two categories, the single woman worker tended to take a back seat in social policy to the wife/mother whom the hegemonic ideology constructed as the dependant of a bread-winning husband/father. The dominant frame in operation at the time, no matter how divergent from social reality,[27] was the conception of the male worker as the head of household and therefore deserving of a 'family wage,'[28] that is, a wage sufficient to support both the man's unwaged children and the children's unwaged, housekeeping mother.[29] This conception would frame the theory informing Leonard Marsh's *Report on Social Security for Canada 1943,* the document regarded as the founding text of 'the welfare state' in Canada.[30]

Hegemonic as this master frame was, it did not completely obscure the existence of women workers nor, provided they were single, totally preclude concern for their welfare. The Left, in particular, admitted the single woman worker into the fold of workers whose interests it sought to protect and advance. But given that the Left was little different from society as a whole in subscribing to the woman as worker/woman as mother dichotomy,[31] it was principally as non-mothers that women and their labour-market interests qualified for the attention of trade union spokesmen and male socialists, communists, and eventually liberals. Usually when trade unionists and left-to-liberal politicians took up the banner of sexual equality, it was for female non-mothers.[32] On the whole, only when thus "desexed"[33] did women workers acquire eligibility for equal treatment. In other words, equality of situation was usually required for women to be considered eligible for equality of treatment. And it was with this understanding of equality between the sexes in mind that J.S. Woodsworth rose in the House, as he did on a number of occasions, to criticize the discrimination according to sex in UI contributions and benefits that was inscribed in the 1935 Act.[34]

In the politically radicalized atmosphere of the Depression, opposition to discrimination on the basis of sex was *de rigeur* among members of the CCF and the CPC. And the "equal treatment of both sexes"[35] as regards contributions and benefits that was incorporated into the 1938 bill reflected the liberal opinion of British expert D. Christie Tait that it was necessary to acknowledge the "increasing reluctance among many people to making such a discrimination in unemployment insurance."[36] The Fifth Convention of the Canadian Federation of Business and Professional Women's Clubs had protested as "unequal pay for equal work" the lower UI contributions and benefits established for girls and women in the 1935 legislation.[37] And the Ottawa Women's Liberal Club had passed a resolution disapproving of "the discrimination between the sexes with regard to the scale of insurance payments and benefits."[38] But the discrimination so signified was less that against dependent wives and mothers than that against single women workers who, in their independent state, were more similar to men. It was possible, in other words, to entertain at one and the same time disapproval of discrimination on the basis of sex and the notion that married women should be supported by their husbands.

Gender in the Flat versus Graded Rates Debate

At the same time, however, the single woman admissible to equality with men on the grounds of independence was crucially different from the large proportion of men in the labour force who were married with dependants.[39] By 1940, those consulted in the revising of the 1938 bill for submission to Parliament were concerned to address the 'social injustice' that they saw entailed in the abandonment of sex categories for setting the rate of contributions and benefits while a flat rate within age categories was retained. Perceived as a 'social injustice' was the flat rate system's non-accommodation of the fact that "men usually have more dependants than women and therefore need a higher benefit."[40] Although both the 1935 Act and the 1938 Bill had provided for dependants' allowances, the amount of allowance was not regarded as sufficient to compensate for the 1938 elimination of the sex-based differential in basic benefit. Clearly, the concept of sexual equality resided uneasily within the master frame of male breadwinner entitled to a 'family wage' to support a dependent wife and children. While the single working woman's independence qualified her for equality with the working man, the married woman's presumed dependence threatened to disqualify her from such equality, and the married male worker claimed a position of more equal than others.[41]

This male claim was based on the concept of the 'family wage.' From its frequent invocations in Commons debates, and from its service as the implicit rationale underpinning dependants' allowances for spouses, one can see that the concept of the 'family wage' was widely accepted as common sense. MPs across party lines invoked the 'family wage' as an ideal or as a principle of social justice. For example, on 12 February 1935, G.D. Stanley of the Conservative Party identified as "the ideal to which [the male worker] strives" the possibility of becoming "self-supporting," which Stanley defined as the condition of a male worker's being able, "during his working years, ... to earn enough to provide for the maintenance of his family during his whole life."[42] On 18 February 1935, Woodsworth of the CCF criticized the capitalist wage system in Canada for the social injustice of "fixing the price of labour" while having "no regard ... to the conditions necessary to maintain the labourer and his wife and family in a state of well-being."[43] And on 9 April 1935, H.B. McKinnon of the Liberal Party made a case for including dependants' allowances in minimum wage legislation on the grounds that "a man with a family of six or seven or eight should be given some consideration over and above what is given to the man who is single."[44]

Civil servant Eric Stangroom of the federal Department of Labour recognized as one of the positive "social effects" of incorporating dependants' allowances within an unemployment scheme the fact that fewer children would be forced into employment, and wives would not be obliged to take on "unsuitable work."[45] Both the 1935 Act and the 1938 draft bill provided for dependants' allowances and allowed that both adults and children could be dependants. The dependant adult was defined in Section 15 (2) of the 1938 draft legislation as "the wife or dependent husband of the insured person, or a female having the care of the dependent children of the insured person."[46] Used without the qualifier "dependent," the term "wife," it should be noted, here bore the social meaning of "dependence" as the very essence of its signification in a way that not even the term "children" did. Moreover, while it was acknowledged that women could have dependent husbands as well as dependent children, it was also assumed by Chief Actuary Watson, among others, that "the dependants of women claimants will be relatively unimportant."[47] Indeed, provision for dependants' allowances was made on the assumption that "the dependants of female wage-earners are relatively few." To support this claim, British data was cited to show that in 1924 only about 2 per cent of working women had adult dependants and only about 2.7 per cent had dependent children.[48] Canadian civil servants assumed, in the complete absence of hard data, that the proportion of female workers with dependent children "would *probably* be lower in Canada as *probably* relatively few women with children are wage earners."[49]

In the discussions surrounding the drafting of the 1940 UI legislation, the question of how to deal in a 'socially just' way with the need of the male head of household for a higher benefit than the single male or female worker turned on the relative merit of a "graded rating" versus the "flat rating schemes" embodied in the 1935 Act and the 1938 Draft Bill.[50] Pivotal to the proposed "graded rating" system was the use of a fixed ratio to allow contributions and benefits to vary in direct relation to income. In other words, the varying amount of contribution to be paid and amount of benefit to be collected were both to be computed in terms of a set proportion of the individual worker's usual earnings.

As early as 1935, Tom Moore of the Trades and Labour Congress of Canada had asked the Senate Committee on Unemployment Insurance to consider "graded benefits 'proportionate to the man's earnings'." William Beveridge had recommended earnings-related contributions and benefits to the British Royal Commission on Unemployment Insurance of 1930-32 (sometimes referred to as the Gregory Commission). The United States had shown a preference for graded rates from the start.[51] By 1938 social policy experts writing in Canada, such as L. Richter in the *Dalhousie Review*[52] and D. Christie Tait in his Report to the Dominion Government,[53] had been criticizing the flat-rate system of contributions and benefits for its unfairness to higher-paid workers. With their deeply entrenched suspicion that the social-insurance recipients would sooner collect benefits than put in a good day's work, many Canadian social-policy drafters and analysts were as wedded to the principle of 'less eligibility' as their British counterparts.[54] In the context of unemployment insurance, honouring this principle meant that the benefit collected had to be set at a level lower than the recipient's usual earnings, otherwise "overinsurance" would occur.[55] Applied within a flat rate system, it meant that contributions and benefits had to be fixed low enough that the insurable worker "earning the lowest rate of wages"[56] would not receive more in UI benefits than his/her normal earnings. According to the 1935 Act and the 1938 Draft Bill, the total benefit possible for a claimant could not exceed 80 per cent of the person's average weekly pay while employed.[57] For so long as they were employed, the more highly-paid insurable workers enjoyed the advantage of contributing a lower proportion of their wages to the UI fund than the less well paid. Once unemployed, however, those who had enjoyed a higher income level would receive in UI benefit a much smaller proportion of their former wages and, as a consequence, would suffer a sharp drop in their standard of living. Following this line of reasoning with respect to Canada's vast regional differences, Labour Minister N.A. McLarty concluded in the Commons debates of 1940 that because "the unemployment benefit can never rise as high as wages, ... the yardstick used to measure UI benefits would necessarily have to be the lowest wages paid in the lowest wage-paid area in the country."[58] It was the graded system's elimination of the leveling effect of the flat-rate system of benefit computation that helped fuel the "strong intellectual argument," noted by Watson in 1940, that the graded system would be more "socially just."[59] Here, clearly, the concept of social justice needs to be read as encompassing the maintenance of wage and salary hierarchies. According to a memo Gerald H. Brown, assistant deputy minister of labour, sent Watson in May 1940, the introduction of graded contributions and benefits would protect the higher standard of living of higher wage earners.[60]

If the existence of wage and salary hierarchies was not perceived as 'socially unjust,' there was some sense that sex-based hierarchies of contribution and benefit might be. The ideology of sexual equality in wages and social benefits was prevalent on the Left, as we have seen, at least insofar as the single female worker could be assimilated to the norm established by the male worker. In 1935, the All Canadian Congress of Labour had raised objections to the system of flat rates graduated "according to age and sex," and recommended its replacement "by a scale of contributions [graded] according to earnings."[61] The 1938 bill had dispensed with sex-based differentiations, but, despite the retention of dependants' allowances, the very removal of sex distinctions in a flat-rate system was seen by some, as mentioned earlier, to violate the principle of the 'family wage,' and penalize the male head of household.[62] The adoption of a system of variable rates, graded according to income, appeared to be the solution to the problem. The differentiation on the basis of sex, by which girls and women in each age group were to pay and receive less in contributions and benefits than boys and men, was "the result," Stangroom reflected in 1939,

> of [a] tradition which has had a bad psychological effect on the efficiency of the woman, who feels she is held cheaply; on the employer, who feels a woman should be paid less; and on the male worker, who feels, from the age of 16 when he enters the scheme, that he is superior by reason of his sex alone.[63]

Stangroom concluded that "an employee contribution equal as to both sexes" should be a feature of any future UI plan contemplated by the Canadian Parliament. Earnings-related contributions and benefits achieved that end and therefore established "a principle more easily defended," for they would not "give to the women wage earners a status of inferiority," as, according to the Ottawa Women's Liberal Club, the 1935 sex-discriminatory provisions had done.[64] Graded contributions and benefits, moreover, "would appeal as more logical and realistic than a division by age and sex."[65] The 1939 response of Watson, the pragmatist, was that "there may, however, be sound reasons for treating men and women technically alike. It certainly does simplify the scheme."[66]

Albeit by 1940, studies showed that the graded system was, in fact, more complicated to administer, in the end it was its potential for creating the illusion of sexual equality that commended the earnings-related system to those concerned with averting charges of sex discrimination. As the May 1940 report comparing flat versus graded rating systems succinctly stated, the latter "dispenses with the sex distinction question, and achieves the same end."[67] In other words, the 1940 adoption of the graded-rates system gave the appearance of formal equality in Canadian UI legislation by eliminating any explicit differentiation in contribution or benefit based on sex. At the same time, however, in the absence of any concurrent social program to change the sexually unequal wage structure of the Canadian labour market, the graded-rate system, calculated as it was in direct relation to individual earnings, implicitly embedded sexual inequality in contributions and benefits into the Canadian unemployment insurance scheme. In the language of the authors of the report outlining the case for the earnings-related system,

> A direct grouping by wages rather than by sex would establish a sounder relationship [between contributions and earnings and between earnings and benefits] which would not be so unfavourable, psychologically, to female labour....

It would, in other words, achieve the desired smoke-and-mirrors effect. At the same time, the report openly acknowledged that the variable-rate system, relative to earnings, would "give public recognition to the common circumstance of lower wages for women as a fixed principle."[68] Given that the report acknowledged that legislated inequality on the basis of sex had a negative psychological effect on women while it simultaneously called for recognition of "the usual difference in wages between men and women" as a matter of "fixed principle," one might paraphrase the report's position as 'No inequality but inequality anyway.' On the one hand, inequality between the sexes would not be explicit in the UI legislation, while on the other there would still be real inequality because women were lower paid than men and would therefore contribute and benefit less.

Provision for Dependants

The earnings-related system, then, was heralded for removing the 'social injustice' of sexual inequality from UI legislation by sleight of hand. Equally important to drafters and supporters was the conviction that the graded rating "does not involve [the] injustice" of penalizing men, who "usually have more dependants than women," as it was believed the flat-rated scheme with no provision for sex categories would have done.[69] Dichotomized into either single female workers or dependent wives and mothers, women as dependants, not independent single women, were the prime objects of social policy throughout the 1930s-1950s, except during the war emergency years. (Women who did not fit into one or the other of these categories tended to fall through the holes of the emerging social security net.) Because the assumption was that most women were dependants, the concept of dependency is the key to understanding many of the gender issues raised in the UI debates.[70] Within the master frame that assigned economic primacy to the man on the grounds of his heading a household of dependants, the claim to dependants' allowances was the logical extension of the claim to a 'family wage.' On this basis, both the 1935 Act and the 1938 UI bill included provisions for dependants' allowances in which a "wife" was by definition classified as a dependant.

Those who were as concerned with expediency as with social justice, like the author of the memo on "The Problem of Dependency in Unemployment Insurance" circulating within the Departments of Labour and Insurance in spring 1940, believed that the 'family wage' should be honoured through provision of dependants' allowances because "the existence of dependants arouses a sense of responsibility in the workman."[71] But for civil servants and their advisors, and the Conservative and Liberal politicians whom they served, the commitment to the 'family wage' and, by extension, dependants' allowances was limited by their concerns about the costs of a social security system, and by their overriding commitment to preserving wage differentials. Throughout the debates on unemployment insurance in Canada, a distinction was drawn between "predictable" and therefore respectable and "insurable" need, on the one hand, and "absolute" need, on the other.[72] UI legislation was never intended to address the latter, the need of the destitute, of the long-term unemployed and of the unemployable. The Dominion Actuary could compare the unemployment insurance scheme proposed in 1940 with the dole, relief, or unemployment assistance and pronounce UI the "soundest socio-economic institution on the whole."[73] But if the first proposed UI legislation had been implemented in 1934 or 1935, a time of high unemployment, it would not have relieved the existing joblessness, as both its authors[74] and its critics[75] well knew. Nonetheless, there were some provisions in the 1935 UI Act, as L. Richter pointed out, that "satisfie[d] the social principle." However restrictedly, they addressed need by providing training and rehabilitation programs, loans for the fares of unemployed men to move to where work was available, and an employment exchange system. Included in the list of provisions addressing need was the "payment of additional benefit for families without any increase of the premium."[76] Asked for his opinion in 1935, an American consultant criticized the inclusion of dependants' allowances in UI plans precisely because they introduced "an element of payment according to need."[77]

By 1940, the issue of whether the new UI bill should or should not include dependants' allowances was muddied by the debate taking place over family allowances.[78] There was a strong belief on the part of some highly placed civil servants in the Departments of Labour, Insurance and Finance that the retention of dependants' allowances in UI legislation and the introduction of family allowances were mutually exclusive. This belief dovetailed with the assumption that the proposed, earnings-related system of setting UI contribution and benefit levels dispensed with the need for dependants' allowances in a UI scheme. It was assumed that, under a graded system that related contributions and benefits directly to earnings, since men earn more, the higher UI benefits they would receive would be sufficient for them to meet their responsibilities as family providers. Dependants' allowances, therefore, could be eliminated. This assumption was used to argue that the graded-rate system would not be more expensive than the flat-rate system because the latter was "accompanied by dependants' allowances" which increased the cost of UI.

Eric Stangroom, in particular, articulated this line of reasoning in a series of memos to Watson in May and June, 1940, on flat versus graded rates and "the problem of dependency." A supporter of an independent scheme of "Family Endowments or Family Allowances regardless of the employment or unemployment status of the breadwinner or breadwinners," Stangroom felt that the retention of dependants' allowances in a UI benefit scheme "would prejudice the introduction of Family Allowance schemes...."[79] Stangroom recognized that having to provide for family dependants had the positive effect of stabilizing a male work force. But in the context of the debate over Family Allowances, Strangroom's desire to detach dependants' allowances from UI led him to argue that dependants' allowances were a matter of need, and need was not a matter to be addressed by Unemployment Insurance.[80] To corroborate his argument, he cited the statistics that

> In Canada between 1934 and 1936, as much as 15.6% of male wage-earners and 49.5% of female wage-earners would not even receive the allowance for an adult dependent [and one dependent child], because their average wage while in employment was less that $12 weekly.[81]

"The truth," he contended, was that "the great need of [Canadian] families" was the result of "a wage situation"; that is, due to pervasive low wages, "need exists in many of the families of the nation *even when the breadwinner is at work.*" In other words, social reality fell far short of the ideal of the 'family wage,' and it was not UI's job to bridge this enormous shortfall. The most "needy" kinds of employment were excluded from the proposed UI scheme anyway, Stangroom pointed out.[82] He feared, moreover, that if dependants' benefits were introduced, they would be difficult to abolish.[83]

Watson, in contrast, held that not providing dependants' allowances in a UI scheme would be difficult, as they were provided under other social insurance measures, such as Workman's Compensation, the Old Age Annuity Scheme in the U.S. Social Security Act, and Canada's Civil Service Superannuation Scheme. Alert to questions of cost, Watson suggested that "there might be advantages in limiting the dependants to children alone rather than including wife and children," but, he conceded, "it might also be difficult to get acceptance for that view."[84] To those who opposed the inclusion of dependants' allowances in the belief that they "would militate against the adoption of family allowances," Watson years later recalled arguing that their inclusion "would hasten rather than retard family allowances."[85] On balance, Watson, ever the pragmatist, recommended "a thorough-going recognition of dependants" in the 1940 UI bill "as in the Act of 1935"[86] to obviate the necessity for additional assistance or relief measures.[87]

Given the prevailing assumption that most women were dependants and were, therefore, to be provided for by men, whether daughters by fathers or wives by husbands, the major channel through which UI coverage was to be extended to women was the provision of dependants' allowances. That the drafters of the UI legislation seriously considered either dispensing with dependants' benefits altogether or not including wives (dependants by definition, as we have seen) says something about the lesser importance, in the eyes of the policy makers, of women relative to men, of wives relative to husbands and of daughters relative to fathers, as well as of the expendability of the 'family wage' principle. Indeed, the debate over UI dependants' allowances versus 'family allowances' was, in large part, a debate over the function of the wage. Although lip service was paid regularly to the principle of the 'family wage,' it was well known that wages did not vary according to need, that is, that dependants' allowances were not built into wages. In a sense, the advocates of 'family allowances' regarded this measure as *the* solution to the non-reality of the 'family wage'. Moreover, dependants' allowances as an integral part of the unemployment insurance benefit package threatened to contravene the 'less eligibility' principle as applied to UI, and cause what bureaucrats and policy analysts of the day called "overinsurance."[88] As Stangroom wrote in his analysis of the problem of dependency in UI, "whatever our decision, it seems that benefits should not exceed wages ... or overinsurance will result, with the danger of malingering."[89] To grant more, in an unemployment insurance benefit package that included dependants' allowances, than a person could earn while in waged or salaried employment would, it was feared, destroy the work incentive.

Initially, dependants' allowances were not a feature of the early drafts of the 1940 UI bill. In the end, partly as a result of representations from labour, particularly Quebec labour, the 1940 UI Act did contain provision for dependants' allowances. They were included in the legislation, however, just as the sex distinctions in contributions and benefits had been excluded from the 1938 bill, by sleight of hand. Watson told the story in 1951. The base benefit rate had been originally set at 40 times the average daily/weekly contribution. A person earning between $5.40 and $7.50 a week and paying a 12 cent weekly contribution would have received a weekly benefit of $4.80. Asked to evaluate the relationship of benefits to contributions in the original 1940 Bill with an eye to increasing the latter to cover dependants' allowances, Watson remembered having found the benefits "to be very considerably in excess of" the contributions. In disagreement with him, however, were those who thought that the rates of benefit were already "so moderate" that they could not possibly be further decreased, but who were "equally reluctant" to propose higher contributions for the sake of dependants' allowances. "Some practical decision had to be reached quickly," Watson recalled in 1951, because "the bill had to go forward into the Senate the next day or perhaps the day after that." The compromise solution was to bring in dependants' allowances through the back door by reducing the base benefit rate from 40 times the average daily/weekly rate of contribution to 34 times for those claimants without dependants, and by allowing only claimants with dependants to receive benefits of 40 times their average contribution.[90] Now, with respect to those covered by UI who had been earning between $5.40 and $7.50 a week, the unemployed person with dependants would receive $4.80 in weekly benefits while the person without, only $4.08.[91]

The "differential on the basis of dependency"[92] thus amounted not to a "15 per cent supplement to [the] base rate" for claimants with dependants, as Struthers describes it,[93] but rather to a reduction to 85 per cent of the base rate for claimants without dependants. In other words, claimants without dependants both were penalized for not having them, and expected to subsidize the 'allowances' for those who did. As it was widely assumed that few women in the labour force had dependants, this measure can hardly be regarded as designed to be of advantage to female workers. At the same time, since the major provision of unemployment insurance for women was to be by way of their dependence on men, to disguise "the differential on the basis of dependency" as a supplement for dependants was not only to mask the cut in the base benefit rate for the single worker but to disregard the real material needs of wives and children living in households organized on the basis of the 'family wage.' Nonetheless, being by definition connected to the labour market only indirectly through their husbands, married women were to have access to unemployment insurance through the dependants' benefits (however meagre) extended to their male providers. As already noted, married women in paid employment did not fit comfortably into the master frame. Upon marriage, women were presumed to enter a state of dependency in which husbands would provide for them. Therefore, for a married woman to claim unemployment insurance was a contradiction in terms or, what was greatly feared, a way to defraud the system. Hovering on the edges of the UI debate in the 1930s was the suspicion that women workers who married would make fraudulent claims. This was the subject of a series of memos exchanged between Watson and Wolfenden in late 1934. Wolfenden clearly delineated two feared scenarios as follows: the woman who had worked long enough to qualify for UI benefits before marriage would, on marriage, leave employment and make claims; or the married woman would continue in paid employment only long enough to qualify for benefits.[94] That both of these cases would have already been covered by the exclusion from benefit of all those who voluntarily severed their employment contract "without just cause" attests to the strength of the fear. The perceived anomalousness (and feared duplicity) of gainfully employed, married women was written into the 1935 Act. Section 25 gave the Unemployment Insurance Commission power to make regulations in respect of "special classes," that is, to impose additional conditions and terms as the commissioners saw fit. This section identified five classes of "anomalies": a) casual workers; b) seasonal workers; c) intermittent workers; d) "married women who, since marriage or in any prescribed period subsequent to marriage, have had less than the prescribed number of contributions paid in respect of them;" and e) piece workers.[95] This section of the 1935 legislation closely followed the British UI Anomalies Act and Regulations of 1931. The framers of Canada's 1938 Bill and 1940 Act, however, felt that the schedule for anomalous cases could be simplified by eliminating both married women and intermittent workers once the "ratio rule," to be discussed below, was built into the UI scheme.

Indirect Methods of Controlling Women's Access to Benefit

In addition to direct, there were also indirect methods of controlling women's access to UI benefit. The remaining five of the seven sets of regulations governing eligibility and coverage all affected women without explicitly mentioning either the female sex or married women. Most importantly, there was, throughout all the drafts from 1935 to 1940, the scheme's inherent bias toward 'the good worker,' the 'good risk.' The framers of the Canadian UI legislation were well aware of the fact that Great Britain's UI scheme had collapsed in the 1920s under the sheer weight of the numbers of unemployed. As the initial drafting in Canada was undertaken at a time of mass unemployment, it is no wonder, then, that the framers exercised great caution, and sought to make eligibility regulations strict and coverage strictly limited. Watson's (and Wolfenden's) preoccupation with actuarial soundness so unmistakably informed the 1935 legislation as to draw fire from CCF critics who attacked the principle as contrary to the interests of workers.[96]

By its thoroughgoing application of a ratio formula that related benefit period to employment and contributory history,[97] the 1938 bill was decidedly framed to reward the steady worker. Moreover, as a summary of the 1938 bill disclosed, the reduction in the number of future benefit days by past claims would penalize the worker who might make what were labelled "trifling claims." In general, the scheme was to function in such a way that "the more he works the greater his benefits."[98] The 1940 legislation retained the "ratio rule," establishing, within a qualifying period of 30 weeks worked over any two-year period, a fixed ratio of five to one between the number of days of paid contributions and the number of days of benefit. Thirty weeks (or 180 days) of employment and contributions within twenty-four months got one six weeks (or 36 days) of benefit. Five years of insurable employment and contributions got one an entire year on UI. As Watson wrote to Arthur MacNamara, Chairman of the Committee on Unemployment Insurance, Dependants' Allowance Board, Department of National Defence, "one important purpose of an unemployment insurance Act ought to be, although not always observed, to give benefit for a good long period to a person who has had a good employment record and then falls on evil days."[99]

Certainly, as Labour Minister McLarty told the House in July 1940, the ratio rule for computing of benefit days was an incentive for "insured persons to try to improve their benefit status by keeping employed."[100] Equally true, as Tait pointed out in discussing the disadvantages of the ratio rule in 1938, was the fact that "the insured worker may be entitled to only a short period of benefit for the simple reason that he has suffered a great deal of unemployment through no fault of his own."[101] Overlooked by (or invisible to) all was the fact that, through no fault of *her* own, the average woman worker was handicapped in the race for 'good worker' status, since circumstances dictated that she had less access than the average male worker either to steady or to long-term insurable employment. Indeed, rather than expressing concern about any possible harmful effects on the woman worker, architects of the 1938 and 1940 legislation heralded as a positive outcome of the ratio rule that it would *disadvantage* married women. Tait, for example, cited as support for the adopting ratio rule an Australian's opinion that it

> would prevent serious anomalies arising from an undue drain on the fund on the part of casual, intermittent and seasonal workers and married women and thus it may avoid the necessity for complicated regulations like the Anomalies regulations in Great Britain.[102]

As we have seen, the schedule for anomalous cases in both the 1938 Draft Bill and the 1940 Act was simplified by the elimination of married women and intermittent workers.

As explicated by Watson in 1934, the proposed UI scheme was designed to alleviate short-term, but not structural, seasonal, or cyclical joblessness.[103] Nor, he could have added, as Tait did in 1938, was it to alleviate the intermittent unemployment of the irregularly employed.[104] In their attempt to negotiate the contradiction between the assumed dependency of wives and the non-realization of the 'family wage,' women, particularly married women, turned to just the sorts of catch-as-catch-can, temporary, and improvised jobs in the 'informal' economy that were deemed uninsurable. And insofar as they did (and had to do) this, women were excluded from unemployment insurance coverage.

According to the 1935 Act, part-time workers were not by definition ineligible, but they were required to contribute for the equivalent of 40 weeks before acquiring eligibility, a condition that a woman working two or three days a week or less would have taken a long time to fulfill.[105] Two changes in the 1940 Act brought some increase in access to benefit for the less regularly employed. One was the reduction of the qualifying period from 40 to 30 weeks worked over two years, and the second was the option of making daily, rather than weekly, contributions towards establishing qualification period. The latter opened the door somewhat to those who would have found it impossible to meet the "continuous employment" requirement of the 1935 legislation.[106] Despite these two changes, the 1940 Act still put UI coverage well beyond the reach of most 'intermittently' or 'irregularly' or 'casually' working women.

In a Canadian economy still heavily reliant on male labour in the primary (and seasonal) industries of agriculture, logging, and fishing, the relegation of seasonal unemployment to the status of an anomaly was bound to affect adversely a large proportion of working men. Furthermore, agricultural labour, logging and fishing were explicitly excluded from insurance coverage, on various grounds, in all the drafted and enacted UI legislation from 1934 to 1940. As part of its mandate to examine the possibility of extending coverage, the Unemployment Insurance Commission began recommending inclusion of such areas of heavy male employment as lumbering, and certain occupations within agriculture, as early as 1945.[107] With the exception of nursing, the excluded categories of employment in which women predominated had to wait almost three decades for inclusion.

The most general principle of exclusion incorporated in the 1930s and 40s UI legislation was the income ceiling. Excluded in the 1940 Act was any employment (in the 1935 Act and 1938 Bill, any non-manual employment) which paid more than $2000 a year.[108] The ruling belief was that, first, the well paid and, second, the securely employed did not have to be insured against the contingency of unemployment, since, in the first case, the person could afford to save enough for a rainy day, and, in the second, unemployment was unlikely. As civil servants were regarded as falling into the second category (the permanently employed), those in the federal and provincial public service as well as municipal employees were all excluded from coverage.[109] The secure employment argument was used also as a rationale for excepting school teachers.[110] Whether in the case of female school teachers or female civil servants, the argument was wholly inappropriate, given that neither teaching nor the civil service meant job security for women. Except during the war, when qualified teachers and civil servants were scarce, the policy of most school boards and provincial and municipal civil services as well as of the federal government itself (until 1955), was to require women to relinquish their positions at marriage or, alternatively, at first pregnancy. Certainly a far tinier proportion of the female than of the male labour force would have been excluded on the basis of earnings exceeding $2000, a condition coincident with the assumption of male independence and female dependence.

In addition to teaching, the two other most salient female-dominated occupations, marked for exclusion from UI coverage in all the bills and enactments from 1934 to 1940 were hospital and private nursing, and domestic service performed in private homes.[111] By one fell swoop, between 30 and 40 per cent of women in the paid labour force were thus denied access to UI coverage. The rationales for exclusion were various, some identical to those regarding male-dominated occupations. The argument advanced for excluding professional nurses, for instance, was that "they collect their own fees," making their relationship to their employer "analogous to that of physician and patient or solicitor and client."[112] While this assimilated nurses to the model of the highly paid male professional, it conveniently overlooked the discrepancy in fee between nurse and doctor or nurse and lawyer. Nursing probationers, on the other hand, were excluded "because they hardly get enough money to clothe themselves."[113] Registered nurses and nurses in training were thus caught between being falsely identified with doctors and lawyers on the one hand, and, on the other, the decision by the original framers of the Canadian unemployment insurance scheme not to include the economically most vulnerable within the scheme's catchment.[114]

While cleaners of clubs and business premises were to be eligible, domestic servants employed in private homes were not.[115] The rationale advanced for their exclusion was administrative difficulty. As McLarty explained to the House in July 1940, their inclusion

> would make the administrative machinery in the matter of inspection so top heavy and complicated that the cost would be out of proportion to the good which would be accomplished.[116]

Agriculture and fishing were also excluded on the grounds that these were occupations carried out far from centres of inspection.[117] Despite the difficulty of supervision, which he conceded, Tait, in his 1938 Report, had argued for reconsidering the exclusion of agriculture, horticulture and forestry, but not of domestic service.[118] The argument of administrative difficulty would prove much more tenacious in the case of domestics than, for instance, in that of loggers or fishermen. One good reason was the perpetual shortage of domestic help. Despite widespread joblessness in the Depression, demand for domestic servants outran supply; and the war only exacerbated the shortage. The administrative argument with respect to paid household labour conveniently disguised the policy of using domestic service as an alternative unemployment insurance scheme for unemployed women.[119] It was an occupation for which, in any case, women were believed to be eminently well-suited.

Another statutory general condition of eligibility for benefit that limited access for women, particularly married women, was the requirement that the claimant be "capable and available for work."[120] For married women, availability was sharply curtailed by the subordination of the wife to the husband in location of residence[121] and, for mothers of young children, by the scarcity of child care facilities. The married woman's lack of mobility, in other words, put geographical limits on her job searching capacity which were as severe as the time limits that child rearing responsibilities imposed on job seeking mothers. Moreover, married women would not have been eligible for the loans provided by the 1935 Act's Section 14 to pay the fares of unemployed workers moving to where work was available.[122] Clearly, the discrimination against women embodied in the regulations regarding availability for work was structural.

Gender and the UI Administrative Structure

Gender was also inscribed in the administrative structure which UI legislation mandated for implementing the scheme. A three-person agency, called the Unemployment Insurance Commission, was created to oversee the entire operation of UI. A dispersed federal bureaucracy of employment service and unemployment insurance offices was to be set up in regional divisions and in cities and towns across Canada. Each region's central office was to act as a clearing house for vacancies and applications for employment and to make this information available to the local offices. Regional insurance officers would be hired to handle unemployment insurance claims. To handle disagreement over claims, the Commission was empowered to set up regional courts of referees and to appoint regional deputy umpires and a national umpire. Provision was also made for the appointment of inspectors authorized to investigate workplaces concerning compliance with UI regulations. To advise and assist the Commission, an Unemployment Insurance Advisory Committee, consisting of a chairman and four to six members, was to be appointed by the Governor in Council.[123]

Not surprisingly, male administrative control of the operation of UI was ensured from the start. It is true that, at the regional and local level, women (if unmarried, of course) could be hired as employment placement or unemployment insurance officers. And during the war, with the male labour shortage, the lifting of the marriage bar, and the creation of the Women's Division of National Selective Service, the labour of both married and unmarried women was drawn upon to fill some of these jobs in many parts of Canada. But, in keeping with the rest of Canadian state structures, within the higher echelons of the UI administration (that is, within the Commission itself, the inspectorate, and the hierarchy of appointees to implement the appeal procedure), no provision was made to ensure that a proportionate number of women would take up positions. The one exception was the Unemployment Insurance Advisory Committee. Although the 1935 Act was silent on the issue of the sex of those appointed to serve, Prime Minister Bennett conceded in the House on February 21, 1935, that, "if it is thought desirable, ... I contemplate that one of the members ... shall be a woman."[124]

And indeed Section 36(1) of the 1938 Draft Bill stipulated that the Unemployment Insurance Advisory Committee (UIAC) should be composed of a chairman and not fewer than four nor more than six other members, "one of whom shall be a woman." For some reason, this stipulation, present in Section 83(1) of the 1940 Act at first reading, was dropped before final passage.[125] Nonetheless, a woman was appointed to the first UIAC formed in December 1940.[126] The aim of having one woman on the UIAC, however, was not to ensure that women workers were represented in proportion to their labour force participation. Instead, this gesture toward sexual equity reproduced a gender asymmetry widespread in western discourses of representation since the 18th century, wherein diversity and plurality have come to characterize the category 'men,' while women have been collapsed into the unified and homogeneous category of 'woman.'[127] Far removed from unemployment insurance as this practice might seem, its relevance can be discerned in the discussion about the composition of the UIAC. Memos exchanged among Commissioners and labour department officials spoke of the need to select representatives of employers, of labour,[128] of government, and one woman. Underlying this search was a conception of men being diverse, and of women being 'all the same.' Quite beyond consideration was the idea that women might also be divided into workers, employers, and government officials, and hence that there might be need to find representatives of women workers, women employers, women government officials. Otherwise dichotomized into women workers in the public sphere and dependent wives in the private domain,[129] women were reduced to a single category when it came to the representation of their public capacities.

Conclusion

On close examination, then, gender pervaded the 1934-40 debate on unemployment insurance, and was inscribed in every clause of the resulting legislation. The indirect limits on women's access to UI benefit derived in large measure (as Diana M. Pearce has argued with respect to unemployment compensation in the U.S.) from the mismatch between the normative worker targeted by the programme, the male breadwinner, and female labour market participation patterns. Less mobile than men, women were less likely to meet the available, able and willing to work requirements of UI regulations. Disproportionately concentrated in low-paying and irregular or intermittent jobs, women would have more difficulty fulfilling the statutory conditions for eligibility: the minimum earnings and minimum work-time qualifications. And as quitting a job voluntarily did not entitle one to unemployment insurance, also disqualified would be any woman who voted with her feet, and left a position because of intolerable work conditions or sexual harassment.[130]

Moreover, women were more or less closed out of the supervisory, adjudicative, inspectorate and decision-making levels of the UI administrative structure. The only possibility for women's needs and interests to receive a hearing was created by the requirement (later dropped) that one of the four to six members of the Unemployment Insurance Advisory Committee be a woman. While Canadian UI legislation contributed to the gendered complementarity of masculine independence and feminine dependence, and to the dichotomization of women into either single workers assimilated to the male norm or dependent wives/mothers, the gendered asymmetry or representation in UI's administrative structure contributed at the same time, paradoxically, to the conceptualization of men as multiple and diverse and to that of women as singular and uniform.

In most depictions of unemployment during the Depression, the plight was viewed as visited directly on men, indirectly on women. The gender crisis thus triggered was a crisis in masculinity, an undermining of what was believed to be the male identity's intrinsic tie to the role of head of household and provider. The parallel discourse on unemployment insurance similarly gave precedence to the wage earning of men, as their income-earning capacity was construed as central to the male's identity both as worker and husband/father. While the Left made liberal gestures toward an ideology of sexual equality, these were constrained by the hegemonic assumptions framing the debate for all participants. Chief among these was the construction of breadwinning as a masculine responsibility, a construction whose normative dimension was intensified in the Depression despite its increased divergence from actuality. A complementary intensification occurred in the renewed enforcement of married women's dependency. In contrast to men's, women's economic and familial identities tended to be viewed as being divided if not contradictory. Separated into single, independent working women on one side, and dependent wives/mothers on the other, women's incorporation into UI provisions was twofold, and their access to unemployment insurance benefit limited in both direct and indirect ways. As workers assumed not to have dependants, women's lower contributions and benefits were only a concern for those disturbed by explicit, formalized sex distinctions. That women's wages were lower than men's was accepted, by government officials, as a fixed characteristic of the labour market. The framers of the UI legislation sought to preserve, not eliminate, wage differentials of both class and gender. That the unemployment insurance scheme would be structured by the inequities women faced in the labour market was largely a matter of indifference to them. As it was assumed that most women would be provided for by a male relative, women's principal access to benefit was to be through the indirect channel of dependants' allowances. The sleight-of-hand provision for dependants in the 1940 Act, however, revealed the hollowness of the government's commitment to the 'family wage.' Ideologically dominant as the concept of the 'family wage' was, its rhetorical deployment by the makers of social policy appears to have functioned more to disenfranchise married women and enforce their dependence than to entitle dependent wives and children to adequate provision.

Notes

The author wishes to thank Paula Bourne for her assistance with the research for this paper, Dr. Jane Lewis for her assistance with its conceptualization, and Philinda Masters for her assistance with its editing. Research for the paper was funded by a grant from the SSHRCC "Women and Work" Strategic Grants Programme.

1. Canada, House of Commons, *Debates,* 22 January 1935, 85. Woodsworth was quoting from the *Winnipeg Free Press,* 18 December 1934.

2. See, for example, Michiel Horn, ed., *The Dirty Thirties: Canadians in the Great Depression* (Toronto 1972); A.E. Safarian, *The Canadian Economy in the Great Depression* (Toronto 1970); H. Blair Neatby, *The Politics of Chaos: Canada in the Thirties* (Toronto 1972).

3. Abraham Albert Heaps, a Labour spokesman, made one of the rare inclusions of women along with men among the unemployed when, in the parliamentary debate on unemployment insurance of January 1935, he referred to the "vast numbers of men and women at present out of work." Canada, House of Commons, *Debates,* 29 January 1935, 288. Beyond Agnes Macphail, one of the only other MPs to express concern for the plight of unemployed women was Charles Grant MacNeil, whose concern for "single, unemployed women transients" focused less on their material deprivation than on their lack of protection from sexual exploitation, which he believed would result in moral ruin and the attendant problems of unmarried motherhood and venereal disease. ("The problem of unmarried mothers is becoming more acute, the problem of illicit alliances is more acute.... the problem of venereal disease is becoming more acute.") Canada, House of Commons, *Debates,* 8 February 1937, 670-1; 2 March 1937, 1434.

4. See Wendy Kozol's analysis of the use by the U.S. New Deal Resettlement Administration (later Farm Security Administration) of photographs of mothers in rags holding children in their arms in the doorways of shacks and other makeshift shelters to symbolize the poor's adherence to patriarchal ideals of family and motherhood, and thereby establish that the poor were deserving of relief. Wendy Kozol, "Madonnas of the Fields: Photography, Gender, and 1930s Farm Relief," *Genders,* 2 (Summer 1988), 1-23.

5. For example, in her study of family violence through examination of the records of child protection agencies in Boston, Linda Gordon has disclosed that social workers "considered the stresses of the Depression as mitigating circumstances of (his) violence as they did not in the case of (her) neglect." Linda Gordon, *Heroes of Their own Lives—The Politics and History of Family Violence: Boston 1880-1960* (New York 1988).

6. In parliamentary debate on the National Employment Commission's provision for a committee on women's employment, Agnes Macphail rose to comment on how little attention the House had paid to the plight of unemployed women. To make her case, she cited the fact that there were no camps for single destitute women as there were for men. "The problem of the young and old unemployed women should be given careful consideration," she argued, "because it has been given very little consideration in the past in connection with any projects to employ unemployed persons on public works and so on. One would almost think," she concluded, "that there was no problem in connection with unemployed women; that it did not exist, when in fact it is a serious problem." Canada, House of Commons, *Debates,* 7 April 1936, 1907-8.

7. James Struthers, *'No Fault of Their Own': Unemployment and the Canadian Welfare State 1914-1941* (Toronto 1983).

8. When I speak of gender as a fundamental category of social historical analysis, I understand gender to encompass all discourses, practices and structures shaping (and shaped by) the prescribed and prevailingly actualized social relations between the sexes. See, among others, Joan Kelly, "The Social Relation of the Sexes: Methodological Implications of Women's History," in *Women, History, and Theory: The Essays of Joan Kelly* (Chicago 1984), 1-18; Joan W. Scott, "Gender: A Useful Category of Historical Analysis," *American Historical Review,* 915 (December 1986), 1053-75; Joan Wallach Scott, *Gender and the Politics of History* (New York 1988).

9. There were only three dissenting votes. See Struthers, *'No Fault',* 129.

10. National Archives of Canada [NAC], RG40, Records of the Department of Insurance, Vol. 24, file 7, Extract from Book II of the Recommendations of the Royal Commission on Dominion-Provincial Relations. Not submitted until February 1940.

11. Struthers, *'No Fault',* 197.

12. Canada, House of Commons, *Debates,* 18 June 1940, 864-5; 11 July 1940, 1532.

13. Not to be confused with Sir Alfred Watson, the British Government Actuary in the 1920s and early 1930s.

14. In a recent article, Alice Kessler-Harris takes a very different approach to the discussion among working people during the Depression as to "who was and was not entitled to work." Conflating gender perception with a notion of separate spheres, Kessler-Harris argues that it was neither of those but rather working people's concern for the integrity of "the family" and a working-class conception of justice that shaped working people's responses to the Depression. "In the code of honour of working people, jobs belonged to the providers." And the concept of the provider could include "widows, single women and married women with unemployed or disabled husbands as well." How does this qualification relate to the popular perception that "a male who worked would ... 'spend his income to the support of his family while the [married?] woman spends for permanent waves, lip sticks'?" Did "males who had other means of support" really face "the same criticism as married women?" Kessler-Harris calls "not gender specific" the perception that men should

be "'men and provide for their mothers, sisters, wives and daughters, and womanhood ... restored to its pedestal motherhood'." What she means is that such a view could be and was held by both men and women. But who would claim that a gender ideology is held by members of only one sex? In her rush to downplay or "decenter" the category of gender, Kessler-Harris sometimes goes too far, as in her claim that "one of the nation's first and most immediate responses [to the Depression-triggered "discussion of who was and was not entitled to work"] was to exclude the spouses of wage earners from the labour force." Male spouses? On the basis of her own evidence, one could conclude that the conception of who deserved employment was as deeply gendered as the notion of "the family" was patriarchal. Alice Kessler-Harris, "Gender Ideology in Historical Reconstruction: A Case Study from the 1930s," *Gender & History*, 1 (Spring 1989), 31-49.

15. NAC, RG 40, Series 3, Vol. 24, file 4, The Employment and Social Insurance Act, Bill 8, Passed by the House of Commons, 12 March 1935.

16. L. Richter, "Limitations of Unemployment Insurance," *Dalhousie Review*, 18 (July 1938), 229-44.

17. NAC, RG 40, Series 3, Vol. 24, file 5, The National Employment Insurance Bill, 1938.

18. NAC, RG 40, Vol. 24, file Unemployment Insurance (6): Drafting 1938 Bill, Watson's Actuarial Report of 15 March 1938.

19. Ruth Roach Pierson, Introduction to Chapter Six, "Paid Work," in Beth Light and Ruth Roach Pierson, eds. and comps., *No Easy Road: Women in Canada 1920s-1960s* (forthcoming).

20. The National Employment Commission's "Summarized Report on Co-ordination of Aid" stated: "Of 3,375,000 women and girls fifteen years of age and over, who might by reason of age be eligible for gainful occupation a large proportion are married and are, therefore, not seeking employment or gainful occupation." NAC, RG 27, Records of the Department of Labour, Vol. 3358, file 12, "Summarized Report on Co-ordination of Aid," 20 March 1937, 39.

21. With reference to postwar Britain, Denise Riley has written that "the dominant rhetoric described the figure of woman as mother and woman as worker as diametrically opposed and refused to consider the possibility of their combination." Denise Riley, "Some Peculiarities of Social Policy concerning Women in Wartime and Postwar Britain," in Margaret Randolph Higonnet, Jane Jenson, Sonya Michel, and Margaret Collins Weitz, eds., *Behind the Lines: Gender and the Two World Wars* (New Haven 1987), 260.

22. NAC, MG 28, I 10 Canadian Council on Social Development, Vol. 63, file 497, Aid to Dependent Mothers and Children in Canada: Social Policy Behind our Legislation, 1942.

23. Those religious orders providing sanctuary for single mothers and their offspring tended to accept the death of the 'illegitimate' infant, the incarnation of the sin of its parents, as a 'blessing.' See Andrée Lévesque, "Deviants Anonymous: Single Mothers at the Hôpital de la Miséricorde in Montreal, 1929-1939," in Katherine

Arnup, Andrée Lévesque and Ruth Roach Pierson, eds., *Delivering Motherhood: Maternal Ideologies and Practices in the 19th and 20th Centuries* (London 1990), 108-25.

24. Veronica Strong-Boag, *The New Day Recalled: Lives of Girls and Women in English Canada, 1919-1939* (Toronto 1988), 62-3.

25. Pierson, Introduction to Chapter Six "Paid Work," in *No Easy Road.*

26. According to Margaret Hobbs' research for her PhD thesis on women and work in the Depression, University of Toronto, forthcoming.

27. See, for an example from the USA, Lois Rita Helmbold, "Beyond the Family Economy: Black and White Working-Class Women During the Great Depression," *Feminist Studies,* 13 (Fall 1987), 629-55. Thanks to Margaret Hobbs for this reference.

28. Ruth Roach Pierson, Introduction to Chapter Five "Unpaid Work," in *No Easy Road;* Hilary Land, "The Family Wage," *Feminist Review,* 6 (1980), 55-77; and Michèle Barrett and Mary McIntosh, "The 'Family Wage': Some Problems for Socialists and Feminists," *Capital & Class,* 11 (1980), 51-72; Martha May, "The Historical Problem of the Family Wage: The Ford Motor Company and the Five Dollar Day," *Feminist Studies,* 8 (Summer 1982), 399-424.

29. Or her substitute. As Sonya Michel has noted with respect to the United States, "public policy during the Depression upheld the ideal of the conventional family with a wage-earning father and housekeeping mother." Sonya Michel, "American Women and the Discourse of the Democratic Family in World War II," in Higonnet *et al., Behind the Lines,* 156.

30. See particularly Leonard Marsh, Part IV: "Family Needs," *Report on Social Security for Canada 1943,* with a new Introduction by the Author and a Preface by Michael Bliss (Toronto 1975), 195-232.

31. A minority within the political Left were sympathetic to the concerns of married women workers. Nonetheless, the view that came to predominate was one that favoured the 'family wage.' See Joan Sangster, *Dreams of Equality: Women on the Canadian Left, 1920-1950* (Toronto 1989).

32. Sangster, *Dreams of Equality.*

33. Riley, "Some Peculiarities of Social Policy concerning Women," 261.

34. Canada, House of Commons, *Debates,* 18 February 1935, 914; 8 March 1935, 1537-8.

35. NAC, RG 40, Series 3, Vol. 24, file 6 (1935-39), A Summary of the 1938 Draft Unemployment Insurance Bill.

36. NAC, RG 40, Vol. 24, file Unemployment Insurance (7), D. Christie Tait, "Report on a Proposed Unemployment Insurance Bill in Canada," n.d. (probably early 1938).

37. NAC, MG 28, I55, Papers of the Canadian Federation of Business and Professional Women's Clubs, Vol. 43, Minute Book 1, Minutes of the 5th Convention, CFBPWC, Calgary, 3-6 July 1935, 9-10.

38. At its 31 January 1935, meeting. NAC, MG 26, K, R.B. Bennett Papers, Vol. 793, Reel M-1461, 503874.

39. According to data used by the Department of Insurance in 1940, 39.8 per cent of male wage-earners were married in 1921 (58.4 per cent were single) and 40.4 per cent were married in 1931 (57.6 per cent were single). NAC, RG 40, Vol. 24, file 6, A Summary of the Draft Unemployment Insurance Bill (1938), January 1940.

40. NAC, RG 40, Series 3, Vol. 24, file 7, "The Principles of Flat and Graded Employee Contributions and Benefit, as Applied to a Projected Canadian Unemployment Insurance Scheme," memo attached to a letter to A.D. Watson from Gerald H. Brown, Assistant Deputy Minister, Department of Labour, 8 May 1940.

41. Catharine MacKinnon has identified the tendency to establish men as the norm against which women are measured as a salient feature of law and other social discourses and institutions. Women, she has written, "have to meet either the male standard for males or the male standard for females." Catharine MacKinnon, *Feminism Unmodified: Discourses on Life and Law* (Cambridge 1987), 71-2. I am grateful to Sherene Razack for bringing this point to my attention in "Feminism and the Law: The Women's Legal Education and Action Fund," PhD thesis, University of Toronto, 1989.

42. Canada, House of Commons, *Debates,* 12 February 1935, 768.

43. Canada, House of Commons, *Debates,* 18 February 1935, 914-15. Apparently Woodsworth was unaware of any contradiction in his espousal in the same speech of a principle of "social justice" that contravened the principle of the 'family wage,' namely that "men and women should receive equal remuneration for work of equal value."

44. Canada, House of Commons, *Debates,* 9 April 1935, 2565-66.

45. NAC, RG 40, Vol. 24, file Unemployment Insurance (6), Eric Stangroom, "Some Aspects and Anomalies of the British Unemployment Scheme as They Might Relate to Possible Canadian Legislation," December 1939.

46. NAC, RG 40, Vol. 24, file Unemployment Insurance (6), "Notes on the Unemployment Insurance Draft Bill (1938)," n.a.

47. NAC, RG 40, Vol. 24, file Unemployment Insurance (6), Watson's Actuarial Report, 15 March 1938.

48. NAC, RG 40, Series 3, Vol. 24, file (6), A Summary of the Draft Unemployment Insurance Bill (1938), January 1940. In 1915 the Fabian Women's Group in Britain had estimated that 50 per cent of working women were partially or wholly maintaining others. The validity of their sample was questioned by B. Seebohm Rowntree and Frank D. Stuart, who put the figure at 12 per cent. Ellen Smith, *Wage Earning Women and their Dependants* (London 1915), and B. Seebohm Rowntree and Frank D. Stuart, *The Responsibility of Women Workers for Dependants* (Oxford 1921). Thanks to Jane E. Lewis for these references.

49. NAC, RG 40, Series 3, Vol. 24, file 6, A Summary of the Draft Unemployment Insurance Bill (1938), January 1940, author's emphasis.

50. NAC, RG 40, Series 3, Vol. 24, file 7, "The Principles of Flat and Graded Employee Contributions and Benefits, as Applied to a Projected Canadian Unemployment Insurance Scheme," memo attached to a letter to A.D. Watson from G.H. Brown, ADM/Labour, 8 May 1940.

51. *Ibid.,* 3.

52. L. Richter, "Limitations of Unemployment Insurance."

53. NAC, RG 40, Vol. 24, file Unemployment Insurance (7), D. Christie Tait, "Report on a Proposed Unemployment Insurance Bill in Canada," probably early 1938.

54. Struthers. *'No Fault',* 6-7, 85, 100, 135, 147, 181, 188, 205, 207, 211-12.

55. NAC, RG 40, Series 3, Vol. 24, file 7, "The Problem of Dependency in Unemployment Insurance," received by Watson from Eric Stangroom, 5 June 1940.

56. NAC, RG 40, Vol. 24, file Unemployment Insurance (7), D. Christie Tait, "Report on a Proposed Unemployment Insurance Bill in Canada," 45.

57. NAC, RG 40, Series 3, Vol. 24, file 7, "The Problem of Dependency in Unemployment Insurance," received by Watson from Eric Stangroom, 5 June 1940.

58. Canada, House of Commons, *Debates,* 16 July 1940, 1786.

59. NAC, RG 40, Series 3, Vol. 24, file 7, Memo. from Watson to Gerald R. Brown, Assistant Deputy Minister, Department of Labour, 6 May 1940.

60. NAC RG 40, Series 3, Vol. 24, file 7, "The Principles of Flat and Graded Employee Contributions and Benefit, as Applied to a Projected Canadian Unemployment Insurance Scheme," memo attached to a letter to Watson from G. H. Brown, ADM/Labour, 8 May 1940. In a comparison of the 1935 and 1940 Acts, the following argument was advanced in support of abandoning the flat rate system of calculating contributions and benefits: "If circumstances compel an insured man to subsist on benefits for several months, the man of high income (within the scope of the Act) will suffer greater hardship than the man of low income because he will have higher obligations in the way of rent and other fixed expenses." NAC, RG 50, Records of the Unemployment Insurance Commission, Vol. 24, file 1-2-2-9, Memorandum of 7 May 1940.

61. Cited by Woodsworth. Canada, House of Commons, Debates, 8 March 1935, 1534.

62. NAC, RG 40, Series 3, Vol. 24, file 7, "The Principles of Flat and Graded Employee Contributions and Benefit, as Applied to a Projected Canadian Unemployment Insurance Scheme," memo attached to a letter to Watson from G. H. Brown, ADM/Labour, 8 May 1940.

63. NAC, RG 40, Vol. 24, file Unemployment Insurance (6), Stangroom's memo re. Some Aspects and Anomalies of the British Unemployment Scheme as They Might Relate to Possible Canadian Legislation, December 1939, 16-17.

64. In resolution passed by the Ottawa Women's Liberal Club on 31 January 1935. NAC, MG 26, K, R.B. Bennett Papers, Vol. 793, Reel M-1461, 503874.

65. *Ibid.*

66. NAC, RG 40, Vol. 24, file Unemployment Insurance (6), Watson's response to Stangroom's Memo. re. British Scheme, 1939, 7.

67. NAC, RG 40, Series 3, Vol. 24, file 7, "The Principles of Flat and Graded Employee Contributions and Benefit, As Applied to a Projected Canadian Insurance Scheme," memo attached to a letter to Watson from G.H. Brown, ADM/Labour, 8 May 1940.

68. *Ibid.*

69. *Ibid.*

70. See Jane Lewis, "Dealing with Dependency: State Practices and Social Realities, 1870-1945," in Jane Lewis, ed., *Women's Welfare, Women's Right* (London 1983), 26-30.

71. NAC, RG 40, Series 3, Vol. 24, file 7, "The Problem of Dependency in Unemployment Insurance," received by Watson from Eric Stangroom, Department of Labour, 5 June 1940.

72. Watson, the Chief Actuary, Department of Insurance, defended the inclusion of dependants' benefits in the 1940 UI plan on the grounds that, although they depended on marital status and dependants, because these variables were taken into account regardless of need in the sense of 'absolute' need, they did not contravene the "insurance principle" of predictable need. NAC, RG 40, Series 3, Vol. 24, file 7, Memo from Watson to G.H. Brown, ADM/Labour, 16 January 1940.

73. *Ibid.*

74. In June 1934, Dominion Actuary Watson more or less advised Bennett that it was an inopportune time to introduce UI. "The plain fact is that until means are found of effecting greater stability than heretofore in social and economic conditions, an unemployment insurance fund is liable to be called upon to bear burdens so uncertain and so incalculable as to set at naught the best considered rates of contributions." NAC, RG 40, Series 3, Vol. 24, file 3, Actuarial Report on Contributions Required under "The Employment and Social Insurance Act," prepared by A.D. Watson, 14 June 1934.

75. In the 1935 debate in the House, Woodsworth criticized the proposed UI legislation for not meeting "the needs of the great mass of the unemployed." Canada, House of Commons, *Debates,* 29 January 1935, 284.

76. L. Richter, "General Principles and European Experience," *The Employment and Social Insurance Bill,* Proceedings of the May 1935 Meeting of the Canadian Economics and Political Science Association, *The Canadian Journal of Economics and Political Science,* 1 (1935), 447. See also A.W. Neill's discussion of Section 14 of the 1935 bill. Canada, House of Commons, *Debates,* 12 February 1935, 771.

77. W.J. Couper, "A Comment From the Point of View of American Opinion," *The Employment and Social Insurance Bill,* Proceedings of the May 1935 Meeting of the Economics and Political Science Association, *Canadian Journal of Economics and Political Science,* 1 (1935), 455.

78. In fact, when Family Allowances were implemented in 1944, even though the cheques were made out to mothers, the amounts were insufficient to counteract the general tendency of Canada's social organization which encouraged women's dependence on men.

79. NAC, RG 40, Vol. 24, file Unemployment Insurance (7), Memo to Watson from Stangroom, 10 May 1940. See also RG 40, Series 3, Vol. 24, file 7, Memo on "The Problem of Dependency in Unemployment Insurance," received by Watson from Stangroom, 5 June 1940.

80. As Eric Stangroom, Department of Labour, responded in a letter dated 17 October 1940, to a query from Angus MacInnis, C.C.F. M.P. from Vancouver, "Personally, I feel that as wages take no account of dependency some system of family allowances might be the proper solution, leaving unemployment insurance to compensate for loss of earnings." NAC, RG 27, Vol. 3454, file 4-1, part 1.

81. NAC, RG 40, Series 3, Vol. 24, file 7, Memo on "The Problem of Dependency in Unemployment Insurance," received by Watson from Stangroom, 5 June 1940. In both the 1935 Act and the 1938 Bill, the total benefit paid to claimants could not exceed 80 per cent of a person's average weekly pay while employed. Thus, for example, under the 1935 Act, a man 21 years of age or older, earning $12 a week, would have been eligible for a maximum benefit package of $9.60 which would have entitled him to draw, beyond the basic benefit of $6.00 for himself, the adult dependant benefit of $2.70 plus benefit for only one dependent child at 90 cents. Because the flat benefit rate for a woman 21 or over was $5.10, while the adult dependant and dependent child benefit rates remained constant, the average weekly pay for an adult working woman would have needed to be approximately $11 in order for her to collect, beyond her own UI benefit, dependants' benefits for one adult and one child.

82. People in low-paid and irregular employment would have faced great difficulty fulfilling the entry requirements for UI under either the 1935 or 1940 Acts or the 1938 draft bill. Introducing a daily rate of contribution option in the 1938 bill and 1940 Act overcame the difficulties with the definition of "continuous employment" encountered when only a weekly contribution was possible, as in the 1935 Act. NAC, RG 50, Vol. 24, file 1-2-2-9, Comparison of 1935 and 1940 Acts, Memorandum from J. MacKenzie, 7 May 1940. The 1940 Act, however, established an earnings floor of 90 cents per day below which a person would not be eligible to collect benefits. NAC, RG 40, Series 3, Vol. 24, file 8, First Reading UI Bill, July 1940, Section 19 (3).

83. NAC, RG 40, Vol. 24, file Unemployment Insurance (7), Memo to Watson from Stangroom, 10 May 1940.

84. NAC, RG 40, Series 3, Vol. 24, file 7, Memo. from Watson to Gerald R. Brown, Assistant Deputy Minister, Department of Labour, 16 January 1940.

85. NAC, RG 40, Series 3, Vol. 26, file 3-25-2, vol. 5, A.D. Watson's Comments on General Review of the UI Act, 1940 by R.G. Barclay, Director of U.I., Parts I & II, as submitted to N. McKellan for comment, 17 February 1951.

86. *Ibid.*

87. NAC, RG 40, Series 3, Vol. 24, file 7, Memo. from Watson to Gerald R. Brown, ADM/Labour, 16 January 1940.

88. NAC, RG 40, Vol. 24, file Unemployment Insurance (6), Eric Stangroom, "Some Aspects and Anomalies of the British Unemployment Scheme As They Might Relate to Possible Canadian Legislation," December 1939, 10, 27.

89. NAC, RG 40, Series 3, Vol. 24, file 7, "The Problem of Dependency in Unemployment Insurance," received by Watson from Eric Stangroom, 5 June 1940.

90. NAC, RG 40, Series 3, Vol. 26, file 3-25-2, vol. 5, A.D. Watson's Comments on General Review of the UI Act, 1940 by R.G. Barclay, Director of UI, Parts I & II, as submitted to N. McKellan for comment, 17 February 1951. The compromise proposal of setting the graded contributions and benefits rate for persons without dependants at 85 per cent of the total for those with dependants was sent to Watson for his appraisal by Gerald H. Brown, ADM/Labour, on 12 July 1940. NAC, RG 40, Series 3, Vol. 24, file 8, letter to Watson from Brown, 12 July 1940.

91. Senator L. Coté was incensed that the differential between those with and those without dependants was so small and threatened to "blow up the whole thing" in the Senate. According to Watson, he was able to reassure the Senator that, "when the opportunity should arise, the differential would be widened." NAC, RG 40, Series 3, Vol. 26, file 3-25-2, vol. 5, Watson's Comments on General Review of the UI Act, 1940 by R.G. Barclay, Director of UI, Parts I & II, as submitted to N. McKellan for comment, 17 February 1951. See also Canada, Senate, *Debates,* 1 August 1940, 412.

92. *Ibid.*

93. Struthers. *'No Fault',* 201.

94. NAC, RG 40, Series 3, Vol. 24, file 2, Wolfenden Memo. re. Married Women, enclosed in a letter to Watson dated 11 December 1934.

95. NAC, RG 40, Series 3, Vol. 24, file 4, The Employment and Social Insurance Act, Bill 8, Passed by the House of Commons, 12 March 1935. The subsequent history of the treatment of married woman workers within UI legislation, complicated, if not to say tortuous, as it is, is the subject of a separate study.

96. Specifically Woodsworth. Canada, House of Commons, *Debates,* 18 February 1935, 915.

97. In a comparison of the 1935 Act and the 1938 bill, Watson singled out, as one of the major differences, the latter's "determination of benefits wholly on the ratio rule principle, instead of partially on that principle as in the 1935 Act and in the British Act." NAC, RG 40, Series 3, Vol. 24, file 8, Memo to MacNamara from Watson, 6 December 1940.

98. NAC, RG 40, Series 3, Vol. 24, file 6, A Summary of the 1938 Draft Unemployment Insurance Bill.

99. NAC, RG 40, Series 3, Vol. 24, file 8, Memo to MacNamara from Watson, 6 December 1940.

100. Canada, House of Commons, *Debates,* 26 July 1940, 1990.

101. NAC, RG 40, Vol. 24, file Unemployment Insurance (7), D. Christie Tait, "Report on a Proposed Unemployment Insurance Bill in Canada," early 1938, 40.

102. *Ibid.,* 42.

103. NAC, RG 40, Series 3, Vol. 24, file 1, Watson's (Revised) Actuarial Report on Contributions, 3 November 1934.

104. NAC, RG 40, Vol. 24, file Unemployment Insurance (7), D. Christie Tait's 1938 Report on UI Bill, 2-6.

105. Frederick George Sanderson, Liberal M.P. for Perth South, Ontario, criticized the Act for its treatment of part-time workers. Canada, House of Commons, *Debates,* 19 February 1935, 990.

106. Canada, House of Commons, *Debates,* 19 July 1940, 1786.

107. NAC, RG 27, Vol. 886, file 8-9-26, part 1, Memo re. Amendments to the Unemployment Insurance Act, 1940, to Chairman and Members of the Unemployment Insurance Advisory Committee from L.J. Trottier, Chief Commissioner, 21 February 1945.

108. First Schedule, Part II (n), 1935 Act: First Schedule, Part II (m), 1938 Draft Bill and 1940 Act.

109. First Schedule, Part II (l), 1935 Act; First Schedule, Part II (k), 1938 Draft Bill and 1940 Act.

110. NAC, RG 40, Vol. 24, file Unemployment Insurance (7), D. Christie Tait's 1938 Report on UI, 32. Another argument developed to justify excepting the teaching profession from UI was that the administration of unemployment insurance was to be organized around an employment service infrastructure, and one could hardly expect a teacher to bypass boards of education and seek placement through an employment office. Canada, House of Commons, *Debates,* 26 July 1940, 1988.

111. First Schedule, Part II, (i), (h), (g), 1935 Act; First Schedule, Part II, (h), (g), (f), 1938 Draft Bill and 1940 Act.

112. Canada, House of Commons, *Debates,* 29 July 1940, 2056.

113. *Ibid.*

114. NAC, RG 40, Series 3, Vol. 24, file 3, Memo. on Excepted Employments, anon., n.d., presumably by Watson in early 1935.

115. Canada, House of Commons, *Debates,* 19 July 1940, 1781.

116. Canada, House of Commons, *Debates,* 26 July 1940, 1988.

117. NAC, RG 40, Vol. 24, file Unemployment Insurance (6), Notes on the Unemployment Insurance Draft Bill (1938), n.a.

118. NAC, RG 40, Vol. 24, file Unemployment Insurance (7), D. Christie Tait, "Report on a Proposed Unemployment Insurance Bill," 27.

119. See Pierson, Introduction to Chapter Six, "Paid Work," in *No Easy Road.*

120. Section 20 (1) (iii) of 1935 Act; Section 16 (1) (iii) of 1938 Draft Bill; and Section 28 (iii) of 1940 Act.

121. According to English Common Law and the Quebec Civil Code, the principle of "the unity of domicile" required that "a wife's domicile, like that of her minor children, [be] that of the husband." It changed as he changed his domicile and not as she changed hers. Indeed, the husband could change his domicile [her "dependent" domicile] against the wife's will "or even without her knowledge." Canada, Royal Commission on the Status of Women in Canada, *Report* (Ottawa 1970), 236-7.

122. Canada, House of Commons, *Debates,* 12 February 1935, 771.

123. NAC, RG 40, Series 3, Vol. 24, file 8, 1940 Bill.

124. Canada, House of Commons, *Debates,* 21 February 1935.

125. NAC, RG 40, Series 3, Vol. 24, file 8, First Reading UI Bill, July 1940; Canada, "The Unemployment Insurance Act, 1940," *Acts of the Parliament of the Dominion of Canada* (Ottawa 1940), c. 44, s. 83 (1).

126. NAC, RG 27, Vol. 163, file 612-01 (68-4), Memo of 3 December 1940 from Minister of Labour recommending appointments to the Unemployment Insurance Advisory Committee. The woman was Miss Estelle Hewson, Secretary of the Border Branch of the Canadian Red Cross, Windsor, Ontario. NAC, RG 50, Vol. 57, file U05— Miss Estelle Hewson, Letter to Dr. W.A. Mackintosh, Chairman, UIC, from Estelle Hewson, 27 December 1940.

127. The Encyclopaedists and philosophes, like Rousseau, called for the diversification of the category of 'man' to reflect the diversity of 'men,' differentiated, as they were seen to be, "by religions, governments, laws, customs, prejudices, climates." Rousseau, *Lettre à D' Alembert* (Garnier-Flamarion edition), 67, quoted in Michèle Le Doeuff, "Pierre Roussel's Chiasmas: from imaginary knowledge to the learned imagination," *Ideology & Consciousness,* 9 (Winter 1981/82), 53. Then the French Revolution abolished the division of society into orders that had applied to women as well as to men and replaced it with a system that drew distinctions among men according to property and occupation but introduced the political treatment of women *en bloc.* It is in that "historic passage from one system of discrimination (by estate) to another (by sex)" that diversity and plurality came to characterize the category 'men' while unity and homogeneity came to characterize the category 'woman.' Le Doeuff, 52.

128. The Unemployment Insurance Act stipulated that "there shall be appointed at least one [member] after consultation with organizations representative of employed persons and an equal number after consultation with organizations representative of employers." "The Unemployment Insurance Act, 1940," s. 83 (3).

129. By definition not in the labour market because not gainfully employed and hence not eligible for unemployment insurance.

130. Diana M. Pearce, "Toil and Trouble: Women, Workers and Unemployment Compensation," *Signs,* 10 (Spring 1985), 439-59.

CHAPTER

10 WILLIAM LYON MACKENZIE KING

If political success is measured by longevity, then Mackenize King's twenty-two years as Canadian Prime Minister make him a very successful politician indeed. Despite this, few Canadian political leaders have received such widely varying treatment at the hands of historians. To some, King represents the epitome of political craftsmanship, the skilled leader with his mind always on the elusive goal of national unity. For those who subscribe to this point of view, King's handling of the conscription issue during the Second World War was his crowning achievement.

King's detractors, among historians, cannot challenge his political success, but they insist that King's goal was less national unity than the success of his own political career, and they argue that the means he used to achieve his ends were petty, unscrupulous, and sometimes immoral. Far from providing the country with strong leadership, he was a model of ambiguity and indecision: "conscription if necessary, but not necessarily conscription."

A further complication for historians, in attempting to assess Mackenzie King, is his somewhat bizarre personality. Shortly after his death, stories about his experiments with spiritualism began to circulate. His extraordinarily extensive diaries, which he had directed should be destroyed after his death (an instruction which his executors decided to ignore), provide a unique insight into the private personality of a political leader.

The first reading in this chapter is by Blair Neatby, author of all but the first volume of the authorized biography of Mackenzie King. In it Neatby argues, in the context of the Great Depression, that King provided real leadership. Although not a radical in any sense, King was "the conciliator in politics" who could hold his government and his party and his country together in a time of crisis.

The second reading, by Colonel C.P. Stacey, is a chapter from a book in which Stacey attempted to analyse what he termed "the private world of Mackenzie King." Some of Stacey's conclusions, particularly those relating to King's sexual proclivities, are controversial and have been challenged. In the reading reprinted here, Stacey examines the question of the extent to which King's public policies were influenced by spiritualism during the Second World War.

The author of the third reading, Joy Esberey, disagrees with Stacey that King led a "a double life." Rather, she claims, "the separation of the private and public King is invalid." Drawing on psychological concepts, she argues that King's political career can only be understood by viewing his public and private lives as integrated rather than contradictory. The private life becomes an explanatory tool rather than something to be explained away.

Suggestions for Further Reading

Dawson, R. MacGregor, *William Lyon Mackenzie King: A Political Biography*. Volume I. Toronto: University of Toronto Press, 1958.

Granatstein, J.L., *Canada's War: The Politics of the Mackenzie King Government*. Toronto: Oxford, 1975.

Neatby, H. Blair, "Mackenzie King and French Canada," *Journal of Canadian Studies*, XI, no. 1 (February 1976), 3-13.

_____, *William Lyon Mackenzie King*, 2 volumes. Toronto: University of Toronto Press, 1963, 1966.

Whitaker, Reginald, "The Liberal Corporatist Ideas of Mackenzie King," *Labour/Le Travailleur*, II (1977), 137-169.

_____, "Political Thought and Political Action in Mackenzie King," *Journal of Canadian Studies*, XIII, no. 4 (Winter 1978-79), 40-60.

WILLIAM LYON MACKENZIE KING: THE CONCILIATOR IN POLITICS

H. Blair Neatby

Mackenzie King is one of the best known and least liked of all our prime ministers. Even today he is a controversial figure; a man who had none of the obvious qualities of a leader and yet a man who survived for an incredibly long time in a very hazardous occupation—he was leader of the Liberal party for almost thirty years and prime minister for over twenty. And not only that, he left an indelible stamp on the country. Whether for good or ill, today's Canada is partly King's making.

From *The Politics of Chaos: Canada in the Thirties* (Toronto: Copp Clark Pitman, 1986), 73-87. Reprinted by permission of Copp Clark Pitman.

Our concern is with the Mackenzie King of the 1930s. Even in those years his contemporaries were puzzled by the man. R.J. Manion, a Conservative opponent, commented that King was unpopular in the House of Commons and among most Canadians. How could such a man win elections? Manion could only suggest that he was an "opportunist, *par excellence*" and also very lucky.[1]

Prominent Liberals were just as ambivalent. J.W. Dafoe of the *Free Press,* for example, was a very partisan critic of R.B. Bennett but he also had reservations about King. Dafoe never sided with the Liberals who wanted to get rid of King—and there were many such Liberals in the early 1930s—but on the other hand he was never prepared to go farther than to say that King, for all his weaknesses, was the best man available. Most party leaders rouse more enthusiasm.

What is the explanation for this ambivalence? The simple answer is that Mackenzie King himself *was* an ambivalent figure. His career is strewn with apparent contradictions and inconsistencies. He seemed to be flabby and indecisive; never yes, never no, always maybe or partly, always the smoke screen of qualifications which concealed any decision, or hid the fact that no decision had been made. And yet this apparently indecisive man picked forceful and powerful colleagues; Gardiner, Dunning, Ralston, C.D. Howe—these men were not nonentities. What is more, King controlled and dominated these men. Ralston he dismissed abruptly, without warning. And C.D. Howe once said that the key to King's career was that King was a leader—a telling remark coming from C.D. Howe! The ambivalence shows up in King's policies too. He posed as a social reformer: the first Minister of Labour, the industrial consultant, the workingman's friend. And yet his record of social legislation is a meagre one, and is as easily explained by political opportunism as by political conviction.

King's political longevity becomes more credible if we begin with his concept of political leadership. King did not believe in imposing his will or his policies on his party; he was not an authoritarian leader like Bennett. King believed that his party, and his cabinet, had to be consulted and had to be convinced before a policy could be adopted. He believed in participatory democracy, at least within the party. This didn't mean that he suppressed his own opinions— quite often it meant that he converted others to the policy he preferred. On other occasions, however, it could mean agreement on a policy or a compromise for which he had little enthusiasm. Political leadership for him was like being a conciliator in labour disputes; the successful conciliator is one who comes to understand the point of view of both sides, and who can thus suggest a compromise or a settlement which both sides can accept. The conciliator is not a passive bystander. He tries to create a satisfactory agreement, a consensus. He contributes his own ideas as well as his techniques for arriving at agreement. Although the final outcome cannot be dictated it is often the result of persuasion.

Mackenzie King's reaction to the depression illustrates his activities as a conciliator. Initially King, like many of his contemporaries, saw the depression as a temporary recession. It could not be ignored but at the same time it did not seem to demand drastic or radical measures. King, in the Liberal tradition, believed at first that the economy would recover with little help from governments. The important thing, from his point of view, was not to obstruct the process but to allow economic laws to operate. Canadian Liberals saw the protective tariff as the worst form of obstruction. By creating artificial barriers to trade, the tariff distorted national economies, and at the same time taxed the poor for the benefit of the rich. It was natural therefore for King in the early 1930s to blame the depression on the tariff which Bennett had just raised to unprecedented levels. Even as late as 1932 King was still focusing on the tariff as the real villain. In the session of that year the Liberal amendment to the budget declared that lower tariffs were "essential to a revival of trade, and improvement of business, and the return of prosperity."

By 1932, however, the traditional emphasis on the tariff no longer satisfied all Liberals. Western Liberals, for example, once so obsessed with the tariff issue, no longer cared. Lower tariffs might reduce the cost of farm machinery but what did this matter when wheat prices were too low to cover the costs of production, much less meet mortgage payments and provide a living? Most westerners by this time had decided that the depression posed new and urgent problems and could only be resolved by new and radical measures. Many of them had come to the radical and almost revolutionary conclusion that the answer lay, not in lower tariffs, but in inflation. Inflation would raise the prices of farm products. It would also raise the prices of the goods which farmers purchased but there would still be a net gain. Most farmers had mortgages on their land and machinery, mortgages based on the inflated prices of the 1920s but which now had to be repaid when dollars were scarce. Inflation, by lowering the value of money, would redress the balance, and make it possible to pay debts in devalued currency. Even in 1932 King had been under strong pressure from western Liberals to go beyond the tariff and opt for some form of inflation. Eastern Liberals were not sympathetic to the idea. They did not represent a debtor community; deliberate inflation was to them shockingly dangerous and even immoral. How could business survive if money had no stable value? There could be no Liberal consensus on inflation under these conditions and so King pacified the westerners by leaving inflation an open question. In the 1932 session at least, the party stayed united on its tariff resolution.

King, however, was sensitive to shifting political currents. Personally he would have been happy to continue to concentrate on the tariff issue; inflation seemed to him morally wrong and unlikely to foster economic recovery. But as party leader he could not ignore the feelings of his western followers. The party must be kept united. If Liberals could not agree to concentrate on the tariff, some new basis of agreement was needed. Inflation did not look like a promising avenue. In addition to King's personal misgivings, it was clear that eastern Liberals would not support that policy.

It was here that King illustrated his capacity for leadership—for his type of leadership. In the fall of 1932 he met with some prominent Liberals, a select group which included Vincent Massey and J.W. Dafoe as well as active politicians like Lapointe and Ralston. They argued about tariff policy, railway policy and, inevitably, about monetary policy. All of these men were Liberals with concern for the underprivileged but also with a healthy respect for free enterprise and existing social institutions. They were not likely to opt for simple panaceas such as printing money. All of them could remember the postwar inflation in Germany a dozen years earlier, when people had gone to the bakery with a wheel-barrow of paper marks for a loaf of bread. But on the other hand, what of the argument that the value of money had already changed during the depression? The depression could be seen as a period of deflation; to say that the prices had declined was only another way of saying that the value of money had increased. Would it be possible to manipulate the money supply to increase prices without having a runaway inflation? How could the money supply be safely adjusted? What about a central bank?

Mackenzie King was intrigued by the possibility. He had once been trained as an economist but he knew little about the complexities of velocity of circulation and rediscount rates, so he consulted Professor Curtis, an economist at Queen's University. From him King learned that a central bank would be necessary if a policy of controlled inflation was ever adopted, but that a central bank did not necessarily mean inflation. Here was the compromise King was looking for. He knew his party could not be united on a policy of inflation but both western and eastern Liberals might be persuaded to agree on the establishment of a central bank. The compromise might be summed up as "inflation if necessary but not necessarily inflation."

It was not enough for King to decide on a policy. Bennett was the kind of leader who announced his decisions in radio broadcasts but for King political leadership involved consultation and discussion. When Parliament reassembled in January of 1933 King therefore announced to caucus that a Liberal platform needed to be hammered out and proposed a number of caucus committees to discuss the various planks. All of the committees—tariffs, railways, social welfare—encountered some difficulty in reaching agreement, but the committee on monetary policy was almost a free-for-all, as he knew it would be. King, however, used all his considerable talent as a conciliator. He attended all the meetings, began by suggesting the central bank as a possible basis of agreement, listened carefully to the contradictory views, drafted what he hoped would be an acceptable policy statement after three weeks, allowed the debate to continue for another two weeks, revised his draft slightly to meet the criticisms and finally got all members of the committee to agree that the draft was at least acceptable—as far as it went. The final consensus was that the Liberal party advocated a central bank. It went farther, however, and also stated that the supply of currency and credit should be determined by the needs of the community.

This was still vague. Liberals might still disagree on what the needs of the community were; but the platform was nonetheless a radical advance in party policy. The Liberal party had affirmed that government should control monetary policy, that it should manipulate currency and credit. Money was no longer sacrosanct; governments on this basis would be as responsible for the supply of money as they were for the level of tariffs or taxes. From King's point of view, what was even more important was that all members of the party had agreed. This policy represented a consensus on which the party was united. It was no mean achievement to have negotiated such a radical shift in policy without alienating any of his followers.

The Liberal platform of 1933 remained the official platform of the party through the election campaign of 1935. It had been difficult enough to arrive at a consensus and King had no urge to open up the Pandora's box and start all over again. In any case, he did not think it was necessary. He was sure that the Liberals would win the next election. It seemed the part of wisdom to be as flexible as possible; to adopt general principles without being committed to specific measures. The party favoured freer trade, closer cooperation with provincial governments, more efficient administration—but few details were spelled out.

It required a good deal of self-confidence to avoid specific promises. Other parties were less reserved. R.B. Bennett had his New Deal. The C.C.F. had its Regina Manifesto of 1933. H.H. Stevens' Reconstruction party was promising a wide range of measures which would restore prosperity. Social Credit had its inflationary panacea. Many Liberals feared that they would suffer defeat if they did not participate in this auction. King, however, was convinced that the Canadian voters had had enough of reckless and unfulfilled promises. He was sure that they would have more respect for a party which offered a stable and responsible administration. In the welter and confusion of three new parties and a Conservative party which had changed its spots, the Liberal party would offer cautious reform. The Liberal slogan in 1935 was "King or chaos." As a slogan it reflected accurately enough the political situation. The Liberal party was the only party with significant support across the country. If it did not win, there would be no majority government. The slogan also reflected King's view that the Liberal party would win without offering anything more specific. The voters confirmed his analysis: they returned 171 Liberals in a House of 245, the largest majority in Canadian history up to that time.

Any slogan, however, is an oversimplification. Chaos was still possible, even with King in office. The multiplicity of parties in 1935 was a reflection of fundamental divisions within the country. One out of every five voters had voted for new parties, radical parties, parties which had not even existed in 1930. And even within the older parties, Conservative and Liberal, there were differences and divisions which had not been resolved. These political divisions were based on deeply rooted divisions within Canada itself. The grievances of western Canada, for example, explain why both the C.C.F. and Social Credit parties drew their strength from that region. The Liberal party itself was a coalition of regional and cultural blocs, and there was no guarantee that it would hold together in the face of the continuing economic crisis.

Mackenzie King, when he returned to office in 1935, had no new or novel policies. In many ways he was still the King of an earlier era. In 1921 he had come into office during an economic recession. His government had economized, it had balanced its budget and even reduced the national debt, it had lowered tariffs and taxes. Within a few years prosperity had returned, and King believed that there was a cause and effect relationship. He was convinced that these policies had brought prosperity once and that similar policies in the 1930s would produce similar results. He did not close the door on new ideas, but he hoped that the tested remedies of the past would still be effective.

He began with the traditional Liberal policy of freer trade. Within three weeks of taking office he had signed a trade agreement with the United States. Negotiations had begun when Bennett was still Prime Minister but Bennett had not been enthusiastic. King had no reservations, although the implications were far-reaching. It was the first formal trade agreement with the United States since the Reciprocity Agreement of 1854 and it marked the turning away from the ever-increasing tariff barriers between the two countries which had reached their peak with the Hawley-Smoot tariff and the Bennett tariff, both in 1930. A further trade agreement was signed three years later, this time involving Great Britain as well as the United States. The trend was clearly towards increased trade with the United States. It is a trend which has continued ever since until today the relationship is almost symbiotic.

Freer trade, especially with the United States, was expected to benefit Canadian producers of natural products by increasing their markets. It was a traditional Liberal policy and the effects would be gradual at best. The same traditional and cautious approach could be seen in the first budget of the new government. No new expenditures were proposed but corporation taxes and the sales tax were increased. The aim was to balance the budget, to have the federal government live within its means.

Even monetary policy scarcely reflected the long-drawn-out discussion over inflation. R.B. Bennett had established a central bank in 1934. The Bank of Canada which he set up was a banker's bank, independent of the federal government and primarily concerned with financial stability. The Liberal government amended the constitution of the Bank of Canada to establish federal control and eventually federal ownership. It was thus in a position to determine the supply of currency and credit on the basis of the needs of the community. Under Graham Towers, however, the Bank of Canada had already established a policy of easy money. Chartered banks had plenty of money to lend at low rates of interest. The policy of easy money was continued but neither Towers nor the government under King was prepared to print more money.

Special measures were introduced for the drought areas on the prairies, where crop disaster continued to be almost the normal way of life. Some marginal crop land was turned back to grazing land and an insurance scheme was introduced to provide some income for farmers in a year of crop failure. The Wheat Board, established under Bennett, was continued under the Liberal government. What improvement there was, however—and there was some—had little to do with federal policies. Crop failures and acreage reductions in Canada and elsewhere in the world gradually eliminated the world wheat surplus and wheat prices increased, although they were still below a dollar a bushel. The price trend was at least encouraging, and if rains would come and if grasshoppers and rust and frost would stay away, the farmers could hope to get off relief.

At this stage there was nothing radical, nothing really novel, nothing that was not consistent with traditional and orthodox Liberalism. The orthodoxy of the new government is most clearly shown in its efforts to economize, to balance the federal budget. The greatest drain on the budget was still the heavy relief expenditures: unemployment relief and farm relief. Soon after taking office King appointed a National Employment Commission, which was asked to do two things. It was to reorganize the administration of all relief expenditures, in the hope that a more centralized and more efficient administration would eliminate duplication and reduce costs. It was also asked to recommend measures which might be taken to create employment opportunities and so remove men from the relief rolls.

The National Employment Commission was not able to introduce many economies. Most of the relief was administered by provincial and municipal governments and, even though the federal government was providing much of the money, there was little the federal government could do to change the system. It was a different story when it came to recommending positive measures to foster employment. The Commission argued that employment was not a local but a national problem. A factory might close down in Hamilton but the cause was elsewhere—in the declining purchasing power in the Maritimes or the prairies perhaps, where men could no longer afford to buy the products of the factory. Two major conclusions were drawn from this analysis. Because the Canadian economy was national and not local or provincial in scope, unemployment must be seen as a national problem. The Commission therefore recommended that the federal government should take over the full cost of unemployment relief. The Commission went much farther, however; it argued that some positive action could be taken to reduce unemployment. Instead of economizing and trying to balance the budget, it recommended increased federal expenditures and reduced taxation in times of depression. The motor of the economy was seen as investment. When private enterprise was not prepared to invest money—when there was a depression—governments should deliberately incur deficits in order to counterbalance the deficiency. John Maynard Keynes had arrived in Canada.

Mackenzie King's initial response to these suggestions was more than negative: it was hostile. He paid little attention to the positive proposals; he was shocked even at the suggestion that the federal government should pay the full cost of unemployment relief. The federal government was having enough trouble meeting its financial obligations as it was; it seemed absurd to aggravate its problems by taking over more responsibilities. King was reacting like a traditional federalist, insisting that both levels of government, federal and provincial, should look after their own affairs. It was at this time, in the fall of 1937, that King decided to set up yet another royal commission—the Rowell-Sirois Commission on Dominion-Provincial Relations. If the federal system was going to be changed it would not be changed unilaterally, by having the federal government volunteer to take on new burdens.

But the positive proposals of the Employment Commission were not forgotten. The 1938 session might be the last session before the next election. King suggested to the Minister of Finance, Charles Dunning, that he plan a pre-election budget. For King this meant a balanced budget, for he was sure that responsible Canadians wanted a government which lived within its means. Charles Dunning agreed; he too believed that government deficits were undesirable, if not immoral. Dunning's first draft of his budget proposed a small surplus.

King and Dunning, however, were surprised to find that some cabinet ministers no longer believed in balanced budgets. Norman Rogers, Minister of Labour, had been converted by the Employment Commission. He argued that Dunning should budget for a deficit and talked of an additional $40 million for public works to inject money into the economy. Dunning threatened to resign if this policy was adopted; Rogers threatened to resign if it wasn't. Other cabinet ministers took sides. It was the kind of situation in which King the conciliator took over. He was not convinced by the arguments but he was, as always, convinced that the party must be kept united. Eventually he proposed $25 million of additional expenditure as a compromise and set up a cabinet committee to decide how the money would be spent.

The budget of 1938 was a turning point in fiscal policy in Canada. For the first time a government had consciously decided to spend money to counteract a low in the business cycle. In addition to the expenditures in the budget the government also offered loans to municipalities for local improvements and passed a National Housing Act to encourage the building of homes. Consistent with this Keynesian approach, the government also reduced some taxes and offered some tax exemptions for private investors. The idea of a static and balanced budget was gone. In its place was a fiscal policy of stimulating economic recovery by government deficits and by direct economic incentives.

The new fiscal policy did not work any miracles. Recovery would not come until the war, when deficit financing and government investment in the economy became a patriotic duty. But the budget of 1938 marks the beginning of a new concept of the role of government in Canada. Until then the federal government had concentrated on providing public services such as railways and canals, police forces and national defence, post offices, and more recently old age pensions and unemployment relief. The taxes it had collected were designed to pay for these services. It had now undertaken a new and significantly different responsibility: that of balancing the total economic investment, private and public, in order to balance the national economy. The implications would be far-reaching. The government budgets of our day are dominated by this new role. Looking back to the 1930s we can now see that it was the most radical and most constructive innovation of that depression decade.

And yet it is still difficult to visualize Mackenzie King as a radical. He was not an innovator; he was not a man with original ideas. Indeed, he still continued to believe that eventually governments should balance their budgets and let free enterprise flourish. Certainly he did not appreciate the significance of the Keynesian revolution. King's strength was in his commitment to a policy of party unity, and in his capacity to accept and adopt new ideas when the alternative was a division within the party. This concept of political leadership had brought King a long way since 1930. On monetary issues he had begun with the certainty that inflation was sin but had come to accept the idea of a central bank which might manipulate currency and credit on the basis of social need. On fiscal policy he had begun with the traditional ideas of a limited role for government with balanced budgets and had come to accept the idea of government responsibility for controlling the level of economic activity.

Under King the Liberal party did respond, gradually and tentatively, to the pressures of a revolutionary decade, and under his leadership it responded without disintegrating into warring factions. To be leader of a still united party four years later was in itself no small achievement. The risk of party schisms had been real. More significant, the party still seemed to have popular support. Mackenzie King's policies had not been dramatic but his concept of political leadership had averted possible chaos.

Notes

1. R.J. Manion, *Life is an Adventure* (Toronto, 1937), p. 290.

WAR: THE PRIME MINISTER SWEARS OFF

C.P. Stacey

The autumn of 1939 brought the war which Canadian politicians, remembering the desperate domestic crisis of 1917, had had particular reason to hope might be averted. The outbreak had a special consequence for Mackenzie King. In effect, he swore off spiritualism for the duration.

On 1 September Hitler, no longer "careful", invaded Poland. On the evening of the 2nd, King and Joan Patteson held at Kingsmere what turned out to be the craziest of all their sessions with the little table.[1] It began with King's father announcing that Hitler was dead: "He was shot by a Pole." King's mother, Laurier, Gladstone, and Max King followed; and William Lyon Mackenzie drew a parallel between himself in 1837 and the German dictator:

> *I did not want to shed a drop of blood*
> *I was driven to desperation*
> *Hitler did not want to have war*
> *He has become desperate.*

At this point there was an interruption. It was 11 p.m. O. D. Skelton telephoned to say that at midnight (London time) the British Cabinet had decided to have Sir Nevile Henderson, the British Ambassador in Berlin, deliver an ultimatum to Germany demanding the withdrawal of German troops from Poland, failing which there would be immediate war. King and Skelton agreed that the British should have allowed more time. King then returned to the table. His father's spirit still asserted that Hitler was dead, and said, "The French and British will agree to a conference when they hear of Hitler's death." King asked, "Are you sure this is not all subconscious thought and desire asserting itself?", but the spirits insisted, and the sitting ended with his mother declaring, "War will be averted."

This very peculiar personal problem added to King's anxieties at this desperate moment. He wrote in his diary:[2]

> ... The real issue:—Christ vs. anti-Christ. I felt strongly tonight, after conversation J. and I had, that there are some things that [as?] Asquith said which we were not meant to know in the sense of attempting to know them by the senses, but which could be known only to Faith. In other words, that the spiritual things must be spiritually discerned; that we must not hope to get the profound spiritual experiences and truths through material agencies. Least of all, must we seek to convince ourselves as to courses of conduct in great decisions by occult means. The Roman Catholic church, I believe, is right in recognizing the existence of phenomena of the kind, but in recognizing its [sic] dangers.

From *A Very Double Life: The Private World of Mackenzie King* (Toronto: Macmillan, 1976), 190-204, 244. Reprinted with the permission of the Master and Fellows of Massey College.

Evil and Good exists [*sic*] in the Hereafter as well as the here and now. Men may be guided by evil spirits or by good spirits....

On 4 September the Prime Minister added a rather formal note to his memorandum of the *séance* of the 2nd:

This all makes perfectly clear either that a lying spirit has come in somewhere, or that sub-conscious wishes dictate the words expressed.—I felt terribly exercised at this for I felt at the time it was not truth, however, that it would serve as a guide to future action & belief as to worth of "automatic writing"— I felt I should perhaps not have sought to use the table to discover the course of events. I had a feeling at the time that it was a sort of betrayal of faith so to do.— Like in Lohengrin.[a] Elsa determined to know what it was not intended she should know—It is faith one must be guided by and intuition—our guide [WLMK Sept. 4]

Here King seems to be repudiating the little table, while reserving judgement as to automatic writing. From this moment the familiar pencilled memoranda of sittings at the little table vanish from King's diary, and references to the table disappear from the text.

The Prime Minister's motives in abandoning the table at this particular point are interesting to speculate upon. The doubts he records about the genuineness of the information it gave him could have arisen at any time, and in fact they had arisen at the time of the knighthoods affair in 1934, "lying spirit" and all. But war is a more serious business than peace, and the leader of a country at war has reason to be especially cautious about the sources of his information and the influences that bear upon him. What is more, he has particular reason to be cautious about his public image. It would have been highly dangerous to King politically at any time if the Canadian public had been informed of his spiritualistic proclivities; with the country at war, it would have been instantly fatal, and King undoubtedly was well aware of it.

It is interesting that King suggested that the table's messages were a product of "subconscious thought"—his own, of course—(though it was surely very simple-minded to ask the spirits about it). Joan had suggested this in 1934. I am left wondering whether, for King, the table had finally become a sort of game, which he enjoyed enormously but did not absolutely believe in, and which he could give up without serious injury to his life.

It should be added that with the outbreak of war King's tolerance for Hitler was at an end. On 23 January 1940, *à propos* of the refusal of General Hertzog of South Africa to believe in Hitler's desire for world domination, he wrote, "I shared that view myself at the time but I have changed it in the light of what has developed since this war began. Germany could not have developed the military machine she has nor proceeded in any way she did unless she were bent on world domination by terror and violence."

---

[a] King had been seeking for explanations of Hitler in the Wagner operas.

The little table was a highly personal and private operation, and very few people apart from King and the Pattesons knew about it. It is questionable whether his secretaries knew, for his records of the *séances* held across it were written by himself in longhand. The danger of the wrong people coming to know about the table was therefore comparatively slight. *Séances* held with mediums were a different matter. When King consulted a medium he was putting his career in her hands and in those of her associates.[b] Moreover, in wartime the steps of a Prime Minister were apt to be dogged by the press even more than in peace. In these circumstances it is not surprising that he severed almost all connection with the spiritualistic fraternity in Britain during the war. He made two wartime visits to London, in 1941 and 1944. In striking contrast with his actions earlier and later, during these visits there were no *séances*. Of his spiritualist friends, the only ones he had contact with were the Duchess of Hamilton and some members of her circle; and none of these contacts seems to have been closer than a telephone conversation. In 1941 he did not even manage to speak to the Duchess (she was trying to get him as he left his hotel to return to Canada), but he sent her a farewell telegram. In 1944 he recorded what appears to have been a telephone talk with her: "She is most understanding. She had hoped to have me meet a number of friends. But realized what the situation was."[3]

In the course of these visits King did not darken the doors of the London Spiritualist Alliance, where before and after he was wont to make arrangements for meetings with mediums. In October 1945, when he had revoked his self-denying ordinance against spiritualism, he went back there again to see Miss Mercy Phillimore, the Secretary of the Alliance. "I was amazed," he wrote, "to learn it was nine years since I had last been there or seen her."[4] He had apparently not been there during his 1937 visit.

The general absence of *séances* from King's diary for the years 1939-45 does not mean that it is a dull or conventional document. It is true that it is basically an enormously valuable dictated record of public business, a detailed day-to-day account of the direction of the Canadian war effort, having as its highlights King's memoranda of his conversations with Churchill, Roosevelt, and other great figures of the crisis. But—well representing the double life that King continued to lead—it continues also to be highly eccentric. It describes—often in King's difficult longhand—his psychic experiences, and in particular his dreams, which he normally terms "visions".[c] Almost every day's diary entry commences

---

[b] I have been assured that many people in Kingston knew of King's consulting a fortune-teller there. But this never reached the newspapers, or if it did it was not published. In spiritualism, as in other matters, King was lucky. The mediums he dealt with were sincere and dedicated people who kept his confidence and were not interested in making money out of him. He would have been an ideal blackmail target, but so far as I know no such attempt was ever made on him.

[c] "Was surprised to find I had been keeping records of visions from 1934, etc., re future—quite clearly recognising later in the day & often in year the vision coming true—(I recall how mother emphasized these are not dreams, they are visions)...." (Diary, 9 Jan. 1938).

with an account of the overnight vision. Frequently, but not always, it stars the deceased members of his family. And frequently King's attempts at interpretation are as curious as the dream. Here, from the early days of the war, is an example taken at random. King records how he felt cold in the night and put an extra quilt on his bed. Then came the vision. He was following a well-known Ottawa lady through the streets of the capital, with an umbrella in his hand. They turned into "a sort of Club or room where a lot of men seemed to be lying in pyjamas.... Suddenly the word 'Mac' and 'Max' came very strongly before me, and I felt at once it was my brother the Doctor who was advising me that it was the covering on me which was causing the damage. The men lying in pyjamas stood for lighter form of bed clothing.... Once I threw off the brown quilt which I had added for the cold, I began to feel relief of body and mind...." King's final conclusion was, "I am quite certain that those who are nearest to me are watching over me hour by hour, and that this was another evidence of it...."[5]

Also increasingly prominent in these wartime diaries is the old obsession with the position of the hands of the clock. Perhaps this and the dreams are compensating King for the loss of the little table. One could give innumerable examples. One is enough. On 25 August 1943 President Roosevelt visited Ottawa; and King wrote a "Memo re hands of clock" as they were at various times that day, beginning with "Exactly 10 past 8 when I looked at clock on waking—straight line", and including "12 noon when noon day gun fired & I read my welcome to President—together", not to mention "25 to 8 when I was handed in my room a letter from Churchill re supply of whiskey to troops ...—both together". Occasionally King is still found consulting the tea-leaves, though not, I think, to discover the future course of the war.[6]

It must further be said—and it will probably surprise nobody—that King's rejection of spiritualism for the duration was not total. Like a drinker who has taken the pledge, but secretly resorts at intervals to the bottle, he occasionally returns to the old ways. The death of Pat I in July 1941, an episode of enormous importance to King, resulted in a *séances* over the little table in which King's parents reported Pat's arrival in the Beyond. They did not mention receiving the "messages of love" that King had entrusted to him. But they described his happy reunion with the Pattesons' dog Derry: "They know all about hunting for rabbits and squirrels." (At this point, Joan remarks, "I hope there are no cats in heaven—it would be hell if there were.") Joan, it is to be feared, did not always take the little table quite as seriously as King.

This sitting was closely followed by two more, arising out of King's plan to visit Britain shortly—another very important matter (flying the Atlantic was novel and serious business for an elderly politician in 1941). In one, Sir Wilfrid Laurier tells him to go by bomber plane and adds that the weather will be bad for flying in September; his mother tells him that Churchill will be delighted to see him ("He likes you very much"); and W. E. Gladstone tells him that the war will be over before Christmas, and that the President loves him, and wants to see him before he goes to England. (That did not happen, but King did have a telephone talk with Roosevelt before he took off.) The other sitting consisted mainly of advice about the will that King was making. All three were recorded in the old way, in pencilled memoranda written by King and placed in the diary.[7] This revival of the table seems to have been a brief and isolated incident.

As with the table, so with *séances* and with mediums. They were rare, but it cannot be said that there were none. Notably, there was one in Toronto in August 1942. King was visiting the office of his publishers, the Macmillan Company of Canada. Conversation with an official of the company revealed that she was a spiritualist and resulted in a spur-of-the-moment *séance* with a "little medium" that evening before the Prime Minister caught the Ottawa train. A galaxy of talent attended: not only King's relations and Laurier, but Queen Victoria, Florence Nightingale, Anne Boleyn, Sir Frederick Banting, Norman Rogers, and others. King had never seen the medium before.[8] One is amazed by his imprudence in putting his career at the mercy of this unknown young woman. It seems likely that he would not have done so had he had more time to think. As always, he was lucky; the story did not get out. But every such episode must have widened the circle of people who knew about the Prime Minister's peculiarities.

In addition to these recorded incidents, we have to reckon with the possibility that others went unrecorded. Did the secret tippler perhaps hold some sessions at the little table without telling the diary? It may be worth while to note something about the record of the epoch-making sitting of 2 September 1939. Except for the pencilled memorandum of it, there is no direct reference to it in the diary. It may be recalled that the text states that King's doubts arose "after conversation J. and I had". This is certainly the table sitting. Elsewhere the text says, "had J. come over for a little *talk, reading and conversation* together" (the italics are mine). The word *conversation* was sometimes used as a synonym for *séance* or *sitting*. Here it was doubtless used to conceal the real meaning from the secretary to whom King was dictating.[d] But when we find King writing, for instance, in 1941, "I spent an hour or so with J. in conversation. Had an exceptionally interesting talk,"[9] is this a concealed reference to a session with the table? It is quite conceivable, but it seems impossible to be certain.

The war's interference with King's spiritualistic activities does not seem to have depressed him. There is no return of the morbid desire for contact with his mother that is found in the diary before the first *séances* with Mrs. Wriedt in 1932. He now thought he knew what he had wished to know. On 18 December 1943, the anniversary of his mother's death, he recalls in some detail the events of 1917, and how he failed to reach Ottawa in time. He proceeds in terms that can only be called triumphant:

---

[d] King dictated his account of the *séances* in Toronto in August 1942 to J. E. Handy, who thus became aware of the Prime Minister's spiritualistic activities, if he had not been before.

My mother is nearer to me today than she was in her last day upon earth and I am nearer to her.... she has come back to me and I have now the assurance that she is at my side and that we will be together for ever.

At the end of this account of Mackenzie King's involvement with the spirit world, one faces the question, so often asked, Did he conduct the affairs of Canada in accordance with what he believed to be advice from the Beyond? And the answer is quite clearly No.

After King's death, reports of his spiritualistic activities at once began to be published, and his friend the Duchess of Hamilton was quoted in print as saying that he "fully appreciated the spiritual direction of the universe and was always seeking guidance for himself in his work".[10] Joan Patteson, who knew him better than anyone else, was much disturbed. She said nothing publicly, but she wrote to Violet Markham at this time, "*never* did he allow his belief to enter into his public life—or [himself to] be guided by anything he found in his search for Reality, as he put it. He looked forward to re-union & he longed to feel that those who loved him, still loved & watched over him & that death did not end but rather began the real life."[11] Mrs. Patteson knew more about King's private than about his public life, but all the evidence fully supports her. Blair Fraser, assiduously interviewing in 1951 the mediums whom King had consulted in the United Kingdom, came to the same conclusion.[12] Blair Neatby, after years of research in the diary and King's other private papers, saw no reason to differ. The spiritual communications King received, he writes, "did no more than confirm his confidence in his own judgment and strengthen his conviction that he was on the right path". He comments on King's "infinite capacity to rationalize, to accept what he wished to believe and to reject the rest".[13]

My own reading leaves me in no doubt of the soundness of these conclusions. A good deal of the evidence has been presented in the foregoing pages. As throughout his life, Mackenzie King in his spiritualistic period was a worried and insecure individual seeking for support. It was support, strength, not advice, that he asked for and received from the spirits. Mainly, he wanted approval, and by a strange coincidence that was what he usually got. The spirits did not, in general, tell him what to do; they told him that what he had done, or what he had decided to do, was right. Thus they sent him on his way with confidence renewed.

Though requests for help are fairly commonly recorded in the diary or in King's notes of *séances,* there are remarkably few requests for advice. At one point however, in January 1935, he did show a tendency to make such requests. He asked Lord Oxford for advice "as to demanding an election", and Oxford told him to try to force one. A week later he asked Laurier to advise him on how long to speak on the Address in reply to the Speech from the Throne; and Sir Wilfrid said, "Speak for an hour and a half.... Speak on trade and labour ... try to touch the high spots only, give up reading figures, or quotations. Try to be humorous, light touches help to relieve the monotony...."[14] I have no doubt whatever that both these replies actually represented plans already formed in King's mind, and now returned to him by his subconscious self with the stamp of approval of two great, dead Liberals. (Humour was an aspiration only; King had always known that he was not capable of it.)[e]

What King would have liked to have, apart from general encouragement, was information about future events. (What politician, what human being, would not?) We have seen him seeking it, in the comic case of the knighthoods in 1934 and in the episode of the election in 1935. In both, the information he received was wrong. The things King got over the little table, I have suggested, came out of his own head; and there were no revelations about the future to be had from there.

King constantly refers to receiving "guidance"; but these references are normally after the fact. After a successful day in Parliament, he is likely to feel that he has been "guided". The examples early in 1935 just given are isolated. Apart from them it would be difficult to find many instances in which he asked one of his correspondents in the Beyond to tell him what to do in a specific situation.

It would be strange, nevertheless, if the irrationalities of King's private world never boiled over into his other world—the rational world of public business. And I believe that this did in fact happen during the greatest political emergency of his career, the Cabinet crisis over conscription in the autumn of 1944.

King told the Governor-General's secretary, after the crisis was over, that it was "wholly the power from beyond" that had saved the day: "I was a mere instrument in working out a higher will."[15] It was a characteristic phrase, though commoner in the privacy of the diary than in conversation. The detailed record in the diary contains no indication, during that long agony, that King felt he was receiving actual guidance. The "little table", we have seen, was not much in use during the war. But to me, at least, the diary does indicate that at one very important point King acted on a basis of intuition rather than reason.

Sir Wilfrid Laurier, it has been made amply clear, was never far from King's mind. And he went into this supreme crisis in 1944 full of memories of the earlier battle over conscription in 1917 and what it had meant for Sir Wilfrid and the Party. When, on 13 October, he received Colonel Ralston's cable telling him that he was returning from England at once in order to raise grave questions, King wrote: "It is a repetition of the kind of thing that led to the creation of the Union government after Borden's return from England [in May 1917]. That will not take place under me."

---

[e]"I cannot be other than earnest. I often wish I could be humourous [sic] but I cannot, it is a decided limitation" (Diary, 20 Jan. 1904).

When trying to write the history of this episode some years ago, I thought I was faced with an interesting conundrum. Ralston told King that the time had come to adopt overseas conscription, and said that if this was not done he would have to resign. For nearly a fortnight King devoted himself to trying to argue Ralston out of resigning. On 26 October he told the Minister of National Defence that it was his duty as a soldier, and his duty under the oath he had sworn as a Minister of the Crown, to remain at his post. And then, on 1 November, when Ralston was still prepared to go on discussing the problem and to seek a compromise, King suddenly and without warning dismissed him from the Cabinet.[16] This seemed to me a little strange; and I examined the diary with care in an attempt to discover just when and why King changed his mind. I thought, and still think, that I found the turning-point on the evening of 30 October.

By this stage of the controversy nerves were certainly fraying. After a long and trying Cabinet meeting, King found awaiting him at Laurier House a telegram from George Fulford, Liberal Member for Leeds. It demanded universal overseas conscription. King remembered Fulford as a strong opponent of his family allowance ("baby bonus") project in the Liberal caucus. Fulford, moreover, though evidently no spiritualist himself, was a son of one of King's close friends in spiritualism, the lady who had introduced him to Mrs. Wriedt; the name Fulford on any document was perhaps likely to have a rather special impact upon him. At any rate the telegram triggered an extraordinary reaction in King's mind. He suddenly became convinced that there was in the Cabinet a conspiracy against him personally. This is what he wrote in the diary:

> This, at once, caused me to feel exactly what the conspiracy is, because I believe it has come to be that. It is not merely a question of conscription. The same men who are for conscription are the same identically as those who opposed most strongly the family allowances and other social reforms in the budget: Ilsley, Ralston, Howe, Macdonald, Crerar and Gibson? [*sic*] It is perfectly plain to me that in pretty much all particulars my position is becoming identical to that of Sir Wilfrid Laurier's [*sic*] where his supposedly strongest colleagues left him, one by one, and joined their political enemies and became a party for conscription. They will find that at this time they have not the Wartimes Election Act to assist them in a campaign....[17]

From this moment, I think, King was determined to dismiss Ralston, presumably because he thought of him as the kingpin of the conspiracy. The difficulty is that the diary never says so; it continues to talk in terms of Ralston's impending *resignation*. But what King *did*, as distinct from what he *wrote*, gives a different impression. The day after the revelation from the Fulford telegram, he sent for General McNaughton and obtained his promise to take the National Defence portfolio if Ralston "resigned". That afternoon he again recorded his conviction that he was the intended victim of a conspiracy: "As I sat in Council, I thought of [*sic*] what was happening to me, was exactly the same as had happened to Sir Wilfrid. I can see this whole thing has been worked out as a plot. Some of the men who were incensed at the proposal at the start are now coming round, being fearful."[18] Yet still he says no word indicating that he has a purely personal counterplot, a plan to strike the conspirators before they can strike him. Why? One explanation occurs to me. Edouard Handy, to whom King dictated the diary, was very, very reliable. But there are some risks that no wise politician takes; and this was the deadliest secret of King's career. Unfortunately, there is no private handwritten diary at this point.

Before the Cabinet met on 1 November, King took steps obviously designed to provide against other conscriptionists leaving with Ralston. He telephoned W. P. Mulock and T. A. Crerar asking them not to commit themselves to anything hasty at the meeting. He did not dare approach J. L. Ilsley and Angus L. Macdonald, Ralston's closest associates, but he did make a curious proposal to the Governor General. He suggested that if Ralston, Ilsley, and Macdonald all resigned, His Excellency should accept Ralston's resignation, but not Ilsley's or Macdonald's, at least for the moment. This would surely have been an interesting constitutional innovation. As the Cabinet was actually assembling for the meeting, King told Louis St. Laurent that McNaughton was willing to take National Defence. This politic hint to his Quebec lieutenant was the only word he had spoken on the subject. As he entered the meeting, having told nobody else—nobody at all—what he intended to do, he had on his side one of the most potent of the principles of war—surprise. Late in the afternoon he exploded his mine; and Layton Ralston gathered up his papers and left the Cabinet room—alone.[19]

If it seems strange that King recorded nothing in advance about his intention to dismiss Ralston, it is at least equally strange that later he denied that he had dismissed him at all. He appears to have denied it in the Cabinet on 7 November, before a tableful of men who had seen it happen; and he denied it in the diary that day and again six days later, although this contradicted the detailed account of the dismissal that he had written in the diary at the time. He had apparently convinced himself that Ralston had carried out his threat of resignation, and that was all.[20] It is all very peculiar, and one wonders what King's colleagues thought about it.

The fact is that there was no Cabinet conspiracy against King. The evidence is now pretty complete—there seems little likelihood that much more will come to light—and none of it supports the conspiracy theory. King himself seems to have recorded no evidence for it. The plot existed only in his mind. It was a product of irrational intuition, in the same class with the information King's dead father gave him about the knighthoods in 1934.[f] And yet I think it

---

[f] King would not have admitted this. See page 192, of *A Very Double Life: The Private World of Mackenzie King* which quotes a passage where he makes a firm distinction between information received over the table and "intuition—our guide". (For full particulars of C.P. Stacey's biography, see p. 378)

is evident that King made it the basis of a great act of policy. The most remarkable thing about the whole affair is that it turned out so well for King. Not only did he survive the crisis, but it left him stronger than ever. I have suggested elsewhere[21] that, though his strategy was non-existent, his tactics in the Ralston case were flawless and typically deadly. I might have added that he was probably the luckiest tactician who has operated in Canada since General Wolfe.

Notes

1. Notes of sitting, Kingsmere, 2 Sept. 1939 (original Diary, 1939, Vol. 133).
2. 2 Sept. 1939.
3. August-September 1941. April-May 1944. See especially 5 and 6 Sept., 1941, and 17 May 1944.
4. 17 Oct. 1945.
5. 18 Sept. 1939.
6. Memo (original Diary, Vol. 145, p. 719). Tea-leaves, e.g., 2 July 1943.
7. Notes of sittings, Kingsmere, The Farm, Wednesday, 16 July 1941; Moorside, 3 Aug. 1941; and (no place), 11 Aug. 1941 (original Diary, Vol. 139). Pickersgill and Forster, *Mackenzie King Record,* Vol. 1, 235.
8. 5 Aug. 1942.
9. 2 Feb. 1941. For more probable case, see Diary, 11 Oct. 1942 (transcribed from "Book F").
10. Article by Fred Archer in *Psychic News* (London), reprinted in *Evening Citizen,* Ottawa, 11 Oct. 1950.
11. 17 Dec. 1950 (Markham Carruthers Papers, M.G. 32, F. 6, P.A.C.).
12. "The Secret Life of Mackenzie King, Spiritualist", *Maclean's,* 15 Dec. 1951.
13. Neatby, 407-8.
14. Notes of sittings, 202 Elgin Street, 6 Jan. 1934 [1935], and 13 Jan. 1935 (Diary, 1935).
15. 8 Dec. 1944.
16. Stacey, *Arms, Men and Governments,* 441-59.
17. 30 Oct. 1944.
18. 31 Oct. 1944.
19. *Arms, Men and Governments,* 456-9.
20. *Ibid.,* 466.
21. *Ibid.,* 459-60.

FRIEND OR FIEND: KING AND HITLER

Joy Esberey

William Lyon Mackenzie King is one of the best known and least understood of all Canadian prime ministers. He was 'to his own great satisfaction ... prime minister longer than any man in British history.'[1] But it is not longevity alone that matters. It has recently been suggested that Mackenzie King's approach to politics 'took such deep roots that people mistook it for politics itself.'[2] This lonely bachelor, apparently devoted to the memory of his mother and obsessed by life beyond the veil, has been described as an enigma, yet has been explained in simple one-dimensional terms. A direct consequence has been the tendency to separate Mackenzie King's private life from his public career, an approach which makes much of his behaviour inexplicable except in the crude terms of hypocrisy or political expediency. This misleading and dysfunctional 'double vision' of King is challenged in this study, which provides a comprehensive analysis of King's personal development and a consideration of selected examples of his political behaviour to demonstrate that the separation of the private and public King is invalid.

Because the impact of his personality is considered to be an essential dimension of King's political actions, it is not enough to rely on selected incidents in King's life or on the obvious Freudian explanations of some of his reactions. Instead I have attempted to trace the development of the main lines of the personality from its roots in the family to its flowering in the adult political leader. To do so the accepted picture of the King family has had to be redrawn to show a more balanced view of King's relationship with his parents, especially his mother, and of his interaction with his siblings. His patterns of behaviour are traced from this source through the search for appropriate sexual and occupational roles to the crisis of identity and its eventual partial resolution in political self. At the same time I give some attention to the development of his attitudes, especially the importance of religion and the cult of money, and to the general perceptual framework, dominated by the idea of the enemy, through which King viewed the world.

The analysis of King's personality is to a considerable extent a study of neurotic tendencies. Most of his apparently bizarre behaviour is explicable in these terms, as are many of the apparent paradoxes in his career. To suggest that King's behaviour reflected neurotic trends is neither to judge nor to condemn. The clinical label is useful only in so far as it is a key to identifying a complex and interrelated set of interactions and defences, which had political as well

From *Knight of the Holy Spirit: A Study of William Lyon Mackenzie King* (Toronto: University of Toronto Press, 1980), 3-8, 208-15, 223-224, 231-232. Reprinted by permission of the University of Toronto Press.

as personal repercussions. It should be noted that these tendencies, while pronounced, were debilitating rather than incapacitating. To the extent that the defences could be related to the constructive facets of his personality, King was able to maintain contact with reality and to function relatively effectively in the uncertain world of politics. To the extent that King failed to achieve his objectives, these time- and energy-consuming defences cannot be dismissed as marginal to understanding his political career.

Selecting an approach for the analysis of personality involved choosing a framework for the study, a level of analysis, and a method of presenting conclusions. For the basic study of King's personality the concept of the life cycle developed by Erik Erikson seemed the most useful.[3] It covers the whole life span of the subject without neglecting the formative years. It gives due attention to the impact of socialization and to environmental factors without losing sight of the epigenetic dimension of the personality. Erikson views the life cycle as a sequence of developmental stages within which conflicts between opposing forces must be resolved. It is a dynamic concept which gives due regard to the place of set-backs and regressions in the total growth pattern termed personality. Perhaps the most important virtue is that the life cycle offers a systematic way of organizing ideas about the growth of personality and it presents specific things to look for, giving a description of the external and internal factors that will indicate a successful or unsuccessful solution to the crisis of each stage. Thus this approach enables one to examine the idiosyncrasies of the personality with some objectivity.

Having selected the framework I then considered the level at which the analysis should be developed. Greenstein suggests 'three overlapping but analytically separable operations: the characterization of phenomenology, the dynamics, and the genesis of personality.'[4] Of these the emphasis was placed on the first two. The phenomenology constituted the basis on which the deeper layers of the analysis are identified and consists of the identification of recurring patterns of behaviour. The dynamics then relate to the circumstances under which these patterns of behaviour become dominant and how the various patterns interact with each other. Although it may be interesting to speculate on the causes of various patterns of response, evidence is lacking on the early years of most political leaders, and as causal answers are not essential to an understanding of personality in action they need be developed no further.

The problem of presenting the personality and relating it to political behaviour was less easily resolved. King's political activity could not be fully covered without having the analysis of the life cycle swamped by a vast sea of detail.[5] I therefore decided to concentrate on presenting those aspects of personality which had important political consequences and to incorporate where necessary additional explanatory material drawn from both Freudian and neo-Freudian sources.[6] As Erikson's work constitutes a bridge between these two schools this compromise did not involve any theoretical incongruity. Although the analysis of King's life and career is arranged in a generally chronological pattern, this study is in no sense a biography. The story of King's life and times has already been told by the historians. This work retreads old ground only when it presents a challenge to existing views.

The application of the insight gained from an understanding of King's personality to his political career also raised methodological problems. Any study of a career as long as King's must be selective. Each incident in his political life is in itself the product of a multi-faceted and complex process and is interrelated to every other incident. Some of these incidents are important enough to the overall pattern of personality development to require detailed analysis; others are not. The criteria for importance are the contribution each incident makes to the general patterns of behaviour which constitute the adult personality and the amount of time and energy the subject expended on each response.

Some of the examples were obvious. The importance of party and party leadership in a parliamentary system of government is such that it can be neglected only by the foolhardy. The fusion of personal and political identity in King's case, however, made it evident that this was one area which could not be ignored. The focus of King's relations with governors general and with his support staff, on the other hand, is important because it was idiosyncratic of King to devote so much personal concern to these matters. The relationship with Buchan is also important as a link in the search for supportive others so characteristic of King's interpersonal relations.

The selection of illustrative material from the field of policy making was more difficult. It was tempting to consider the dramatic developments of the 1940s when the war, the conscription crisis, and the social-welfare policy proposals of the post-war period dominate the field. But these events climaxed rather than characterized his career, and since they are already well documented in existing literature an interested reader would have little difficulty applying the insight of the psycho-analytical study to these examples. I therefore restricted my choice to those areas where the type of explanation that personality studies offer would be most helpful. One of the subjects that conventional explanations have not explained satisfactorily is why King persisted in emphasizing the tariff issue long after it had ceased to be of popular concern. This study offers an explanation along with a consideration of the apparent ambiguities in King's relation with the British government. The visit to Hitler and King's attitude to personal diplomacy were selected to illustrate the consistency of behavioural patterns in King's career and the way in which such well-entrenched actions were not always politically efficacious.

The discussion of these events must of necessity be limited, and the structural and environmental components of the interaction are given less attention than the psychological necessities. This emphasis is not reductionist but a logical progression from the original objective. In attempting to demonstrate the connection between personality and political behaviour emphasis must be given to psychological elements. Nowhere in this study do I suggest that only psychological explanations are needed to understand King's political behaviour. I do maintain, however, that the personality variable is crucial to this understanding. I suggest that the inner psychology of the leader ensured that particular sets of circumstances produced specific results and that another leader given the same set of circumstances might have chosen another course. The settlement of the dispute over the relative importance of personal and environmental factors must await detailed studies of specific incidents in which both variables are adequately examined. This study aims only to provide the basis for the personality dimension of such works. Similarly, within the limits of this study, it was not possible to offer any conclusions about the contribution King's personality made to his success. Discussion of this problem would involve an examination of the whole Canadian political process, the electoral system, and the historical climate of the times. My aim is to illuminate the psyche in action in the political field, not to rewrite the history of the 1920s and 1930s, although to the extent that King and the Liberal party dominated these decades the two cannot be completely separated. The study makes heavy demands on the reader because it assumes some knowledge of the incidents and individuals mentioned. The focus at all times is on King and the complexities of his personality.

Obviously, King's diary constitutes an essential source for any study of his personality, but it should not be the only source. An equal amount of attention must be given to the family and personal letters in the King papers. King was an enthusiastic and diligent correspondent throughout his life and often devoted dozens of pages in his letters to incidents that only merited a few lines in the diary. Much that is obscure in the diary can be explained in the light of letters written at the time and subsequently returned to King.[7]

It is equally clear that neither source can be taken at face value. They constitute a complex integration of King as he was and King as he wished to be. It is the analyst's task to sift the 'real' self from the 'idealized' self, and the defence mechanisms from the factual descriptions. This is a complex process and one can do little more now than identify the signals of inner conflict—fatigue, inconsistent reactions, repetition—hidden under the surface narration of feelings and events.

It is possible that King's diary represented a substitute 'wife-confidante' but it is not clear that it was intended to be a secret.[8] The first entry in the first volume (6 September 1893) expressed the hope that 'the reader may be able to trace how the author has sought to improve his time.' And the sentiment is repeated the following January and at various places throughout the volumes. Even when King went so far as to declare, 'this journal is strictly private,' as he did on the fly leaf in 1902, he continued to write 'and none should look upon its pages save with reverent eyes.' Obviously, strictly private in King's view did not mean for his eyes only.

Nevertheless, a diary is a personal rather than a public work, and the author is less concerned with communicating with others than with a personal record and self-evaluation; consequently, large sections of the entries are ambiguous or even obscure. In reading a diary, it is essential to seek the author's meanings rather than impose standard or preconceived ideas on the material. Thus a certain circularity is inevitable: without the diary, it is impossible to present an accurate picture of King's personality, but without a clear view of King's personality it is impossible to understand the diary. A simple phrase—'tonight was practically wasted'—means little in itself without some understanding of what the individual considers a waste of time, an understanding that might be obtained, for example, by comparing his intentions with his actions.

In interpreting the diary it is helpful to keep in mind that King was essentially Victorian in his outlook and responses. Anyone familiar with the writings of nineteenth-century evangelical Christians will have little difficulty with the style of the King diaries. They show the same emotionalism, the same extensive use of Christian symbolism, the same 'conscious record of sins,' the compulsive self-examination, and concern for mental and spiritual well-being that dominated the private papers of such people.[9] This piety is as much a part of King's personality as his pragmatism in later years. These were not two different faces of the same man; they were an integrated whole. But the integration was often imperfect and it required a great deal of psychic energy to maintain. The diary was one of the avenues wherein this endeavour could be sustained: 'I am taking up this diary again as a means of keeping me true to my true purpose ... it has helped to clear me in my thoughts and convictions ... I shall seek to be true in what I record in its pages ... revealing a desire to work ... to make the will of God prevail among men, to achieve personal righteousness, truth in thought & word, purity in heart, constancy and courage in action.'[10] It was the earnest Christian rather than the scholar or the politician who set the tone of the diary.

Friend or Fiend: King and Hitler

King's visit to Hitler in 1937 was probably the most controversial of all his actions in external relations, yet it was also the action most characteristic of his personal style. He had shown great faith in the efficacy of face-to-face contact in industrial conflict, and his association of industrial and international disputes would ensure that his thoughts would turn in this direction as the European situation became more threatening. His impulsive interview with Mussolini in 1928 had set a precedent which could be followed. King had taken the opportunity while in England in 1936 to propose such private negotiations to Prime Minister Baldwin, and the following year he discussed the desirability of such meetings of heads of states with Franklin Roosevelt.[11]

King's early enthusiasm for summit diplomacy, later to become an important facet of international relations, was in part derived from his perception of the European situation. On 15 June 1936 he had observed in his diary that: 'The European situation as it is today has nothing to compare with it at any time. No man can have to do with public affairs without feeling the necessity of coming to grips with it first hand.' In one sense the European situation offered a perfect example of a problem which he felt uniquely qualified to resolve—the building of confidence through the 'personal individual effort ... [of] men of different countries.'[12] He hoped that his talents as an intermediary could lead others to seek his aid. At the beginning of the year he had noted: 'I would be happy beyond words were I called on to intervene in the European situation. It would be the greatest joy of my life—but it seems too great a mission to expect.'[13]

His belief that through intervention he could avert war had a national as well as a personal component. He sought to make Canada's voice heard in 'a situation which threatens to engulf her in a world war and which, by being heard, might prevent such an appalling possibility.'[14] His confidence was derived from a simplistic view of both the European crisis and Hitler: a situation viewed in terms of juvenile personal associations and a projection onto the German leader of his own hopes and desires. His decision is best considered in his own words:

> I had been born in Berlin in Canada, in a county which had several communities of German names, and had represented that county in Parliament. Had also lived one winter in Berlin and felt I knew the best sides of the German people ... if I were talking to Hitler I could reassure him what was costing him friends was the fear which he was creating against other countries. That there was not so far as Canada, for example, and other parts of the Empire were concerned, any thought of continued enmity toward Germany but a desire to have friendly relations all around.
>
> On talking the matter over with Skelton, he still feels very strongly that it would be resented in Canada; that it would only be flattering Hitler by having him feel that some more persons were coming to him; that he was so much of an anglo-maniac, that nothing could influence him. That his speech three months ago that he was following his star of destiny just as a somnambulist walks in his sleep, showed how completely mystical he was, and unwilling to view anything to influence him in any way from different sides.
>
> My own feeling is that I made Canada's position vis-à-vis Europe and Great Britain, very plain, that to go to Germany might undo a little of the solid position in which I had already placed matters by creating doubts and suspicions as to what underlay the visit of Germany. It might also seem to obligate us to side with the British, should war come later. The Jingo press of Canada might misconstrue it all. My feeling, therefore, is that while I feel I could do some good and might do a great deal at this juncture, unless something should come up before I go away which would give a real reason for going, it might be better not to take the risk involved ...[15]

The following year he reconsidered this verdict when in the course of discussions with the German ambassador the possibility of an interview with Hitler arose. King accepted the invitation and with the approval of Chamberlain made the trip to Berlin.

The outcome of the visit was predetermined by two personal factors. King had throughout his life demonstrated a tendency to be very impressed by and enthusiastic about new situations. His enthusiasm often later gave way to misgivings and disappointment, but King made only one visit to Berlin. In the light of his determination to avoid overseas entanglements and his belief that peace was still a viable alternative, King was already strongly predisposed to see Hitler in a favourable light. It has already been observed that an individual's commitment to a particular course of action creates unconscious barriers to information that threatens this belief. Hitler did not fit into the category of enemy as long as he was willing to listen to King and to appear to accept King's interpretation of the issues.

The structure of the interview only reinforced this predisposition. A great deal of the diary record of the encounter focuses on the physical surroundings and appearance of Goering and Hitler, and the whole entry reflects King's personal satisfaction in the formal courtesy and laudatory tones of such diplomatic occasions. He did not hesitate to read personal approval into the slightest gestures, observing that 'Hitler nodded his head as much as to say that he understood,' and 'he would turn and look at me sideways and would smile in a knowing way as much as to say you understand what I mean.'[16] There was none of the lack of courtesy, the personal invective, the criticism of the opponent that King associated with the enemy.

To a man obsessed with signs and divine guidance there were many auguries of God's purpose. His Bible reading the day of the meeting was by chance just that chapter that he had read to his mother prior to her death. His day was filled with meetings and symbols associated with 'witnesses' and parallels. He could believe that 'it would seem to be the day for which I was born—Berlin 1874.' Nor did King have any difficulty with the German leader, and noted: 'while he was talking ... I confess I felt he was using exactly the same argument as I had used in the Canadian Parliament last session.'[17]

In his summary King stressed Hitler's mysticism, his deeply religious nature, his humble origins, and the fact that he was 'a teetotaller, and also a vegetarian, unmarried, abstemious in all his habits and ways.' These were the characteristics of the virtuous not of the enemy, as was the need for 'quiet and nature to help him think out the problems of his country.' A man who had so much in common with Mackenzie King, who could look 'most direct at me in our talks together,' who 'never once became the least bit restless during the talk,' could not be other than 'eminently wise.'[18]

King saw and heard only those things that he needed to see: 'a genuine patriot,' a 'simple peasant,' a man 'with whom it should be possible to work with a good deal of trust and confidence,' and was completely duped.[19] Once he returned to Canada he did not find it difficult to find further evidence to reinforce his original misperception:

> I felt I wanted to read to Joan something re Hitler, to talk of his life. I had cut out recently articles concerning him. I am convinced he is a spiritualist—that he has a vision to which he is being true—His going to his parents' grave at the time of his great victory—or rather achievement—the annexation of Austria was most significant—I read aloud from Gunther's Inside Europe, concerning his early life—his devotion to his mother—that Mother's spirit is I am certain his guide and no one who does not understand this relationship—the worship of the highest purity in a mother can understand the power to be derived there from—or the guidance. I believe the world will yet come to see a very great man—mystic in Hitler. His simple origin & being true to it in his life—not caring for pomp—or titles, etc., clothes—but reality—His dictatorship is a means to an end—needed perhaps to make the Germans conscious of themselves—much I cannot abide in Nazism—the regimentation—cruelty—oppression of Jews—attitude towards religion etc., but Hitler ... the peasant—will rank some day with Joan of Arc among the deliverers of his people, & if he is only careful may yet be the deliverer of Europe. It is no mere chance that I have met him, & von Ribbentrop & Goering & the others I did—it is part of a mission I believe ... 'Divine Commission Fulfilled' says Hitler etc. The world scoffs at these. They are given in ridicule—but they are I believe true—He is a pilgrim—his love of music—of Wagner Opera—his habits abstinence, purity, vegetarian, etc., all evidence of the mystic who is conscious of his mission & lives to it. Strange this bringing together of Hitler & Bunyan, both I believe are meant to guide me at this time to the purpose of my life—which I believe to be to help men to know the secret of the path to peace, in industrial & international relationships—If I can only live to that they will know I have been with Him that end will be achieved. I pray God I may so live that men see that I have been with him.[20]

It is important not to downgrade the influence of King's meeting with Hitler merely because subsequent events proved King's perceptions of the man to be so wrong. Despite his attempts to transcend the limits of his finite existence King was no more omniscient than any other mortal; rather his personal defence made him even more liable to misinterpretation than others. Nevertheless, it is possible to agree with Nicholas Mansergh that this misperception of Hitler's intent made little difference to King's actions: 'essentially it was the situation in Canada, not the situation in Europe that determined his approach.'[21] And he was able to confront Hitler with Canada's intentions. This does not detract from the emphasis which King placed on this personal impression and which could have affected his sense of the imminence of danger. He steadfastly held to the belief that his view of Hitler was the correct one. He told Tweedsmuir the following year: 'I shall be interested in knowing whether it is not agreed [by Chamberlain and Halifax] that my little visit to Berlin, a year ago, was not helping to inspire a little more in the way of confidence ... I think you will agree that what I told you of different attitudes and probable developments was not wide of the mark.'[22] A few months later King observed: 'I believe, however, that it will be found in the end that Hitler is for peace, unless unduly provoked.'[23]

King could respond enthusiastically to Munich because he believed he had been instrumental in it. In many ways it seemed that Chamberlain was a substitute for King himself. Throughout 1937 King had dwelt in his private record on his capacity as a conciliator in a world where such a need was clearly visible. In October, in the course of interpreting one of his visions he had written.

> I am sure all this struggle is to help me in the field of international relations. It is to enable me to speak with conviction on the application of the Principles that make for Peace being a condition of mind and heart, in the nation as the individual, resulting from application of right principles bringing into being right policies in the former & right conduct in the latter—till we all 'become of one mind,' from 'being like minded'—This seems to me to be the process of spiritual evolution, from *being like minded to Christ thro' him, becoming one with God.* In this way the soul preserves its individuality and identity, and finds both preserved as they lose themselves in God, unless we lose our lives, we cannot find them. Instead of a multitude of souls, we become one soul with the One soul.[24]

He wondered about the possibility of leading a mission to Japan and told Tweedsmuir: 'How grateful I am that Chamberlain went to see Hitler! You may recall how strongly I urged these personal contacts. While it is not yet clear that war will be avoided, it is altogether certain that but for Chamberlain's meeting with Hitler we all should have been in the throes of a world war today.'[25] As Violet Markham sadly observed to Tweedsmuir, 'Hitler I fear pulled a good bit of wool over our friend Rex's eyes.'[26]

King's responses, however distasteful to some Canadians today, were perfectly consistent with his general beliefs. King was an appeaser by conviction rather than as an expedient, and his actions need to be judged in the context of Martin Gilbert's position: 'Appeasement, both as an attitude of mind and as a policy, was not a silly or treacherous idea in the minds of stubborn, gullible men, but a noble idea, rooted in Christianity, courage and commonsense.'[27] It was a policy in which, through patient and conciliatory reactions, men would be given an opportunity to declare themselves with the forces of good or those of evil. King had repeated in a public broadcast in 1936 the views he had expressed in *Industry and humanity.*

Fundamentally, the world struggle of today is one between the contending forces of good and evil. It is a part of the never-ending conflict between the forces activating those who, by their thoughts of others, and their unselfish acts, are seeking to further 'the law of Peace, Work and Health,' and the forces actuating those who, by their greed and selfish ambitions, are furthering 'the law of Blood and Death.'[28]

In times of stress King was inclined to consider some of his British allies among the latter rather than the former. King's tendency to see old threats and dangers would be accentuated by suggestions such as the proposal for an imperial war conference or cabinet. In 1936 he had been preparing himself for possible conflict by 'going pretty carefully through Lloyd George's "War Memories" ... I owe it to the country and to my work to anticipate ... the matters to be given consideration "prior to or in the event of war".'[29] Inevitably in times of stress King was dominated by the tensions of the past as much as by the problems of the present, but because he had surrounded himself with able men this perceptual difficulty did not seriously affect his capacity to lead.

The war with all its serious complications was at the same time a great triumph for King. His success in bringing a united Canada into the war has been described as 'one of the outstanding achievements of Commonwealth statesmanship.'[30]

Notes

1. Nicholas Mansergh, *The Commonwealth experience* (London 1969), 17.
2. William Christian and Colin Campbell, *Political parties and ideologies in Canada* (Toronto 1974), 2.
3. Erik H. Erikson, *Childhood and society* (Middlesex, Eng. 1965); *Insight and responsibility* (New York 1964); *Identity, youth, and crisis* (New York 1968); *Identity and the life cycle* (New York 1959); *Young man Luther* (New York 1968); *Gandhi's truth* (New York 1969).
4. F.I. Greenstein, *Personality and politics* (Chicago 1969), 65.
5. J.E. Esberey, 'Personality and politics: a study of William Lyon Mackenzie King' (unpublished PH D thesis, University of Toronto 1974).
6. Karen Horney, *The neurotic personality of our times* (New York 1937); *Neurosis and human growth* (New York 1950); *Our inner conflict* (New York 1945). Helen Deutsch, *Neurosis and character types* (New York 1965). O. Fenichel, *The psychoanalytical theory of neurosis* (New York 1945). G. Mahl, *Psychological conflict and defense* (New York 1971). D. Shapiro, *Neurotic styles* (New York 1965).
7. The main source of primary material on King is the W.L. Mackenzie King collection in the Public Archives of Canada (PAC). There are extensive references to King in other collections in this repository. Among published sources one would note: R. MacGregor Dawson, *William Lyon Mackenzie King, a political biography, 1874-*

1923 (Toronto 1958); H. Blair Neatby, *William Lyon Mackenzie King, 1924-1932* (Toronto 1963); *William Lyon Mackenzie King, 1932-1939* (Toronto 1976). F.A. McGregor, *The fall & rise of Mackenzie King* (Toronto 1962). J.W. Pickersgill and D.F. Forster, eds, *The Mackenzie King record,* 4 vols (Toronto 1968-70). Earlier volumes of interest include: H.S. Ferns and B. Ostry, *The age of Mackenzie King* (Toronto 1955); H.R. Hardy, *Mackenzie King of Canada* (Toronto 1949); Andrew Haydon, *Mackenzie King and the Liberal party* (Toronto 1930); Bruce Hutchinson, *The incredible Canadian* (Toronto 1952); O.E. McGillicuddy, *The making of a premier* (Toronto 1922); Norman Rogers, *Mackenzie King* (Toronto 1935). University of Toronto published a microfiche edition of King's diaries in two parts, 1893-1931 in 1974 and 1932-47 in 1980.

8. J.L. Granatstein, *Canada's war: the politics of the Mackenzie King government 1939-1945* (Toronto 1975), v.

9. C.P. Stacey, *A very double life, the private world of Mackenzie King* (Toronto 1976), 11.

10. Diary, 1 Jan. 1902.

11. Diary, 5 Mar. 1937.

12. WLMK to Buchan, 8 Sept. 1936 (BP).

13. Diary, 5 Jan. 1936.

14. Diary, 15 Jan. 1936.

15. Diary, 1 Oct. 1936.

16. Diary, 29 June 1937.

17. Ibid.

18. Ibid.

19. WLMK to Anthony Eden, 6 July 1937.

20. Diary, 17 Mar. 1938.

21. Mansergh, *Commonwealth experience,* 382.

22. WLMK to Buchan, 23 July 1938 (BP).

23. WLMK to Buchan, 6 Sept. 1938 (BP).

24. Diary, 18 Oct. 1937.

25. WLMK to Buchan, 20 Sept. 1938 (BP).

26. Violet Markham to Buchan, 20 Aug. 1939 (BP).

27. Martin Gilbert, *The roots of appeasement* (London 1966), 3.

28. J. Eayrs, *In defence of Canada: appeasement and rearmament* (Toronto 1965), xi.

29. WLMK to Buchan, 24 Aug. 1936 (BP).

30. Mansergh, *Commonwealth experience,* 284.

CHAPTER

11 THE EVACUATION OF THE JAPANESE CANADIANS

After the outbreak of war in 1914 the Canadian government found itself under increasing public pressure to deal with the perceived threat to the security of the state from "enemy aliens," particularly those of German and Austro-Hungarian birth. During the course of the war such persons were subject to discrimination and harassment. Many were placed in internment camps. Then, in 1917, voters of enemy alien birth who had been naturalized in Canada after 1902 were disenfranchised. Given the large population of recent immigrants, it was perhaps natural that the Canadian government would experience difficulty in finding an appropriate balance between democratic rights and legitimate concern about national security. Certainly it failed to do so.

Despite this experience, the Canadian government seemed no better prepared to deal with this problem during the Second World War. Although various groups within Canadian society were affected, the most celebrated—many would argue notorious—case was that of the Japanese Canadians in British Columbia. Evacuated into the interior in 1942, their property was confiscated, and many were threatened with deportation at the end of the war. It should be remembered that many of the Japanese Canadians were Canadian citizens who had been born in Canada.

In the first reading in this unit, a chapter from his book on attitudes towards orientals in British Columbia, Peter Ward dismisses out-of-hand any suggestion that the Japanese-Canadians posed a security risk. "No significant evidence of Japanese treachery could be seen at this time," he wrote. "Nor would any be discovered at a later date." Rather, he finds the explanation for the anti-Japanese furore in British Columbia in long-standing racial prejudices there, whipped up by wartime anxieties.

This interpretation has been challenged by J.L. Granatstein and Gregory Johnson. While they agree that the Japanese-Canadians were victims of racism, they argue that there were legitimate "military and intelligence concerns" which, after the attack on Pearl Harbor in early December 1941, could have been used as a justification for the evacuation.

Suggestions for Further Reading

Adachi, Ken, *The Enemy That Never Was: A History of the Japanese-Canadians*. Toronto: McClelland and Stewart, 1976.

Roy, Patricia, "British Columbia's Fear of Asians, 1900-1950," *Histoire sociale / Social History*, XIII, no. 25 (May 1980), 161-172.

_____, "The Soldiers Canada Didn't Want: Her Chinese and Japanese Citizens," *Canadian Historical Review*, LIX, no. 3 (September 1978), 341-358.

_____, "'White Canada Forever': Two Generations of Studies," *Canadian Ethnic Studies*, XI, no. 2 (1979), 97-109.

Roy, Patricia, et al., *Mutual Hostages: Canadians and Japanese during the Second World War*. Toronto: University of Toronto Press, 1990.

Sunahara, Ann Gomer, *The Politics of Racism: The Uprooting of Japanese Canadians during the Second World War*. Toronto, James Lorimer, 1981.

EVACUATION

Peter Ward

Between late 1937 and early 1942 resurgent nativism once more flooded white British Columbia. Three waves of anti-Orientalism swept across the province, in 1937-38, 1940, and 1941-42, each of them of several months' duration. The third was by far the greatest in magnitude. Indeed, its crest was broader and higher than that of any previous racial outburst in the history of the province. Never before had west coast whites been so intensely aroused. Never before had their protests been so vociferous. Never before had they confronted the federal government with such insistent demands. And in the end, never before had the response of Ottawa been as drastic as it was on this occasion.

The Japanese were the sole targets of these three new outbursts. While anti-Chinese sentiment found intermittent voice in British Columbia during the 1930s, mounting anti-Japanese prejudice had largely eclipsed it since the last days of Chinese immigration. During the depression years images of Japanese militarism came to dominate white attitudes toward the Japanese. To growing numbers of British Columbians, Japan seemed bent on a program of conquest

From *White Canada Forever: Popular Attitudes and Public Policy toward Orientals in British Columbia* (Montreal: McGill-Queen's University Press, 1978), 142-166, 193-198. Reprinted by permission of McGill-Queen's University Press.

which might well sweep the entire north Pacific rim. On this account the Japanese minority on the west coast appeared more threatening than ever. In the eyes of white observers, its unwillingness to abandon Japanese culture was proof of continuing loyalty to the new Japanese Empire, and even more unsettling was the inference that the Japanese immigrant community harboured subversive elements, men and women who would undermine the nation's defence efforts in the event of war with Japan. At bottom, of course, these assumptions were variations of the longstanding popular belief in Asiatic unassimilability. They had been buried in white racial thought since the Russo-Japanese war. What brought them to the fore during the early 1930s was the resumption of Japan's military adventures in Manchuria. Her subsequent attack on China in 1937 placed them in even sharper relief.

It was the invasion of China in the summer of 1937 that touched off the first of these incidents. In Canada reports of this aggression provoked the first strong outburst of anti-Oriental feeling in a decade. Much of it was directed at Japan herself. Across the nation indignant Canadians boycotted Japan's products and protested her war atrocities.[1] Meanwhile British Columbians aimed new barbs at the local Japanese. Animus was most intense in coastal centres—especially Vancouver and Victoria, and their surrounding districts—where provincial nativism traditionally had been strongest. To some extent the Japanese were made scapegoats of Japan's militarism. But many whites also saw in them another cause for concern, for the attack fused old racial antipathies with vague, new anxieties in the minds of west coast residents. Suddenly the region's longstanding fears of isolation and vulnerability were stirred to life again, and this new, tense atmosphere breathed fresh life into the community's dormant racial hostility. At the same time the menace inherent in the Japanese image was once again confirmed. Japan, it was presumed, had designs on British Columbia. Rumour had it that hundreds of illegal Japanese immigrants were present on the coast, that Japanese spies and military officers lived surreptitiously in the community, and that a potential Japanese fifth column was growing in the province. The result was a new upsurge of anti-Asian sentiment.

Archdeacon F. G. Scott, a popular Anglican wartime padre, precipitated the new outbreak in mid-November 1937, one week after the Japanese had taken Shanghai. In a widely reported interview with the *Toronto Daily Star* he suggested that Japanese officers were living, disguised, in fishing villages along the west coast.[2] A few coastal residents ridiculed Scott's claims. Others, however, vouched for their truth, and his supporters won the day for a public outcry followed in the wake of his remarks. Capt. MacGregor Macintosh, a Conservative member of the legislature, first endorsed Scott's report and then, early in 1938, raised charges of widespread illegal Japanese immigration.[3] Led by A. W. Neill, by now a perennial foe of the Oriental immigrant, provincial members of Parliament from all parties demanded a halt to Japanese immigration.[4] Simultaneously Alderman Halford Wilson urged Vancouver City Council to limit the number of licenses for Japanese merchants and to impose zoning restrictions upon them.[5] Meanwhile Vancouver's major daily newspapers launched their own anti-Japanese campaigns.[6] In Ottawa the prime minister received a flurry of protest notes while the outspoken Alderman Wilson's mail brought him letters of support.[7] The chief object of public concern was the persistent rumour that hundreds of illegal Japanese immigrants were living in the province, a tale made all the more credible by memories of serious immigration frauds which had been discovered early in the decade.

Judged in the light of previous anti-Oriental incidents, this was not a major outburst. Its central figures, Wilson and Macintosh, made no attempt to organize a protest movement. They merely spent their energies in making public demands for more restrictive legislation. Nor was popular hostility as intense as it had been in the past. Because the level of animosity was relatively low and dynamic organizational leadership was absent, this precluded the development of a major racial crisis. Nevertheless all signs pointed to increasing public tension, and the weight of this concern was soon felt in Ottawa.

Prime Minister Mackenzie King was loath to grasp such a nettle as this. King probably wished to placate British Columbia's nativists, or at least quiet them if he could. At the same time, he was subject to countervailing pressures. He was anxious not to embarrass British interests in Asia by taking any initiative which might provoke Japanese ire. Japan's renewed militarism had heightened his own inherent sense of caution. But demands from the west coast grew so insistent that ultimately he could not ignore them. Urged first by Premier T. D. Pattullo of British Columbia and then by Ian Mackenzie, the only west coast representative in the cabinet, King early in March 1938 promised a public enquiry into rumours of illegal Japanese entrants.[8]

But the mere promise of an investigation did not still demands for an end to Japanese immigration. Macintosh went even further and called for the repatriation of all Japanese residents in Canada, regardless of their citizenship.[9] On March 24 the Board of Review charged with the investigation held its first public hearing in Vancouver. During the next seven weeks it conducted a series of additional meetings in major centres throughout the province, and once the hearings commenced, popular unease appeared to dissipate. The hearings themselves put an end to scattered public protest by offering a forum to the vociferous. Furthermore, the meetings forced critics to prove their allegations or remain silent, and many chose the latter refuge. Public concern subsided to such an extent that when the board concluded, early in 1939, that rumours of illegal Japanese immigration had been greatly exaggerated, its report attracted little notice.[10]

But while hostility ebbed appreciably, it was not completely dispelled, and for the next two years the west coast Japanese remained the targets of rumour, suspicion, and criticism. Repeated calls rang out for an end to all Japanese immigration (now fallen to less than 60 per year) while the Vancouver City Council tried to restrict the number of trade licenses issued to Orientals.[11] Then, in the spring of 1940, the second wave of animosity began to well up. In this instance the anxious wartime atmosphere created by Canada's recent belligerency heightened traditional prejudices and aggravated racial tensions in west coast society. At the same time, and for the same reason, Japan's Asian military campaign again began to rouse concern. The growth of general unease once more strengthened feelings of vulnerability and insecurity in the community. Prompted by mounting anxiety, the cry went up that illegal Japanese immigrants were infiltrating the country; renewed demands were made for an end to all Japanese immigration as well as for stronger Pacific coast defences. Tales of the Japanese subversive threat also circulated freely.

It was Alderman Halford Wilson who headed this new campaign of protest. Throughout the summer of 1940 he warned of Japanese subversion and called for closer restrictions on all Japanese residents.[12] Wilson still made no attempt to organize a popular movement, but he did remain the most insistent of the Japanese community's critics. Apart from himself, it is difficult to know for whom Wilson actually spoke. Few British Columbians in 1940 were willing to follow his lead in public. Yet he was by no means the only outspoken public figure and undoubtedly there were many whites who endorsed the general thrust of his remarks, if not their specific aim. Certainly his crusade was a measure of the times for anti-Japanese nativism was once more on the rise,[13] and in Ottawa as well as Victoria this resurgence soon became a source of some concern.[14] The worry was that Wilson's comments might put the torch to public discontent and touch off racial disorder. According to C. G. Power, the minister of national defence for the air, who visited the west coast early in the fall, public feeling was "running high" and the "danger of anti-Japanese outbreaks was serious."[15]

While provincial and federal authorities grew increasingly alarmed at the prospect of racial turmoil, senior military officers in British Columbia were also concerned by the presence of Japanese on the coast. Intelligence officers had kept watch on the Japanese community since 1937 and from the outset had accepted the prevailing assumption that Japanese residents, regardless of their citizenship, would endanger national security in time of war. As early as June 1938 the Department of National Defence had explored the prospect of widespread Japanese wartime internment.[16] In 1940, during the summer's crest of popular anti-Japanese feeling, the Pacific Command's Joint Service Committee approved contingency plans to meet both an external Japanese attack and an internal Japanese insurrection. The committee also endorsed an intelligence report which warned of possible sabotage by the west coast Japanese fishing fleet. Japanese residents, it reported, "could very easily make themselves a potent force and threaten the vital industries of British Columbia." If war broke out, the committee believed, every Japanese resident in British Columbia should be considered a potential enemy.[17]

On the other hand the RCMP tended to minimize the Japanese threat. Since 1938 officers in "E" Division, stationed in Vancouver, had also kept the Japanese under surveillance. In 1940 they assigned three constables to observe the community and also employed Japanese informants. On the basis of continual investigation, the force concluded that Japanese residents posed no real threat to Canada. On the contrary, it observed what it believed to be convincing evidence of Japanese loyalty to Canada. Signs of this were especially clear in the community's strong support for Victory bond drives and Red Cross work, the Nisei desire to volunteer for military service, and the widespread Japanese wish not to arouse white antagonism. "This office," the Officer Commanding at Vancouver reported late in October 1940, "does not consider that the Japanese of British Columbia constitute a menace to the State."[18]

Was there substance to this apparent threat of Japanese subversion? The Board of Review in 1938 had found no proof of wholesale illegal immigration. Nor had the RCMP discovered any indication of serious danger, and surely this was the organization best able to judge.[19] It had scrutinized the Japanese community more carefully than had any other agency. Neither military intelligence nor popular rumour was founded on such close observation, and the claims of each should be judged accordingly. All available signs pointed in one direction only: no significant evidence of Japanese treachery could be seen at this time. Nor would any be discovered at a later date. The threat of Japanese subversion was created by the union of traditional racial attitudes and perceptions shaped by the fears and anxieties conjured up by war. Yet despite its insubstantial basis, the threat was real enough to many British Columbians, and it was the goad which stirred popular animus to life once more.

This resurgence of anti-Japanese sentiment again placed the King government in an uncomfortable position. Whatever it felt about the demands of west coast nativists, more than ever, in the summer of 1940, it wished to avoid irritating Japan as this might jeopardize British interests in the Pacific, if not induce war itself. Moreover, by this time Canada was preoccupied by the European conflict and presumably the federal government wished to avoid distractions. Therefore it hesitated as long as seemed possible before taking action. But by September 1940, when rumours first were heard that Oriental Canadians would be included in the first call for military service, the question could no longer be ignored. Just as Japan announced her alliance with the Axis powers, these reports provoked a sharp cry of protest. Bowing before the rising winds of criticism, the Cabinet War Committee omitted Asian Canadians from the first draft and then formed a special committee to investigate the question of Orientals and British Columbia's security.[20]

The committee soon confirmed that anti-Japanese feeling was high in the province and that this, rather than Japanese subversion, was the greatest potential source of danger to the community. Its major recommendations were therefore aimed at reducing public tension. In order to scotch persistent rumours of illegal Japanese immigration, it urged a new registration of all Japanese residents, both citizens and aliens alike. It also proposed the creation of a standing committee of prominent British Columbians to advise the government on problems relating to Orientals in British Columbia.[21] For their part, because of the delicate state of Anglo-Japanese relations, King and his cabinet were anxious to avoid even the threat of civil disorder in British Columbia, and they implemented the recommendations in the hope of restoring public calm. Intent on disarming British Columbia's nativists, the government included MacGregor Macintosh on the Standing Committee. And in order to reassure the Japanese, it nominated Professor H. F. Angus, the long-time champion of full civil rights for second-generation Japanese Canadians.[22]

If the King government hoped its new initiative would calm popular fears, however, it must soon have been disabused of its optimism. During the first half of 1941 the public temper remained aroused, and there were signs that some British Columbians were growing even more suspicious of the Japanese. Agitation continued, even though no credible leadership had emerged to give protest a focus. Halford Wilson kept up his one-man campaign, now repeatedly urging that in the interest of national security all Japanese fishing boats should be sequestered.[23] The state of tension remained a source of concern to federal officials who still feared a racial incident. Wilson was singled out as the chief cause for alarm, and unsuccessful efforts were made to persuade him to keep silent.[24] Meanwhile, in military circles fear of public disturbance was matched by continued suspicion of the Japanese themselves. As an intelligence report noted in July 1941, widespread Japanese sabotage was unlikely in the event of war, but it remained a possibility unless proper security precautions were taken and the Japanese themselves were protected from white provocation.[25]

In the final months before Pearl Harbor was bombed, racial tensions began to abate. Nevertheless conditions remained favourable to a new anti-Japanese outburst. Influenced by the community's xenophobia, its traditional racial cleavage, and its anxieties borne of war and isolation, white British Columbians continued to suspect their Japanese neighbours. The west coast Japanese could not be trusted. Their allegiance was in doubt. Given the opportunity, it was assumed, some among them would betray the province to the enemy. For its part the federal government, while alarmed by the Japanese problem, was ill-prepared to meet the issue head on. It feared that Japan might use a racial disturbance as a *casus belli,* but aside from forming the Standing Committee it had done very little to prevent an outbreak.

The third and final wave of hostility, in force and amplitude surpassing all previous racial outbursts, was touched off in December 1941 by Japan's assault on Pearl Harbor. This sudden, dramatic attack roused the racial fears and hostilities of white British Columbians to heights never before attained. In turn they loosed a torrent of racialism which surged across the province for the next eleven weeks. This outbreak of popular feeling demanded an immediate response from the King government. In attempting to placate white opinion it offered a succession of policies, each one aimed at further restricting the civil liberties of the west coast Japanese. As it proved, nothing short of total evacuation could quiet the public outcry.

The outbreak of war with Japan immediately raised the problem of public order for the King government because it greatly increased the likelihood of violent anti-Japanese demonstrations in British Columbia. It also created a new enemy alien problem, for the declaration of war altered the status of many Canadian residents of Japanese origin.[26] Faced with the prospect of racial incidents as well as that of an alien menace, the Dominion government quickly took preemptive action. A few hours after war was declared, thirty-eight Japanese nationals were interned on the grounds that they might endanger the community. At the same time the west coast Japanese fishing fleet was immobilized. On the advice of the RCMP, all Japanese-language newspapers and schools voluntarily closed their doors. Meanwhile Prime Minister King, senior police and military officers, and Vancouver's major newspapers all reassured the public and called for calm. As King told the nation in a radio address on December 8, "the competent authorities are satisfied that the security situation is well in hand. They are confident of the correct and loyal behaviour of Canadian residents of Japanese origin."[27]

But many west coast whites were not so easily mollified. Neither prompt federal action nor loyal protestations from leading Japanese did much to assuage their concern. War's outbreak once more opened the floodgates of fear and hostility. As a result the west coast quickly resumed its attack on the province's Japanese. Once again enmity was strongest in and around Vancouver and Victoria, long the province's two focal points of anti-Asian sentiment. In the week following Pearl Harbor some Japanese in Vancouver were victimized by scattered acts of vandalism. Several firms began discharging their Japanese employees. Fear of Japanese subversion again spread in the province.[28] In private, British Columbians began protesting to their members of Parliament. The weight of public concern also bore down on provincial newspapers. Columnist Bruce Hutchison informed the prime minister's office that at the *Vancouver Sun,* "we are under extraordinary pressure from our readers to advocate a pogrom of Japs. We told the people to be calm. Their reply was a bombardment of letters that the Japs all be interned."[29]

To encourage calm, police, government, and military officials issued further assurances that the Japanese problem was well in hand.[30] But their statements seemed to have little effect. Popular protest continued to grow, and in response alarm in government and military circles increased too. On December 20 F. J. Hume, chairman of the Standing Committee, told King:

> In British Columbia particularly, the successes of the Japanese to date in the Pacific have to a great extent inflamed public opinion against the local Japanese.

People here are in a very excited condition and it would require a very small local incident to bring about most unfortunate conditions between the whites and Japanese.[31]

Maj.-Gen. R. O. Alexander, commander-in-chief of the Pacific Command, was also concerned.

The situation with regard to the Japanese resident in British Columbia is assuming a serious aspect. Public feeling is becoming very insistent, especially in Vancouver, that local Japanese should be either interned or removed from the coast. Letters are being written continually to the press and I am being bombarded by individuals, both calm and hysterical, demanding that something should be done.[32]

Alexander feared that public demonstrations, which according to rumour were to be held in the near future, might lead to racial violence.

After a brief lull over Christmas the public outcry grew more strident than ever. Increasing numbers of west coast whites, regardless of all reassurance, were certain that the local Japanese community endangered west coast security. By early January 1942 patriotic societies, service clubs, town and city councils, and air raid precaution units, most of them on Vancouver Island or in the Vancouver area, had begun to protest.[33] Repeatedly they urged that all Japanese, regardless of citizenship, be interned as quickly as possible. Other spokesmen suggested somewhat less drastic action, but whatever the precise demands of the public, they all assumed the need for some form of Japanese evacuation. And with each passing day opinion seemed to grow more volatile. Even moderates like J. G. Turgeon, Liberal MP from Cariboo, were alarmed at the seeming danger. On January 6 he warned the prime minister:

The condition in this province is dangerous, so far as the Japanese are concerned. If the Government do not take drastic action, the situation will get out-of-hand. The Government will suffer, and so will the Japanese, personally and through destruction of property.

I am therefore forced to recommend that very strong measures to [*sic*] taken,—and quickly. Either delay, or lack of thorough action, may cause violence.[34]

Under heavy pressure, both popular and political, the federal government ordered yet another review of the Japanese problem. On January 8 and 9, 1942, a committee of federal and provincial government, police, and military officials met in Ottawa to discuss means of allaying west coast alarm. The central question explored was whether or not the Japanese should be removed from coastal areas; but the meeting could not agree on an answer. Several representatives who had just arrived from British Columbia, together with Ian Mackenzie, the meeting's chairman, argued that all able-bodied male Japanese nationals should immediately be removed. The majority of the delegates, however, few of whom had recently been in British Columbia, opposed such drastic action. Consequently the meeting submitted a moderate report which suggested both an extension of existing minor restrictions on the liberties of all Japanese and the creation of a quasi-military work corps for Canadian Japanese who wished to support the war effort.[35]

But the conference's report was only one opinion. From British Columbia there came ever more insistent demands for an evacuation program, and within the cabinet Ian Mackenzie, King's closest political friend from the province, pressed for such a solution.[36] Consequently, when the government announced its revised plans on January 14, the new policy bore the unmistakable imprint of west coast opinion. The King government accepted most of the Ottawa conference's proposals, but in addition it proposed to remove all enemy aliens, regardless of age, sex, or nationality, from protected areas soon to be defined in British Columbia. The program was aimed primarily at Japanese nationals although it embraced Germans and Italians as well. The statement also promised that a Japanese Civilian Corps would soon be formed for work on projects deemed in the national interest.[37] The covert hope was that Japanese Canadian men would volunteer for it in large numbers, thus permitting the government to remove them from the protected areas without an unpleasant resort to compulsion.[38]

It was felt that, by yielding to some of the west coast's demands, the partial evacuation policy would calm British Columbian fears. Concerned for the safety of Canadian prisoners in Japan's hands, anxious to avoid needless expense and disruption in time of war, and touched with a lingering sense of justice and humanity, the King government refused to make further concessions. But the plan was also rather equivocal in that it neither defined the protected areas nor promised when evacuation would begin. In effect, it still gave the federal government considerable freedom of action. For a few, brief moments the gesture seemed satisfactory. Premier John Hart of British Columbia, whose government had already demanded similar measures, applauded the decision and the *Vancouver Sun* praised the King government's common sense. The storm of protest abated temporarily.[39]

Within ten days, however, agitation began to increase once again. The public outcry mounted throughout February until, during the last week of the month, it reached unprecedented volume. Pressed by the irrational fear of enemy subversion, thousands of west coast whites petitioned Ottawa for the immediate evacuation of all Japanese. Individuals, farm organizations, municipal councils, civil defence units, constituency associations, service clubs, patriotic societies, trade unions, citizens' committees, chambers of commerce—even the Vancouver and District Lawn Bowling Association—all demanded the total evacuation of Japanese from coastal areas.[40] One group of prominent Vancouver residents telegraphed Ian Mackenzie that, "owing to wide spread public alarm over enemy aliens on the Pacific coast and especially respecting those astride vital defence points and with a view to stabilizing public opinion and in the interest of public safety," they urged the immediate evacuation of all Japanese.[41] Never before had west coast race relations been so seriously strained.

Parliament reconvened on January 22 as the racial crisis mounted. Members of Parliament from British Columbia, no doubt as concerned as their protesting constituents, began to press for total evacuation. Howard Green, the Conservative member from Vancouver South, opened the attack in the Commons on January 29.[42] The threat of Japanese treachery confronted the Pacific coast, he said, and therefore all Japanese should be removed from the province. During the next three weeks other British Columbian members made similar claims in the House. In private they were even more insistent. On January 28 British Columbians in the Liberal caucus demanded that Japanese Canadians who failed to volunteer for the Civilian Corps be evacuated as quickly as possible. In succeeding weeks, as popular protest reached its greatest heights, King faced successive demands for relocation from provincial politicians, Conservative, Liberal, and independent alike.[43]

Meanwhile government officials in British Columbia sustained their pressure as well. At the height of the popular outcry the attorney-general of British Columbia told Ian Mackenzie:

> Events have transpired recently which add to the danger we have always been subjected to by the presence of Japanese on this Coast.
> I cannot urge too strongly the seriousness of this situation and the danger the people of British Columbia feel upon this matter.
> Nothing short of immediate removal of the Japanese will meet the dangers which we feel in this Province.[44]

At the same time the minister of labour campaigned for total evacuation. The lieutenant-governor informed the prime minister that he had "rarely felt so keenly about any impending danger as I do about the Japanese on this coast being allowed to live in our midst." He suggested that at the very least Japanese males be quickly interned. Since mid-January senior officers of the Pacific Command had grown more concerned as well. By the time public protest reached its peak, they too subscribed to demands for total evacuation.[45]

It was Ian Mackenzie who ultimately bore the brunt of this storm of protest. First he received warnings and notes of alarm, then petitions urging evacuation, and finally demands that he resign. But on this matter Mackenzie had long shared the concern of his constituents. In the first weeks after the outbreak of war he grew convinced that all able-bodied Japanese men should be removed from strategic areas. In consequence he considered the partial evacuation policy inadequate. He also believed that the April 1 deadline was too remote. As pressure upon him grew, Mackenzie's alarm at the instability of public opinion increased in like proportion. On February 22, when news reached him of a series of mass protest meetings planned for March 1, his anxiety reached a peak.[46] Two days later he informed cabinet colleagues of the heated state of west coast opinion and of a call for his own resignation. As he told the minister of justice:

> The feeling in British Columbia in regard to the Japanese is so aflame that I consider we should take the necessary powers (if we have not got them now) to remove Canadian Nationals, as well as Japanese Nationals, from the protected areas.
>
> I have no report on how the Vancouver Corps has succeeded, but I greatly fear *disorder* from reports actually received, unless all able-bodied males of Japanese origin are immediately evacuated.[47]

Publicly Mackenzie appeared unperturbed, urging calm on his west coast correspondents, but privately he was extremely exercised.[48]

Within the cabinet others shared something of Mackenzie's alarm, particularly his concern for possible public disturbances. The prime minister agreed that there was "every possibility of riots" on the west coast, and feared that in such an event there would be "repercussions in the Far East against our own prisoners." The situation was awkward, he recognized, because "public prejudice is so strong in B.C. that it is going to be difficult to control."[49] Under such heavy external pressure, and alarmed by the evident danger of racial violence, the federal government finally took decisive action. On February 24, only hours after Mackenzie had written his warning to cabinet colleagues, the government approved an enabling measure which permitted total evacuation. Three days later the announcement was made that all persons of Japanese ancestry would have to leave the protected zones.[50] The King government had once more capitulated to public pressure.

In his *Theory of Collective Behavior,* Neil J. Smelser provides a model for the study of hostile public outbursts.[51] He suggests that five basic factors influence the development of mass hostility. First, the social setting must provide conditions which are conducive to the rise of such a movement. A second important component is that of social strain, the dynamic element which generates and sustains the hostile outburst. Its precipitating factors are a third influence for they crystallize hostility in the form of a social movement. Fourth, the structure and organization of the movement thus mobilized give the outburst its precise form. Finally, opposing influences usually attempt to contain the outbreak by employing various techniques of social control. In reference to this particular outburst of hostility, Smelser's model offers a useful tool of social analysis for, when viewed within this framework, the psychological forces which underlay the events of these eleven weeks assume a greater clarity.

That the structure of west coast society was conducive to this outburst there can be no doubt. British Columbia's traditional racial cleavage, in recent years marked by strong anti-Japanese feeling, had created enduring racial tensions which perpetually tended toward outbreaks of racial animosity within the white community. No obstacles prevented the general acceptance of racial prejudices. On the contrary, the strength of the consensus encouraged widespread espousal of these negative beliefs. White society aired its biases openly and often, and its pronouncements met with virtually no contradiction. Racism was further legitimated by discriminatory law and custom, both of which enforced differential patterns of treatment among white and Oriental citizens. Thus the racial assumptions of west coast whites, the product of long-standing strains in race relations, created a climate of public opinion in the province which tended toward this eruption. The fact that similar minor incidents had occurred in recent years simply increased the likelihood that an outburst would occur.

In this instance, of course, the precipitating factor was North America's engagement in war on the Pacific, an event which suddenly imposed complex psychological strains upon white British Columbians. Owing to war in Europe, the level of generalized public anxiety in the province was already well above peacetime norms by December 7, 1941. Pearl Harbor raised this level appreciably, and in the following weeks a further increase took place.

In itself, the opening of a new theatre of war was an additional source of unease because it raised new uncertainties in an already war-troubled world. More specifically, the ambiguity which enveloped Japan's military activities in the weeks after December 7 also conditioned the growth of anxiety. The startling number of her targets, the suddenness of her assaults, the speed of her military expansion, and the seeming ease of her victories surprised and frightened many west coast whites. The enemy seemed everywhere in the Pacific. No one knew where he might next attack and some feared it would be British Columbia. In such conditions civil defence preparations themselves became a source of unease for they reflected the assumption that a Japanese attack was indeed imminent. During the first week of war air raid precaution units were called for duty, defence regulations were posted, and nightly blackouts were enforced. Far from offering reassurance, these activities further unsettled an already apprehensive public.

In the weeks that followed, a series of military reverses continued to play on west coast fears. By mid-January Japanese troops had overrun much of Malaya, the Philippines, Burma, and British North Borneo. They had occupied Thailand, captured Hong Kong (taking more than 1,600 Canadian troops prisoner), sunk Britain's most modern battleship, and crippled her Pacific fleet. Late in January they had laid siege to the island of Singapore. News of this swift succession of decisive victories dominated the front pages of the provincial press. These accounts repeatedly emphasized that Japanese subversion and fifth column activity had played a central role in Japan's program of conquest. Already convinced of their own vulnerability, British Columbians grew more alarmed when worse news succeeded bad, and increasingly hostile toward the Japanese minority. The combined effect of Japanese militarism and the province's legacy of racial tension was to reveal the old image of the Yellow Peril in a new and lurid light. As many British Columbians peered through the fog of their anxieties, they saw little but the menacing outline of Japanese subversion. A growing sense of crisis narrowed their perceptions, which in turn intensified public unease. Thus social tensions and racial imagery were mutually reinforcing. Had British Columbians seen their Japanese neighbours clearly, they would have observed an isolated, defenceless minority, gravely alarmed by its plight and anxious to demonstrate its loyalty to Canada. But fear and prejudice obscured their vision. The local Japanese seemed nothing but a grave and growing threat.

A further sign of mounting social pressure was the increasing incidence of rumours of Japanese subversion. Some told of Japanese who owned high-powered vehicles and short wave equipment, who lived near sites of great strategic value, who swelled with insolent pride at Japan's successive victories. Others hinted at active Japanese disloyalty, and in the hothouse atmosphere of growing public tension stories grew to outlandish proportions. Military intelligence officers were informed in mid-January that Japanese in Vancouver had fixed infra-red and ultraviolet beacons on their roofs, devices which, when viewed through special binoculars, would guide enemy flights over the city.[52] Rumour is usually the product of serious social and psychological stress,[53] and these persistent rumours were one more indication of the growing racial crisis on Canada's west coast. The outbreak of war with Japan had spread a grave sense of looming threat among west coast whites. Yet for all its immediacy the threat remained somewhat vague and nebulous. The enemy was identified; his whereabouts were not. Rumours helped resolve this ambiguity. They suggested that some of the enemy were very close at hand. While this in itself was cause for concern, it also helped to clarify the confusion of war with a distant, elusive power. Because rumours singled out the nearest available enemy, they helped reduce the ambiguity which had spawned them in the first place. Once in circulation, they too stirred the ever-widening eddies of hostility and alarm.

It seems clear that a further, immediate reason for the renewed upsurge of protest in February was that many British Columbians, anxious for total evacuation, had misinterpreted the government's policy announcement of January 14. The *Sun* had taken it to mean that "all Japanese and other enemy aliens" were to be removed from protected areas, an assumption shared by several British Columbia members of Parliament. "My understanding," wrote Ian Mackenzie, "was that all able-bodied, adult enemy aliens would have to be removed from protected areas. My further understanding was also that all able-bodied *Canadian nationals* would have to be moved, but that *first* they should be given an opportunity to volunteer in the Civilian Corps."[54] Added complications arose from the failure of the federal government to implement its program immediately. Neither the evacuation plans nor the designated protected areas were announced until January 23, and the delay itself provoked some concern. When finally announced, the plans indicated that evacuation was not to be completed before April 1, a date which seemed far too remote to those who believed the Japanese threat was imminent. Once the plans were made public there was a further delay while the relocation machinery was set up. The task of arranging to move, house, and care for several thousand Japanese proved a time-consuming one and it was complicated further by the strong opposition of residents in the British Columbian interior, especially the Okanagan Valley, to proposals that all the Japanese be settled inland.[55] Several times the immediate departure of Japanese from Vancouver was announced and then postponed. Consequently few, if any, Japanese left their homes before mid-February. In the eyes of concerned west coast whites the government's partial evacuation policy increasingly seemed a mixture of confusion, delay, and prevarication. It appeared that Ottawa did not understand, let alone sympathize with, British Columbia's predicament.

Three elements thus combined to generate social strain in the province after the bombing of Pearl Harbor: reports of Japan's military campaigns in Asia, rumours of impending Japanese attack on British Columbia, and federal delays in implementing the wholesale evacuation policies advocated on the west coast. The first two projected a Japanese military threat to the province and assumed that the local Japanese community would play a subversive role in the anticipated conflict. The third expressed the frustrations of whites when the precautions they deemed necessary were not immediately taken. In each case the roots of this strain were fundamentally psychological.

The pattern of mobilization of this outburst is also revealing, for, by and large, British Columbians reached their conclusions about the Japanese menace with little prompting. More or less simultaneously, thousands recognized an obvious threat and identified the equally obvious solution. In the generation of this consensus, neither popular leaders nor popular journalism played a predominant role. Halford Wilson and MacGregor Macintosh, once the two chief critics of the west coast Japanese, were submerged beneath the rising tide of hostility. In fact, the protest movement had no preeminent leaders whatsoever. Nor did provincial papers become leaders of opinion, even though some took up the popular cry. During the crisis west coast journalism helped sustain the prevailing mood, but most papers merely reflected the popular mind. In other words the outburst was both widespread and largely spontaneous.

The very structure of the protest movement supports this contention for it clearly revealed how extensive was the anti-Japanese consensus. Although public anxiety had flared up immediately after Pearl Harbor, no effective anti-Japanese movement began to emerge until late January. In its earliest stage protest was random; it had no central leadership and no institutional focus. When the movement did begin to take form, protest was mobilized concurrently by a broad range of the traditional social, economic, administrative, and political organizations already entrenched in British Columbia. The Provincial

Council of Women, the Vancouver Real Estate Exchange, the Canadian Legion in Gibson's Landing, the Kinsmen's Club of Victoria, the North Burnaby Liberal Association, the BC Poultry Industries Committee, the Corporation of the District of Saanich, the National Union of Machinists, Fitters, and Helpers (Victoria Local Number 2), and scores of other similar groups all pressed their demands for evacuation. Not only did these organizations represent major interest groups in the province, but their influence cut across most social, economic, and political bounds in west coast society. They represented the interests and opinions, the fears and hostilities of tens of thousands of British Columbians. If there were some provincial whites who did not share prevailing attitudes, they remained largely silent in the face of the consensus.

In addition, the forces opposing the outburst were relatively weak. In this case ultimate responsibility for control rested with the King government. Throughout the eleven-week crisis its chief concern remained constant: to reduce the level of racial tension in west coast society. For King and those of his ministers who were preoccupied with the problem, the first task was to prevent the torrent of racist rhetoric from spilling over into overt violence. Beyond that they wished to moderate racial hostility. But they had few tools at their disposal with which to achieve these ends. Physical protection of the minority by police or military forces was never seriously considered. Nor, save in a limited way, was counter-publicity used to refute the claims of the nativists and encourage public calm. Instead the government employed appeasement to mollify British Columbia. Its first step, taken immediately, was a policy of selective internment and increased restrictions on Japanese civil liberties. The second was a plan to remove that segment of the Japanese population which seemed most immediately dangerous. The third and final step was wholesale evacuation. As a means of attaining the primary goal of lower social strain, the King government selected this as the path of least resistance. Whether any alternative policy could have succeeded is now a moot point.

That the King government chose this solution is not at all surprising, for west coast opinion weighed down upon a group of politicians quite susceptible to prejudice against Asians. Ever since Confederation, anti-Orientalism had pervaded the political culture of the province beyond the Rockies and on many occasions provincial representatives had thrust their opinions upon Ottawa. Usually their words had received a fairly sympathetic hearing, and past governments had repeatedly acquiesced in their major demands. Ian Mackenzie, on whom much of the burden of west coast opinion fell in 1942, had long been confirmed in his anti-Asian sentiments, though not outspokenly so, and on the eve of war in the Pacific most British Columbian politicians held the same convictions that he did. Consequently, when anti-Japanese feeling welled up after Pearl Harbor, they shared the public's growing concern and transmitted it with alacrity to Parliament and cabinet.

In Ottawa Mackenzie King also faced the rising tide of protest. His experience with west coast hostility toward Asians had been longer and more intimate than that of any other federal politician. In 1907 and 1908 he had held three royal commissions to investigate Oriental immigration and racial disturbances in Vancouver. In the 1920s and 1930s, as prime minister, he was repeatedly confronted by the issue. As was usual with King, his comments on the Oriental problem were always extremely circumspect. Prior to his premiership he had concluded that the roots of west coast tensions were economic, not racial, and he envisaged their satisfactory resolution through negotiation with Asian nations to seek mutually acceptable immigration levels.[56] In office, he proceeded to use both diplomacy and legislation to restrict immigration from China and Japan. During the later 1930s, however, when anti-Japanese feeling increased on the west coast, King felt constrained from any further restrictive action by international tensions. His view of the issue after the outbreak of war with Japan remains unclear. He did not share the anxieties of west coast residents, yet he ultimately accepted the possibility of a Japanese invasion of British Columbia.[57] Probably his primary concern was for the instability of west coast opinion and the threat to public order which it posed. If subsequent government policy is any measure of his thought, he was willing to adopt any expedient that would reduce public tension.

When the final announcement was made, the province did not immediately breathe a sigh of collective relief. Tension remained high for several days thereafter. In Ottawa Ian Mackenzie believed that public disorder was still possible. Slowly, however, the strain of racial crisis began to ease. The two mass meetings held on March 1 were quiet and orderly. Mackenzie received a note of praise from supporters in Vancouver. The flood of protests to Ottawa began to recede.[58]

When the cabinet approved the order which permitted evacuation, the editors of the *Sun* looked forward to the day the move would be complete. They hoped that the coast was "Saying Goodbye, Not Au Revoir" to the Japanese.[59] But while some had undoubtedly seen the crisis as a chance to solve the province's Japanese problem for all time, this scarcely explains the previous weeks' outburst of hostility. War with Japan had sharpened the animus, narrowed the vision, and intensified the fears of a community already profoundly divided along racial lines. In the minds of west coast whites, intimations of vulnerability and isolation had long nursed a sense of insecurity, and after Pearl Harbor many British Columbians had felt themselves exposed as never before to attack from Japan. In addition, they had grown convinced that the resident Japanese were a threat to the community's security. These beliefs had virtually no foundation in fact. In essence they were facets of the traditional Japanese image held by white British Columbians, stereotypes further distorted in the heat of war. Its fears fed by these perceptions, the west coast loosed a torrent of hostility. Sensitive to the public temper, and alarmed by the prospect of racial disturbance, the federal government attempted preventative action. But neither minor restrictions on civil liberties nor the promise of partial relocation satisfied west coast whites. They demanded total Japanese evacuation. In the end their wishes were met.[60]

By promising total relocation the new federal policy removed the apparent threat to provincial security which had prompted the outburst of mass hostility. But while white tempers were defused on Vancouver Island and in the lower mainland, in many interior communities they were further aroused. As numbers of Japanese refugees moved eastward on their own, and as the prospect increased that thousands of evacuees would be sent to inland locations, whites in many centres raised a new chorus of protest. From the Okanagan, for example, came claims that Japanese infiltration was "assuming alarming proportions and if not forthwith stopped will create serious defence and economic problems in the Valley."[61] They were accompanied by a call for the removal of all Japanese who had recently entered the valley and for the complete prohibition of any further Japanese arrivals. Whites in other inland cities and towns made similar demands. For those in charge of the evacuation program the problem was serious. As the chairman of the British Columbia Security Commission telegraphed Ian Mackenzie, "protests from interior points are such that without government intervention for necessity of cooperation from them it will be practically impossible for us to evacuate Japanese to any of these points."[62] Similarly, plans to move evacuees east of the Rockies encountered vociferous local opposition, especially in southern Alberta where some Japanese were to be sent in order to work district sugar beet crops.[63]

These subsequent flare-ups provided a basis in public opinion for the many legal restrictions which hedged round the lives of the evacuees. While inherent in the logic of the evacuation plan, two new dimensions of federal policy, further curbs on Japanese civil liberties and the alienation of Japanese property, were also extensions of those deep-rooted racist sentiments brought to the fore by recent events. Although the high pitch of popular protest was not sustained throughout the war, nativism continued to lie close to the surface of west coast society. It lurked behind federal initiatives to repatriate Japanese at the end of World War II. It encouraged plans to disperse the remaining minority throughout several provinces. And it delayed the granting of the franchise to Japanese Canadians once the war had concluded.

Yet, more openly than ever before, a small but growing number of whites simultaneously declared support for the Japanese minority. Campaigns by whites in favour of Oriental civil rights were not entirely new by the 1940s. During the interwar years, to a very limited extent, west coast attitudes toward Asians had begun to liberalize. British Columbia trade unionism gradually abandoned its intense nativism. Undoubtedly racism persisted within the labour movement, but union leaders and policies were no longer outspokenly anti-Oriental and limited support for racial equality could be found in union circles. Of greater importance was the fact that Asian minorities had gained a political voice for the first time during the 1930s; the CCF took their cause to the public; calling for the franchise for second-generation Orientals, albeit with due regard for the party's political fortunes. Liberal protestantism also lost its obsession with the seeming need to assimilate Asiatics and commenced open advocacy of minority group interests. Together these various developments marked the dawn of a reassessment of traditional white assumptions about the Asian immigrant in British Columbia, and it was on these foundations that the first shift in attitudes during and after World War II was based.

The wartime advocates of the Japanese-Canadian cause demanded just treatment for all evacuees and urged positive government policies to extinguish anti-Orientalism forever. In the forefront of this movement were a handful of Protestant clergy and laymen and a few members of the CCF. Early in 1942 they formed the Vancouver Consultative Council, a group of between thirty and forty men and women from civil libertarian backgrounds.[64] Soon they were joined by the Fellowship for a Christian Social Order, a Christian socialist organization with branches in Toronto, Vancouver, and other Canadian cities. Both groups denounced racism and campaigned for government action to eliminate discrimination and encourage Japanese integration into Canadian society. They believed that the only way to solve the racial problem for all time was to disperse the Japanese community throughout Canadian society. In the words of Dr. Norman F. Black, a leading member of the VCC:

> We feel very strongly that our Japanese problem can be solved only by prompt and systematic geographic and occupational dispersion ... *we foresee bloodshed on the streets of Vancouver* if, at the termination of the war, twenty thousand or ten thousand or even five thousand homeless and workless Japanese and Canadians of Japanese ancestry suddenly crowd back into this locality when war passions are still surging. The reasons for such anxiety are too manifest to require explanation. And we feel that, unless in the meantime these people have established real homes and become absorbed into the general currents of Canadian economic and social life, an intrinsically hopeless situation will inevitably develop.[65]

Similar sentiments were echoed by the provincial CCF.[66]

Late in the war this movement broadened as leaders of the second-generation Japanese joined church groups, civil libertarians, and CCF politicians in a protest against the federal disenfranchisement of those Japanese Canadians who lived outside the province of British Columbia.[67] An even more vigorous campaign opposed the King government's plan for mass Japanese deportation, a policy intended to send to Japan some 10,000 persons of Japanese ancestry who during 1944 and 1945 had declared their wish to go and had not retracted their decision before the Pacific war had ended; the majority of them had subsequently changed their minds and thus were to be deported against their will. In this instance protest was marshalled by Japanese-Canadian civil rights groups and the Co-operative Committee on Japanese Canadians, a Toronto-based coalition of local and national organizations, among them churches, youth clubs, trade unions, welfare councils, the YMCA, YWCA, and civil liberties associations. This was by far the most vigorous opposition yet mounted against anti-Oriental government policies. Ultimately it was successful for the King government relented and repatriated only those who still wished to be sent.[68]

These campaigns marked a fundamental shift in white attitudes toward Orientals, the first in the lengthy history of their presence in Canada. In British Columbia and across Canada liberal views on race relations were suddenly ascendant. In the later 1940s nativists still voiced their views in public but they were clearly on the defensive. One sign of this change in public opinion was the relative swiftness and ease with which discriminatory legislation was dismantled. The federal government repealed the Chinese Immigration Act in 1947, although sharp limitations on the number of entrants were to continue for years. Of greater symbolic significance was the removal of the franchise restrictions which had long been imposed upon all Asiatics. Chinese and East Indian Canadians gained the vote both provincially and federally in 1947. After a further two-year delay, symptomatic of greater white prejudice, Japanese Canadians were also given the franchise. Soon all of the legal disabilities affecting Orientals had been removed. By the early 1950s discrimination in law against residents of Oriental ancestry was a thing of the past. Undeniably nativism still lurked in white British Columbia, but its public spokesmen had vanished. Lacking public legitimacy, racial discrimination was henceforth forced to assume its many subtler forms.

The motives which lay beneath this major change in public opinion are too complex for analysis here. But among the many possibilities, four seem especially significant. First, and of most immediate importance, the end of the war and the Japanese dispersal had finally erased the image of a Japanese menace in Canada. Henceforth this minority group ceased to seem a military and economic threat. As a result, those attitudes which had once formed the core of anti-Japanese feeling could no longer be maintained. Second, the post-war revelations of German war atrocities cast racist doctrines into unprecedented disrepute in western societies. This revulsion underlay the growing trend toward public declarations of basic human rights, ideals which found open expression in the United Nations' charter and the liberal internationalist rhetoric of the postwar years. So articulate were the champions of this new idealism and so pervasive were their beliefs that by the early 1950s they had reduced Canadian nativists to virtual silence. In the third place, China had been a wartime partner of the Allies and this may have encouraged more positive public attitudes toward the Chinese in Canada, in any case a group which had already ceased to seem a major threat in the eyes of most British Columbians.

Finally, acculturation had greatly reduced the social distance between whites and Asians, particularly those of the second generation. In defiance of all that nativists had long predicted, the Chinese, Japanese, and East Indians had in varying degrees absorbed the social and cultural norms of western Canadian society. Thus they had taken great strides toward eliminating the fundamental source of British Columbian racism. The unassimilable Oriental was becoming assimilated.

Notes

1. A. R. M. Lower, *Canada and the Far East—1940* (New York: Institute of Pacific Relations, 1940), pp. 23-28.
2. *Sun,* Nov. 17, 1937.
3. *Sun,* Nov. 24, 1937; *Colonist,* Jan. 19, 1938.
4. Canada, *Commons Debates,* Feb. 17, 1938, 550-75.
5. *Province,* Feb. 22, 1938.
6. *Province,* Feb. 2, 17, 18, and 24, 1938; *Sun,* Feb. 10, 12, 14, and 28, 1938.
7. Two representative letters to King are: Dr. R. S. Hanna to King, Feb. 14, 1938, King Papers, MG 26, J2, vol. 147, file I-209; Forgotten Native of Japanada to King, n.d., ibid. Letters to Wilson in 1938 can be found in the Wilson Papers, vol. I, file 1.
8. Pattullo to King, Jan. 26, 1938, King Papers, MG 26, J1, vol. 256, 218388-89; Mackenzie to King, Feb. 26, 1938, ibid., vol. 253, 216060; King to Mackenzie, Mar. 1, 1938, ibid., 216062-63A.
9. *Sun,* Mar. 23, 1938.
10. The Board of Review estimated that about 120 Japanese were then living illegally in the province. Board of Review [Immigration], *Final Report,* Sept. 29, 1938, p. 38.
11. British Columbia, *Journals,* Dec. 9, 1938, 120; *Sun,* Oct. 12 and 18, 1938.
12. H. L. K[eenleyside], Memorandum, June 11, 1940, Department of External Affairs Records, vol. 2007, file 212, pt. I; *Province,* Aug. 7 and 15, 1940.
13. See also Wilson Papers, vol. I, file 4; *Sun,* June 29 and Aug. 10, 1940; *Province,* Aug. 21 and 24, 1940.
14. K[eenleyside], Memorandum, June 11, 1940, External Affairs Records, vol. 2007, file 212, pt. I; J. G. Turgeon to King, Aug. 7, 1940, King Papers, MG 26, J1, vol. 297, 252824-25; King to E. Lapointe, Aug. 8, 1940, ibid., 252828.
15. Canada, Privy Council, Minutes and Documents of the Cabinet War Committee, vol. II, Minutes, Oct. 8, 1940, 2, PAC.
16. L. R. LaFleche to F. C. Blair, June 2, 1938, Canada, Department of National Defence Records, file H.Q. 6-0-7, Department of National Defence Archives, Ottawa.

17. Brig. C. V. Stockwell to the Secretary, Department of National Defence, Sept. 4, 1940, Defence Records, file H.Q.S., v.s. 38-1-1-1, vol. 5.

18. Supt. C. H. Hill to the Commissioner, Aug. 25, 1938, Canada, Immigration Branch Records, vol. 86, file 9309, vol. 16; Asst. Comm. R. R. Tait to Keenleyside, Oct. 28, 1940, External Affairs Records, vol. 2007, file 212, pt. I. The entire contents of this file substantiate the observations made in this paragraph.

19. The RCMP did, however, identify a small number of Japanese who might endanger the state in time of war and these individuals were arrested and detained immediately after war on Japan was declared.

20. Pattullo to King, Sept. 23, 1940, King Papers, MG 26, J1, vol. 293, 248363; King to Pattullo, Sept. 27, 1940, T. D. Pattullo Papers, vol. 70, file 4, 21, PABC; Wilson to the Finance Committee, City of Vancouver, Sept. 24, 1940, Wilson Papers, vol. I, file 4; A. D. P. Heeney, Memorandum for the Prime Minister, Sept. 27, 1940, King Papers, MG 26, J4, vol. 361, file 3849.

21. Report and Recommendations of the Special Committee on Orientals in British Columbia, December 1940, typescript, King Papers, MG 26, J4, vol. 361, file 3849. The committee also recommended that, because testimony before it almost unanimously favoured a complete end to Japanese immigration, the government should forbid it when the international situation permitted the move. This recommendation was not published because King feared it might strain existing relations with Japan and inflame anti-Oriental opinion in British Columbia. Canada, Privy Council, vol. IV, Minutes, Jan. 2, 1941, 8-9; Keenleyside to G. Sansom, [Jan. 3, 1941] External Affairs Records, vol. 1868, file 263, pt. IV; Additional Statement by the Members of the Special Committee on Orientals In British Columbia for consideration by the Prime Minister and members of the Cabinet War Committee, n.d., King Papers, MG 26, J1, vol. 307, 259432-33.

22. Keenleyside to King, Dec. 2, 1940, King Papers, MG 26, J1, vol. 289, 244808-10.

23. *Province,* Jan. 9 and Feb. 11, 1941; *Times,* Feb. 26, 1941; *Sun,* Apr. 8 and July 26, 1941. One sign of growing suspicion was the increasing sensitivity of west coast whites to Japanese using cameras. For example see *Free Press,* Feb. 8, 1941.

24. Keenleyside to Comm. S. T. Wood, Feb. 20, 1941, External Affairs Records, vol. 2007, file 212, pt. II; Asst. Comm. F. J. Mead to the Commissioner, Feb. 28, 1941, ibid.; H. F. Angus to Mayor F. J. Hume, July 25, 1941, ibid.

25. F/O W. A. Nield, Report on the State of Intelligence on the Pacific Coast with Particular Reference to the Problem of the Japanese Minority, July 27, 1941, Defence Records, file H.Q., S67-3, vol. 1.

26. All Japanese nationals immediately became enemy aliens and restrictions imposed upon them were also imposed upon all Japanese Canadians naturalized after 1922.

27. Forrest E. La Violette, *The Canadian Japanese and World War II: A Social and Psychological Account* (Toronto: University of Toronto Press, 1948), p. 44; Declaration of the Existence of a State of War Between Canada and Japan, Dec. 8, 1941, King Papers, MG 26, J5, D58190-94; *Sun,* Dec. 8, 1941; *Free Press,* Dec. 8, 1941; *Province,* Dec. 8, 1941.

28. After Pearl Harbor the major daily newspapers in Vancouver and Victoria published a steady stream of letters on the Japanese problem, most of which voiced suspicion of the west coast Japanese and demanded federal action to remove the threat which they posed. For reports of vandalism see *Province,* Dec. 8, 9, and 11, 1941. For rumours of Japanese subversion see Weekly Internal Security Intelligence Report, Dec. 13, 1941, Western Air Command, Defence Records, file H.Q. S67-3, vol. 1. With the exception of fishermen, most Japanese who lost their jobs were soon reabsorbed by the labour market. Hill, Intelligence Report, Dec. 16, 1941 and Jan. 13, 1942, External Affairs Records, file 3464-G-40, Department of External Affairs, Archives Branch (EAA).

29. Hutchison to Pickersgill, [Dec. 16, 1941], King Papers, MG 26, J4, vol. 347, 239219-20.

30. *Province,* Dec. 19, 1941; Hill to the Commissioner, RCMP, Dec. 20, 1941, External Affairs Records, file 3464-H-40C, EAA.

31. Hume to King, Dec. 20, 1941, External Affairs Records, vol. 1868, file 263, pt. IV, PAC.

32. Alexander to Chief of the General Staff, Dec. 30, 1941, Defence Records, file H.Q. 6-0-7. Alexander's concern was shared by those officers commanding Canada's Pacific coast naval and air forces. Commodore W. J. R. Beech to the General Officer Commanding-in-Chief, Pacific Command, Dec. 27, 1941, ibid.; Air Commodore L. F. Stevenson to the Secretary, Department of National Defence for Air, Jan. 2, 1941, Defence Records, file H.Q., S67-3, vol. 1. In Ottawa the Chief of the General Staff did not subscribe to these fears. Lt. Gen. K. Stuart to Keenleyside, Dec. 26, 1941, External Affairs Records, file 3464-H-40C, EAA.

33. Petitions to the federal government can be found in King Papers, MG 26, J2, vol. 294, file P-309, vol. 14; Ian Mackenzie Papers, vol. 24, file 70-25, vol. 1; ibid., vol. 25, file 70-25, vols. 2 and 3; ibid., vol. 25, file 70-25E, PAC; External Affairs Records, file 773-B-1-40, pts. I and II, EAA.

34. Turgeon to King, Jan. 6, 1942, ibid., pt. I.

35. Conference on the Japanese Problem in British Columbia, Minutes, Jan. 8 and 9, 1942, External Affairs Records, vol. 1868, file 263, pt. IV, PAC, Mackenzie to King, Jan. 10, 1942, Mackenzie Papers, vol. 32, file x-81; Keenleyside to Mackenzie, Jan. 10, 1942, ibid. The minority recommendation for partial evacuation was appended to the report.

36. Mackenzie to King, Jan. 10, 1942, ibid.; Pacific Command to National Defence Headquarters, Jan. 12, 1942, telegram, Defence Papers, file H.Q. 6-0-7.

37. Statement of the Prime Minister, Jan. 14, 1942, Mackenzie Papers, vol. 24, file 70-25, vol. 1. Two protected zones were ultimately defined. The larger embraced the area west of the Cascade Mountains, a range which ran parallel to the coast about 100 miles inland. The smaller encompassed the city of Trail and vicinity.

38. Mackenzie to B. M. Stewart, Jan. 23, 1942, Mackenzie Papers, vol. 32, file x-81, vol. 2; Keenleyside to Mackenzie, Jan. 26, 1942, ibid.; Keenleyside, "The Japanese Problem in British Columbia," Memorandum to N. A. Robertson, Jan. 27, 1942, ibid.

39. *Sun,* Jan. 14, 1942; the lull was obvious to military intelligence officers in British Columbia. Maj. H. C. Bray to the Director, Military Operations and Intelligence, National Defence Headquarters, Jan. 29, 1942, Canada, Department of Labour Papers, Lacelle Files, vol. 174, file 614.02:11-1, vol. 1, PAC.

40. See above, n. 33.

41. M. C. Robinson and others to Mackenzie, Feb. 23, 1942, Mackenzie Papers, vol. 25, file 70-25, vol. 2.

42. *Commons Debates,* Jan. 29, 1942, 156-158.

43. Mackenzie to Robertson, Jan. 28, 1942, Mackenzie Papers, vol. 32, file x-81, vol. 2; E. W. Mayhew to King, Feb. 12, 1942, King Papers, MG 26, J1, vol. 330; G. G. McGeer to King, Feb. 13, 1942, Gerald Grattan McGeer Papers, box 2, file 9, PABC; O. Hanson and others to King, Feb. 21, 1942, King Papers, MG 26, J1, vol. 336.

44. R. L. Maitland to Mackenzie, Feb. 17, 1942, Mackenzie Papers, vol. 32, file x-81, vol. 2.

45. G. S. Pearson to A. Macnamara, Feb. 17, 1942, Labour Records, Lacelle Files, vol. 174, file 614.02:11-1, vol. 2; *Sun,* Feb. 16, 1942; Lt. Gov. W. C. Woodward to King, Feb. 11, 1942, King Papers, MG 26, J1, vol. 336; Alexander to the Secretary, Chiefs of Staff Committee, Feb. 13, 1942, Defence Records, Chiefs of Staff Committee, Miscellaneous Memoranda, vol. 3, February 1942; Joint Services Committee, Pacific Coast, Minutes, Feb. 19 and 20, 1942, ibid.

46. Mackenzie to L. St. Laurent, Feb. 14, 1942, Mackenzie Papers, vol. 24, file 70-25, vol. 1; Mackenzie to King, Feb. 22, 1942, King Papers, MG 26, J1, vol. 328.

47. Mackenzie to St. Laurent, Feb. 24, 1942, Mackenzie Papers, vol. 25, file 70-25, vol. 2. At the same time Mackenzie sent similar letters to colleagues King C. G. Power, J. L. Ralston, A. Macdonald, and H. Mitchell.

48. Mackenzie to J. R. Bowler, Feb. 26, 1942, ibid.

49. King Diary, Feb. 19, 1942, King Papers, MG 26, J13.

50. Order in Council P.C. 1486, Feb. 24, 1942; *Commons Debates,* Feb. 27, 1942, 917-20.

51. (New York: Free Press, 1962), chap. VIII.

52. Weekly Internal Security Intelligence Report, Jan. 17, 1942, Western Air Command, Defence Records, file H.Q. S67-3, vol. 1. For another example of rumour see Gwen Cash, *A Million Miles from Ottawa* (Toronto: Macmillan, 1942), pp. 25-26.

53. On the nature and significance of rumour see Gordon W. Allport and Leo Postman, *The Psychology of Rumor* (New York: Russell and Russell, 1965), especially chap. II.

54. *Sun,* Jan. 14, 1942; Mackenzie to Stewart, Jan. 23, 1942, Mackenzie Papers, vol. 32, file x-81, vol. 2. The emphasis was Mackenzie's.

55. Although some fruit and vegetable growers in the Okanagan Valley requested Japanese workers for the duration of the war in order to ease the wartime labour shortage, the proposal roused a strong outburst of bitter opposition in the valley. Protest was channelled through municipal councils, newspapers, boards of trade, and dissenting farm organizations. Proposals that the Japanese be moved east of the

Rockies met opposition from several provincial governments. *Penticton Herald,* Jan. 15, 22, and 29, 1942; *Kelowna Courier,* Jan. 22 and Feb. 12, 1942; Keenleyside, Memorandum for Robertson, Feb. 4, 1942, External Affairs Records, file 3464-G-40, EAA.

56. W. L. Mackenzie King, *Industry and Humanity: A Study in the Principles Underlying Industrial Reconstruction* (Toronto: Thomas Allen, 1918), pp. 75-76.

57. King Diary, Feb. 20, 23, and 24, 1942, King Papers, MG 26, J13.

58. Cash, *A Million Miles,* p. 33; *Province,* Mar. 2, 1942; *Colonist,* Mar. 3, 1942; A. Thompson to C. N. Senior, Feb. 27, 1942, Mackenzie Papers, vol. 25, file 70-25, vol. 2.

59. *Sun,* Feb. 26, 1942.

60. While racial tensions swelled in British Columbia after Pearl Harbor, a similar crisis occurred on the American Pacific Coast. There, as in Canada, residents in coastal areas who were of Japanese origin, were forced to move inland to camps constructed for their reception. The American decision for evacuation, however, was based solely on military considerations and was taken by military officers who had been given a free hand by President Roosevelt. There seems to have been no collaboration between the Canadian and American governments in the decision-making process, and, while the events of the two evacuations ran in close parallel, neither country's policy appears to have had much influence upon that of the other. For accounts of the American evacuation see Morton Grodzins, *Americans Betrayed: Politics and the Japanese Evacuation* (Chicago: University of Chicago Press, 1949); Stetson Conn, "The Decision to Evacuate the Japanese from the Pacific Coast (1942)," *Command Decisions,* ed. Kent Roberts Greenfield, prepared by the Office of the Chief of Military History, Department of the Army (New York: Harcourt, Brace, 1959), pp. 88-109; Roger Daniels, *Concentration Camps USA: Japanese Americans and World War II* (New York: Holt, Rinehart and Winston, 1972).

61. E. W. Barton to Stirling, Mar. 6, 1942, Mackenzie Papers, vol. 24, file 67-25, vol. 1.

62. A. Taylor to Mackenzie, Mar. 4, 1942, telegram, ibid.

63. *Lethbridge Herald,* Mar. 17 and 19, 1942.

64. Interview with Rev. Howard Norman, July 26, 1973.

65. Black to G. Dorey, Jan. 4, 1943, United Church of Canada, Board of Home Missions, United Church Archives, Toronto.

66. Grace MacInnis and Angus MacInnis, *Oriental Canadians—Outcasts or Citizens?* (n.p., n.d.), pp. 17-20.

67. Carol F. Lee, "The Road to Enfranchisement: Chinese and Japanese in British Columbia," *BC Studies,* no. 30 (Summer 1976), p. 52.

68. Ibid., 60; La Violette, *The Canadian Japanese and World War II,* chaps. X and XI.

THE EVACUATION OF THE JAPANESE CANADIANS, 1942: A REALIST CRITIQUE OF THE RECEIVED VERSION

J.L. Granatstein and G.A. Johnson

The popularly accepted version of the evacuation of the Japanese Canadians from the Pacific Coast in 1941-1942 and the background to it runs roughly like this. The white population of British Columbia had long cherished resentments against the Asians who lived among them, and most particularly against the Japanese Canadians. Much of this sprang from envy of the Japanese Canadians' hard-work and industry, much at the substantial share held by Japanese Canadians of the fishing, market gardening and lumbering industry. Moreover, white British Columbians (and Canadians generally) had long had fears that the Japanese Canadians were unassimilable into Canadian society and, beginning early in this century and intensifying as the interwar period wore on, that many might secretly be acting as agents of their original homeland, now an aggressive and expansionist Japan. Liberal and Conservative politicians at the federal, provincial and municipal levels played upon the racist fears of the majority for their own political purposes. Thus when the Second World War began in September 1939, and when its early course ran disastrously against the Allies, there was already substantial fear about "aliens" in British Columbia (and elsewhere) and a desire to ensure that Japanese Canadians would be exempted from military training and service. The federal government concurred in this, despite the desire of many young Japanese Canadians to show their loyalty to Canada by enlisting.

After 7 December 1941 and the beginning of the Pacific War, public and political pressures upon the Japanese Canadians increased exponentially. Suspected subversives were rounded up by the RCMP in the first hours of the war, and over the next ten weeks a variety of actions took place that resulted in the seizure of fishing vessels, arms, cars, cameras, radio transmitters and short-wave receivers owned by Japanese Canadians, and then escalated through the evacuation from the coast of male Japanese nationals between the ages of 18 and 45 to the removal of all Japanese, whether Canadian citizens by birth or naturalization and regardless of age or sex, into the interior. The legalized theft of the property of these Japanese Canadians then followed, and even before the war ended the government moved to deport large numbers to Japan. These events occurred despite the facts that the RCMP and Canada's senior military officers considered the removal of the Japanese from the coast unnecessary, there

From Norman Hillmer, *et al.*, (eds.), *On Guard for Thee: War, Ethnicity, and the Canadian State, 1939-1945* (Ottawa: Canadian Committee for the History of the Second World War, 1988), 101-129. Reprinted by permission of the Canadian Committee for the History of the Second World War.

being no credible military or security threat; that the responsible politicians in Ottawa, and particularly Ian Mackenzie, BC's representative in the Cabinet, knew that the Japanese Canadians posed no threat to national security and acted out of a desire to pander to the bigotry of some whites or for political motives relating to the conduct of the war at home.

This bald summary is based on such books as Ken Adachi's *The Enemy that Never Was* (Toronto, 1976), the second volume of Hugh Keenleyside's *Memoirs* (Toronto, 1982), and Ann Gomer Sunahara's *The Politics of Racism* (Toronto, 1981), as well as on the National Association of Japanese Canadians' brief to the federal government, *Democracy Betrayed: The Case for Redress* (1985). There are variations of emphasis in these accounts, naturally enough, but the received version is a composite that does not pay much attention to these differences.

That Canadians should be interested in the events of 1942 is understandable. That they should attempt to fix blame for the events of those days is no less so, and historians, whose trade obliges them to rummage with more or less science through the past, have not been immune from this tendency. It is the responsibility of historians, however, to try to put themselves back into the circumstances of the past and, while never becoming apologists for the horrors of those times, to seek to understand why people acted as they did. This paper is an attempt to do precisely that, and to look afresh at some points which are encompassed in the received version of the 1942 evacuation and open for examination and some which are not.

The Intelligence Services

The first question that must be raised, and one that has not been asked before, is this: what resources did Ottawa's civil, military and police authorities have on the West Coast before the outbreak of war to secure information about the 22,000 Japanese Canadians living in British Columbia? The answer is readily available.

The responsibility for internal security rested with the RCMP, assisted as necessary by the armed forces.[1] In July 1941, five months before the outbreak of war with Japan, the RCMP's "E" Division responsible for the Pacific Coast had on its staff three persons concerned with gathering intelligence on the Japanese Canadians in British Columbia: a sergeant who did not speak Japanese, a constable who did, and a civilian translator. These three were in charge of the "active personnel intelligence work on enemy and potential enemy aliens and agents." There was, in addition, a lieutenant-commander at Naval Headquarters in Esquimalt charged with intelligence duties who was "greatly interested in the Japanese problem generally," but who had many other tasks. The Royal Canadian Air Force's intelligence section in the province, which like the Royal Canadian Navy's had a wide range of duties over and above collecting information on Japanese Canadians, consisted of two officers, both of whom had lived in Japan and spoke Japanese. The senior officer, a Squadron Leader Wynd, however, could read Japanese only with difficulty; whether his colleague was any more fluent is uncertain. The army's intelligence on the coast was in the hands of two very busy officers, neither of whom spoke Japanese. In addition, the British Columbia Provincial Police had four officers working in the Japanese-Canadian community. Cooperation between the various services was hampered by RCMP regulations that forbade the Mounties to share information with their colleagues without first securing permission from Ottawa headquarters. Even so, the West Coast Joint Intelligence Committee had been created to coordinate the information collected by the military and police.[2] There is one additional point worth mentioning: the British intelligence services had some representation on the West Coast, and there exists in RCMP files one very long (and very inflammatory) report on "Japanese Activities in British Columbia," prepared by someone unnamed for William Stephenson's British Security Coordination.[3]

This intelligence presence did not amount to very much. As Hugh Keenleyside of the Department of External Affairs, a British Columbian who had served in the Legation in Japan and who was genuinely sympathetic to the Japanese Canadians, wrote in June 1940, there was a danger of subversive activities on the part of some elements in the Japanese community. "The police," he went on, "are not in a position to ferret out the dangerous Japanese as they have done with the Germans and Italians; they have lines on a few Japanese who might be expected to take part in attempts at sabotage.... But that would not really solve the problem."[4] Even, therefore, in the view of someone in a position to know (and understand), the intelligence information gathered on the Japanese Canadians was strictly limited, the officers involved pathetically few in number and largely baffled by the impenetrability of the Japanese language and the tendency of the Japanese Canadians to stay together, separate, and (with good historical reasons) not to trust whites.

The discussion thus far has said nothing about the quality of the information gathered. The available intelligence evidence on the Japanese Canadians is very slim (and the Privacy Act prevents us from seeing whatever else there might be), but we can state with confidence that when the RCMP looked at Communist questions, towards which it had a definite *idée fixe,* or the activities of suspected Nazis in this period, its work was far from competent.[5] In November 1939, J.W. Pickersgill of the prime minister's office complained that the force could not distinguish between facts and hearsay, or discriminate between legitimate social and political criticism and subversive doctrine. There was, moreover, "no suggestion that there is any co-ordination with Military Intelligence, or with the Immigration authorities, or with the Department of External Affairs, or even with the Censorship." More disturbing still to Pickersgill was "the evidence of a total lack of the capacity, education and training required for real intelligence work...."[6] Whether the RCMP's efforts on the Japanese Canadians were any better remains speculative, at least until all the files are open to research; the existing documents offer no grounds for optimism.

There is little more information available on the quality of military intelligence gathered. But as the regular forces before the war were tiny and as military intelligence, a skill requiring years of preparation, was not among the best-developed areas of the permanent forces, there is no reason to believe that the army, navy or air force by 1941 were any less clumsy or more sophisticated in their ability to gather and assess information on the Japanese Canadians than the RCMP. Evidence for this conclusion is suggested by the efforts of the Examination Unit, a secret operation of External Affairs and National Defence set up under the shelter of the National Research Council, among other things to attempt to decipher Japanese diplomatic and military wireless messages in response to a British request before Pearl Harbor. As the just declassified manuscript history of the Examination Unit notes, two people were engaged for this purpose in August 1941, a Mr. and Mrs. T.L. Colton. "It was hoped that Mrs. Colton, who was very well educated in Japanese but could not handle translation into English, might be able to explain the contents of messages to her husband who could then write them out in English. This system," the history notes dryly, "did not prove very satisfactory" and the Coltons were replaced in April 1942.[7]

In this atmosphere of improvisation and amateurism, many of the available reports by the RCMP and the military on the Japanese Canadians tended to focus on investigations of alleged "unlawful drilling [with weapons]" by male Japanese Canadians, reports of caches of Japanese rifles and ammunition, and accounts of suspicious fishing parties of well-dressed Japanese who did not appear to be fishermen. Rumours, plain and fanciful.[8] On the other hand, there were just as many assertions offered with great confidence that 95 percent of Japanese Canadians were law abiding and satisfied with their lot in Canada and that "No fear of sabotage need be expected from the Japanese in Canada." That last statement by Assistant Commissioner Frederick J. Mead of the RCMP, one of the Mounties' specialists in security matters and Communist subversion, was, he added, "broad [but] at the same time I know it to be true."[9]

Mead was soon a member of the British Columbia Security Commission where, activist *Nisei* (or second generation Canadian Japanese) correctly believed, he depended on intelligence from Etsuji Morii, a man suspected of blackmailing other Japanese Canadians and a notorious underworld figure. Morii was in turn the Commission's appointed chairman of the "Japanese Liaison Committee," whose mandate was to convey news and information in 1942 to the community.[10] As Mead was the senior RCMP official on the coast early in 1942, he was almost certainly the main source for RCMP Commissioner

S.T. Wood's defence of Morii and his assertion to William Stephenson (in response to the British Security Coordination report mentioned earlier) in August 1942 that "we have searched without letup for evidence detrimental to the interests of the state and we feel that our coverage has been good, but to date no such evidence has been uncovered."[11] The RCMP's firmly-stated position may have been correct, but again the small size of its resources and the lack of sophistication of all its operations in this period tend to raise doubts. From 45 years distance, the fairest thing that can be said is that the RCMP had uncovered relatively little hard information about possible subversion among the Japanese Canadians before 7 December 1941, if there were indeed subversive intentions within the community, because it lacked the competence and skills to do so. Moreover, much of the information that the RCMP had before and after that date came from sources that even many Japanese Canadians considered self-interested and tainted.

The Role of the Japanese Consulate

Such intelligence information as there was tended to agree that the Japanese Consulate in Vancouver was the focus of Japanese nationalism, propaganda and possible subversive activities in BC. One RCMP report surveying the general activities of the Japanese Canadians noted that the Consul and his staff regularly visited areas where Japanese Canadians lived to deliver speeches and to talk privately with individuals about the Tokyo government's views of world events. One RCAF intelligence officer was sufficiently alarmed by these activities to tell his superior that he considered British Columbia's Japanese Canadians to be "directly under the control of the Japanese Government through their consul at Vancouver."[12] The Consul was also thought to exercise considerable influence on the local Japanese language schools and press. Roles of these sorts, of course, were well within the bounds of diplomatic niceties. And since, under Japanese law, *Nisei* born abroad before 1924 were considered as Imperial subjects, while those born abroad after that date could register at Japanese consulates and secure Japanese citizenship in addition to their status as British subjects, the Consul in Vancouver had substantial work to do in dealing with the approximately 7,200 Japanese nationals, 2,400 naturalized British subjects, and the unknown (but very large) number of Japanese Canadians holding dual citizenship in the BC community.[13] A military intelligence paper surveying the situation on the coast added that the Consul "through his agents, and through the Japanese schoolmasters, and the Japanese patriotic societies cultivates a strong Japanese spirit and a consciousness among the BC Japanese of being 'sons of Japan abroad' rather than Canadian citizens."[14] That was no different than the role of the Italian and German consuls in this pre-war period.

There were, however, grounds for believing that in this instance the Japanese Consulate's officials had duties of a more dangerous kind. On 28 February 1941, Vincent Massey, the high commissioner in London, reported to Prime Minister Mackenzie King that "reliable information of a most secret character" had revealed that "official Japanese circles" were taking great interest in the British Columbia Coast. "Reference is also made to large number of Japanese settled in British Columbia and on Western Coast of United States, who are all said to have their duties,"[15] an ominous phrase.

The source of that information was possibly Britain's Government Code & Cypher School which had been reading some Japanese military and diplomatic messages since the 1920s,[16] or more probably "Magic," the name given by the Americans to their armed forces' decryption operation that in January 1941 had cracked the "Purple" code used for the most secret Japanese diplomatic traffic. Britain and the United States soon started to cooperate in reading Japanese codes, and by the spring of 1941 the two countries had pooled their intelligence.[17] The Americans also began reading their hitherto unbroken files of Japanese messages back to 1938.

The decryption team had intercepted important telegrams from the Foreign Office in Tokyo to the Japanese Embassy in Washington dated 30 January 1941, which gave the *Gaimusho*'s orders to its officials in North America to de-emphasize propaganda and to strengthen intelligence gathering. Special reference was made to "Utilization of our 'Second Generations' [Nisei] and our resident nationals" and to the necessity for great caution so as not to bring persecution down on their heads. Those messages were copied to Ottawa and Vancouver as "Minister's orders"—instructions, in other words, that were to be carried out in Canada just as in the United States. The Consulate's success in carrying out these orders remains unknown.

A further message from Tokyo to Washington, dated 15 February 1941, was also sent to Ottawa and Vancouver as a "Minister's instruction." In this telegram, the Foreign Ministry specified the "information we particularly desire with regard to intelligence involving US and Canada," especially the strengthening of Pacific Coast defences, ship and aircraft movements. In a telegram the day before, the Consulate in Vancouver was instructed to pay special attention to paragraph 10 of the order to Washington: "General outlooks on Alaska and the Aleutian Islands, with particular stress on items involving plane movements and shipment of military supplies to those localities." The next month, the Consulate was asked to report on RCN ship movements. Whether these particular telegrams were the basis for Massey's despatch to Ottawa is unclear.[18]

A thorough search of the "Magic" intercepts in the United States National Archives makes clear that at least as early as 1939 intelligence and counter-intelligence work was carried on from the Vancouver Consulate, exactly as was taking place in the Japanese Consulates all over the United States and throughout the Western Hemisphere. As we have seen, the 1941 telegrams also stress efforts to involve the resident nationals and the second generation *Nisei,* at whom radio broadcasts from Tokyo had been deliberately aimed for some years. How much, if anything, Ottawa knew of all this, beyond the RCMP's suspicions and the information conveyed in the Massey telegram, is still indeterminate. But surely there was ample justification in the light of the Massey telegram for the government to have increased surveillance on the Consulate and the Japanese-Canadian community. There is no sign that it did so.[19]

One contemporary assessment of the Canadian situation by an RCAF intelligence officer noted that "espionage and subversive activity is largely carried on by a few key Japanese working under the Consul and *seriously* involves only a few—say 60 at most—Japanese individuals." This same officer then tried to assess the response of Japanese Canadians in the event of war, particularly if the Japanese authorities instructed them to engage in sabotage, and if such orders were reinforced by "disorderly demonstrations of white antipathy." His answer was that "No one knows; but no one in his senses would take a chance on Japanese loyalty under those circumstances."[20]

The Pre-War Pro-Japan Actions of Japanese Canadians

If that sounds harsh, there were reasons why it should not. Throughout the 1930s and especially after 1937, Japan had aggressively expanded its influences in northern China, and the Imperial Japanese Army had campaigned with great brutality in that country. The Japanese government, naturally enough, tried to put the best face possible on its actions, and it encouraged the creation and spread of propaganda on its behalf abroad, something in which Japanese Canadians directly assisted by writing and distributing leaflets. The most widely distributed pamphlet, dated 1 October 1937 and published by the Canadian Japanese Association, the largest Japanese-Canadian association with over 3,000 members, was "Sino-Japanese Conflict Elucidated," a far from unbiased examination of the struggle in China, despite its claim to be circulated "in the interests of truth, to meet unfair and untrue propaganda." Moreover, money, comforts for the troops, medical supplies and tin foil were collected for Japan by first generation *Issei* and second generation *Nisei* groups.[21] There was, of course, nothing remotely improper about this, and other ethnic groups in Canada at that time (Italians, say, during the Italo-Ethiopian war) and more recently (Jews during the Arab-Israeli wars, for example) have acted similarly in comparable circumstances.

But the wholly justifiable outrage in Canada over such incidents as the brutal rape of Nanking, with its estimated 200,000 or more dead (and Japanese army assaults on Canadian missionaries stationed there) led many Canadians to boycott Japanese products and to call upon the federal government to take steps to cease strategic metal exports to Japan. Such measures were eventually taken.[22] And the *New Canadian,* the newspaper of British Columbia's *Nisei,* began publication in late 1938, noted its founder, Edward Ouchi, the General Secretary of the main *Nisei* organization, the Japanese Canadian Citizens' League, to counter the "vicious" anti-Japanese propaganda of North American Chinese that was hurting Japanese-Canadian businesses. Although the newspaper did not offer frequent support for Japan's war in China in its pages, it did give close and favourable coverage to the activities of the Consul in Vancouver and even ran an occasional rotogravure section of propagandistic photographs on life in Japan.[23]

Inevitably Japanese-Canadian support for Japan's war on China focussed much attention upon the *Issei* and *Nisei.* As Professor Henry Angus of the University of British Columbia wrote in October 1940:

> The young Japanese understand the position well enough. At first they (in all good faith I think) distributed a good deal of pro-Japanese, anti-Chinese propaganda. Now they say, "we are not responsible for what Japan may do." I tell them that they have unfortunately made people feel that they are identified with Japan by their action in distributing propaganda, and that it is very difficult to find a way of removing this impression.[24]

Angus was always very sympathetic to the Japanese Canadians (and after he had joined External Affairs, he and Hugh Keenleyside would find themselves under attack in Parliament because of the vigour of their resistance to the evacuation in January and February 1942),[25] but he was surely correct in his assessment. Even such supportive British Columbia politicians as CCF Member of Parliament Angus MacInnis agreed.[26] The Japanese Canadians by their support for Japan "impaired [their] standing with those circles most disposed to press [their] cause," Professor Angus lamented.[27]

We can say today that Canadians should have understood the difficulties that a small minority would have faced in not supporting its belligerent mother country in those days in the late 1930s and early 1940s. But after the Pearl Harbor attack and the fall of Hong Kong, British Columbians, already predisposed to expect the worst of the Japanese Canadians and motivated by deep-rooted racism against them, and Canadians generally could not reasonably have been expected to make such judgements. Many Japanese Canadians had supported Japan against China before 7 December and few, if any, had opposed her; after Pearl Harbor, China was an ally and Japan an enemy. Therefore, the supporters of Japan before 7 December were now supporters of Canada's enemy and possibly (or probably) disloyal, particularly as there seemed no way of distinguishing the active few from the passive majority. The syllogism was flawed (and certainly the vast majority of German and Italian Canadians had been treated far differently in the comparable circumstances of September 1939 and June 1940), but few were prepared to challenge its logic.

Norman Robertson, the under secretary of state for external affairs, a British Columbian and no bigot, expressed something of the same reasoning when he told Pierrepont Moffat, the American minister to Canada, on 8 December 1941 that "the Government had hoped not to have to intern all Japanese. However, this might be very difficult in view of the treacherous nature of the Japanese attack, [and] the evidences of premeditation...."[28] Robertson's description of the attack mirrored the public's response: "In the wake of Pearl Harbor, the single word favoured by Americans as best characterizing the Japanese people," John Dower has noted, "was 'treacherous'...."[29]

In August 1944, Prime Minister King told the House of Commons that "no person of Japanese race born in Canada has been charged with any act of sabotage or disloyalty during the years of war." In his account, Ken Adachi added that "no alien Japanese or naturalized citizen had ever been found guilty of the same crime."[30] Those statements are undoubtedly true, but they do not tell the whole story.

Thirty-seven or 38 Japanese nationals were arrested and interned by the RCMP at the outbreak of the war, presumably because they were thought to be engaged in espionage or subversive activities. None of the standard accounts offers any detailed information on the allegations against or the fate of these people.[31]

More important, it seems certain that support for Japan remained strong among some Japanese Canadians after the war began. The *Issei* Takeo Nakano, in his book *Within the Barbed Wire Fence,* notes that "We Japanese, largely working-class immigrants, were, generally speaking, not given to sophisticated political thinking. Rather we had in common a blind faith in Japan's eventual victory." John J. Stephan's study, *Hawaii Under the Rising Sun,* cites the conclusions of Japanese historians Nobuhiro Adachi and Hidehiko Ushijima that most first-generation Japanese in Hawaii remained loyal to Japan: "even among those who considered the Pearl Harbor attack a betrayal were many who believed in and hoped for an ultimate Japanese victory.... Radio reports of Japanese advances ... confirmed for many their motherland's invincibility." Nakano's book demonstrates that the same response existed in British Columbia, and even Sunahara notes that the Japanese vice-consul encouraged some Japanese Canadians to seek internment as a gesture of support for Japan.[32] Those of Japanese origin, of course, formed a greater proportion of the Hawaiian population (about 35 percent) than did the Japanese Canadians in British Columbia (about three percent). Moreover, at this point it is impossible to determine if the links between the Japanese Canadians and Japan were stronger or weaker than those between Hawaiian Japanese and the mother country. These two factors could certainly have affected the situation.

Nakano also underlines the presence in the Japanese-Canadian community of a substantial number of hard-liners or *gambariya,* "best described as rebels against the treatment they were receiving in time of war. The *Nisei gambariya* were protesting such unjust treatment of Canadian citizens," he continues, an understandable response. He goes on, however, to note that "the *Issei gambariya* firmly believed in Japan's eventual victory and looked forward to the Canadian government's enforced compensation to them."[33] That attitude is less understandable if the revised version is to be accepted. More than 750 *gambariya,* a fairly substantial number of the approximately 9,000 adult males over the age of sixteen in a BC community of 22,000, were interned at Angler in Northern Ontario, and Nakano, in part as a result of misunderstanding, he says, ended up there as well. Nakano's story is stylistically elliptical, but it rings true. None of the historical accounts make much mention of the *gambariya,* other than to skirt the evidence by saying that there were some who refused to have anything to do with the evacuation or to cooperate with the Canadian authorities.

Perhaps a last word here should belong to Stephan, whose study of Hawaii is an exemplary and sensitive one. "It has been common to write about Hawaii's Japanese before and during the Second World War as if their 'loyalty' were a self-evident, quantifiable phenomenon," he said. "In the justifiable impulse to indict the relocation of West Coast Japanese and Japanese Americans ... writers have in many cases dealt simplistically with what is full of complex nuances and ambiguities."[34] Those comments apply with equal force to the Canadian accounts, almost all of which have been remarkably one-dimensional.

The Role of the Military in the Evacuation

There is no doubt that senior officers of the armed forces and the RCMP in Ottawa were remarkably unperturbed by the presence of large numbers of Japanese Canadians in British Columbia.[35] General Maurice Pope, the vice chief of the General Staff, attended the Conference on the Japanese Problem in British Columbia in Ottawa on 8-9 January 1942, which brought together representatives from British Columbia, the federal bureaucracy, and political figures, and his memoir provides the standard account. The navy, he wrote, had no fears, now that the Japanese-Canadian fishing fleet was in secure hands; the RCMP expressed no concern, and Pope himself, offering the army position, said that if the RCMP was not perturbed, "neither was the Army." Pope adds that several days after the meeting adjourned, the angry and frightened British Columbians who had attended "must have got busy on the telephone" for "we received an urgent message from the [Army's] Pacific Command recommending positive action against the Japanese in the interests of national security. With the receipt of this message, completely reversing the Command's previous stand," the minister of national defence, Colonel J.L. Ralston, "was anything but pleased."[36]

The evidence simply does not support Pope's account. While it is clear that the Department of National Defence's representatives on the Special Committee on Measures to be Taken in the Event of War With Japan agreed in mid-1941 with the Committee's recommendation to Cabinet that "the bulk of the Japanese population in Canada can continue its normal activities,"[37] and while it is equally certain in mid-December the Chiefs of Staff Committee told the Cabinet War Committee that fears of a Japanese assault on BC were unwarranted,[38] there is absolutely no doubt that the military commanders *in* British Columbia and the military members of the Permanent Joint Board on Defence were seriously concerned about the possible threat posed by the Japanese-Canadian population both before and after 7 December 1941. The real question that remains unanswered is why in this instance the generals, admirals and air marshals in Ottawa were so ready to ignore the advice of their commanders in the field.

Certainly the military advice from BC was completely unambiguous. The Joint Service Committee, Pacific Coast, the key coordinating military body that brought together the three service commanders in British Columbia, had prepared plans in July 1940 for preventive actions directed at the Japanese Canadians in the event of war with Japan.[39] The Committee also recommended on 17 June 1941 that "the Japanese population [of approximately 230] residing in the vicinity of the Royal Canadian Air Force Advanced Base at Ucluelet [on the West Coast of Vancouver Island] should, in the event of an emergency, be evacuated for reasons of security. It was felt that similar steps should be taken in connection with Japanese resident near other important defence areas, and particularly those established near air bases." There were about two hundred Japanese Canadians living at Port Alice near the Coal Harbour RCAF base and the same number in Prince Rupert near another air station. The Committee's recommendations had been forwarded to the Chiefs of Staff Committee in Ottawa no later than 20 September 1941.[40]

In addition, the RCN on the coast had long been concerned with the fleet of up to 1,200 fishing vessels operated by Japanese Canadians. In 1937, for example, the Navy's staff officer (intelligence) at Esquimalt had said that "The fact that there are a large number of Japanese fishermen operating in British Columbia waters ... and having a thorough and practical knowledge of the coast, is in itself a matter of some concern to the Naval authorities."[41] In August 1941, the naval officer commanding on the coast asked Ottawa for authority to round up the fishing boats in the event of war. The Department of External Affairs refused to agree to this *in toto,* however, and in October orders were issued for seizure only of boats "owned and operated by Japanese *nationals.*" "Vessels owned and operated by British subjects of Japanese origin," the RCN was told, "will only be interfered with where there are positive grounds for suspicion, comparable to those which would justify the internment of a British subject of Japanese origin."[42] When war came five weeks later, those orders would be overridden in the urgency of the moment.

Furthermore, before the outbreak of war in the Pacific, both the Canadians and the Americans worried about the concentration of Japanese Americans and Canadians living along the common coastline. The Joint Service Committee, Pacific Coast, had urged Ottawa on 20 September 1941 to coordinate any actions with Washington. In its opinion, "inequality in the treatment of persons of Japanese race in the territories of the Dominion of Canada and the United States would be liable to prove a source of danger to the effective prosecution of such measures of control as may be ordered by either government and to furnish grounds for grievance by the persons immediately concerned."[43] The Permanent Joint Board on Defence at its meeting on 10-11 November at Montreal had also considered the question of the "population of Japanese racial origin." Just as the Joint Service Committee on the West Coast had urged, the Canadian and American members agreed that there should be consultation to produce "policies of a similar character in relation to these racial groups" if war with Japan broke out. The aim was "a practicable coincidence of policy."[44] That did not imply evacuation from the Pacific Coast, but it did suggest that there was a shared realization of a "problem." And as John Hickerson, the senior State Department official regularly concerned with Canadian affairs, noted after that PJBD meeting, it would "cause the Canadians considerable political difficulty in British Columbia if we adopted more rigid treatment of Japanese in California than that prescribed in British Columbia." That, he added, is why the Canadians suggest "that at the proper time there be consultation" between the two governments "with the view to adopting similar policies in Canada and in continental United States."[45]

After Pearl Harbor, but before the Conference in Ottawa, the three senior officers on the coast wrote to Ottawa with their views. Major-General R.O. Alexander, the GOC of Pacific Command, told the chief of the General Staff on 30 December that he believed "internment of Japanese males between the ages of 18 and 45, their removal from the coast and their organization into paid units on public works ... would be advisable." Such action, Alexander added, "might prevent inter-racial riots and bloodshed, and will undoubtedly do a great deal to calm the local population." There is no doubt that General Pope saw this letter, because he sent a copy of it to Hugh Keenleyside of the Department of External Affairs and Keenleyside wrote back to him with suggestions on 3 January—before the "Japanese Problem" conference in Ottawa took place.[46]

The senior RCAF officer in BC shared the view of his army colleague. Air Commodore L.F. Stevenson informed RCAF headquarters in Ottawa on 2 January that security "cannot rest on precarious discernment between those who would actively support Japan and those who might at present be apathetic." If the government had doubts about the wisdom of moving the Japanese out,

Stevenson said, "I suggest a strong commission be appointed immediately to ... obtain the opinion of a good cross section of the BC public and the officers charged with the defence of the Pacific Coast." The senior naval officer agreed, Commodore W.J.R. Beech telling his headquarters on 27 December that "Public opinion is very much against the Japanese all over the Queen Charlotte Islands and in view of the strategic position of these Islands I would strongly recommend that all the Japanese be removed."[47]

All three officers stressed public opinion at least as much as military needs, and it is reasonable to assume that their positions often put them in close contact with politicians and journalists likely to be pressing for stern action. But this does not alter the fact that the responsible military commanders in British Columbia, after 7 December and before the Ottawa conference, called for removal of the Japanese Canadians from all or part of the coastal region; so too had their staffs urged removal before 7 December from the vicinity of military bases and after Pearl Harbor from coastal areas of the province.[48] Moreover, on 13 February 1942, the Joint Services Committee, Pacific Coast, decided that in view of "the deterioration of the situation in the Pacific theatre of war ... the continued presence of enemy aliens and persons of Japanese racial origin [in the coastal areas] constitutes a serious danger and prejudices the effective defence of the Pacific Coast of Canada."[49] And as late as 26 February, the RCN commanding officer on the coast was advised by his security intelligence officer that "The removal of all Japanese from this coastal area would undoubtedly relieve what is becoming more and more a very dangerous situation from the point of view of sabotage and aid to the enemy as well as the great danger of development of inter-racial strife."[50] Again, public opinion was given equal weight with the fear of sabotage, but it is significant that this advice was proffered after adult male Japanese citizens living on the coast had been ordered inland.

Even after the great majority of Japanese Canadians had been cleared from the government's designated defence zone, moreover, substantial concern was expressed repeatedly by the American military and by the US members of the Permanent Joint Board on Defence on 26-27 May and 1 September 1942 at the relocation of Japanese Canadians inland to road camp sites near railway lines or other strategic points. Under pressure, the Canadian government then acted to resolve matters to reassure its ally. Similar concerns had been expressed in June 1942 in the British Security Coordination report.[51]

An additional factor that played an unquantifiable but important part in events in BC were the reports that Japanese living in Hawaii, Hong Kong and Malaya had helped the attacking Japanese forces.[52] Undoubtedly the lurid tales of fifth column activities from Europe in 1940 also fed popular fears. The Hawaii stories eventually proved to be mere rumours, but their impact was great in the first months of 1942. In Hong Kong and particularly in Malaya, however, there was substantial truth to the reports in January and February that local Japanese had hidden arms and ammunition, planted explosive charges at military installations, docks and ships, and sniped at troops, as well as providing information to the invaders.[53] It is virtually immaterial if the stories were true; what is important is that they circulated widely among a generally anti-Japanese public and a fearful military that were prepared to believe them. As the *Vancouver Sun* put it on 2 January 1942, "we may expect Japanese civilians to do all in their power to assist the attacker."[54]

Finally, the stories, all too true, of the brutality of the Japanese victors towards captured Allied servicemen and civilians had substantial impact on both the public and political leaders. As early as 12 February, telegrams from London to Ottawa spoke of atrocities against captured Hong Kong prisoners and of deplorable conditions in the POW camps. Within the week, Cabinet ministers in Ottawa were talking about the fate of the Hong Kong force with their intimates, and on 10 March, the widespread rumours were given official sanction by statements in Parliament in London and Ottawa. The "devilish" Japanese, or so M.J. Coldwell of the CCF said in the House of Commons, would be punished after the war for their atrocities. The Canadian Japanese, wholly innocent of the crimes of the Imperial Japanese Army, nonetheless were denied sympathy as a result.[55]

Was There a Military Threat to the Coast?

Whether there was a direct military threat to the coast from the Imperial Japanese forces is also worth some consideration, if only because the received version denies any. In September 1941, RCAF headquarters in Ottawa had been confident that the United States Navy was the ultimate guarantor of the safety of the Pacific Coast: "Unless the United States Navy is seriously defeated or loses its northern bases," Air Vice Marshal G.M. Croil told his Minister, C.G. Power, all Canada had to do was remain in "watchful readiness" on the West Coast.[56] With that attitude in the ascendant, the coast of British Columbia was left "poorly defended," the words employed to describe matters by Robert Rossow, Jr., the American Vice-Consul in Vancouver, in August 1941.[57] After Pearl Harbor, however, the worst possible case seemed to have occurred, and Canada was largely unprepared. Certainly there were few modern aircraft, few ships and relatively few trained soldiers in the area until the outbreak of war,[58] and it took some time before more could be rushed to the coast.[59] That caused concern.

So too did the course of the war. The Japanese hit Pearl Harbor on 7 December and simultaneously attacked Malaya, Hong Kong, the Philippines and Wake and Midway Islands. On 8 December, Japan occupied Thailand, captured Guam on 13 December, Wake on 24 December, and Hong Kong on 25 December. Manila fell on 2 January, Singapore followed on 15 February, a staggering blow to the British position in Asia (and something that frightened British Columbia[60]) and the Imperial Japanese Navy crushed an allied fleet in the Java Sea on 27 February, the date that the Canadian government's decision to move all Japanese Canadians inland was in the newspapers. Closer to home, a Japanese submarine had shelled Santa Barbara, California on 23 February, two days later the "Battle of Los Angeles" took place with much ammunition expended against (apparently) imaginary targets, and there were submarine attacks on points in Oregon. (On 20 June a Japanese submarine shelled Estevan point on Vancouver Island.) The Dutch East Indies and most of Burma were then captured in March, capping an extraordinary four months of conquest.

At the beginning of June, the Japanese launched what H.P. Willmott, the leading historian of Pacific war strategy, called "their main endeavour, a twin offensive against the Aleutians," designed to draw the American fleet to battle to protect their territory, "and against the western Hawaiian Islands," intended to lead to an invasion once the Americans' Pacific Fleet had been destroyed. At least two plans for such an invasion existed before and after the attack on Pearl Harbor, and one plan saw the capture of Hawaii "as preparatory to strikes against the United States mainland."[61] (Whether attacks against the Canadian Coast were intended remains unclear until such Japanese military records that survived the war are searched.) Dutch Harbor, Alaska was attacked by carrier-based aircraft on 3 June as part of this plan. Four days later Kiska and Attu in the Aleutian Islands were taken.

Although in retrospect the American naval victory at Midway in June, aided beyond measure by "Magic" intercepts, put an end to the Hawaiian adventure and truly marked the beginning of the end for Japanese imperial ambitions as a whole, its significance was not quite so apparent in mid-1942 as it has since become. Certainly the Canadian government did not slacken its defence efforts on the coast after the American victory. In mid-February 1942, a military appreciation prepared by the chiefs of staff for the minister of national defence's use at a secret session of Parliament noted that "probable" Japanese strategy included containing "North American forces in America" by raids on the North American Pacific seaboard. "Possible" enemy aims included an "invasion of the West Coast of North America," although the chiefs noted that "Under present conditions" such invasion was "not considered to be a practicable operation of war."[62]

The next month, with the Japanese forces seemingly roaming at will throughout the Pacific and with the politicians anxious to satisfy the public clamour for stronger local defences in British Columbia, the chief of the General Staff in Ottawa was estimating the possible scale of a Japanese attack on the Pacific Coast to be two brigades strong (i.e., two Japanese regiments of three battalions each or approximately 5,200 to 6,000 men), and he was recommending the raising of new forces.[63] At the beginning of April, President Roosevelt used the occasion of the first meeting of the Pacific Council, made up of representatives of all the belligerent allies, to say that he had invited Canada because "he thought that Canada might do more than she was now doing."[64] That disturbed Ottawa, perhaps because it mirrored British Columbia public opinion so clearly, and Mackenzie King hastened to discuss the matter with the president.[65]

Later that month, after Lieutenant Colonel James Doolittle's B-25 bombers, launched from the carrier *Hornet,* had hit Tokyo, Canadian intelligence reports predicted that enemy aircraft carriers would launch retaliatory attacks against the West Coast in May.[66] By June, there were nineteen battalions on the coast, a response to Japan's invasion of the Aleutians and continued and growing public concern. Even so, the military commanders were far from satisfied. The Joint Canadian United States Services Committee at Prince Rupert believed that military strength in the area was "entirely inadequate against many types of attack that are possible and probable from the West."[67] The air officer commanding on the coast asked for sixteen squadrons to deal with the maximum scale of attack by battleships, cruisers and carrierborne aircraft. There were also blackouts and dimouts, and active plans underway in July and August 1942 for the evacuation of Vancouver Island and the lower mainland in the event of a Japanese attack.[68]

The Cabinet War Committee was assured by the chief of the General Staff in late September that he saw "no reason to fear any invasion from the Pacific Coast at present time,"[69] but two months later the Combined Chiefs of Staff, the highest Allied military authority, determined that while "carrier-borne air attacks and sporadic naval bombardment" were the most probable form of attack, the possibility of "a small scale destructive raid cannot be ignored." By that, the British and American planners meant "a force comprising 10/15 fast merchant ships carrying up to two brigades."[70] And as late as March 1943, there was a flurry of reports of Japanese activity in North American waters that stirred fears about a possible attack of the precise sort the planners had anticipated.[71] In other words, and contrary to the arguments of those who have argued that there was never any threat from Japan to the coast and hence no justification on grounds of national security for the evacuation of the Japanese Canadians, there *was* a credible—if limited—military threat into 1943.

The intent of this paper was to present some new and re-state some old evidence on several aspects of the Japanese-Canadian question. What has our account done to the received version? It has pointed to the gross weaknesses of and wishful thinking in RCMP and military intelligence about the Japanese Canadians. It has demonstrated irrefutably that the Japanese Consulate in Vancouver had orders from the Foreign Ministry to employ British Columbia *Nisei* in information collection or spying. It has called into question the advice of the military planners in Ottawa, brought forward once more the widespread concerns of the senior officers and staff planners of all three armed forces in

British Columbia, and argued that there was a limited but credible military threat to North America from early 1942 into 1943 from the Imperial Japanese forces. It has noted that the attitudes of some Japanese Canadians by their support for Japan's war with China before 7 December 1941 raised understandable concerns on the part of British Columbians and Canadians generally. And although the attitudes of Japanese Canadians before and during the war have yet to be thoroughly studied despite all the work on the subject, Nakano's memoir is important for its account of the wartime attitudes and divisions in the community and especially so because of its resonance with Stephan's account of Hawaii. Finally, although little has been made of this here, it is certainly germane to recall that there was a war on and that Canada and its Allies were losing it at the beginning of 1942. As the civil libertarian and historian Arthur Lower wrote in October 1941, "The temper of the Canadian people seems to be becoming more and more arbitrary and we are fast losing whatever tolerance and magnanimity we once possessed."[72] That explains much that happened.

None of this alters the conclusion that the Japanese Canadians were victims of the racism of the society in which they lived and an uncaring government that failed to defend the ideals for which its leaders claimed to have taken Canada and Canadians to war. Even so, this paper does maintain that there were military and intelligence concerns that, in the face of the sudden attack at Pearl Harbor, could have provided Ottawa with a justification for the evacuation of the Japanese Canadians from the coast. The government in December 1941 was unaware of much of the data that has since emerged, and even if it had had it all, it simply lacked the assessment capability to put it together. If it had had the information and the intelligence capacity to appraise it properly, the arguments for evacuation would certainly have appeared far stronger than they already did.

However arguable this case, there is, of course, no necessary connection between the later confiscation of property and the still later effort to deport the Japanese Canadians and the reasons for the evacuation that seemed compelling to some in January and February 1942. The anger that persists at the evacuation might be misplaced; that at the confiscation of property and the attempt at deportation still seems wholly justifiable. In any case, this paper should demonstrate that there remains ample room for further work, broader interpretations and, perhaps, a changed emphasis in this area of research.

Notes

1. National Archives of Canada (NA), Department of National Defence Records, mf reel 5257, f. 8704, "Instructions for the Guidance of General Officers Commanding-in-Chief Atlantic and Pacific Commands," 26 February 1941

2. NA, Department of External Affairs Records, vol. 2007, f. 1939-212, pt. 2, "Report on the State of Intelligence on the Pacific Coast with Particular Reference to the

Problem of the Japanese Minority," 27 July 1941; Department of National Defence Records, vol. 11913, "Japanese" file, Cmdr Hart to R.B.C. Mundy, 21 August 1940

3. PAC, RCMP Records, declassified report, "Japanese Activities in British Columbia" and attached correspondence. See also External Affairs Records, vol. 2007, f. 1939-212, pt. 2, "Report on the State...."

4. External Affairs Records, vol. 2007, f. 1939-212, pt. 1, Keenleyside to H.F. Angus, 28 June 1940. After the order to remove the Japanese from the coast, Keenleyside noted that American "control of enemy aliens seems to be rather more severe than ours while their action with regard to their own citizens is somewhat less severe than ours." *Ibid.*, Acc. 83-84/259, box 171, f. 2915-40, pt. 1, Keenleyside to Wrong, 14 March 1942

5. See, e.g., Robert H. Keyserlingk, " 'Agents Within the Gates': The Search for Nazi Subversives in Canada During World War II," *Canadian Historical Review,* LXVI (June 1985), 216-17; J.L. Granatstein, *A Man of Influence* (Ottawa, 1981), pp. 81ff; Reg Whitaker, "Official Repression of Communism During World War II," *Labour/Le Travail,* XVII (Spring 1986), 137 and *passim.*

6. NA, W.L.M. King Papers, "Note on a War-Time Intelligence Service," 27 November 1939, f. C257903ff. We are indebted to Professor W.R. Young for this reference.

7. Department of National Defence Records, Declassified Examination Unit Files, memorandum for chairman, Supervisory Committee, 15 August 1941, Lt C.H. Little memorandum, 18 April 1942, Draft History, chapter VI, "Japanese Diplomatic Section," 1

8. The spy scares in British Columbia sound much the same as those in Britain before the Great War. See Christopher Andrew, *Secret Service* (London, 1985), 34ff.

9. Department of National Defence Records, vol. 11917, f. 5-1-128, 1938-9, RCMP report, 3 June 1938; *ibid.,* vol. 11913, "Japanese" file, "Vancouver" [an agent] to Cmdr Hart, 30 June and 13 July 1940; External Affairs Records, vol. 2007, f. 1939-212, pt. 2, RCMP report, 29 July 1941; Ann Sunahara, *The Politics of Racism* (Toronto, 1981), 23

10. See Roy Miki, ed., *This is My Own: Letters to Wes & Other Writings on Japanese Canadians, 1941-48 by Muriel Kitagawa* (Vancouver, 1985), 98-9.

11. RCMP Records, declassified material, Commissioner S.T. Wood to Stephenson, 5 August 1942

12. Department of National Defence Records, vol. 3864, f. N.S.S. 1023-18-2, vol. 1, memorandum, F/L Wynd to senior air staff officer, 24 June 1940

13. External Affairs Records, vol. 2007, RCMP report, 29 July 1941. Under a Japanese law of 1899, Japanese men liable for military service did not lose Japanese nationality upon naturalization abroad unless they had performed their military service. After 1934, Canada would not accept Japanese for naturalization without certification that they had completed military service. See *ibid.,* Acc. 83-84/259, box 171, f. 2915-40, pt. 3, memorandum, "Postwar Treatment of Japanese in Canada," n.d.; John J. Stephan, *Hawaii Under the Rising Sun* (Honolulu, 1984), 24; and Ken Adachi, *The Enemy That Never Was* (Toronto, 1976). Adachi, 175, says that in 1934 86 percent of *Nisei* were dual citizens. The population numbers used here are those in the

Report and Recommendations of the Special Committee on Orientals in British Columbia, December 1940 (copy in NA, Privy Council Office Records, vol. 1, f. C-10-3), not those of the 1941 Census which were, of course, not available at the time.

14. External Affairs Records, vol. 2007, f. 1939-212, pt. 2, "Report on the State...." See also the pamphlet by the Vancouver unit of the Fellowship for a Christian Social Order, "Canada's Japanese" (Vancouver [1942?]), 7-8, with its explanation of the role of the Consulate.

15. External Affairs Records, f. 28-C(s), Massey to prime minister, 28 February 1941. This telegram was discussed by the Cabinet War Committee, the key comment being that by Angus L. Macdonald, the minister of national defence (naval services), that there was "little danger of serious attack by Japan" on the Pacific Coast. Privy Council Office Records, Cabinet War Committee Minutes, 5 March 1941. This type of attitude presumably was responsible for the fact that, as late as July 1941, as we have seen above, the RCMP still had only three people responsible for Japanese- Canadian questions. For a plausible hypothesis on how the information might have reached Massey—from US under secretary of state, S. Welles, to the British ambassador, Halifax, to London and thence to Massey—see Ruth Harris, "The 'Magic' Leak of 1941 and Japanese-American Relations," *Pacific Historical Review*, L (1981), 83.

16. Andrew, 261, 353; Ronald Lewin, *The American Magic* (New York, 1982), 44ff

17. *Ibid.*, 45-6

18. United States National Archives (USNA), General Records of the Department of the Navy, RG 80, "Magic" Documents, box 56, Tokyo to Washington, 30 January 1941 (2 parts); *ibid.*, Tokyo to Washington, 15 February 1941; *ibid.*, Los Angeles to Tokyo, 9 May 1941; *ibid.*, Tokyo to Vancouver, March 1941. USNA, Records of the National Security Agency, RG 457, "Magic" Documents, SRH 018, SRDJ nos. 1233-4, 1246-9, 1370, 1525, Vancouver to Tokyo, 7, 14 July, 11, 19 August 1939. Some of this information is contained in *The "Magic" Background to Pearl Harbor* (Washington, 1977), I, no. 131, and especially no. 135, which is the Tokyo to Vancouver, 14 February 1941, telegram referred to. See also *New York Times,* 22 May 1983, and Gregory A. Johnson's doctoral research paper, "Mackenzie King and the Cancer in the Pacific" (York University, 1984).

19. Indeed, as late as 21 October 1941, and despite the Massey telegram referred to above, Hugh Keenleyside, the assistant under secretary of state for external affairs, told the under secretary that "While it might be possible to find Japanese nationals in British Columbia against whom some meagre suspicion exists, there is certainly no Japanese national at large in that Province or elsewhere in Canada against whom any really convincing case can be made out." That comment likely reflected both RCMP advice, which is suspect, and Keenleyside's own extensive knowledge. Whether his certainty was justified—in the light of the Consulate's activities—is another question. D.R. Murray, ed., *Documents on Canadian External Relations,* vol. VIII: *1939-41,* pt. 2 (Ottawa, 1976), 1169

20. External Affairs Records, vol. 2007, f. 1939-212, pt. 2, "Report on the State...." Cf. H.F. Angus' critique of this report in Department of National Defence Records, f. 212-39c, 15 August 1941, and his memorandum of an interview with the officer, F/O Neild,

15 August 1941. We are indebted to Professor Patricia Roy for the Angus critique. It is worth noting that even missionaries shared alarmist views. A United Church China missionary, in Vancouver in January 1941, wrote that "I have had too much experience with the Japanese to trust them ... there is a war in progress and we in Vancouver are in the front line. And the front line is no place for thousands of enemy citizens." United Church Archives, Board of Foreign Missions, Honan, box 11, f. 174, Stewart to Reverend Armstrong, 20 January 1942

21. Adachi, 184-5. Membership figures for the Canadian Japanese Association are in University of British Columbia Archives, Japanese Canadian Collection, Miyazaki Collection, f. 6-4. A copy of the pamphlet is in *ibid.*, P.H. Meadows, Japanese Farmers Association Papers.

22. Granatstein, 98ff; King Papers, f. C144716ff, contains petitions and other material on Canadian policy to Japan after 1937. See also Murray, 1203ff, for extensive documentation on metals export policy.

23. Ed Ouchi, ed., *'Til We See the Light of Hope* (Vernon, BC, 1982[?]), 70. *The New Canadian* is available in the UBC Archives. For support for the war, see the 20 October 1939 issue; on the consul, see, e.g., 8 September 1939. The rotogravure section began in late 1939 and ran well into 1940. On the economic boycott launched by Chinese groups, see UBC Archives, *Chinese Times* translations for 1937.

24. NA, J.W. Dafoe Papers, Angus to Dafoe, 15 October 1940. Mackenzie King told the Japanese minister to Canada in January 1941 that Japanese Canadians would not be called up for NRMA service: "he must remember that Japan and China were at war and we might be encouraging a little civil war if we supply both Chinese and Japanese with rifles etc., in BC at this time. He laughed very heartily at that." King Papers, Diary, 8 January 1941

25. University of British Columbia, Special Collections, H.F. Angus Papers, vol. 1, folder 2, draft memoir, 320-1; H.L. Keenleyside, *Memoirs of Hugh L. Keenleyside,* vol. II: *On The Bridge of Time* (Toronto, 1982), 171

26. University of British Columbia Archives, Special Collections, MacInnis Papers, Box 54A, f. 8, MacInnis to the Canadian Japanese Association, 11 December 1937; *ibid.*, f. 12, MacInnis to T. Umezuki, 18 April 1939. The CCF did not live up to its ideals once the Pacific War started and the BC party supported removal of Japanese Canadians. See Werner Cohn, "The Persecution of Japanese Canadians and the Political Left in British Columbia, December 1941—March 1942," *BC Studies,* LXVIII (Winter 1985-6), 3ff.

27. H.F. Angus, "The Effect of the War on Oriental Minorities in Canada," *Canadian Journal of Economics and Political Science,* VII (November 1941), 508

28. Harvard University, J. Pierrepont Moffat Papers, "Memorandum of Conversations with Mr. Norman Robertson ...," 8 December 1941

29. John W. Dower, *War Without Mercy: Race and Power in the Pacific War* (New York, 1986), 36. See also Christopher Thorne, *Racial Aspects of the Far Eastern War of 1941-1945* (London, 1982) and chapter II of his *The Issue of War* (London, 1985).

30. Canada, House of Commons *Debates,* 4 August 1944, 5948; Adachi, 276

31. RCMP Records, "Japanese Activities in British Columbia," Appendix 6, lists the names. Adachi, 199, says 38 were arrested. Sunahara, 28, agrees.

32. Takeo Nakano, *Within the Barbed Wire Fence* (Toronto, 1980), 8; Sunahara, 70; Stephan, 171

33. Nakano, 44-45. Sunahara, 69, says that many *Nisei gambariya* had been educated in Japan.

34. Stephan, 177

35. To what extent the post-7 December military response was a reflection of pre-war contempt for Japanese military capabilities remains unknown. Dower, 98ff, discusses the responses of the American and British military and civilians both before and after the outbreak of war.

36. Maurice Pope, *Soldiers and Politicians* (Toronto, 1962), 176-8. Escott Reid, who attended the Conference for the Department of External Affairs, later wrote that delegates from BC "spoke of the Japanese Canadians in a way that Nazis would have spoken about Jewish Germans. I felt in that room the physical presence of evil." "The Conscience of a Diplomat: A Personal Testament," *Queen's Quarterly,* LXXIV (Winter 1967), 6-8

37. External Affairs Records, Acc. 83-84/259, box 115, f. 1698-A-40, "Report of Special Committee ...," July 1941. Ottawa had not always been so calm. The Joint Staff Committee at Defence Headquarters on 5 September 1936 had foreseen circumstances in which "the Western Coast of Canada will be within the area of hostilities and is likely to be attacked not only by Japanese naval and air forces, but, in the case of important shore objectives, by Japanese landing parties operating in some strength." An abridged version of the document is in James Eayrs, *In Defence of Canada,* vol. II: *Appeasement and Rearmament* (Toronto, 1965), 213ff. Two years later Defence Headquarters had concluded that "there was a problem of possible sabotage in wartime and recommended that Japanese Canadians not be allowed to purchase property adjacent to areas of military importance." Cited in John Saywell, "Canadian Political Dynamics and Canada-Japan Relations: Retrospect and Prospect," 26, a paper published in Japanese only ("Nikkakankei No Kaiko To Tembo," *Kokusai Seiji* (May 1985), 121-36)

38. W.A.B. Douglas, *The Creation of a National Air Force,* vol. II: *The Official History of the Royal Canadian Air Force* (Toronto, 1986), 405. The British and American planners meeting at the Arcadia conference later in December agreed. *Ibid.,* 410. On 29 December 1941, the chief of the General Staff told the Cabinet War Committee that he had just returned from the Pacific Coast where he found the military and police more concerned with the possibility of attacks on Japanese Canadians than with subversion. Cabinet War Committee Minutes, 29 December 1941. The enormous difficulties that the military would have faced in dealing with racist attacks on Japanese Canadians should not be underestimated: the limited number of trained troops in the area and the very real problem of using white troops against white British Columbians in defence of Japanese Canadians would have frightened any realistic commander.

39. Department of National Defence Records, vol. 2730, f. HQS-5199X, "Memorandum of the Joint Service Committee, Pacific Coast, on the matter of the Defences of the Pacific Coast of Canada," 12 July 1940

40. *Ibid.,* vol. 3864, f. N.S.S. 1023-18-2, vol. 1, N.A. Robertson to LCol K.S. Maclachlan, 14 August 1941; *ibid.,* vol. 2730, f. HQS-5199X, "Memorandum of the Joint Service Committee, Pacific Coast, on the Subject of Dealing With Persons of Japanese Origin in the Event of an Emergency," 20 September 1941. See Peter Ward, *White Canada Forever* (Montreal, 1978), 145, which notes that as early as June 1938, the military were thinking of widespread wartime internment of Japanese Canadians. The numbers near RCAF stations are from NA, Ian Mackenzie Papers, vol. 32, f. X-81, Commander Parsons to Attorney General Maitland, 17 February 1942.

41. Department of National Defence Records, vol. 3864, f. N.S.S. 1023-18-2, vol. 1, "Extract from Report on Japanese Activities on the West Coast of Canada," 10 March 1937. See also Privy Council Office Records, vol. 3, f. D-19-1 Pacific Area, for AVM Croil's "Appreciation of the Situation Likely to Arise on the West Coast ...," 11 September 1941.

42. External Affairs Records, Acc. 83-84/259, box 115, f. 1698-A-40, memorandum for Robertson, 21 October 1941. London soon urged that as many Japanese fishing vessels as possible be seized in the event of war. External Affairs Records, f. 28-C(s), secretary of state for dominion affairs to prime minister, 23 October 1941

43. National Defence Records, vol. 2688, f. HQS-5199-1, vol. 1, "Memorandum of the Joint Service Committee, Pacific Coast, on the Subject of Dealing with Persons of Japanese Origin in the Event of an Emergency," 20 September 1941

44. USNA, Department of State Records, RG 59, PJBD Records, box 14, meeting 12

45. *Ibid.,* 842.20 Defense/140 1/2, Hickerson to Hackworth, 2 December 1941. We are indebted to Professor Robert Bothwell for this reference.

46. RCMP Records, vol. 3564, f. C11-19-2-24, General Alexander to CGS, 30 December 1941; *ibid.,* Keenleyside to Pope, 3 January 1942

47. Mackenzie Papers, vol. 32, f. X-81, "Extracts from Secret Letters," 30, 27 December 1941. See also C.P. Stacey, *Six Years of War* (Ottawa, 1955), 169, and W.A.B. Douglas, "The RCAF and the Defence of the Pacific Coast, 1939-1945," an unpublished paper presented to the Western Studies Conference, Banff, Alberta, January 1981, 8.

48. Department of National Defence, Directorate of History, f. 193.009 (D3), Pacific Command, Joint Service Committee, minutes, 9 January 1942

49. Department of National Defence Records, Acc. 83-84/216, f. S-801-100-P5-1, minutes of Joint Service Committee, Pacific Coast, 13 February 1942

50. *Ibid.,* vol. 11767, f. PC019-2-7, P.A. Hoare to commanding officer, 26 February 1942. The Joint Service Committee recommended on 20 February that all aliens and all Japanese regardless of age and sex should be removed from certain areas on the coast, particularly those near defence installations and in isolated areas. Cited in Patricia Roy, "Why Did Canada Evacuate the Japanese?" unpublished paper, 6-7

51. USNA, Records of US Army Commands, RG 338, box 4, f. 291.2, contains ample evidence of US concern from April 1942; RCMP Records, declassified material, "Japanese Activities in British Columbia." See also Department of National Defence Records, mf. reel 5258, f. 8704-11, for indications of National Defence's concern about sabotage in August 1942 and especially the vice chief of the General Staff's fear that the RCMP lacked "a realistic appreciation of the present danger of sabotage." *Ibid.,* General Murchie to Ralston, 19 August 1942

52. Mackenzie papers, vol. 32, f. X-81, BC Police Commissioner T.W.S. Parsons to Attorney General Maitland, 17 February 1941: "With these people neither Canadian birth nor naturalization guarantees good faith. Something to remember in the case of invasion or planned sabotage."

53. On Pearl Harbor, see Roger Daniels, *Concentration Camps USA: Japanese Americans in World War II* (New York, 1972), 36-8 and Gordon W. Prange, *Pearl Harbor: The Verdict of History* (New York, 1986), 348ff; on Hong Kong, see Stacey, 467, Oliver Lindsay, *The Lasting Honour* (London, 1978), 28, Carl Vincent, *No Reason Why* (Stittsville, 1981), 137, 139 and 146, and Ted Ferguson, *Desperate Siege: The Battle of Hong Kong* (Toronto, 1980), 57, 127-8, 137-9; on Malaya, see Ian Morrison, *Malayan Postscript* (London, 1942), 32-3, and the book by the British official historian of the war in Asia, General S. Woodburn Kirby, *Singapore: The Chain of Disaster* (New York, 1971), 30, 37, 152, 251, as well as the British Security Coordination report cited above from declassified RCMP records.

54. *Vancouver Sun,* 2 January 1942

55. External Affairs Records, Acc. 83-84/259, box 160, f. 2670-D-40, high commissioner in Great Britain to secretary of state for external affairs, 12 February 1942; Queen's University Archives, T.A. Crerar Papers, Crerar to J.W. Dafoe, 20 February 1942; Montreal *Gazette,* 11 March 1942. See also *Times* (London), 13 March 1942.

56. Privy Council Office Records, vol. 3, f. D-19-1, Pacific Area, memorandum, AVM Croil to minister for air, 11 September 1941

57. Department of State Records, 842.20 Defense/100, "Observations on the General Defense Status of the Province of British Columbia," 1 August 1941

58. See Stacey, 165ff, and Department of National Defence Records, vol. 2730, f. HQS-5199X, "Memorandum of the Joint Service Committee, Pacific Coast, on the Matter of the Defences of the Pacific Coast of Canada," 12 July 1940; Privy Council Office Records, vol. 3, f. D-19-1, Pacific Area, appreciations of 18 November 1941 and 10 December 1941.

59. See, e.g., Dafoe Papers, Bruce Hutchison to Dafoe, January 1942; Mackenzie Papers, vol. 30, chief of air staff to minister for air, 16 March 1942 and various memoranda.

60. Dower, 112, notes that, as the Japanese victories continued through early 1942, "Suddenly, instead of being treacherous and cunning, the Japanese had become monstrous and inhuman ... invested in the eyes of both civilians and soldiers with superhuman qualities."

61. The best accounts of Pacific war strategy are H.P. Willmott, *Empires in the Balance* (Annapolis, 1982) and *The Barrier and the Javelin* (Annapolis, 1983). On the Aleutian and Midway plans, see Willmott, *Barrier,* chapter 3; Stephan, chapters 6-7. Note,

however, Willmott's cool assessment of the difficulties Japan would face in trying to take Hawaii. *Empires,* 437. The importance of the Aleutian thrust was seen by the Americans' Special Branch, Military Intelligence Service, based on an analysis of "Magic" traffic. See USNA, RG 457, box 2, SRS-668, supplement to Magic summary, 30 July 1942, and on the Special Branch, Lewin, 141ff. One interesting assessment of the Japanese attack in the Aleutians was offered to Japanese Ambassador Oshima in Berlin by General von Boetticher, a former military attach_ in Washington: "the Aleutian attack has closed the only practicable route for an attack on Japan and is a serious threat to Canada and the West Coast." *Ibid.,* box 1, SRS-640, Magic summary, 26 June 1942

62. NA, J.L. Ralston Papers, vol. 72, Secret Session file, chiefs of staff appreciation, 19 February 1942

63. Stacey, 171. See also Cabinet War Committee Minutes, 18 February 1942, and National Defence Records, vol. 2688, f. HQS-5159-1, vol. 2, "Report of Meeting Held at Headquarters, 13th Naval District Seattle, ... 6 March 1942," where Canadian and American commanders agreed with the Canadian estimates of scales of attack and suggested that "nuisance raids" were most likely. Additional information on defence preparations is in John F. Hilliker, ed., *Documents on Canadian External Relations,* vol. IX: *1942-1943* (Ottawa, 1980), 1162ff. For a good example of hindsight 20/20 vision on the impossibilities of a Japanese attack on the coast, see Adachi, 207-8.

64. Privy Council Office Records, vol. 14, f. W-29-1, "First Meeting of the Pacific Council in Washington," n.d. [1 April 1942] and attached documents

65. *Ibid.,* "Memorandum re Prime Minister's Visit to Washington, April 14th to 17th, 1942"

66. Department of National Defence Records, vol. 11764, f. PC05-11-5, naval message to NOI/C, Vancouver and Prince Rupert, 29 April 1942

67. *Ibid.,* vol. 11764, f. PC010-9-18, memorandum, "Defence of the West Coast," 7 July 1942

68. See *Vancouver Sun,* 10 August 1942; *Vancouver Province,* 13 August 1942; documents on External Affairs Records, Acc. 83-84/259, box 216, f. 3942-40; Douglas, *Creation,* 354. We are indebted to Professor John Saywell for his recollections of this period on Vancouver Island and to his father's book, John F.T. Saywell, *Kaatza: The Chronicles of Cowichan Lake* (Sidney, BC, 1967), 197-8, which briefly details the role of the Pacific Coast Militia Rangers, a force largely of skilled woodsmen and hunters.

69. King Papers, f. C249469, memorandum for file, 25 September 1942. See also Cabinet War Committee Minutes, 25 September 1942, where the chief of the General Staff said he would be "surprised" if the Japanese attacked the coast.

70. USNA, RG 218, Records of the US Joint Chiefs of Staff, mf. reel 10, f. 39322ff, Combined Chiefs of Staff, "Probable Maximum Scale of Attack on West Coast of North America," CCS 127, 29 November 1942. See also *ibid.,* f. A4024ff, CCS 127/1, "Probable Scale of Attack on the West Coast of North America," 16 January 1943. Not until August 1943 (in CCS 127/3) did the Combined Chiefs declare the possibility

of any serious attack on the coast "very unlikely." Douglas, *Creation,* 368-9. C.P. Stacey's comment in *Arms, Men and Governments* (Ottawa, 1970), 46, that "No informed and competent officer ever suggested that the Japanese were in a position to undertake anything more than nuisance raids" seems exaggerated in the light of the CCS papers. It is worth recalling that the Canadian raid on Dieppe involved about 5,000 men and was intended, among other purposes, to lead the Nazis to strengthen the French Coast at the expense of the Eastern front. The Japanese planners could (and should?) have been thinking similarly. Certainly a raid in force would have resulted in a massive public demand for the stationing of more troops on the coast; indeed, the simple prospect of such a raid did lead to the strengthening of defences.

71. Department of National Defence Records, vol. 11764, f. PC05-11-7, naval messages, 30-31 March 1943. This may have been based on false information. A secret US Federal Communications Commission project had reported on landing barges in the area; Washington discounted these reports but turned the information over to Canada, which sent them to the West Coast and then back into the American intelligence net where "they were believed to be authentic. Hence military action was ordered." See USNA, RG 457, SRMN-007, memorandum, 19 April 1943.

72. Lower to Frank Underhill, 15 October 1941, quoted in Doug Owram, *The Government Generation* (Toronto, 1986), 263

CHAPTER
12 THE NEW MIDDLE CLASS AND THE QUIET REVOLUTION IN QUEBEC

In the last half century, Québécois intellectuals, and especially Québécois historians, have been fascinated with the concept of the bourgeoisie, the middle class. As examined in volume one of this series, much of the historiographical debate on the Conquest has centred on whether, over the course of its history, New France developed a "normal" colonial bourgeoisie, and, if so, the impact on it of the British take-over. With respect to the first half of the nineteenth century, the nature of the "new", professional middle class which then appeared has also become a matter of contention. Was it genuinely reformist, or politically progressive and socially conservative, or some variation thereof? What direction did it take in the wake of the failed rebellions of 1837-1838?

Part of the fascination with the bourgeoisie was the fact that, in the Western world since the late eighteenth century, the middle class has been perceived as the carrier of nationalist ideologies. The type of nationalism dominant at any given time, it is argued, has depended largely upon the nature of the particular bourgeoisie in place. The defensive *la survivance* brand of nationalism which characterized late nineteenth- and early twentieth-century French Canada, for example, has been attributed to the conservative, largely clerical-professional elite which set the values of the society for nearly a century. Rejecting modernization and the materialistic culture that went along with it, this elite embraced a backward-looking agrarian, Catholic and anti-statist posture, much, according to its detractors, to the detriment of Québécois society as a whole.

With regard to the post-World War II era in Quebec history, the matter of the bourgeoisie has once again become the subject of debate. At issue this time are the origins and implications of what has popularly become known as the "Quiet Revolution" in the 1960s. For many analysts this period witnessed a socio-economic and demographic revolution in the province which led to the creation of yet another "new" middle class. Materialist and secular in education and outlook, this new bourgeoisie was strongly attached to the burgeoning Québécois state, seeing it as the only vehicle possible for the *rattrapage* that must occur to ensure Québécois development. Presenting the case in support of this interpretation of the "Quiet Revolution" is Marc Renaud, in an article entitled "Quebec's New Middle Class in Search of Social Hegemony: Causes and Political Consequences" which first appeared in 1978. Countering Renaud is William Coleman, whose full interpretation is to be found in his 1984 book, *The Independence Movement in Quebec*. Excerpted here is part of his introduction in which he challenges the "new middle class" thesis of Renaud as well as variations of it put forward by other analysts.

Suggestions for Further Reading

Behiels, Michael, *Prelude to Quebec's Quiet Revolution*. Montreal: McGill-Queen's University Press, 1985.

Blais, Andre, and Kenneth McRoberts, "Public Expenditure in Ontario and Quebec, 1950-1980: Explaining the Differences," *Journal of Canadian Studies*, XVIII, no. 1 (Spring 1983), 28-53.

Borins, Sanford F., "Capital Accumulation and the Rise of the New Middle Class," *The Review of Radical Political Economics*, XII, no. 1 (Spring 1980), 17-34.

Coleman, William D., *The Independence Movement in Quebec, 1945-1980*. Toronto: University of Toronto Press, 1984.

Fortin, Gerald, "Le nationalisme canadien-français et les classes sociales," *Revue d'histoire de l'Amérique française*, XXII, no. 4 (mars 1969), 525-534.

Fournier, Pierre, *The Quebec Estabiishment*. Montreal: Black Rose Books, 1976.

Gagnon, Alain G., and Khayam Z. Paltier., "Toward *Maître chez nous*; the Ascendancy of a Balzacian Bourgeoisie in Quebec", *Queen's Quarterly*, XCIII, no. 4 (Winter 1986), 731-749.

Jones, Richard, *Community in Crisis*. Toronto: McClelland and Stewart, 1972.

McRoberts, Kenneth, *Quebec: Social Change and Political Crisis* (3rd ed.). Toronto: McClelland and Stewart, 1988.

_____, "The Sources of Neo-Nationalism in Quebec," *Ethnic and Racial Studies*, VII, no. 1 (January 1984), 55-85.

Niosi, Jorge, *La bourgeoisie canadienne: la formation et le développement d'une classe dominante*. Montreal: Boreal Express, 1980.

Pinard, Maurice, and Richard Hamilton, "The Class Bases of the Independence Movement: Conjectures and Evidence," *Ethnic and Racial Studies*, VII, no. 1 (January 1984), 20-54.

Trofimenkoff, Susan, *The Dream of Nation: a Social and Intellectual History of Quebec*. Toronto: Gage, 1983.

QUEBEC'S MIDDLE CLASS IN SEARCH OF SOCIAL HEGEMONY: CAUSES AND POLITICAL CONSEQUENCES

Marc Renaud

Introduction

In the last three decades, Quebec has experienced social change to an extent and with a depth perhaps unparalleled in western countries. As a Canadian ambassador to Paris suggested, the recent transformation of Quebec society seems to be "the most rapid industrial, social, educational and religious revolution in the Western world."[1]

An overview of the most often cited indicators will permit an appreciation of the thoroughness of this change.[2] While two-thirds of the Quebec population lived in cities in 1950, more than 80 percent did in 1971, with the largest increases in the Montreal region, which half the population now inhabits. The Catholic Church was in 1960 the key institution of social control well as the moral authority and often, indirectly, the political authority. It was also the power holder, if not always the owner, in health, education, and social-welfare organizations. Ten years afterwards, it had been almost totally relegated to its spiritual role, with a sharp decline in the number of people engaging in religious orders, a drastic drop in the level of religious practice, and the state takeover of the health, education, and social-welfare fields. While there were about 2,000 new sacerdotal vocations per year in the late 1940s, only about 100 were recruited in 1970.[3] While roughly 80 percent of the population practised its religion in 1960, in urban areas only 15 percent to 35 percent still do so now. This was paralleled by a substantial and extremely brusque decline in the birth rate, moving from 30 births per 1,000 population to 28 in 1959, to 14 in 1974. During the same period (1950-1974), the divorce rate increased eighteenfold and the suicide rate increased to 4.4 times the 1950 rate!

From *The International Review of Community Development,* New Series, 39/40 (1978), 1-36. Reprinted by permission of *The International Review of Community Development.*

The organization of the polity also profoundly changed. Provincial government expenditures multiplied by 32 during this period, with the most visible and important increments due to massive state interventions during the Quiet Revolution (1960-65).[4] The traditionally dominant political party, the Union Nationale—which held power from 1936 to 1939 and from 1944 to 1960—gradually lost its importance in the popular vote, to be replaced by the Parti Québécois, which with an entirely different political base took power in November 1976.[5] In the 1960s, public administration was totally reshaped: from parochial and paternalist in style and highly decentralized in its structures, it became centralized, bureaucratic, and typically "modern." A series of events accounts for this change: the growth of the human-service sectors (education, health, and welfare), the government takeover of these sectors, the reorganization of all ministries, the greater involvement of the state in the economy (for example, creation of state enterprises, government involvement in industrial sectors, and the creation of planning agencies), and the creation of a multitude of other government boards and agencies. In 1960 the Quebec provincial public sector employed 36,000 people, while in 1971 almost 350,000 people were employed in its administration, in public enterprises and in health and educational services—that is, an increase from 2 percent to 15 percent of the labour force. And this is a gross underestimate of the number of people paid by provincial tax money and by state enterprises. The expenditures of the federal, provincial, and municipal public sectors in Quebec have grown, according to recent estimates, from 33.4 percent of the Quebec GNP at market prices in 1961 to 45.8 percent in 1970, with the Quebec public sector accounting for 31.8 percent of the GNP in 1970 as compared to 17.9 percent in 1961.[6] The most noticed result of this febrile growth has been a democratization of the access to the previously Church-controlled and highly elitist educational system and a substantial improvement in the access of poorer strata to health services,[7] along with an extremely intense, although not necessarily successful, reshuffling of jobs, personnel, and organizations.

Position of the Question

Except for the brusque character of these changes and the dramatic downfall of the Catholic Church, Ontario, the neighbouring and comparable province, has experienced similar transformations. In particular, contrary to what is often believed, the expansion of the provincial and municipal public sectors for the economy has followed quite similar paths in all provinces and has meant a similar quantitative development of the state. Further, this expansion was in all provinces associated with a change in the ideologically dominant institutions, from religious and rural ones to secular and urban-based political and social ones.

In general, however, in all provinces except Quebec, this expansion did not mean much more than a change in the organization of the economy linked to the worldwide transformation of capitalism into its "post-industrial" or "advanced" stages. The state directly employed many more people, social security policies were much more extensive and progressive, Keynesian economic policies became widespread, the state organizational apparatus was modernized, and the coercive legal and fiscal powers of the governments were increased. But, all things considered, this expansion did not fundamentally alter the basic matrix of interest groups and class relationships within each province. Therefore, it did not look "revolutionary," as it seemingly did in Quebec.

In fact, although the tangible outputs of governmental actions have not markedly differed among provinces, these same actions in Quebec have taken on a colouring that contrasts sharply with what has occurred in the Anglophone provinces. What is particular to Quebec is not the changes per se, but its style of problem solving. In other words, Quebec has evolved what may be termed its own distinctive strategy of reform. The growth of the presence of government in Quebec was accompanied by a rhetoric so strongly social democratic, stated objectives of reform so sweeping, and such legislative authoritarianism, that one is forced to recognize the distinctive character of government intervention in Quebec.

In all countries where the structure of the economy is monopolistic, the technocratic point of view that everything needs administrative rationalization is bound to emerge and to confront individualistic, entrepreneurial, or market-oriented points of view. As many have said, the state is bound to grow and to institutionalize more and more aspects of social relations. In Quebec after 1960, not only did the technocratic point of view emerge, but—contrary to elsewhere—it gradually totally dominated and penetrated the state along with social-democratic ideals. Reform after reform, the heralding of fundamental objectives, the systematic recourse to the powers of coercion, and reorganization of the state permitted this point of view of take over the political management of problems and crises, thus determining the emergence of unique political dynamics and of a distinctive political culture.

This strategy of reform boils down to a typical three-act play for government actions.[8] The characteristic initial reaction of the Quebec government to the various social ills or to heavy public pressure has almost always been to arouse seemingly boundless hopes and expectations. Unlike the other Canadian provinces, Quebec has summoned numerous commissions of inquiry and policy-making bodies to elaborate, often in enough detail to be convincing, policies inspired by the desire to rationalize the allocation of resources and by the great social-democratic ideals of our times—equality of opportunity, heritage preservation, collective ownership of natural resources, democratization and regionalization of decision-making, comprehensive medical care, and so on.

The second step in government action, following the policy recommendations and the resulting expectations and co-optations, consists in implementing with lightning speed extremely ambitious plans of total reorganization, restructuring, and reshuffling. This has been done almost solely through the coercive mechanisms of legislation, without extended public debate, pilot projects, or other unusual procedures for gradual change. Here again we can see at work a style of political problem solving that is radically different from anything to be found elsewhere in Canada, where the accent is put on pilot projects and other ad hoc or "muddling through" procedures.

According to the scenario, the third act opens a few years later, when it turns out that the reforms have fallen short of their objectives, not only because they bore few solutions to the social problems they were supposed to solve, but also because they were far removed from the many social-democratic ideals they promised to fulfill. The often gaping void separating the ideal from the actual objectives and their operationalization would then become the yeast for the increasingly complex crises to come.

Clearly, this is what happened for the reforms in the education, health, and welfare fields. Whatever the political party in power, the same technocratic and highly ambitious, yet only partially successful, crisis-solving style has by and large pervaded government actions in these fields. The story is different for economic reforms. During the Quiet Revolution, exactly the same scenario was followed. Electric-power companies were nationalized. State financial enterprises were created, along with many public enterprises in the productive sectors. And central and regional planning agencies were set up—all of this in a context of profound economic reform. Afterwards, with the Johnson, Bertrand, and Bourassa administrations (1966-76), these organizations, except for a few, received much less support from government officials. A move away from the development of an indigenous state capitalism seems to have occurred: the overall government strategy shifted back to subsidizing foreign-owned enterprises, as incentives for their investments, thus lending credence to the hypothesis that the political base of these administrations was quite different from the one that supported the Liberal Party in the early 1960s and the Parti Québécois in the 1970s.

If this analysis is correct, the important question is the following: how can we explain the distinctive character of Quebec state interventions? How can we understand that, in general, technocratic elites and ideologies have had in Quebec an unparalleled status and legitimacy? How does one explain that, after so many years of passivity and conservatism, the Quebec state suddenly decided with such determination to pursue social-democratic objectives that undoubtedly present a leftist outlook by North American political standards?

There is an emerging consensus among Quebec sociologists to view the Quiet Revolution and later government reforms as the result of two interacting factors. First, there was the deeply felt need in various segments of the population to upgrade Quebec infra- and superstructures to catch up with the rest of North America economically, politically, and culturally. The 1957 economic depression, combined with the political pressures emerging from a structurally rapidly changing population, forced the Quebec government to modernize society to insure economic growth, full employment, and social peace. Second, a newly formed petty bourgeoisie could take advantage of this situation and more or less consciously manoeuvre to replace the Church as the locally dominant hegemonic group.[9] This search for hegemony would be the key feature of class relationships in Quebec in the 1960s and the 1970s. Within this new petty bourgeoisie, two segments are often distinguished: one, the neo-capitalist faction, is linked to private capital and is represented by the Liberal Party in the 1970s; the other, the technocratic faction, is tied to the new managerial roles in a monopolistic economy and can be found in Quebec especially in the top echelons of the public sector. The Parti Québécois is its political representative.

The purpose of this paper is to further specify this hypothesis, especially for understanding the distinctive reform strategy of the Quebec government. For reasons of conceptual clarity,[10] I prefer the term, "new middle class" to "new petty bourgeoisie." Needless to say, my argument here will be a highly tentative one. As Barrington Moore has stated, "All that the social historian can do is point to a contingent connection among changes in the structure of society." And, given the complexity of the issues to be addressed, their contemporary character and the lack of systematically gathered data, we can only hope to develop a plausible interpretation of the exceptional dominance of technocratic ideologies and elite groups, coloured as they are by social democratic ideas, in Quebec's political arena.

Summary of the Argument

The most plausible and all-embracing hypothesis to explain the distinctive problem-solving style of the Quebec state during the 1960s and 1970s is the emergence of a new middle class with a definite stake in the expansion of the state apparatus and the latter's legitimacy in society. The following summarizes this hypothesis.

Contrary to Anglophone provinces, the expansion of the state in Quebec occurred in a political and economic context that radically altered the pattern of class relations. Quebec's political economy can be schematically characterized by the following idiosyncratic elements.

First, there have been profound structural changes in Quebec's economy since the end of the Second World War, with the numbers of white-collar workers and skilled manual labourers growing in leaps and bounds compared to the number of unskilled and agricultural jobs. The result has been an impressive surge in the upward mobility of the French-speaking segment of the Quebec population, and an equally impressive increase in the college and university enrolment figures. This trend gathered momentum and, by the mid-1960s, thousands and thousands of young graduates were out looking for jobs.

Second, the private sector of the Quebec economy is less dynamic than in Ontario or British Columbia in terms of productivity, ability to attract new investment, and job-generating power. There is a general agreement among economists[11] to say that the Quebec economy has suffered a relative decline since the Second World War, compared to other Canadian provinces, especially because of this weak manufacturing sector and its heavy reliance on the primary and tertiary sectors for economic growth.

Third, the doors to upper and middle management in the largely English-Canadian and American private corporate world have remained for the most part shut for those who are of French origin, even when they have the same qualifications as their English-speaking colleagues. Several reasons have been suggested for this: the private economy was not expanding quickly enough, many enterprises were absentee owned and controlled, and the institutionalized networks of the business community systematically favoured the recruitment of people speaking the language of the incoming capital.

Unlike most other Canadians, French-speaking Quebeckers have been determined to work in their own province whatever the job situation may be. The politico-economic conjuncture in the 1960s and 1970s consequently conferred on the growth of the state apparatus in Quebec dynamics that are distinctive in the Canadian context. Given that the state turned out to be one of the only sources of job openings for the growing proportion of university graduates among the French-speaking population, had the civil service and public sector not expanded, the gap between English- and French-speaking Quebeckers would have continued to widen, since the already scarce upper- and middle-echelon jobs of the private economy were closed to the Francophones. The Quebec state was therefore the only institutional base capable of providing prestigious and well-paid jobs for educated French-speaking Quebeckers. In other words, these people had no choice but to orient themselves toward the state sector of the economy—that is, government, government-owned corporations and autonomous state-managed agencies, and industries or organizations directly or indirectly dependent on the state. In the other Canadian provinces, more and more individuals also became university educated, but, contrary to Quebec, the state was not the almost sole purveyor of jobs for them. They could also work in the private sector of the economy and, if they could not find job satisfaction within their native province, they could always go elsewhere in English-speaking North America.

University- or technically-trained Francophones can in fact be said to constitute a class in the sense that their academic capital provides them with commonly shared levels of market capacity and with a set of objective common interests in seeing the state evolve, by various means, interesting (i.e., prestigious, powerful, and well-paid) jobs for them. Although this class is by and large composed of the people classified by census statisticians as "professional and technical labour," it is not merely a statistical aggregate. It is not simply the addition of individuals with certain attributes, such as a certain level of education, certain types of occupations, a given level of income, and so on. It is in fact a social collectivity grounded in the material order in a fairly identifiable fashion: specifically, by the similar symbolic skills brought by its members to the labour marketplace. Such a new middle class exists in all Canadian provinces, but in Quebec it has the supplementary cohesiveness-inducing constraints of a relatively closed and declining private economy. That is, contrary to its English-speaking counterpart, it is bound to view and use the Quebec state as its only leverage for survival.

The Quebec new middle class is not a "ruling class" or a "bourgeoisie" in the Marxist sense. That is, it is not part of this core group of families who own not only the larger part, but also the socially and culturally most determinant part of the world economy, the monopoly sector. It does not own the means of production in the private economy. The ruling class is for the most part foreign in origin, either English Canadian or American, and its enterprises often are absentee-owned and controlled.

The Quebec state with varying intensity throughout its history has had to act in ways that support foreign dominance, either directly (for example, subsidization of multinational enterprises for their investments) or indirectly (socialization of certain costs of production on public works, for example, to compensate for the lack of dynamism of the private economy). State spending has to behave in such a way in order to maintain the growth of the economy and low levels of unemployment.

This reality is undoubtedly harmful for the immediate interest of most of the fractions of the new middle class, but the latter are hard pressed to express their opposition lest they undermine the Quebec state itself. From time to time, when the economic context permits, some of these factions succeed in manoeuvring themselves into the position of being able to allocate resources in the manufacturing or the financing sectors of the economy, by socializing the purchase price or the investment capital necessary for creating this or that enterprise and nationalizing its profits. Such state actions may have the effect both of providing some new-middle-class elites with the power to allocate resources and of stimulating employment and economic growth to the satisfaction of both the general population and of the capitalist bourgeois class. Generally speaking, however, the new middle class most forcibly seeks to acquire real (if limited) hegemony at the local level in those sectors—especially human services—where the state has the freest hand.

Any action that has the effect of extending the quantitative and qualitative influence of the state serves the interests of this class. The new middle class has consequently produced a political culture that favours high-profile wide-ranging reorganizations that draw on, in the highly politicized context of Quebec, broad social-democratic and nationalist aspirations. Even though state intervention sometimes provokes short-term conflicts among petty-bourgeois factions (among "technocrats," "professionals," and "neo-capitalists," for instance), there is a common class interest in the self-preservative and self-promoting virtues of increased state initiative, and they spare no pains to impress on the population the idea that the Quebec state is the only collective lever it has. As an ex-Minister of Industry and Commerce said, given the weakness of the private economy and the general leverage of the Quebec state, Quebec would now be on the verge of creating a "socialism by default." This means the appropriation of key economic enterprises by the state and the enactment of thorough bureaucratic reforms aimed at equalizing the distribution of wealth and income in the society.

Against such a backdrop, when technocratic elite groups such as the dominant members of the Parent (education reform) or Castonguay-Nepveu (health and social-welfare reforms) commissions appear for one reason or another on the scene and formulate policies involving highly visible organizational shakeups, premised on larger social-democratic policies for Quebec society, they are automatically greeted with broad social support and open arms in civil service circles. No matter what short-term tensions these elite groups may cause, general class interest dictates that they be provided sweeping power and the legitimacy they need, inasmuch as they contribute to the quantitative *and* qualitative expansion of the state apparatus. This is why these groups have little trouble in obtaining broad cabinet and National Assembly approval for speedy and far-reaching reform, however authoritarian the legislation and regulations enacted may be.

In the very different context of Ontario, for instance, comparable groups have not been legitimized in this way nor received comparable powers. Of course, a new middle class also exists in Ontario, but the state apparatus is not its only means of survival and thus there are no social forces that push for unconditional support to technocratic elites whose aim is to extend state control. To put it another way, it is inconceivable, in a context like that of Ontario, that an elite group like the Castonguay-Nepveu Commission could succeed in completely controlling an entire sector of government activity and imposing its own blue-print for change and its own way of doing things. Again, this is not to say that such groups do not exist in Ontario—quite the contrary. But, given the politico-economic conjuncture in this province, their social status could not be as high and their ideologies could not penetrate the state as thoroughly as they have in Quebec.

To clarify the maze of numbers and events that will now be presented in support of this argument, figure 1 diagrams the structure of the argument just summarized: each point in figure 1 will be documented in the alphabetical order presented.

FIGURE 1   The Development of the New Middle Class

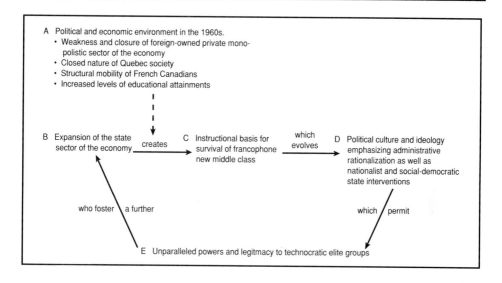

The Evolution of Quebec's Political Economy

The discussion of the evolution of Quebec's economy will use the classification categories developed by James O'Connor in *Fiscal Crisis of the State*.[12] I will distinguish among the *monopolistic* sector, the market or competitive sector, and the state sector. The first sector is highly monopolistic in concentration of ownership and in economic behaviour (like uses of price fixing). It requires large amounts of fixed capital invested per worker and it is involved in wide-scale markets. Important features of this sector are the high wages and salaries paid, the stable levels of employment, and the tendency toward vertical as well as horizontal integration of production and distribution processes. The market or *competitive* sector was once the largest economic sector, but it is now declining in importance. It is characterized by its lower levels of productivity, smaller-scale production, local or regional markets, lower ratios of capital invested per worker, lower unionization rate, lower wages and salaries, and more unstable levels of employment. Agriculture, construction, retail-trade, and personal-service enterprises are typically part of this sector of the economy. O'Connor also divides up the *state* sector into two categories: production of goods and services organized by the state itself (for instance, mail, education, public health, welfare, and other social services) and production organized by industries owned by the state (state industrial enterprises) or under contract with the state (such as military equipment and supplies, highway construction).

1920-1945: Competitive Capitalism and the Arrival of Foreign Industry

It was not until the end of the Second World War that fundamental changes in the Quebec economy began. After the war, a massive migration took place to the major cities and foreign—especially American—monopoly capital moved in at an accelerated speed causing the occupational structure to change considerably. Quebec history from about 1900 to the mid-1940s has been thoroughly described elsewhere[13] and there is no need for us to discuss it in other than outline form.

This period was characterized by the fact that most French Canadians were engaged in petty commodity production, mostly in agriculture but also in small-scale industry. Priests, doctors, and lawyers were the local elites, in control of almost all the political, social, and cultural organizations of the community. During this period, foreign capital and its industries began to install themselves in Quebec, but this did not have any impact on the social organization of Quebec.

In fact, till the late 1940s, foreign and local capital largely remained two separate worlds, as they were fulfilling complementary functions. As Guindon has argued,[14] Anglo-Canadian and American industries moved into a society faced with the economic burden of the demographic surplus[15] of French-Canadian rural society. In relieving this acute population surplus, they could accumulate capital by exploiting Quebec's natural-resource base and its cheap labour without encroaching on the traditional social organization of Quebec society or its traditional elites. Furthermore, the foreign group could itself fill the management and technical levels of industry with little conflict, for French Canadians provided only the semi-skilled and unskilled labour.[16] As for French-Canadian society, the absorption of surplus labour by foreign industry permitted its distinctive political and religious elite, its political and social institutions anchored to the rural parish, and its petty commodity-production economy to survive despite the changes in the surrounding material order.[17]

1945-1960: The Growth of the Monopoly Sector and its Consequences

With more and more Francophones working within foreign industry and with the increasing monopolistic characteristics of this industry, the complementarity of functions and the convergence of interests between Quebec's traditional elites and foreign entrepreneurs gradually disappeared. By the early 1950s, the Quebec economy had changed so much that the traditional social order had stopped being reproduced, despite the length of time it took for this fact to be politically and socially felt.

By the early 1960s, while French Canadians comprised more than 80 percent of Quebec's population and owned 50 percent of the enterprises, they controlled only 15 percent of the value added in Quebec industry while some of the 13 percent of English Canadians and a few Americans controlled 85 percent.[18] In other words, French-Canadian ownership and control was almost entirely limited to the much less profitable competitive sector of the economy, while English-Canadian and other foreign interests owned and controlled the profitable monopolistic sector.

The ex-president of the Economic Council of Canada, André Raynauld, has done research on industrial enterprises in Quebec in 1961. His results confirm that the Quebec economy is characterized by a French-Canadian competitive sector and a foreign monopolistic sector. He writes:

> French-Canadian establishments were at the one extreme in every respect. Foreign establishments were at the other extreme in every respect and Other Canadian establishments were in between. With regard to *size,* Foreign establishments were seven times larger than French Canadian, and four times larger than Other Canadian by *value added.* The *average output* per man was 6500, 8400, and 12000 dollars respectively for French-Canadian, Other Canadian and Foreign establishments. *Wages and salaries* in French-Canadian establishments were 30 percent below those in Foreign, and 12 percent below those in Other Canadian establishments....[19]

French-Canadian-owned enterprises, with few exceptions in 1961, were within the competitive or market sector. French-Canadian ownership was concentrated in agriculture, construction, retail trade, and services. According to the Royal Commission on Bilingualism and Biculturalism:

> Francophones are owners and proprietors in large proportions in agriculture and to a lesser degree in the service fields and retail trade. In wholesale they play a still smaller role, while in finance and manufacturing they account for about one-fourth of the total. Moreover, within manufacturing itself, the pattern of ownership is also uneven. In small-scale manufacturing, such as the production of wood products, Francophones predominate; but in fields requiring large capital investment and highly advanced technology, such as the manufacture of chemicals and petroleum products, they play virtually no role in ownership or control.[20]

Foreign-owned enterprises constituted Quebec's major enterprises, in terms of value added and outputs. These enterprises can be classified in three main categories. First, from this earlier phase of industrialization, largely created by the National Policy of the federal government in the 1870s, Quebec has inherited secondary industries in labour-intensive sectors (textile, wood, shoes, and other finished products). Second, in the mid-1930s, primary industries began to appear exploiting Quebec's natural resources (pulp and paper, primary metallic industries). Finally, later on, some large American high-technology enterprises (automobile, electrical equipment) came in, but at an extremely slow pace compared to Ontario.[21] Almost all these enterprises are owned and controlled by American and English-Canadian interests.[22] The second and third categories are largely part of the American monopolistic sector. The first category shows to a lesser extent similar monopolistic features.

Weakness of this Economy

This general structure of the economy in the early 1960s (much of it is still the same) had key economic and social consequences. The economy had two overwhelming characteristics. In the first place, as just seen, the profitable monopolistic sector was almost entirely owned by foreign interests, while the fairly large and unprofitable competitive sector was French-Canadian owned. Second, since the monopolistic sector, with the complicity of Quebec traditional elites, was built on the requirements of foreign interests and their industries, it appeared almost only where high profits could be made. Foreign enterprises therefore exploited Quebec's natural-resource base and cheap labour. In those industrial sectors where labour was abundant and therefore cheap, labour-intensive light consumer-goods industries developed. The dynamism of these enterprises has now considerably declined. Extremely few durable-goods and producer-goods industries have replaced them, even though such enterprises would have been necessary to generate new investments and create new jobs. The combination of a fairly large competitive sector and a partially weak monopolistic sector in light consumer-goods industries means that a relatively large proportion of workers are employed in slow-growth and low productivity industries.

This situation accounts for the general weakness of Quebec's economy in contrast to that of Ontario. Here are a few indices of this relative decline of Quebec's economy. Fewer people worked in the Quebec manufacturing sector in 1971 than in 1961, while this number has increased on the average all over Canada.[23] In fact, as a task force to the Department of Industry and Commerce recently noted, new jobs in Quebec tend not be created in the nonvalue-producing tertiary sector alone, contrary to Ontario:

> About 230,000 jobs have been created between 1966 and 1971, among which 133,000 are in "personal social service and others" and 22,000 in the public administration. More than 90 percent of the new jobs are due to the growth of the tertiary sector. During the same period, approximately 50,000 jobs have disappeared in equal parts in construction and in the primary sector, in particular forestry and mining. This means a net creation of 180,000 jobs; that is 36,000 on the average each year in comparison with 85,600 for Ontario (428,000 total for this five-year period).[24]

Further, Quebec consistently had 50 percent of the bankruptcies in Canada, while its GNP accounted for only 25 percent of Canada's GNP.[25] Quebec always had a 20 percent to 50 percent higher unemployment rate than the Canadian average, usually twice as high as Ontario. Over the last two decades, the personal income per capita in Quebec has been 12 percent to 15 percent lower than the Canadian mean, and between 23 percent to 30 percent lower in Ontario. The discrepancies between Quebec and English Canada are even clearer if we disaggregate according to ethnicity. André Raynauld has shown that French Canadians were among the most poorly paid workers in Quebec in 1961, ranking twelfth in labour income in a list of 14 ethnic groups. He writes: "The most remarkable fact ... is that French-Canadian labour income was 12 percent below the overall average in every province except Quebec, where it was 40 percent below the overall provincial average. In absolute terms, the gap was about 1000 dollars a year in Canada as a whole, and 2000 dollars in Quebec."[26]

Eliminating the effects of several factors (age, sex composition of labour force, education, occupation, employment status, region, and labour-force participation) on this discrepancy, he found that ethnicity still accounted for more than 50 percent of the income differential. French Canadians, because they are French Canadians and for no other reason, earn much less than their English-Canadian counterparts in Quebec.

The Closure of the Top Corporate World to French Canadians and the Closed Nature of Quebec Society

Not only was this structure of the economy weak for generating investments and for creating employment, but it also did not provide employment for university- or technically trained Francophones. On the one hand, the competitive sector does not possess high-income, high-prestige, and high-power jobs. The competitive sector is largely composed of small enterprises of self-employed individuals and a few workers. On the other hand, the top corporate world was and is closed to Francophones. Entries at the top of the occupational hierarchy were and are blocked to French Canadians, whatever their level of education. This has both historical and sociological grounds.

Both because of the "language" of the incoming capital and in view of their earlier higher levels of education, successive English-Canadian generations have always been better placed in the occupational hierarchy. As a consequence, they are still at an advantage over French Canadians for high-income and high-power jobs in the monopolistic sector. English Canadians have systematically preceded French Canadians in their patterns of social mobility, thus blocking the entry of French Canadians in the top jobs of the private economy. Whatever the levels of education now achieved by French Canadians, the institutionalized networks of the big-business community tend to omit French Canadians. Examples of these networks are the well-known links between Anglophone universities and enterprises in the monopoly sector. The Royal Commission on Bilingualism and Biculturalism has noted:

Because of their higher educational level, their position in the occupational structure, and their original position as leaders of Quebec's industrialization, the Anglophones have always been better prepared than the Francophones to enjoy the benefits of the province's economic development. Once socio-economic patterns have been established, they tend to be self-perpetuating; the momentum favouring the Anglophones was never matched in the Francophone community.[27]

As a consequence, very few French Canadians could be considered part of a corporate elite. Porter[28] estimated this group to be 51 persons in 1951 (or 6.7 percent of the Canadian corporate elite at that time). Milner and Milner[29] and Clement[30] estimate that in 1971, while French Canadians constituted a third of the Canadian population, this group included only 65 persons (or 8.4 percent of the Canadian corporate elite). In Milner and Milner's words:

> We looked at those Quebec firms controlled by French Canadians, borrowing the results of a study[31] which selected from these firms a sample of the two largest banks, the two largest trust companies, the six largest industries, the three largest insurance companies, and the three largest finance companies. There are 216 positions on the boards of directors of these enterprises held by 163 persons. Of these 163 persons, 65 (40%) hold 118 (54%) of the 216 positions. These men hold among themselves 50% of the directorships of the insurance companies, 68% of the trust companies, 43% of the six industries, and 72% of the banks. These 65 persons thus are a good approximation of the French-Canadian economic elite.... Over half of this elite was educated in two schools: Collège Sainte-Marie and Jean de Brébeuf.[32]

It is important to add here that, notwithstanding the enormous fiscal and legal efforts of the Quebec state in the late 1960s to raise the level of education among Francophones and to enforce French as the language of work in Quebec, the private economy remained closed to Francophones. This runs counter to the popular belief that, with the increased levels of educational attainments of the Quebec population and the corollary rejection of the self-defeating rural and Catholic ideology, French Canadians could be in a position to make significant inroads into the private monopolistic economy.

Wallace Clement has presented convincing evidence to counter this belief. Noticing that the number of French Canadians in the economic elite had risen only from 51 to 65 from 1951 to 1971, he writes:

> This means a net increase of only 14 more French Canadians or 1.7 percent more of the elite population over the last 20 years. These have not been uneventful years in French-Anglo relations; quite the contrary, they were supposed to contain the "new awakening" (a loaded phrase which somehow assumes the French have themselves been their own barrier to gaining equality and not their position vis-à-vis the dominant Anglos) and the "quiet revolution" of the 1960s and the not-so-quiet revolution of recent years. In spite of ideological statements to the contrary, the French have not made significant inroads into the economic world.[33]

He then cites the research of Presthus[34] to show that not only have the French not made it to the very top of the corporate world, but they also did not make gains in the middle range and smaller corporations:

> A recent study based on 12,741 names of executives from some 2,400 companies operating in Canada listed in the 1971 *Directory of Directors* found only 9.4 percent to be French Canadians. This is only about one percent more than are to be found in the economic elite and includes many corporations much smaller than the 113 dominant ones which are the basis of this study.[35]

Further evidence of the restricted mobility of Francophones into the private economy is provided by a study of the Institut International D'économie Quantitative. It shows that, in 1971, 28 percent of the top management jobs in the private economy earning above $20,000, 28 percent of the middle management occupations earning between $15,000 and $19,999, and 48 percent of lower-level management positions earning between $5,000 and $14,999 were held by Francophones, while French Canadians constituted 75 percent of the labour force in 1971.[36] In other words, the proportion of Francophones occupying any level of management in the private economy is considerably smaller than the proportion of Francophones in the overall labour force. An analysis of the 1971 census has even shown that, at a same level of managerial occupation, French Canadians earn 11 percent less than their English-Canadian counterparts.[37]

To sum up, university- and technically trained Francophones were in the early 1960s and still by the mid-1970s confronted with the following situation: a fairly large competitive economy with practically no appropriate job for their training and a monopolistic economy with only a few job outlets, either because enterprises are absentee owned and controlled or because some of them are in such obsolete industrial sectors that they do not expand enough to provide new jobs. When a position does open up, because of the historically determined linkages between the Anglophones and the business community, it tends to be given to an Anglophone. Almost the only job outlets therefore seem in the state sector of the economy.

One could object that, given this situation, French Canadians have incentives to go to work elsewhere in Canada or North America, as was the case for many French-Canadian unskilled labourers during the 1920s and the Depression years, but the situation was quite different then. In the 1920s and 1930s, the surplus labour of rural Quebec was such that is could not be entirely absorbed by incoming industry. In the 1960s and 1970s, we are talking about a different kind of people, individuals who have over 15 years of formal education and who correctly believe that they have the skills necessary for the top jobs at least as much as their Anglophone counterparts. In such cases, cultural barriers impose considerable restrictions on geographic mobility much more than they did in the 1920s or 1930s. The French-Canadian situation is different from that experienced by Canadians in the poorer Atlantic provinces. Maritimers who do not find jobs in their native province will tend to look for jobs anywhere on the North American continent. A corresponding Québécois, unless he or she accepts the disturbing emotional consequences of becoming an expatriate, is almost glued to Quebec's territory, whatever the job outlets.

Evidence for this phenomenon is overwhelming. For instance, reporting on a study of Quebec engineers, the Royal Commission on Bilingualism and Biculturalism wrote:

> Although 80 percent of the Francophone engineers in our Montreal sample thought Quebec offered them the best opportunities, only nine percent of the Anglophones agreed with them; almost half the Anglophone engineers named the United States instead. There are indications that the situation is changing, but the evidence is consistent in showing a lower mobility rate and a lesser willingness to move on the part of Francophone engineers and their wives. If they work for a large corporation, the consequence of this difference is the same for the managers—a slower rate of promotion. For those who work in small firms of Francophone-owned institutions, this effect, though not as pronounced, is still at work.[38]

Further, if we look at some aggregated migration statistics,[39] the same phenomenon is visible: Quebec loses proportionally fewer inhabitants than any other province and received the smallest relative proportion of internal migrants. Ontario receives many more internal migrants and few leave the province, because of the economic wealth and immense job opportunities it offers. If these data could be analysed by ethnic origin, it is probable that even fewer Québécois would appear to be leaving the province.

In this sense, Quebec is a closed society for the Francophone segment of its population. However unfulfilling the job opportunities and whatever one's political opinions, Quebec, in a real sense, is a nation, the borders of which are not easily passed.

The Structural Mobility of French Canadians and the Increased Levels of Education

After the war, the politico-economic situation in Quebec changed somewhat. A great number of French Canadians had left the agricultural rural world to become unskilled or semi-skilled labourers in foreign industry. Many of the small commodity producers who in a former era had derived quite a good standard of living from their farms, retail stores, or crafts shops also joined the ranks of the increasingly urban working class. None of them was educated enough to occupy managerial, professional, or technical positions. During this period, English Canadians occupied the entire top managerial, professional, and technical occupations within industry.

From the 1930s to the early 1960s, two parallel phenomena took place. On the one hand, since Francophones increasingly filled the bottom positions of the occupational hierarchy and since more and more Anglophones filled the top positions of this hierarchy, French Canadians as an ethnic group were in fact getting proletarianized, in the sense of increasingly having nothing else to sell but their labour power. On the other hand, with the expansion of the monopoly sector and the corollary changes in the occupational structure (technical, clerical, and skilled tasks becoming quantitatively more important than unskilled and primary labour) came a structural mobility of French Canadians. That is, quite independently of their own volition and uniquely because of changes in the structure of the demand for labour, many French Canadians began to perform better-paid and somewhat more prestigious tasks. With such a structural mobility, French Canadians began to enjoy better standards of living and began to aspire for better jobs for themselves and their children. More and more people enrolled in school and great pressure was put on the state to facilitate the financial and geographical access to education.

The data that follow are unsatisfying because of the varying definitions of occupational categories used in different research studies and because of the lack of built-in comparability between the studies; however, they are the only published data available. However crude, they provide approximate empirical evidence for the phenomena just described.

The widening of the gap in the occupational hierarchy between Anglophones and Francophones in Quebec is well illustrated by an analysis performed by John Porter.[40] He compared the percentage of over- or underrepresentation of French and British males in various occupational categories, according to census data in 1931, 1951, and 1961. I have corrected for some slight computational errors in Porter's results and I have computed the same information for 1971. Because census statisticians have redefined certain occupational categories during this period, the results have only an indicative value.[41]

These data show that from 1931 to 1961 Quebeckers of British origin have increasingly been overrepresented at the professional and technical levels, moving from +5 percent to +7.2 percent. Conversely, the French have become more and more underrepresented in this group, moving from -0.9 percent to -1.5 percent. A similar evolution also seems to have occurred in the category "manager" between 1951 and 1961. For primary and unskilled jobs, although the gap has not been widened as much between 1931 and 1961, French Canadians have been constantly overrepresented, moving from 0.3 percent to 1.1 percent in 1961, to 1.3 percent in 1971. For the other occupational levels, there seems to have been a levelling off of the differences between the two groups, both increasingly tending towards the overall male labour-force distribution.

In other words, between 1931 and 1961, there seems to have been a widening gap between Anglophones and Francophones. This view is also confirmed by Rocher and de Jocas' analysis[42] of intergenerational mobility of sons in 1954. It showed that the relative proportion of English Canadians was increasing in nonmanual tasks and decreasing in manual jobs. In Rocher and de Jocas' sample, the gap in the top two categories (liberal professions and high management; semi-professionals and middle management) was, in 1954, increasing from 9.5 percent for the father to 15.2 percent for the sons, in favour of the Anglophones, while manual workers were increasingly French in origin, the gap moving from 14.3 percent to 29.3 percent.

In the 1971 census, the overall picture changed considerably. For all the occupational categories listed, the distribution of Anglophones and Francophones tended towards the overall labour-force distribution. While the gap for "professionals and technicians" had been widening between 1931 and 1961, it is reduced by more than a half in 1971, the British moving from an overrepresentation of +7.2 percent in 1961 to only +3.2 percent in 1971, the French moving from an underrepresentation of -1.5 percent to -0.8 percent, for a reduction of the difference from 8.7 percent in 1961 to 4.0 percent in 1971. Although this might only be an artifact of the census redefinitions, a similar, yet less drastic, phenomenon seems to have occurred for "managers." The gap between Francophones and Anglophones in primary and unskilled jobs diminished from 7.0 percent to 3.6 percent.

The same phenomenon has been noticed by Jacques Dofny and Muriel Garon-Audy,[43] who studied the intergenerational mobility of sons in 1964, which they compared with the identical study of Rocher and de Jocas for sons in 1954. In 1964, the gap between Anglophones and Francophones was significantly reduced for all categories except "semi-professionals and middle managers," for "skilled and semi-skilled workers," and for "personal services." They concluded:

> In summary, for reduction of the gaps between French Canadians and English Canadians from the generation of fathers to the generation of sons in contrast to what was observed in 1954 (in 1954, in 6/8 cases the gap was increasing between the two ethnic groups; in 1964, on the contrary, the gap is decreased in 5/8 cases) would underline an acceleration of mobility for French Canadians.[44]

Sociologists call this phenomenon "structural" mobility, as opposed to "individual" mobility. Dofny and Garon-Audy have attempted to quantify its importance. French Canadians have recently experienced an enormous social mobility, much more so than the French Canadians studied in 1954 by Rocher and de Jocas or the English Canadians surveyed in 1964: 75.1 percent of the French Canadians studied in 1964 (with 50 percent upwardly mobile, 15 percent downwardly mobile, and 10 percent mobile to approximately equivalent jobs) have been mobile with respect to their fathers' occupational status, as compared to 64.1 percent in 1954 (35 percent upwardly mobile, 20 percent downwardly mobile, and 10 percent mobile to equivalent jobs) and to 66.0 percent of the Anglo-Canadians in 1964. Yet, this recent social mobility of French Canadians is to an important extent solely attributable to changes in the occupational structure—from primary and unskilled labour to skilled and white-collar tasks—that is, the mobility was structural rather than individual. Nearly half (45.0 percent) of the observed mobility among French Canadians in 1964 is structural, compared to a fourth (27.6 percent) of the observed mobility in 1954.

The Porter, Rocher/de Jocas, and Dofny/Garon-Audy data underline a key phenomenon. They seem to show that the gap between Anglophones and Francophones, which had been widening between 1930 and 1960, was transferred during the 1960s to higher levels in the occupational hierarchy because of the structural changes in the economy. The 1971 census data indicate that this gap has perhaps even begun to diminish, with proportionally more French Canadians entering managerial, professional, and technical jobs. In other words, while for a long time it looked as if the whole French-Canadian ethnic group was being increasingly proletarianized, the 1971 census shows, it seems, that an important class cleavage is appearing within the Francophone community in Quebec. Given the closure of the private monopolistic economy to French Canadians, this can only be attributable to the expansion of the Quebec state sector of the economy. The expansion of the state sector opened up new possibilities for mobility and thus probably did reduce the income, prestige, and power gap between Anglophones and Francophones.

But before we examine this specific issue, let us consider an important correlate of the structural changes in the economy: the rise of education among French Canadians. This phenomenon explains why proportionally more Francophones could by the 1960s aspire to professional, managerial, or technical jobs.

The transition of capitalism into its monopolistic advanced stages is associated with increased levels of education in the population. The increasing complexity of industrial tasks, the expanding needs for regulatory jobs, the growth of the human service sector, and so on all demand high levels of formal training. It took Quebec Francophones a decade or two longer than Anglophones to realize this, partly because their low-level jobs did not require many years in school; partly because it was culturally assumed that academic studies were valuable only to those who wished to become priests, doctors, or lawyers; and partly because of the extremely elitist structure of the Church-controlled educational system. In the 1950s, with the increasingly individually felt changes in the economy, things began to change.

Jacques Brazeau[45] has noted that between 1950 and 1960 the percentage of the population between the ages of five and twenty-four who attended school rose from 53 to 62; attendance in grades 9 to 12 more than doubled and, beyond Grade 12, it increased by more than 50 percent. Yet, the educational sector was incapable of coping with demands for massive school enrolment, as a consequence of the high costs and maldistribution of educational facilities. In 1960, Quebec had the tenth rank among Canadian provinces in secondary schooling (actually, one out of two Quebec adults had less than seven years of school), but it had the fourth rank for the proportion of its population holding a university diploma. That this system was ill equipped to fit the needs of children from low-income families is manifested by the fact that the retention rate in Quebec—defined as the enrolment in Grade 11 as a percentage of Grade 2 nine years earlier—was the lowest in Canada (33 percent).[46] The educational reforms of the 1960s resulted from such pressures and the retention rate jumped to 70 percent in 1967, placing Quebec in the fifth-highest rank among the ten Canadian provinces. Furthermore, while the Quebec education sector had been oriented for generations towards training in the liberal professions and in the humanities, proportionally more students now enrol in those fields that were not so long ago reserved for Anglophones (sciences, engineering, and the like), so that the overall school enrolment picture for Francophones increasingly tends to look more like Ontario's.[47]

To sum up, by the early 1960s, quite a few French Canadians had the formal training enabling them to fulfill top managerial, professional, and technical jobs in the economy and, after the educational reforms of the mid-1960s, their number considerably increased. In effect, a new middle class was born—that is, a social collectivity characterized by the fact that only the certified academic capital of its members, as opposed to the classical monetary capital provides them with bargaining powers on the labour market. This new middle class is, in essence, different from Quebec's old middle class and traditional elites whose power and status derived above all from their position vis-à-vis the religious order.

In the early 1960s, this new middle class was confronted with a private economy quite incapable of generating new job outlets and quite inhospitable to certified French-Canadian skills. The expansion of the state in this context came as a miracle. It provided job outlets to university- and technically-trained French Canadians, thus securing the survival of that class within Quebec.

The Expansion of the State Sector of the Economy

As we have seen, all over Canada, the 1950s and the 1960s witnessed an enormous expansion of the state sector of the economy. This expansion is mainly the expansion of the provincial and local state sectors. Both the provincial and the municipal governments have enormously increased their gross general expenditures[48] in comparison with the federal government: from $101.35 per capita on the average in 1954-55 to $802.54 in 1971-72 for the provinces; from $58.37 in 1952 to $437.64 in 1971 for municipalities; and from $314.99 in 1954-55 to $844.65 in 1971-72 for the federal government.[49] Provincial and municipal expenditures took an increasing share of personal income, while federal expenditures remained fairly constant. In seventeen years, the provinces and the municipalities increased their gross general expenditures by 800 percent, while the federal increased its by less than 300 percent.

The growth of the provincial level of administration is largely attributable to the expansion of state-controlled social services, which are taking an increasing share (from a half in 1950 to two-thirds in 1970) of an otherwise rapidly increasing total budget. In fact, the administration responsibility for social-welfare services has shifted almost entirely to provinces. While 34 percent of consolidated expenditures for health (after elimination of transfer payments between administrations) was assumed by the federal administration in 1947-48, only 2.8 percent was in 1970-71. The situation is identical for education (2.8 percent in 1970-71) but differs for welfare expenditures (where 73.4 percent were federal).[50] Overall, the priorities for provincial expenditures have shifted from roads and agriculture to health and education.

There is, besides governmental administrations, a second important element in the state sector: state enterprises. While the gross general expenditures per capita at the provincial level of government have expanded on the average in Canada by five times during the 1960s, the assets per capita of state enterprises have increased on the average in all Canadian provinces by four times during the same period.[51]

In general, these statistics underestimate the importance and the rate of expansion of the state sector of the economy, for they only partially include the economic activity derived from contracts of various private enterprises with the state. For instance, in Quebec, the economic activity—linked to Expo '67, to the massive construction of schools in the 1960s, hospitals, nursing homes, the Manic and James Bay projects, and the Olympics—is only partially accounted for in the previously presented statistics.

Now, if we compare the evolution of provincial finances, Quebec is strikingly different in three respects. First, because of Quebec's weaker economic structure, the share of provincial and municipal expenditures within personal income is considerably higher than in Ontario and in the other provinces on the average.[52] The consolidated provincial-municipal expenditures represented a relatively equivalent per capita expenditure, but 34.9 percent of Quebec personal income in 1971, as compared to 27.5 percent in Ontario and 30.9 percent across Canada.

Second, the growth of the state sector in Quebec has really only begun in 1960 with the Liberal party administration, while the 1950s had been the take-off point for Ontario.[53] This is evident in the evolution of provincial and municipal expenditures. It is also evident in the growth of the assets of provincial state enterprises. In the 1960s, there was a sevenfold increase of these assets in Quebec, as compared with a threefold increase in Ontario and a fourfold increase on the average among Canadian provinces, so that these assets represented

$6,604,432,000 in 1971 in Quebec (or $1095.63 per capita) and $6,443,001,000 in Ontario (or $836.43 per capita). As a result of this febrile creation and expansion of state enterprises in Quebec, their assets as of 1971, both in absolute terms and per capita, were the highest among all Canadian provinces.

Third, because the growth of the state sector in Quebec gained momentum only in the 1960s, the current public debt in Quebec is much higher than in Ontario. From 1960 to 1968, Quebec's direct debt (the government's) has increased by five times (Ontario, about 1.5 times) and the indirect debt (debt guaranteed to other parts of the state, such as state enterprises) by three times (while in Ontario it remained about the same).[54] In other words, the fiscal efforts were spread out over the 1950s and 1960s in Ontario, but they were condensed into the 1960s for Quebec.

These differences boil down to one sociological observation: the state sector of the economy is qualitatively, if not in strict quantifiable fiscal terms, more important in Quebec than in the other provinces. Since its expansion has been more sudden in its timing, more extensive in its nationalization and creation of enterprises, and more costly to its taxpayers, the state inevitably achieved a much greater presence in people's minds than anywhere else in Canada. This is to say that the state has expanded not only quantitatively, but also qualitatively. This has been well expressed by Claude Morin, a former high state official and minister of intergovernmental affairs in the Parti Québécois government:

> In the eyes of French-speaking Quebeckers, Ottawa and Quebec have no authority over each other; each administration is autonomous in its areas of jurisdictions; sometimes their activities are complementary, and if conflicts arise, the Government of Quebec is *a priori* in the right.... The common denominator of views in the other provinces is that the federal government is the "national" government; neither the Newfoundlander nor British Columbian questions this basic postulate.... An English-speaking provincial political figure, even a Premier, is considered to have received a promotion if he becomes a federal Cabinet minister. In Quebec, for a politician to move from the Quebec to the federal arena is no longer necessarily a promotion; the two are considered of similar significance.[55]

Because of this, the intensity of the feelings towards the actions of the Quebec government is incomparably higher in Quebec than elsewhere in Canada, as indicated by such things as the virulence of public debates, the much higher amount of press coverage, or the popular imagery surrounding political figures. In this context, given the general ideology surrounding this expansion—which we will describe later—the Quebec state can easily appear as the collective lever for the upward mobility of all the Québécois people, independently of who in fact most tangibly benefits from this expansion of the state.

The Quebec State as the Institutional Basis for the New Middle Class

With more and more French Canadians being university educated but incapable of finding appropriate jobs, the gap between Anglophones and Francophones would have widened to a historically unparalleled, socially explosive proportion. But the state sector did expand and did provide job outlets for a vast proportion of the new middle class. In so doing, it became the institutional basis for the existence of this class.

The available evidence to support this hypothesis is quite scattered and unsystematic. Yet it describes the issue from so many different angles that it makes a rather convincing case for the assertion that the Quebec state has evolved into the main locus for the local hegemony of a Quebec Francophone new middle class.

A first line of evidence is the following. If we break down the 1971 census category "professional and technical" into occupational specialties, we notice that Anglophones are overrepresented in the natural sciences, engineering, architecture, mathematics, and related fields (+18.8 percent); the Francophones, underrepresented (-6.8%). Health and education are, however, significantly overrepresented by Francophones (+1.9% and +3.3 percent, respectively, for French Canadians; -7.6 percent and -8.4 percent, respectively, for Anglophones).[56] Because census statisticians presented disaggregated data of this sort only in 1971, longitudinal data are unavailable.

This pattern of over- and underrepresentation is not surprising. Health, education, and religion have traditionally been the only institutional sectors where mobility from bottom to top was conceivable for French Canadians. Similarly, because of their earlier association with monopolistic enterprises, Anglophones have until recently been more prone to specialize in and to work in hard-science fields.

What is important, however, is that the health and education fields are now almost totally under the jurisdiction of the Quebec state. With the hospitalization insurance plan, the educational reforms, the medical-insurance plan, and the reorganization of welfare services, almost all of the social services have become part of the state sector of the economy. The same has not occurred for the hard-science field. Further, the majority of the new jobs created within Quebec during the 1960s have been in social services. Health, education, and welfare employment has almost doubled, while the absolute number of people employed in manufacturing has slightly diminished. Making the reasonable assumption that the growth of employment in the state-controlled social services occurred for Anglophones and Francophones in proportion to their relative number in the overall population, this would mean that a large proportion of the

Quebec new middle class went to work in these areas and thus in the state sector of the economy. In other words, the emergence of Quebec's new middle class was directly associated with the growth of the state's social-services agencies and departments.

A second line of evidence comes from the comparative examination of the location of work of various professional groupings of both ethnic origins. The Royal Commission on Bilingualism and Biculturalism investigated this question in the mid-1960s. It writes:

> Even among candidates with the educational qualifications suited to careers in industrial management, there appear to be substantial differences between Francophones and Anglophones as to where they actually choose, or are chosen to work. For instance, in 1964, commerce graduates of McGill were employed in industry to a greater extent than graduates of the École des Hautes Études Commerciales.... The membership list of the Institute of Chartered Accountants of Quebec showed a similar pattern of employment. More than 90 percent of the chartered accountants employed by the provincial and municipal government were Francophones; in industry and commerce less than 40 percent were Francophones. Among both commerce graduates and chartered accountants, however, there was a trend among the younger Francophones towards greater participation in the private sector. Even so, Anglophones still outnumbered Francophones to a considerable extent among the younger employees.

The same is true for engineers and scientists:

> The proportion of Francophone engineers working in private industry in 1963 was similarly low; only 25% of Francophone engineers compared with 78% of Anglophone engineers, were employed in this sector.... The pattern of employment of science graduates from Francophone universities among industrial sectors has many of the same features as that of Francophone engineers. Among scientists employed by provincial and municipal governments, 85% were Francophones. Their proportion was much lower in teaching (43%), the federal government (39%) and non-salaried professional services (32%). Like the engineers, they had low proportions in the large mining and manufacturing sectors (14%) and in construction, transportation, and communication (13%).[57]

The engineers' situation could be looked at from another angle. While one of the biggest electrical power companies employed only 20 Francophone engineers out of 175 in 1963 prior to being nationalized, Montreal Quebec Hydro (nationalized in 1944) had 190 Francophone engineers out of 243 at the same date.[58] We can reasonably assume that the nationalization of all electrical power companies has been conducive to the hiring of Francophone as opposed to Anglophone engineers. The situation in Montreal Quebec Hydro in 1963 has probably gradually been extended to the entire hydro field after nationalization. Again, this would show that the expansion of the state has served Quebec's new middle class.

This observation is strengthened by a third piece of evidence. The Centre de Sondage of the Université de Montréal conducted a study in 1973 on behalf of the Commission d'Enquête sur la situation de la langue française et sur les droits linguistiques au Québec (Gendron Commission). In this study, an inquiry was made into the location of work in a stratified random sample of Quebec university graduates. It showed that, on the aggregate, 25.6 percent of Anglophone university graduates in all fields worked for the Quebec government,[59] while 53.8 percent of Francophones did. In younger cohorts, the proportion is even higher: 65.3 percent of Francophone graduates and 33.8 percent of Anglophones work for the Quebec government. In other words, two-thirds of Francophones who graduated from university in the 1960s worked in the Quebec state sector of the economy, while one-third of Anglophones did. For those who had graduated from university before the early 1960s, the comparable figures were: about one-half of Francophones and one-fifth of Anglophones worked for the government.

Finally, not only has the expansion of the state provided, in gigantic proportions, job outlets to university-trained Francophones, but is also seems to have provided them with high incomes, perhaps even more so than if they had worked in a comparable job in the private sector of the economy. The relative income position of workers in the state sector considerably increased in the 1960s, while the income status of workers in the private sector either remained stable or decreased. It is remarkable that the entrance of a given occupational category in the state sector (for Quebec, physicians and surgeons in 1970, teachers in 1964, employees of institutions in 1961 for the most part) has meant a considerable amelioration of their relative income status in the following years. While workers in the state sector over the decade increased their declared incomes by at least one and a half times in constant dollars (two and one-third in current dollars), workers in the private sector have only very slightly increased their incomes.[60] Exactly the same phenomena occurred in Ontario, but, contrary to Quebec, they did not almost exclusively apply to a social collectivity whose survival depended on state expansion.

In short, all the evidence seems to point to the fact that state expansion has provided job outlets to the majority of educated Francophones within Quebec. It has created jobs that presumably were much more powerful, prestigious, and well-paid than the jobs the same individuals could have found in the private sector of the economy. To repeat, the expansion of the state and the creation of new job outlets within it are not unique to Quebec. The same phenomenon has occurred in all provinces and quantitatively perhaps to a comparable degree. What is peculiar to Quebec is that this expansion served as the almost sole institutional basis for the Francophone new middle class as a whole.

State Interventions and Their Ideology

It would be false to say that state expansion benefited only Quebec's new middle class. For one thing, it helped to modernize considerably the economic infrastructure, to the benefit mainly of the capitalist owning class. The Quiet Revolution can indeed by viewed partially as state interventions aimed at socializing the costs of production of the monopolistic sector, despite the fact that profits were to be privately appropriated in foreign hands. As Milner and Milner write:

> While the reforms of the period were genuine and did transform Quebec society, they operated only at the middle level. The basic pattern of economic control, investment, and development was, except for a few adjustments, basically left untouched. Foreign interests were dominant and indeed many of the reforms were designed to encourage even further foreign takeover by providing the owing class with a modern economic infrastructure. As such there was a definite limit on the changes which the architects of the Quiet Revolution could accomplish, beyond what meant attacking the basic economic system root and branch. For the Liberals, being as always a party supporting and supported by big business, such a possibility was dismissed out of hand.[61]

In fact, never was this Quiet Revolution intended to go to the root economic causes of social inequalities between Anglophones and Francophones and among the Francophone population:

> From our vantage point today, we can make out the significant weaknesses at the base of Quiet Revolution. While it opened up the world of ideas to all possibilities, it limited changes in structure to those which meant catching up with North America. Those spheres of society which had been held back under the older order were permitted to expand and grow. The schools, the media, the arts, all experienced a renaissance and soon became the locus for the spread and discussion of the new ideas. The changes, though fundamental in relation to the older order, did not at any point challenge the underlying economic structure of Quebec. And when some intellectuals and writers were no longer content to rail against Ottawa and devise even more complex constitutional schemata, but instead chose to attack the economic system head on; and when these new ideas began to receive attention and consideration among the students and trade unionists—then the authorities decided that things had simply gone too far. "Law and Order" came back into style.[62]

Furthermore, many state interventions only derived from the imperatives to strengthen the economy and to maintain full employment: the government simply had to do something about the high rates of unemployment, the lack of investment, the comparatively declining growth of Quebec total production, and so on. As many economists have indicated, the Quebec GNP has progressed at a high rate despite a relative decrease in private investments, because of massive public investments:

Let us remember that, during the period 1961-67, public works such as Manic-Outardes (important dam construction), the construction of the Montreal subway, and the preparation of Expo '67 have sustained growth and carried along the private sector. The construction of schools and hospitals between 1967 and 1970 has permitted to [Quebec] escape catastrophe. Finally, since 1971, the preparation of the Olympic Games, the prolongation of the Montreal subway, the construction of Mirabel airport, and the James Bay project are above all responsible for economic growth. Consumption has also been largely sustained by governments. Subsidies of all kinds (transfer payments) have increased, over the last 10 years, at the annual rate of 20% and they now represent in Quebec more than 15% of personal income.[63]

In consequence, two journalists were able to write that "every new brick put up in Quebec costs as much to the taxpayer as it costs the private investor."[64] In fact, a task force to the Department of Industry and Commerce estimated that in Quebec over three-quarters of the jobs created between 1966 and 1972 were linked to government actions, while the proportion is much smaller in Ontario.

Yet, despite these imperatives to maintain the growth of the economy, certain government interventions seemed to be more directly aimed at correcting the social makeup of the Quebec private economy and at providing top control jobs to members of the new middle class.

James Iain Gow has noted that, while the Duplessis regime in nineteen years (1936-40, 1944-1960) had created only five new departments (among which only two remained stable), eight regulatory boards, and one state enterprise:

> The 1960s have seen a much more febrile activity as far as the creation of new administrative institutions is concerned. In six years, the Lesage administration has created six departments, three regulatory boards, eight state enterprises and nine consultative councils. The impetus was followed by the Union Nationale Administrations between 1966 and 1970, with the creation of five new departments, seven regulatory boards, five public enterprises and three consultative councils.[65]

Jean-Jacques Simard has likewise tried to compute the quantitative growth of the state apparatus. He writes:

> The Quebec government includes 23 departments among which only one, the Department of Revenue, has not changed vocation since 1960, 55 consultative boards which were nearly all born in the same period, nine judiciary institutions, and 63 organizations aimed at economic management and regulation. Of the 148 para-governmental organizations, 126 date back only 15 years. The growth of the 250 school boards, the CEGEP, universities and schools, the thousand and more municipal councils, the thousand health and social welfare institutions ... brought about in the name of coordination and coherence, was proportional to the increase of the financial, administrative and political dependency of these organizations on the upper echelons of government.[66]

All these councils, departments, boards, and enterprises provided previously unexisting high-prestige and high-power jobs for university-trained Francophones. This is indicated, for instance, by the number of people involved in new managerial tasks in the Quebec civil service between 1964 and 1971 (economists, sociologists, social workers, psychologists): it increased by more than 400 percent, while the traditional professional personnel of the government (like doctors and engineers) increased only by 20 percent.[67]

A similar job-creating process seems to have occurred through the economic reforms. To sustain production in some declining French-Canadian industries and to encourage an indigenous capitalism, the Société Générale de Financement was created. Electrical power companies were bought up. To create a public fund out of individual savings, the Caisse de Dépôt et de Placement was created. New enterprises were created to venture into value-producing sectors, such as steel, mining, petroleum, forestry, and so on. In all these cases, the costs of maintaining, buying up, or creating enterprises have been socialized, the profits (if any) nationalized, and the high-power control jobs appropriated by members of the new middle class.

Economist Albert Breton suggested in 1964 that the creation of such jobs may well have been their sole purpose:

> The nationalization of private assets is aimed at providing high-income jobs for nationals, rather than at other objectives connected with rasing social income, such as control of monopoly, increased investment in industries displaying external economies, or purchases of high-yielding public or social goods. This implication is borne out by the most important act of the new nationalist government of Quebec, namely, the nationalization of eleven private power companies.... This decision was not a decision about investing in electricity but one about investing in ethnicity. When the decision was made, it was not decided to consider the flow of rewards to society as a whole but only to a group within society ... the new middle class in Quebec.... [The same is true for the Société Générale de Financement where] the resources which could have been invested to increase the social income of the community have been used ... to keep already existing high-income jobs for the same middle class.[68]

In retrospect, this view is clearly an overstatement. As Carol Jobin has shown, the main impetus behind the nationalization of Quebec private electrical power companies was the inability of these companies to expand in a way that would have been profitable to them.[69] And yet the growth of Quebec's economy required such as expansion. That the new middle class benefited from this nationalization is secondary to the economically determined constraints imposed on the government to further expand the hydro field.

The creation of planning agencies and programs has also provided new job openings and a new mystique about the role of the state. During the 1960s, Quebec evolved broad programs and instituted highly advertised supervisory agencies. Their impact seems to have been negligible as far as tangibly developing Quebec's economy and reducing regional disparities, but they were important for creating prestigious jobs for Francophones. As political scientist Jacques Benjamin has written:

> Everything that has been undertaken in the last twelve years in the field of planning has only an emotive value; Quebec, it seems to me, must first control its economy in one way or the other (directly or indirectly) before creating plans. To first instigate a mystique of the plan and then to control the economy is the same as putting the cart before the horse. For the last twelve years, we have been working backward. We have consciously put the emphasis on the concept of planning while it would have been more fruitful to pay attention to the instruments; the "fever from France" has invaded the offices of the first planners; we wanted to apply the French model integrally to Quebec, while Quebec did not even possess some of the instruments enabling it to operationalize its plans, especially the control of the economy, the coordination between state departments and even political stability in 1968-70.[70]

The reforms of health, education, and welfare displayed gigantic reorganizations but a comparable lack of tangible benefits to the overall population. Although they did considerably facilitate the financial and, to a certain extent, geographical access to medical and educational services, they did not achieve the far-reaching social-democratic ideals that had been put forward. The education reforms were to be conducive to an extensive democratization of education, with new pedagogical relationships, the suppression of class differentials between types of schooling, a decentralization of management to regions, and parents' involvement in decision making. The changes actually implemented have fallen considerably below expectations. The health and social-welfare reforms were to institutionalize a new, more social approach to health and disease, decentralization of decision making to regions and institutions, and worker and consumer participation in the management of these institutions. The reality was again short of what had been promised. The net results of these reforms were huge reorganizations and administrative reshuffling that in a sense did rationalize the allocation of resources. But, above all, these reforms seem either to have maintained or reinforced the powers and privileges of various categories of Francophone professionals, or to have created new interesting jobs for university-trained individuals in the state bureaucracy.

The Unparalleled Status and Legitimacy of Technocratic Elite Groups

This overview of the main interventions of the Quebec state during the 1960s and the 1970s is rapid and oversimplifies several points. Yet, it underlines a key phenomenon. Because the Quebec state is virtually the sole institutional basis for the new middle class, this class has evolved a unique nationalist and social-democratic political culture. The old all-encompassing rhetoric of bishops in the Church has been superseded by an equally far-reaching rhetoric of elite members of the new middle class in the state, but with a different content. As the religious symbols of the past have helped traditional elites maintain their social status in Quebec traditional society, the nationalist and social-democratic ideals of new-middle-class elites now legitimize and reinforce their recently acquired dominance over an increasingly unionized and politicized population. Nationalism is not new in Quebec politics, but its association with social-democratic ideals is. It is this association between nationalism and a mild form of socialism that characterizes the ideology of Quebec's new middle class. Under different forms and with different emphases, both the Liberal party and the Parti Québécois—at different points in its history for the former and more consistently for the latter—have put forward such an ideology.

Such a political culture camouflages the objective interest of this class while at the same time legitimates intervention into more and more aspects of social life through an administratively rational problem-solving approach, thereby furthering its hegemony as a class.

This is not to say that this class manoeuvres in some conspiratorial manner, as if totally conscious of its interests or unconstrained by larger social, political, and economic forces. This is not to say either that administrative rationalization is useless. Quite the contrary: it is sometimes absolutely imperative. The point is that, because expansion of the state serves its interests, the new middle class will support all actions that will produce huge reorganizing, restructuring, reshuffling, *independently* of the objective necessity and feasibility of such transformations. This is so because both the quantitative (budget increase, growth of civil service employees and of the assets of state enterprises, and so on) and the qualitative (involvement in the greatest possible number of areas of social life, increase in the prestige and importance of professional expertise in the government, and increase of the visibility of the state) expansion of the state serves its search for jobs and a local hegemony. In this context, technocratic elite groups and ideologies that share the political culture of the new middle class are bound to be endowed with a status, a legitimacy, and political powers unseen in the rest of Canada, thus providing Quebec with a distinctive strategy of social change.

Conclusion

The combination of the objective material interests of a class in seeing the Quebec state sector of the economy expand quantitatively and qualitatively as well as its self-fulfilling ideological emphasis on nationalism and social-democracy, as argued here, is the most plausible explanation for the distinctive character of Quebec state interventions. There has developed in Quebec a systemic logic, so to speak, that has endowed the inevitable expansion of the state with hopes and expectations far beyond what could be delivered in a capitalist economy and under the present system of national government. Yet it did introduce new political dynamics, the results of which one would be hard pressed to predict. It introduced a new "social imagery" that could lead to a further technocratic and professional takeover or—because of the frustrations, inequities, and fiscal problems the reforms have brought on—it may lead to the tangible implementation of the ideals as advertised. Under the guise of deprofessionalizing through consumer and worker participation, of debureaucratizing through decentralization of decision making, and of repatriating the collective heritage and patrimony through nationalization and creation of state enterprises, government actions have in fact led to a further professionalization, bureaucratization, and concentration of powers and privileges. This contradiction may be managed to the advantage of those who benefit from it, but it may also, in the long run, assume a liberating character.

Notes

1. Quoted in Edmond Orban, "Indicateurs, concepts et objectifs" in *La modernisation politique du Québec,* edited by Edmond Orban (Quebec: Boréal Express, 1976), 7.

2. Unless otherwise noted, these indicators are taken from the various essays in E. Orban, ed., *La modernisation politique du Québec* and from Gary Caldwell and B. Dan Czarnocki, "Un rattrapage raté: Le changement social dans le Québec d'aprés-guerre, 1950-1974: une comparaison Québec/Ontario," *Recherches Sociographiques* XVII, 1 (1977): 9-58.

3. Denis Monière, *Le développement des idéologies au Québec des origines à nos jours* (Montreal: Éditions Québec-Amérique, 1977), 328.

4. For a discussion of these expenditures consistent with the argument developed in this article, see Daniel Latouche, "La vraie nature ... de la Révolution tranquille," *Revue Canadienne de Sciences Politiques* VII, 3 (Sept. 1974): 525-35.

5. Here is the share of popular vote for the Union Nationale and the Parti Québécois in the last seven elections: 1956 (UN: 51.5%); 1960 (UN: 46.6%); 1962 (UN: 42.1%); 1966 (UN: 40.9%); 1970 (UN: 20.0%; PQ: 23.6%); 1973 (UN: 5.0%; PQ: 30.2%); 1976 (UN: 18.2%; PQ 41.4%). For analyses of these elections, see for instance Vincent Lemieux, ed., *Quatre élections provinciales* (Quebec: Presses de l'Université Laval, 1969); V. Lemieux, M. Gilbert, and A. Blais, *Une élection de réalignement* (Montreal: Cahiers de Cité libre, Éd. du Jour, 1970); or Robert Boily, "Genèse et développement des partis politiques au Québec," in *La modernisation politique du Québec,* 79-100. For a somewhat positive history of the Union Nationale and its leader, Maurice Duplessis, see Conrad Black, *Duplessis,* (Montreal: Les éditions de l'Homme, 1977).

6. Given the available data, it is impossible to regionalize the effects of federal spending and to estimate with any precision the total amount of spending by the public

sector in a given year in a given province. Therefore, it is difficult to estimate the part of each province's GNP (or more precisely the Gross National Expenditure, which is equivalent) accounted for by government spending. For tentative estimates, see Kemal Wassef, "La situation du gouvernement du Québec dans les affaires économiques de la province" (unpublished manuscript, Confédération des Syndicats Nationaux, October 1971); and B. Roy-Lemoine, "The Growth of the State in Quebec" in *The Political Economy of the State: Quebec / Canada / U.S.A.,* edited by D. Roussopoulos (Montreal: Black Rose Books, 1973), 59-87.

7. For the health services, see A.D. McDonald, J.C. McDonald, and P.E. Enterline, "Études sur l'assurance-maladie du Québec," and André Billette, "Santé, classes sociales et politiques redistributive," both in *Sociologie et Sociétés: La gestion de la santé* IX, 1 (April 1977): 52-92.

8. I documented this scenario for health reforms in Marc Renaud, "Réforme ou illusion? Une analyse des interventions de l'État québécois dans le domaine de la santé," *Sociologie et Sociétés: La gestion de la santé* IX, 1 (April 1977): 127-52. Further evidence of the omnipresence of this scenario can be found in a variety of publications. See, for instance, *Une certaine révolution tranquille* (Montreal: Éd. La Presse, 1975); Kenneth McRoberts and Dale Posgate, *Quebec: Social Change and Political Crisis* (Toronto: McClelland and Stewart, 1976); Pierre Doray, "Une pyramide tronquée: les politiques de sécurité du revenu pour les retraités" (M.Sc. thesis, Département de sociologie, Université de Montréal, 1978); Diane Poliquin-Bourassa, "La réforme de l'éducation: phase II" in *Premier mandat,* edited by Daniel Latouche, vol. II (Montreal: Éditions de l'Aurore, 1977): 15-26; and Michel Pelletier and Yves Vaillancourt, *Les politiques sociales et les travailleurs, Les années 60* (Montreal: available from the authors, 1974).

9. Although present in the literature for a long time (e.g., Hubert Guindon, "Social Unrest, Social Class and Quebec's Bureaucratic Revolution" in *Social Stratification in Canada,* edited by J.E. Curtis and W.G. Scott (Toronto: Prentice-Hall, 1973), this hypothesis has been systematized by Gilles Bourque and Nicole Frenette in "La structure nationale québécoise," *Socialisme québécois* 21, 2 (1970): 109-56. A similar hypothesis has simultaneously been developed in Luc Racine and Roch Denis, "La conjoncture politique depuis 1960," ibid.: 17-78. Using different paradigms (in the sense of Robert R. Alford, "Towards a Critical Sociology of Political Power" in *Stress and Contradictions in Modern Capitalism,* edited by Léon Lindberg (Lexington, 1975): 145-60) a vast series of authors have expanded on a similar hypothesis. See, for instance, Anne Legaré, *Les classes sociales au Québec* (Montreal: Presses de l'Université du Québec, 1977); Pierre Fournier, *The Quebec Establishment: The Ruling Class and the State* (Montreal: Black Rose Books, 1976); Marcel Fournier, "La question nationale: les enjeux," *Possibles* 1, 2 (Winter 1977): 7-18; Daniel Latouche, "La vraie nature", Denis Monière, *Le développement des idéologies au Québec.*

10. For a discussion of these terms, see Anthony Giddens, *The Class Structure of Advanced Societies* (New York: Harper and Row, 1973).

11. See, for instance, Pierre-Paul Proulx, ed., *Vers une problématique globale du développement de la région de Montréal* (Montreal: CRDE, June 1976); P. Fréchette,

R. Jouandet-Bernadat, and J.P. Vézina, *L'économie du Québec* (Montreal: Les Éditions HRW Ltée, 1975); Ministère de l'Industrie et du Commerce, *Une politique économique québécois* (Quebec, Jan. 1974). This is also confirmed by the study of G. Caldwell and B.D. Czarnocki, "Un rattrapage raté."

12. James O'Connor, *The Fiscal Crisis of the State* (New York: St. Martin's Press, 1973); for further conceptual development, see his *The Corporations and the State: Essays in the Theory of Capitalism and Imperialism* (New York: Harper and Row, 1975).

13. See, for instance, the essays published in Marcel Rioux and Yves Martin, eds., *French-Canadian Society* (Toronto: McClelland and Stewart, 1964). See also Denis Monière, *Le développement des idéologies au Québec*, and Maurice Saint-Germain, *Une économie à libérer: le Québec analysé dans ses structures économiques* (Montreal: Presses de l'Université de Montréal, 1973).

14. Hubert Guindon, "The Social Evolution of Quebec Reconsidered" in *French-Canadian Society*, 137-61, and his "Social Unrest, Social Class and Quebec's Bureaucratic Revolution."

15. French Canadians had one of the highest birth rates in the industrialized world. Now it is among the lowest in Canada. See Jacques Henripin, "From Acceptance of Nature to Control: The Demography of the French Canadians since the Seventeenth Century," in *French-Canadian Society*, 204-15. See also Bureau de la statistique du Québec, *Tendances passées et perspectives d'évolution de la fécondité au Québec* (Quebec, 1976).

16. Some violent strikes have, however, occurred after the war. For a sociological analysis of these, see Hélène David, "La grève et le bon Dieu: la grève de l'amiante au Québec," *Sociologie et Société* I, 2 (Nov. 1969): 249-76, and "L'état des rapports de classe au Québec de 1945 à 1967," *Sociologie et Société* VII, 2: 33-66. On the beginnings of trade unionism, see Louis Maheau, "Problème social et naissance du syndicalisme catholique," *Sociologie et Société* I, 1 (May 1969), and Louis-Marie Tremblay, *Le syndicalisme québécois: idéologies de la CSN et de la FTQ 1940-1970* (Montreal: Presses de l'Université de Montréal, 1972).

17. Examples of the convergence of interests between the Church, political leaders, and "foreign" entrepreneurs abound. For instance, the Roman Catholic hierarchy supported simultaneously foreign corporations and French-Canadian workers in the development of trade unions. The actions of political leaders are even clearer as manifest in the proxy battle for the St-Lawrence Corporation, the 99-year leases to Iron Ore and others. For more examples, see the appendices to the manifestoes of the Quebec trade unions (translated in Daniel Drache, ed., *Quebec: Only the Beginning* (Toronto: New Press, 1972), and in *Quebec Labour* (Montreal: Black Rose Books, 1972). On the relations between political leaders and the corporate world, the most systematic study is Pierre Fournier, *The Quebec Establishment*. See also Union des Travailleurs du Papier et du Carton Façonnés, *Les Tigres de Carton* (Montreal: Éditions Québécoises, n.d.); Groupe de Recherches Économiques, *Les Compagnies de Finance* (Montreal: Éditions Québécoises, n.d.).

18. André Raynauld, *La propriété des enterprises au Québec* (Montreal: Presses de l'Université de Montréal, 1974), 78.

19. André Raynauld, "The Quebec Economy: A General Assessment" in *Quebec Society and Politics: Views from the Inside*, edited by Dale C. Thomson (Toronto: McClelland and Stewart, 1973), 152, my emphasis.

20. Report of the Royal Commission on Bilingualism and Biculturalism, Book III, *The Work World* (Ottawa: Queen's Printer, 1969), 447.

21. For descriptions of this industrial structure, see Gilles Lebel, *Horizon 1980: une étude sur l'évolution de l'économie du Québec de 1946 à 1968 et sur ses perspectives d'avenir* (Quebec: Ministère de l'Industrie et du Commerce, 1970); and P. Fréchette et al., *L'économie du Québec*.

22. For an examination of foreign dominance over the Canadian economy, see Kari Levitt, *Silent Surrender* (Toronto: Macmillan, 1970); R. Laxer, ed., *Canada Ltd., The Political Economy of Dependency* (Toronto: McClelland and Stewart, 1973); Wallace Clement, *Continental Corporate Power* (Toronto: McClelland and Stewart, 1977); T. Naylor, *The History of Canadian Business* (Toronto: Lorimer, 1975). For an examination of foreign dominance over the Quebec economy, see André Raynauld, *La propriété des enterprises au Québec*; Jorge Niosi, "Le gouvernement du PQ, le capital américain et le contrôle canadien" (unpublished paper, Département de sociologie, Université du Québec à Montréal, 1978); and Arnaud Sales, "La différenciation nationale et ethnique de la bourgeoisie industrielle au Québec," and "Le gouvernement du Parti Québécois et les pouvoirs économiques" (unpublished papers, Département de sociologie, Université de Montréal, 1978). As Niosi and Sales have convincingly shown, despite foreign dominance, an identifiable *grande* bourgeoisie exists among the Francophone segment of the Quebec population, but it is comparatively small and concentrated in specific economic sectors.

23. *Canadian Census*, 1961, vol. III, part 2, table 9; *Canadian Census*, 1971, vol. III, part 4, table 10.

24. Ministère de l'Industrie et du Commerce, *Une Politique Economique Québécoise* (mimeographed, 1974), 18.

25. Ibid., 9.

26. André Raynauld, *La propriété des entreprises au Québec*, 147.

27. Report of the Royal Commission on Bilingualism and Biculturalism, 81.

28. John Porter, "The Economic Elite and the Social Structure in Canada" in *Canadian Society*, edited by B.R. Blishen, F.E. Jones, K.D. Naegele and J. Porter (Toronto: Macmillan, 1961). 486-500.

29. Sheilagh Hodgins Milner and Henry Milner, *The Decolonization of Quebec: An Analysis of Left-Wing Nationalism* (Toronto: McClelland and Stewart, 1973).

30. Wallace Clement, *The Canadian Corporate Elite: An Analysis of Economic Power* (Toronto: McClelland and Stewart, 1975).

31. André Raynauld, *La Propriété des entreprises au Québec*.

32. Milner and Milner, *The Decolonization of Quebec*, 71.

33. Clement, *The Canadian Corporate Elite*, 233-34.

34. Robert Presthus, *Elite Accommodation in Canadian Politics* (Cambridge: Cambridge University Press, 1973).

35. Clement, *The Canadian Corporate Elite*, 234. As Pierre Fournier has argued in "Les tendances nouvelles du pouvoir économique au Québec," *Le Devoir,* 9 and 10 juin 1976, there is something intrinsically misleading in this approach. Generally, it tends to underestimate the importance of the French-Canadian bourgeoisie because it computes only the number of persons on corporate boards, a number likely to be substantially increased by legislation forcing French as the language of work in Quebec. Further, since these data are limited to the corporate world, they do not include this segment of the Quebec bourgeoisie linked to the co-operative movement (Mouvement Desjardins, Coopérative Fédérée, Coopérative agricole de Granby) and to state enterprises (like Sidbec, Dosco, and the Société Générale de Financement).

36. Tore Thonstad with C. Fluet and C. Ross, *Simulations de la pénétration des francophones parmi les cadres du secteur privé au Québec, 1971-1986*, Études réalisées pour le compte de la Commission d'enquête sur la situation de la langue française et sur les droits linguistiques au Québec (L'éditeur officiel du Québec, February 1974).

37. Dominique Clift, "French Elite Lags in Salary Scale," *La Presse* (1975).

38. Report of the Royal Commission on Bilingualism and Biculturalism, 488.

39. M.V. George, *Internal Migration in Canada: Demographic Analyses* (Ottawa: Statistics Canada, 1970).

40. John Porter, *The Vertical Mosaic: An Analysis of Social Class and Power in Canada* (Toronto: University of Toronto Press, 1965).

41. For reasons of space, all tables have been dropped from this article. For further detail, see Marc Renaud, "The Political Economy of the Quebec Health-Care Reforms" (Ph.D. thesis, University of Wisconsin, Madison, 1976), 411-28.

42. Guy Rocher and Yves de Jocas, "Inter-Generation Occupational Mobility in the Province of Quebec," *The Canadian Journal of Economics and Political Science* 23, 1 (Feb. 1957).

43. Jacques Dofny and Muriel Garon-Audy, "Mobilités Professionnelles au Québec," *Sociologie et Societé* I, 2 (Nov. 1969): 277-302.

44. Ibid., 287.

45. Jacques Brazeau, "Quebec's Emerging Middle Class" in *French Canadian Society*, 296-306.

46. Ian Adams, William Cameron, Brian Hill, and Peter Penz, *The Real Poverty Report* (Edmonton: Hurtig, 1971), 219.

47. See Hélène Ostiguy, "Statistiques détaillées relatives à l'enseignement supérieur" (unpublished manuscript, Université de Montréal, Département de Sociologie, September 1971).

48. Gross general expenditures reflect the administrative burden of a given level of government. Net general expenditures reflect the fiscal burden. From an account-

ing point of view, the difference is constituted by the following items: (1) All revenues of institutions coming under the government; (2) revenues in the form of interests, premiums, and discounts; (3) grants-in-aid and shared-cost contributions; (4) all capital revenue. These revenues are deducted from the corresponding gross expenditures to obtain the net general expenditures.

49. Statistics Canada, *Federal Government Finance, Revenue and Expenditure, Assets and Liabilities* (Catalogue no. 68-211), *Provincial Government Finance, Revenue and Expenditure* (Catalogue no. 68-207), *Local Government Finance, Revenue and Expenditure, Assets and Liabilities* (Catalogue no. 68-204).

50. Research and Statistics Division, Department of National Health and Welfare, *Government Expenditures on Health and Social Welfare—Canada, 1927-1959* (Social Security Series, memorandum no. 16, Ottawa, 1961), 45; and Canadian Tax Foundation, *The National Finance 1973-74*, 24.

51. Statistics Canada, *Provincial Government Enterprise Finance* (Catalogue no. 61-204); *Federal Government Enterprise Finance* (Catalogue no. 61-203).

52. Statistics Canada, *Consolidated Government Finance—Federal, Provincial and Local Governments, Revenue and Expenditures* (Catalogue no. 68-202).

53. For systematic summaries of the evolution of Ontario, see a series of publications issued by the Ontario Economic Council and entitled *The Evolution of Policy in Contemporary Ontario*.

54. *Annuaire du Québec* (1971), 733.

55. Claude Morin, "The Gospel According to Holy Ottawa" in *Quebec Society and Politics: Views from the Inside*, edited by Dale C. Thomson (Toronto: McClelland and Stewart, 1973), 210.

56. *Canadian Census*, 1971, vol. 3, part III, table 5.

57. Report of the Royal Commission on Bilingualism and Biculturalism, 474-75.

58. Pierre-Paul Gagné, "L'Hydro et les Québécois: l'histoire d'amour achève," *La Presse* (13 June 1975), A-8.

59. The Quebec state is here defined as the provincial and municipal governmental bureaucracies as well as the electricity and the relevant parts of the education and health-care fields. It does not include state enterprises other than Hydro-Québec.

60. Department of National Revenue, *Taxation Statistics, Analysing the Returns of Individuals for the 1960, 1965, 1970, 1972, 1974, Taxation Year and Miscellaneous Statistics*, table 9.

61. Milner and Milner, *The Decolonization of Quebec*, 169.

62. Ibid., 191-92. A similar observation is expressed in Gérald Bernier, "Le cas québécois et les théories du développement politique et de la dépendance," in *La modernisation politique du Québec*, 19-54; and in Denis Monière, *Le développement des idéologies au Québec*, chap. 8.

63. Translated from Jean-P. Vézina, "Le développement économique: les enjeux en cause" in *Premier mandat*, 51.

64. Rhéal Bercier and Robert Pouliot, "Le pénible apprentissage de l'état québécois en matière de croissance: la charrue avant les boeufs ..." *La Presse* (14 June 1975), A-7.

65. Translated from James Iain Gow, "L'évolution de l'administration publique du Québec 1867-1970" (unpublished paper, Département de Sciences Politiques, Université de Montréal), 37. See also his "Modernisation et administration publique" in *La modernisation politique du Québec*, 157-86.

66. Translated from Jean-Jacques Simard, "La longue marche des technocrates," *Recherches Sociologiques* XVIII, 1 (1977), 119.

67. Ibid., 122.

68. Albert Breton, "The Economics of Nationalism," *The Journal of Political Economy* (1964), 382, 384, and 385.

69. Carol Jobin, "La nationalisation de l'électricité au Québec en 1962" (M.A. thesis, Université du Québec à Montréal, 1974).

70. Translated from Jacques Benjamin, *Planification et politique au Québec* (Montreal: Les Presses de l'Université de Montréal, 1974), 114.

INTRODUCTION

William D. Coleman

The future of Canada as a political community is uncertain. In these rather puzzling days in the twilight of the twentieth century, supposedly Canada's century, this is one of the few facts about which Canadians agree. The hopes and dreams of this country's leaders at the turn of the century, hopes and dreams raised by the startling economic expansion that resulted from the wheat boom, now seem rather naïve and archaic. We are troubled peoples. The Maritime provinces, it now appears, were at the zenith of their strength on the eve of Confederation. The branch plant industries of southern Ontario suffer chronic whiplash from the constant stops and starts prompted by the European and Japanese challenges to American domination of the world capitalist system. The northern parts of this same province are classic victims of the 'staple trap' and hence are haunted by visions of that old Canadian phenomenon, the ghost town. The prairie provinces continue their century-long struggle to free themselves of the Ontario 'empire,' whether by seeking a fair return in the grain trade or maintaining control of natural resources. British Columbia lives on with the instability and unemployment that characterize any economy built on the extraction and export of a limited number of natural resources.

The most politically developed challenge to Canada as an entity and hence the most immediate is the movement for political sovereignty in the province of Quebec. The questions and issues raised by this movement are important not only because of their implications for the future of the Canadian political com-

From *The Independence Movement in Quebec, 1945-1980* (Toronto: University of Toronto Press, 1984), 3-20, 229-231. Reprinted by permission of the University of Toronto Press.

munity but also because they overlap to a degree with the problems being experienced by other regions in the country. The political understanding, if any, reached with Quebec will colour the resolution of many of these other difficulties. Accordingly, the Quebec referendum of May 1980 was only a step, an indicator of relative support for and hence power of the actors involved. It resolved little. The *indépendantistes* are a political force of some importance for the immediate future. They have constructed a political voice, the Parti québécois, which is already unique in its strength and its staying power in the history of Quebec. It is more successful than the Parti national of Mercier, the Action libérale nationale, the Bloc populaire, and the Ralliement créditiste. It has a popular basis that is unlikely to be undermined in the short run.

The political question posed by the movement for political sovereignty is relatively clear. Within the boundaries of the province of Quebec is found a society that social scientists term 'ethnically pluralist.' It is composed of several cultural communities, one of which, the French, is predominant. The French-language community has lived in Quebec for close to four hundred years, and through its well-developed sensitivity to the history of those years, its religious tradition, its language, and its self-consciousness it views itself as a nation. From within that community has grown a political movement that wishes to endow Quebec and by implication this community with a sovereign state. To a degree, the shape and form of this state remain unclear but this uncertainty takes nothing away from the fundamental character of the change being envisaged.

The independence movement in Quebec has survived for over twenty years. Some might even say it has become stronger with each passing year. Despite these years and despite the continued viability of the movement, our understanding of it remains poor. When asked why there is such a strong indépendantiste movement in Quebec, the political scientist and the man in the street usually shrug and mutter something about an impatient middle class or about the French always being impatient. There have been studies of the Quiet Revolution, of the Parti québécois, and of nationalism in general, yet there have been few attempts to reflect upon the rise of the independence movement in a more comprehensive fashion. The object of this study is to try to accomplish this very task. I am presenting a wide-ranging study of political change in Quebec in the post-war period in order to suggest some reasons why there has been a thriving independence movement there since the early 1960s.

Three Current Explanations

A first and important step in the pursuit of this task will be the analysis of the policies, events, and thinking of the period that has come to be called the Quiet Revolution. The series of changes set in motion during this period were the catalyst to the independence movement. They sparked a reaction among a number of social groups and classes that was to grow quickly into a political movement. It therefore becomes disconcerting when one surveys the explanations for the Quiet Revolution and finds rather striking differences. The more successful explanations have focused upon a social class or classes and seen the rise of one or more of these as critical to understanding the Quiet Revolution. Unfortunately there appear to be major differences over which class is the 'motor' or the 'spark' for change. One group argues that a 'new middle class' is the generator of change in Quebec. Another group places the emphasis on a class variously described as a bourgeoisie francophone, a bourgeoisie québécoise, or a bourgeoisie autochtone. Still another group emphasizes a rise in influence at this time of the English-Canadian bourgeoisie in Quebec.

The existence of three quite different explanations for the remarkable turn of events in Quebec between 1959 and 1965 is unsatisfactory if only because it was out of these events that the independence movement came. Eventually, I shall show that each of these three explanations captures a part of the reality and that all can be drawn upon in fashioning an interpretation of the Quiet Revolution. My analysis then will begin with a critical review of these three explanations. From this critical review I will draw conclusions concerning how my own analysis must proceed. In the remainder of this introductory chapter, therefore, the inadequacies of the existing explanations will be noted and an outline of the approach to be used in this study will be presented.

Hypothesis I: The new middle class   The more widely accepted explanation, particularly among English-Canadian social scientists, of the series of changes that have occurred in Quebec since 1945 rests on the conceptual shoulders of a mostly francophone, new middle class. This class is composed of the white-collar workers who staff the bureaucracies of ecclesiastical, political, and economic institutions. The explanation based on this class is most fully developed in the writings of Hubert Guindon, Charles Taylor, and Kenneth McRoberts and Dale Posgate.[1] These authors begin with the seemingly indisputable fact that the traditional political institutions of Quebec society—particularly those involved in the administration of education and social services—had reached a crisis by 1960. The institutions simply no longer seemed able to meet the needs of the citizens of Quebec. They were seen as corrupt, moribund, and inefficient.

Partly from within these institutions, under the guidance of progressive clerics, and partly from without, where new institutions had arisen in labour, communications, and the co-operatives, there emerged, it is argued, a new middle class. It was more modern in its thinking and more progressive in its ideas than Quebec's traditional middle class of professionals and clerics. In the critical years from 1959 to 1965, this new class challenged successfully the traditional middle class for control of the provincial state and the social and educational bureaucracies. It mounted the challenge through the agency of a revitalized Parti libéral du Québec. The Parti libéral narrowly defeated the foundering Union nationale, the supposed agent of the traditional middle class, in the 1960 election. The new premier, Jean Lesage, had gathered an équipe de tonnerre which included the former Liberal leader, Georges-Émile Lapalme, the journalist René Lévesque, Paul Gérin-Lajoie, and, later, Pierre Laporte and Eric Kierans. This team carried out the 'administrative revolution' desired by the new middle class. It moved to create a competent civil service, an expanded educational system, a publicly controlled health care system, and a series of economic institutions to give the new class a toehold in Quebec's economy.

In so moving, the Parti libéral is seen as helping to redress a lag that had developed between Quebec's political development and its social and economic development. Economically and socially Quebec was an urban, industrial society; politically it was a nineteenth-century fiefdom. The arrival of the Liberals then, it is said, ended the tenure of Duplessis's Union nationale, which had been more and more holding the province back politically during the post-war period. In breaking this hold and giving rein to the new middle class, the Liberals ushered in what has been termed the 'Quiet Revolution.' The supporters of the new-middle-class hypothesis caution, however, that this was a revolution mainly in the realm of ideology, of the mind. It was a revolution marked by the final rejection of the vision of Quebec as a society with a rural vocation, as a unanimously Catholic, defiantly spiritual entity. It meant the exuberant espousal of a philosophy of épanouissement, that is, of growth, development, and openness to industrial society. Quebec was viewed as a plural society and as a society in a hurry to make up lost time. The provincial government was hailed as the moteur principal, the leader in the movement forward.

This ideological revolution, which was conceived by the new middle class and promoted by its agent, the Parti libéral, raised expectations that were to be dashed on the shoals of the economic and political reality of Quebec. The established corporations did not open their doors to the new middle class and did not provide a francophone milieu in which their employees could work. The federal government was not ready to hand over to this class the full range of fiscal and monetary powers it desired in order to reorient Quebec along a new path of economic development and it was not eager to have francophones in its own bureaucracy. The result, so the story goes, was the fracturing of the Parti libéral into two forces, one more technocratic, more radical and dedicated to political independence, the other more economically conservative and committed to a retooling of the federal system. The struggle henceforth was between these two fractions of the new middle class and their agents, the Parti québécois and the Parti libéral.

However persuasive this explanation might appear, it merits criticism on several grounds. First, the principal agent of change in this explanation is a social class. Social classes, it must be cautioned, become agents or are mobilized to become political actors only under special circumstances. There must first be a group of individuals who occupy relatively similar positions in a particular mode of production. In addition, these individuals must be in positions where they can become conscious of their similar position and perhaps similar plight. Second, then, this consciousness develops when these individuals are opposed as a group by another class. Classes are formed into cohesive actors on the political stage through struggles with other classes. For the new-middle-class hypothesis to be valid, then, that class would need to have found itself in these special circumstances. It would have to have been in a structural position that would enable it to become a class. It would also have to have been placed in a political situation where it was likely to be mobilized as a class. Yet during the critical period for this explanation, 1959 to 1965, it is very doubtful that these circumstances existed.

1/ If one examines closely Quebec's institutions at the end of the 1950s, one finds little evidence of individuals having positions in society that would form the structural base for a new middle class. There was no coterie of francophone white-collar workers at the middle levels of large private corporations. In the established education and social service bureaucracies, there was no structural unity that would tend to create the conditions for such a class. Educational institutions were controlled partly by the church and partly by the state.[2] Those under ecclesiastical control operated somewhat independently of each other, being organized along diocesan lines, and being controlled by various orders.[3] The church had a virtual monopoly on institutions in the social sphere, but here again the various institutions were organized separately for each diocese and were operated by a panoply of religious orders. In both educational and social organizations, the use of lay personnel was increasing rapidly, but the ranking administrative positions remained firmly in clerical hands even at this date. These latter positions would certainly have been part of the nucleus of any new middle class, but there is little evidence to suggest that the clerics involved were imbued with the ideology of épanouissement in sufficient members to have joined such a nucleus. The reaction to such modest reforms as were suggested by Frère Untel would suggest the contrary.[4]

The proponents of this hypothesis however would counter by arguing that a factor giving unity to the new middle class was its claim to power and status based on its monopoly of specialized, modern social science knowledge.[5] But where was this knowledge attained? The occupants of these bureaucracies had been educated under the traditional, classics-oriented education system in Quebec. The social sciences were hardly the important force in the universities (still controlled by the church) that they were to be a decade hence. The numbers of social science graduates during the 1950s were neither high nor growing.[6] The expansion that took place in the civil service in the 1950s drew in the main from those with twelve years of education or less.[7] Even in the education system, teachers had not been introduced to this modern social scientific knowledge. Quebec's standards for entry into the teaching profession required only a year of normal school beyond grade 11. Even then, in 1958, 48 per cent of the teachers in Quebec did not meet this minimum standard.[8] Normal schools themselves were in a deplorable state; the professors there earned less than teachers themselves, who were already poorly paid.

If one turns the spotlight on institutions outside these traditional bureaucracies, evidence of a structural base for a new middle class is more encouraging but hardly compelling. In the labour field, it was clear that some cadres in the Confédération des travailleurs catholiques du Canada (CTCC) had had a training in the social sciences.[9] Yet their involvement in the labour movement brought them closer to the working class than to the supposed new class. Further, their numbers were not large. The larger Fédération des travailleurs du Québec (FTQ) did not have cadres with a similar training. Most of its officials had worked up to leadership positions from the shop floor. There did seem to be a new breed of journalist in Quebec, particularly at Radio-Canada, but the numbers here are very small. Similarly one notes a shift to a more technical orientation in the Union catholique des cultivateurs (UCC) and the co-operatives. Still, farmers are not usually considered to be members of the new middle class. The co-operatives remained under the considerable conservative influence of the church. The latter institution still exercised significant influence over Quebec society in the late 1950s. For example, it took the somewhat renegade CTCC seven years to remove the word 'Catholic' from its name. The Corporation des instituteurs et institutrices catholiques, the teachers' union, actually became more confessional and corporatist in ideology as the decade progressed.[10]

To summarize, the existence, at a structural level, of a new middle class at the dawn of the Quiet Revolution is not as obvious as has been assumed. In some sense, it is more sensibly argued that the new middle class was a product of the reforms of the 1960s [other] than their instigator.[11] The provincial state, in rationalizing the education and social service systems and in founding a series of public corporations during the 1960s, may have created this class in its wake.

2/ Not only is the structural position of this class in doubt, but also its existence as a conscious political agent. I have argued that individuals tend to be mobilized as a class only in opposition to other classes. The new-middle-class thesis postulates that this new class was mobilized politically in order to struggle against a traditional middle class of clerics, farmers, doctors, and lawyers that held power under Duplessis. However, little evidence of such a struggle can be adduced. Guindon himself, writing in 1960, points out that the new class was working with traditional elites.[12] Similarly, the 1960 political stance of the Parti libéral, the supposed agent of the new middle class, was not one that invited a struggle with the traditional middle class. On the contrary, the party borrowed a page from Duplessis's Union nationale and presented the electorate a platform founded on the notion of political autonomy for Quebec.[13] François-Albert Angers, a spirited representative of the traditional middle class, described that platform as 'le meilleur programme autonomiste et nationaliste dans le sens le plus positif du mot depuis les jours du Bloc Populaire; probablement, le meilleur programme du genre présenté par un des deux partis traditionnels.'[a] [14] His words hardly sound like those of a member of a class that has just been ousted from power. Rather he actually speaks of victory. 'Dans ces conditions on peut considérer que l'option nationaliste vient d'emporter l'une de ses plus grandes, de ses plus significatives victoires depuis le début du siècle.'[b] [15] In short, not only is the structural basis of the new middle class questionable, but also the conflict that was supposed to have forced it into the political arena was little in evidence.

3/ The first two arguments, then, against the hypothesis of a new middle class are based on observations that suggest that the conditions usually necessary for the rise of such a class as a political force were not present in Quebec in the late 1950s. A third major weakness of the hypothesis is related to the very theoretical framework from which the concept of a new middle class emerged. This concept was not an inspiration that arose simply from the patient observation of Quebec society. Rather the central role given to this class followed logically from the theoretical framework and the concepts brought to the study of Quebec by the social scientists concerned. The theoretical framework in question had been fashioned to describe a process of political development and political modernization. It was gradually elaborated, starting in the 1950s, principally by American social scientists who wished to gain some understanding and to give some direction to the many movements of national liberation occurring in the Third World at the time.[16] Using the concepts of this framework, they evaluated these movements according to the degree to which they took their societies from a traditional status to a modern one. Whether the traditional society was characterized by using the pattern variables of the sociologist Talcott Parsons or by using the more elaborated concepts of the Comparative Politics group of the American Social Sciences Research Council, it was clear that the modern status envisaged was very much akin to that of a Western liberal democracy.

Usually, within these models the catalyst to development is a native elite that has been trained by the outgoing colonial power. This élite is therefore well-schooled in the principles of liberal democracy, is familiar with Western-style administrative procedures, and as a result is sufficiently self-confident and motivated to want to rule on its own. It seeks to engineer the independence of its people by mobilizing a mass population whose expectations already have been rising with increased exposure to Western culture.

---

[a] the best platform concerning autonomy and nationalism in the best sense of the word since the days of the Bloc Populaire; probably the best platform of this kind proposed by one of the two traditional parties.

[b] Under these conditions, we can assume that the nationalist option has just won one of its greatest and most important victories since the beginning of the century.

The new-middle-class hypothesis then was a logical outgrowth of the application of this framework to Quebec. Quebec was seen as a traditional society. American sociologists had already studied the French community in Quebec as an example of a 'folk culture' and hence considered it under the same light they had used to study peasant societies in Mexico and elsewhere.[17] The folk culture notions had influenced French-Canadian sociological thinking as well.[18] It was a short step to see the changes that began to manifest themselves at the end of 1950s as a movement to modernize a traditional society with a paternalistic and authoritarian political culture. The agent of these changes, the counterpart of the restless native élites of the Third World, was, of course, the new middle class, a class schooled in 'modern social science' and devoted to rationalized bureaucratic administration.

The successful application of this theoretical approach depends in part on whether Quebec should be treated as analogous to the emerging nations of the Third World. There are a number of reasons why such treatment is misleading. The people of Quebec have had a measure of self-rule for over a century that goes considerably beyond that which was possessed by the Third World colonies that achieved independence in the post-war period. It has enjoyed a parliamentary system of government that is as advanced in its development as any in the Western world. The Quebec economy, whatever its structural irregularities, shares in the advanced capitalist economy of North America in ways that most Third World countries can only dream of. The popular classes in Quebec consist in the main of an industrialized labour force that is considerably more skilled and more highly paid than the labour forces in the Third World nations in question. The rate of literacy, the degree of urbanization, the family structure, the place of religion, and any number of other indicators mark post-war Quebec as an integral part of the First and Second worlds and as no closer to the Third World than any other Western nation.

Hence an indication of how inappropriate the application of this framework is to Quebec is the treatment given by the analysts concerned to the period prior to the Liberal victory in 1960. The Quebec of the 1950s under the rule of Duplessis and the Union nationale is presented in many respects as a traditional society of the nineteenth century. The provincial state is described as committed to laissez-faire capitalism, as predisposed to avoid intervention in the economy at virtually any cost, and as unwilling to accept trade unionism. The conduct of politics is described variously as paternalistic, corrupt, authoritarian, and élitist. The education system with its clerics and its classical colleges is frowned upon as a throwback to the Ancien Régime in France. The society was considered to be largely dominated by a set of beliefs that stressed the virtues of the rural life, the advantages of the corporatism of the papal encyclicals, and the evils of the materialism of the American way of life. This tendency to view Quebec as 'traditional' and 'backward' is a logical outgrowth of the theoretical framework being used.

Such a description of Quebec in the period from 1945 to 1960 ignores many important events and changes that were taking place. Subsequent analysis in this book will show that the gap between the Quebec of Duplessis and the Quebec of Lesage and Johnson is much narrower than has been presumed. The education system, for example, was not completely church-controlled under Duplessis as is so often assumed. The provincial bureaucracy actually grew more in the 1950s than it did in the early 1960s. Jean-Louis Roy has pointed out that there was ongoing evaluation of many aspects of social policy with substantial reforms being considered and at times even implemented in the immediate post-war period.[19] He remarks on the important educational role and non-traditional character of such institutions as the CTCC, the Association professionel des industriels (API), the co-operative movement, and the universities, and one might add the Union catholique des cultivateurs (UCC) and the provincial Chambre de Commerce.[20]

It is also unsettling that this presentation of the Duplessis period as that of a grand noirceur coincided with the interpretation of history promoted by the Liberal government of Jean Lesage and such liberal intellectuals as Trudeau, Pelletier, and others involved in the Rassemblement in the 1950s.[21] Even more disconcerting, the concepts and rhetoric of national liberation often linked to theories of development were adopted freely by members of the Lesage government. The 1962 provincial election campaign, the campaign where the slogan 'Maîtres chez nous' was popularized, was fought using the language of liberation found in the Third World.[22] It is sometimes troubling when the language and thinking of social scientists are shared with the politicians of the day. The capacity of the social scientist to stand back, reflect, and if need be criticize is undercut. Furthermore, the probability increases that his or her work may come to be used by and to serve the existing authorities. In the study of Quebec, the sharing among politicians and social scientists of similar notions of development, modernization and liberation is indicative of the susceptibility of both to American concerns for development in the Third World and the intellectual debates these concerns spawned. The coincidence in perspective nonetheless is an additional factor that weakens the new-middle-class hypothesis as an explanation of events in post-war Quebec.

Hypothesis II: The 'bourgeoisie autochtone'   In recent years, a second hypothesis about change in post-war Quebec has been suggested that challenges the theory based on the new middle class. Dorval Brunelle has argued that the central problem that gave rise to the Quiet Revolution was not the rising expectations of a new middle class but economic conditions that threatened the existence of a mainly francophone employer class owning mainly small and medium-sized enterprises.[23] He documents the rising strength of American multinational corporations in Quebec's economy in the years following the

Second World War. He notes the tendency of these enterprises to penetrate further and further into the local economy of the French-speaking community. This penetration gradually eliminated many small firms and promised continuation of these processes in the years to come. The resulting concentration raised the question whether there would be a role and a place for the existing French-Canadian bourgeoisie. Brunelle writes that this question was critical because if a role and place were not found for this class, then the future of capitalist production in Quebec might itself become doubtful.

Whereas Duplessis had paid little attention to this class, the Lesage Liberals, in this view, took its concerns very much to heart. Shortly after their arrival in power, the Liberals created a body called the Conseil d'orientation économique du Québec. Such an organization had long been the dream of the French-Canadian bourgeoisie. In a short time span, the Council developed a series of proposals that were to mark the early years of the Quiet Revolution. It advanced the notion of mixed enterprises, state and private interests collaborating in major economic projects. Such major new economic agents of the 1960s based on this concept, the Société générale de financement, the Sidérurgie du Québec (Sidbec), and the Société québécoise d'exploration minière (Soquem), were all then recommended by the Council. Thus, Brunelle concludes, the ambiguous coalition of the state and a weakening, ethnically homogeneous fraction of the bourgeoisie produced a series of progressive changes (a revolution) within the capitalist system (hence quiet). He writes: 'Ce sera là le *projet* ... de la bourgeoisie canadienne-française, un projet ambigu s'il en est, puisqu'il amènera les représentants de cette bourgeoisie à être à la fois nationalistes et pro-américains, à la fois fédéralistes et autonomistes, à la fois pour l'empire qu'exerce l'enterprise privée mais aussi en faveur de la solution bureaucratique.'[c] [24]

According to Brunelle these new public enterprises and the staff increases they and other reforms generated in the provincial civil service created the new middle class. The desire for modernization and revitalization shown by the francophone business class helped spur the drive to educational reform. The new public educational system as well sowed the seeds of a new middle class. This class thus was the product of the Quiet Revolution and not its initiator, in this view.

These arguments by Brunelle form a serious challenge to the orthodox explanation of change in post-war Quebec. To a degree, in the chapters that follow in this book, they will be expanded upon and amplified. The role of the French-speaking businessman in the changes of the early 1960s has been overlooked in the existing studies. This failing is significant, I shall show, because this par-

---

[c] In the eyes of the French-Canadian bourgeoisie, this will be *the* project even though it is also ambiguous; it will cause the representatives of this bourgeoisie to be both nationalists and pro-American, federalists and for independence, for the control possessed by private enterprise and for bureaucratic solutions, all at the same time.

ticular class was active not only in directing the economic reforms of the Quiet Revolution but also in promoting important constitutional change, reforms in federal-provincial policy-making, and the idea of publicly controlled education.

Yet Brunelle's explanation is limited in scope. If one were to rely solely upon it, it would be difficult to account for the rise of the independence movement in the 1960s. What is clear is that the independence movement did not grow out of this class. The francophone business class in Quebec has been a consistent and staunch supporter of federalism. Its members from the beginning have seen independence as a threat to their access to the wider Canadian market and as a possible catalyst to economic deterioration within the province. In part, I shall argue, the independence movement has been a movement that arose in opposition to this class and its proposals. Brunelle does us the service of identifying the French-Canadian business class as being in the forefront of the Quiet Revolution. The issue that we are left with then is the consequences of the success of this class on the political plane.

Hypothesis III: Competition   A third hypothesis that has emerged quite recently appears to be opposed to both of the previous explanations. Like the theory based on the new middle class, this third hypothesis is global in scope. Gilles Bourque and Anne Legaré have proposed an explanation that focuses principally on what they call three 'fractions' of the bourgeois class.[25] 'Fraction' is a Marxist term that may be interpreted to mean a subdivision or a branch of a particular class. Bourque and Legaré suggest three bourgeois fractions are essential for understanding the political development of Quebec since the Great Depression. The first fraction is the non-monopoly, Quebec-based bourgeoisie.[26] Its members are owners of small enterprises that are highly competitive with each other and that are oriented primarily to the regional Quebec market. They have their roots in the main in the francophone community. The second fraction is the monopolistic Canadian bourgeoisie. Its members own or manage large corporations that operate mainly in oligopolistic markets that are Canada-wide in scope. It contains disproportionately many English-speaking Canadians. The third fraction is a monopoly, imperialist bourgeoisie. Its members are owners or managers of large transnational corporations that also operate under oligopoly conditions but on a global rather than a national basis. Its membership is said to be disproportionately high in Americans.

Bourque and Legaré describe the political history of Quebec by centering their analysis on the relations among these three fractions and their respective influence on the provincial government. They write that during the years 1936-60, the tenure of Duplessis's Union nationale (except for a Liberal interlude during the war), the provincial government was dominated by a power bloc comprising the non-monopoly, Quebec-based fraction and the imperialist fraction. The Union nationale, as a party, promoted and defended the interests of small francophone entrepreneurs by ensuring that they were given the business of providing the infrastructure needed by the imperialist fraction that was sweeping Quebec in search of natural resources. For example, local entrepreneurs were given the task of building the roads that were needed by the large foreign corporations to get access to resources. The Quebec-based capitalists were able to maintain this favoured position because the Union nationale had managed to add the paysans, the small Quebec farmers, as a supporting class. This coalition of social forces with their substantial financial resources assured the party electoral dominance. In promoting the interests of the indigenous small entrepreneurs, the party thus relegated the Canada-based bourgeois fraction to a position of lesser influence.

By 1960, however, the argument continues, the expansion of commercial farming had led to a substantial decline in the numbers of paysans and with it the electoral base of the Union nationale began to crumble. The ascension to power of the Liberals with their national power base turned the tables by replacing the Quebec-based fraction in the power bloc by the Canada-based fraction. The Quiet Revolution, in this view, is a series of reforms designed to bring Quebec's educational and social services in line with those available elsewhere in Canada to facilitate the expansion of English-Canadian capital in Quebec. Quebec is not seen as becoming more autonomous in this period as is usually assumed but as becoming more integrated into Canadian society as a whole. The Canada-based fraction achieved a dominant position electorally by enlisting the support of the working class. The expansion of the Canada-based fraction was seen to promise more jobs and more security for industrial workers. The Liberals promised and implemented reforms in labour relations that gave a certain security and legitimacy to organized labour. In doing so, they distinguished themselves from the Union nationale, which had confronted the labour movement at every turn.

According to Bourque and Legaré, and contrary to Brunelle then, the Quebec-based fraction of the bourgeoisie went into a period of relative decline with the onset of the Quiet Revolution. Similarly, the party that had defended its interests, the Union nationale, also began its descent into eventual oblivion. In the latter part of the 1960s, however, elements from this fraction concerned about its demise helped forge a new political vehicle, the Parti québecois. According to these authors, the Parti québecois grew out of two movements supported by the petite bourgeoisie, the Rassemblement pour l'indépendance nationale (RIN) and the Regroupement national, and one supported by the Quebec-based capitalist class, the Mouvement Souveraineté Association (MSA). The new party was to emerge, however, as being primarily dedicated to the interests of the Quebec-based capitalist class. Using a nationalist ideology that highlighted the oppression of the French by the English, the Parti québecois added sufficient voters from the working class to its petty bourgeois support to forge an electoral coalition that was to carry it to power in 1976. Accordingly, these authors see strong parallels between the Union nationale of Duplessis and the Parti québecois of Lévesque and Parizeau. Both parties promote the interests of the Quebec-based bourgeoisie at the expense of the Canada-based bourgeoisie; both are subservient to the imperialist fraction.

This latter explanation diverges from the new-middle-class hypothesis on several key points. The Quiet Revolution was not ushered in by a new middle class but by the establishment of a dominant position on the part of a Canada-based monopoly bourgeoisie. Power was transferred in 1960 not from a traditional middle class to a new middle class, but from a Quebec-based non-monopoly bourgeoisie to this large Canada-based bourgeoisie. The independence movement was the inspiration not of a new middle class but of a coalition between the middle classes and the Quebec-based bourgeoisie. Similarly, this explanation appears to contradict that put forth by Brunelle, who argues that 1960 marked the ascension of the regional capitalist class and not its demise. In this study, it will be argued that Bourque and Legaré point to an important dimension of the Quiet Revolution, its attempt to integrate Quebec more fully into North American capitalism. However, it shall be argued also that their interpretation of the class forces behind this attempt is too simplistic and in the end inadequate.

The Missing Dimension   One might be tempted to play down the differences among the explanations just described by casting them as ideological. The new-middle-class hypothesis grew out of a perspective that held Western rationalized, liberal democracy up as the standard of progress. Bourque and Legaré, in contrast, begin with a Marxist problematic that sees liberal democracy as a political form fashioned to realize the interests of the capitalist class. These fundamental differences in perspective and assumptions do affect how the world is viewed and which phenomena are emphasized. However, the differences here are not just in values. Brunelle also works within the Marxist framework, and his conclusions seem to be at odds with those of Bourque and Legaré. Further, Bourque and Legaré were well aware of the new-middle-class hypothesis and examined it using their categories and found it empirically wanting. The proponents of the theory of the new middle class were certainly well aware of what they would call the English-Canadian business élite in Quebec, but they did not see this élite as a key factor in accounting for the Quiet Revolution.

In short, it will be my view that each of these explanations points to important lacunae in the other, and aspects of each are complementary to the other. One of the tasks of this book will be to show the nature of this interdependence. To do so, however, it will be necessary to add a second dimension to the analysis found in each of these three competing explanations, that of ideology. All of them take as their starting point a social class. They assume that this social class exists and is reasonably conscious of its interests as a class. I prefer to begin more ambiguously and to treat the existence of classes as an empirical question. Social classes, in the sense of conscious social actors, are formed through conflict and mobilization that take place not only in the economy but also in the political arena and the realm of ideas. The full analysis of a society that takes social class as a central starting point must leave open the possibility that classes do not exist but may be formed in the context of struggle. Each of the three explanations examined above has explored the dimension of struggle in the economy and in the political sphere. None has paid enough attention to the world of ideas and of ideologies and how these help form social classes. This gap is quite surprising, because most social scientists agree that many of the most critical changes in post-war Quebec were changes in ideology, in views of the world. The examination of the realm of ideology will be central to understanding fully the rise of the independence movement.

The Ideological Dimension

During the Duplessis years, a series of important developments altered the ideology of opinion-makers in French-speaking society. In several institutions of Quebec's francophone community that had been established relatively recently and were not under complete ecclesiastical control, the individuals involved embarked upon an interesting process of self-reflection. I speak here first of the various Catholic Action organizations such as the Jeunesse étudiante catholique (JEC), the Ligue ouvrière catholique (LOC), and the Jeunesse ouvrière catholique (JOC). These organizations, which had first developed in Europe as part of the church's response to industrialization and which were supported by Pius XI in the encyclical *Quadragesimo Anno* published in 1931, brought an important change to the Catholic church in Quebec. They were the first institutions concerned with the temporal social problems of the lay Christian to be led by laymen. The clergy played only an advisory role. I refer also to the Confédération des travailleurs catholiques du Canada (CTCC) under the leadership of Gérard Picard, who became its president in 1946, and Jean Marchand, who became its general secretary in 1947, and to the co-operative movement, which was strongly influenced by Père Georges-Henri Lévesque, founder of the Social Sciences faculty at Université Laval. Another more informal organization was the group of literati who formed around the *Refus global* manifesto published in 1948. Working in these milieux, individuals were better able to view the church from an external perspective. They came to realize that a monolithic ideology dominated the thinking and orientation of the French-speaking community's economic, political, social, and religious institutions. Such a realization allowed them to see the dominant ideology in relation to others. Once this process of reflection was begun new vistas of thought and new perspectives on society began to emerge. A reading of journals in Quebec in the late 1940s and the 1950s shows this prospect generated immense excitement in many intellectual circles.

In most studies of Quebec during this period, this shift in consciousness is well-documented. The later rise to prominence of Pierre Trudeau, Jean Marchand, and Gérard Pelletier has led social scientists to pore back over the pages of *Cité libre,* the struggles of the CTCC, and the movement against Duplessis.[27] What is less often remarked upon, however, is that these changes occurred simultaneously with some intense reflection upon the traditional values and culture of French Canadians.

Throughout his tenure as premier, Duplessis engaged in a series of battles with the federal government in order to defend the autonomy of Quebec. In one of the more important of these battles, as part of his political game, he commissioned a study into Quebec's constitutional problems. The report of the fabled Tremblay Commission was a remarkable intellectual achievement. Its four volumes are an exemplar of powerful prose, cogency, and brilliant logic.[28] It was written by some of the most capable intellectuals of the traditional élites of the French-speaking community. These commissioners defined explicitly what in their view was unique and valuable in the culture of French-speaking society in Quebec. In particular, they singled out the community's dedication to spiritual values, its unique classical education system, its private, church-controlled and -inspired social welfare institutions, and its rural, agricultural heritage. They were committed to preserving these institutions and practices which they saw to be the product of centuries of development. They sketched out a political program complete with detailed political demands that in their view had to be followed if this unique culture were to survive.

That these particular commissioners should follow such a course is not surprising, and knowledge of it is hardly new to the scholarly community. Nevertheless, what is not remarked upon often is that the political program of the Tremblay Commission became the basis, the cornerstone, of political strategy by the government of Quebec throughout the 1960s and into the 1970s. It may be argued that the various movements for independence and for renewed federalism that have emerged since are all variations on the Tremblay theme.

This conclusion is important because the dynamic of social change outside the political arena during the 1960s was not in a direction that would have been welcomed by the Tremblay Commission. The questioning of the dominant ideology in the French-speaking society and with it the growing criticism of the extensive penetration of the church into the social fabric of the community that I mentioned above led to the promotion of an idea that was heresy to the commission, that of pluralism. Increasingly intellectuals and opinion leaders argued that the French-speaking community was not homogeneous, that it supported a variety of ideologies, and that its institutions should be more adapted to this situation. As consciousness of division within the community increased, there was a tendency to examine more closely institutions in English Canada and the United States as possible models for use in a plural society.

What is essential to note here is that the very social and educational structures and the very penetration of the church into the community's life that were being scrutinized with a critical eye had been defined by the Tremblay Commission as the hallmarks, the foundations, of the unique culture of Quebec's French-speaking society. Furthermore, these structures had been championed because they represented a shield against the North American society that now was being examined with interest. It was on the assumption that these structures needed to be protected and preserved that the Tremblay commissioners had constructed their political program.

Throughout the 1960s and 1970s, there was an interesting contradiction between the political reforms being implemented and the program or strategy being used for their implementation. The political program elaborated with painstaking care by the Tremblay commission was being used to alter fundamentally the very institutions the program had been designed to protect. The commission was correct in defining a strategy designed to affect fundamentally traditional institutions but in doing so it also opened the possibility that its strategy could be used to affect these institutions in ways it never intended. The rapid attack on traditional institutions that came at this time led directly to the growth of the independence movement when largely foreign borrowings were put in their place.

The independence movement has arisen because the political changes in the early 1960s undermined several basic institutions and practices of traditional French-Canadian civilization. The institutions and practices that replaced the old did not renew French-Canadian civilization but contributed to its further demise. Perhaps no factor illustrates this process better than the place of language in political struggles and ideological debate. By the late 1960s, with the 'reform' of educational and social welfare institutions and the withdrawal of the church into more strictly spiritual realms, the most evident distinguishing characteristic of the French-speaking community became its language. The struggle to preserve a distinctive culture became in many instances a struggle to preserve the use of French. Whereas language had earlier been one of several foundations of French-Canadian civilization, by the late 1960s it often appeared to be the only visible foundation left.

I will show, that the policies on language pursued by governments beginning in the mid-1960s had the effect of undermining the French language as a cultural foundation. The policies developed have transformed French from an informal language not used in several key spheres of economic life into a standard language helping to integrate the French-Canadian community into the dominant culture of North America. French, which had been one of several barriers restricting contact between les Canadiens français and les autres has become the policy instrument for breaking barriers among the several cultural communities in Quebec. The struggle for autonomy outlined by the Tremblay

Commission had been a struggle to preserve the culture of a single community. The struggle for autonomy in the 1970s was a struggle to integrate several cultures through the use of a common language, French. If language is being increasingly lost as a tool for cultural preservation, should we be surprised to find individuals saying a break has to be made, new powers must be garnered, a society has to be rethought if it is to continue at all?

Aim of This Study

This study will outline and weave together this series of cultural and ideological changes with the development of social classes. I have only indicated the blueprint for the analysis to follow. In giving this emphasis to the ideological dimension, I am indicating that it has a significant autonomy from the mode of economic production and the organization of social classes. The degree of autonomy will vary over the period being studied. What will become clear is that after the period of the supposed Quiet Revolution, that is after 1965, social classes increasingly become the dominant actors on the political stage. The political confrontation and disputes in the period leading up to 1965 have the effect of creating social classes and hence of fostering class struggle. After 1965, the discussion of cultural and ideological change can have meaning only if it focuses upon social classes.

This study will demonstrate that Quebec society has redefined itself in fundamental ways in the post-war period. In embarking upon this process of reflection and redefinition, the members of this society have become increasingly divided. They have divided along class lines, with the capitalist class on one side, the working class on the other, and the various sections of the petty bourgeoisie shifting constantly between the two. They have also divided along lines of language and of ethnicity. It is a matter not simply of the English versus the French, but also of tensions among vocal smaller groups such as the Jewish, Italian, Greek, Inuit, Cree, and Haitian communities. The members of the French-speaking community themselves are divided along religious lines. The movement toward secularization and toward a plural Quebec society is strongly opposed by many who see Catholicism as still an integral part of any French community in Quebec and by others who wish to use Catholicism to preserve some mythic ideal of a unique people living in Quebec.

The movement toward political independence is a phenomenon of too much complexity to be treated as the vehicle of a particular class pursuing its own particular interests. The movement is a coalition of various classes and groups who agree that the first step to a better future society is the achievement of political sovereignty. They agree on this first step for different reasons. In the interests of the political success of the movement, these differences are quite deliberately played down. The means have gradually been elevated to the status of an end in itself. Keeping the coalition together has been a remarkable political achievement in the face of these differences. The fact that the coalition has not broken up is an indicator of the depth of the grievances of the various partners. They strongly desire political independence. A promising future is not possible without it. The ultimate contribution of this study then will be to move from a discussion of the increasing divisions within Quebec society to provide some suggestions why many of these divisions have been overcome in a single political movement advocating radical change. The understanding of both these divisions and this unity is necessary before a satisfactory understanding of the independence movement can be attained.

Notes

1. See Hubert Guindon 'The Social Evolution of Quebec Reconsidered' *Canadian Journal of Economics and Political Science* XXVI (November 1960) 553-61; 'Social Unrest, Social Class and Quebec's Bureaucratic Revolution' *Queen's Quarterly* LXXI (summer 1964) 150-62; 'Two Cultures: An Essay on Nationalism, Class and Ethnic Tensions' in R. Leach ed *Contemporary Canada* (Durham, NC, 1967); Charles Taylor 'Nationalism and the Political Intelligentsia: A Case Study' *Queen's Quarterly* LXXII (spring 1965) 150-68; Kenneth McRoberts and Dale Posgate *Quebec: Social Change and Political Crisis* (Toronto 1976). For a recent analysis of events based on this hypothesis by French-Canadian political scientists, see G. Bergeron and R. Pelletier ed *Le Québec en devenir* (Montreal 1980).

2. The provincial government administered a series of vocational schools and technical colleges. These were attached to different government departments, such as Agriculture, Lands and Forests, Mines, and the Provincial Secretary.

3. Thus the various classical colleges were not integrated systematically into any network. It was not until 1953 that the Fédération des collèges classiques was formed to represent their interests. It was set up to defend the collèges in the face of increasing criticism in the post-war period and to put more pressure on the provincial government to provide them with adequate grants. Duplessis had, to a certain degree, administered grants to individual collèges on a patronage basis.

4. Frère Untel was the pseudonym used by a teaching brother, Jean-Paul Desbiens, who wrote a scathing critique of the church's role in education in Quebec. The critique began with a letter to *Le Devoir* in 1959. André Laurendeau, then editor of the paper, invited Untel to elaborate on his letter. The series of criticisms was then published in a book entitled *Les Insolences du Frère Untel* (Montreal 1960). The book became a best seller, with over one hundred thousand copies being sold. The book was not greeted warmly by the church hierarchy or by Untel's superiors. He was sent on a study trip to Europe shortly thereafter.

5. McRoberts and Posgate *Quebec* 102

6. Enrolment in the social sciences in francophone universities remained between 400 and 500 students throughout the 1950s. In 1958-9, 423 students were enrolled.

After that year, the numbers began to increase steadily. By 1964, the figure had almost tripled, to 1,293; Canada, DBS, *Survey of Higher Education* Catalogues 81-402, 81-518, 81-211.

7. See Gérard Lapointe *Essais sur la fonction publique québécoise,* Documents of the Royal Commission on Bilingualism and Biculturalism, No. 12 (Ottawa 1970).

8. Jean-Louis Roy *La Marche des Québécois: le temps des ruptures 1945-1960* (Montreal 1976) 256

9. For example, Jean Marchand, secretary general of the CTCC during the 1950s and president 1961-5, and Marcel Pépin, Marchand's successor, were both educated at the Faculty of Social Sciences at Université Laval.

10. Roy *La Marche* 325

11. This is a point made by Dorval Brunelle. See his book *La Désillusion tranquille* (Montreal 1978) 79-80.

12. Guindon 'The Social Evolution'

13. See Jean-Louis Roy *Les Programmes électoraux du Quebec* II (Montreal 1971) 378-88.

14. François-Albert Angers 'Éditorial' *L'Action nationale* L no 1 (1960) 9-10

15. *Ibid*

16. This approach is most fully developed in a series of studies sponsored by the Comparative Politics Committee of the Social Science Research Council in the United States. Prominent contributors in this series were Leonard Binder, James S. Coleman, Joseph LaPalombara, Lucien Pye, Dankwart Rustow, Sidney Verba, Robert E. Ward, and Myron Weiner. Gabriel Almond was an important early inspiration to this group. The series was published by Princeton University Press.

17. See for example the studies by Horace Miner, *St.-Denis, A French Canadian Parish* (Chicago 1939), and Everett Hughes, *French Canada in Transition* (Chicago 1945).

18. These influences are particularly evident in the earlier works of Marcel Rioux and to a lesser extent those of Jean-Charles Falardeau. The use of the concept of a folk society was the subject of an academic debate in Quebec in the 1950s, with the chief protagonists being Marcel Rioux and Philippe Garigue, then dean of the Faculty of Social Sciences at the Université de Montréal. For a flavour of this debate, see Marcel Rioux, 'Remarques sur les valeurs et les attitudes des adolescents d'une communauté agricole du Québec' *Contributions à l'étude des sciences de l'homme* no 3 (1956) 133-143; 'Kinship Recognition and Urbanization in French Canada' in Rioux and Y. Martin ed. *French Canadian Society* (Toronto 1964); 'Remarks on the Socio-Cultural Development of French Canada' in ibid.; Philippe Garigue 'Change and Continuity in French Canada' in ibid.; 'Mythes et réalités dans l'étude du Canada français' *Contributions à l'étude des sciences de l'homme* no 3 (1956) 123-32.

19. Roy *La marche* part I

20. For a useful examination of the Chambre de Commerce de la Province de Québec, see Monique Odstricil 'La Chambre de Commerce de la Province de Québec, 1935-1970: Une étude d'un groupe de pression,' MA thesis, Carleton University, 1974.

21 The Rassemblement was a group founded in 1956 with the object of educating the people of Quebec about democracy. It sought to be above party politics, although its major goal was the end of the rule of Duplessis. Trudeau and Marchand were prominent figures in the group.

22. For example, the following quotation is drawn from the 1962 platform of the PLQ: 'Le peuple du Québec a confiance, comme ont confiance *toutes* les nations jeunes qui, un jour, ont résolu de s'affirmer ... Pour la première fois dans son histoire, le peuple du Québec peut devenir maître chez lui! L'époque du colonialisme économique est révolue. Nous marchons vers la libération! Maintenant ou jamais! MAÎTRES CHEZ NOUS!!!'

23. This hypothesis is developed in Brunelle *La Désillusion tranquille.*

24. *Ibid* 102

25. Gilles Bourque and Anne Legaré *Le Québec: La question nationale* (Paris 1979)

26. This class in terms of its definition is very similar to the entity that is at the centre of Brunelle's analysis.

27. Trudeau and Pelletier founded *Cité libre* in 1950 and in the early years of the journal wrote several articles critical of the church. Marchand, at this time, was general secretary of the CTCC and Pelletier, editor of the newspaper *Le Travail,* published weekly by the CTCC. Trudeau served some time as a researcher for another labour organization, the Fédération des unions industrielles du Québec, a fact that is less well known.

28. Quebec, Royal Commission of Inquiry on Constitutional Problems *Report* (Quebec 1956). The commission was headed by Judge Thomas Tremblay.

CHAPTER
13 E. HERBERT NORMAN, CANADA AND THE COLD WAR

On April 4, 1957, the Canadian ambassador to Egypt, E. Herbert Norman, climbed to the roof of a nine-storey Cairo apartment building, carefully removed his glasses, watch, and jacket, and jumped to his death on the street below. Norman's suicide sent shock waves throughout Canada and sparked a multi-layered controversy that continues to this day. At one level the controversy bears on Norman himself, on his guilt or innocence with respect to the charges of being a Communist spy in the service of a foreign power, presumably the Soviet Union. More generally, the incident raises questions about the impact of the "Red Scare" on Canada in the late 1940s and early 1950s, about the Cold War mentality that it spawned, and about the Canadian-American relationship during that era.

The immediate circumstances surrounding the Norman suicide are relatively well known. Less than a month before, in March 1957, Norman's name had surfaced in the investigations of the U.S. Senate Subcommittee on Internal Security, dedicated to ferreting out "Red" subversives in high governmental places in the United States and elsewhere. The charges that Norman was a Communist and a threat to Western security were not new ones. Indeed, he had previously undergone two internal security checks by the RCMP, first in October 1950, and again in January 1952. The latter, in fact, had been prompted by accusations made by another witness before that same U.S. Subcommittee on Internal Security. According to notes which Norman left at the time of his death, he was not prepared to go through yet another round of interrogations which were sure to follow the latest allegations. Suicide seemed the only way out.

While what immediately precipitated the Norman suicide may be reasonably clear, less certain (and heatedly debated) are his ultimate motives in choosing this drastic course of action. Was Norman really a Communist spy who feared what another, more intense investigation would reveal? Was he even perhaps the "Fifth Man" so long sought by British Intelligence? Or, was he an innocent Canadian victim of the McCarthyite witchhunts of the 1950s, hounded to death by American innuendo and false accusations? The readings presented here take very different positions on these questions, and rely upon very different kinds of evidence. Indeed, an important aspect of the modern phase of the Norman controversy revolves around the quality of scholarship on the subject. In particular, the two major protagonists, Roger Bowen and James Barros, have been accused of faulty, even misleading, craftsmanship. With respect to all readings on this topic, students should examine carefully the general interpretations and the detailed evidence upon which they are based.

Following in an older tradition of writers such as Charles Taylor, Roger Bowen defends Norman, arguing that his was in reality "murder by slander." In *No Sense of Evil Espionage: The Case Of Herbert Norman*, Chapter 9 of which is reproduced here, James Barros takes the opposite tack, maintaining that there is sound evidence to conclude that Norman's admitted affiliation with the Communist Party had extended well beyond his days as a student at Cambridge University in the mid-1930s, and that that affiliation was much more than simply benign intellectual curiosity. The most recent pronouncement on the subject is that of J.L.Granatstein and David Stafford in their book, *Spy Wars*. Granatstein and Stafford are neither so convinced of Norman's guilt as Barros, nor of his innocence as Bowen, characterizing him as a "casualty of the cold war."

Suggestions for Further Reading

Barros, James, *No Sense of Evil Espionage: The Case of Herbert Norman*. Toronto: Deneau, 1986.

Bothwell, Robert, and J.L. Granatstein, "Introduction," *The Gouzenko Transcripts*. Ottawa: Deneau, 1982.

Bowen, Roger W., *Innocence Is Not Enough The Life and Death of Herbert Norman*. Armonk, New York: M.E. Sharpe Inc., 1986.

Bowen, Roger W. (ed.), *E.H.Norman: His Life and Scholarship*. Toronto: University of Toronto Press, 1984.

Cuff, R.D., and J.L.Granatstein, "Looking Back At The Cold War," in *Ties That Bind* (2nd ed.). Toronto: Samuel Stevens Hakkert and Co., 1977.

English, John, *Shadow of Heaven: The Life of Lester Pearson, Vol.I: 1897-1948*. Toronto: Lester & Orpen, Dennys, 1989.

Granatstein, J.L. and David Stafford, *Spy Wars*. Toronto: Key Porter Books Ltd., 1990.

Smith, Denis, *Diplomacy of Fear: Canada and the Cold War 1941-1948*. Toronto, University of Toronto Press, 1988.

Taylor, Charles, "Herbert Norman," in *Six Journeys: A Canadian Pattern*. Toronto: Anansi, 1977.

COLD WAR, MCCARTHYISM, AND MURDER BY SLANDER: E.H. NORMAN'S DEATH IN PERSPECTIVE

Roger W. Bowen

Probably no event in recent years involving Canadian-United States relations aroused such a wave of indignation and resentment in Canada as the suicide on April 4 in Cairo of Canadian Ambassador E. Herbert Norman. The general belief was that charges of communism against Mr. Norman, which were revived by the Subcommittee of the United States Internal Security Committee, were directly or indirectly responsible for his death. Canadians were indignant because the charges were regarded as false, as well as because the tactics employed by the Subcommittee were considered reprehensible and unwarranted interference in Canadian affairs.[1] So reads a 'confidential' dispatch sent to the State Department by the American ambassador to Canada two weeks after Norman's fatal leap from a nine-story Cairo apartment building in April 1957. Concerned exclusively with the 'Canadian Reactions to the Suicide of Ambassador E. Herbert Norman,' this dispatch catalogued the plethora of charges which Canadian newspapers levelled against the American government, ranging from 'guilt by association' and 'character assassination' to 'trial by smear.' Extensively quoted was a Toronto *Globe and Mail* article which claimed that 'the smear of Norman was just one more example of a long series of insults and injuries [inflicted] by the Americans' on Canada.[2] The highly emotive cries of 'witch-hunt' and 'murder by slander' that issued forth even from the halls of Parliament were similarly recorded in the dispatch to State. Yet the Americans fully understand that while the moral outrage expressed by press and public was no doubt genuine, it could not be sustained, particularly as the moral issue involved was being transmogrified into a political one.[3]

    During the first week after Norman's death, Secretary of State for External Affairs Lester 'Mike' Pearson said nothing to indicate that the charges of communism levelled against Norman by the American Senate subcommittee might be grounded in historical fact, but instead remained silent as press reports recalled Pearson's 1951 defense of Norman when the same subcommittee had

---

From Roger W. Bowen (ed.), *E.H. Norman: His Life and Scholarship* (Toronto: University of Toronto Press, 1984), 46-71. Reprinted by permission of the University of Toronto Press.

first alleged Norman's previous association with the Communist party. Pearson had then, on 9 August 1951, reported that the 'security authorities of the Government' had given Norman 'a clean bill of health' and personally praised Norman for being 'a trusted and valuable official of the department.'[4] Seen in this light in 1957 after Norman's death, the expressions of moral outrage by the press seem altogether reasonable. Equally reasonable, and much applauded by the Canadian press, was Pearson's 10 April official note of protest to the American government that threatened to cease providing security information on Canadians unless the American executive branch could guarantee that future congressional investigatory bodies would be denied unrestricted access. But two days later, and following repeated reaffirmations by the Senate that its information on Norman was correct, the man who could hardly wait to be prime minister, John Diefenbaker, turned the 'Norman affair' into a political football in this election year.[5]

Diefenbaker asked Pearson in Parliament whether the American allegations were 'untrue, unjustified, and had no basis in fact.' Pearson finally came clean on 12 April, replying: 'To say there was no truth in statements about Mr. Norman's past associations would have deceived the country.' Pearson was then pummelled by the press. A typical response to his admission was a 15 April editorial in the Montreal *Gazette* which accused him of having exercised bad judgment in 1951 by giving the public a 'misleading impression' about Norman's involvement in the Communist party. Pearson tried defending himself in an article in the same newspaper two days later. Referring to the 1950-51 RCMP investigation of Norman, Pearson said, 'I concluded that he had had, as a student, ideological beliefs which were close to some brand of Communism. I also concluded, 'Pearson went on, 'that he regretted these earlier associations and beliefs and had voluntarily abandoned them by the time he entered the Canadian Foreign Service.'[6]

Yet despite his attempts to offer a defence of his position, Pearson's credibility had been damaged. Mr Low, leader of the Social Credit party, summed up Opposition sentiment, and perhaps public sentiment as well, when he said to Mr. Pearson, 'The Minister is letting us know something that he has withheld ever since 1951.'[7] A 'confidential' American dispatch from Ottawa to Washington at this time further explains the effect of Pearson's truth-telling: 'The opposition position on the Norman case has undergone a fundamental change in the last few days. From a position of supporting the Government in its defense of Mr. Norman and in its protests to the United States, it has now accused the government of using the protests for political purposes and of withholding information on the case.'[8] In the more personal terms of how these disclosures affected the way Norman would be remembered by the Canadian public afterwards, the image of Norman as martyr for Canadian nationalism was replaced by Norman the communist.

A secondary but by no means less important consequence of the politicization of Norman's death was the impact it had on Canada's foreign policy. As James Eayrs suggests, some of Canada's more prominent Anglophiles began to call into question the Liberal government's policy under Pearson of volunteering Canadian military forces for peacekeeping purposes in the Middle East.[9] Norman after all had been Canada's ambassador to Egypt until his death. Now critics could point to a one-time communist negotiating with a suspected pro-Russian Egyptian President (Nasser) towards the undoing of Mother England's noble attempt to prevent the Suez Canal from being nationalized. Moreover, now that Pearson's credibility had been damaged by the Norman affair, evidence suggesting that Pearson had also seemed to be all too sympathetic towards Egyptian nationalism (and, conversely, prejudiced against Israel) took on a new light, especially as Pearson himself was being attacked by McCarthyite innuendo. Arthur Blakney reported in the *Gazette* that 'there have been veiled suggestions that the Subcommittee [on Internal Security] could—if it were bent on causing trouble—release secret testimony by ex-communist Elizabeth Bentley tagging Mr. Pearson as a man who was far too close to the inside of wartime communist espionage rings.' The same report also asserted that Pearson could have been 'a source of information to communist espionage rings during the war.'[10] State Department records from this period show that the Americans took these allegations seriously. That the allegations against Pearson, as well as against Robert Bryce for that matter, were not made public by the Senate subcommittee can likely be attributed to pressure placed on the Senate by the State Department, which wished to avoid another Norman affair.[11]

In this sense, the reputations of Pearson and Bryce were not assaulted by the Americans *because of* Norman's death, or rather because of the politicization of Norman's death by both the Americans and the Canadians. But because Norman's death was so politicized, his life was in the process stripped of all meaning. For with Pearson's admission that Norman had once been 'some brand' of communist, the McCarthyites, who had tried him for his past associations, seemed vindicated and the public's memory of Norman formed unidimensionally around the ideological imprint of 'communist.' Only recently have North Americans started to rethink Norman's death in terms of his life and scholarship. Initiated first by a scholarly study of Norman's Japan-related writings by the American 'New Left' scholar John Dower and then a sensitive but excessively psychological treatment by Canadian journalist Charles Taylor,[12] Canadians seem more prepared today to consider Norman's life in the complex terms it deserves. Yet just as political events in 1957 seemed to conspire to obfuscate the meaning of his life and death, so too does the rise of a new 'red scare' threaten once again to distort the real meaning of the Norman tragedy.

Over the past several years, it seems, every reported espionage case in North America or Britain invariably refers to Norman. Most recently, Norman's name re-emerged in the context of the Hambleton case which 'proved,' says the popular weekly magazine *Maclean's,* 'that Canada is enmeshed in the international espionage game.'[13] Similarly, when in March 1980 Sir Roger Hollis, chief of British counter-espionage from 1956 to 1965, was accused of having been a 'mole' for the Soviets, Norman was again mentioned by the Canadian press. So too in 1979 was he mentioned in the context of the discovery that Anthony Blunt might have been the 'fourth man' in a Soviet spy ring consisting of Guy Burgess, Donald Maclean, and Kim Philby, all of whom were Norman's contemporaries in Cambridge in the 1930s. And for those swept away by what *Maclean's* calls Canada's 'mood of paranoia,'[14] the publication of Chapman Pinscher's *Their Trade Is Treachery* in 1981 put to rest any lingering doubts about Norman. Therein Pinscher states unequivocally that Norman, along with John Watkins, Canada's ambassador to the Soviet Union between 1954 and 1956, served as a spy for the Soviets.

Old questions have therefore been asked with renewed interest in recent years: Was Norman the long-sought 'fifth man' in a Soviet spy ring? Was he simply a vanquished traitor rather than a victimized martyr? Was he accurately labelled by the Senate subcommittee and just poorly protected by Pearson? Or rather, from an entirely different perspective—one that is supportive of Pearson's 1951 judgment—are not these accusatory questions, offered as they are during a period of heightened political conservatism and fear of communism, simply old grist for neo-McCarthyite mills?

The latter is a rhetorical question and the abbreviated account of Norman's adult life which follows is an attempt to substantiate the claim of Norman's 'innocence.' I emphasize 'innocence' now so there will be no misunderstanding. For some people, belief in Marxism will always remain a 'crime,' albeit of a lesser order than membership in the Communist party. Norman was 'guilty' of both prior to joining External Affairs in 1939, and probably for a good while after that time he still subscribed to a Marxist-humanist vision of historical change. Let it also be mentioned now that after surveying over eight hundred pages of FBI documents, over a hundred pages of State Department material, hundreds of pages of External Affairs files, and all the material held by U.S. Army Intelligence and U.S. Navy Intelligence, I can quite confidently assert that there is not one shred of evidence to suggest that Norman ever served the Soviets or any other foreign country as a spy. Instead, as I shall try to show, this heretofore classified material reveals only that a great many Americans suspected disloyalty on Norman's part because of the people with whom he associated and the ideas he professed. Of course, to believe that any American had the right to attribute 'disloyalty' to any individual Canadian suggests a presumptuousness and arrogance that some Canadians, especially Lester Pearson, saw at that time and decried as a violation of Canada's sovereign rights. As much as anything, the terrible lesson of Norman's death is that he was prosecuted in America by Americans who were ideologically trapped by Cold War, McCarthyite fears. But the deeper meaning of his death can only be captured by looking at his life. To this account, in dangerously abbreviated form, I now turn.

Student Years

By the time Norman was sixteen years old he was already a serious student of Karl Marx. His early correspondence shows that while he, the son of a missionary, could in no way accept Marx's 'unchristian spirit,' he none the less found Marx's condemnation of 'ironfisted capital' appealing. In justifying to his older brother his attraction to Marx's ideas, he quoted an epigram attributed to the King of Sweden: 'If a man under 30 had never been a socialist, he had no heart, and if a man over 30 was a socialist, he had no head!'[15] Still under thirty in 1933, six years later Norman was quoting Marx and Reinhold Niebuhr with equal facility in order to justify revolution in capitalist society. 'Capitalism,' he wrote, 'is now pure stupidity; its historic role has long been finished and is acting contrary to civilization.' 'Reason and Humanity,' he told his brother, 'cannot come about without revolution, so tightly and firmly will the acquisitive society in power fight to preserve its privileges.'[16]

Such was Norman's state of mind when he left Canada with a Victoria College B.A. in the autumn of 1933 for Trinity College in Cambridge, England. Within a month of enrolling, Norman attached himself to the liveliest young socialist group then active in England. He noted in one letter that once he mentioned to other students he had read John Strachey's *The Coming Struggle for Power,* 'you are granted a sesame into their company.'[17] The company to which Norman was admitted was the Cambridge University Socialist Society, then dominated by the young and brilliant radical John Cornford. A class list shows that Guy Burgess, Donald Maclean, Anthony Blunt, and James Klugmann were among Norman's classmates. Kim Philby had already graduated that spring. But it was under Cornford's political guidance that Norman wrote of experiencing an 'intellectual rebirth' upon renouncing 'infantile Canadian Marxism.' 'Under his [Cornford's] tutelage,' Norman proudly wrote four years later, 'I entered the party. I not only respected him and his gifts, both intellectual and political, but loved him.'[18]

He returned to North America in 1935 and the following year entered graduate school at Harvard. Besides working for a doctorate in Asian studies, he involved himself in collecting money and goods to be sent to the anti-Franco Spanish rebels; he helped organize a Canadian affiliate of the American Friends of the Chinese People, an organization supporting Mao's forces; he joined a Marxist study group that included Robert Bryce, later to become an Ottawa mandarin, and Tsuru Shigeto, today a well-known economist in Japan; and he aided Phillip Jaffe, who in the mid-forties was indicted for communist spy activities during the time he headed *Amerasia,* a magazine openly sympathetic to what are now known as 'national liberation movements.' According to Jaffe, Norman was at this time a member of the Canadian Communist party.[19]

By late 1939 Norman was in the process of completing his doctoral dissertation, entitled *Japan's Emergence as a Modern State* and published under the same title in 1940 by the Institute of Pacific Relations. Regarded by most Japanologists today as a pathfinding effort,[20] his book was singular for its heavy reliance upon secondary histories by Japanese Marxist writers; and remarkable for its unabashed use of Marxist terminology in explaining Japan's transition from the feudal epoch to an exploitative capitalist era. This work was followed by another IPR publication, *Soldier and Peasant in Japan* (1943), an unpublished monograph called 'Feudal Origins of Modern Japan' (1944), and in 1949 a biography of Tokugawa period utopian rebel Ando Shoeki, whom Norman likened to seventeenth-century English egalitarians John Lilburne and Gerrard Winstanley. All these later works shared with *Japan's Emergence* a striking left-leaning, anti-authoritarian message that was embellished by an iconoclastic radical tone and analysis.

Norman's first writings had a political relevance and impact too important to overlook. His first two books particularly brought him a tremendous amount of acclaim and notoriety in the field of Asian studies. Owen Lattimore, for instance, wrote in 1945 about Norman: 'Widely read in Japanese sources, this young Canadian is already the most authoritative contemporary analyst of Japan's economy, society, and government. He is to some extent a disciple, and in a sense the successor, of Sir George Sansom.'[21] In October, 1945, this very quotation was incorporated into a memorandum to General Thorpe, counter-intelligence chief of the occupation forces of Japan, recommending Norman to the general's attention. A handwritten postscript was added, interestingly, noting that 'Dr. Norman would be too modest to bring this evaluation of his own work to anyone else's attention. Owen Lattimore is, of course, one of the outstanding American writers on China, now a professor at Johns Hopkins University.'[22]

Norman's writings, in other words, earned him the attention and respect of scholars and military people alike. But this prominence was a mixed blessing. Once Thorpe was replaced by General Willoughby, who turned his office into a 'loyalty board' (as we shall see), and people like Owen Lattimore became a target of McCarthyism—or in other words as political power shifted to right-wing forces—Norman's writings and the fame they earned him were turned into evidence of infamy and disloyalty. Should this be difficult to believe, one has only to look at the 17 April 1957 'Summary of Bureau [FBI] Files Re Egerton Herbert Norman' which cites 'Norman's Published Writings for IPR and *Amerasia*' and 'Owen Lattimore "Impressed" with Norman's Work' as two major pieces of evidence against Norman. Ironically, except for one section on 'Norman's Participation in Marxist Discussion Group at Harvard, 1937,' there is nothing in this 'top secret' document about Norman's involvement in Marxist groups during his student years.[23]

Foreign Service Years

Shortly after joining External Affairs in late 1939, Norman was sent to Japan to serve as a language officer in the Canadian embassy. After the outbreak of war, he and the other embassy officials were interned until June 1942, when through a prisoner exchange with the Japanese government they were repatriated to Canada. It was right after the trip home that the FBI first intruded into Norman's life. Upon disembarking from the SS *Gripsholm* he was interviewed by an FBI agent regarding information he might have to offer about 'other passengers.' As he had none to offer, says the 5 September 1942 report, the interview was brief, and the report concluded with the words: 'failure to develop any derogatory information through a personal interview with the subject.'[24] Norman's FBI file was started.

It was added to in 1946, though the event which prompted the newest report occurred in November 1942 in Cambridge, Massachusetts. On 9 November, Norman had contacted the FBI in Boston for the purpose of 'securing from them the property of Tsuru [Shigeto],' Norman's graduate school friend of several years earlier. According to the FBI report, Norman produced a calling card of Tsuru as evidence of his authority to take possession of the property. The report read, 'Norman first claimed to be on an official mission for the Canadian government to obtain the books of Tsuru for the use of the Canadian government in a special investigation. He indicated that he held diplomatic immunity. Norman stated that he was on a highly confidential mission and could not divulge the details of the mission.' Norman likely had only a vague idea about what Tsuru's property comprised, and probably did not know that the FBI had already completed a thorough inventory of Tsuru's possessions. In fact, they consisted of Senate reports on munition hearings, communist propaganda materials, correspondence on the Young Communist League, and so on. Norman most likely gained some appreciation of the sorts of materials involved during his conversation with the FBI agents from whom he was trying to secure Tsuru's possessions. The agent's report reads: 'Later on, during the conversation, Norman changed his story and indicated that he did have a personal interest in the possessions of the subject [Tsuru] and that he was not actually on a special mission for the Canadian Government to obtain this material.'[25]

Norman had been caught in a lie—one, moreover, that made him look all the worse because of the sort of communist materials involved. Without going into details, suffice it to say that this incident followed Norman for the rest of his life.

Several hundred pages of FBI reports on this episode appear periodically in Norman's file over the next fifteen years. As late as 1957, interest on the part of the U.S. Senate subcommittee in Tsuru and the Tsuru-Norman connection remained strong. In fact, on 27 March 1957, a week before Norman's death, Japanese citizen Tsuru *voluntarily* testified before the Senate subcommittee regarding his relationship with Norman (and Robert Bryce) in the Harvard Marxist study group.[26] For Norman, this must have been the ultimate betrayal. A generous interpretation might have it that in 1942, the thirty-one-year-old Norman, who was after his repatriation involved in a very sensitive intelligence work aimed against imperialist Japan,[27] risked a great deal to help his Japanese friend by retrieving materials the content of which, if reported to the Japanese wartime government, would most certainly have put Tsuru in prison.

It is easy to imagine that Norman felt compelled to dissemble before the FBI agents precisely because his job in Ottawa from late 1942 until the end of the war involved security and intelligence matters concerned with the war against Japan. Assisting a Japanese national, even a leftist, at this time could have seriously compromised his position with External. Regardless, it must be concluded that this run-in with the FBI was not reported to Ottawa because Norman kept his security job until the end of the war.

Norman's duties at External changed within a month of Japan's surrender when Norman Robertson, under-secretary of state, gave Norman a new assignment to assist in the work of assembling and repatriating liberated Canadians in the Far East. He was sent first to the Philippines, and then to Japan, and was expected back in Ottawa by late September or early October. 'There could not be a better man for the assignment,' wrote Owen Lattimore upon learning of Norman's Far Eastern duty.[28] Apparently the American occupiers thought the same, for in late September or early October the supreme commander for the Allied powers in Tokyo sent a request to Ottawa, asking that Norman be permitted to remain in Japan and serve as a civilian head of an American army counter-intelligence unit. 'We were particularly asked to leave him there awhile, and I agreed rather reluctantly,' wrote H.H. Wrong, acting under-secretary, in late October 1945.[29]

The young thirty-four-year-old Norman was clearly enthusiastic and thrilled with his new assignment; he wrote his wife at this time: 'You have no idea how terribly busy I have been the last two weeks, yet never so excitingly busy in my life. My present position is head of the Research and Analysis Branch of the Counter-Intelligence Section of GHQ—and it is every bit as interesting as it sounds. My boss, the head of CIS, is General Thorpe—a frank, blunt, rough-tongued soldier but so accepts suggestions with so much ease and affability that sometimes it quite astounds me.'[30]

His assignment, as it later became clear, was a precarious one. A major part of his task, defined by the Americans, was first to help arrange for the release of long-imprisoned Japanese radicals who had opposed Japan's war effort—some were communists and Norman was later slandered for assisting in their release—and secondly, to interrogate them. Among those working with him was John K. Emmerson, who himself was later a victim of McCarthyism. A few years later their duty came to be regarded as a 'crime' when Eugene Dooman, who during the war had served as chairman of the Far Eastern subcommittee of the State-War-Navy Coordinating Committee, testified in 1951 that the official attention given by Norman and Emmerson to these Japanese communists served to enhance the public regard for the communists to such an extent that they were able to recruit '100,000' new members. But for Norman, in that job of releasing the imprisoned Japanese communists he was simply following the orders of General MacArthur. Innocently, he wrote of the experience: 'I have never enjoyed anything so much as being able to tell them [the prisoners] that according to General MacArthur's orders they were to be released within a week ... Later we had the opportunity to interview them at greater length and after a few days at liberty they were able to give us political information on current affairs of the utmost interest.'[31]

The work was exhausting, he wrote, often necessitating ten-hour days. What pleasures he enjoyed during this period, he told his wife, came from the occasional tennis game, conversations with Japanese intellectuals, and the close personal associations he had with noted Asian specialists then in Japan such as T.A. Bisson, Bill Holland, Owen Lattimore, John K. Emmerson, and Shigeto Tsuru, all figures who later figure prominently in the McCarthyite witch-hunt directed at the Institute of Pacific Relations. In another letter (25 November 1945) Norman mentions seeing Jack Service as well, one more Far Eastern expert whose career was badly damaged by the infamous 'China Lobby.'

During this very early phase of the occupation, when the essential policy was to demilitarize and democratize the Japanese state, Norman was enamoured of the MacArthurian radical messianic zeal that prosecuted militarists and protected democrats. Norman easily accepted MacArthur's judgment that the occupation was a 'spiritual revolution' wherein 'freedom is on the offensive, democracy is on the march.'[32] In his own words, Norman believed that MacArthur was 'following a course designed to give the Japanese the maximum opportunity to develop their own democratic institutions.'[33] At the same time, Norman retained a healthy scepticism about the possibility of imposing democracy from above, a view reinforced by his superiors in Ottawa. Dr Hugh Keenleyside, Norman's superior at the Far Eastern desk during the war, believed in late 1945 that 'there is nothing in MacArthur's record to lead one to think that he has any serious interest in democracy and all that should mean.' Keenleyside worried that the 'enlightened policy' towards both China and Japan of men like John Carter Vincent—later victimized by McCarthyism—in the State Department would be undercut by MacArthur who could not 'know just where the convenience of supporting the old order should be sacrificed to the *necessity* of encouraging a growth of economic as well as political democracy.'[34] Although early on in the occupation Norman tried to dispel such doubts held by Ottawa ('No one is more fully aware of the need for the Japanese to take hold and to perform the task [of democratization] than General MacArthur'),[35] he later echoed doubts similar to those of his superiors once MacArthur 'reversed course' and partially 'de-democratized' Japan. Nevertheless, by the end of his first tour of duty, his pro-occupation views and actions had earned the genuine respect of his commander, General Thorpe, MacArthur's first chief of counter-intelligence. Upon Norman's departure from Japan, General Thorpe wrote the prime minister of Canada, MacKenzie King, on 31 January 1946: 'I should like to express to you my personal appreciation of Dr. Norman's services. His profound knowledge of Japan, his brilliant intellectual attainments and his willingness to give his utmost to our work has made his contributions to the success of the occupation one of great value. During his tour of duty with us, Dr. Norman has won the respect and admiration of all who have been associated with him. It will be difficult, indeed, to fill the vacancy left by his departure.'[36]

In January 1946, given a respite from the occupation, Norman was assigned to the office of Canada's ambassador to the United States, Mike Pearson, who also was serving as Canada's chief representative to the Far Eastern Commission (FEC), the Allied powers' organization that was *nominally* in charge of overseeing the occupation of Japan. Norman was Pearson's first secretary and the alternate Delegate to the FEC. But when by mid-1946 it had become clear that Norman's talents were being wasted by serving on the powerless FEC, on Pearson's initiative he was reassigned to head Canada's mission to occupied Japan. Pearson wrote to the secretary of state: 'As Mr. Norman is a distinguished Japanologist and served for a time on General MacArthur's staff in Tokyo and later as Canadian delegate on the FEC during its tour of Japan, it was felt that it would be easier to get SCAP's cooperation if Mr. Norman was named head of the mission, and that he was the best man we could send.'[37] MacArthur personally accepted this argument. On 2 August 1946, Norman departed aboard the SS *General Meigs* from Vancouver and arrived in Yokohama on 14 August as Canada's head of the liaison mission. There Norman remained until October 1950 when, in the words of Arthur Menzies, until recently Canada's ambassador to China, he was recalled 'following certain inquiries undertaken as a result of allegations concerning Norman's communist connections.'[38] Thereafter began the nightmare that ended only with his death.

The political atmosphere of the occupied Japan to which Norman returned in August 1946 had changed from the early period which was so evangelically democratic in tone. Occupied Japan of late 1946 can best be characterized by quoting General MacArthur's 'Statement on the First Anniversary of Surrender.' MacArthur made it clear that occupied Japan had become enmeshed in the emerging Cold War, which he depicted as 'dread uncertainty arising from impinging ideologies which now stir mankind.' MacArthur asked, 'Which concept will prevail?' The choice for the Japanese was clear: 'principles of right and justice and decency' or the evil of 'the philosophy of an extreme radical left' that could prove seductive to a nation afflicted by 'generations of feudalistic life.'[39] As far as Norman was personally concerned, once MacArthur began yielding to Cold War rhetoric, his chief witch-hunter, General Willoughby, was permitted to conveniently forget that the Japanese communists whom Norman and Emmerson released in 1945, in order to serve as a countervailing force to rightist tendencies in Japan, had been freed and encouraged to organize political parties and labour unions by MacArthur himself. Unknown to Norman, General Willoughby began investigating Norman as a 'security matter' in October 1946, two months after Norman's return to Japan.[40]

None the less, from all accounts Norman and MacArthur enjoyed a healthy, mutually respectful relationship during much of Norman's last four years in Japan. Though critical of some of MacArthur's policies, Norman admired the general for the missionary zeal he still brought to this crusade for democratization, and MacArthur for his part seemed to have genuinely respected Norman's expertise as a Japanologist. Charles Kades, then a high-ranking functionary in Government Section (G-1) and one of the architects of Japan's constitution, wrote:

> So far as General MacArthur is concerned, I know of my own knowledge that they [EHN and MacArthur] were on excellent terms ... It is my recollection that the first person in GHQ General MacArthur spoke to after the Emperor visited him in the Embassy was Herb Norman, which perhaps is some measure of his closeness to the Commander-in-Chief, and in my opinion Mr. Norman's memoranda and oral advice were very favourably received and influential ... There is no doubt Herb Norman influenced me ... and I frequently turned to him for advice ... When I needed additional personnel for the Government Section who were experts on Japan, he recommended that I try to secure the assignment of then Captain (U.S.N.) Sebald.[41]

Sebald later became America's ambassador to Japan.

For his part, Norman no less admired MacArthur, and seemed to enjoy an intimacy with the General that few might expect. Some of Norman's letters to the general began with 'My Dear General MacArthur,' even as late as July 1950, after the Korean War broke out. One of Norman's then junior advisors in the Canadian mission recently told me the story about MacArthur's personal appearance at Canada's Dominion Day celebration in 1947. MacArthur, who on record was a teetotaller and non-smoker, accepted both a drink and a cigarette from Norman before the two men retired onto the veranda of the legation for a private chat.

Norman's private communiqués to Ottawa, a few of his public speeches, and his private correspondence with the general, however, clearly show that

Norman was not uncritical of the man and many of his policies. In a confidential memo to External, dated 28 January 1948, and in response to MacArthur's second anniversary message, Norman wrote: 'The ideas which he stressed in the message were not new and could be criticized for not admitting the slightest possibility that any grounds of criticism of the occupation existed.'[42] He further observed, in referring to emerging Cold War realignments, that MacArthur's policies were designed 'to tie [Japan's] economy to that of the United States.'[43] In a different communiqué of the same year to Ottawa he warned that democratic reform was being undone because of MacArthur's policies aimed at 'de-purging' war criminals: 'Some of the most powerful political forces in Japan today are those commanded by former leaders who have been purged but still exert an indefinable but nonetheless potent influence behind the scenes.'[44]

Publicly, Norman was saying to Japanese audiences that 'there would seem to be dangers inherent in the tendency of the occupation to think of democracy as something institutional.' Institutional reforms, he said, 'were imposed on Japan from the top. These reforms, admirable in themselves, were not initiated by the Japanese, hence they could scarcely command the deepest loyalty ... It is safe to say that not all the changes of the occupation will remain.' In the same speech Norman questioned MacArthur's pronouncement that Japan had by 1948 undergone a 'spiritual revolution' in the name of democracy. He queried, 'If democracy can be measured by written laws, he [MacArthur] was right, but can it be?' The mistakes of the occupation authorities, he said, grew out of the Cold War which prompted policy that would 'favour the interests of the conservatives in Japan who could be counted upon to be anti-communist.' The result was a 'watering down' of most progressive reforms undertaken earlier on.[45]

Privately, in his letters to MacArthur, Norman also raised questions about the wisdom of certain occupation policies. One of the best examples was his questioning, on humanitarian grounds, of the sentences imposed on two Japanese 'war criminals,' Shigemitsu Mamoru and Togo Shigenori. In pleading for commutation of their sentences, which MacArthur had personally endorsed the day before (22 November 1948), Norman defended his recommendation by saying, 'This may not be legal reasoning but I think at least it has in it a quality of common sense and humanity.' Reduction of their sentences, he further argued, 'will reveal to the Japanese public in a practical manner that the victorious powers are not motivated by a general and indiscriminate sense of revenge.' Norman ended his letter saying, 'I feel that I am carrying out my obligations to my government and also following the dictates of my conscience.'[46] Though MacArthur did not heed Norman's advice on this issue, neither does it appear that he bore Norman a grudge for questioning his wisdom, for three months later MacArthur personally recommended to Ottawa that Norman's rank be upgraded to minister. Lester Pearson, by then secretary of state, immediately endorsed MacArthur's recommendation, adding in a note to the general,

'[Norman's] cordial relations with you have resulted in benefits to your Headquarters, as well as to the Government of Canada.'[47] In thanking the general for this vote of confidence, Norman sent MacArthur an autographed copy of his new book, *Ando Shoeki,* and MacArthur responded to this gesture of goodwill by urging Norman to write a general article on Japan, past and present.[48]

But outside the relationship of mutual respect, goodwill, and cooperation between MacArthur and Norman, suspicions regarding Norman's 'loyalty' to the occupation were being voiced. As mentioned earlier, General Willoughby, head of counter-intelligence (G-2) and a notorious right-winger who reputedly said of Franco of Spain that he was 'the second best general in the world,' began investigating Norman for his past communist sympathies. Why Willoughby chose Norman as a target can easily be guessed. One reason stems from Norman's strong criticism of many in MacArthur's staff whom he accused of incompetence or indifference. Norman bemoaned what he termed the loss 'of the old crusading zeal that characterized the earlier phase of the occupation,' and the emerging, 'rather blind and unquestioning faith in all the policies that have emanated from SCAP and a somewhat intolerant impatience with any doubts as to whether there is a discrepancy between the theory and implementation of occupation policy.'[49] He especially regretted the reversal in land reform policy—these democratic advances had been reversed by American 'disinterested officials' and the 'very mediocre and in some cases painfully inept performance of an increasingly conservative Japanese bureaucracy.'[50] In large part the cause of these problems could be found, Norman wrote in a report of February 1950, in the contradiction inherent in the occupation: 'A brief review of the fate of the post-war government of Japan will show that a parliamentary democracy is scarcely compatible with a military occupation.'[51] Shortly thereafter, Norman's assessment was, if anything, even more negative: 'As the year wore on it became more and more evident that GHQ, SCAP, believed it could secure the economic and political stability of Japan by placing its confidence in, and giving support to, the more conservative social forces at work here. This development cast before it a shadow over the future of liberal democracy; it gave hope to the "old guard." '[52]

If Norman's official expression of such sentiments was not responsible for Willoughby's investigation of him, then some of Norman's activities and associations were, once Willoughby began organizing his 'loyalty boards' in order to search for 'leftists and fellow-travellers' working for the occupation. And, of course, once America 'lost' China to Maoist communism, the 'loyalty boards' began operating at a feverish rate. Suddenly, all Far Eastern experts, especially those who advised the State Department, came under suspicion. FBI reports, among which there was one on Norman, were sent to Willoughby from Washington. It was then remembered that Norman had earlier in the occupation worked with Japanese communists; that he was a friend to such Japanese socialist scholars as Hani Goro, and to American Far Eastern experts Owen Lattimore, Bill Holland, T.A. Bisson, Emmerson, and others. Subsequently, it was also learned that Norman had involved himself in organizing a Japan branch of the Institute of Pacific Relations, which for Willoughby was 'a spy ring for Russian Communists,' and 'heavily weighted with known leftists in control positions.'[53] And in 1947, Norman brazenly travelled to an IPR conference in England. The 'evidence' began mounting: he wrote four articles for *Amerasia* in 1937 and 1938, six for *Far Eastern Survey* (1939-45), and six for *Pacific Affairs* (1943-49). These were allegedly 'communist-inspired' journals. Then, after the outbreak of the Korean War, according to speculation in the press, Norman criticized Willoughby's faulty intelligence reports which rejected the possibility of Chinese intervention in Korea. But the *coup de grace*, according to one U.S. security report, was the discovery by the Government of Canada of 'certain communist connections, especially with Israel Halperin,'[54] a Russian-Jewish *émigré* who had been implicated by Igor Gouzenko, the Russian embassy cipher clerk who defected in Ottawa in 1945. Halperin had once shared a dormitory room with his friend Norman in the early thirties when both were undergraduates at the University of Toronto, and later kept in touch it would seem; Norman's phone number was found by the RCMP in Halperin's personal notebook.

The Gouzenko-Halperin-Norman connection had not been made until August 1950 when the FBI asked Counter-Intelligence (G-2) to initiate an investigation of persons listed in the address book of Israel Halperin. The investigation showed, or rather the connection was made for the first time, that in addition to Norman's name appearing in the address book, so too was Tsuru Shigeto's. Suddenly, the 1942 interrogation of Norman by the FBI over his attempt to secure Tsuru's possessions took on renewed relevance. This information was communicated to the FBI, which in turn sent it on to Ottawa. With little advance warning, Norman was abruptly recalled from Japan on 19 October 1950 on the basis of a 17 October report compiled by the RCMP and most certainly based largely on the G-2 and FBI information.[55] On the basis of these reports, Norman was subjected to intermittent interrogation by the RCMP over a six-week period, ending in late November.

'A pile of bricks does not make a house,' to cite one of Norman's favourite quotations: the evidence against Norman, though considerable, was insufficient and inconclusive. And so the RCMP 'cleared' Norman, noting in a 1 December 1950 report that the original 17 October RCMP report that prompted his recall and which had been sent to the FBI, was no longer valid. The newest report said: 'Of the numerous points supplied at the time, the majority have been absolutely determined to be in error. The remaining few have not been confirmed nor does there appear to be any answer to them.'[56] The most damning comment to appear in the second RCMP report read: 'The worst possible conclusion we can arrive at is the very apparent naivete in his relationships with his fellow man.'[57] The December report also concluded that the October report's findings should be discounted; this too was communicated to the FBI.

But for Norman's sense of well-being, the judged validity or invalidity of the early report mattered little. By all accounts, from both friends and family members, the experience had been terrifying and emotionally exhausting. Though one of his interrogators told me not long ago that Norman had 'stood up' well to the questioning, Norman's close associates say he was still recounting the nightmare years later, especially after the second Senate attack came in 1957.

Shortly after the interrogation ended, he was made head of the American and Far Eastern division, a position he held until July 1952. It was unfortunate that External Affairs retained this archaic combination of American *and* Far Eastern affairs in one division, for in August 1951, when Asianist and ex-communist Karl Wittfogel testified before a Senate subcommittee that Norman was a communist, American State Department figures expressed alarm that a communist was in charge of American affairs in the Department of External Affairs, entitled as he was to inspect 'top secret' material. Ottawa was outraged by this public disclosure and immediately issued a protest, claiming Norman had been 'given a clean bill of health' and remained 'a trusted and valuable official of the Department.'[58] Unofficial Canadian reaction to the McCarran committee disclosures was no less swift and angry. Harold Greer, writing for the *Toronto Daily Star,* suggested that the 'smearing' of Dr Norman was the result of 'vendetta' on the part of Major General Willoughby who had been angered by Norman's objections to the increasingly undemocratic policies of the MacArthur occupation of Japan. The Toronto *Globe and Mail* demanded that 'the Federal Government protest strongly to Washington against the manner in which the Canadian diplomat was smeared with the allegations of Communist sympathies.' The *Globe and Mail* further asserted that in this instance 'the Washington witch-hunt' had insulted Canadian national integrity by not working quietly through regular diplomatic channels; Washington, the newspaper claimed, was treating Canada like a 'poor relation living in the porter's lodge on Uncle Sam's estate.' The *Ottawa Citizen* echoed these remarks, saying that 'the U.S. Congressmen show as much contempt for Canada's sovereignty as the Soviet Union does for Bulgaria's.' The *Citizen* attack ended: 'U.S. Senators would do the cause of world freedom a great service if they confined their star chamber procedures to their own citizens.'[59]

Pearson sought to erase the smear by discrediting the 'unimpressive and unsubstantiated statements by a former Communist [Wittfogel],' before announcing at the conclusion of a press conference on 16 August that Norman would serve as his chief advisor to the 4 September San Francisco Conference on the Japan Peace Treaty.

Politically, however, a 'clean bill of health' only serves to remind the 'once-afflicted' of the disease. Norman confided to a friend in the aftermath of the 1951 publicity, 'You can't wash off the poison of a smear from your emotions.' 'How can you,' he asked in desperation, 'fight back against this sort of thing?'[60] Deeply depressed at losing the sine qua non attributes of a successful diplomat, his private anonymity and his public reputation, Norman passively resigned himself to unattractive and out-of-the-way foreign service positions during the next few years. After a closet post in Ottawa, Norman went off to New Zealand in 1953 as high commissioner for, in the words of one high-ranking Canadian diplomat still in service today, 'a rest and cure.' 'For someone of Herb's calibre,' this same diplomat remarked, 'New Zealand was exile.' Norman, of course, knew this, and suffered diplomatic convalescence passively. Hence, his hopes were renewed when in 1956 Lester Pearson told him of his political resurrection, namely that he was being sent to a diplomatic hot spot, Egypt, as ambassador. According to many who were closest to him at that time, this new and promising assignment served to lift the cloud of depression still troubling Norman, sending him into Egypt filled with enthusiasm and high hopes of being able to make an important contribution to the cause of world peace.

And contribute he did by establishing a relationship of trust with President Nasser following the invasion of Egypt by Israel, England, and France in October 1956. From Norman's dispatches to Ottawa during this period of the Suez crisis, it is clear that his intervention with Nasser was crucial in securing Egyptian acceptance of a United Nations—Canadian peacekeeping force to be stationed in the Sinai. As late (in his life) as 14 March 1957, Norman's personal intercession with Nasser, in this case a late night visit to Nasser's holiday retreat, had the effect of clearing the way for additional Canadian troops to occupy the battle zones.[61] It is something more than mere historical irony that at the same time as Norman was meeting late at night with Nasser to work for peace in the Middle East, in Washington Norman's old American friend from the early days of the occupation, John K. Emmerson, was undergoing congressional hearings before being appointed to serve as political counsellor in Paris. It was in the course of those hearings that Emmerson mentioned something that members of Congress had not known, that E. Herbert Norman was then serving as Canada's ambassador to Egypt and minister to Lebanon. Emmerson also remarked that he had had the opportunity of meeting with Norman during his stay in Beirut in the fall of 1956. In Emmerson's words, 'the statement was like a shock wave: the sharp investigators [Senators Jenner and Watkins, and Counsel Robert Morris] had not known where Norman was and what he was doing. Both senators asked me to repeat it. Morris asked the senators if they would like to see the evidence in the security files that Norman was a communist. He proceeded to read into the record reports about Norman's communism, laying stress on statements by a former communist, Karl August Wittfogel, that Norman had been a member of a summer Communist study group in 1938 and that he had been identified as a member of the Communist party in 1940.'[62]

Clearly, the record from which Counsel Morris read was the October 1950 RCMP report, the one discredited and superseded by the December 1950 RCMP report which also had been sent to Washington. But no matter; the full text of this meeting between Emmerson and his Senate interrogators was released to the press at 4:30 PM on 14 March. 'Senators Probe Canadian Envoy,' newspaper headlines read, the same 'Canadian Envoy' who was at the very same time meeting with President Nasser in order to ensure peace in the Middle East. Old charges, old evidence, but inserted into a new situation: Would internal saboteurs, 'stab-in-the-back' leftists cause the 'loss' of Egypt from the 'free world' as they had with China? The McCarthyite defenders of freedom, the architects of a new kind of organized stupidity, answered a resounding 'No!' Norman had to go. And thus began the public persecution of Norman that led to his jump from a downtown Cairo apartment building.

Conclusion

But was it 'murder by slander' as some have alleged? Was Norman guiltless of the charges of 'communism'? Had he been slandered?

The answer to these questions, according to official Canadian records, is a yes qualified only by the admission of youthful left-wing sympathies. According to official American records, the answer is an unqualified no. There is, as we have seen, support for both positions. Norman was undoubtedly a communist during his early years, but there is no evidence to suggest he remained a communist during his time as a foreign service officer. Yet there is evidence to suggest he was something of a radical-liberal who believed in, among other things, non-intervention, self-determination for all peoples, popular democracy, and the value of 'national liberation movements.' He supported, for example, what he called 'emergent Arab nationalism,' as a popular struggle for independence, even as he criticized Nasser for demagoguery. Before that he supported the rise of the Japanese Communist party and the labour movement because he saw them as positive countervailing forces to lingering fascist tendencies in the Japanese body politic and as the bearers of a historical, verifiable democratic undercurrent in Japan's past. For similar reasons, earlier in his life he was drawn to support democratic forces in Spain's civil war and communist forces in China's struggle. History, he believed, was on the side of the forces of liberation, and as a historian of transnational background he felt compelled to back those whom he believed were struggling for principles that transcended petty nationalism. That his conception of freedom conflicted with the ahistorical and ultranationalistic McCarthyite conception can be of no surprise to anyone.

Finally, as a Canadian diplomat in a world dominated by American power and U.S.-USSR ideologically based schisms, Norman was especially vulnerable to McCarthyism. Nor was he alone. A secret U.S. Foreign Service dispatch and other sources recently released under the Freedom of Information Act show, as we have seen, that other Canadians were similarly being targeted by McCarthyism at this time, the three most prominent names being Robert Bryce, clerk of the Privy Council; Arthur Menzies, until recently Canada's ambassador to China; and Lester Pearson himself. Bryce had once shared with Norman involvement in a Marxist study group at Harvard and had introduced Tsuru to

Norman; Menzies had along with Norman joined the Canadian Friends of the Chinese People in the late thirties; and Pearson had helped prevent the Americans from getting Igor Gouzenko to testify in Washington. It may very well be that the international furor raised by Norman's death actually served to protect these other distinguished Canadians from McCarthyism.

But perhaps the more important point to be made about Norman's death was made by Lester Pearson: 'The issue before us, is not only the tragedy of one man, victimized by slanderous procedures in another country and unable to defend himself against them. There is the broader question of principle involved—the right, to say nothing of the propriety, of a foreign government to intervene in our affairs ... Such intervention is intolerable.'[63]

Norman's tragic death can be understood in similar terms, perhaps no less appropriate, as defined by George Grant in his influential *Lament for a Nation*.[64] Grant's book is a lament for the loss of his nation's identity to the all-consuming American leviathan to the south. Norman's story is in a very real sense a story of Canada's loss of one of its own to this same giant, the story of how one Canadian fell victim to the American behemoth run amok.

The imagery is apt, for it reminds us that giants may be both gentle and savage. Canadians no doubt benefit when the giant is gentle and protective, but they will suffer when it feels threatened and strikes out, blindly, even at its friends. Norman was the giant's victim, not really its target as some advocates of a conspiracy theory might suggest. Norman was a victim of its blind fear, albeit a fear expressed in a slow, methodical, organized, though sensibly stupid manner, much in the fashion of a blind person searching for his cane. That the blind giant struck out in fear, hurting friends in the process, might be forgiveable except for the fact that the blindness was self-inflicted.

Notes

1. Department of State, dispatch no. 875, 18 April 1957, file no. 601/42274/4-1857. All American records cited in this paper were obtained through the Freedom of Information Act.

2. Appearing in the *Globe and Mail* on 11 April 1957.

3. Hence, we read in a 17 April 1957 telegram from the American ambassador to Canada to the secretary of state: 'Believe strong Canadian line re exchange security information motivated by domestic political considerations as well as by widespread bitter feelings resulting from Norman suicide. Pearson's detailed statement in Parliament and publicity given to exchange of notes [between U.S. and Canadian governments] would appear aimed at meeting political exigencies rather than at solving basic problem. April 16 speech by conservative leader Diefenbaker indicated intention conservative opposition use Norman affair as political ammunition in election campaign already underway' ('Confidential' telegram, file no. 601.4274/4-1057).

4. Quoted in a U.S. 'Confidential' memorandum, 14 August 1951, State Department document file no. 742.001/8-1451.

5. See note no. 3; and Department of State dispatch 892, 25 April 1957, file no. 601.4274/4-2557.

6. The *Gazette* editorial and Pearson's reply appear in their entirety in 'The Strange Case of Mr. Norman,' *U.S. News and World Report,* 26 April 1957, 153-54. See also 'The Pearson Case,' *Globe and Mail,* 19 April 1957.

7. Reported in 'Confidential' dispatch, 18 April 1957, American embassy in Ottawa, file no. 601.4274/4-1857.

8. The American ambassador's assessment in ibid.

9. See James Eayrs, ed., *The Commonwealth and Suez* (New York, Toronto: Oxford University Press 1964), 382-8, 416-21.

10. Blakney's article was quoted extensively in U.S. embassy dispatch (Ottawa) of 18 April 1957, file no. 601.4274/4-1857.

11. Department of State, file nos. 601.4274/4-1557; 601.4274/6-958; 601.4274/5-2658. See also 'Intolerable Incident,' *Newsweek,* 22 April 1957, 64. FBI Chief Hoover stated in a secret memorandum of 10 April 1957, 'I want complete summaries of all we have on Norman and Pearson.' FBI file no. 100-346993-73.

12. John W. Dower, *Origins of the Modern Japanese State: Selected Workings of E.H. Norman* (New York: Pantheon 1975); Charles Taylor, *Six Journeys: A Canadian Pattern* (Toronto: Anansi 1977): 107-51

13. *Maclean's,* 13 December 1982, 29

14. Ibid.

15. Personal correspondence to brother Howard Norman, 11 July 1927

16. Ibid., 15 May 1933

17. Ibid., 21 October 1933

18. 3 March 1937; Cornford had recently been killed in action in the Spanish Civil War.

19. Personal correspondence, from Jaffe to the author, 25 February 1978

20. See the articles by John W. Hall and George Akita in *Journal of Japanese Studies* 3, no. 2 (Summer 1977), and Herbert Bix's rejoinder in the same *Journal,* vol. 4, no. 2 (Summer 1978).

21. Owen Lattimore, *Solution in Asia* (Boston: Little, Brown and Company 1945), 38, n. 4

22. No. 201 miscellaneous file, Department of External Affairs, no. 53038440; memorandum dated 22 October 1945

23. FBI file no. 100-346993-73

24. FBI file no. 100-346993-x; the interrogation actually took place on 25 August 1942.

25. FBI file no. 100-346993-2, dated 16 October 1946

26. Tsuru's testimony is quoted at length in the FBI's 'Summary of Information,' file no. 100-346993-73.

27. It appears that Norman's work between 1942 and the end of the war involved the translation and interpretation of captured and/or intercepted Japanese war documents. In the summer of 1943 or 1944 he arranged for security clearance for such work for his older brother who also read Japanese language material with facility.

28. Owen Lattimore to Hugh Keenleyside, 5 September 1945; External Affairs file no. 50061-40 (hereafter External Affairs will be rendered EA)

29. H.H. Wrong to Hugh Keenleyside, 20 October 1945, EA no. 104-C-34

30. Correspondence, 26 October 1945

31. Ibid.

32. Supreme Commander for the Allied Powers (SCAP) *Political Reorientation of Japan II* (Washington, DC: U.S. Government Printing Office), 737, 756

33. Correspondence to his wife, 26 October 1945

34. Correspondence, Hugh Keenleyside to Norman Robertson, under-secretary of state, 4 September 1945; EA 104-CD-34

35. From his speech on 'Japan in Evolution,' given in New York on 16 March 1946 to the Foreign Policy Association

36. EA 50061-40, vol. 3/4-1

37. Ibid., 30 May 1946

38. Personal communication to the author, 20 February 1978

39. SCAP, *Political Reorientation of Japan II,* 756

40. The case remained open until 11 March 1947 and was reopened in May 1950; FBI file no. 100-346993.

41. Personal communication to author, 18 January 1979

42. EA 4606-F-2-40

43. Ibid.

44. EA 4606-E-8-40, vol. 1, 19 January 1948

45. 'Japan since Surrender' (unpublished typescript, 13 pp, 1951?)

46. 23 November 1948 (This letter can be found in the MacArthur Archives, Norfolk, Virginia.)

47. 9 February 1949

48. Norman letter to General MacArthur, 28 February 1949 (MacArthur Archives)

49. EA 10848-10, 26 October 1949

50. EA 10463-B40, 11 August 1949, 4

51. EA 10463-B40

52. Annual Review of Events in Japan for 1950, EA 4606-F-40, part I

53. See note 2 in the 'Conclusion' to this volume.

54. Department of State, 20 March 1957, file no. 601.4274/3-2057

55. Correspondence between G-2 and the FBI between August and October 1950, and references to communication with Ottawa by both, lend credence to this conclu-

sion. Memo from GHQ, Far East Command, to G-2, Washington, 30 November 1950; reference to CIA involvement noted in 30 November 1950 memo from Lt Col Roundtree to Willoughby, G-2, GHQ, inter-office memorandum; and FBI file memorandum, 1 November 1950, file no. 100-346993-6.

56. This finding is one of several incorporated into a review of the Norman case by the American embassy in Ottawa, dated 25 April 1957, file no. 601.4274/4-2557.

57. Quoted in memorandum from U.S. Department of Justice, Ottawa, Liaison office, 7 December 1950, from Glenn H. Bethel to director, FBI, file no. 100-346993-24.

58. See no. 4.

59. All of the above newspapers' remarks are found in a 'restricted' dispatch from Ottawa to Washington, dated 20 August 1951; file no. 310.342/8-2051 XR 742.001.

60. Quoted by Sidney Katz, in *Maclean's,* 28 September 1957.

61. EA, 15 March 1957, file no. 50366-40 (A thirty-year rule restricting quotation prohibits specific citations.)

62. John K. Emmerson, *The Japanese Thread: A Life in the U.S. Foreign Service* (New York: Holt, Rinehart, Winston 1978), 334-5

63. House of Commons, 10 April 1957

64. George Grant, *Lament for a Nation: The Defeat of Canadian Nationalism* (Toronto: McClelland and Stewart 1965)

SUICIDE

James Barros

The suggestion that Norman's tragic death on April 4, 1957 was due to the actions of the Senate Subcommittee on Internal Security now raises some doubts that this was what drove him to take his own life. A close examination of events before and after he committed suicide shows that the reasons for it are far more complex than would appear at first glance.

The Senate Subcommittee's release on March 14, 1957 of Emmerson's testimony of March 12 included the excerpts from the Summary of Information prepared for General Willoughby in mid-April 1951. This Summary of Information was an amalgam of FBI and RCMP information.[1] The release of the testimony led to a defense of Norman by Pearson which was as forceful as it had been six years earlier. Indeed, in March-April 1957, Pearson was fully supported, at least initially, by the parliamentary opposition leader and future prime minister John Diefenbaker. The opinions of an aroused Canadian public and a press sympathetic to Norman were echoed across the border, although

From *No Sense of Evil Espionage: The Case of Herbert Norman* (Toronto: Deneau, 1986), 143-57, 235-37. Reprinted by permission of Deneau Publishers & Company Ltd.

some of the American reaction may have been politically motivated. Ottawa quickly lodged an official protest. Washington was seemingly embarrassed, and though Norman, at first, was "upset," as his deputy Arthur Kilgour subsequently told Ottawa, he was also "somewhat detached."

Morally and politically, Norman's position appeared to be virtually unassailable as the confident tone of his March 19 messages of thanks to both Pearson and Diefenbaker seemed to indicate. Pearson then wrote a personal letter of support in return, which appears to show that he had not only won the government's endorsement but also that of his colleagues and friends. In fact, Pearson's initial comments in the House of Commons had led the embassy staff in Cairo, as well as others, to consider the Norman matter closed. What more could anyone have asked for?

Norman's work habits appeared normal. He never mentioned the Senate Subcommittee to Kilgour, and later inquiries by the embassy staff led to the reasonable conviction that there had been "no sudden and drastic change" in his behavior. Then about March 21, a week after Emmerson's testimony was released, he showed "signs that he was preoccupied." His secretary "found him somewhat tense," he appeared to lose interest in important matters, yet still adhered to the usual daily schedule. The first recorded occasion when his conduct attracted attention was a reception on March 22, for the Director General of the Food and Agriculture Organization. Norman "appeared to several people to be quite upset."

It was not until several days later, on March 25, when he broached the subject of the subcommittee's activities to Kilgour who, much later informed External Affairs that he thought that day had "marked perhaps a turning point" in Norman's demeanor. Complaining that the people in Washington were still after him, he produced a newspaper clipping dealing with a statement by the subcommittee's counsel Judge Morris. Referring to Pearson's protest to Washington, the judge had declared that he would press ahead and present, through reputable witnesses and reliable evidence and documentation, those underlying facts that impinged on the United States' security. Kilgour tried to assure Norman the statement was in character with the judge's attitude, and that he saw no reason to believe that his name would resurface. Norman then noted that when Emmerson had previously been investigated in Washington, he had written an affidavit attesting to Emmerson's character. This was not so, as the particular affidavit dealt only with the events that took place at Fuchu prison in October 1945.[2] He reasoned that when the subcommittee had reopened the case, it must have been angered by the affidavit it had found in Emmerson's file. He also maintained that although his acquaintanceship with various individuals—Owen Lattimore especially—had been raised during his own "investigation" in Ottawa, it had not come up in the subcommittee's previous hearings. There is no documentary evidence to support the fact that Norman was ever questioned about Owen Lattimore in Ottawa. While it is true that the subcommittee was not aware of most of his acquaintances, it did know about his relationship with Lattimore during the postwar period when they were both in Tokyo.[3] Norman then observed that the thought that the subcommittee "might be able to reveal apparently *new information disturbed him very much.*"[4] He added that he found it discouraging to work so hard and then to have something like this develop.

For the next several days he continued to work in his office. Then on March 28, during an informal luncheon at the Young Women's Christian Association, "a decisive change" was noted. Though all the Canadians were seated at a single small table, it did not go unnoticed that Norman "scarcely took part in the conversation and in fact did not appear to be mentally with us," Kilgour subsequently wrote. He also had begun closing his office door which had not been his usual practice, and was sometimes seen scribbling on foolscap sheets of paper or resting on his office couch; in fact, some of the embassy staff thought he looked ill.

On the morning of March 29 he arrived at his office and then asked one of the embassy's Egyptian employees to open the door that led to the roof of the chancery building. Though the ambassador told the employee that he was not needed, he, nevertheless, decided to accompany him. Norman walked around the roof, looking over the sides, and particularly at the highest point which was directly over the garage.

On the same day it was announced in the Egyptian press that Tsuru had been interviewed by the subcommittee. The embassy staff agreed that the news should not be brought to Norman's attention, although he subsequently asked Kilgour if anything further had developed. He answered in the negative to save his chief additional anguish. Although Kilgour never found out whether Norman had ever learned that the subcommittee had again commenced inquiries about him, it would be safe to assume that in a cosmopolitan city such as Cairo, especially in the circle in which Norman moved, it was only a matter of time before the subcommittee's activities would have become known to him. Mrs. Norman later admitted to Kilgour that Herbert had told her that the subcommittee "probably would eventually interview" Tsuru, since he was temporarily teaching at Harvard University. The fact that he was aware of Tsuru's presence at Harvard prompted an RCMP officer to scribble in the margin of Kilgour's report that Norman "must have still been in touch with him."

For the next three days Kilgour saw virtually nothing of his chief. It appears that he had driven out of Cairo to get away from it all. On at least one occasion he was accompanied by a friend who said Norman had slept in the car a great deal of the time and that he had declared he could sleep for an entire year.

On April 1 and 2 Norman was up and about holding talks with senior Egyptian officials. He still appeared "preoccupied though no more than previously."[5] By this point, Tsuru's public testimony to the subcommittee had been released. Norman admitted to the Canadian journalist King Gordon that he had never been as depressed as he had been during the last weeks. He was convinced that the old communist charge would be revived, and that Judge Morris' boast that nothing would obstruct the subcommittee's investigatory work was a sure sign that a new inquiry was about to be initiated. He dwelt on what he euphemistically called his 1950 investigation, admitting that it had not been inquisitorial, only terribly thorough. Convinced that the RCMP had passed on his file to the FBI, he now feared that the FBI, in cahoots with the sub-committee, might extract information out of context and distort whatever was in his file. These comments to Gordon were, of course, deceptive in the extreme, for Norman well knew from his January 1952 interrogation by Messrs. Guernsey, McClellan, and Glazebrook that the most damaging information about him had been supplied to the RCMP by M15, and not by the FBI. Denigrating the English cousin, however, was less productive than denigrating the American neighbor.

According to Gordon, Norman had no fear that new information might emerge in any renewed investigation. He was very satisfied with the "thor-oughness" of the previous one, although he claimed that it had been an ordeal both physically and psychically. He thought that others might become unjustly enmeshed because of the distortions. He also observed that these congressional investigations had no limits when they were intent on destroying someone's name. As an example, he cited the Senate Subcommittee's use of a letter writ-ten in September 1940 by William Holland of the Institute of Pacific Relations, stating that any "secret message" to Institute member Philip Lilienthal in Tokyo might be sent in care of Herbert Norman at the Canadian Legation. What Holland seemingly had wanted to say was that any communications not meant for the attention of the Japanese branch of the Institute of Pacific Relations—Lilienthal's mailing address in Tokyo—were to be sent to Norman, in view of growing Japanese criticism of the Institute's excessively pro-Chinese attitude. Norman claimed that he had not known about Holland's letter until it was mentioned in the subcommittee's hearings, and that he naturally would never have agreed to his proposal.

He also thought that External Affairs might be embarrassed if he were once more involved in the subcommittee's questionable activities, despite Pearson's and the Department's complete support. Yet, he felt that neither Ottawa nor Washington could deflect its intentions, if it decided to press for a renewed investigation; as an afterthought, he mentioned that he had awak-ened the previous night thinking that to be innocent was not sufficient, adding that he had been both conscientious and very discreet in executing his ambas-sadorial mission. If the question again were to surface he would chuck it all and retire to the country. He characterized the congressional investigations and those who conducted them as "evil." His use of the word evil, according to Gordon, was interesting for he spoke it as if it were an "incarnate" object, some-thing able to destroy life and the world.[6]

At 8:30 the following morning, April 2, Norman visited his Egyptian physician, Dr. Halim Doss. He stayed with him until 10:30, and again visited him that same afternoon between 3:00 and 5:30 p.m. He told the doctor the whole story of his relationship with the subcommittee, and "how he was *worried* about its further investigations."[7] Mentioning that he had discussed the matter with Arthur Kilgour who had minimized the subcommittee's current activities, he felt that the FBI "contained some vicious elements who might not hesitate to frame him if they were able to do so." He spoke of Alger Hiss who had probably been "framed," and that his only mistake had been to deny that he knew Whittaker Chambers—a statement he could not retract.

It is true that the FBI, like any other security organization should be kept on a tight leash, yet the thought that it would attempt to "frame" Norman is preposterous, just as his comments about Alger Hiss border on the absurd, even if they were, no doubt, shared at the time by many from the "Liberal Left." Hiss had been found guilty by twenty of the twenty-four jurors who had sat at both his trials. Despite the fact that he had been defended by America's best legal talent, and had invoked every appeal process the American federal system of law had to offer, all his appeals were rejected. Predictably, if Alger Hiss had been charged in Canada he would have been convicted under the draconian strictures of the Official Secrets Act, after facing a judiciary which was and still is, generally, far more conservative than its American counterpart.

Although Dr. Doss insisted that Norman was exaggerating the subcommittee's actions, noting that it had made no further comments, Norman pointed out that it was working behind closed doors. He then showed him about twelve pages of notes he had written. Some were on the embassy's blue air mail stationery and, according to Dr. Doss' disclosure, they resembled the text of a note found after Norman's suicide. The doctor understood, he later told Kilgour, that Norman had subsequently burned them.

Dr. Doss felt that his patient suffered from a "tremendous sense of guilt." He had, in fact, brought this to his attention. He correctly concluded that "he must have had a very strong religious upbringing." Norman had also maintained that "he had *never* been a communist but during his student days he had become very interested in communism because of its international aspects,"[8] casually observing, in this connection, that Soviet Russia had stood up to Nazi Germany. Kilgour later admitted to Ottawa that he had had a similar conversation with Norman, and that both he and Dr. Doss had assured him that there was no reason to take these prewar experiences so seriously, because many intelligent people had walked the same road. According to the doctor, Norman felt that he had "let the Canadian Government down because it previously had said that he had never been a communist but now he was afraid that a [sub]committee in Washington might show that he had *almost* been a communist."[9] The fear that obviously stalked him was that of public exposure.

The following day, April 3, Norman did not appear at the office, but he telephoned Kilgour to invite him to lunch and a chat, since they had not had an opportunity to talk to each other for several days. Since Kilgour had a prior engagement, he visited with him before lunch for approximately an hour. Kilgour thought he looked "quite weary," and Norman observed that the Washington investigation "had got him down." It was Kilgour's impression that he was unaware that Tsuru had testified, as he talked of the previous RCMP investigation and how tiring it had been. He repeated the assertion that the RCMP had been fed information by the FBI—no mention of MI5—recalling that during the Ottawa investigations he had been asked if he knew a certain Cambridge University economist. When he had said he did, it had taken several hours of questioning to satisfy the RCMP. Available documentary evidence shows that no questioning took place on the subject. Norman also claimed that John Foster Dulles had told him in Tokyo that the only thing Alger Hiss had done was not to cooperate with the FBI. Kilgour surmised that he might have "actually expected another prolonged inquiry." Indeed, "he mentioned the possibility of being recalled to Ottawa for investigation—the result of which might be that he was not properly cleared." Ultimately, the discussion led to the mutual decision that Norman should take an immediate holiday in Spain.

Since the Normans and Arthur Kilgour were planning to attend a Japanese movie that evening, Kilgour was invited for dinner. The proposed holiday was discussed before dinner, and an appropriate draft message to External Affairs on the subject was prepared. Kilgour was to review it the following morning, amend it if necessary and, after Norman's approval, dispatch it to Ottawa. After dinner they picked up two of the Normans' friends, and during the showing of the movie, the ambassador supplied some explanations about its contents. Entitled "Mask of Destiny," it dealt with the self-destruction of the leading character; although his fate had been decided, he was, nevertheless, unable to control the flow of events. During the movie and over drinks afterwards, Norman appeared to feel better, taking an active part in the conversation,[10] and even making arrangements to play croquet the following afternoon.[11]

It was not to be, for on the morning of April 4 he ended his life by jumping off the roof of an eight-storey apartment building. How much seeing the Japanese film the night before may have contributed toward the chemistry of his suicide is an imponderable, as his inspection of the chancery's roof had occurred several days before....

Mrs. Norman strongly denied that Herbert had ever discussed suicide either with her or with Dr. Doss. Indeed, in conversations with others he may have appeared depressed or uneasy, but had never spoken of taking his life. Mrs. Norman wanted this fact conveyed to Lester Pearson—which it was—and also to Prime Minister Louis St. Laurent. What Herbert had discussed with Dr. Doss, according to Mrs. Norman, were his vexations and disquiet over what had developed. She feared that anything said by Herbert's physician might be twisted and overstated.[12] Interestingly, Pearson never publicly discussed the information relayed to him by Mrs. Norman. To have spoken of it would have undercut the notion that Norman had been driven to his death, solely by the activities of the Senate Subcommittee. Politically, it was wiser, even more advantageous, to ignore it and perpetuate the myth. America—specifically the Senate Subcommittee—would be the convenient whipping boy.

But what did Norman supposedly say before his death? According to the Senate Subcommittee report for 1957, the CIA had in its file an April dispatch from a highly reliable source in Cairo stating that on the night before he took his life, he had dined with a physician. He had informed him that he feared Prime Minister St. Laurent was not supporting him and that a Royal Commission of Inquiry would be established. If called to testify "he would have to implicate 60 to 70 Americans and Canadians and that he couldn't face up to it and that he was going to destroy himself."[13]

Before making a textual exegesis of this purported CIA dispatch it should be pointed out that the CIA never denied the existence of a dispatch resembling the text cited by the Senate Subcommittee. Moreover, no agency, no department of the American government, nor the White House have ever denied it. The Diefenbaker government subsequently refuted the existence of any record indicating that prior to Norman's suicide, the St. Laurent government had intended to establish a Royal Commission of Inquiry. The possibility that there may have been unofficial discussions within the government about such a commission was unfortunately never investigated.[14] Nevertheless, there was silence on the American side, especially by the CIA which usually is quick to deny even the most far-fetched story that tangentially might concern it.

However, like any information conveyed through several sources, this CIA dispatch, assuming it exists and had not got its Egyptian events muddled, has obviously undergone some distortion. There is no evidence that Norman dined with any physician on the evening of April 3. He saw Kilgour before lunch and that evening he and his wife dined with him. Then, accompanied by friends they went to see the Japanese movie. Apart from Norman's alleged observation that Prime Minister St. Laurent was not supporting him, the other comment credited to him in the purported conversation with a physician, was about his fear that a "Royal Commission of Inquiry" would be struck and, if called as a witness, his testimony would implicate sixty to seventy Americans and Canadians. Supposing the intelligence and knowledge of the alleged physician with whom he was said to have dined were above average, that individual would have had to be very sophisticated to conjure up the phrase "Royal Commission of Inquiry." Without fear of contradiction, it therefore can be asserted that the nature of such a specialized government body would have been unknown to almost every American and, undoubtedly, to almost every Egyptian. In this instance, the words could only have been voiced by a Canadian or someone familiar with analogous British royal commissions. Only Norman himself could have made such a comment. In line with his remarks about St. Laurent, one can only conclude that the purported conversation had, at least some basis in fact, and that some sort of conversation therefore may have taken place. Only a Royal Commission of Inquiry, with its draconian powers, could have posed questions and would have insisted on the kind of replies that no Senate Subcommittee would have been able to emulate because of lack of jurisdiction and in view of Norman's diplomatic immunity.

The reported conversation, undoubtedly, took place in Cairo between Norman and another individual. Whether he was a physician or someone else is unclear. We know that similar comments were made by him to Kilgour who then reported them to External Affairs: "he mentioned the possibility of being recalled to Ottawa for investigation—the result of which might be that he was not properly cleared."[15]

Ten years later a chronology of the events leading up to Norman's suicide was drafted. It seemingly included all the relevant telegrams sent to and received from Cairo. Nowhere is there a message, either from Louis St. Laurent or Lester Pearson discussing such possibilities.[16]

The only message that we know came from Ottawa was Pearson's handwritten note, sent about a week before Norman's suicide.[17] He might have commented on St. Laurent's uneasiness or he may have made some remarks which, though innocent, may have sufficed to unnerve Norman.

Norman's scribbled suicide notes are so enigmatic that they offer no clear picture of why he actually took his own life. The prudent and reasonable person is placed in the unenviable position of having to weigh and judge jottings made only minutes before his self-destruction, in light of what we now know of his past record. These notes, therefore, must be dissected with the greatest of care.

In the longest, intended for External Affairs, he speaks about being "overwhelmed" by his "consciousness of sin." He asks for God's forgiveness and goes on to say that time and access to the record would show to anyone "impartial" that he was "innocent" of the main allegation, namely, of having conspired or acted against the security of Canada or that of any other state. Claiming never to have violated the secrecy oath as a member of External Affairs, he states that he felt the issue would be obfuscated and twisted. He was exhausted by all of it and, though innocent, was faced by formidable forces. He thought it was better to end it all now than to face further calumny. He then begs for his family's forgiveness.

External Affairs would naturally be upset by the implications of his suicide, the scribbled note continues, but he trusts that an impartial and thorough study would support his "innocence." At this very moment, and because he liked his work in External Affairs, he would, with alacrity, confess to any security breach he may have made. He observes that his weakness has been "illusion," and his chief flaw "naivete." It had been naive of him to think that it was sufficient to be innocent of any act that contravened security. External Affairs, he contends, was aware of his "error," but he had committed no crime. He concludes the note by stating that he was unworthy of his wife whose loyalty had sustained him throughout trials and disappointments.[18]

Then there is the note to his brother Howard, a man who had never lost his belief in Christianity and who, over the years, had been at odds with Herbert about his sequential views of life.[19] Although Norman never specifically mentions the Senate Subcommittee by name, he says that he had been "overwhelmed by circumstances and had lived under illusions too long." Stating that Christianity was the only true road, he asks for Howard's forgiveness because things were not as black as they appeared, though, God knows, they were bad enough.

For what should Howard have forgiven him? Was it for straying from the true Christian path or for planning to take his own life? The answer is unclear. Herbert again claims that he had never betrayed his oath of secrecy, observing that guilt by association had begun to crush him. He was praying to God for forgiveness if it was not too late ... Yet, why should guilt by association have necessitated God's forgiveness?

In a second note to his brother and sister-in-law, he again pleads innocence, and once more dwells on his own weak Christianity and how it had, nevertheless, helped to sustain him during the previous days.[20]

The fourth note is addressed to his wife. In it he contends that he could no longer live with himself and was unfit to live at all. The short note concludes that he lacked hope of meriting any sympathy.

That Herbert Norman was a sensitive and civilized human being who cared for his fellowmen is attested to in the fifth note addressed to the Swedish minister; it is the shortest and most macabre. He begs forgiveness for choosing his apartment building as the place from which to take the fatal plunge, explaining that it was the only one which would allow him to avoid endangering someone below.[21]

At this point it might be appropriate to examine the qualities potential candidates had to have in the 1930s after having been talent spotted for recruitment by the Communist Party and the Russian intelligence services. The types of persons in whom they were interested were the well-meaning and those who were moved by idealism. The 1946 Royal Commission described them as people who had "a burning desire to reform and improve Canadian society according to their lights." If properly groomed and cultivated through "study groups" and the appropriate literature, such as the periodical *New Masses* to which Norman had subscribed, they would gradually develop what the Royal Commission called "a sense of divided loyalties" or, in extreme cases, "a transferred loyalty." This process was assisted by whatever "sense of internationalism" would have motivated the potential recruit. He was encouraged to develop feelings of loyalty toward an "international ideal," rather than to any particular foreign state. "This subjective internationalism" was then linked through courses of indoctrination and by appropriate Russian propaganda "with the current conception of the national interests" of Soviet Russia and "the current doctrines and policies of Communist Parties throughout the world."[22]

As we have seen, Norman possessed all the right qualities, as even at the bitter end he made sure that no one else suffered. He also had succumbed, for various reasons—some peculiarly Canadian—to the ideological siren of secular optimism and human perfectibility. This probably was the "sin" to which he alluded in his suicide note to External Affairs. Unlike his brother Howard, he had believed in a false god for so long that that sin was partly redeemed by discovering—at the very end—the staying power of his weak Christianity. This may also, at least partially, explain why the Senate Subcommittee was not specifically mentioned in the notes, and was perhaps only hinted at in the remark that he faced formidable forces, although he was innocent. Was this omission due to his perception that the subcommittee was less at fault than he himself because of his prior activities?

He claims to have lived under an illusion and that he had shown naiveté, that he could not live with himself, was unfit to live, and lacked any hope of meriting sympathy. He says he is innocent of having violated Canada's security and his oath of secrecy, yet his silence about any association with the Communist Party is deafening. Surely, this would have been the time to categorically deny that he was or had ever been a member. He did not do so. Why? Because that part of the *mea culpa* curtain had to be kept tightly drawn. Knowing as we do that he was or had been a member, what are we to make of his denials of all the allegations made against him? Because, to admit even the remotest association with communist elements quickly would have placed in doubt all his other statements.

Norman believed in the great march of history which is part and parcel of communist scripture. No matter what he did, no matter how illegal it was, it could be justified ideologically and psychologically. The laws of communism's dialectical materialism were higher than those governing Canada, higher than any secrecy oath, and greater than thoughts of national security. Moreover, one should differentiate, as Norman had not done, between conveying to unauthorized individuals "secret information" covered by the secrecy oath and "privy information" not covered by that oath. If secret and/or privy material was conveyed by Norman to Moscow during the war when Canada and Soviet Russia were allied, he could have rationalized that Canada's security was not being compromised. However, even if he had passed nothing that was either secret or privy, his denials would not have covered his actions as an agent of disinformation and/or of influence. As pointed out in Brian Crozier's book *Strategy for Survival,* in the United Kingdom and in some other Western states as well—and that would include Canada—*"it is not a punishable offence to be a Soviet agent of influence, even a conscious and paid one."*[23] (Italics in the original.)

The question of whether or not Norman was an agent of influence must have bothered the mandarins at External Affairs because, almost two weeks after he had committed suicide, someone in its Middle East Division sent a report to Glazebrook's Defense Liaison II, stating that a selection of Norman's telegraphic reports on political matters had been examined and that a cursory check had been made of his Cairo dispatches. Their quality was considered "outstanding," and no trace had been found that showed any inclination on Norman's part "to sympathize with Communist ideology or practice." On the contrary, in contact with Egyptians and other Arabs, it appeared that he had gone to some trouble to warn them of the dangers which Russian penetration would, in the end, pose to their governments and the peoples of the Middle East. Norman consciously seemed to have developed wide-ranging sources among Egyptians, Arabs, and the diplomatic corps in Cairo, and he had close and friendly relations with the Indian ambassador. This, the report maintains, illustrated that he had not hesitated to pursue any "useful channel," even though he "must have realized that evidence of contact with and dependence on 'neutralist' sources increased his personal vulnerability to irresponsible charges." Of the materials examined only three telegrams had been dispatched after March 14, when the Senate Subcommittee released Emmerson's executive session testimony.[24]

The Middle East Division's analysis is somewhat naive. No agent of influence would have been foolish enough to reveal anything in a telegram or dispatch. Of value to his true masters would have been the type of advice he might have tendered to his government and perhaps to others who could have been influenced by it. What Norman supposedly had said to Egyptians and other Arabs is virtually non-verifiable. Therefore, the Middle East Division's contribution would have been far more significant if his advice to Ottawa on how to handle Middle East events had been juxtaposed with Russian objectives in the region, particularly in Egypt.

Thus, Norman's deep commitment to the cause may help explain his inability to acknowledge the enormity of the evil that had stalked the Russian landscape, expecially during the Stalin era and, subsequently, other regions of the world.

One writer sympathetic to Herbert Norman said about him in 1977 that his "outright naiveté" was "linked to his lack of any strong sense of evil."[25] Three years earlier, almost the same comments were made many miles south of the 49th parallel by a stepson about his stepfather who he considered to have been a "severely repressed and morally rigid person." The stepson recalled that he was "a man capable of inflicting great suffering on himself in order to protect others at all costs." Moreover, until his stepfather's conviction and imprisonment, the stepson asserted he " 'had no sense of evil.' " That man was Alger Hiss.[26] The same characteristics were also noted in the longtime Canadian KGB agent Hugh Hambleton who was convicted in Great Britain under the Official Secrets Act. He, too, never seemed to have been "interested, and never would be, in making any moral judgement of the Soviet regime."[27]

This is not the time to examine the traits which appear to run like threads through the psyches of many who have served the Russian behemoth; let others who follow delve into the matter. If they wish to do so, they might consider the words of the Israeli novelist Amos Oz who said, " ' Whoever ignores varying degrees of evil is bound to become a servant of evil.' "[28]

What exactly were the "overwhelming circumstances" that had decided Herbert Norman to take his own life? Unexpectedly, after a long silence, the Senate Subcommittee on Internal Security again became interested in him, especially after Emmerson's testimony. Some days later, Patrick Walsh attempted to contact Pearson to present a brief dealing with Norman's communist background.[29] Is it possible that Walsh's overtures were mentioned in Pearson's handwritten note to him? Then Tsuru testified before the subcommittee, although Norman apparently was not aware of it. This is possible but not probable, considering the circles in which he moved in Cairo. Even if we discount his purported comments about the establishment of a Royal Commission of Inquiry, he had after all, mentioned to Kilgour "the possibility of being recalled to Ottawa for investigation."

Although Arnold Heeney had been made Canadian Ambassador to Washington by this time, Pearson was still in harness directing External Affairs, and there were others in positions of influence who, in the past, had been sympathetic to Norman's plight. The relative immunity he had enjoyed in the past would probably continue into the future, as long as the Senate Subcommittee desisted from delving into his background and activities. Was it lining up a new surprise witness? Testimony by Jaffe would be damaging in the extreme. Norman undoubtedly knew that he had broken with the American Communist Party and the extreme Left in the late 1940s. Was someone else being groomed to testify against him? Who else was there, and what new evidence might surface, even without the subcommittee's initiatives? Other information it might uncover could again lead to interrogations by Messrs. Guernsey, McClellan, and Glazebrook. That had to be avoided at all costs.

As in Edgar Allan Poe's classic, *The Pit and the Pendulum,* Norman had escaped several brushes with the pit of destruction. But like on the narrator of Poe's tale of horror, the "walls" were closing in and forcing him inexorably toward the pit. The walls, in this case, were the mounting testimony against him and the fear of possible further revelations concerning his past activities, some of them suspicious. In line with information supplied by the RCMP, the FBI, and MI5, they might have led to a fuller and more vigorous interrogation than the one he had experienced in 1952. Buttressed by a full RCMP field investigation, the façade he had so carefully and cleverly constructed over the years would collapse. Aware of this distinct possibility and dreading, no doubt, that his unmasking would expose others, including perhaps influential friends, Norman decided to commit suicide. Of all the bleak options he may have had, taking his own life must have appeared the least objectionable. No doubt, he was well aware of E. M. Forster's 1930s credo, mouthed by Anthony Blunt and dear to the heart of the Left, "that betraying one's friend was worse than betraying one's country."[30]

Notes

1. See Chapter 7, p. 107.
2. Unless cited otherwise, what follows is based on a report by Norman's deputy Arthur Kilgour, about the events in Cairo before and after Norman's suicide. Kilgour to Léger, April 10, 1957, Norman File, RCMP (CSIS) Papers. Kilgour's subsequent version of these days is slightly inaccurate, based as it was on memory. Arthur Kilgour, "On Remembering Herbert Norman," in Roger W. Bowen (ed.), *E. H. Norman: His Life and Scholarship* (Toronto: University of Toronto Press, 1984), p. 77. See also Charles Taylor, *Six Journeys: A Canadian Pattern* (Toronto: Anansi, 1977), p. 147. As to the affidavit, see E[gerton] H[erbert] N[orman] to Glazebrook, March 12, 1952, and the attached documents especially the affidavit, Norman File, RCMP (CSIS) Papers.
3. See Chapter 4, p. 41.
4. Italics added. Kilgour to Léger, April 10, 1957, Norman File, RCMP (CSIS) Papers.
5. Kilgour to Léger, April 10, 1957, Norman File, RCMP CSIS Papers.
6. King Gordon to [Pearson], April 7, 1957, Vol. 44, Pearson Papers, MG 26, N1, PAC. On Holland's letter, see Hearings, *Institute of Pacific Relations,* Part 1 (July 25, 26, 31, August 2 and 7, 1951), pp. 320-321, and *ibid.,* Part 14 (May 2, June 20, 1952), pp. 5030-5031.
7. Italics added.
8. Italics added.
9. Italics in the original.
10. Kilgour to Léger, April 10, 1957, Norman File, RCMP (CSIS) Papers.
11. Taylor, p. 147.
12. Holmes to Pearson, July 18, 1957, Vol. 44, Pearson Papers, MG 26. N1, PAC.
13. Committee on the Judiciary, *Internal Security Annual Report for 1957,* p. 101 fn.
14. Canada, Parliament, House of Commons, *Debates, Official Report,* 24th Parliament, 1st Session, Vol. I (May 15-16, 1958) (Ottawa: Queen's Printer, 1958), pp. 92, 137-138.
15. This chapter, p. 149.
16. Chronology—Part II, February 23, 1967, Norman File, External Affairs Papers.

17. See Chapter 7, pp. 111-112.

18. Kilgour to External Affairs, No. 260, April 6, 1957, Norman File, External Affairs Papers.

19. H[oward] Norman to Pearson, April 13, 1957, Vol. 44, Pearson Papers, MG 26, N1, PAC.

20. Taylor, p. 149.

21. Kilgour to External Affairs, No. 259, April 6, 1957, Norman File, RCMP (CSIS) Papers.

22. Report of the 1946 Royal Commission on Espionage in Canada, pp. 72-73. On the *New Masses,* see Chapter 4, p. 36.

23. Italics in the original. Brian Crozier, *Strategy of Survival* (New Rochelle, New York: Arlington House, 1978), p. 136.

24. Middle East Division to D[efense] L[iaison] II, April 17, 1957, Norman File, External Affairs Papers.

25. Taylor, p. 119.

26. Allen Weinstein, *Perjury: the Hiss-Chambers Case* (New York: Knopf, 1978), pp. 526-527.

27. Leo Heaps, *Hugh Hambleton, Spy. Thirty Years with the KGB* (Toronto: Methuen, 1983), p. 53.

28. *The New York Times,* January 16, 1986, p. 17.

29. See Chapter 7, p. 111.

30. Andrew Boyle, *The Fourth Man* (New York: The Dial Press/James Wade, 1979), p. 384.

CHAPTER
14 THE MOSAIC, LIMITED IDENTITIES AND NATIONAL PURPOSE

All nation states suffer through stages of euphoria and depression, and while politicians are usually praised or damned for this, the process is multi-dimensional and frequently influenced by international trends. Canada in the 1990s faces an uncertain future, with alienation and fragmentation commonplace. Discontent is neither new nor unique for, as Peter Waite observed of 1867, "Canada did not begin well," yet it survived and prospered. It may be, as Frank Underhill suggested in an article in *The Centennial Review*, that dissatisfaction is simply the "Canadian Way of Being Unhappy." The complexity of the current world order, however, combined with the dissolution of fixed patterns in and among nations, reminds us that idealization of the status quo may be the first stage of its disintegration.

Much of Canadian history centres on the expedients adopted to overcome the problem of national unity. French-English relations have, of course, "run like a mountain" through our history, and so far accommodations have been found. Regional divisions were inherited in 1867 and have been both solved and further complicated by successive generations. Class divisions have been alternately denied and exploited. The composition of the population itself has been altered. In the twentieth century the term "mosaic" was popularized as a concession to a growing change as well as a rejection of the American "melting pot." While the notion had some validity, it was more form that substance, for as late as 1947

Prime Minister William Lyon Mackenzie King declared: "The people of Canada do not wish to make a fundamental alteration in the character of their population through mass immigration."

Despite that government policy, the immigrants of the 1950s and 1960s contributed to unprecedented ethnic diversity, though English-French dominance was unchallenged, and the Royal Commission on Bilingualism and Biculturalism was an attempt to strengthen "the equal partnership between the two founding races, taking into account the contribution made by other ethnic groups to the cultural enrichment of Canada." An unexpected by-product of that Commission was the increased visibility of those "other ethnic groups" and their demands for a place at the table. About the same time the Native people finally began to assert themselves with claims that questioned the validity of the dominant society.

One result of the Royal Commission was Prime Minister Pierre Elliot Trudeau's announcement in 1971 that "a policy of multiculturalism within a bilingual framework commends itself to the Government as the most suitable means of assuring the cultural freedom of Canadians." If the hope was to satisfy everyone, including the natives, it was a case of too little and too late. If offended as much as it pleased and ignored the native peoples. By that time, moreover, even academics had begun to think of Canada's "limited identities" rather than any national ideal.

During the 1970s and 1980s a great tide of alienation burst over a fragile Canada. In its wake were the regions, the separatists, the ethnic groups, the workers, the natives, the women, the poor, the refugees, the children, the students, the elderly, the sick, the criminals and their victims. The diversity in aspirations of these groups may be so great as to render common goals unobtainable. On the other hand, a dispassionate view might see all this as exaggeration. The three readings included here represent samples from an endless spectrum. The first by Menno Boldt and J. Anthony Long is a detached view of "Tribal Traditions and European-Western Political Ideologies: The Dilemma of Canada's Native Indians." The second is an overview of "Ethnic Identity" from *"Coming Canadians": An Introduction to a History of Canada's Peoples* by Jean R. Brunet with Howard Palmer. The final selection is by Reginald W. Bibby, who is alarmed by the thrust of our limited identities, suggesting that "not a few times in history the unsound has been mistaken for the profound." The fragmentation "may well result in the production of individual mosaic fragments." This in turn could be among "the most serious threats to social life in Canada."

Suggestions for Further Reading

Bercuson, David Jay and Phillip A. Buckner, eds., *Eastern and Western Perspectives: Papers from the Joint Atlantic Canada / Western Canadian Studies Conference.* Toronto: University of Toronto Press, 1981.

Buckner, Phillip A., "'Limited Identities' and Canadian Historical Scholarship: An Atlantic Provinces Perspective," *Journal of Canadian Studies*, XXIII, nos. 1 & 2 (Spring/Summer 1988), 177-198.

Burnet, Jean, "Myths and Multiculturalism," *Canadian Journal of Education* IV, 4 (1979), 43-58.

Careless, J.M.S., "'Limited Identities' in Canada," *Canadian Historical Review*, L, no. 1 (March 1969), 1-10.

_____, "Limited Identities - Ten Years Later," *Manitoba History*, (Spring, 1976), 3-9.

Getty, Ian A.L. and Antoine S. Lussier, eds., *As Long as the Sun Shines: A Reader in Canadian Native Studies*. Vancouver: University of British Columbia Press, 1983.

McCormick, Peter, "Regionalism in Canada: Disentangling the Threads," *Journal of Canadian Studies*, XXV, no. 2 (Summer 1989), 5-21.

Pratt, Larry and Garth Stevenson, eds., *Western Separatism: The Myths, Realities and Dangers*. Edmonton: Hurtig, 1981.

Rasporich A.W., ed., *The Making of The Modern West: Western Canada Since 1945*. Calgary: University of Calgary Press, 1984.

Underhill, Frank, "The Canadian Way of Being Unhappy," *The Centennial Review*, X, no. 4 (Fall 1966), 446-461.

TRIBAL TRADITIONS AND EUROPEAN-WESTERN POLITICAL IDEOLOGIES: THE DILEMMA OF CANADA'S NATIVE INDIANS

Menno Boldt and J. Anthony Long

In their quest for political and cultural self-determination, Indian leaders in Canada have adopted the European-Western concept of sovereignty as the cornerstone of their aspirations. They advance claims to inherent sovereignty in order to establish the legal, moral and political authority that will allow them to nurture and develop their traditional tribal customs, values, institutions and social organization. Thus, the concept of sovereignty represents for the current generation of Indian leaders a means to an end, rather than an end in itself.[1]

Recently, Indian leaders have taken their claim to inherent sovereignty into the international arena in an attempt to bring external political pressure to bear on the Canadian government. They feel that the more "enlightened norms" of international law and the United Nations' covenants on political and cultural self-determination will bolster their case for sovereignty, and will serve to counteract the negative treatment their claims have received at the hands of Canadian judges and policy-makers.

From *The Canadian Journal of Political Science* XVII, no. 3 (September 1984), 537-53. Reprinted by permission of *The Canadian Journal of Political Science*.

This study addresses the question: How does the European-Western idea of "sovereignty" complement traditional tribal Indian customs, values, institutions and social organizations? This question implies more than a linguistic or semantic analysis. It goes to the very heart of Indian culture. We approach this question by examining the implications and pitfalls of sovereignty for traditional Indian customs, values and institutions. We then proceed to explore alternative ideas for achieving political and cultural self-determination.

Before proceeding, however, three important points need to be made. First, our statements about traditional Indian society refer to the period prior to European-influenced change. The analysis, of course, has relevance for contemporary Indian society since many traditional values have persisted even in the face of systematic and coercive measures taken by European colonizers and their successors to eliminate these values. But, more significantly, there is a strong cultural nationalist movement among Indians aimed at reinstituting many traditional values and customs.

Second, we use the term "tribe" to refer to a type of social organization rather than a level of political jurisdiction. Historically, Indian tribes were autonomous and self-sufficient social groupings. The Indian Act organized Indians into legal entities called bands. But Indian people today still recognize the concept of tribe, just as they still recognize the concept of Indian nation. In our usage both "bands" and "nations" qualify as tribal societies.

Finally, although we use the term "Indian" we do not intend to imply that Canada's indigenous tribes constitute a single people in any sociocultural or political sense. Great diversity exists among tribes with respect to language, political styles, cultural heritage, and so on. However, there is now emerging a national cultural-political unity movement among Canada's Indians,[2] and there exist today, as there have always existed, cultural traits and values which traditionally have been shared by most Indian tribes. These include reaching decisions by consensus, institutionalized sharing, respect for personal autonomy and a preference for impersonal controls over behaviour.[3]

Tribal Traditions and the Concept of Sovereignty

Youngblood-Henderson has noted that, for Indians, sovereignty is "a matter of the heart"—an emotional, not an intellectual concept.[4] This probably helps to explain why their conceptions of how sovereignty would function in a tribal context are still embryonic and inchoate. In fact, much of the emotional appeal that sovereignty holds for Indians stems from its vagueness. It allows them to project onto it a promise of most of their political, sociocultural and economic aspirations without a rigorous consideration of the adequacy of their resources and instrumentalities for achieving it. Also, the ambiguity of the concept averts factionalism within Indian society, as each group is free to infer its preferred meanings and objectives.

Indian leaders, in their discussion of sovereignty, focus attention almost exclusively on its instrumentality for checking the intrusion of *external* authority and power into their social and political structures and territory. That is, sovereignty is very narrowly conceived of as a strategy to free themselves from external intrusions into their society. In their preoccupation with the goal of self-determination they overlook almost entirely the significance that the doctrine of sovereignty potentially has for ordering *internal* tribal authority and power relationships. Thus, Indian leaders have ignored the latent peril that the idea of sovereignty may hold for their traditional tribal customs, values, institutions and social organization. But, if they are going to advocate sovereignty as the foundation of their contemporary and future goals Indian leaders need to consider its implications for the central values of their tribal traditions—the very values they seek to protect. These values will not be preserved if the concept of sovereignty is inconsistent with their cultural legacy.

The potential consequences of sovereignty for Indian tribal traditions must be evaluated in the context of some key ideas contained in European-Western doctrines of sovereignty, namely, the concepts of authority, hierarchy and a ruling entity; and the notions of statehood and territoritality.

Authority, Hierarchy and a Ruling Entity

The concept of *authority* is critical to any analysis of how the European-Western doctrine of sovereignty can function in the context of indigenous North American forms of the "band," "tribe" or "nation." Bodin and Hobbes wrote of sovereignty as it if were equivalent to absolute and perpetual authority derived either from God or the people. For Locke and Rousseau sovereignty arose from absolute authority derived from the voluntary agreement of independent wills (contract of association) delegating their authority to the government, the fiduciary sovereign.[5] Common to both of these conceptions of sovereignty, and generally implied in all European-Western concepts of sovereignty, is a principle of authority defined as the supreme, if not absolute and inalienable, power by the ruling entity to make decisions and to enforce them, if necessary, through sanctions or coercion.

Invariably linked with this principle of authority is the idea of a *hierarchy* of power relationships. This association between hierarchy and authority is exemplified in Haller's theory that authority is the base of sovereignty, and that sovereignty arises from the natural superiority of one over another.[6] Haller reasons that equals will not obey equals, hence sovereignty can only be exercised in a state of inequality where the stronger rules. For Haller this represented a universal law of nature—even among the birds of the air and the beasts of the forest the stronger always rules. This assumption of a hierarchy of authority relationships is general not only in traditional European doctrines of sovereignty but is also evident in contemporary conceptions of "popular sovereignty."

The European-Western assumption of hierarchical authority relationships implies a *ruling entity,* that is, a particular locus for sovereign authority. In European society this precept found expression in the authority of rulers. In fact, much of the philosophical debate about sovereignty has focussed on the appropriate locus for sovereign authority.[7] Even in the ideal sense of popular sovereignty, that is where authority is derived from the people, this authority, once it is delegated by the people, must be lodged somewhere. Thus, terms like "political rulers," "decision-makers," "government," and so on, are used to distinguish those who exercise authority from the rest of the members of society. These terms imply that an identifiable subset of the members of the total society have the power of authority in their hands.[8]

How do these three key ideas—authority, hierarchy and a ruling entity—contained in European-Western concepts of sovereignty fit into traditional Indian society? In examining the question we want to stress that our discussion of authority, hierarchy and government in traditional Indian society has reference to the basic political culture of most tribes. We are not suggesting that everywhere, without exceptions, North American Indians adopt the same model.

Taking the idea of authority first, we note that the history and experience of North American tribal societies were very different from those of European societies. The European-Western notion of a sovereign authority had its origins in the system of feudalism and the associated belief in the inherent inequality of men. The indigenous peoples of North America, however, never experienced feudalism and most believed in the equality of men. In the Hobbesian doctrine of sovereignty, authority was deemed necessary to protect society against rampant individual self-interest. But in Indian tribal society individual self-interest was inextricably intertwined with tribal interests; that is, the general good and the individual good were taken to be virtually identical.[9] Laslett's "onion skin" analogy aptly illustrates the mythical quality of individuality in traditional Indian society. To apprehend the individual in tribal Indian society, he says, we would have to peel off a succession of group-oriented and derived attitudes as layers of onion skin. The individual turns out to be a succession of metaphorical layers of group attributes which ends up with nothing remaining.[10]

Indians traditionally defined themselves communally[11] in terms of a "spiritual compact" rather than a social contract.[12] The "tribal will" constituted a vital spiritual principle which for most tribes gained expression in sharing and cooperation rather than private property and competition. This obviated the need for sovereign authority to sustain the integrity of the society against the centrifugal forces of individual self-interest. Thus, the political and social experiences that would allow Indians to conceive of authority in European-Western terms simply did not exist, nor can it be reconciled with the traditional beliefs and values that they want to retain.

The idea of hierarchical power relationships contained in European-Western concepts of sovereignty is, likewise, irreconcilable with Indian history and experiences. In European thought the Enlightenment concept of egalitarianism emerged as a reaction and response to excesses resulting from the hierarchical doctrine of sovereignty. Egalitarianism was imposed on, and interacted with, the hierarchical concept of sovereign authority to produce more humane political structures. In traditional Indian society, however, the idea of egalitarianism did not emerge as a reaction to excesses of hierarchical authority. Equality was derived from the Creator's founding prescription. The creation myth held that, from the *beginning,* all members of the tribe shared and participated *equally* in all privileges and responsibilities. In their dealings with the British Crown, Indian representatives always used images of equality such as "links in a chain" or "going down the road together."[13] Neither the members of the tribe nor outsiders who studied them found images of hierarchical political authority. The exercise of hierarchical authority would have been viewed as a device to deprive the people of equality.[14]

Traditional Indian beliefs and values also clash with the concept of a ruling entity—that is, a dichotomy of ruler(s) and the ruled.[15] In Europe, even after the Enlightenment, it was not authority per se that came under question but rather who should exercise authority. New arrangements for exercising authority were devised including election and delegation. Most Indian tribes, however, did not accept that any man or agency had by virtue of any qualities, inherent or by transfer, the right to govern others, even in the service of the tribal good. The people ruled collectively, as a tribe, exercising authority as one body with undivided power, performing all functions of government. The tribe was not held to be the result of a contract among individuals, or between ruler(s) and ruled, but of a divine creation by the Creator. No human being was deemed to have control over the life of another. Therefore, the authority to rule could not be delegated to any one man or subset of members of the tribal group. This denial of personal authority extended even to the notion of transferring the right to govern within specified fixed limits. *Any* arrangement that would separate the people from their fundamental, natural and inalienable right to govern themselves directly was deemed illegitimate.

In place of personal authority, hierarchical power relationships, and a ruling entity, the organizing and regulating force for group order and endeavour in traditional Indian society was *custom* and *tradition.*[16] Put another way, Indians invested their customs and traditions with the authority and power to govern their behaviour.[17] Customs were derived from the Creator. They had withstood the test of time and represented the Creator's sacred blueprint for survival of the tribe. By implication, therefore, everyone must be subject to custom; everyone, equally, came under the same impersonal authority. By unreservedly accepting custom as their legitimate guide in living and working together they alleviated the need for personal authority, a hierarchical power structure and a separate ruling entity to maintain order. Customary authority protected individuals from self-serving, capricious, and coercive exercise of power by contemporaries. Since customs are not readily changed, or new ones quickly created, authority was not easily or expediently expanded.

In the traditional myths, custom had a source and sanction outside the individual and the tribe. It was the handiwork of the Creator. Conformity to custom was a matter of religious obedience that accorded with the generally accepted moral standards of the tribe and it was not deemed necessary to appoint agents with authority to enforce custom. Custom carried authority of the type that Rees calls of a "moral kind,"[18] that is, it obliges individuals, by conscience, to obey. This is quite different from law which is a dictum accompanied by an effective sanction.[19] Rule by custom, without a separate agency of enforcement, was possible in traditional Indian society because a face-to-face society can maintain order with few but broad general rules known to everyone. When large gatherings of diverse bands occurred (for the Sun Dance, for example) it was customary to temporarily make one of the Indian "societies" a peace-keeper.[20]

Rituals confirmed custom by investing it with a spiritual quality whose authority was rooted in a sacred beginning, a founding in the past. Through consecrated rituals the testimony of the ancestors, who first had witnessed the sacred founding, was passed from one generation to the next. Arendt[21] has identified a similar concept of order in the Roman image of the pyramid which did not reach up hierarchically, but into the past—a past that was sanctified.

The absence of personal authority, hierarchical relationships, and a separate ruling entity carried profound implications for the exercise of leadership in Indian society. For example, elders played an essential and highly valued function by transmitting the Creator's founding prescriptions, customs and traditions. Yet they had no formal authority. The elders merely gave information and advice, never in the form of a command. The elders were revered not because of their power or authority, but because of their knowledge of the customs, traditions and rituals, and because of their ancestral links with the sacred beginning. Chiefs, like elders, also led without authority. Their personality or skills as warrior, hunter, and so on, would gain them a following, but the Chief was on the same level as the followers—personal domination over others did not exist. In fact, most tribes had a multiplicity of chiefs at any one time, each without sanctioning powers beyond personal charisma and proven ability. Even in the heat of battle a warrior had the option of participating or not, without prejudice. Self-direction (autonomy), an aristocratic prerogative in European society, was everyone's right in Indian society.[22]

An interesting model of nonauthoritarian leadership is contained in Paul-Louis Carrier's "coach-driver" analogy.[23] In his analogy Carrier proposes that in a liberal state of affairs the government is like a coach-driver, hired and paid by those whom he drives. The coach-driver conveys his patrons, but merely to the destination and by the route they choose. To an uninformed observer the coach-driver may appear to be the real master, but this is an illusion. Carrier's model of nonauthoritarian leadership only approximates the traditional Indian conception of leadership. In tribal Indian society leadership was more aptly symbolized by the relationship of a military drummer to his company. The drummer can establish a cadence but he has no authority to require individuals in the company to march to it. That authority comes from an "external source." For Indians this external source was always to be found in their sacred customs. Significantly, unlike Carrier's "coach-driver" who is subordinate to his patrons, the Indian leader, like the drummer, is not subordinate to the dictates of those who march to his beat. He is responsible only to the "external authority," that is the sacred tribal customs and traditions.

Government without rulers requires special procedures. The mechanism used in traditional Indian society was direct participatory democracy and rule by consensus. This implies an adequate level of agreement amongst all who share in the exercise of authority. Custom provided the mechanism to ensure that order did not break down through failure to achieve consensus.[24]

Statehood and Territoriality

In addition to the concepts of authority, hierarchy and a separate ruling entity, the European-Western doctrine of sovereignty subsumes two more ideas with special implications for Indian tribal traditions: the notions of statehood and territoriality. Merriam points out that, while an unresolved debate exists amongst scholars as to whether sovereignty is an essential characteristic of the state, all theorists of sovereignty implicitly, if not explicitly, assume that statehood is an essential and indispensable requirement for sovereignty to exist.[25] F. F. Hinsley has asserted that the emergence of the state as a form of rule is, by definition, a necessary condition for the exercise of sovereignty.[26]

Indian tribes, prior to colonization, held an independent self-governing status which is best defined as "nationhood," not "statehood." In place of the "myth of a state" they had a "myth of the nation." As *nations* of people they regulated their internal and external relations. But, essentially unlike *states,* their foundation of social order was not based on hierarchical authority wielded by a distinct central political entity. Whereas the state represents a structure of hierarchical political authority imposed upon the community, the tribes, while they were highly organized, had not undergone the separation of the state from the community. They lacked separate state forms and government institutions. But it is a mistake to view traditional Indian nations as though they were at some primitive stage of development undergoing a transition to statehood. As noted earlier, authority and order in tribal Indian society rested on custom and the directly spoken will of the community. Indian nations had no need for statehood and the condition of hierarchical authority that statehood implies. Their community performed all of the necessary political functions: it kept the peace, preserved individual life, and protected its members from injustice, abuse and arbitrary actions by any of their number.

The concept of *territoriality* is also fundamental to European-Western doctrines of sovereignty and statehood. Briefly expresses this as follows:

> At the basis of international law lies the notion that a state occupies a definite part of the surface of the earth, within which it normally exercises ... jurisdiction over persons and things to the exclusion of other states. When a state exercises an authority of this kind ... it is popularly said to have sovereignty over the territory.[27]

Although Indian leaders today place great emphasis on land claims and their irrevocable rights to reservation lands, this represents a concession to European-Western political-legal influence. Traditionally, Indian notions of territoriality were not conceived of in terms of precisely fixed territorial boundaries. Tribes existed as spiritual associations that transcended narrow issues of territory.[28] The basis for nationhood was their community, not a fixed territory or geographically defined citizenship.[29] Most tribes had no concept of private or collective land ownership. They believed all land belonged to the Creator who had made the land for *all* life forms to use in harmony. This belief imposed certain restraints on tribes in their territorial claims and in their relationship to each other.

The lack of precisely delineated and recognized territorial borders between tribes occasionally produced conflicts over hunting privileges, but tribes fought mainly over access to game in the territories not the territories themselves. Even when they were at war with each other Indian tribes displayed an abiding respect for each other's autonomy and community. As Ahenakew points out, "it was unknown among the First Nations that one nation could by force deprive another nation of its right to self-determination and to sufficient lands and resources to maintain the lives of its people."[30] Because the notion of territoriality did not have primacy for them, victorious tribes did not colonize vanquished tribes in the way European states did. In short, whereas the European-Western concept of sovereignty was based on authority by the state over a piece of territory, clearly demarcated by boundaries, Indians traditionally based their concept of nationhood on their social community.

Implication of Aspirations to Sovereignty for Indian Culture

Indians in Canada are opting for sovereignty because they view it as the most promising doctrine for protecting their ancestral heritage from encroachment by external influences and powers. They want sovereignty not to justify indigenous coercive authority within their communities but, rather, to exclude the sovereign authority of the Canadian government.

As part of their political-legal justification for sovereignty, and to convince the Canadian government and the international community that their claim to sovereignty is legitimate, contemporary Indian leaders are reconstructing and reinterpreting their tribal history and traditional culture to conform to the essential political and legal paradigms and symbols contained in the European-Western concept of sovereign statehood. They are raising the fiction that Indian societies, prior to European contact, had hierarchically structured governments that exercised authority through a ruling entity as do states, and were in possession of territories clearly defined by political boundaries.[31] To rationalize their claim to sovereignty, Indian leaders are resorting to highly selective assumptions about the traditional exercise of authority by tribal groups; assumptions that contradict the images Indians hold of their traditional aboriginal reality when they are not specifically making a political-legal case for tribal sovereignty. As we have argued, sovereignty was not relevant to their internal or external relationships. Furthermore, all claims to inherent tribal sovereignty, as distinct from claims to nationhood, are necessarily hypothetical ones since, historically, the European conception of sovereignty was not in the linguistic apparatus of Indians. It should be emphasized that this does not represent a cynical manipulation of political concepts so much as a misguided reinterpretation of traditional aboriginality.

By resorting to the expedient claim of inherent sovereign statehood, Indian leaders are legitimizing European-Western philosophies and structures of authority and decision-making within contemporary Indian communities. Most Indian communities initially opposed the imposition of European-Western models of elected "democratic government" and the associated bureaucratic administrative structures. They protested the hierarchical structures that relegated most tribal members to the periphery of decision-making. Yet, by adopting the European-Western ideology of sovereignty, the current generation of Indian leaders is buttressing the imposed alien authority structures within its communities, and is legitimizing the associated hierarchy comprised of indigenous political and bureaucratic elites. This endorsement of hierarchical authority and a ruling entity constitutes a complete rupture with traditional indigenous principles. It undermines fundamental and substantial distinctions between traditional Indian and European political and cultural values. The legal-political struggle for sovereignty could prove to be a Trojan Horse for traditional Indian culture by playing into the hands of the Canadian government's long-standing policy of assimilation.[32]

An Exploration of Alternative Models of Self-Determination

The Canadian government and native Indians must find a way of coexisting that will allow each to preserve that which it deems essential to its survival and identity. The Canadian government has made clear that it will not accept full independence or absolute sovereignty for Canada's Indians.[33] For most

Indians, on the other hand, assimilation into Canadian culture and politics is repugnant and unacceptable. Thus, the acceptable model for a relationship between the federal government and Canada's Indians lies somewhere between assimilation and sovereignty.

Most Indian peoples are committed to a separate social system with corresponding networks of social institutions that are congruent with their historical tribal arrangements, and that are based on their traditional identity, language, religion, philosophy and customs. The Canadian government, while it is rigidly opposed to any concept of sovereignty and separate statehood for Indians, is ready to accept Indian self-government. The challenge for Indian leaders is to develop a model of self-government that is acceptable to the Canadian government, yet will give them internal self-determination without compromising fundamental traditional values. The option of pluralism suggests itself.

In his analysis of pluralism Kenneth McRae[34] identifies three uses of the term: first, that of the British political pluralists (J. N. Figgis, Harold Laski and G. D. H. Cole) who viewed pluralism primarily in terms of alternative foci of citizen loyalties with respect to the sovereign state; second, that put forward by the American writers (A. F. Bentley, David Truman, Robert Dahl and others) which contains the central idea of countervailing but overlapping interest groups competing in policy formation, and, third, that expressed in the literature on colonial and post-colonial societies (J. S. Furnival, M. G. Smith, Leo Kuper and Pierre van den Berghe) which posits two or more social systems and associated constitutional networks within one political system. This latter use of pluralism, which allows for the presence of several nations within one sovereign state, is evident in the "consociational school" (notably Arend Lijphart, Gerard Lehmbruch, Hans Doalder, Jurg Steiner, and Val Lorwin).[35] A consociational arrangement is a significant step short of separation and sovereignty. Theoretically, it could accommodate the essential political requisites of both Indians and the Canadian government, but it compromises traditional Indian values because of its emphasis on rule by elites.

For Indians the issue is not one of choosing between different forms of sovereignty. All forms of sovereignty, whether monistic or pluralistic, involve the hierarchical exercise of authority by a ruling entity and are therefore incompatible with the cultural heritage they seek to preserve. A more promising political model can be found in the works of Vernon Van Dyke.[36] Briefly stated, Van Dyke challenges the "two-level theory of rights."[37] He proposes that rights are not simply a question of the individual and the state but that ethnic communities meeting certain criteria should be considered as unities (corporate bodies) with moral rights and legal status accorded them as *groups* rather than as *individuals*. He proposes that ethnic communities, not only states, are entitled to be regarded as right-and-duty bearing entities. Traditional European-Western concepts of sovereignty provide no place for groups in the state. European philosophers such as Hobbes and Locke emphasized the role of the *individual* in his relationship to the sovereign state. Western liberal political theorists have continued this emphasis on the relationship between individual and state. Robert Nisbet identifies this as the most influential philosophy of freedom in modern Western society.[38]

Van Dyke advocates a more complex paradigm, one that would permit both group and individual rights, legal and moral, to exist side by side. The objective is not to downplay equal treatment for individuals but to extend to groups equal rights to preserve their integrity. This model implies the principle that a *nation of people* have an intrinsic and inalienable collective right to self-determination. This principle, as Van Dyke points out, had legitimate status in the League of Nations Charter and now enjoys the same status in the United Nations Charter, where the moral, if not legal right to self-determination by *nations of people* is upheld.[39] While one possible outcome of the exercise of the right of nations to self-determination is sovereign statehood, it is clear that other arrangements are possible.[40] Van Dyke cites Puerto Rico, which has chosen commonwealth status.

How does Van Dyke's model fit the historical and contemporary status of Indian tribes? Prior to colonization, Indian tribes operated as independent stateless nations, in their own right; not a derived, delegated or transferred right, but one that came into existence with the group itself. Under the Indian Act and by historical convention Indian tribes in Canada have retained their special group-based status and rights.[41]

Indians also constitute nations of peoples according to social science criteria. Walker Connor[42] defines the essence of a nation "as a psychological bond that joins a people and differentiates it, in the subconscious conviction of its members, from all other people in a most vital way."[43] He adds, in another context, that "national consciousness is therefore accompanied by a growing aversion to being ruled by those deemed aliens."[44] Other social scientists have defined a nation as "a social group which shares a common ideology, common institutions and customs and a sense of homogeneity."[45] The very high level of cultural uniqueness and homogeneity of Indian tribal groups not only strengthens their political integration as nations, but also acts as a barrier to political integration into Canadian society. The fact that Indian cultural uniqueness has become politicized has created an additional serious obstacle to integration into the larger society. Clearly, Indian tribes meet the criteria of nationhood. Indians' first loyalty is to their own group. They believe themselves to be nations.

Van Dyke's paradigm provides a framework within which the Canadian government and Indians may be able to negotiate internal self-determination that will provide Indians the opportunity to retain their group differences without sovereignty. The component unit representing native people would be the "nation," based on traditional cultural and linguistic communities. The Indian nations would function in a constitutionally defined and guaranteed relationship with the provincial and central governments. Both the Canadian state and the

Indian nations would be subject to domestic arrangements specified by general rules or particular treaty agreements regulating the relationship between them.

Indian peoples would be subject to Canadian sovereignty and control over their external affairs but there would be constitutionally defined limits to Canadian control over Indian internal affairs. Although the Canadian government, pursuant to agreements, would continue to exercise some indirect control over individual Indians (for example, in the area of criminal law), in those matters not covered by agreement or treaty, Indian nations would be paramount in setting policies over their own territories and people within their territories. They would exercise jurisdiction over their legal, political, social and economic institutions.

The Canadian federal system provides an institutional framework for accommodating Van Dyke's paradigm. It could be acceptable to the Canadian government because Indian nationhood does not require sovereignty, statehood or separation. It does not threaten the territorial integrity or impair the sovereignty of the Canadian state. The Indian minority would not be seen in competitive terms because it would not have equal weight to the majority. Negotiated limits would place Indians in a position where they could not significantly change the existing distribution of power. In fact, most Indians would shy away from exercising reciprocal authority over the broader, non-Indian political community. Their basic desire is for self-government over their own affairs, not participation in the governing of the rest of Canada through representation in Canada's Parliament or provincial legislatures.

Resolution of common problems or conflicts between the Canadian government and Indian nations could occur through political and administrative mechanisms involving consultative negotiations. Such a model, imbedded as a constitutionally guaranteed principle, would allow Indians the freedom they need to build the sort of communities they desire. Furthermore, by avoiding the issue of sovereign statehood this model conforms approximately to the United Nations' ambiguous strictures on self-determination of peoples.[46] This gives it greater legal, political and moral validity.[47]

Conclusion

The most critical political and legal objections of the Canadian government are directed at Indian claims to European-Western-style sovereign statehood, not at the principle of self-determination. In a struggle to achieve sovereign statehood Indian people could very well provoke a full-scale power struggle with the Canadian government. Such a struggle would consume their limited human, political and economic resources in a futile exercise and could create a backlash in which the "nationhood" option might be eliminated. Furthermore, whereas the Indian condition of economic dependence is a serious constraint on aspirations to sovereign statehood, there is no necessary incompatibility between the current economic dependent status of Canadian Indians and a claim to nationhood. Perhaps more important for Indians than the political-economic *feasibility* of autonomous nationhood is its *compatibility* with their traditional beliefs. Autonomous nationhood, unlike sovereign statehood, would allow Indians to preserve traditional beliefs, values, customs and institutions, and to integrate these with emergent contemporary group interests.

For its part the Canadian government is confronted with two alternatives. It can continue its thinly disguised, much-despised policy of assimilation or, alternatively, it can adopt a policy of meaningful self-determination for Indian tribes. The Canadian government has a moral if not a legal obligation to deal justly and humanely with the Indian people. Should it deny their historical and legitimate claim to nationhood through political or legal stratagems, Indian feelings of injustice will persist. These feelings will inhibit improvement in their economic, social and political condition. If this situation is allowed to fester it could erupt in extra-legal actions culminating in violence.[48] If, however, Indians are accorded "nation" status within the Canadian federation, and are dealt with fairly and honourably, such an arrangement could foster a sense of mutual trust, it could depoliticize cultural divergency and, in the long term, ease cultural cooperation with Canadian society. Thus, native Indian loyalties might, over time, be voluntarily transferred to Canadian society.

Notes

1. The claim to tribal sovereignty is regularly asserted by Indian leaders in Canada and is virtually always explicit in the written representations that provincial and national Indian organizations have made to the Canadian government. For example, see Assembly of First Nations, "Memorandum Concerning the Rights of First Nations and the Canadian Constitution," June 16, 1982; Federation of Saskatchewan Indians, "Indian Nationhood and Indian Government," 1977; *Proceedings of the Indian Government Development Conference* (Ottawa: National Indian Brotherhood, 1979); Union of British Columbia Indian Chiefs, "Indian Nations: Determination or Termination," October 1980; and Assembly of First Nations, "Opening Remarks for Presentation by David Ahenakew, National Chief, Assembly of First Nations to the First Ministers' Conference on Aboriginal Rights," March 15, 1983. The consensus among Indian leaders at the band level regarding inherent sovereignty was also strongly evidenced in the testimony of 567 witnesses, representing Indian bands from every province, before the Special Committee on Indian Self-Government of the House of Commons. The Committee has stated that witnesses unanimously rejected the federal government's proposed band-government bill principally because that proposal involved a delegation of power rather than a recognition of the sovereignty of Indian First Nations' governments. See *Indian Self-Government in Canada,* report of the Special Committee on Indian Self-Government, House of Commons, October 20, 1983, 24.

2. Menno Boldt, "Intellectual Orientations and Nationalism Among Indian Leaders in an Internal Colony: A Theoretical and Comparative Perspective," *British Journal of Sociology* 33 (1982), 484-510; "Enlightenment Values, Romanticism and Attitudes Toward Political Status: A Study of Native Indian Leaders in Canada," *Canadian Review of Sociology and Anthropology* 18 (1981), 545-65.

3. Nancy Oestreich Lurie, "The Contemporary American Indian Scene," in Eleanor B. Leacock and Nancy Oestreich Lurie (eds.), *American Indians in Historical Perspective* (New York: Random House, 1971), 443-46.

4. James Youngblood-Henderson, "Comment," in W. R. Swagerty (ed.), *Indian Sovereignty: Proceedings of the Second Annual Conference on Problems and Issues Concerning American Indians Today* (Chicago: Newberry Library, 1979), 71-72.

5. Charles E. Merriam, Jr., *History of the Theory of Sovereignty Since Rousseau* (New York: AMS Press, 1968), 83; and Sir Ernest Barker, *Essays on Government* (2nd ed.; Oxford: Clarendon, 1960), 100.

6. Merriam, *History of the Theory of Sovereignty Since Rousseau,* 65.

7. See W. J. Stankewicz, "Sovereignty as Political Theory," *Political Studies* 24 (1966), 142.

8. David Easton, "The Perception of Authority and Political Change," in Carl J. Friedrich (ed.), *Authority* (Cambridge, Mass.: Harvard University Press, 1958), 184.

9. See *A Basic Call to Consciousness: The Hau de no san nee Address to the Western World* (Rooseveltown, N.Y.: Akwesasne Notes, 1977); and Alfonso Ortiz, "Summary," in W. R. Swagerty (ed.), *Indian Sovereignty.*

10. Peter Laslett, "The Face to Face Society," in Peter Laslett (ed.), *Philosophy, Politics and Society* (Oxford: Blackwell, 1963), 167.

11. Frances Svensson, "Liberal Democracy and Group Rights: The Legacy of Individualism and Its Impact on American Indian Tribes," *Political Studies* 27 (1980), 421-39.

12. Youngblood-Henderson, in W. R. Swagerty (ed.), *Indian Sovereignty,* 77.

13. Ibid., 58.

14. It is worth noting that many of the values termed "enlightenment" values have been found by various students of native Indian society to be indigenous, in approximate form and in varying degrees, to the cultures of many native tribes in North America. See for example, C. E. Hamilton, *Cry of the Thunderbird: The American Indian's Own Story* (New York: Macmillan, 1950); J. B. MacKenzie, *The Six Nations Indians in Canada* (Toronto: Hunter Rose, 1896), 35; J. D. Forbes, *The Indians in American Past* (Englewood Cliffs: Prentice-Hall, 1964); George Catlin, in M. Ross (ed.), *Episodes From Life Among the Indians and Last Rambles* (Norman, Oklahoma, 1959); M. W. Smith, *Indians of the Urban North-West* (New York: Columbia University Press, 1949), 13; and A. M. Josephy, Jr., *The Indian Heritage of America* (New York: Bantam Books, 1968), 119. See also, in this connection, Menno Boldt, "Social Correlates of Romanticism: A Study of Leadership in an Internal Colony," *Ethnic Groups* 3 (1981), 307-32. It is a matter of historical record that philosophers from Montaigne to Rousseau were influenced by what they un-

derstood to be the enlightened state of North American Indians. Egalitarianism was the most prevalent, though not the universal, model. See, for exceptions, Philip Drucker, *Indians of the Northwest Coast* (Garden City, N.Y.: Natural History Press, 1963), chap. 4. For such exceptional tribes sovereignty does not hold all of the cultural contradictions that we identify in this article.

15. Walter B. Miller, "Two Concepts of Authority," *American Anthropologist* 57 (1955), 271-89.

16. Ibid.

17. In European-Western society we have something akin to this notion of authority in what Friedrich has called "procedural authority." Somewhat along this same line, the Americans substituted the impersonal authority of the Constitution for the personal authority of George III. Carl J. Friedrich, "Authority, Values, and Policy," in Friedrich (ed.), *Authority,* 54.

18. W. J. Rees, "The Theory of Sovereignty Restated," in Peter Laslett (ed.), *Philosophy, Politics and Society,* 58.

19. Merriam, *History of the Theory of Sovereignty Since Rousseau,* 138.

20. R. H. Lowie, "Property Rights and Coercive Powers of Plains Indians," *Journal of Legal and Political Sociology* 1 (1943), 59-71.

21. Hannah Arendt, "What Was Authority?" in C. J. Friedrich (ed.), *Authority,* 102-04.

22. Michael Dorris, "Twentieth Century Indians: The Return of the Natives," in Raymond L. Hall (ed.), *Ethnic Autonomy, Comparative Dynamics: The Americas, Europe and the Developing World* (New York: Pergamon Press, 1979), 71.

23. Yves R. Simon, "Sovereignty in Democracy," in W. J. Stankiewicz (ed.), *In Defense of Sovereignty* (New York: Oxford University Press, 1969), 244.

24. This is possible only in face-to-face societies such as the Indian tribes were. See Laslett in Peter Laslett (ed.), *Philosophy, Politics and Society,* 158, for a discussion of the characteristics of such societies.

25. Merriam, *History of the Theory of Sovereignty Since Rousseau,* 202-03.

26. Frances F. Hinsley, *Sovereignty* (London: C. A. Walls, 1966), 16.

27. Quoted in Keith W. Werhan, "The Sovereignty of Indian Tribes: A Reaffirmation and Strengthening in the 1970's," *Notre Dame Lawyer* 54 (1978), 5-25.

28. Michael E. Melody, "Lakota Myth and Government: The Cosmos as the State," *American Indian Culture and Research Journal* 4 (1980), 1-19.

29. Laslett characterizes this de-emphasis of territoriality as one of the defining characteristics of the political form of a face-to-face society, because geographically defined borders are not suited for nor capable of giving a sense of political consciousness or identity to the members of such groups. That is why Indians retained their sense of nationhood even during the forced mass-migrations. They carried their concept of "nationhood" on their backs. See Laslett, in Peter Laslett (ed.), *Philosophy, Politics and Society.*

30. David Ahenakew, "Aboriginal Title and Aboriginal Rights: The Impossible and Unnecessary Task of Identification and Definition." 1984.

31. *A Basic Call to Consciousness,* and Saskatchewan Federation of Indians, "Indian Nationhood and Indian Government," 1977.

32. We are not here advocating the reconstructionist anthropologists' position that Indians should change into what they once were. But, neither should they be forced to adopt alien political ideas that distort what they value most in their cultural heritage. They should be free to adopt a model of government that will preserve what they value in their cultural traditions.

33. Government of Canada, "Opening Statement by the Prime Minister of Canada, The Right Honourable Pierre Elliott Trudeau to the Constitutional Conference of First Ministers on the Rights of Aboriginal Peoples," March 15, 1983, 16.

34. Kenneth D. McRae, "The Plural Society and the Western Political Tradition," this JOURNAL 12 (1979), 677-78.

35. For a discussion of consociationalism in Canada see Herman Bakvis, *Federalism and the Organization of Political Life: Canada in Comparative Perspective* (Kingston: Institute of Intergovernmental Relations, Queen's University, 1981), 62-189; and Kenneth D. McRae (ed.), *Consociational Democracy: Political Accommodation in Segmented Societies* (Toronto: McClelland and Stewart, 1974), 253-99.

36. See Vernon Van Dyke, "Human Rights and the Rights of Groups," *American Journal of Political Science* 18 (1974), 725-41; "Justice as Fairness: For Groups?", *American Political Science Review* 69 (1975), 607-14; "The Individual, the State, and Ethnic Communities in Political Theory," *World Politics* 29 (1977), 343-69; "Collective Entities and Moral Rights: Problems in Liberal-Democratic Thought," *Journal of Politics* 44 (1982), 21-40.

37. Van Dyke, "Human Rights and the Rights of Groups."

38. Robert A. Nisbet, *Community and Power* (New York: Oxford University Press, 1962), 224.

39. Additionally, a major treaty has been in force for Canada since August 1979. Article of the Covenant on Civil and Political Rights provides that:
    1. All peoples have the right of self-determination. By virtue of that right they freely determine their political status and freely pursue their economic, social and cultural development.
    2. All peoples may, for their own ends, freely dispose of their natural wealth and resources without prejudice to any obligations arising out of international economic cooperation, based upon the principle of mutual benefit, and international law. In no case may a people be deprived of its own means of subsistence.
    3. The States Parties to the present Covenant ... shall promote the realization of the right of self-determination and shall respect that right, in conformity with the provisions of the Charter of the United Nations.

    As a party to this covenant, Canada is obliged to report on the "measures ... adopted which give effect to the rights recognized" (Article 40[1]) to a body set up under the treaty called the Human Rights Committee.

40. See also, Wendell Bell, *Jamaican Leaders: Political Attitudes in a New Nation* (Berkeley: University of California Press, 1964); *The Democratic Revolution in the*

West Indies: Studies in Nationalism, Leadership and the Belief in Progress (Cambridge, Mass.: Schenkman, 1967); "New States in the Caribbean: A Grounded Theoretical Account," in S. N. Eisenstadt and Stein Rokkan (eds.), *Building States and Nations: Analysis by Region,* Vol. 2 (Beverly Hills: Sage, 1975); and "Equality and Social Justice: Foundations of Nationalism in the Caribbean," *Caribbean Studies* 20 (1980), 5-36.

41. The European colonizer's position on Indian sovereignty has been inconsistent and opportunistic; see F. Jennings, "Sovereignty in Anglo-American History," in W. R. Swagerty (ed.), *Indian Sovereignty,* and Keith W. Werhan, "The Sovereignty of Indian Tribes," 5-25. Initially, to avoid conflict amongst themselves, European powers introduced the doctrine of "discovery" to regulate competition for colonial territory. Subsequently, this doctrine was used as justification for declaring sovereignty over Indians on grounds that they were savages, they did not work the land, and had no civil government; see A. S. Keller, O. J. Lissitzyn and F. J. Mann, *Creation of Rights of Sovereignty Through Symbolic Acts 1400-1800* (New York: Columbia University Press, 1958). At the same time, in order to avoid war and risk defeat, the British ostensibly recognized Indian tribes as sovereign nations and negotiated treaties with them. It is important to note that British claims to sovereignty over Indians were never based on "consent of the people." Even today, although they live in a "representative democracy," so far as Indians in Canada are concerned, the Canadian government does not derive its powers to govern Indians from the consent of the Indian people.

42. Walker Connor, "Ethnic Nationalism as a Political Force," *World Affairs* 133 (1970), 91-97; "Nation-Building or Nation-Destroying," *World Politics* 24 (1972), 319-55; and "A Nation is a Nation, is a State, is an Ethnic Group is a ... ," *Ethnic and Racial Studies,* 1 (1978), 377-400.

43. Connor, "A Nation is a Nation ... ," 379.

44. Connor, "Ethnic Nationalism as a Political Force," 93.

45. Jack C. Plano and Ray Olton, *The International Relations Dictionary* (New York: Holt, Rinehart and Winston, 1969).

46. Rupert Emerson, "Self-Determination," *American Journal of International Law* 65 (1971), 459-75.

47. Barker asserts that on moral and practical grounds sovereignty cannot exist for a "nation" which is a minority within a state. Because, if every national group in the world were assumed to be entitled to sovereign statehood it would create chaos and threaten the authority of existing sovereign states. See Sir Ernest Barker, *Principles of Social and Political Theory* (Oxford: Clarendon Press, 1951), 139. Furthermore, the claim that Indian tribes existed as "sovereign states" is vulnerable to the argument that if ever they had such a status, they have now suffered a total loss of sovereignty because their paramount legislative authority has been effectively usurped by another state. The claim that they existed, and continue to exist, as "nations" is not as vulnerable to such an argument.

48. Menno Boldt, "Philosophy, Politics and Extralegal Action: Native Indian Leaders in Canada," *Ethnic and Racial Studies* 4 (1981), 205-21.

ETHNIC IDENTITY

Jean Burnet with Howard Palmer

In Canada it is common to reply to the question "Who are you?" in ethnic terms. Immigrants in the past were sometimes not aware of an ethnic identity when they arrived, seeing themselves only as coming from a village or at most a province, or as adherents of a particular religion. They became ethnically conscious as they were thrust into association with others who shared their language and culture or their physical traits or both, and were accorded a common label and common treatment. But they usually knew of some people from whom they sharply distinguished themselves. More recently, with the salience of ethnicity throughout the world and with the sophistication of many immigrants, people have had an ethnic identity on arrival, and an attitude toward it, either as a burden to be cast off or as a treasure to be passed on to their children. With the passage of time and of generations, both the content and the meaning of the immigrants' ethnic identities change. Whether they continue to consider themselves in the same way or begin to couple the word "Canadian" with the old label, or to call themselves simply "Canadian," the ethnic aspect of their selves and their lives is transformed. Their children and their children's children have a different sense of ethnic identity and manifest it in different ways.

The sense of ethnic identity is difficult to gauge. It is essentially subjective or internal, but it has external aspects that are frequently used as indices. It is for the external aspects that governmental aid is sought and recently has been frequently obtained. The relationship between the external and internal aspects of identity is extremely complex: the feelings of ethnic identity of individuals may or may not be in line with objective criteria defining ethnicity.

For white ethnic groups, among the most conspicuous external manifestations have been language, folklore, cuisine, and sports. Ancestral languages, however important or unimportant in the past, have recently been given primacy as ethnic symbols because of the salience of language in industrial and post-industrial societies and, in particular, the salience of language in Canada since it became officially bilingual in 1969. Languages have been considered to be inseparable from cultures, and linguistic transfer has been deemed to be loss of language and culture. Languages have played a crucial role in many of the white ethnic groups as vehicles for other elements of culture. They have served as means of unifying the groups: people who have spoken regional dialects have, through learning the standard version of their language, come not only to enlarge the number of those recognized as their ethnic fellows but also to iden-

From *"Coming Canadians": An Introduction to a History of Canada's Peoples* (Toronto: McClelland and Stewart, 1988), 212-22. Reprinted by permission of the Minister of Supply and Services.

tify with linguistically dependent aspects of the high culture of their homeland. Languages have been boundary markers, for unless they are world languages they are exclusive to the group.

The descendants of peasant immigrants with high rates of illiteracy, unaccustomed to give importance to linguistic matters, have become keenly interested in linguistic retention. Ukrainians are perhaps exceptional because of the perceived threat to their language in their homeland: their concern about their language in the schools and in the media has been unremitting. The abolition of bilingual schools in Manitoba and the punishment of children for speaking Ukrainian in Prairie schools have played a prominent part in the litany of grievances of Ukrainians against Canadian governments and society. The recent introduction of heritage languages into the curricula of the public schools and the introduction of bilingual Ukrainian-English education in the city of Edmonton have been viewed as triumphs.

Not only schools but families and churches have been crucial to the transmission of ancestral languages. The term "mother tongue" is often interpreted as indicative of the role of the family: the mother, because of her contact with the young child, is seen as having the duty to pass on the ancestral tongue. In an immigrant group, the myriad other duties devolving on the mother hamper her endeavours in regard to language teaching. One of the results of the mother's role in some groups, such as the Armenian and the Jewish, is that women have been allowed to teach language classes while being barred from many other occupations outside the home. In settled communities the old also play a role in transmitting language and culture, as storytellers to the young, but the absence of grandparents is another obstacle to the teaching of the ancestral language in many immigrant households.

The church has frequently regarded its well-being as tied to the traditional language. Sometimes this language is not in everyday use: through centuries, Hebrew was the language of Judaism, too holy for daily use, until it became the language of Israel; in some sects high German was the language of the religious texts and services while low German was used in other aspects of life; until the 1960's Latin was employed in many Catholic religious rituals. But churches have been among the most dedicated sponsors of language classes for children, and priests and pastors have been among the teachers of such classes.

However cherished the mother tongue is, among first-generation immigrants comprehension of one of the country's official languages and fluency in speaking it have been crucial for economic and social adjustment. Spokespeople for immigrants have been much concerned about opportunities to acquire knowledge of the official languages. They have pointed out that workers in segregated occupations and women in the home have often lacked such opportunities. It has been rare, though not unknown, that people have protested that the teaching of English and French has infringed on the rights of another language in Canada.

Knowledge of ancestral languages declines sharply from generation to generation. Research has shown that fluency in non-official languages is virtually confined to first-generation immigrants, and that in the third and succeeding generations the majority have no knowledge at all of the ancestral tongue. On the other hand, even in the third generation most people profess to be in favour of the retention of ancestral languages by their children. The chief reason all generations give for favouring retention is, however, not the keeping up of customs or traditions, nor communication with other members of one's ethnic group. Rather, it is the economic and cultural advantage of knowing more than one language.[1]

Linguistic transfer does not necessarily mean a renunciation of ethnic identity. The Canadian-born may claim the right to select their own symbols of identity and resist pressure from their elders to give primacy to language. How long and how intensely they retain identification with their ancestral group once they have adopted another language may vary greatly from group to group, but the linguistic versatility of Jews and the ethnic retention in spite of linguistic transfer of Scots and Irish indicate that language is not always essential.

One of the ways other than language that members of ethnic groups have had of displaying their ethnic identity has been by maintaining their folkloric heritage and transmitting it from one generation to another. Few belonged wholly to a folk culture or society before coming to Canada: even many eastern Europeans who came out during the Sifton era had been migrant labourers to industrial cities or had had contact with migrant labourers and thus with city ways. They often learned folk arts in Canada, as symbols of their heritage, rather than having retained them. So, among South Asians, music and folk dance have become important community phenomena; among Japanese Kabuki dance, flower arranging, and paper folding are taught and practised; Ukrainians have bandura orchestras and teach embroidery and the painting of Easter eggs. The intellectuals of the group often profess to scorn "red boots multiculturalism" and "dancing in church basements" as trivial or frivolous. Nonetheless, folklore has proved to be extremely persistent.

Several explanations can be given for this persistence. Folklore has great symbolic value:

> Generally, the folklore symbolizes an era in which the people, now in danger and in too much contact with others, were alone and showed their traditional culture in a more pure form. The heroes of lore are thought to have possessed the true virtues, the virtues that distinguish this people from others. The true German of folklore was unspoiled by foreign influences, whether Roman or Jewish. He was set up as a model for the new, restored, true German. Something like this is happening in the Zionist movement, too, where a hardy, sometimes belligerent, athletic Jewish youth is set up both as the original and as the true model for the future.[2]

It is also eminently suited to display before those who do not belong to the ethnic group. Ethnic dancing and instrumental music in particular have become the stock in trade of ethnic or multicultural festivals. A study sponsored by the Multicultural Directorate of the Department of the Secretary of State in 1982 found that in a representative sample of approximately 6,000 folkloric performing arts groups from across Canada, most performances, while they mark special occasions or holidays of the group's own ethnic community, are for general audiences rather than the ethnic community only, and substantial numbers of performances are also for other people's festivals or galas and for special Canadian events and national days.[3]

Certain forms of folklore, such as music, dance, and theatre, have appeal to the young. The Multiculturalism Directorate's study indicated that passing the culture on to children and youth ranked high among reasons for participating in the performing arts. It also showed that in fact the performers tended to be concentrated among those under thirty-five years old. The folkloric performing arts thus are a means of transmitting some of the cultural symbols of the group to new generations so that social networks are established on an ethnic basis and chances of endogamous marriage are increased.

That the folklore thus transmitted is symbolic rather than part of a functioning folk culture is shown by periodic attempts to "purify" it or "make it more authentic." A functioning culture changes and adapts. Weeding out Canadian variants in favour of old country form indicates that the folklore reflects only a museum culture.

One frequent type of change not resisted is the transmutation of elements of folklore into "high culture." Many immigrants have not been familiar with the high culture of their homeland: to southern Italian peasants, for example, Leonardo da Vinci, Michelangelo, Dante, and Verdi have meant little. But they and their children have learned of the homage the world pays to such immortals and have come to take pride in them. Immigrant and native-born artists in various fields who contribute to high culture have been cherished by their ethnic groups, and have on occasion incorporated the folk symbols of those groups into their work. The symbols have thus become part of a more universal heritage.

The same might be said for ethnic foods, whether everyday dishes or *haute cuisine*. They also have become symbolic and, likewise, are suited to sharing and to becoming part of wider Canadian custom. In Canada in the 1980's ethnic bakeries, food stores, and restaurants multiply and flourish. Members of many ethnic groups have not been able to maintain their dietary patterns in their homes for lack of ingredients or lack of time for preparation. They have had to limit their ethnic dishes to ceremonial occasions, or to indulge in them only in restaurants. There the general public shares in the dishes, and the dishes are modified to meet the more general tastes.

Foods, ways of cooking and serving them, and meals have been important experiences in the lives of all immigrants. Food, of course, is intimately related to the family. Fasting and feasting are also religious rituals of great importance. The familial and religious connotations of ceremonial meals, such as Christmas and Easter dinners, and of fasting, in Judaism and Islam as well as Christianity, result in memories of eating and drinking and fasting as part of a social group being among the most poignant recollections of childhood.

Ethnic entrepreneurs have taken advantage of the situation to establish businesses. Markets serving a particular ethnic group or groups from a particular region; bakeries; butchers at which the religious prescriptions of a group and the customs concerning kinds and cuts of meats and seasoning of sausages can be maintained; fishmongers; restaurants—all these have contributed to the rise of businessmen in the occupational and income structure. Bread was a staple for many European peoples and came to be endowed with rich cultural and religious symbolism; hence, bakeries have sprung up in most immigrant areas. In Toronto, for example, by 1912 there were ten small Jewish bakeries producing bread and rolls in the Ward, the area bounded by Yonge, University, Queen, and Dundas. In the 1920's, as the community spread out, so did the bakeries; they began also to serve non-Jewish immigrants from eastern Europe. In the 1930's the dispersion continued, the bakeries began to show some specialization along class lines, a variety of cakes and pastries began to be offered, and the clientele was extended beyond Jewish and eastern European immigrants to include Canadians of all origins. The war accelerated and accentuated these trends, and the 1940's and 1950's were a time of prosperity. They also brought competition, as more recent arrivals began to set up their own small family-run bakeries.

The Estonians were among those who quickly saw that the influx of continental European immigrants offered an opportunity to suppliers of European-type breads. A number of them established small bakeries in Toronto and Hamilton, and some of the bakeries soon grew into sizable enterprises. In the 1960's many new German and Italian bakeries were established, and these offered competition to the Estonian businesses; in the 1970's all the Estonian bakers retired except one.[4] Bakers often did not pass their businesses on to their children: in both the Jewish and the Estonian groups the children of bakers, though they worked in the shops in their youth, tended to go on to higher education and to enter professions.

Ethnic restaurants have ranged from "greasy spoons" to luxurious dining places. At one extreme are cafés and grills in which hamburgers, hotdogs, and sandwiches are served to the public but special soups and stews and sausages are prepared for the owner's family and acquaintances; at the other extreme are restaurants in expensive locations that advertise their exotic character in their service, menu, décor, and prices. In all cases the dishes on the menu have been modified, not simply by the unavailability of ingredients (in the 1970's and

1980's, transportation and refrigeration have made most foodstuffs accessible everywhere), but by the necessity of appealing to the tastes of the public as well as those of the appropriate ethnic group.

The Chinese were early in making the restaurant business an ethnic specialty. For them, at the turn of the century, it was an alternative to the laundry business; it required somewhat greater initial outlay than a laundry but offered a larger return. As Chinese spread eastward from British Columbia they set up restaurants in small towns, where sometimes the restaurateur was the only Chinese, and in large cities. Usually they were inexpensive eating places serving Western-style foods, and their owners had to fight the discrimination visited upon Asians. For example, by-laws restricted them to certain areas and laws made it illegal for white women to work in Chinese restaurants. But they prospered nonetheless, and restaurants in Chinatowns serving Chinese-style food in the 1930's and 1940's began to enjoy a vogue that has continued to the present. Nowadays, not simply Chinese cookery but styles of cooking from various provinces of China are offered.

Macedonians also have made of restaurant-keeping something of an ethnic specialty in the Toronto area, where they have concentrated. It is said that during World War I a quarrel broke out between Canadian soldiers and a Greek restaurant owner, which led the soldiers to wreck a number of Greek-owned restaurants. After this incident many Greeks sold their restaurants, and large numbers of Macedonians who had been working in the restaurants bought them. A study of Macedonian restaurants in Toronto in the 1970's, while unable to establish the exact number of Macedonian-owned restaurants, refers to estimates ranging from 600 to two-thirds of all restaurants in Toronto.[5]

Before World War II, eating in restaurants was not a major aspect of Canadian life. With urbanization and industrialization, eating outside the home has become much more general. The burgeoning of ethnic restaurants in all large cities has led to emphasis on food as one of the prime areas of ethnic differentiation. French, Italian, Japanese, Korean, Vietnamese, Moroccan, and many other types of restaurants have come to enjoy great popularity. Sometimes a restaurant offers more than one ethnic cuisine, Chinese and Middle Eastern, for example, or Ukrainian, Polish, and German.

Although they are less often singled out as expressions of group identity than folklore or cuisine, sports and athletics have been important parts of the tradition of many ethnic groups and have been transplanted to Canada by early arrivals. Ethnic sports associations and athletic achievements for a long time attracted little notice because they lay outside the North American mainstream. Only a few outstanding individuals of non-British origin, such as Bobbie Rosenfeld, a Russian-born Jewish athlete whose many achievements included winning a silver medal at the 1928 Olympics, became household names. But sports were important within ethnic communities as means of holding the loyalty of the young, particularly the young men. Churches often recognized the role of sports and offered the use of their premises for gymnastics or sponsored basketball, baseball, and hockey teams. Political movements also saw the utility of sports, and a workers' sports movement throve in the 1920's and 1930's among Canadian Communists.[6]

Since World War II, the people who have immigrated from every corner of the earth have brought their sports traditions with them. Finns, Czechs, and Estonians have brought modern and rhythmic gymnastics, for example, the West Indians have revivified cricket, originally brought to Canada by upperclass Britishers, and the East Asians have made karate and tai chi popular. Above all, soccer has won a place as a Canadian sport, not so well publicized and patronized as hockey, baseball, and football, perhaps, but taught in the schools and played in leagues at a number of levels. Harney describes the ethnic aspect of soccer in the Toronto region in the 1970's:

> ... in the Toronto and District Soccer League in the early 1970s, more than three-quarters of the seventy-eight teams had ethnic emblems, colours, and/or specifically national associations in their names. Among the teams were Panhellenic, First Portuguese, Croatia, Serbia White Eagle, Toronto Falcons, Hungaria and Heidelberg. Rivalries were along ethnic and sub-ethnic lines, and although sports should be either a substitute for or a mock and harmless form of warfare between nations, the National Soccer League had to stop its season prematurely in 1974 because of violence among players and fans of competing South Slav teams.[7]

In addition to supporting Canadian teams emblematic of their ethnic group, through television people are able to follow the soccer exploits of teams in their homelands. Italy's 1982 soccer victory in the World Cup occasioned an outburst of joy in the Italian community of Toronto, the largest in Canada, that has become legendary. It has been estimated that half a million people assembled on the streets to celebrate the victory.

However, sports and athletics are not simply expressions of group identity. Teams bearing ethnic designations have often selected players in terms of ability rather than ethnicity, so that matches that appear to be inter-ethnic actually pit polyethnic teams against one another. Similarly, in professional team sports, individuals of outstanding ability have been sources of pride for their ethnic group, but at the same time those individuals have been subject to de-ethnicization or ethnic transfer.

Most permanent external symbols of ethnic identity are physical traits. A person can change his or her behaviour, including linguistic behaviour; he or she cannot change skin colour, hair form, or other physical characteristics except by procedures that are often painful and costly. Thus it has been possible to single out members of the visible minorities for discrimination. Their numbers in the country were for long kept low by immigration regulations, and those who were admitted were denied full participation in Canadian society. Blacks, South

Asians, Chinese, and Japanese developed their own communal structures and retained some of their distinctive behaviour patterns. They were given little opportunity to think of themselves as Canadians. Black Canadians whose ancestors came to Canada in the seventeenth and eighteenth centuries and Chinese, Japanese, and South Asian Canadians whose grandfathers or great-grandfathers immigrated in the late nineteenth century and early twentieth centuries complain of being asked where they came from.

However, visibility is not clear-cut. Sensitivity to physical differences and knowledge of the appearance of members of different ethnic groups vary. Some ethnic groups are considered at times to be and at other times not to be visibly distinguishable from the bulk of the population.[8] Individual members of some groups can "pass" as members of the dominant white groups. Further, inter-marriage can decrease physical differences from the rest of the population: the high rates of intermarriage among Japanese Canadians have led to fears that, without renewal of immigration, they might disappear as a visible group. In addition, it is possible that in time the conception of a Canadian may be broadened and redefined so that black and Asian Canadians are not as frequently asked where they come from, as they now tend to be. As their numbers and their social and economic status increase they may become increasingly recognized as Canadians.

Ethnic self-identification is usually examined in terms of the survival of ethnic groups, and change of ethnic identity is seen as loss. It can instead be seen as transfer. In most cases, to cease to regard oneself as Polish or Greek or Danish is to begin to regard oneself as Canadian, or as both Canadian and a member of an ethnic group. In some cases, however, individuals may lose one identity without acquiring another: "I don't know what I am" is a complaint of some second-generation immigrants.

Efforts to probe the internal aspects of identity have usually centred on the question, "To what ethnic group do you feel you belong?" In a study of ancestral languages carried out in 1973, which included no one of British or French ethnic origin, people were asked how they usually throught of themselves and were given four options, ranging from an ethnic label to Canadian. In a sample, two-thirds of which was composed of immigrants and almost 20 per cent of which was composed of people who had been in Canada less than ten years, "17.3 per cent identified themselves with an ethnic label (`Chinese,' `Dutch,' and so on), 44.5 per cent identified themselves with a dual label (Chinese-Canadian, or `Canadian of Chinese origin,' and so on), and the remaining 35.4 per cent identified themselves simply as `Canadians.' "[9]

A more recent study, conducted in Metropolitan Toronto between 1977 and 1979, used a sample of men and women between the ages of eighteen and sixty-five who were in the labour force or were students. It employed an Ethnic Identity Index, based on "(1) the respondents' self-definition in terms of the hyphenated or unhyphenated ethnic or Canadian label, (2) the importance the respondents place on their ethnicity, (3) the respondents' perception of closeness of one's ethnic ties." The range of index scores was from 3, indicating high ethnic identity, to 8, indicating low ethnic identity. The scores do not, of course, show the degree to which a strong Canadian identity has emerged. Of the groups surveyed in the first generation, the West Indians had a score of 3.94, the Chinese 4.35, the Italians 4.37, the Jewish 4.44, the Ukrainians 4.61, the English 5.12, the Portuguese 5.26, and the Germans 5.73.[10]

Generation is usually considered to be the chief factor affecting ethnic identity. First-generation immigrants often have cultural and linguistic badges they cannot shed even if they wish to; second-generation immigrants may still have, or feel they have, distinctive marks, but even more commonly have a feeling of being divided or being in transition; members of the third and later generations, unless they have visible characteristics linking them to their ancestral group, have a choice of identifying themselves with that group or simply being Canadian. In a study carried out in 1969-71 in eighteen ethno-religious bloc settlements in north-central Saskatchewan, all Hutterites favoured preservation of ethnic identity, but among Doukhobors, Ukrainian Catholics, Ukrainian Orthodox, Mennonites, Scandinavians, French, and German Catholics there was a steady increase from the first through the second and third generations in the proportion not favouring identity preservation.[11] In the Metro Toronto study, the indices for the groups that included three generations in all cases but one increased regularly. For Germans, the index in the second generation dipped to 5.57 but in the third generation this rose to 7.69, the highest index attained by any group.[12]

The significance of generation is made most evident among the Japanese, where different terms are used for the different generations. The immigrants are Issei, their children are Nisei, their grandchildren are Sansei. Since most immigration of Japanese to Canada before 1967 occurred from 1904 to 1914, the generational names also indicate roughly the age of the person and the outstanding historical events experienced.

Important as it is, generation is not the sole factor influencing ethnic identity. Through the years, questions in the Canadian census have given prominence to ethnic origin. Periodically efforts were made to remove the questions, or to allow people to answer Canadian or American. However, spokespeople for various ethnic groups fought against such efforts: in 1961 members of the Legislative Assembly of Quebec threatened to call upon French Canadians to boycott the census or answer Negro to the question about ethnic origin if Canadian and American were accepted as answers.[13] The question has continued to be asked, with the difference that in 1981 it no longer specified that origin should be reckoned on the male side. Having to claim an ethnic origin, and knowing that it was entered in official records, has accentuated ethnic consciousness. It is ironic that immigration statistics ceased to be kept regarding ethnic origin in the late 1960's when the Royal Commission on Bilingualism and Biculturalism had brought ethnicity to the forefront in Canada.

Surnames also have an effect. The bearers of surnames that are not of British origin are often asked what the origin of the name is and are approached for support by ethnic organizations that make assumptions about origin based on names. In 1986 it was revealed that "foreign-sounding" names on court dockets were routinely checked by immigration officers looking for illegal aliens. Researchers sometimes propose surnames as found in telephone directories or on voters' lists or assessment roles as the basis for sampling an ethnic group, or employ names as clues to the immigration and settlement of ethnic groups.

Names are, however, an uncertain guide to ethnic identity. They may be changed fairly easily. Sometimes in the past immigration officers simplified names or changed them completely for convenience; immigrants later also simplified or changed their surnames, especially (according to two studies of name-changing carried out in Ontario in the early 1960's[14]) Slavic immigrants. Such changes in many cases, but not all, reflect changes in ethnic identity; sometimes individuals or their descendants revert to the original family names.

Although the legal process of changing one's name by deed poll is easy, the psychological process may be extremely difficult. When attempts were made to Anglicize the names of the Armenian orphans known as the Georgetown boys in 1923, one boy said of another, "... do you see that boy sitting on the end of this row? He lost his father and mother, his home and country—everything that is dear to a boy's heart. All he has left of his past is his name. Please sir, you won't take that away from him, will you?" As a result the attempt at name-changing was abandoned.[15] In the case of one Italian immigrant, the Anglicizing of his name from Veltri to Welch has been blamed for his mental illness and early death.[16]

Discrimination based on name, appearance, or accent against members of various ethnic groups has heightened ethnic consciousness; it has also exerted pressure toward discarding an ancestral ethnic identity. The novelist John Marlyn has described how the protagonist of *Under the Ribs of Death*, Sandor Hunyadi, the Canadian-born son of a cultured Hungarian immigrant growing up in Winnipeg in the 1920's, was led by discrimination to turn away from the values of his father and to change his name to Alex Hunter so that nobody would be able to tell that he had ever been a foreigner.[17] The signal discrimination against enemy aliens, especially Germans, during World War I and against Japanese Canadians during World War II appears to have led in the first instance to many denials of reprobated ethnic origins and in the second to avoidance of ethnic communities and institutions and to intermarriage.

The policy of multiculturalism also has contradictory effects. It has been interpreted as encouraging retention of ancestral ethnic identity, culture, and language, and has been criticized either for attempting to do so or for doing so inadequately. At the same time, it involves programs designed to remove barriers to full participation in Canadian society and to promote interchange between different ethnic groups: thus, to the degree that it succeeds, it facilitates development of a Canadian identity. The contradiction reflects a paradox in the aims of ethnic groups. They want both to remain distinctive and to have equality, as collectivities and as individuals, with others. However, the question must be posed whether more than marginal differentiation, or symbolic ethnicity, is possible in an egalitarian pluralism. Critics of the policy of multiculturalism accuse it of ignoring issues of economic and political power in favour of cultural issues. They assume that the two kinds of issues can be separated. The assumption is erroneous: "Cultures ... differ in nothing more than in the skill, work habits and goals which they instill into the individual."[18] Hard choices must be made whether stress will be put upon preservation of differences or equality; the choices will be made by individuals rather than by collectivities.

Notes

1. O'Bryan *et al., Non-Official Languages.*
2. Everett C. Hughes, *The Sociological Eye: Selected Papers* (Chicago and New York: Aldine Atherton, 1971), p. 186.
3. The Levy-Coughlin Partnership, "The National Survey of Folkloric Performing Arts Groups," Prepared for the Multiculturalism Program of the Government of Canada, 1982.
4. Aun, *The Political Refugees,* p. 58.
5. Harry Vjekoslav Herman, *Men in White Aprons: A Study of Ethnicity and Occupation* (Toronto: Peter Martin Associates, 1978), p. xiii.
6. Bruce Kidd, "The Workers' Sports Movement in Canada, 1924-40: The Radical Immigrants' Alternative," *Polyphony,* 7, 1 (1985), pp. 80-88.
7. Robert F. Harney, "Homo Ludens and Ethnicity," *Polyphony,* 7, 1 (1985), pp. 9-10.
8. Doug Daniels, "The White race is shrinking: perceptions of race in Canada and some speculations on the political economy of race classification," *Ethnic and Racial Studies,* 4, 3 (1981), pp. 353-56.
9. O'Bryan *et al., Non-Official Languages,* p. 97.
10. Wsevolod W. Isajiw, "Ethnic Identity Retention," Ethnic Pluralism Paper No. 5 (Toronto: Centre for Urban and Community Studies, University of Toronto, 1981), pp. 47-49.
11. Alan Anderson and Leo Driedger "The Mennonite Family: Culture and Kin in Rural Saskatchewan," in Ishwaran, ed., *Canadian Families,* p. 166.
12. Isajiw, "Ethnic Identity Retention," p. 49.
13. *Globe and Mail,* 18 January 1961.

14. Canadian Institute of Cultural Research, *Ethnic Change of Name, Ontario—A Pilot Study* (Toronto: Canadian Institute of Cultural Research, 1965); Brenda Conway, "A Study of Factors Involved in Name Changing by Members of Ethnic Minorities" (M.A. thesis, University of Toronto, 1966).

15. Jack Apramian, "The Georgetown Boys," *Polyphony,* 4, 2 (1982), pp. 44-45.

16. John Potestio, "The Memoirs of Giovanni Veltri," *Polyphony,* 7, 2 (1985), p. 14.

17. John Marlyn, *Under the Ribs of Death* (Toronto: McClelland and Stewart, 1957).

18. Hughes, *The Sociological Eye,* p. 75.

OUR PREDICAMENT

Reginald W. Bibby

Introduction

The 1990s are a time of startling changes worldwide. Late 1989 saw the dismantling of the Eastern bloc, with Poland, Hungary, Czechoslovakia, East Germany, and Romania severing their ties with Communism and declaring their autonomy. The Soviet Union, on the heels of its unexpected 1989 policies of economic reform (*perestroika*) and critiquing of the old (*glasnost*), announced in early 1990 the end of its single-party system. China may well be the next Communist giant to regroup. In Latin America, Panamanian dictator Manuel Noriega was ousted in favor of a democratic government, while Daniel Ortega was handed a stunning upset in an unprecedented free election in Nicaragua. Other countries, including El Salvador, could soon follow. In South Africa, Nelson Mandela emerged after twenty-seven years of political captivity and declared that apartheid would soon be a thing of the past. The Middle East perhaps will be the next place where the curtain will rise on the unforeseen.

The pervasive theme in these dramatic political developments is that of *freedom.* At the collective level, people are saying that they want the freedom to govern themselves, to develop their economies, to enhance their overall quality of life. Closely tied to the theme of freedom is the theme of *the individual.* At the personal level, men and women are saying that they want to be free from oppressive regimes, free to express themselves, free to work, to worship, to travel, to share in what their nations and the world have to offer, free to become everything that they as individuals are capable of being.

Closely tied to the themes of freedom and the individual is a third important emphasis—*pluralism.* Sheer diversity, nationally and globally, makes pluralism

From *Mosaic Madness: The Poverty and Potential of Life in Canada* (Toronto: Stoddart, 1990), 1-15. Reprinted by permission of Stoddart Publishing Co. Limited.

a descriptive term: we have many "pluralistic" societies; internationally, we have a "pluralistic" planet. As a policy, pluralism contributes to collective and personal freedom by legitimizing diversity. It resolves the question of how different individuals who want to be free can live in community. Pluralism diplomatically and optimistically declares that the whole is best served by the contribution of varied parts.

Nationwide and worldwide, such a policy translates into an emphasis on coexistence, versus conquest or assimilation. Pluralism's call for tolerance and respect frequently takes the form of statements about human rights. Expressed nationally, it means that Californians are expected to coexist on U.S. turf with Mexican Americans, that ethnic groups in the Soviet Union no longer need to pretend that they don't exist, that Blacks and Whites in South Africa can live as equals in an integrated society, that minority-group members in Canada no longer need to change their names and cultures if they want to "fit in." Expressed globally, it means that war and domination of societies no longer are appropriate. Cultural obliteration in the form of both intolerance and alleged enlightening is likewise an unacceptable violation of the norms of planetary pluralism. Customs and languages, worldviews and religions, are not to be tampered with.

The three themes of freedom, the individual, and pluralism are joined by a fourth centrally important characteristic—*relativism*. The free expression of the individual and groups is made possible only by suspending value judgments about how people live. *Truth* and *best* are not listed in the pluralism dictionary. The only truth is that everything is relative. "Cultural relativism" is accepted as a given; those who dare to assert that their culture is best are dubbed ethnocentric; those who dare to assert that they have the truth are labeled bigots. Truth has been replaced by personal viewpoint.

Many observers are heralding these significant worldwide developments as indications of a new era in world history. What lies ahead, they say, are unprecedented peace and affluence. Social forecasters John Naisbitt and Patricia Aburdene, for example, maintain that "the great unifying theme at the conclusion of the twentieth century is the triumph of the individual. Threatened by totalitarianism for much of this century," say the two authors, "individuals are meeting the millennium more powerful than ever before."[1] As for the future, they write: "On the threshold of the millennium ... we possess the tools and the capacity to build utopia here and now.... Within the hearts and minds of humanity, there has been a commitment to life, to the utopian quest for peace and prosperity for all, which today we can clearly visualize."[2]

Our planet is indeed moving toward worldwide freedom, led by the emancipated individual. That freedom is being made possible by pluralism and relativism. It all sounds progressive, for many exciting, and for the likes of Naisbitt and Aburdene a cause for celebration.

But hold on everybody—the victory party is premature. Since the 1960s, one country has been leading the world in advocating freedom through pluralism and relativism. It has been carrying out something of a unique experiment in trying to be a multinational society, enshrining coexistence and tolerance. The preliminary results are beginning to appear. The news is not that good.

Societies on the verge of implementing pluralistic ideals would do well to take a good look at this important case example. The country? *Canada.*

Our Predicament

On an ordinary September night in 1988, a far from ordinary event took place. A man from Canada did something no other human had previously done. He blazed down a track in Korea in the fastest time ever, and a nation enjoyed a rare moment of collective ecstasy as he leaned over and accepted the gold. The fact that he was assisted by a banned drug soon transformed jubilant celebration into painful disappointment and anger. Millions who had passionately cheered now passionately chided. Some reminded the critics that any young man might well have broken under the pressure of such gigantic national expectations. In the end, Ben Johnson seems to have done what was best for Ben Johnson. And a nation walked away. Did Ben Johnson have any obligation to Canada? Did Canada have any obligation to Ben Johnson? Was it wrong for him to break the rules? Was it wrong to have any rules? Was it wrong only because he got caught?

In Victoria just a few weeks earlier, Canada's largest Protestant denomination acknowledged that sexual orientation should not be a barrier to full participation in the Church. Practicing homosexuals could be ordained as Christian ministers. While some applauded the United Church decision as prophetic, large numbers of members and adherents felt betrayed, and some threatened to leave. The controversy continues into the 1990s. If individual faith is tied to religious community, what happens when one's group does not represent one's views? Is the individual led by God? Is the group led by God? Is no one led by God? Is truth just an outdated illusion, replaced in our time by personal preference?

Canadians were no better prepared to respond to an international controversy that erupted in early 1989 after an author attacked a major religion and found himself condemned to die. It was an unlikely matchup—Salman Rushdie vs. Ayatollah Khomeini—with a worldwide audience looking on. Is ultimate good found in being open to unlimited expression, or are there times when such expression is purchased at the price of others' pain, and therefore must be denied? Does freedom of expression include the freedom to assail what some cherish or, in turn, to assail the assailer ... and then to assail the assailer of the assailer? Is there no limit to such a regression of individual rights, some boundary that preserves what is socially important?

Then there was the turban controversy. In 1989, the federal Solicitor General announced that the face of the RCMP would be altered to better reflect the changing nature of Canadian society. Variations to the uniform would be considered; Sikhs might be allowed to wear turbans. A great outcry was heard, particularly from western Canada. Some people, including the Prime Minister, saw the protest as blatant racism. Others maintained that the changes represented the dismantling of one of the cherished symbols of Canadian life. In a pluralistic society, is it possible to have *any* collective symbols that do not offend the cultural inclinations of some? Is it possible to have consensus on anything at a national level? Does the invitation to come to Canada carry an expectation that accommodations will be made to our culture? Are we expecting more of ourselves than other people would expect of us in their countries?

The June 1990 failure to ratify the Meech Lake accord renewed speculation that Quebec would abandon its traditional place in Canada. After three years of doomsday proclamations and mounting anxiety, Canadians were left, not with a positive outcome, but with more uncertainty than ever about the country's future. Is such ongoing strain really necessary? Can Quebec and the rest of Canada not decide what is best for each other? When will Quebec decide what it wants from Canada? When will the rest of Canada respect Quebec's wishes and get on with life? How long must we live in such political limbo, giving our resources and energies to such debilitating "nation-building"?

Incidents and issues such as these are a reflection of a crisis in social life that Canadians are experiencing from coast to coast. It's more than Meech Lake; together or apart, Canada and Quebec will continue to experience the crisis. It's more than Free Trade or the GST. It's more than federalism or regionalism, racism or sexism. It's almost Canadian sacrilege to say it, but still it needs to be said: the crisis stems from the unintended consequences of the policy that is our pride and joy—*pluralism.*

The Heralded Mosaic

Faced with the problem of creating a society in which people of varied linguistic and cultural backgrounds can live together, Canadians have decided to convert a demographic reality into a national virtue. We have decreed that what is descriptively obvious should be prescriptively valued. Canada, we have concluded, will be a multinational society, a multicultural mosaic of people from varied backgrounds who will have the freedom to live as they see fit.

Freedom for Everyone In this country, there will be no pressure, as there is in some other countries—notably the United States—to discard one's cultural past, and conform to the dominant culture. The name of the Canadian cultural game is not *melting* but *mosaic.* Our premier spokesman for a multinational

Canada, Pierre Elliott Trudeau, eloquently expressed things this way: "Canada ... is a human place, a sanctuary of sanity in an increasingly troubled world. We need not search further for our identity. These traits of tolerance and courtesy and respect for our environment and one another provide it. I suggest that a superior form of identity would be difficult to find."[3] The central goal of Canadian life has become harmonious coexistence, the central means equality and justice. We aspire to accept and respect the ideas and lifestyles of one another, to be equitable and fair. Beyond mere platitudes, Canada has enshrined good intentions in bilingual and multicultural policies, along with a Charter of Rights and Freedoms.

In Canada, we decry any signs of racism or bigotry, exploitation or abuse. We have written laws into our criminal code that prohibit the willful promotion of hatred against any identifiable group. Our social scientists—going back at least to Carleton University's John Porter and his *Vertical Mosaic* of 1965—have given preeminent attention to issues of equality and justice as they affect minorities, women, the poor, and others. The media instill in us the primacy of such issues by consistently treating charges of racism or unfair treatment as front-page news.

Few events have more dramatically disclosed the importance that Canada officially gives to equality than the national soul-searching that followed the tragic slaying of fourteen young women at the University of Montreal in November 1989. As Canadians, we have aspired to coexistence; there is no place here for disrespect, let alone hatred. The charges of rampant sexism and misogyny in the aftermath of Montreal left the nation dazed. What was being attacked was not our Achilles heel but our heart. Peaceful coexistence has been our national dream. In Montreal, that dream was interrupted by a nightmare.

Canada might not be among the world's elite nations, especially when we compare ourselves with our giant cousin to the south. But we like to believe that we have one special thing going for us—our mosaic. Joe Clark's oft-cited phrase sums up our self-image: "We are a community of communities." Such an endorsement of pluralism, we have believed, gives us a social system and a social outlook that is right for the day. As two York University sociologists, Linda Hunter and Judith Posner, put it, "Canada as a whole presents a neutral, affable face that distinguishes the country, for example, from its more exuberant and aggressive neighbor.... Canada's gentler cultural presence may be ahead of its time."[4]

There we have it: a country comprised of diversified groups that together comprise a mosaic—except there's more. Our emphasis on *individual* freedom means that, beyond the cultural groups that comprise the national mosaic, we also have individual mosaic pieces within each group. If the prophet Ezekiel saw "wheels within wheels" as he looked toward the heavens, those looking toward Canada today see "mosaics within mosaics."

Our mosaics have not stopped with the sphere of intergroup relations. Pluralism at the group and individual levels has become part of the Canadian psyche. Some time ago it left its cultural cradle. The pluralism infant has been growing up in the past three decades. It has been traveling across the country, visiting our moral, religious, family, educational, and political spheres. We now have not only a cultural mosaic but also a moral mosaic, a meaning system mosaic, a family structure mosaic, a sexual mosaic. And that's just the shortlist. Pluralism has come to pervade Canadian minds and Canadian institutions.

Everywhere it has traveled, pluralism has left behind its familiar emphases—tolerance, respect, appreciation for diversity, the insistence that individuals must be free to think and to behave according to their consciences. The result is that ours has become a society in which everything seems possible.

Improving the Truth Pluralism translates into emancipated groups and emancipated individuals. Indispensable to such a posture is the accompanying declaration that all viewpoints are equally valid and that all pursuits are equally noble.

Such legitimization of diverse choice has been provided by the widespread acceptance of *relativism*. Absolutists assert that truth transcends cultures and individuals. In contrast, relativists assert that viewpoints reflect the social and intellectual settings from which people come. "Truth" is socially constructed. Consequently, the origin of ideas is not mysterious; ideas can be traced back to social locations.

The emphasis on relativism grew out of the laudable desire of nineteenth-century social scientists to describe foreign cultures in the cultures' own terms. Marriage and sexual practices in Polynesia, for instance, should be described in Polynesian terms, rather than in terms that flow from Western assumptions and practices. Many philosophers made similar efforts. Ethical relativism, for example, recognizes that fundamental differences in ethical views and practices fall along cultural lines, with no one position necessarily transcending all cultures.

In Canada, pluralism articulates the pathway to group and individual freedom. But relativism plays the important role of providing the rationale for freedom of thought and behavior. If pluralism is the pitcher, relativism is the center-fielder. Relativism pronounces that it is appropriate and ideal that a culture encourage a wide variety of views and lifestyles. Pluralism establishes choices; relativism declares the choices valid.

It all sounds reasonable and logical, maybe even a shade ingenious. The picture that emerges, according to sociologist Carol Agòcs, is one of Canadian culture as an intricate tapestry of many hues, woven from the strands of many cultures.[5] At its best, Canada stands as a model to the world, a nation that can be a home to people of all nations and cultures, a microcosm of the harmony and peace that are possible when cultural diversity is tolerated and respected.

But then again, not a few times in history the unsound has been mistaken for the profound.

Too Much of a Good Thing　　Social life has always required a balance between the individual and the group. It also has required a balance between encouraging choice and insisting on the careful evaluation of choices in order to determine which positions are better, best, and true.

Since the 1960s, Canada has been encouraging the freedom of groups and individuals without simultaneously laying down cultural expectations. Canada has also been encouraging the expression of viewpoints without simultaneously insisting on the importance of evaluating the merits of those viewpoints. During the past thirty years, colorful collages of mosaics have been forming throughout Canadian life. Our expectation has been that fragments of the mosaic will somehow add up to a healthy and cohesive society. It is not at all clear why we should expect such an outcome.

To encourage individual mosaic fragments may well result in the production of individual mosaic fragments—and not much more. The multiculturalism assumption—that a positive sense of one's group will lead to tolerance and respect of other groups—has not received strong support, notes McGill University sociologist Morton Weinfeld. The evidence, he says, "suggests a kind of ethnocentric effect, so that greater preoccupation with one's own group makes one more distant from and antipathetic to others."[6]

The evaluation research, however, has just begun. The official enshrinement of pluralism is a fairly recent development, dating back only to 1969 in the case of bilingualism, 1971 for multiculturalism, and 1982 for the Charter of Rights and Freedoms. The truth of the matter is that we know very little about the effects of pluralism on our culture as a whole. We also don't have the luxury of being able to look to other countries to get some sneak previews of how things will turn out. While other societies may be pluralistic in the sense that they are culturally diverse, virtually no other country actually declares itself "multicultural." England, for example, is culturally varied, but people are expected to be "English"—however culturally inflated that concept may be. Similarly, the United States is culturally diverse, but there has been a historical sense that people who come to America become Americans, regardless of how much they may value the cultures of their homelands. Demographer Myron Weiner comments that societies are rarely open to the arrival of persons with racial or ethnic characteristics different from their own.[7] Consequently it is no exaggeration to say that Canada is a world leader in enshrining multinationalism and multiculturalism. "In a sense," says sociologist Roderic Beaujot of the University of Western Ontario, "Canada is trying something unique and needs to ensure that this continues to be a successful experiment."[8]

The early returns for pluralism's impact on life in this country are just now starting to come in. The preliminary results indicate that pluralism is having some significant, unanticipated consequences. For starters, our rights are outdistancing our rules. Armed with our new Charter, groups and individuals are insisting that they are entitled to the right to equal expression, participation, and prosperity. Racial minorities, women, the elderly, and the disabled are working hard to combat inequities. Individuals are invoking the Charter as they square off on every topic imaginable—abortion, homosexuality, knowingly transmitting AIDS, euthanasia, blood transfusions, the spreading of hatred, crosses in Remembrance Day celebrations, Sunday shopping, religion in the schools, female participation in sports, the wearing of turbans, membership in private clubs, age- and gender-based insurance rates, mandatory breathalyzer tests, mandatory wearing of seat belts, displaying excessive tattoos, being drunk in a public place, gun controls, opposition to all-White male regiments, and on and on.

As George Bain put it, in his nationally syndicated column of June 16, 1990: "... Canadians have a lamentably limited capacity to see a national interest broader than the membership list of the occupational, economic, cultural, ethnic, gender, environmental, or other groups with which they identify in spirit if not formally."

Given our emphasis on equality and justice, it's fair enough that we Canadians insist on our rights. However, when our own rights conflict with another person's rights—as is increasingly the case—we obviously have a problem. Something has to give. Unfortunately, pluralism Canadian-style is showing a limited ability to provide a way out.

Resolving Conflicting Rights   One possibility is for both of us to give a little and seek a solution where we both win, where we both get as much as is socially possible of what we want. In popular parlance, the goal is a win-win outcome. But the current Canadian obsession with group and individual rights doesn't seem to include the inclination to give up much of anything. People seem to want a total victory, "a blow-out." Many Canadians come precariously close to equating "win-win" with the forfeiting of integrity, "win-lose" with the triumph of right.

The abortion debate is a case in point. Both sides have shown little sign of being willing to settle for anything less than a shutout of the opposition. Nothing short of a win-lose situation will do. For politicians, the abortion debate is a no-win issue because everyone wants a win-lose outcome, including many politicians themselves. Following the May 1990 Commons' passing of the new abortion legislation, Justice Minister Kim Campbell told reporters, "We have found some common ground." But anti-abortionist Liberal Don Boudria said, "If the government thinks this issue is going to go away, it is mistaken." Pro-abortionist Dawn Black of the NDP predicted that women would "continue to struggle" until they are "fully equal, participating citizens in this country."[9]

Future historians will note with interest that we applauded a Charter of Rights and Freedoms [see table 1] but had no counterbalancing Charter of Social Responsibility. As long as we ourselves won, we frequently were content to blank our opponents.

TABLE 1 Crisis? What Crisis?

	% Agreeing					
	NAT	BC	PR	ONT	QUE	ATL
In general, the Charter is a good thing for Canada.	81	76	79	82	89	80
The Charter of Rights will strengthen Canadian national identity.	63	58	62	59	66	71
The idea that everyone has a right to their own opinion is being carried too far these days.	38	34	35	32	48	40

Source: *Charter Survey,* York University, 1987.

If win-win is out of the question, a second logical way to resolve conflicting rights might be to introduce an outside standard to determine which position is the more correct or appropriate. The problem here however is that relativism has decreed that all viewpoints have equal value.

No one viewpoint is superior to or more accurate than others; no one lifestyle is more valid than others. To live by the sword of relativism, which sanctioned collective and individual pluralism, may also be to die by it.

In Canada, truth has become little more than personal opinion. "It's all relative," declare Canadians from British Columbia to Newfoundland. Consequently, we aren't sure how to respond to Ben Johnson, to homosexuals who want to be ordained, to writers whose works upset others, to the desire to preserve valued cultural symbols. Relativism has slain moral consensus. It has stripped us of our ethical and moral guidelines, leaving us with no authoritative instruments with which to measure social life. Our standards for evaluating ideas and behavior have been restricted to our local cultural and religious domains. Those same historians who never found our charter of social responsibility will further note that we were a country that was a champion of choice, that we triumphantly discarded the idea that there are better and best choices in favor of worshipping choice as an end in itself.

A Cause for Pause If we don't resolve our difficulties by pursuing a win-win solution or by using an outside ethical standard, the remaining recourse is the courthouse. And, in case no one has noticed, that's where we are increasingly ending up. As we approach the new century, we find ourselves playing a disorganized social game. We are stressing individual rights over social rules and hiring legal technicians as our referees. Our team spirit—our social spirit—is frequently nonexistent. The Canadian social game is also bogging down because we are cheering for all plays instead of the best plays. In declaring everything equal, we are ceasing to explore what is better and best, personally and socially. The attention given to the individual's rights and potential has been extremely important in this century, but it has become increasingly detached from what is socially beneficial, resulting in excessive *individualism*.

Together, individualism and relativism make social life difficult indeed, in the long run perhaps impossible. Individualism focuses on the individual to the detriment of the group. Relativism, taken to an extreme, erases agreement on the norms that are essential to social life.

Unbridled individualism and relativism are obviously not new problems. But conditions do not have to be new in order to be destructive. Moreover, conditions that don't go away may well be more threatening to societies at some points in history rather than at others. In our time, excessive individualism and relativism may well be two of the most serious threats to social life in Canada. With the movement of many of the world's nations toward greater freedom and individualism and toward pluralism and relativism, there is good reason to believe that the threat to social life will become increasingly global as well.

In its zeal to promote coexistence, Canada may find itself a world leader in promoting the breakdown of group life and the abandonment of the pursuit of the best. Individually, we have been emancipated; socially, we are in disarray. Despite a generally high level of affluence, Canadians these days seem frustrated, restless, and nervous. Author Pierre Berton recently said, "I haven't seen the country as mean-spirited since the Depression." In April 1990, Montreal *La Presse* columnist Lysianne Gagnon wrote, "Obviously the mood of the country is terrible." In the same month, *Winnipeg Free Press* editor John Dafoe described the nation as "fractious," saying that the most disturbing thing is "a certain lack of community. People seem to be very wrapped up in their own problems."[10] *Maclean's* editor Kevin Doyle summed things up this way: "At a time when the world seems to be on the brink of a new era of hope and change and freedom, symbolized by the events in Eastern Europe and the Soviet Union, Canadians [seem] to be blocked in a time warp, isolated and anxious about the future."[11]

Such is the madness characterizing the country today. It has an important history.

Notes

1. John Naisbitt and Patricia Aburdene, *Megatrends 2000* (New York: William Morrow, 1990) p. 298.

2. *Ibid.,* p. 322 and p. 3.

3. Cited in Kevin J. Christiano, "Federalism as a Canadian National Ideal: The Civic Rationalism of Pierre Elliot Trudeau," Unpublished paper.

4. Linda Hunter and Judith Posner, "Culture as Popular Culture," in Michael M. Rosenberg, William B. Shaffir, Allan Turowetz and Morton Weinfeld (eds.), *An Introduction to Sociology,* 2nd, ed. (Toronto: Methuen, 1987), p. 104.

5. Carol Agòcs, "Ethnic Group Relations," in James Teevan (ed.), *Basic Sociology: A Canadian Introduction,* 2nd, ed. (Scarborough: Prentice-Hall, 1987), p. 187.

6. Morton Weinfeld, "Ethnic and Race Relations," in James Curtis and Lorne Tepperman (eds.), *Understanding Canadian Society* (Toronto: McGraw-Hill Ryerson, 1987), p. 600.

7. Myron Weiner, "International Migration and International Relations," in *Population and Development Review,* 11 (1985) pp. 441-455.

8. Roderic Beaujot, "Canada's Demographic Profile," in James Curtis and Lorne Tepperman (eds.), *Understanding Canadian Society* (Toronto: McGraw-Hill Ryerson, 1988), p. 57.

9. Canadian Press, May 29, 1990.

10. Canadian Press, April 30, 1990.

11. *Maclean's,* January 1, 1990.

Name Index